Pro T-SQL 2012 Programmer's Guide

Third Edition

Jay Natarajan
Rudi Bruchez
Scott Shaw
Michael Coles

Pro T-SQL 2012 Programmer's Guide

ISBN-13 (pbk): 978-1-4302-4596-4

ISBN-13 (electronic): 978-1-4302-4597-1

President and Publisher: Paul Manning
Lead Editors: Jonathan Gennick and Kate Blackham
Technical Reviewer: Robin Dewson
Editorial Board: Steve Anglin, Ewan Buckingham, Gary Cornell, Louise Corrigan, Morgan Ertel, Jonathan Gennick, Jonathan Hassell, Robert Hutchinson, Michelle Lowman, James Markham, Matthew Moodie, Jeff Olson, Jeffrey Pepper, Douglas Pundick, Ben Renow-Clarke, Dominic Shakeshaft, Gwenan Spearing, Matt Wade, Tom Welsh
Coordinating Editor: Mark Powers
Copy Editors: Michele Bowman and Kimberly Burton-Weisman
Compositor: SPi Global
Indexer: SPi Global
Artist: SPi Global
Cover Designer: Anna Ishchenko

Distributed to the book trade worldwide by Springer Science+Business Media New York, 233 Spring Street, 6th Floor, New York, NY 10013. Phone 1-800-SPRINGER, fax (201) 348-4505, e-mail orders-ny@springer-sbm.com, or visit www.springeronline.com.

For information on translations, please e-mail rights@apress.com, or visit www.apress.com.

Apress and friends of ED books may be purchased in bulk for academic, corporate, or promotional use. eBook versions and licenses are also available for most titles. For more information, reference our Special Bulk Sales–eBook Licensing web page at www.apress.com/bulk-sales.

Any source code or other supplementary materials referenced by the author in this text is available to readers at www.apress.com/9781430245964. For detailed information about how to locate your book's source code, go to www.apress.com/source-code.

I dedicate this book to my son, Satya.

—Jay Natarajan

I dedicate this book to my family and all their patience.

—Scott Shaw

Contents at a Glance

Contents

About the Authors

Jay Natarajan has more than 15 years of experience in the SQL Server space. Her skills lie in both the design and the implementation arenas, having architected and deployed complex solutions for enterprise customers. She joined Microsoft Consulting Services in 2008. She holds a bachelor's degree in mechanical engineering from the University of Madras. Jay currently lives in Atlanta with her husband, Chad, and their son Satya.

Rudi Bruchez is an independent consultant and trainer based in Paris, France. He has 15 years of experience with SQL Server. He has worked as a DBA for CNET Channel, a subsidiary of CNET.com, at MSC (Mediterranean Shipping Company) headquarters in Geneva, and at Promovacances, an online travel company in Paris. He has provided consulting and audits, as well as SQL Server training since 2006. As SQL Server evolves into a more complex solution, he tries to make sure that developers and administrators continue mastering the fundamentals of the relational database and the SQL language. He coauthored a bestselling French-language book on the SQL language, and published the only French-language book on SQL Server optimization. He can be contacted at www.babaluga.com.

Scott Shaw went from a starving literature major to a well-fed but sleep-deprived IT professional. After filling a wall with certifications ranging from Oracle to Microsoft server, he found his niche in SQL Server. Scott has more than 12 years of experience working in information technology, and now spends his days and nights managing hundreds of virtual SQL servers for a large Midwest healthcare organization while writing articles and presenting speeches for the always-generous SQL community. Scott lives in Saint Louis, Missouri, with his wife and two children. He has a master's degree in English and comparative literature, and a master's degree in management information systems. Scott has taught classes in T-SQL for Washington University's CAIT program. He presents topics for SQLSaturday. He is a frequent contributor to MSSQLTips.com and spoke at the inaugural PASS SQLRally in Orlando, Florida, in November 2011.

Michael Coles has more than a decade's worth of experience designing and administering SQL Server databases. He is a prolific writer of articles on all aspects of SQL Server, particularly on the expert use of T-SQL, and he holds MCDBA and MCP certifications. He graduated magna cum laude with a bachelor's degree in information technology from American Intercontinental University in Georgia. A member of the United States Army Reserve, he was activated for two years following 9/11.

About the Technical Reviewer

Robin Dewson has been hooked on programming ever since he bought his first computer, a Sinclair ZX80, in 1980. He has worked with SQL Server since version 6.5, and with Visual Basic since version 5. Robin is a consultant based in London, where he has lived for nearly eight years. He also develops a rugby-related web site and maintains his own site at Fat-Belly.com.

Acknowledgments

First, I would like to thank Tejaswi Redkar, my colleague and mentor, who connected me with Apress and gave me the confidence to write. Without his encouragement, I am not sure if I would have ventured this journey. I would like to thank the Apress team, especially Jonathan Gennick and Mark Powers, for giving me the opportunity and putting up with me as a first-time writer. Robin Dewson, our technical reviewer, helped me tremendously to shape the content of this book. I would like to thank my husband and my son for their patience when I was unavailable—most evenings and weekends—while writing the book. I especially appreciate my husband for proofreading and correcting countless mistakes, even when he was tired and busy.

Speaking on a personal front, this book, my career, and everything I do and am today is due to my parents. They made sacrifices along the way to give me opportunities they never had. They allowed me to chase my dreams. I am always thankful for their support. I would also like thank my mentors—Rick Hines, Robert E. Avery, Lou Carbone, Robert Skoglund, John Nisi, and Lenny Fenster—for their guidance and help in shaping my career. Last but not least, I want to thank *you* for purchasing this book. Hopefully, it will provide you overview and direction as you develop solutions using SQL Server 2012.

—Jay Natarajan

I would simply like to thank my family for their support. Thank you also to my coauthors and the Apress team. It has been a real pleasure to work with you.

—Rudi Bruchez

Introduction

In the mid-1990s, when Microsoft parted ways with Sybase in their conjoint development of SQL Server and started developing Windows NT versions, it was almost a whole different product. When version 6.5 was released in 1996, it was starting to gain credibility as an enterprise-class database server. It still had rough management tools and only core functionalities, and some limitations that are forgotten today, like fixed size devices and the inability to drop table columns. It was doing anyway what a database server is designed for: storing and retrieving data for client applications. There was already enough to learn for anyone new to the relational database world. A lot of concepts had to be understood, like foreign keys, stored procedures or triggers, and of course, the dedicated language, T-SQL, a baffling experience for every newcomer. Writing SELECT queries sometimes involves a lot of head-scratching. But when we—developers—eventually mastered all that, we still had to keep up with additions made by Microsoft to the database engine with each new version, and some of them were not for the faint of heart, like .NET database modules, support for XML and the XQuery language or even a full implementation of symmetric and asymmetric encryption. These additions are today core components of SQL Server. Because an RDBMS (Relational DataBase Management Server) like SQL Server is one of the most important elements of the IT environment, we need to make the best of it, which implies a good understanding of the more advanced features. We have designed this book with the goal of helping T-SQL developers get the absolute most out of the development features and functionality in SQL Server 2012. We will cover all of what's needed to master T-SQL development, from the management and development tools to performance tuning. We hope you will enjoy it and it will help you to become a pro SQL Server 2012 developer.

Whom This Book Is For

This book is intended for SQL Server developers who need to port code from prior versions of SQL Server, and those who want to get the most out of database development on the 2012 release. You should have a working knowledge of SQL, preferably T-SQL on SQL Server 2008 or 2005, as most of the examples in this book are written in T-SQL. In this book, we will cover some of the basics of T-SQL, including some introductory concepts like data domain and three-valued logic—but this is not a beginner's book. We will not be discussing database design, database architecture, normalization, and the most basic of SQL constructs in any kind of detail. Apress offers a beginner's guide to T-SQL 2012 that does that. We will be focusing here on topics of advanced SQL Server 2012 functionalities, which assume a basic understanding of SQL statements like INSERT and SELECT. A working knowledge of C# and the .NET Framework is also useful (but not required), as two chapters are dedicated to .NET client programming and .NET database integration. Some examples in the book will be written in C#. When C# sample code is provided, it is explained in detail, so an in-depth knowledge of the .NET Framework class library is not required.

How This Book Is Structured

This book was written to address the needs of four types of readers:

- SQL developers who are coming from other platforms to SQL Server 2012

- SQL developers who are moving from prior versions of SQL Server to SQL Server 2012

- SQL developers who have a working knowledge of basic T-SQL programming and want to learn about advanced features

- Database Administrators and nondevelopers who need a working knowledge of T-SQL functionality to effectively support SQL Server 2012 instances

For all types of readers, this book is designed to act as a tutorial that describes and demonstrates T-SQL features with working examples, and as a reference for quickly locating details about specific features. The following sections provide a chapter-by-chapter overview.

Chapter 1

Chapter 1 starts this book off by putting SQL Server 2012's implementation of T-SQL in context, including a short history of T-SQL, a discussion of T-SQL basics, and an overview of T-SQL coding best practices.

Chapter 2

Chapter 2 gives an overview of the tools that are packaged with SQL Server and available to SQL Server developers. Tools discussed include SQL Server Management Studio (SSMS), SQLCMD, SQL Server Data Tools (SSDT), and SQL Profiler, among others.

Chapter 3

Chapter 3 introduces T-SQL procedural code, including control-of-flow statements like IF...THEN and WHILE. In this chapter, we also discuss CASE expressions and CASE-derived functions, and provide an in-depth discussion of SQL three-valued logic.

Chapter 4

Chapter 4 discusses the various types of T-SQL user-defined functions available to encapsulate T-SQL logic on the server. We talk about all forms of T-SQL-based user-defined functions, including scalar user-defined functions, inline table-valued functions, and multistatement table-valued functions.

Chapter 5

Chapter 5 covers stored procedures, which allow you to create server-side T-SQL subroutines. In addition to describing how to create and execute stored procedures on SQL Server, we also address a thorny issue for some—the issue of why you might want to use stored procedures.

Chapter 6

Chapter 6 introduces all three types of SQL Server triggers: classic DML triggers, which fire in response to DML statements; DDL triggers, which fire in response to server and database DDL events; and logon triggers, which fire in response to server LOGON events.

Chapter 7

Chapter 7 discusses SQL Server encryption, including the column-level encryption functionality introduced in SQL Server 2005 and the newer transparent database encryption (TDE) and extensible key management (EKM) functionality, both introduced in SQL Server 2008.

Chapter 8

Chapter 8 dives into the details of common table expressions (CTEs) and windowing functions in SQL Server 2012, which feature some improvements to the OVER clause to achieve row-level running and sliding aggregations.

Chapter 9

Chapter 9 discusses T-SQL data-types, first with some important things to know about basic data-types, like how to handle date and time in your code, and then with advanced data types and features, like the hierarchyid complex type, and the FILESTREAM and filetable functionality.

Chapter 10

Chapter 10 covers the full-text search (FTS) feature and advancements made since SQL Server 2008, including greater integration with the SQL Server query engine and greater transparency by way of FTS-specific data management views and functions.

Chapter 11

Chapter 11 provides an in-depth discussion of SQL Server 2012 XML functionality, which carries forward the new features introduced in SQL Server 2005 and improves upon them. We cover several XML-related topics in this chapter, including the xml data type and its built-in methods, the FOR XML clause, and XML indexes.

Chapter 12

Chapter 12 discusses XQuery and XPath support in SQL Server 2012, including improvements on the XQuery support introduced in SQL Server 2005, like support for the xml data type in XML DML insert statements and the let clause in FLWOR expressions.

Chapter 13

Chapter 13 introduces SQL Server catalog views, which are the preferred tools for retrieving database and database object metadata. This chapter also discusses dynamic management views and functions, which provide access to server and database state information.

Chapter 14

Chapter 14 is a discussion of SQL CLR Integration functionality in SQL Server 2012. In this chapter, we discuss and provide examples of SQL CLR stored procedures, user-defined functions, user-defined types, and user-defined aggregates.

Chapter 15

Chapter 15 focuses on client-side support for SQL Server, including ADO.NET-based connectivity and the newest Microsoft ORM (Object-Relational Mapping) technology, Entity Framework 4.

Chapter 16

Chapter 16 discusses SQL Server connectivity using middle-tier technologies. Since native HTTP endpoints are deprecated since SQL Server 2008, we discuss them as items that may need to be supported in existing databases but should not be used for new development. We focus instead on possible replacement technologies, such as ADO.NET Data Services and IIS/.NET Web Services.

Chapter 17

Chapter 17 discusses improvements to server-side error handling made possible with the TRY...CATCH block. We also discuss various methods for debugging code, including using the Visual Studio T-SQL debugger. This chapter wraps up with a discussion of dynamic SQL and SQL injection, including the causes of SQL injection and methods you can use to protect your code against this type of attack.

Chapter 18

Chapter 18 provides an overview of performance-tuning SQL Server code. This chapter discusses SQL Server storage, indexing mechanisms, and query plans. We wrap up the chapter with a discussion of a proven methodology for troubleshooting T-SQL performance issues.

Appendix A

Appendix A provides the answers to the exercise questions that we've included at the end of each chapter.

Appendix B

Appendix B is designed as a quick reference to the XQuery Data Model (XDM) type system.

Appendix C

Appendix C provides a quick reference glossary to several terms, many of which may be new to those using SQL Server for the first time.

Appendix D

Appendix D is a quick reference to the SQLCMD command-line tool, which allows you to execute ad hoc T-SQL statements and batches interactively, or run script files.

Conventions

To help make reading this book a more enjoyable experience, and to help you get as much out of it as possible, we've used the following standardized formatting conventions throughout.

C# code is shown in code font. Note that C# code is case sensitive. Here's an example:

```
while (i < 10)
```

T-SQL source code is also shown in code font, with keywords capitalized. Note that we've lowercased the data types in the T-SQL code to help improve readability. Here's an example:

```
DECLARE @x xml;
```

XML code is shown in code font with attribute and element content in bold for readability.

Some code samples and results have been reformatted in the book for easier reading. XML ignores whitespace, so the significant content of the XML has not been altered. Here's an example:

```
<book publisher="Apress">Pro SQL Server 2012 XML</book>:
```

▨ **Note** Notes, tips, and warnings are displayed like this, in a special font with solid bars placed over and under the content.

SIDEBARS

Sidebars include additional information relevant to the current discussion and other interesting facts. Sidebars are shown on a gray background.

Prerequisites

This book requires an installation of SQL Server 2012 to run the T-SQL sample code provided. Note that the code in this book has been specifically designed to take advantage of SQL Server 2012 features, and some of the code samples will not run on prior versions of SQL Server. The code samples presented in the book are designed to be run against the AdventureWorks 2012 sample database, available from the CodePlex web site at http://www.codeplex.com/MSFTDBProdSamples. The database name used in the samples is not AdventureWorks2012, but AdventureWorks, for the sake of simplicity.

If you are interested in compiling and deploying the .NET code samples (the client code and SQL CLR examples) presented in the book, we highly recommend an installation of Visual Studio 2010. Although you can compile and deploy .NET code from the command line, we've provided instructions for doing so through the Visual Studio Integrated Development Environment (IDE). We find that the IDE provides a much more enjoyable experience.

Some examples, such as the ADO.NET Data Services examples in Chapter 16, require an installation of IIS (Internet Information Server) as well. Other code samples presented in the book may have specific requirements, such as the Entity Framework 4 samples, which require the .NET Framework 3.5. We've added notes to code samples that have additional requirements like these.

Apress Website

Visit this book's apress.com webpage at http://www.apress.com/9781430245964 for the complete sample code download for this book. It is compressed in a zip file and structured so that each subdirectory contains all the sample code for its corresponding chapter.

We and the Apress team have made every effort to ensure that this book is free from errors and defects. Unfortunately, the occasional error may have slipped past us, despite our best efforts. In the event that you find an error in the book, please let us know! You can submit errors to Apress by visiting http://www.apress.com/9781430245964 and filling out the form under the "Errata" tab.

CHAPTER 1

■ ■ ■

Foundations of T-SQL

SQL Server 2012 is the latest release of Microsoft's enterprise-class database management system (DBMS). As the name implies, a DBMS is a tool designed to manage, secure, and provide access to data stored in structured collections within databases. T-SQL is the language that SQL Server speaks. T-SQL provides query and data manipulation functionality, data definition and management capabilities, and security administration tools to SQL Server developers and administrators. To communicate effectively with SQL Server, you must have a solid understanding of the language. In this chapter, we will begin exploring T-SQL on SQL Server 2012.

A Short History of T-SQL

The history of Structured Query Language (SQL), and its direct descendant Transact-SQL (T-SQL), begins with a man. Specifically, it all began in 1970 when Dr. E. F. Codd published his influential paper "A Relational Model of Data for Large Shared Data Banks" in the Communications of the Association for Computing Machinery (ACM). In his seminal paper, Dr. Codd introduced the definitive standard for relational databases. IBM went on to create the first relational database management system, known as System R. It subsequently introduced the Structured English Query Language (SEQUEL, as it was known at the time) to interact with this early database to store, modify, and retrieve data. The name of this early query language was later changed from SEQUEL to the now-common SQL due to a trademark issue.

Fast-forward to 1986 when the American National Standards Institute (ANSI) officially approved the first SQL standard, commonly known as the ANSI SQL-86 standard. Microsoft entered the relational database management system picture a few years later through a joint venture with Sybase and Ashton-Tate (of dBase fame). The original versions of Microsoft SQL Server shared a common code base with the Sybase SQL Server product. This changed with the release of SQL Server 7.0, when Microsoft partially rewrote the code base. Microsoft has since introduced several iterations of SQL Server, including SQL Server 2000, SQL Server 2005, SQL Server 2008 R2, and now SQL Server 2012. In this book, we will focus on SQL Server 2012, which further extends the capabilities of T-SQL beyond what was possible in previous releases.

Imperative vs. Declarative Languages

SQL is different from many common programming languages such as C# and Visual Basic because it is a *declarative language*. To contrast, languages such as C++, Visual Basic, C#, and even assembler language are *imperative languages*. The imperative language model requires the user to determine what the end result should be and also tell the computer step by step how to achieve that result. It's analogous to asking a cab driver to drive you to the airport, and then giving him turn-by-turn directions to get there. Declarative languages, on the other hand, allow you to frame your instructions to the computer in terms of the end result. In this model, you allow the computer to determine the best route to achieve your objective, analogous to just telling the cab driver to take you to the airport and trusting him to know the best route. The declarative model makes a lot of sense when you consider that SQL Server is privy to a lot of "inside information." Just like the cab driver who knows the shortcuts, traffic conditions, and other factors that affect your trip, SQL Server inherently knows several methods to optimize your queries and data manipulation operations.

Consider Listing 1-1, which is a simple C# code snippet that reads in a flat file of names and displays them on the screen.

Listing 1-1. C# Snippet to Read a Flat File

```
StreamReader sr = new StreamReader("c:\\Person_Person.txt");
string FirstName = null;
while ((FirstName = sr.ReadLine()) != null) {
Console.WriteLine(s); } sr.Dispose();
```

The example performs the following functions in an orderly fashion:

1. The code explicitly opens the storage for input (in this example, a flat file is used as a "database").

2. It then reads in each record (one record per line), explicitly checking for the end of the file.

3. As it reads the data, the code returns each record for display using `Console.Writeline()`.

4. And finally, it closes and disposes of the connection to the data file.

Consider what happens when you want to add or delete a name from the flat-file "database." In those cases, you must extend the previous example and add custom routines to explicitly reorganize all the data in the file so that it maintains proper ordering. If you want the names to be listed and retrieved in alphabetical (or any other) order, you must write your own sort routines as well. Any type of additional processing on the data requires that you implement separate procedural routines.

The SQL equivalent of the C# code in Listing 1-1 might look something like Listing 1-2.

Listing 1-2. SQL Query to Retrieve Names from a Table

```
SELECT FirstName FROM Person.Person;
```

■ **Tip** Unless otherwise specified, you can run all the T-SQL samples in this book in the AdventureWorks 2012 sample database using SQL Server Management Studio or SQLCMD.

To sort your data, you can simply add an ORDER BY clause to the SELECT query in Listing 1-2. With properly designed and indexed tables, SQL Server can automatically reorganize and index your data for efficient retrieval after you insert, update, or delete rows.

T-SQL includes extensions that allow you to use procedural syntax. In fact, you could rewrite the previous example as a cursor to closely mimic the C# sample code. These extensions should be used with care, however, since trying to force the imperative model on T-SQL effectively overrides SQL Server's built-in optimizations. More often than not, this hurts performance and makes simple projects a lot more complex than they need to be.

One of the great assets of SQL Server is that you can invoke its power, in its native language, from nearly any other programming language. For example, in .NET you can connect and issue SQL queries and T-SQL statements to SQL Server via the System.Data.SqlClient namespace, which we will discuss further in Chapter 15. This gives you the opportunity to combine SQL's declarative syntax with the strict control of an imperative language.

SQL Basics

Before we discuss developments in T-SQL, or on any SQL-based platform for that matter, we have to make sure we're speaking the same language. Fortunately for us, SQL can be described accurately using well-defined and time-tested concepts and terminology. We'll begin our discussion of the components of SQL by looking at *statements*.

Statements

To begin with, in SQL we use statements to communicate our requirements to the DBMS. A statement is composed of several parts, as shown in Figure 1-1.

Figure 1-1. *Components of a SQL Statement*

As you can see in the figure, SQL statements are composed of one or more *clauses,* some of which may be optional depending on the statement. In the SELECT statement shown, there are three clauses: the SELECT clause, which defines the columns to be returned by the query; the FROM clause, which indicates the source table for the query; and the WHERE clause, which is used to limit the results. Each clause represents a primitive operation in the relational algebra. For instance, in the example, the SELECT clause represents a relational *projection* operation, the FROM clause indicates the *relation,* and the WHERE clause performs a *restriction* operation.

■ **Note**   The *relational model* of databases is the model formulated by Dr. E. F. Codd. In the relational model, what we know in SQL as *tables* are referred to as *relations*, hence the name. *Relational calculus* and *relational algebra* define the basis of query languages for the relational model in mathematical terms.

ORDER OF EXECUTION

Understanding the logical order in which SQL clauses are applied within a statement or query is important when setting your expectations about results. While vendors are free to physically perform whatever operations, in any order, that they choose to fulfill a query request, the results must be the same as if the operations were applied in a standards-defined order.

The WHERE clause in the example contains a *predicate,* which is a logical expression that evaluates to one of SQL's three possible logical results: true, false, or unknown. In this case, the WHERE clause and the predicate limit the results to only rows in which the ContactId equals 1.

The SELECT clause includes an expression that is calculated during statement execution. In the example, the expression EmailPromotion * 10 is used. This expression is calculated for every row of the result set.

SQL THREE-VALUED LOGIC

SQL institutes a logic system that might seem foreign to developers coming from other languages like C++ or Visual Basic (or most other programming languages, for that matter). Most modern computer languages use simple two-valued logic: a Boolean result is either true or false. SQL supports the concept of NULL, which is a placeholder for a missing or unknown value. This results in a more complex three-valued logic (3VL).

Let us give you a quick example to demonstrate. If we asked you the question, "Is *x* less than 10?" your first response might be along the lines of, "How much is *x*?" If we refused to tell you what value *x* stood for, you would have no idea whether *x* was less than, equal to, or greater than 10; so the answer to the question is neither true nor false—it's the third truth value, *unknown*. Now replace *x* with NULL and you have the essence of SQL 3VL. NULL in SQL is just like a variable in an equation when you don't know the variable's value.

No matter what type of comparison you perform with a missing value, or which other values you compare the missing value to, the result is always unknown. We'll continue the discussion of SQL 3VL in Chapter 3.

The core of SQL is defined by statements that perform five major functions: querying data stored in tables, manipulating data stored in tables, managing the structure of tables, controlling access to tables, and managing transactions. All of these subsets of SQL are defined following:

- *Querying:* The SELECT query statement is a complex statement. It has more optional clauses and vendor-specific tweaks than any other statement, bar none. SELECT is concerned simply with retrieving data stored in the database.

- *Data Manipulation Language (DML):* DML is considered a sublanguage of SQL. It is concerned with manipulating data stored in the database. DML consists of four commonly used statements: INSERT, UPDATE, DELETE, and MERGE. DML also encompasses cursor-related statements. These statements allow you to manipulate the contents of tables and persist the changes to the database.

- *Data Definition Language (DDL):* DDL is another sublanguage of SQL. The primary purpose of DDL is to create, modify, and remove tables and other objects from the database. DDL consists of variations of the CREATE, ALTER, and DROP statements.

- *Data Control Language (DCL):* DCL is yet another SQL sublanguage. DCL's goal is to allow you to restrict access to tables and database objects. DCL is composed of various GRANT and REVOKE statements that allow or deny users access to database objects.

- *Transactional Control Language (TCL):* TCL is the SQL sublanguage that is concerned with initiating and committing or rolling back *transactions*. A transaction is basically an atomic unit of work performed by the server. The BEGIN TRANSACTION, COMMIT, and ROLLBACK statements comprise TCL.

Databases

A SQL Server *instance*—an individual installation of SQL Server with its own ports, logins, and databases—can manage multiple *system databases* and *user databases*. SQL Server has five system databases, as follows:

- resource: The resource database is a read-only system database that contains all system objects. You will not see the resource database in the SQL Server Management Studio (SSMS) Object Explorer window, but the system objects persisted in the resource database will logically appear in every database on the server.

- `master`: The `master` database is a server-wide repository for configuration and status information. The `master` database maintains instance-wide metadata about SQL Server as well as information about all databases installed on the current instance. It is wise to avoid modifying or even accessing the `master` database directly in most cases. An entire server can be brought to its knees if the `master` database is corrupted. If you need to access the server configuration and status information, use catalog views instead.

- `model`: The `model` database is used as the template from which newly created databases are essentially cloned. Normally, you won't want to change this database in production settings, unless you have a very specific purpose in mind and are extremely knowledgeable about the potential implications of changing the `model` database.

- `msdb`: The `msdb` database stores system settings and configuration information for various support services, such as SQL Agent and Database Mail. Normally, you will use the supplied stored procedures and views to modify and access this data, rather than modifying it directly.

- `tempdb`: The `tempdb` database is the main working area for SQL Server. When SQL Server needs to store intermediate results of queries, for instance, they are written to `tempdb`. Also, when you create temporary tables, they are actually created within `tempdb`. The `tempdb` database is reconstructed from scratch every time you restart SQL Server.

Microsoft recommends that you use the system-provided stored procedures and catalog views to modify system objects and system metadata, and let SQL Server manage the system databases. You should avoid modifying the contents and structure of the system databases directly through ad hoc T-SQL. Only modify the system objects and metadata by executing the system stored procedures and functions.

User databases are created by database administrators (DBAs) and developers on the server. These types of databases are so called because they contain user data. The AdventureWorks2012 sample database is one example of a user database.

Transaction Logs

Every SQL Server database has its own associated transaction log. The transaction log provides recoverability in the event of failure and ensures the atomicity of transactions. The transaction log accumulates all changes to the database so that database integrity can be maintained in the event of an error or other problem. Because of this arrangement, all SQL Server databases consist of at least two files: a database file with an `.mdf` extension and a transaction log with an `.ldf` extension.

THE ACID TEST

SQL folks, and IT professionals in general, love their acronyms. A common acronym in the SQL world is ACID, which stands for "atomicity, consistency, isolation, durability." These four words form a set of properties that database systems should implement to guarantee reliability of data storage, processing, and manipulation.

- *Atomicity:* All data changes should be transactional in nature. That is, data changes should follow an all-or-nothing pattern. The classic example is a double-entry bookkeeping system in which every debit has an associated credit. Recording a debit-and-credit double entry in the database is considered one "transaction," or a single unit of work. You cannot record a debit without recording its associated credit, and vice versa. Atomicity ensures that either the entire transaction is performed or none of it is.

- *Consistency:* Only data that is consistent with the rules set up in the database will be stored. Data types and constraints can help enforce consistency within the database. For instance, you cannot insert the name Meghan in an `int` column. Consistency also applies when dealing with data updates. If two users update the same row of a table at the same time, an inconsistency could occur if one update is only partially complete when the second update begins. The concept of isolation, described in the following bullet point, is designed to deal with this situation.

- *Isolation:* Multiple simultaneous updates to the same data should not interfere with one another. SQL Server includes several locking mechanisms and isolation levels to ensure that two users cannot modify the exact same data at the exact same time, which could put the data in an inconsistent state. Isolation also prevents you from even reading uncommitted data by default.

- *Durability:* Data that passes all the previous tests is committed to the database. The concept of durability ensures that committed data is not lost. The transaction log and data backup and recovery features help to ensure durability.

The transaction log is one of the main tools SQL Server uses to enforce the ACID concept when storing and manipulating data.

Schemas

SQL Server 2012 supports database schemas, which are logical groupings by the owner of database objects. The AdventureWorks2012 sample database, for instance, contains several schemas, such as HumanResources, Person, and Production. These schemas are used to group tables, stored procedures, views, and user-defined functions (UDFs) for management and security purposes.

■ **Tip** When you create new database objects, like tables, and don't specify a schema, they are automatically created in the default schema. The default schema is normally dbo, but DBAs may assign different default schemas to different users. Because of this, it's always best to specify the schema name explicitly when creating database objects.

Tables

SQL Server supports several types of objects that can be created within a database. SQL stores and manages data in its primary data structures, tables. A table consists of rows and columns, with data stored at the intersections of these rows and columns. As an example, the AdventureWorks HumanResources.Department table is shown in Figure 1-2.

	DepartmentID	Name	GroupName	ModifiedDate
1	1	Engineering	Research and Development	2002-06-01 00:00:00.000
2	2	Tool Design	Research and Development	2002-06-01 00:00:00.000
3	3	Sales	Sales and Marketing	2002-06-01 00:00:00.000
4	4	Marketing	Sales and Marketing	2002-06-01 00:00:00.000
5	5	Purchasing	Inventory Management	2002-06-01 00:00:00.000
6	6	Research and Development	Research and Development	2002-06-01 00:00:00.000
7	7	Production	Manufacturing	2002-06-01 00:00:00.000
8	8	Production Control	Manufacturing	2002-06-01 00:00:00.000
9	9	Human Resources	Executive General and Administration	2002-06-01 00:00:00.000
10	10	Finance	Executive General and Administration	2002-06-01 00:00:00.000
11	11	Information Services	Executive General and Administration	2002-06-01 00:00:00.000
12	12	Document Control	Quality Assurance	2002-06-01 00:00:00.000
13	13	Quality Assurance	Quality Assurance	2002-06-01 00:00:00.000
14	14	Facilities and Maintenance	Executive General and Administration	2002-06-01 00:00:00.000
15	15	Shipping and Receiving	Inventory Management	2002-06-01 00:00:00.000
16	16	Executive	Executive General and Administration	2002-06-01 00:00:00.000

Figure 1-2. Representation of the HumanResources.Department Table

In the table, each row is associated with columns and each column has certain restrictions placed on its content. These restrictions comprise the *data domain*. The data domain defines all the values a column can contain. At the lowest level, the data domain is based on the data type of the column. For instance, a smallint column can contain any integer values between −32,768 and +32,767.

The data domain of a column can be further constrained through the use of check constraints, triggers, and foreign key constraints. Check constraints provide a means of automatically checking that the value of a column is within a certain range or equal to a certain value whenever a row is inserted or updated. *Triggers* can provide similar functionality to check constraints. *Foreign key constraints* allow you to declare a relationship between the columns of one table and the columns of another table. You can use foreign key constraints to restrict the data domain of a column to only include those values that appear in a designated column of another table.

RESTRICTING THE DATA DOMAIN: A COMPARISON

In this section, we have given a brief overview of three methods of constraining the data domain for a column. Each method restricts the values that can be contained in the column. Here's a quick comparison of the three methods:

- Foreign key constraints allow SQL Server to perform an automatic check against another table to ensure that the values in a given column exist in the referenced table. If the value you are trying to update or insert in a table does not exist in the referenced table, an error is raised. The foreign key constraint provides a flexible means of altering the data domain, since adding or removing values from the referenced table automatically changes the data domain for the referencing table. Also, foreign key constraints offer an additional feature known as cascading *declarative referential integrity (DRI)*, which automatically updates or deletes rows from a referencing table if an associated row is removed from the referenced table.

- Check constraints provide a simple, efficient, and effective tool for ensuring that the values being inserted or updated in a column are within a given range or a member of a given set of values. Check constraints, however, are not as flexible as foreign key constraints and triggers since the data domain is normally defined using hard-coded constant values.

- Triggers are stored procedures attached to insert, update, or delete events on a table. Triggers can also be set on changes to an object's structure. Both DDL and DML triggers provide a flexible solution for constraining data, but they may require more maintenance than the other options since they are essentially a specialized form of stored procedure. Unless they are extremely well designed, triggers have the potential to be much less efficient than the other methods as well. Triggers to constrain the data domain are generally avoided in modern databases in favor of the other methods. The exception to this is when you are trying to enforce a foreign key constraint across databases, since SQL Server doesn't support cross-database foreign key constraints.

Which method you use to constrain the data domain of your column(s) needs to be determined by your project-specific requirements on a case-by-case basis.

Views

A view is like a virtual table—the data it exposes is not stored in the view object itself. Views are composed of SQL queries that reference tables and other views, but they are referenced just like tables in queries. Views serve two major purposes in SQL Server: they can be used to hide the complexity of queries, and they can be used as a security device to limit the rows and columns of a table that a user can query. Views are expanded, meaning that their logic is incorporated into the execution plan for queries when you use them in queries and DML statements. SQL Server may not be able to use indexes on the base tables when the view is expanded, resulting in less-than-optimal performance when querying views in some situations.

To overcome the query performance issues with views, SQL Server also has the ability to create a special type of view known as an *indexed* view. An indexed view is a view that SQL Server persists to the database like a table. When you create an indexed view, SQL Server allocates storage for it and allows you to query it like any other table. There are, however, restrictions on inserting, updating, and deleting from an indexed view. For instance, you cannot perform data modifications on an indexed view if more than one of the view's base tables will be affected. You also cannot perform data modifications on an indexed view if the view contains aggregate functions or a DISTINCT clause.

You can also create indexes on an indexed view to improve query performance. The downside to an indexed view is increased overhead when you modify data in the view's base tables, since the view must be updated as well.

Indexes

Indexes are SQL Server's mechanisms for optimizing access to data. SQL Server 2012 supports several types of indexes, including the following:

- *Clustered index:* A clustered index is limited to one per table. This type of index defines the ordering of the rows in the table. A clustered index is physically implemented using a b-tree structure with the data stored in the leaf levels of the tree. Clustered indexes order the data in a table in much the same way that a phone book is ordered by last name. A table with a clustered index is referred to as a *clustered table,* while a table with no clustered index is referred to as a *heap.*

- *Nonclustered index:* A nonclustered index is also a b-tree index managed by SQL Server. In a nonclustered index, *index rows* are included in the leaf levels of the b-tree. Because of this, nonclustered indexes have no effect on the ordering of rows in a table. The index rows in the leaf levels of a nonclustered index consist of the following:

  - A nonclustered key value

- A row locator, which is the clustered index key on a table with a clustered index, or a SQL-generated row ID for a heap

- Nonkey columns, which are added via the INCLUDE clause of the CREATE INDEX statement

- *Columnstore index:* A columnstore index is a special index used for very large tables (>100 million rows) and is mostly applicable to large data warehouse implementations. A columnstore index creates an index on the column as opposed to the row and although they allow for efficient and extremely fast retrieval of large data sets. Tables with columnstore indexes are required to be readonly.

A nonclustered index is analogous to an index in the back of a book.

- *XML index:* SQL Server supports special indexes designed to help efficiently query XML data. See Chapter 10 for more information.

- *Spatial index:* A spatial index is an interesting new indexing structure to support efficient querying of the new geometry and geography data types. See Chapter 2 for more information.

- *Full-text index:* A full-text index (FTI) is a special index designed to efficiently perform full-text searches of data and documents.

You can also include nonkey columns in your nonclustered indexes with the INCLUDE clause of the CREATE INDEX statement. The included columns give you the ability to work around SQL Server's index size limitations.

Stored Procedures

SQL Server supports the installation of server-side T-SQL code modules via *stored procedures (SPs)*. It's very common to use SPs as a sort of intermediate layer or custom server-side *application programming interface (API)* that sits between user applications and tables in the database. Stored procedures that are specifically designed to perform queries and DML statements against the tables in a database are commonly referred to as *CRUD (create, read, update, delete)* procedures.

User-Defined Functions

User-defined functions (UDFs) can perform queries and calculations, and return either scalar values or tabular result sets. UDFs have certain restrictions placed on them. For instance, they cannot utilize certain nondeterministic system functions, nor can they perform DML or DDL statements, so they cannot make modifications to the database structure or content. They cannot perform dynamic SQL queries or change the state of the database (i.e., cause side effects).

SQL CLR Assemblies

SQL Server 2012 supports access to Microsoft .NET functionality via the SQL Common Language Runtime (SQL CLR). To access this functionality, you must register compiled .NET SQL CLR assemblies with the server. The assembly exposes its functionality through class methods, which can be accessed via SQL CLR functions, procedures, triggers, user-defined types, and user-defined aggregates. SQL CLR assemblies replace the deprecated SQL Server extended stored procedure (XP) functionality available in prior releases.

■ **Tip**　Avoid using XPs on SQL Server 2012. The same functionality provided by XPs can be provided by SQL CLR code. The SQL CLR model is more robust and secure than the XP model. Also keep in mind that the XP library is deprecated and XP functionality may be completely removed in a future version of SQL Server.

Elements of Style

Now that we've given a broad overview of the basics of SQL Server, we'll take a look at some recommended development tips to help with code maintenance. Selecting a particular style and using it consistently helps immensely with both debugging and future maintenance. The following sections contain some general recommendations to make your T-SQL code easy to read, debug, and maintain.

Whitespace

SQL Server ignores extra whitespace between keywords and identifiers in SQL queries and statements. A single statement or query may include extra spaces and tab characters, and can even extend across several lines. You can use this knowledge to great advantage. Consider Listing 1-3, which is adapted from the HumanResources.vEmployee view in the AdventureWorks2012 database.

Listing 1-3. The HumanResources.vEmployee View from the AdventureWorks2012 Database

```
SELECT e.BusinessEntityID, p.Title, p.FirstName, p.MiddleName, p.LastName, p.Suffix, e.JobTitle,
pp.PhoneNumber, pnt.Name AS PhoneNumberType, ea.EmailAddress,

p.EmailPromotion, a.AddressLine1, a.AddressLine2, a.City, sp.Name AS StateProvinceName,
a.PostalCode, cr.Name AS CountryRegionName, p.AdditionalContactInfo

FROM HumanResources.Employee AS e INNER JOIN Person.Person AS p ON p.BusinessEntityID =
e.BusinessEntityID INNER JOIN Person.BusinessEntityAddress AS bea ON bea.BusinessEntityID =
e.BusinessEntityID INNER JOIN Person.Address AS a ON a.AddressID = bea.AddressID INNER JOIN
Person.StateProvince AS sp ON sp.StateProvinceID = a.StateProvinceID INNER JOIN
Person.CountryRegion AS cr ON cr.CountryRegionCode = sp.CountryRegionCode LEFT OUTER JOIN
Person.PersonPhone AS pp ON pp.BusinessEntityID = p.BusinessEntityID LEFT OUTER JOIN
Person.PhoneNumberType AS pnt ON pp.PhoneNumberTypeID = pnt.PhoneNumberTypeID LEFT OUTER JOIN
Person.EmailAddress AS ea ON p.BusinessEntityID = ea.BusinessEntityID
```

This query will run and return the correct result, but it's very hard to read. You can use whitespace and table aliases to generate a version that is much easier on the eyes, as demonstrated in Listing 1-4.

Listing 1-4. The HumanResources.vEmployee View Reformatted for Readability

```
SELECT
  e.BusinessEntityID,
  p.Title,
  p.FirstName,
  p.MiddleName,
  p.LastName,
  p.Suffix,
  e.JobTitle,
  pp.PhoneNumber,
  pnt.Name AS PhoneNumberType,
  ea.EmailAddress,
  p.EmailPromotion,
  a.AddressLine1,
  a.AddressLine2,
  a.City,
```

```
  sp.Name AS StateProvinceName,
  a.PostalCode,
  cr.Name AS CountryRegionName,
  p.AdditionalContactInfo
FROM HumanResources.Employee AS e INNER JOIN Person.Person AS p
  ON p.BusinessEntityID = e.BusinessEntityID
INNER JOIN Person.BusinessEntityAddress AS bea
  ON bea.BusinessEntityID = e.BusinessEntityID
INNER JOIN Person.Address AS a
  ON a.AddressID = bea.AddressID
INNER JOIN Person.StateProvince AS sp
  ON sp.StateProvinceID = a.StateProvinceID
INNER JOIN Person.CountryRegion AS cr
  ON cr.CountryRegionCode = sp.CountryRegionCode
LEFT OUTER JOIN Person.PersonPhone AS pp
  ON pp.BusinessEntityID = p.BusinessEntityID
LEFT OUTER JOIN Person.PhoneNumberType AS pnt
  ON pp.PhoneNumberTypeID = pnt.PhoneNumberTypeID
LEFT OUTER JOIN Person.EmailAddress AS ea
  ON p.BusinessEntityID = ea.BusinessEntityID;
```

Notice that the ON keywords are indented, associating them visually with the INNER JOIN operators directly before them in the listing. The column names on the lines directly after the SELECT keyword are also indented, associating them visually with the SELECT keyword. This particular style is useful in helping visually break up a query into sections. The personal style you decide upon might differ from this one, but once you have decided on a standard indentation style, be sure to apply it consistently throughout your code.

Code that is easy to read is easier to debug and maintain. The code in Listing 1-4 uses table aliases, plenty of whitespace, and the semicolon (;) terminator marking the end of the SELECT statement to make the code more readable. Required in some instances, it is a good idea to get into the habit of using the terminating semicolon in your SQL queries.

■ **Tip** Semicolons are required terminators for some statements in SQL Server 2012. Instead of trying to remember all the special cases where they are or aren't required, it is a good idea to use the semicolon statement terminator throughout your T-SQL code. You will notice the use of semicolon terminators in all the examples in this book.

Naming Conventions

SQL Server allows you to name your database objects (tables, views, procedures, and so on) using just about any combination of up to 128 characters (116 characters for local temporary table names), as long as you enclose them in single quotes ('') or brackets ([ ]). Just because you *can*, however, doesn't necessarily mean you *should*. Many of the allowed characters are hard to differentiate from other similar-looking characters, and some might not port well to other platforms. The following suggestions will help you avoid potential problems:

- Use alphabetic characters (A–Z, a–z, and Unicode Standard 3.2 letters) for the first character of your identifiers. The obvious exceptions are SQL Server variable names that start with the at sign (@), temporary tables and procedures that start with the number sign (#), and global temporary tables and procedures that begin with a double number sign (##).

- Many built-in T-SQL functions and system variables have names that begin with a double at sign (@@), such as @@ERROR and @@IDENTITY. To avoid confusion and possible conflicts, don't use a leading double at sign to name your identifiers.

- Restrict the remaining characters in your identifiers to alphabetic characters (A–Z, a–z, and Unicode Standard 3.2 letters), numeric digits (0–9), and the underscore character (_). The dollar sign ($) character, while allowed, is not advisable.

- Avoid embedded spaces, punctuation marks (other than the underscore character), and other special characters in your identifiers.

- Avoid using SQL Server 2012 reserved keywords as identifiers. You can find the listing here: http://msdn.microsoft.com/en-us/library/ms189822.aspx.

- Limit the length of your identifiers. Thirty-two characters or less is a reasonable limit while not being overly restrictive. Much more than that becomes cumbersome to type and can hurt your code readability.

Finally, to make your code more readable, select a capitalization style for your identifiers and code, and use it consistently. Our preference is to fully capitalize T-SQL keywords and use mixed-case and underscore characters to visually "break up" identifiers into easily readable words. Using all capital characters or inconsistently applying mixed case to code and identifiers can make your code illegible and hard to maintain. Consider the example query in Listing 1-5.

Listing 1-5. All-Capital SELECT Query

```
SELECT P.BUSINESSENTITYID, P.FIRSTNAME, P.LASTNAME, S.SALESYTD
FROM PERSON.PERSON P INNER JOIN SALES.SALESPERSON SP
ON P.BUSINESSENTITYID = SP.BUSINESSENTITYID;
```

The all-capital version is difficult to read. It's hard to tell the SQL keywords from the column and table names at a glance. Compound words for column and table names are not easily identified. Basically your eyes have to work a lot harder to read this query than they should, which makes otherwise simple maintenance tasks more difficult. Reformatting the code and identifiers makes this query much easier on the eyes, as Listing 1-6 demonstrates.

Listing 1-6. Reformatted, Easy-on-the-Eyes Query

```
SELECT
    p.BusinessEntityID,
    p.FirstName,
    p.LastName,
    sp.SalesYTD
FROM Person.Person p INNER JOIN Sales.SalesPerson sp
    ON p.BusinessEntityID = sp.BusinessEntityID;
```

The use of all capitals for the keywords in the second version makes them stand out from the mixed-case table and column names. Likewise, the mixed-case column and table names make the compound word names easy to recognize. The net effect is that the code is easier to read, which makes it easier to debug and maintain. Consistent use of good formatting habits helps keep trivial changes trivial and makes complex changes easier.

One Entry, One Exit

When writing SPs and UDFs, its good programming practice to use the "one entry, one exit" rule. SPs and UDFs should have a single entry point and a single exit point (RETURN statement). The following SP retrieves the ContactTypeID number from the AdventureWorks2012 Person.ContactType table for the ContactType name passed into it. If no ContactType exists with the name passed in, a new one is created, and the newly created ContactTypeID is passed back. Listing 1-7 demonstrates this simple procedure with one entry point and several exit points.

Listing 1-7. Stored Procedure Example with One Entry and Multiple Exits

```
CREATE PROCEDURE dbo.GetOrAdd_ContactType
(
    @Name NVARCHAR(50),
    @ContactTypeID INT OUTPUT
)
AS
    DECLARE @Err_Code AS INT;

    SELECT @Err_Code = 0;

    SELECT @ContactTypeID = ContactTypeID
    FROM Person.ContactType
    WHERE [Name] = @Name;

    IF @ContactTypeID IS NOT NULL
    RETURN;      -- Exit 1: if the ContactType exists

    INSERT
    INTO Person.ContactType ([Name], ModifiedDate)
    SELECT @Name, CURRENT_TIMESTAMP;

    SELECT @Err_Code = 'error';
    IF @Err_Code <> 0
        RETURN @Err_Code;   -- Exit 2: if there is an error on INSERT

    SELECT @ContactTypeID = SCOPE_IDENTITY();

    RETURN @Err_Code;       -- Exit 3: after successful INSERT
GO
```

This code has one entry point, but three possible exit points. Figure 1-3 shows a simple flowchart for the paths this code can take.

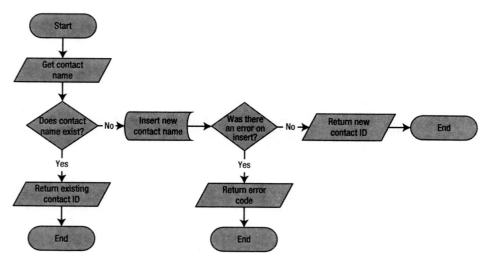

Figure 1-3. *Flowchart for Example with One Entry and Multiple Exits*

As you can imagine, maintaining code such as in Listing 1-7 becomes more difficult because the flow of the code has so many possible exit points, each of which must be accounted for when you make modifications to the SP. Listing 1-8 updates Listing 1-7 to give it a single entry point and a single exit point, making the logic easier to follow:

Listing 1-8. Stored Procedure with One Entry and One Exit

```
CREATE    PROCEDURE    dbo.GetOrAdd_ContactType
(
        @Name NVARCHAR(50),
        @ContactTypeID INT OUTPUT
)
AS
        DECLARE @Err_Code AS INT;
        SELECT @Err_Code = 0;

        SELECT @ContactTypeID = ContactTypeID
        FROM Person.ContactType
        WHERE [Name] = @Name;

        IF  @ContactTypeID  IS  NULL
        BEGIN
        INSERT
        INTO  Person.ContactType  ([Name],  ModifiedDate)
        SELECT  @Name,  CURRENT_TIMESTAMP;
        SELECT @Err_Code = @@error;
        IF  @Err_Code  =  0    -- If  there's an error, skip next
        SELECT  @ContactTypeID  =  SCOPE_IDENTITY();
        END
        RETURN @Err_Code;   -- Single exit point
GO
```

Figure 1-4 shows the modified flowchart for this new version of the SP.

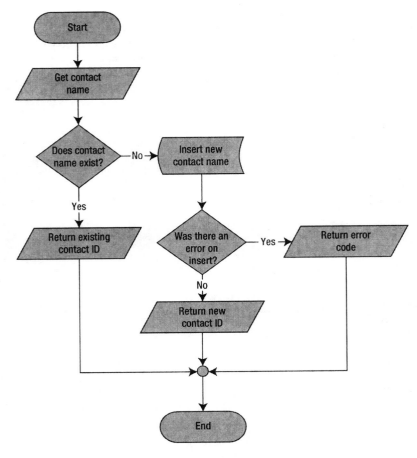

Figure 1-4. *Flowchart for Example with One Entry and One Exit*

The one entry and one exit model makes the logic easier to follow, which in turn makes the code easier to manage. This rule also applies to looping structures, which you implement via the WHILE statement in T-SQL. Avoid using the WHILE loop's CONTINUE and BREAK statements and the GOTO statement; these statements lead to old-fashioned, difficult-to-maintain spaghetti code.

Defensive Coding

Defensive coding involves anticipating problems before they occur and mitigating them through good coding practices. The first and foremost lesson of defensive coding is to always check user input. Once you open your system up to users, expect them to do everything in their power to try to break your system. For instance, if you ask users to enter a number between 1 and 10, expect that they'll ignore your directions and key in ; DROP TABLE dbo.syscomments; -- at the first available opportunity. Defensive coding practices dictate that you should check and scrub external inputs. Don't blindly trust anything that comes from an external source.

Another aspect of defensive coding is a clear delineation between exceptions and run-of-the-mill issues. The key is that exceptions are, well, exceptional in nature. Ideally, exceptions should be caused by errors that you can't account for or couldn't reasonably anticipate, like a lost network connection or physical corruption of your application or data storage. Errors that can be reasonably expected, like data entry errors, should be captured before they are raised to the level of exceptions. Keep in mind that exceptions are often resource intensive, expensive operations. If you can avoid an exception by anticipating a particular problem, your application will benefit in both performance and control. In fact, SQL Server 2012 offers a valuable new error handling feature called THROW. The TRY/CATCH/THROW statemetns will be discussed in more detail in Chapter 17.

The SELECT * Statement

Consider the SELECT * style of querying. In a SELECT clause, the asterisk (*) is a shorthand way of specifying that all columns in a table should be returned. Although SELECT * is a handy tool for ad hoc querying of tables during development and debugging, you should normally not use it in a production system. One reason to avoid this method of querying is to minimize the amount of data retrieved with each call. SELECT * retrieves all columns, whether or not they are needed by the higher-level applications. For queries that return a large number of rows, even one or two extraneous columns can waste a lot of resources.

Also, if the underlying table or view is altered, columns might be added to or removed from the returned result set. This can cause errors that are hard to locate and fix. By specifying the column names, your front-end application can be assured that only the required columns are returned by a query, and that errors caused by missing columns will be easier to locate.

As with most things, there are always exceptions—for example, if you are using the FOR XML AUTO clause to generate XML based on the structure and content of your relational data. In this case, SELECT * can be quite useful, since you are relying on FOR XML to automatically generate the node names based on the table and column names in the source tables.

▓ **Tip** SELECT * should be avoided but if you do need to use it always try to limit the data set being returned. One way of doing so is to make full use of the T-SQL TOP command and restrict the number of records returned. In practice though you should never write SELECT * in your code—even for small tables. Small tables today could be large tables tomorrow.

Variable Initialization

When you create SPs, UDFs, or any script that uses T-SQL user variables, you should initialize those variables before the first use. Unlike some other programming languages that guarantee that newly declared variables will be initialized to 0 or an empty string (depending on their data types), T-SQL guarantees only that newly declared variables will be initialized to NULL. Consider the code snippet shown in Listing 1-9.

Listing 1-9. Sample Code Using an Uninitialized Variable

```
DECLARE @i INT; SELECT @i=@i+5; SELECT @i;
```

The result is NULL, a shock if you were expecting 5. Expecting SQL Server to initialize numeric variables to 0 (like @i in the previous example) or an empty string will result in bugs that can be extremely difficult to locate in your T-SQL code. To avoid these problems, always explicitly initialize your variables after declaration, as demonstrated in Listing 1-10.

Listing 1-10. Sample Code Using an Initialized Variable

```
DECLARE @i INT=0; -- Changed this statement to initialize @i to 0
SELECT @i=@i+5;
SELECT @i;
```

Summary

This chapter has served as an introduction to T-SQL, including a brief history of SQL and a discussion of the declarative programming style. We started this chapter with a discussion of ISO SQL standard compatibility in SQL Server 2012 and the differences between imperative and declarative languages, of which SQL is the latter. We also introduced many of the basic components of SQL, including databases, tables, views, SPs, and other common database objects. Finally, we provided our personal recommendations for writing SQL code that is easy to debug and maintain. We subscribe to the "eat your own dog food" theory, and throughout this book we will faithfully follow the best practice recommendations that we've asked you to consider.

The next chapter provides an overview of the new and improved tools available out of the box for developers. Specifically Chapter 2 will discuss the SQLCMD text-based SQL client (originally a replacement for osql), SSMS, SQL Server 2012 Books Online (BOL), and some of the other available tools that make writing, editing, testing, and debugging easier and faster than ever.

EXERCISES

1. Describe the difference between an imperative language and a declarative language.

2. What does the acronym *ACID* stand for?

3. SQL Server 2012 supports five different types of indexes. What are they?

4. Name two of the restrictions on any type of SQL Server UDF.

5. [True/False] In SQL Server, newly declared variables are always assigned the default value **0** for numeric data types and an empty string for character data types.

CHAPTER 2

Tools of the Trade

SQL Server 2012 comes with a wide selection of tools and utilities to make development easier as enhancing productivity of the developers is one of the key areas of focus in SQL Server 2012. In this chapter, we will introduce some of the most important tools for SQL Server developers, including SQL Server Management Studio (SSMS) and the SQLCMD utility, SQL Server Data Tool add-ins to Microsoft Visual Studio, SQL Profiler, Database Tuning Advisor, Extended Events, and SQL Server 2012 Books Online (BOL). We will also introduce supporting tools like SQL Server Integration Services (SSIS), the Bulk Copy Program (BCP), and the AdventureWorks 2012 sample database, which we will use in examples throughout the book.

SQL Server Management Studio

Back in the heyday of SQL Server 2000, it was common for developers to fire up the Enterprise Manager (EM) and Query Editor GUI database tools in rapid succession every time they sat down to write code. Historically, developer and DBA roles in the DBMS have been highly separated, and with good reason. DBAs have historically brought hardware and software administration and tuning skills, database design optimization experience, and healthy doses of skepticism and security to the table. On the other hand, developers have focused on coding skills, problem solving, system optimization, and debugging. This separation of powers works very well in production systems, but in development environments developers are often responsible for their own database design and management. Sometimes developers are put in charge of their own development server local security.

SQL Server 2000 EM was originally designed as a DBA tool, providing access to the GUI (graphical user interface) administration interface, including security administration, database object creation and management, and server management functionality. QUERY EDITOR was designed as a developer tool, the primary GUI tool for the creation, testing, and tuning of queries.

SQL Server 2012 continues the tradition begun with SQL Server 2005 by combining the functionality of both of these GUI tools into a single GUI interface known as SSMS. This makes perfect sense in supporting real-world SQL Server development, where the roles of DBA and developer are often intermingled in development environments.

Many SQL Server developers prefer the GUI administration and development tools to the text-based query tool SQLCMD to build their databases, and on this front SSMS doesn't disappoint. SSMS offers several features that make development and administration easier, including the following:

- The integrated, functional Object Explorer, which provides the ability to easily view all the objects in the server and manage them in a tree structure. The added filter functionality helps the users narrow down the objects that they want to work with.

- The color coding of scripts, making editing and debugging easier.

- Enhanced keyboard shortcuts that have made searching faster and easier. Additionally users have the ability to map predefined keyboard shortcuts to stored procedures that are used most often.

- The SQL Server Management Studio supports two keyboard shortcut schemes, keyboard shortcuts from SQL Server 2008 R2 and Microsoft Visual Studio 2010.

- Usability enhancements such as the ability to zoom text in the query editor by holding the ctrl key and scroll to zoom in and out. Users can now drag and drop the tabs–true multi-monitor support as well.

- Breakpoint validation prevents setting a breakpoint at invalid locations.

- The T-SQL code snippets are templates that can be used as starting point to build T-SQL statement in scripts and batches.

- The T-SQL debugger Watch and Quick watch windows support watching T-SQL expressions now.

- The graphical query execution plans are the bread and butter of the query optimization process. They greatly simplify the process of optimizing complex queries, quickly exposing potential bottlenecks in your code.

- The project management and code version control integration have been introduced, including integration with Team Foundation Server (TFS) and Visual SourceSafe version control systems.

- The SQLCMD mode allows you to execute SQL scripts using SQLCMD, taking advantage of SQLCMD's additional script capabilities like scripting variables and support for AlwaysON feature.

SSMS also includes database and server management features, but we will limit the discussion of this section to some of the most important developer-specific features.

IntelliSense

IntelliSense is a feature that was introduced in SQL Server 2008. When coding, you often need to look up the language elements such as functions, table names, or column names to complete the code. This feature allows the SQL Editor to help you to automatically complete the syntax input based on partial words. To enable IntelliSense, go to Tools -> Options -> Text Editor -> Transact-SQL -> IntelliSense. Figure 2-1 demonstrates how the IntelliSense feature suggests the language elements based on the first letter.

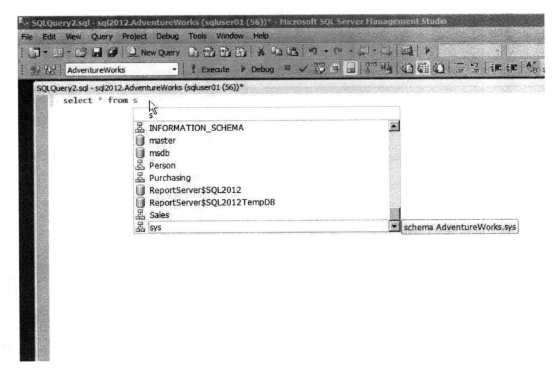

Figure 2-1. *Using IntelliSense Feature to Complete the SELECT Statement*

Code Snippets

Code snippets are not a new concept to the programming world. Visual Studio developers are very familiar with this feature, and since SQL Server 2012 is built on the Visual Studio 2010 shell, SQL inherits this functionality as well. During the development cycle, often the developer uses a set of T-SQL statements multiple times throughout the code being worked on. It would be much more efficient to access a block of code that contains the common code elements such as `create stored procedure` or `create function` to help the developer build on top of the code block. Code snippets are building blocks of code the developer can use as a starting point when building the T-SQL scripts. This feature can aid developer productivity while increasing reusability and standardization by enabling the development team to use existing templates or to create and customize a new template.

Code snippets help provide a better editing experience of T-SQL code, but additionally the snippet is a XML template that can be used for development to guarantee consistency across the development team. Code snippets can fall under any of these three categories–expansion snippets, surround snippets, and custom snippets. Expansion snippets list the common outline of T-SQL commands such as Select, Insert or Create Table statements. Surround Snippets allow constructs such as `while`, `if else` or `begin end` statements. Custom snippets allow custom templates that can be invoked via the snippet menu. You can create a custom snippet and add to the server by importing the snippet using the Code Snippet Manager. Once you add a custom snippet, the Custom Snippets category will appear in the Code Snippet Manager.

To access the code snippets, select the Code Snippets Manager from the Tools menu. Figure 2-2 shows the Code Snippet Manager interface which can be used to add, remove, or import the code snippets.

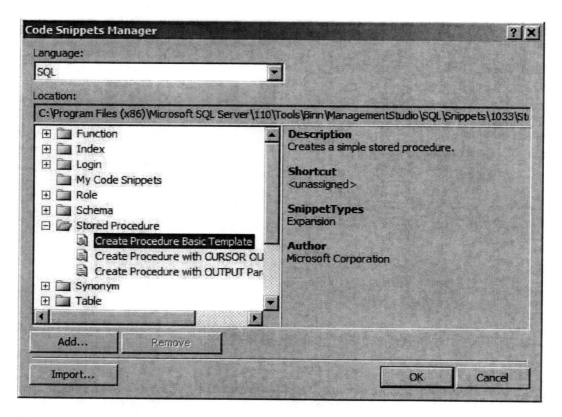

Figure 2-2. *Code Snippet Manager*

To insert a code snippet within the T-SQL Editor, right click and select Insert Snippet or use Ctrl K + X. Figure 2-3 demonstrates how to invoke the Insert and Surround command with snippets.

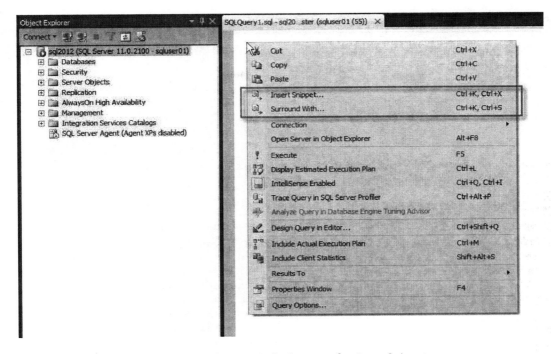

Figure 2-3. *Right Click in the T-SQL Editor to Invoke Command to Insert Snippets*

Once the insert snippet command is invoked, you have the option to choose the templates based on the SQL object types such as Index, Table, Function, Login, Role, Schema, Stored Procedures, Triggers, custom snippets, etc. Figure 2-4 shows how to insert a snippet.

Figure 2-4. *Insert Snippet*

Once the snippet is inserted into the T-SQL editor, the fields that need to be customized are highlighted, and you can use the tab key to navigate through the highlighted tokens. If you mouse over the highlighted token, you will notice that the tooltip provides additional information about the token. Figure 2-5 shows the CREATE TABLE snippet invoked in the T-SQL Editor along with the tooltip that lists the field description.

```
CREATE TABLE dbo.Sample Table
(
    column_1 int
    column_2 int NULL
);
```

Name of the table

Figure 2-5. *Adding CREATE TABLE Snippet with Tooltip Demonstrated*

Keyboard Shortcut Schemes

If we ask the question, "What is the shortcut key to execute queries?" to both an SQL user and Visual Studio user, we are bound to receive two different answers, as it is Ctrl + E for SQL users and Ctrl + Shift + E for Visual Studio users. Since most application developers are primarily Visual Studio users, it would be prudent to have an option to pick the keyboard shortcut schemes for the users who are familiar with the tool they have been using. Another advantage of defining and standardizing the keyboard shortcut schemes at the "team" level helps the team members to not execute wrong actions in the team environment. SQL Server 2012 offers two keyboard shortcut schemes: the default setting that is the SQL Server 2012 shortcut scheme, and the Visual Studio 2010 shortcut scheme. To change the keyboard shortcut settings, click Tools -> Options -> Environment -> Keyboard. Figure 2-6 shows the option to change the keyboard mapping scheme.

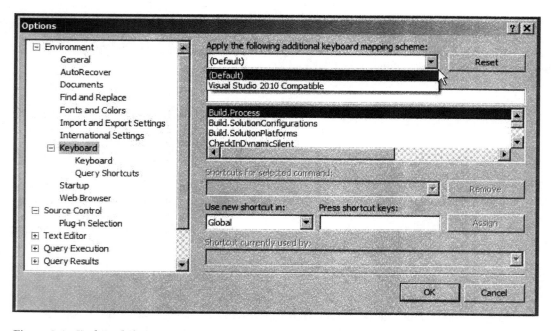

Figure 2-6. *Keyboard Shortcut Mapping Scheme*

T-SQL Debugging

SQL Server 2012 introduces enhancements to T-SQL debugging by providing the ability to set conditional breakpoints, meaning the breakpoint is invoked only if a certain expression is evaluated. T-SQL debugging also extends support for expression evaluation in watch and quick watch windows. You also have the capability to specify the hit counts, meaning you can specify how many times a breakpoint can be hit before it is invoked. Breakpoints can also be exported from one session to the other. The watch and quick watch window supports T-SQL expressions as well. Figure 2-7 shows the debug screen with output and quick watch windows.

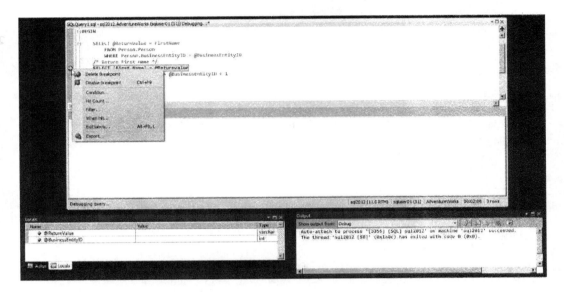

Figure 2-7. *T-SQL Debugging with the Locals and Output Windows*

A breakpoint can now be placed on individual statements within a batch, and they are context-sensitive. When a breakpoint is set, SQL validates the breakpoint location and immediately provides feedback if the breakpoint is set on an invalid location. For example, if the breakpoint is set on a comment, you will get a feedback that it is an invalid breakpoint, and if you try to set a breakpoint for one of the lines in a multi-line statement, it will add the breakpoints to all the lines.

A Datatip is another debugging enhancement that has been added in SQL Server 2012 to help you track the variables and expressions within the scope of execution better while debugging by providing ability to "pin" the Datatip to keep the Datatip visible (even when the debug session is restarted). When debugger is in the break mode, if you mouse over a T-SQL expression that is being evaluated, you will be able to see the current value that of that expression. Figure 2-8 shows the breakpoint and Datatip.

```
SQLQuery1.sql - sql2012.AdventureWorks (sqluser01 (51)) Debugging...*
  ⊟BEGIN

    ⊟    SELECT @ReturnValue = FirstName
            FROM Person.Person
            WHERE Person.BusinessEntityID = @BusinessEntityID
         /* Return First name */
         SELECT 'First Name' = @Returnvalue
         SELECT @BusinessEntityID = @b  @Returnvalue  🔍 ▾ Ken  ⊏⊐
    END
```

Figure 2-8. *Breakpoints and Datatip*

■ **Note**   The user login must be part of sysadmin role on the SQL Server instance in order to use the T-SQL debugging capabilities.

SSMS Editing Options

SSMS incorporates and improves on many of the developer features found in Query Editor. You can change the editing options discussed in this section via the Tools -> Options menu.

SSMS includes fully customizable script color coding. The default font has been changed to fixed font type Consolas, and the background color has now been changed to blue to match Visual Studio 2012. You can now customize the foreground and background colors, font face, size, and style for elements of T-SQL, XML, XSLT, and MDX scripts. Likewise, you can customize just about any feedback that SSMS generates, to suit your personal taste.

You can set other editing options such as word wrap, line number display, indentation, and tabs for different file types based on their associated file extensions. SSMS lets you configure your own keyboard shortcuts to execute common T-SQL statements or SPs.

By default, SSMS displays queries using a tabbed window environment. If you prefer the classic multiple-document interface (MDI) window style, you can switch the environment layout to suit your taste. You can also change the query results' output style from the default grid output to text or file output.

Context-Sensitive Help

Starting with SQL Server 2012, the product documentation is available online (MSDN/TechNet) to make sure the content is up-to-date. If you want to access the product documentation from your local computer, you have to download the help catalogs and set up help viewer. To configure the documentation, go to the Help menu and select Manage Help Settings. This will launch Help Library Manager; then scroll down to the SQL Server 2012 section and click Add next to the documentation you want to download. If the documentation is already available in your system, the Help Library Manager will update the catalog's index with the SQL Server documentation.

To access context-sensitive help, just highlight the T-SQL or other statement you want help with and press F1. You can add Help pages to your Help Favorites or go directly to MSDN. Figure 2-9 shows the result of calling context-sensitive help for the CREATE TABLE statement.

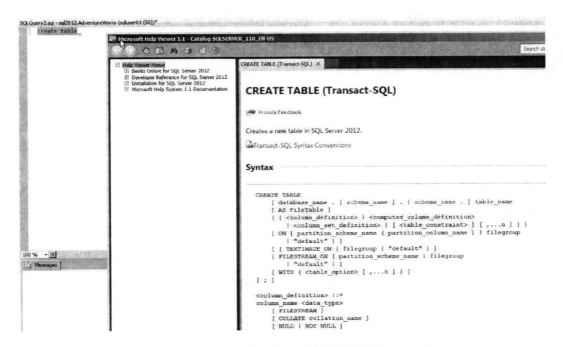

Figure 2-9. *Using SSMS Context-sensitive Help to Find CREATE TABLE Statement*

SSMS Help has several options that allow you to control help functionality and presentation. You can, for example, use the SSMS Integrated Help Viewer, which was shown in Figure 2-9, or you can use the External Online Help Viewer. The Help Options window of the Help Viewer settings allows you to set the preference to use online or offline help; it is shown in Figure 2-10.

Figure 2-10. *Using the Help Viewer Settings to Personalize SSMS Help*

Help Search rounds out the discussion of the help functionality in SSMS. The Help Search function automatically searches several online providers of SQL Server-related information for answers to your questions. Your searches are not restricted to SQL Server keywords or statements; you can search for anything at all, and the Help Search function will scour registered websites and communities for relevant answers. Figure 2-11 shows the results of using Help Search to find XQuery content and articles.

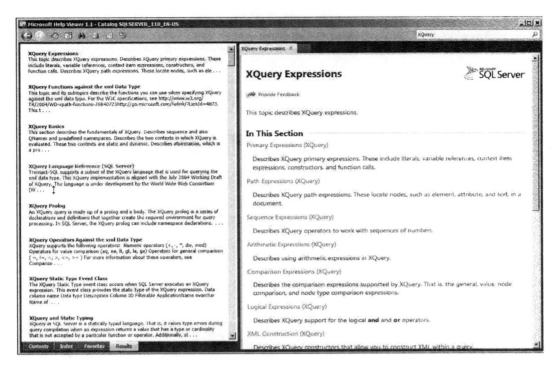

Figure 2-11. *Using the Help Search to Find Help on XQuery*

Graphical Query Execution Plans

SSMS offers graphical query execution plans similar to the plans available in Query Editor. The graphical query execution plan is an excellent tool for aiding and optimizing query performance. SSMS allows you to view two types of graphical query execution plans: estimated and actual. The *estimated* query execution plan is SQL Server's cost-based performance estimate of a query. The *actual* execution plan is virtually identical to the estimated execution plan, except that it shows additional information like actual row counts, number of rebinds, and number of rewinds when the query is run. Sometimes the actual execution plan may differ from the estimated execution plan and this may be due to changes in indexes or statistics or parallelism or in some cases the query may use temporary tables or DDL statements. These options are available via the Query menu. Figure 2-12 shows an estimated query execution plan in SSMS.

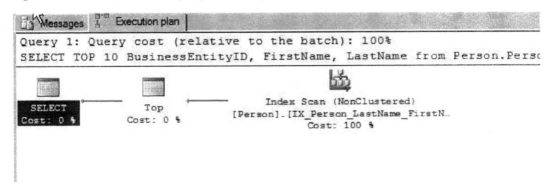

Figure 2-12. *Estimated Query Execution Plan for a Simple Query*

In addition, you can right-click the Execution Plan window and choose to save the XML version of the graphical query plan to a file. SSMS can open these XML query plan files (with the extension .sqlplan) and automatically show you the graphical version. In addition to this, the properties window of the SQL Server 2012 query plan now contains details regarding the MemoryGrantInfo, OptimizerHardwareDependentProperties, and warnings about the data that can affect plans. Figure 2-13 shows a sample properties window for the query plan. You also have an option to view the Execution Plan in XML format by right-clicking the Execution Plan window and choosing Show Execution Plan XML option.

Figure 2-13. *Sample Properties Window for a Simple Query*

Along with the execution plan you can also review the query statistics and network statistics in the Client Statistics tab. This is extremely useful for remotely troubleshooting performance problems with slow-running queries.

Project Management Features

SSMS incorporates new project management features familiar to Visual Studio developers. SSMS supports solution-based development. This allows you to create solutions that consist of projects, which in turn contain T-SQL scripts, XML files, connection information, and other files. By default, projects and solutions are saved in your My Documents\SQL Server Management Studio\Projects directory. Solution files have the extension .ssmssln, and project files are saved in an XML format with the .smssproj extension. SSMS incorporates a Solution Explorer window similar to Visual Studio's Solution Explorer, as shown in Figure 2-14. You can access the Solution Explorer through the View menu.

Figure 2-14. Viewing a Solution in the SSMS Solution Explorer

SSMS can take advantage of source control integration with Team Foundation Server (TFS) to help you manage versioning and deployments. To use SSMS's source control integration, you have to set the appropriate source control options in the Options menu. The Options window is shown in Figure 2-15.

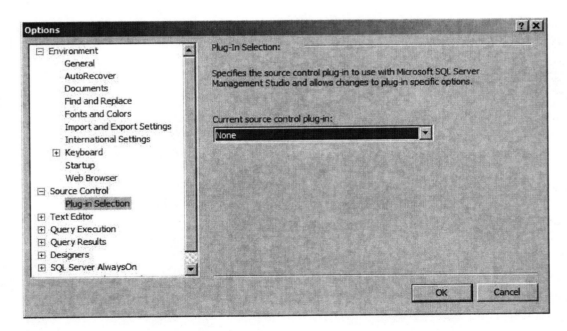

Figure 2-15. Viewing the Source Control Options

■ **Note** To use SSMS with TFS, you will need to download and install the appropriate Microsoft Source Code Control Interface (MSSCCI) provider from Microsoft. Go to www.microsoft.com/, search for "MSSCCI," and download either the Visual Studio Team System 2010 or 2012 version of the MSSCCI provider, depending on which version you're already using.

After you create a solution and add projects, connections, and SQL scripts, you can add your solution to TFS by right-clicking the solution in the Solution Explorer and selecting Add Solution to Source Control.

To check out items from source control, open a local copy and choose Check Out for Edit. You'll find options for checking out items from source control on the File ➤ Source Control menu. After checking out a solution from TFS, SSMS shows you the pending check-ins, letting you add comments to, or check in, individual files or projects.

The Object Explorer

The SSMS Object Explorer lets you view and manage database and server objects. In the Object Explorer, you can view tables, stored procedures (SPs), user-defined functions (UDFs), HTTP endpoints, users, logins, and just about every other database-specific or server-scoped object. Figure 2-16 shows the Object Explorer in the left-hand pane and the Object Explorer Details tab on the right.

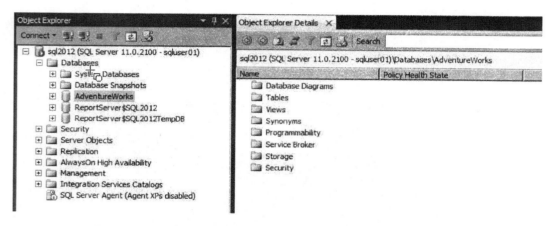

Figure 2-16. *Viewing the Object Explorer and the Object Explorer Details Tab*

Most objects in the Object Explorer and the Object Explorer Details tabs have object-specific pop-up context menus. Right-clicking any given object will bring up the menu. Figure 2-17 shows an example pop-up context menu for database tables.

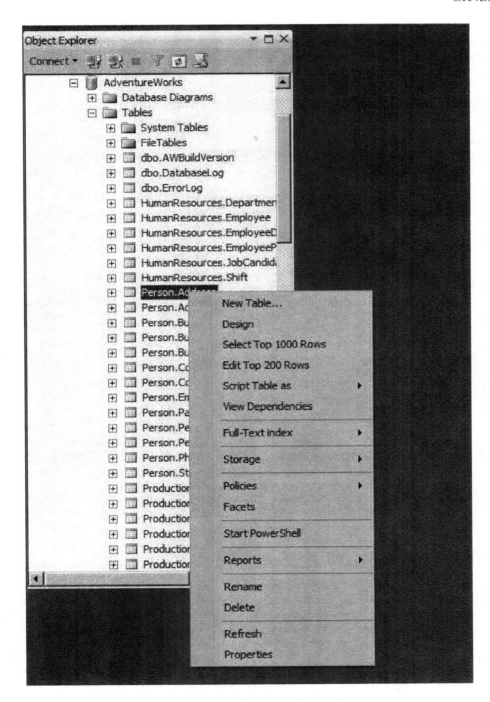

Figure 2-17. *Object Explorer Database Table Pop-up Context Menu*

Object Explorer in SQL Server 2012 allows developers to filter specific types of objects from all the database objects. To filter the objects, type the text with optional wild card characters in the Object Explorer Details window and hit enter. Optionally you can filter the objects using the Filter icon on the Object Explorer Details toolbar as well. Figure 2-18 shows an example of filtering objects named with "person."

Figure 2-18. *Object Explorer with Database Objects Filtered on Person*

The SQLCMD Utility

The SQLCMD utility was originally introduced in SQL Server 2005 as an updated replacement for the SQL 2000 osql command-line utility. You can use SQLCMD to execute batches of T-SQL statements from script files, individual queries or batches of queries in interactive mode, or individual queries from the command line. This utility uses SQL Server Native Client to execute the T-SQL statements.

■ **Note**   Appendix D provides a quick reference to SQLCMD command-line options, scripting variables, and commands. The descriptions in the appendix are based on extensive testing of SQLCMD and differ in some areas from the descriptions given in BOL.

SQLCMD offers support for a wide variety of command-line switches, making it a flexible utility for one-off batch or scheduled script execution. The following command demonstrates the use of some commonly used command-line options to connect to an SQL Server instance named SQL2012 and execute a T-SQL script in the AdventureWorks database. The command uses some of the more common command-line options, including -S to specify the server\instance name, -E to indicate Windows authentication, -d to set the database name, and -i to specify the name of a script file to execute. The command-line switches are all case sensitive, so -v is a different option from -V, for instance.

```
sqlcmd -S SQL2012 -E -d AdventureWorks -i "d:\scripts\ListPerson.sql"
```

SQLCMD allows you to use scripting variables that let you use a single script in multiple scenarios. Scripting variables provide a mechanism for customizing the behavior of T-SQL scripts without modifying the scripts' content. You can reference scripting variables that were previously set with the -v command-line switch, the SQLCMD :setvar command (discussed in the next section), or via Windows environment variables. You can also use any of the predefined SQLCMD scripting variables from within your scripts. The format to access any of these types of scripting variables from within your script is the same: $(variable_name). SQLCMD replaces your scripting variables with their respective values during script execution. Listing 2-1 shows some examples of scripting variables in action.

Listing 2-1. Using Scripting Variables in an SQLCMD Script

```
-- Windows environment variable
SELECT '$(PATH)';
```

```
-- SQLCMD scripting variable
SELECT '$(SQLCMDSERVER)';
-- Command-line scripting variable -v COLVAR = "Name" switch
SELECT $(COLVAR)
FROM Sys.Tables;
```

Because scripting variables are replaced in a script wholesale, some organizations might consider their use a security risk because of the possibility of SQL injection-style attacks. For security reasons, some might choose to use the -x command-line option which disables variable substitution to turn this feature off.

An example of an SQLCMD scripting variable is the predefined SOLCMDINI scripting variable, which specifies the SQLCMD startup script. The startup script is run every time SQLCMD is run. The startup script is useful for setting scripting variables with the :setvar command, setting initial T-SQL options such as QUOTED_IDENTIFIER or ANSI_PADDING, and performing any necessary database tasks before other scripts are run.

In addition to T-SQL statements, SQLCMD recognizes several commands specific to the application. SQLCMD commands allow you to perform tasks like listing servers and scripting variables, connecting to a server, and setting scripting variables, among others. Except for the batch terminator GO, all SQLCMD commands begin with a colon (:). SQLCMD can also be run interactively. To start an interactive mode session, run SQLCMD with any of the previous options that do not exit immediately on completion.

■ **Note**   SQLCMD options such as -o, -i, -Z, and -? exit immediately on completion. You cannot start an interactive SQLCMD session if you specify any of these command-line options.

During an interactive SQLCMD session, you can run T-SQL queries and commands from the SQLCMD prompt. The interactive screen looks similar to Figure 2-19.

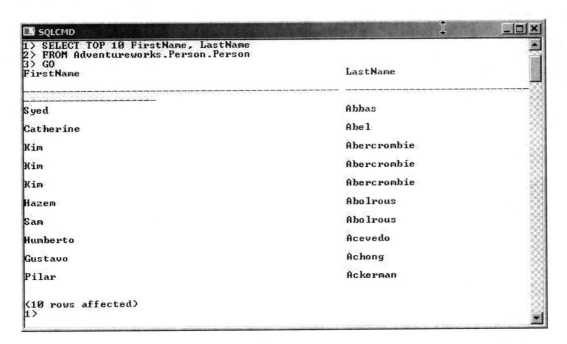

Figure 2-19. *Sample Query Run from the SQLCMD Interactive Prompt*

The SQLCMD prompt indicates the current line number of the batch (1>, 2>, etc.). You can enter T-SQL statements or SQLCMD commands at the prompt. T-SQL statements are stored in the statement cache as they are entered; SQLCMD commands are executed immediately. Once you have entered a complete batch of T-SQL statements, use the GO batch terminator to process all the statements in the cache.

SQLCMD has support for the new alwayson feature. You can use the switch –K to specify the Listener name.

There has been a behavior change for SQL CMD FOR XML as well. In SQL 2008, text data that contained a single quote was always replaced with an apostrophe. This behavior change has been addressed in SQL Server 2012. Additionally, legacy datetime values with no fractional seconds will not return three decimal digits; however, other date time data types are not affected.

SQL Server Data Tools

SQL Server 2012 ships with a new developer toolset named SQL Server Data Tools which serves as a replacement for Business Intelligence Development Studio (BIDS). In the highly competitive business world, the top 3 challenges today's developers face are collaboration, targeting different database platforms with the same codebase, and code stability. SQL Server Data Tools is designed to help with these top challenges. SQL Server Data Tools provides a platform to help you with providing database development experience declaratively. To help with this experience, the tool also enables you to add validations at design time and not at runtime. A common pitfall for developers is that errors are discovered during runtime which are not apparent and do not surface during design time, and SSDT serves to eliminate this issue. The developer is able to code, build, debug, package, and deploy the code without leaving the tool. The tool is also edition aware. For example, if you are developing code for SQL Azure, the tool knows that you cannot use sequence objects. This type of built-in intelligence within the tool is key to a faster effective development so that the developer does not discover the issue during runtime which would require re-architecting the application.

SSDT can be used for connected development and disconnected development in case of a team project. Figure 2-20 shows the New Project window, which is based on the familiar SSMS Object Explorer.

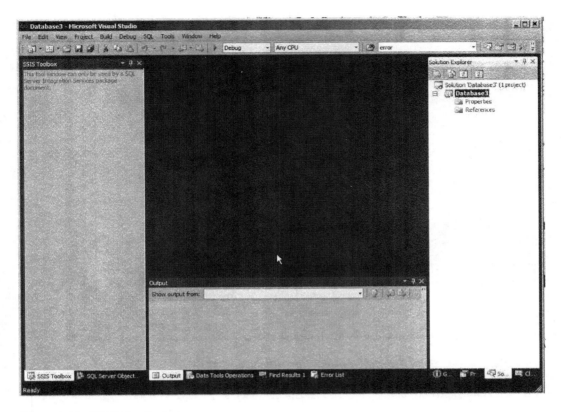

Figure 2-20. *SSDT New Project*

You will be able to create the object and buffer the object editing, and you can also see that the T-SQL IntelliSense is leveraged in this development experiences as well. Once you are able to finalize the development you can choose the platform to deploy and the project will be deployed with a single click.

SQL Profiler

SQL Profiler has been the primary tool for analyzing SQL Server performance. If you have a performance problem but aren't sure where the bottleneck lies, SQL Profiler can help you rapidly narrow down the suspects. SQL Profiler works by capturing events that occur on the server and logging them to a trace file or table. The classes of events that can be captured are exhaustive, covering a wide range of server-side events, including T-SQL and SP preparation and execution, security events, transaction activity, locks, and database resizing.

When you create a new trace, SQL Profiler allows you to select all of the events you wish to audit. Normally, you will narrow this list down as much as possible for both performance and manageability reasons. Figure 2-21 is a sample trace that captures T-SQL-specific events on the server.

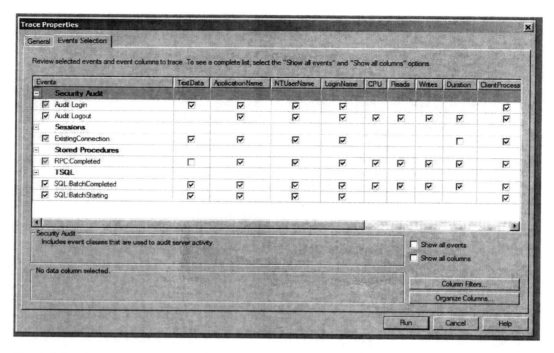

Figure 2-21. *Preparing to Capture T-SQL Events in SQL Profiler*

Once a trace is configured and running, it captures all of the specified events on the server. A sample trace run using the T-SQL events is shown in Figure 2-22.

Figure 2-22. *Running a Trace of T-SQL Events*

As you can see in the example, even a simple trace with a relatively small number of events captured can easily become overwhelming, particularly if run against an SQL Server instance with several simultaneous user connections. SQL Profiler offers the Column Filter option, which allows you to eliminate results from your trace. Using filters, you can narrow the results down to include only actions performed by specific applications or users, or those activities relevant only to a particular database. Figure 2-23 shows the Edit Filter window, where trace filter selections are made.

Figure 2-23. Editing Filters in SQL Profiler

SQL Profiler offers several additional options, including trace replay and the ability to save trace results to either a file or a database table. SQL Profiler is vital to troubleshooting SQL Server performance and security issues.

Extended Events

In these days it is common to have many complex systems with hundreds of cores that support applications with scale out model with a set of SQL Servers. These SQL Servers that support the complex applications are using various SQL Server features such as compression to reduce storage costs and high availability and disaster recovery features to make the application highly available. For such a complex system performance monitoring is vital and Extended Events is designed to handle these complex situations without adding any additional performance penalty to diagnose issues in these systems. Extended Events (XEvents) is one of the diagnostic tools that was introduced in SQL 2008, and it received a makeover in SQL Server 2012 with a new GUI interface to enable ease of use. XEvents is a lightweight asynchronous eventing system that can retrieve information based on the events being triggered in the SQL engine. You can use Extended Events to track both high-level issues such as query execution or blocking in the server, and also low-level issues that are very close to the SQL Server code such as how long it took for the spinlocks to back off as well. Extended Events can be used to collect additional data on any event and perform predefined actions such as taking a memory dump when these events happen; for example, you may be working with an application where the developer requests that you take a memory dump when a specific query executes.

Results from the Extended Events can be written to various targets and one such target is Windows trace file. If you have an application which is gathering the diagnostic information from IIS, and you want to correlate the data from SQL Server, writing to Windows trace file will make the debugging much easier. The event data that has been written to the Windows trace file can be viewed using tools such as Xperf or tracerpt. As with any diagnostic tool, the data that is being collected can be saved to multiple locations including the file system, tables, and windows logging simultaneously. Figure 2-24 shows the Extended Events user interface.

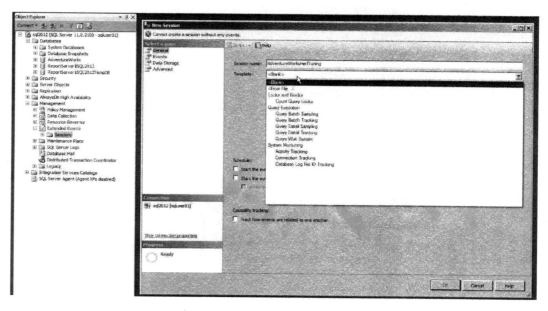

Figure 2-24. *Extended Events New Session*

Extended Events has been implemented by SQL Engine, Merge replication, Analysis services, and Reporting Services in SQL Server 2012. In some of the components like Analysis services, it is just targeted information and not a complete implementation.

Extended Events UI is integrated with Management Studio and we have a separate node in the tree called Extended Events. You can create a new session by right clicking the Extended Events node and selecting the session. Extended events sessions can be based on predefined templates or you can create the session by choosing specific events.

Extended Events offers a rich diagnostic framework that is highly scalable and offers the capability to collect little or large amounts of data in order to troubleshoot a given performance issue. Another reason to start using XEvents is simply because SQL Profiler has been marked for deprecation. We will discuss Extended Events in detail in Chapter 18.

SQL Server Integration Services

SSIS was introduced in SQL Server 2005 as the replacement service for SQL Server 7.0 and 2000 Data Transformation Services (DTS).

SSIS provides an enterprise class Extract Transform Load (ETL) tool that allows you to design simple or complex packages to pull data from multiple sources and integrate them into your SQL Server databases. It also provides rich BI integration and extensibility. In addition to data transformations, SSIS provides SQL Server-specific tasks that allow you to perform database administration and management functions like updating statistics and rebuilding indexes.

SSIS divides the ETL process into three major parts: control flow, data flow, and event handlers. The *control flow* provides structure to SSIS packages and controls execution via tasks, containers, and precedence constraints. The *data flow* imports data from various sources, transforms it, and stores it in specified destinations. The data flow, from the perspective of the control flow, is just another task. However, the data flow is important enough to require its own detailed design surface within a package. *Event handlers* allow you to perform actions in response to predefined events during the ETL process. Figure 2-25 shows a simple SSIS data flow that imports data from a table into a flat file.

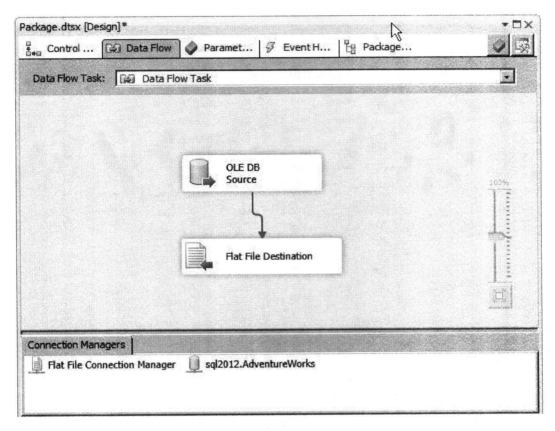

Figure 2-25. *Data Flow to Import Data from a Table to Flat File*

SSIS is a far more advanced ETL tool than DTS, and you will find that it provides significant improvements in features, functionality, and raw power over the old DTS tools.

The Bulk Copy Program

While not as flashy or feature-rich as SSIS, BCP is small, fast and can perform simple imports with no hassle. BCP is handy for generating format files for BCP and other bulk import tools, for one-off imports where a full-blown SSIS package would be overkill, and for exporting data from database tables to files and for backward compatibility when you don't have the resources to devote to immediately upgrading old BCP-based ETL processes. Figure 2-26 shows a simple command-line call to BCP to create a BCP format file and a listing of the format file. The format files generated by BCP can be used by BCP, SSIS, and the T-SQL BULK INSERT statement.

```
C:\Windows\system32\cmd.exe

C:\Users\Public>bcp adventureworks.person.person format null -S SQL2012 -T -fper
son.fmt -c

C:\Users\Public>copy person.fmt con
10.0
13
1       SQLCHAR        0        12      "\t"      1    BusinessEntityID
2       SQLCHAR        0        4       "\t"      2    PersonType
                    SQL_Latin1_General_CP1_CI_AS
3       SQLCHAR        0        3       "\t"      3    NameStyle
4       SQLCHAR        0        16      "\t"      4    Title
                    SQL_Latin1_General_CP1_CI_AS
5       SQLCHAR        0        100     "\t"      5    FirstName
                    SQL_Latin1_General_CP1_CI_AS
6       SQLCHAR        0        100     "\t"      6    MiddleName
                    SQL_Latin1_General_CP1_CI_AS
7       SQLCHAR        0        100     "\t"      7    LastName
                    SQL_Latin1_General_CP1_CI_AS
8       SQLCHAR        0        20      "\t"      8    Suffix
                    SQL_Latin1_General_CP1_CI_AS
9       SQLCHAR        0        12      "\t"      9    EmailPromotion
10      SQLCHAR        0        0       "\t"      10   AdditionalContactInfo
11      SQLCHAR        0        0       "\t"      11   Demographics
12      SQLCHAR        0        37      "\t"      12   rowguid
13      SQLCHAR        0        24      "\r\n"    13   ModifiedDate
        1 file(s) copied.

C:\Users\Public>
```

Figure 2-26. *Generating a Format File with BCP*

SQL Server 2012 Books Online

Books Online (BOL) is the primary reference for SQL Server programming and administration. SQL Server 2012 introduces the Help Viewer piece from the VS2010 shell and does not include BOL along with the default setup. During the SQL installation, you have an option to choose the documentation feature which in turn will install the help viewer.

You also have the option to install the BOL from an online resource. You can access a locally installed copy of BOL or you can access it over the Web at Microsoft's website. The help documentation can be found at http://www.microsoft.com/download/en/details.aspx?id=347.

Figure 2-27 shows a search of a local copy of BOL.

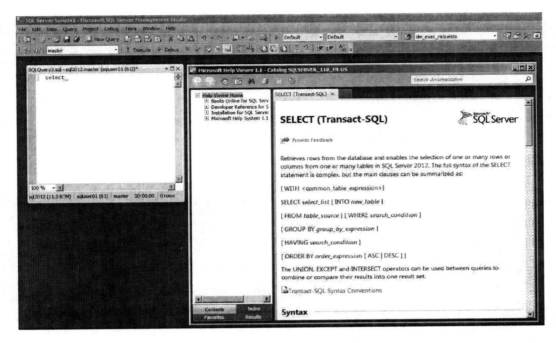

Figure 2-27. *Searching Local BOL for Information on the SELECT Statement*

You can get updates for BOL at www.microsoft.com/sql/default.mspx. The online version of SQL Server 2012 BOL is available at http://msdn.microsoft.com/en-us/library/ms130214.aspx. Also keep in mind that you can search online and local versions of BOL, as well as several other SQL resources, via the Help Search function discussed previously in this chapter.

■ **Tip** Microsoft now offers an additional option for obtaining the most up-to-date version of BOL. You can download the latest BOL updates from the Microsoft Update site, at http://update.microsoft.com/microsoftupdate. Microsoft has announced plans to refresh BOL with updated content more often, and to integrate SQL Server developer and DBA feedback into BOL more quickly.

The AdventureWorks Sample Database

SQL Server 2012 has two main sample databases: the AdventureWorks OLTP and Adventure-Works Data Warehouse databases. In this book, we will refer to the AdventureWorks OLTP database for most samples. Microsoft now releases SQL Server sample databases through its CodePlex website. You can download the AdventureWorks databases and associated sample code from www.codeplex.com/MSFTDBProdSamples.

■ **Note** We highly recommend that you download the SQL Server AdventureWorks 2012 OLTP database so that you can run the sample code in this book as you go through each chapter.

Summary

SQL Server 2012 includes several of the tools we've come to expect with any SQL Server release. In this chapter, we've provided an overview of several tools that will be important to you as an SQL Server 2012 developer. The tools discussed include the following:

- SSMS, the primary GUI for SQL Server development and administration

- SQLCMD, SSMS's text-based counterpart

- SSDT, integrated tool for developers

- SQL Profiler, which supplies event capture and server-side tracing capabilities for analyzing SQL Server performance and auditing security

- Extended Events, lightweight asynchronous event-based troubleshooting tool

- SSIS, the primary ETL tool for SQL Server 2012

- BCP, a command line-based bulk import tool

- BOL, the first place to look when trying to locate information about all things SQL Server

- AdventureWorks, the freely available Microsoft-supplied sample database

These topics could easily fill a book by themselves (and many, in fact, have). In the following chapters, we will review the SQL Server 2012 features in detail.

EXERCISES

1. SSDT is an SQL development tool. What is the purpose of this tool?

2. [Choose all that apply] SQL Server 2012 SSMS provides which of the following features:

   a. Ability to add code snippets and customize them

   b. An integrated Object Explorer for viewing and managing the server, databases, and database objects

   c. IntelliSense, which suggests table, object, and function names as you type SQL statements

   d. Customizable keyboard mapping scheme for Visual Studio users

3. SSIS is considered what type of tool?

4. [True/False] SQLCMD can use command-line options, environment variables, and SQLCMD :setvar commands to set scripting variables.

5. [Choose one] BCP can be used to perform which of the following tasks:

    a. Generating format files for use with SSIS

    b. Importing data into tables without format files

    c. Exporting data from a table to a file

    d. All of the above

6. What is one feature that Extended Events offers that SQL profiler does not?

7. What are the target platforms that can be deployed using SSDT?

CHAPTER 3

■ ■ ■

Procedural Code and CASE Expressions

T-SQL has always included support for procedural programming in the form of control-of-flow statements and cursors. One thing that throws developers from other languages off their guard when migrating to SQL is the peculiar three-valued logic (3VL) we enjoy. In Chapter 1 we introduced you to SQL 3VL and we will expand on this topic further in this chapter. SQL 3VL is different from most other programming languages' simple two-valued Boolean logic. We will also discuss T-SQL control-of-flow constructs, which allow you to change the normally sequential order of statement execution. Control-of-flow statements allow you to branch your code logic with statements like IF...ELSE..., perform loops with statements like WHILE, and perform unconditional jumps with the GOTO statement. We will also introduce CASE expressions and CASE-derived functions that return values based on given comparison criteria in an expression. Finally, we will finish the chapter by explaining a topic closely tied to procedural code: SQL cursors.

■ **Note**   Technically the T-SQL TRY...CATCH and the newer TRY_PARSE and TRY_CONVERT are control-of-flow constructs but these are specifically used for error handling and will be discussed in Chapter 17 which describes error handling and dynamic SQL.

Three-Valued Logic

SQL Server 2012, like all ANSI-compatible SQL DBMS products, implements a peculiar form of logic known as 3VL. 3VL is necessary because SQL introduces the concept of NULL to serve as a placeholder for values that are not known at the time they are stored in the database. The concept of NULL introduces an unknown logical result into SQL's ternary logic system. We will introduce SQL 3VL with a simple set of propositions:

- Consider the proposition "1 is less than 3." The result is logically true because the value of the number 1 is less than the value of the number 3.

- The proposition "5 is equal to 6" is logically false because the value of the number 5 is not equal to the value of the number 6.

- The proposition "*X* is greater than 10" presents a bit of a problem. The variable *X* is an algebraic placeholder for an actual value. Unfortunately, we haven't told you what value *X* stands for at this time. Because you don't know what the value of *X* is, you can't say the statement is true or false; instead you can say the result is unknown. SQL NULL represents an unknown value in the database in much the same way that the variable *X* represents an unknown value in this proposition, and comparisons with NULL produce the same unknown logical result in SQL.

Because NULL represents unknown values in the database, comparing anything with NULL (even other NULLs) produces an unknown logical result. Figure 3-1 is a quick reference for SQL Server 3VL, where p and q represent 3VL result values.

p	q	p AND q	p OR q
TRUE	TRUE	TRUE	TRUE
TRUE	FALSE	FALSE	TRUE
TRUE	UNKNOWN	UNKNOWN	TRUE
FALSE	TRUE	FALSE	TRUE
FALSE	FALSE	FALSE	FALSE
FALSE	UNKNOWN	FALSE	UNKNOWN
UNKNOWN	TRUE	UNKNOWN	TRUE
UNKNOWN	FALSE	FALSE	UNKNOWN
UNKNOWN	UNKNOWN	UNKNOWN	UNKNOWN

p	NOT p
TRUE	FALSE
FALSE	TRUE

Figure 3-1. *SQL 3VL Quick Reference Chart*

As mentioned previously, the unknown logic values shown in the chart are the result of comparisons with NULL. The following predicates, for example, all evaluate to an unknown result:

```
@x = NULL
FirstName <> NULL
PhoneNumber > NULL
```

If you used one of these as the predicate in a WHERE clause of a SELECT statement, the statement would return no rows at all—SELECT with a WHERE clause returns only rows where the WHERE clause predicate evaluates to true; it discards rows for which the WHERE clause is false or unknown. Similarly, the INSERT, UPDATE, and DELETE statements with a WHERE clause only affect rows for which the WHERE clause evaluates to true.

SQL Server provides a proprietary mechanism, the SET ANSI_NULLS OFF option, to allow direct equality comparisons with NULL using the = and <> operators. The only ISO-compliant way to test for NULL is with the IS NULL and IS NOT NULL comparison predicates. We highly recommend that you stick with the ISO-compliant IS NULL and IS NOT NULL predicates for a few reasons:

- Many SQL Server features like computed columns, indexed views, and XML indexes require SET ANSI_NULLS ON at creation time.

- Mixing and matching SET ANSI_NULLS settings within your database can confuse other developers who have to maintain your code. Using ISO-compliant NULL-handling consistently eliminates confusion.

- SET ANSI_NULLS OFF allows direct equality comparisons with NULL, returning true if you compare a column or variable to NULL. It does not return true if you compare NULLs contained in two columns, though, which can be confusing.

- To top it all off, Microsoft has deprecated the SET ANSI_NULLS OFF setting. It will be removed in a future version of SQL Server, so it's a good idea to start future-proofing your code now.

IT'S A CLOSED WORLD, AFTER ALL

The *closed-world assumption (CWA)* is an assumption in logic that the world is "black and white," "true and false," or "ones and zeros." When applied to databases, the CWA basically states that all data stored within the database is true; everything else is false. The CWA presumes that only knowledge of the world that is complete can be stored within a database.

NULL introduces an *open-world assumption (OWA)* into the mix. It allows you to store information in the database that may or may not be true. This means that an SQL database can store incomplete knowledge of the world—a direct violation of the CWA. Many relational management (RM) theorists see this as an inconsistency in the SQL DBMS model. This argument fills many an RM textbook and academic blog, including web sites like Hugh Darwen and C. J. Date's "The Third Manifesto" (www.thethirdmanifesto.com/), so we won't go deeply into the details here. Just realize that many RM experts dislike SQL NULL. As an SQL practitioner in the real world, however, you may discover that NULL is often the best option available to accomplish many tasks.

Control-of-Flow Statements

T-SQL implements procedural language control-of-flow statements, including such constructs as BEGIN...END, IF...ELSE, WHILE, and GOTO. T-SQL's control-of-flow statements provide a framework for developing rich server-side procedural code. Procedural code in T-SQL does come with some caveats, though, which we will discuss in this section.

The BEGIN and END Keywords

T-SQL uses the keywords BEGIN and END to group multiple statements together in a statement block. The BEGIN and END keywords don't alter execution order of the statements they contain, nor do they define an atomic transaction, limit scope, or perform any function other than defining a simple grouping of T-SQL statements.

Unlike other languages, such as C++ or C#, which use braces ({ }) to group statements in logical blocks, T-SQL's BEGIN and END keywords do not define or limit scope. The following sample C# code, for instance, will not even compile:

```
{
int j=10; } Console.WriteLine (j);
```

C# programmers will automatically recognize that the variable j in the previous code is defined inside braces, limiting its scope and making it accessible only inside the braces. T-SQL's roughly equivalent code, however, does not limit scope in this manner:

```
BEGIN
    DECLARE @j int = 10;
END
PRINT @j;
```

The previous T-SQL code executes with no problem, as long as the DECLARE statement is encountered before the variable is referenced in the PRINT statement. The scope of variables in T-SQL is defined in terms of command batches and database object definitions (such as SPs, UDFs, and triggers). Declaring two or more variables with the same name in one batch or SP will result in errors.

■ **Caution** T-SQL's BEGIN and END keywords create a statement block but do not define a scope. Variables declared inside a BEGIN. . .END block are not limited in scope just to that block, but are scoped to the whole batch, SP, or UDF in which they are defined.

BEGIN. . .END is useful for creating statement blocks where you want to execute multiple statements based on the results of other control-of-flow statements like IF. . .ELSE and WHILE. BEGIN. . .END can also have another added benefit if you're using SSMS 2012 or a good third-party SQL editor like ApexSQL Edit (www.apexsql.com/). In advanced editors like these, BEGIN. . .END can alert the GUI that a section of code is collapsible, as shown in Figure 3-2. This can speed up development and ease debugging, especially if you're writing complex T-SQL scripts.

Figure 3-2. BEGIN...END Statement Blocks Marked Collapsible in ApexSQL Edit

---

■ **Tip** Although it's not required, we like to wrap the body of CREATE PROCEDURE statements with BEGIN. . .END. This clearly delineates the bodies of the SPs, separating them from other code in the same script.

The IF...ELSE Statement

Like many procedural languages, T-SQL implements conditional execution of code using the simplest of procedural statements: the IF...ELSE construct. The IF statement is followed by a logical predicate. If the predicate evaluates to true, the single SQL statement or statement blocked wrapped in BEGIN...END is executed. If the predicate evaluates to either false or unknown, SQL Server falls through to the ELSE statement and executes the single statement or statement block following ELSE.

▓ **Tip** A predicate in SQL is an expression that evaluates to one of the logical results true, false, or unknown. Predicates are used in IF...ELSE statements, WHERE clauses, and anywhere that a logical result is needed.

The example in Listing 3-1 performs up to three comparisons to determine whether a variable is equal to a specified value. The second ELSE statement executes if and only if the tests for both true and false conditions fail.

Listing 3-1. Simple IF...ELSE Example

```
DECLARE @i int = NULL;
IF @i = 10
    PRINT 'TRUE.';
ELSE IF NOT (@i = 10)
    PRINT 'FALSE.';
ELSE
    PRINT 'UNKNOWN.';
```

Because the variable @i is NULL in the example, SQL Server reports that the result is unknown. If you assign the value 10 to the variable @i, SQL Server will report that the result is true; all other values will report false.

To create a statement block containing multiple T-SQL statements after either the IF statement or the ELSE statement, simply wrap your statements with the T-SQL BEGIN and END keywords discussed in the previous section. The simple example in Listing 3-2 is an IF...ELSE statement with statement blocks. The example uses IF...ELSE to check the value of the variable @direction. If @direction is ASCENDING, a message is printed, and the top ten names, in order of last name, are selected from the Person.Contact table. If @direction is DESCENDING, a different message is printed, and the bottom ten names are selected from the Person.Contact table. Any other value results in a message that @direction was not recognized. The results of Listing 3-2 are shown in Figure 3-3.

Listing 3-2. IF...ELSE with Statement Blocks

```
DECLARE @direction NVARCHAR(20) = N'DESCENDING';

IF @direction = N'ASCENDING'
BEGIN
        PRINT 'Start at the top!';

        SELECT TOP (10)
        LastName,
        FirstName,
        MiddleName
        FROM Person.Person
        ORDER BY LastName ASC;
END
ELSE  IF @direction = N'DESCENDING'
```

```
BEGIN
        PRINT 'Start at the bottom!';

        SELECT TOP (10)
        LastName,
        FirstName,
        MiddleName
        FROM Person.Person
        ORDER BY LastName DESC;
END
ELSE

        PRINT '@direction  was not recognized!';
```

	Last Name	First Name	Middle Name
1	Zwilling	Michael	J.
2	Zwilling	Michael	J
3	Zukowski	Jake	NULL
4	Zugelder	Judy	N.
5	Zubaty	Patricia	M.
6	Zubaty	Carla	J.
7	Zimprich	Karin	NULL
8	Zimprich	Karin	NULL
9	Zimmerman	Tiffany	E
10	Zimmerman	Marc	NULL

Figure 3-3. The Last Ten Contact Names in the AdventureWorks Database

The WHILE, BREAK, and CONTINUE Statements

Looping is a standard feature of procedural languages, and T-SQL provides looping support through the WHILE statement and its associated BREAK and CONTINUE statements. The WHILE loop is immediately followed by a predicate, and WHILE will execute a given SQL statement or statement block bounded by the BEGIN and END keywords as long as the associated predicate evaluates to true. If the predicate evaluates to false or unknown, the code in the WHILE loop will not execute and control will pass to the next statement after the WHILE loop. The WHILE loop in Listing 3-3 is a very simple example that counts from 1 to 10. The result is shown in Figure 3-4.

Listing 3-3. WHILE Statement Example

```
DECLARE @i int=1;
WHILE @i <= 10
BEGIN
    PRINT @i;
    SET @i=@i+1;
END
```

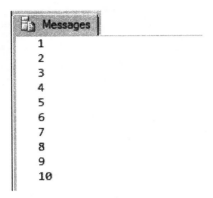

Figure 3-4. *Counting from 1 to 10 with WHILE*

■ **Tip** Be sure to update your counter or other flag inside the WHILE loop. The WHILE statement will keep looping until its predicate evaluates to false or unknown. A simple coding mistake could create a nasty infinite loop.

T-SQL also includes two additional keywords that can be used with the WHILE statement: BREAK and CONTINUE. The CONTINUE keyword forces the WHILE loop to immediately jump to the start of the code block, as in the modified example in Listing 3-4.

Listing 3-4. WHILE…CONTINUE Example

```
DECLARE @i int=1;
WHILE @i <= 10
BEGIN
    PRINT @i;
    SET @i=@i+1;

CONTINUE; -- Force the WHILE loop to restart

PRINT 'The CONTINUE keyword ensures that this will never be printed.';

END
```

The BREAK keyword, on the other hand, forces the WHILE loop to terminate immediately. In Listing 3-5, BREAK forces the WHILE loop to exit during the first iteration so that the numbers 2 through 10 are never printed.

Listing 3-5. WHILE…BREAK Example

```
DECLARE @i int=1;
WHILE @i <= 10
BEGIN
    PRINT @i;
    SET @i=@i+1;
```

```
    BREAK; -- Force the WHILE loop to terminate

    PRINT 'The BREAK keyword ensures that this will never be printed.';
END
```

■ **Tip**   BREAK and CONTINUE can and should be avoided in most cases. It's not uncommon to see a WHILE 1 = 1 statement with a BREAK in the body of the loop. This can always be rewritten, usually very easily, to remove the BREAK statement. Most of the time, the BREAK and CONTINUE keywords introduce additional complexity to your logic and cause more problems than they solve.

The GOTO Statement

Despite Edsger W. Dijkstra's best efforts at warning developers (see Dijkstra's 1968 letter, "Go To Statement Considered Harmful"), T-SQL still has a GOTO statement. The GOTO statement transfers control of your program to a specified label unconditionally. Labels are defined by placing the label identifier on a line followed by a colon (:), as shown in Listing 3-6. This simple example executes its step 1 and uses GOTO to dive straight into step 3, skipping step 2. The results are shown in Figure 3-5.

Listing 3-6. Simple GOTO Example

```
PRINT 'Step 1 Begin.';
GOTO Step3_Label;

PRINT 'Step 2 will not be printed.';

Step3_Label:
PRINT 'Step 3 End.';
```

Figure 3-5. *GOTO Statement Transfers Control Unconditionally*

The GOTO statement is best avoided, since it can quickly degenerate your programs into unstructured spaghetti code. When you have to write procedural code, you're much better off using structured programming constructs like IF. . .ELSE and WHILE statements.

The WAITFOR Statement

The WAITFOR statement suspends execution of a transaction, SP, or T-SQL command batch until a specified time is reached, a time interval has elapsed, or a message is received from Service Broker.

▨ **Note** Service Broker is an SQL Server messaging system. We don't detail Service Broker in this book, but you can find out more about it in *Pro SQL Server 2008 Service Broker*, by Klaus Aschenbrenner and Remus Rusana (Apress, 2008).

The WAITFOR statement has a DELAY option that tells SQL Server to suspend code execution until one of the following criteria is met or a specified time interval has elapsed. The time interval is specified as a valid time string in the format hh:mm:ss. The time interval cannot contain a date portion; it must only include the time, and it can be up to 24 hours. Listing 3-7 is an example of the WAITFOR statement with the DELAY option, which blocks execution of the batch for 3 seconds.

WAITFOR CAVEATS

There are some caveats associated with the WAITFOR statement. In some situations, WAITFOR can cause longer delays than the interval you specify. SQL Server also assigns each WAITFOR statement its own thread, and if SQL Server begins experiencing *thread starvation*, it can randomly stop WAITFOR threads to free up thread resources. If you need to delay execution for an exact amount of time, you can guarantee more consistent results by suspending execution through an external application like SSIS.

In addition to its DELAY and TIME options, you can use WAITFOR with the RECEIVE and GET CONVERSATION GROUP options with Service Broker-enabled applications. When you use WAITFOR with RECEIVE, the statement waits for receipt of one or more messages from a specified queue.

When you use WAITFOR with the GET CONVERSATION GROUP option, it waits for a conversation group identifier of a message. GET CONVERSATION GROUP allows you to retrieve information about a message and lock the conversation group for the conversation containing the message, all before retrieving the message itself.

A detailed description of Service Broker is beyond the scope of this book, but *Accelerated SQL Server 2008*, by Rob Walters et al. (Apress, 2008) gives a good description of Service Broker functionality and options still applicable to SQL Server 2012.

Listing 3-7. WAITFOR Example

```
PRINT 'Step 1 complete. ';
GO

DECLARE @time_to_pass nvarchar(8);
SELECT @time_to_pass=N'00:00:03';
WAITFOR DELAY @time_to_pass;
PRINT 'Step 2 completed three seconds later. ';
```

You can also use the TIME option with the WAITFOR statement. If you use the TIME option, SQL Server will wait until the appointed time before allowing execution to continue. Datetime variables are allowed, but the date portion is ignored when the TIME option is used.

The RETURN Statement

The RETURN statement exits unconditionally from an SP or command batch. When you use RETURN, you can optionally specify an integer expression as a return value. The RETURN statement returns a given integer expression to the calling routine or batch. If you don't specify an integer expression to return, a value of 0 is returned by default. RETURN is not normally used to return calculated results, except for UDFs, which offer more RETURN options (we will detail these in Chapter 4). For SPs and command batches, the RETURN statement is used almost exclusively to return a success indicator, failure indicator, or error code.

WHAT NUMBER, SUCCESS?

All system SPs return **0** to indicate success, or a nonzero value to indicate failure (unless otherwise documented in BOL). It is considered bad form to use the RETURN statement to return anything other than an integer status code from a script or SP.

UDFs, on the other hand, have their own rules. UDFs have a flexible variation of the RETURN statement, which exits the body of the UDF. In fact, a UDF *requires* the RETURN statement be used to return scalar or tabular results to the caller. You will see UDFs again in detail in Chapter 4.

■ **Note**   There are a couple of methods in T-SQL to redirect logic flow based on errors. These include the TRY...CATCH statement and the THROW statement. Both statements will be discussed in detail in Chapter 17.

The CASE Expression

The T-SQL CASE function is SQL Server's implementation of the ISO SQL CASE expression. While the previously discussed T-SQL control-of-flow statements allow for conditional execution of SQL statements or statement blocks, the CASE expression allows for set-based conditional processing inside a single query. CASE provides two syntaxes, *simple* and *searched*, which we will discuss in this section.

The Simple CASE Expression

The simple CASE expression returns a result expression based on the value of a given input expression. The simple CASE expression compares the input expression to a series of expressions following WHEN keywords. Once a match is encountered, CASE returns a corresponding result expression following the keyword THEN. If no match is found, the expression following the keyword ELSE is returned, and NULL is returned if no ELSE keyword is supplied.

Consider the example in Listing 3-8, which uses a simple CASE expression to count all the AdventureWorks customers on the West Coast (which we arbitrarily defined as the states of California, Washington, and Oregon). The query also uses a CTE (common table expression) which we will discuss more thoroughly in Chapter 8. The results are shown in Figure 3-6.

Listing 3-8. Counting West Coast Customers with a Simple CASE Expression

```
WITH  EmployeesByRegion(Region)
AS
(
    SELECT
        CASE sp.StateProvinceCode
        WHEN 'CA' THEN 'West Coast'
        WHEN 'WA' THEN 'West Coast'
        WHEN 'OR' THEN 'West Coast'
        ELSE 'Elsewhere'
        END
    FROM  HumanResources.Employee e
    INNER JOIN Person.Person p
        ON e.BusinessEntityID = p.BusinessEntityID
        INNER JOIN Person.BusinessEntityAddress bea
            ON bea.BusinessEntityID = e.BusinessEntityID
        INNER JOIN Person.Address a
            ON a.AddressID = bea.AddressID
        INNER JOIN Person.StateProvince sp
            ON sp.StateProvinceID = a.StateProvinceID
    WHERE sp.CountryRegionCode = 'US'
)
SELECT  COUNT(Region) AS NumOfEmployees, Region
FROM    EmployeesByRegion
GROUP  BY Region;
```

	NumOfEmployees	Region
1	6	Elsewhere
2	278	West Coast

Figure 3-6. *Results of the West Coast Customer Count*

The CASE expression in the subquery compares the StateProvinceCode value to each of the state codes following the WHEN keywords, returning the name West Coast when the StateProvinceCode is equal to CA, WA, or OR. For any other StateProvinceCode in the United States, it returns a value of Elsewhere.

```
SELECT CASE sp.StateProvinceCode
        WHEN 'CA' THEN 'West Coast'
        WHEN 'WA' THEN 'West Coast'
        WHEN 'OR' THEN 'West Coast'
        ELSE 'Elsewhere'
    END
```

The remainder of the example simply counts the number of rows returned by the query, grouped by Region.

A SIMPLE CASE OF NULL

The simple CASE expression performs basic equality comparisons between the input expression and the expressions following the WHEN keywords. This means that you cannot use the simple CASE expression to check for NULLs. Recall from the "Three-Valued Logic" section of this chapter that a NULL, when compared to anything, returns unknown. The simple CASE expression only returns the expression following the THEN keyword when the comparison returns true. This means that if you ever try to use NULL in a WHEN expression, the corresponding THEN expression will not be returned. If you need to check for NULL in a CASE expression, use a searched CASE expression with the IS NULL or IS NOT NULL comparison operators.

The Searched CASE Expression

The searched CASE expression provides a mechanism for performing more complex comparisons. The searched CASE evaluates a series of predicates following WHEN keywords until it encounters one that evaluates to true. At that point, it returns the corresponding result expression following the THEN keyword. If none of the predicates evaluates to true, the result following the ELSE keyword is returned. If none of the predicates evaluates to true and ELSE is not supplied, the searched CASE expression returns NULL.

Predicates in the searched CASE expression can take advantage of any valid SQL comparison operators (e.g., <, >, =, LIKE, and IN). The simple CASE expression from Listing 3-8 can be easily expanded to cover multiple geographic regions using the searched CASE expression and the IN logical operator, as shown in Listing 3-9. This example uses a searched CASE expression to group states into West Coast, Pacific, and New England regions. The results are shown in Figure 3-7.

Listing 3-9. Counting Employees by Region with a Searched CASE Expression

```
WITH  EmployeesByRegion(Region)
AS
(
    SELECT
        CASE WHEN sp.StateProvinceCode IN ('CA', 'WA', 'OR') THEN 'West Coast'
        WHEN sp.StateProvinceCode IN ('HI', 'AK') THEN 'Pacific'
        WHEN  sp.StateProvinceCode  IN  ('CT',  'MA', 'ME', 'NH', 'RI', 'VT')
        THEN 'New England'
        ELSE 'Elsewhere'
        END
    FROM  HumanResources.Employee e
    INNER JOIN Person.Person p
        ON e.BusinessEntityID=p.BusinessEntityID
        INNER JOIN Person.BusinessEntityAddress bea
            ON bea.BusinessEntityID=e.BusinessEntityID
        INNER JOIN Person.Address a
            ON a.AddressID=bea.AddressID
        INNER JOIN Person.StateProvince sp
            ON sp.StateProvinceID=a.StateProvinceID
    WHERE sp.CountryRegionCode='US'
)
SELECT  COUNT(Region) AS  NumOfCustomers,  Region
FROM    EmployeesByRegion
GROUP  BY  Region;
```

Figure 3-7. *Results of the Regional Customer Count*

The searched CASE expression in the example uses the IN operator to return the geographic area that StateProvinceCode is in: California, Washington, and Oregon all return West Coast; and Connecticut, Massachusetts, Maine, New Hampshire, Rhode Island, and Vermont all return New England. If the StateProvinceCode does not fit in one of these regions, the searched CASE expression will return Elsewhere.

```
SELECT
    CASE WHEN sp.StateProvinceCode IN ('CA', 'WA', 'OR') THEN 'West Coast'
        WHEN sp.StateProvinceCode IN ('HI', 'AK') THEN 'Pacific'
        WHEN sp.StateProvinceCode  IN ('CT',  'MA', 'ME', 'NH', 'RI', 'VT')
        THEN 'New England'
        ELSE  'Elsewhere'
    END
```

The balance of the sample code in Listing 3-9 counts the rows returned, grouped by Region. The CASE expression, either simple or searched, can be used in SELECT, UPDATE, INSERT, MERGE, and DELETE statements.

A CASE BY ANY OTHER NAME

Many programming and query languages offer expressions that are analogous to the SQL CASE expression. C++ and C#, for instance, offer the ?: operator, which fulfills the same function as a searched CASE expression. XQuery has its own flavor of if...then...else expression that is also equivalent to the SQL searched CASE.

C# and Visual Basic also supply the switch and Select statements, respectively, which are semi-analogous to SQL's simple CASE expression. The main difference, of course, is that SQL's CASE expression simply returns a scalar value, while the C# and Visual Basic statements actually control program flow, allowing you to execute statements based on an expression's value. The similarities and differences between SQL expressions and statements and similar constructs in other languages provide a great starting point for learning the nitty-gritty details of T-SQL.

CASE and Pivot Tables

Many times, business reporting requirements dictate that a result should be returned in pivot table format. Pivot table format simply means that the labels for columns and/or rows are generated from the data contained in rows. Microsoft Access and Excel users have long had the ability to generate pivot tables on their data, and SQL Server 2012 supports the PIVOT and UNPIVOT operators introduced in SQL Server 2005. Back in the days of SQL Server 2000 and before, however, CASE expressions were the only method of generating pivot table-type queries.

And even though SQL Server 2012 provides the PIVOT and UNPIVOT operators, truly dynamic pivot tables still require using CASE expressions and dynamic SQL. The static pivot table query shown in Listing 3-10 returns a pivot table-formatted result with the total number of orders for each AdventureWorks sales region in the United States. The results are shown in Figure 3-8.

Listing 3-10. CASE-Style Pivot Table

```
SELECT
    t.CountryRegionCode,
    SUM
    (
        CASE WHEN t.Name = 'Northwest' THEN 1
        ELSE    0
        END
    ) AS        Northwest,
    SUM
    (
        CASE WHEN t.Name = 'Northeast' THEN 1
        ELSE    0
        END
    ) AS        Northeast,
    SUM
    (
        CASE WHEN t.Name = 'Southwest' THEN 1
        ELSE    0
        END
    ) AS        Southwest,
    SUM
    (
        CASE WHEN t.Name = 'Southeast' THEN 1
        ELSE    0
        END
    ) AS        Southeast,
    SUM
    (
        CASE WHEN t.Name = 'Central' THEN 1
        ELSE    0
        END
    ) AS  Central
FROM  Sales.SalesOrderHeader soh
INNER  JOIN  Sales.SalesTerritory  t
    ON  soh.TerritoryID = t.TerritoryID
WHERE  t.CountryRegionCode  =  'US'
GROUP  BY  t.CountryRegionCode;
```

	CountryRegionCode	Northwest	Northeast	Southwest	Southeast	Central
1	US	4594	352	6224	486	385

Figure 3-8. *Number of Sales by Region in Pivot Table Format*

This type of static pivot table can also be used with the SQL Server 2012 PIVOT operator. The sample code in Listing 3-11 uses the PIVOT operator to generate the same result as the CASE expressions in Listing 3-10.

Listing 3-11. PIVOT Operator Pivot Table

```
SELECT
    CountryRegionCode,
    Northwest,
    Northeast,
    Southwest,
    Southeast,
    Central
FROM
(
    SELECT
        t.CountryRegionCode,
        t.Name
    FROM  Sales.SalesOrderHeader  soh
    INNER JOIN Sales.SalesTerritory t
        ON  soh.TerritoryID = t.TerritoryID
    WHERE t.CountryRegionCode = 'US'
) p
PIVOT
(
    COUNT (Name)
    FOR  Name
    IN
    (
        Northwest,
        Northeast,
        Southwest,
        Southeast,
        Central
    )
) AS pvt;
```

On occasion, you might need to run a pivot table-style report where you don't know the column names in advance. This is a dynamic pivot table script that uses a temporary table and dynamic SQL to generate a pivot table, without specifying the column names in advance. Listing 3-12 demonstrates one method of generating dynamic pivot tables in T-SQL. The results are shown in Figure 3-9.

Listing 3-12. Dynamic Pivot Table Query

```
-- Declare variables
DECLARE @sql nvarchar(4000);

DECLARE @temp_pivot table
 (
  TerritoryID int NOT NULL PRIMARY KEY,
  CountryRegion nvarchar(20) NOT NULL,
  CountryRegionCode nvarchar(3) NOT NULL
 );
```

61

```
-- Get column names from source table rows
INSERT INTO @temp_pivot
 (
  TerritoryID,
  CountryRegion,
  CountryRegionCode
 )
 SELECT
  TerritoryID,
  Name,
  CountryRegionCode
  FROM Sales.SalesTerritory
  GROUP BY
     TerritoryID,
     Name,
     CountryRegionCode;

-- Generate dynamic SQL query
SET @sql=N'SELECT' +
    SUBSTRING(
       (
         SELECT N', SUM(CASE WHEN t.TerritoryID=' +
           CAST(TerritoryID AS NVARCHAR(3)) +
         N' THEN 1 ELSE 0 END) AS '+QUOTENAME(CountryRegion) AS "*"
         FROM @temp_pivot
         FOR XML PATH('')
    ), 2, 4000) +
    N' FROM Sales.SalesOrderHeader soh ' +
       N' INNER JOIN Sales.SalesTerritory t ' +
       N' ON soh.TerritoryID=t.TerritoryID; ' ;

-- Print and execute dynamic SQL
PRINT @sql;

EXEC (@sql);
```

	Northwest	Northeast	Central	Southwest	Southeast	Canada	France	Germany	Australia	United Kingdom
1	4594	352	385	6224	486	4067	2672	2623	6843	3219

Figure 3-9. *Dynamic Pivot Table Result*

The script in Listing 3-12 first declares an *nvarchar* variable that will hold the dynamically generated SQL script and a table variable that will hold all of the column names, which are retrieved from the row values in the source table.

```
-- Declare variables
DECLARE @sql nvarchar(4000);
```

```
DECLARE @temp_pivot table
 (
  TerritoryID int NOT NULL PRIMARY KEY,
  CountryRegion nvarchar(20) NOT NULL,
  CountryRegionCode nvarchar(3) NOT NULL
 );
```

Next, the script grabs a list of distinct territory-specific values from the table and stores them in the @temp_pivot table variable. These values from the table will become column names in the pivot table result.

```
-- Get column names from source table rows
INSERT INTO @temp_pivot
 (
  TerritoryID,
  CountryRegion,
  CountryRegionCode
 )
 SELECT
  TerritoryID,
  Name,
  CountryRegionCode
  FROM Sales.SalesTerritory
  GROUP BY
     TerritoryID,
     Name,
     CountryRegionCode;
```

The script then uses FOR XML PATH to efficiently generate the dynamic SQL SELECT query that contains CASE expressions and column names generated dynamically based on the values in the @temppivot table variable. This SELECT query will create the dynamic pivot table result.

```
-- Generate dynamic SQL query
SET @sql=N'SELECT' +
    SUBSTRING(
       (
         SELECT N', SUM(CASE WHEN t.TerritoryID=' +
           CAST(TerritoryID AS NVARCHAR(3)) +
         N' THEN 1 ELSE 0 END) AS '+QUOTENAME(CountryRegion) AS "*"
         FROM @temp_pivot
         FOR XML PATH('')
    ), 2, 4000) +
    N' FROM Sales.SalesOrderHeader soh ' +
       N' INNER JOIN Sales.SalesTerritory t ' +
       N' ON soh.TerritoryID=t.TerritoryID; ' ;
```

Finally, the dynamic pivot table query is printed out and executed with the T-SQL PRINT and EXEC statements.

```
-- Print and execute dynamic SQL
PRINT @sql;

EXEC (@sql);
```

63

Listing 3-13 shows the dynamic SQL pivot table query generated by the code in Listing 3-12.

Listing 3-13. Autogenerated Dynamic SQL Pivot Table Query

```
SELECT SUM
(
    CASE  WHEN  t.TerritoryID  =  1  THEN      1
        ELSE 0
    END
) AS   [Northwest],
SUM
(
    CASE  WHEN  t.TerritoryID  =  2  THEN      1
        ELSE 0
    END
) AS   [Northeast],
SUM
(
    CASE  WHEN  t.TerritoryID  =  3  THEN      1
        ELSE 0
    END
) AS  [Central],
SUM
(
    CASE  WHEN  t.TerritoryID  =  4  THEN      1
        ELSE 0
    END
) AS   [Southwest],
SUM
(
    CASE  WHEN  t.TerritoryID  =  5  THEN      1
        ELSE 0
    END
) AS   [Southeast],
SUM
(
    CASE  WHEN  t.TerritoryID  =  6  THEN      1
        ELSE 0
    END
) AS  [Canada],
SUM
(
    CASE  WHEN  t.TerritoryID  =  7  THEN      1
        ELSE 0
    END
) AS  [France],
SUM
(
    CASE  WHEN  t.TerritoryID  =  8  THEN      1
        ELSE 0
    END
) AS  [Germany],
```

```
SUM
(
    CASE  WHEN  t.TerritoryID  =  9  THEN         1
          ELSE 0
    END
)  AS  [Australia],
SUM
(
    CASE  WHEN  t.TerritoryID  =  10  THEN        1
          ELSE 0
    END
)  AS  [United Kingdom]
FROM  Sales.SalesOrderHeader soh
INNER  JOIN  Sales.SalesTerritory  t
    ON  soh.TerritoryID = t.TerritoryID;
```

▓ **Caution**   Anytime you use dynamic SQL, make sure that you take precautions against *SQL injection*—that is, malicious SQL code being inserted into your SQL statements. In this instance, we're using the QUOTENAME function to quote the column names being dynamically generated to help avoid SQL injection problems. We'll cover dynamic SQL and SQL injection in greater detail in Chapter 17.

The IIF Statement

SQL Server 2012 simplifies the standard CASE statement by introducing the concept of an IIF statement. You get the same results as you would using the CASE statement but with much less code. Those familiar with Microsoft .NET will be glad to see the same functionality is now part of T-SQL.

The syntax is simple. The command takes a Boolean expression, a value when the expression equates to true and a value when the expression equates to false. Listing 3-14 show two examples. One example uses variables and the other uses table columns. The output for both statements is shown in Figure 3-10.

Listing 3-14. Examples Using the IIF statement

```
--Example 1. IIF Statement Using Variables

DECLARE @valueA int = 85
DECLARE @valueB int = 45

SELECT IIF (@valueA < @valueB, 'True', 'False') AS Result

--Example 2. IIF Statement Using Table Column

SELECT IIF (Name in ('Alberta', 'British Columbia'), 'Canada', Name)
FROM [Person].[StateProvince]
```

	Result
1	False

	(No column name)
1	Ain
2	Aisne
3	Alabama
4	Alaska
5	Canada
6	Allier
7	Alpes (Haute)
8	Alpes-de-Haute P...
9	Alpes-Maritimes
10	American Samoa
11	Ardèche
12	Ardennes
13	Ariège

Figure 3-10. *Partial Output of IIF Statements*

CHOOSE

Another logical function introduced in SQL Server 2012 is the CHOOSE function. The CHOOSE function allows you to select a member of an array based on an integer index value. Simply put, the CHOOSE function lets you select a member from a list. The member you select can either be based off a static index value or computed value. The syntax for the CHOOSE function is as follows:

```
CHOOSE ( index, val_1, val_2 [, val_n ] )
```

If the index value is not an integer (let's say it's a decimal), then SQL will convert it to an integer. If the index value is out of range for the index, then the function will return a NULL. Listing 3-15 shows a simple example and Figure 3-11 shows the output. The example uses the integer value of the PhoneNumberTypeID to determine the type of phone. In this case the phone type is defined in the table so a CHOOSE function would not be necessary but in other cases the value may not be defined.

Listing 3-15. Example Using the CHOOSE Statement

```
SELECT p.FirstName,
       pp.PhoneNumber,
       CHOOSE(pp.PhoneNumberTypeID, 'Cell', 'Home', 'Work') 'Phone Type'
FROM Person.Person p
JOIN Person.PersonPhone pp
ON p.BusinessEntityID=pp.BusinessEntityID
```

	FirstName	PhoneNumber	Phone Type
1	Syed	926-555-0182	Work
2	Catherine	747-555-0171	Cell
3	Kim	334-555-0137	Work
4	Kim	919-555-0100	Work
5	Kim	208-555-0114	Cell
6	Hazem	869-555-0125	Work
7	Sam	567-555-0100	Work
8	Humberto	599-555-0127	Cell
9	Gustavo	398-555-0132	Cell
10	Pilar	1 (11) 500 555-0132	Cell
11	Pilar	577-555-0185	Work
12	Aaron	417-555-0154	Cell
13	Adam	129-555-0195	Home
14	Alex	346-555-0124	Cell
15	Alexandra	629-555-0159	Home

Figure 3-11. *Partial Output of CHOOSE Statement*

COALESCE and NULLIF

The COALESCE function takes a list of expressions as arguments and returns the first non-NULL value from the list. The COALESCE function is defined by ISO as shorthand for the following equivalent searched CASE expression:

```
CASE
WHEN expressionl IS NOT NULL THEN expression! WHEN expression IS NOT NULL THEN expression
[ ... " ] END
```

The following COALESCE function example returns the value of MiddleName when MiddleName is not NULL, and the string No Middle Name when MiddleName is NULL:

```
COALESCE (MiddleName, 'No Middle Name')
```

The NULLIF function accepts exactly two arguments. NULLIF returns NULL if the two expressions are equal, and it returns the value of the first expression if the two expressions are not equal. NULLIF is defined by the ISO standard as equivalent to the following searched CASE expression:

```
CASE WHEN expressionl=expression2 THEN NULL
ELSE expressionl
END
```

NULLIF is often used in conjunction with COALESCE. Consider Listing 3-16, which combines COALESCE with NULLIF to return the string This is NULL or A if the variable @s is set to the character value A or NULL.

Listing 3-16. Using COALESCE with NULLIF

```
DECLARE @s varchar(10);
SELECT @s = 'A';
SELECT COALESCE(NULLIF(@s, 'A'), 'This is NULL or A');
```

T-SQL has long had alternate functionality similar to COALESCE. Specifically, the ISNULL function accepts two parameters and returns NULL if they are equal.

COALESCE OR ISNULL?

The T-SQL functions COALESCE and ISNULL perform similar functions, but which one should you use? COALESCE is more flexible than ISNULL and is compliant with the ISO standard to boot. This means that it is also the more portable option among ISO-compliant systems. COALESCE also implicitly converts the result to the data type with the highest precedence from the list of expressions. ISNULL implicitly converts the result to the data type of the first expression. Finally, COALESCE is a bit less confusing than ISNULL, especially considering that there's already a comparison operator called IS NULL. In general, we recommend using the COALESCE function instead of ISNULL.

Cursors

The word *cursor* comes from the Latin word for *runner,* and that is exactly what a T-SQL cursor does: it "runs" through a result set, returning one row at a time. Many T-SQL programming experts rail against the use of cursors for a variety of reasons—the chief among these include the following:

- Cursors use a lot of overhead, often much more than an equivalent set-based approach.
- Cursors override SQL Server's built-in query optimizations, often making them much slower than an equivalent set-based solution.

Because cursors are procedural in nature, they are often the slowest way to manipulate data in T-SQL. Rather than spend the balance of the chapter ranting against cursor use, however, we'd like to introduce T-SQL cursor functionality and play devil's advocate to point out some areas where cursors provide an adequate solution.

The first such area where we can recommend the use of cursors is in scripts or procedures that perform administrative tasks. In administrative tasks, the following items often hold true:

- Unlike normal data queries and data manipulations that are performed dozens, hundreds, or potentially thousands of times per day, administrative tasks are often performed on a one-off basis or on a regular schedule like once per day.
- Administrative tasks often require calling an SP or executing a procedural code block once for each row when performing administrative tasks based on a table of entries.
- Administrative tasks generally don't need to query or manipulate massive amounts of data to perform their jobs.
- The order of the steps in which administrative tasks are performed and the order of the database objects they touch are often important.

The sample SP in Listing 3-17 is an example of an administrative task performed with a T-SQL cursor. The sample uses a cursor to loop through all indexes on all user tables in the current database. It then creates dynamic SQL statements to rebuild every index whose fragmentation level is above a user-specified threshold. The results are shown in Figure 3-12. Be aware that your results may return different values for each row.

Listing 3-17. Sample Administrative Task Performed with a Cursor

```
CREATE PROCEDURE dbo.RebuildIndexes
@ShowOrRebuild nvarchar(10)=N'show',
@MaxFrag decimal(20, 2)=20.0
AS
BEGIN
-- Declare variables
SET NOCOUNT ON;

DECLARE
    @Schema nvarchar(128),
    @Table nvarchar(128),
    @Index nvarchar(128),
    @Sql nvarchar(4000),
    @DatabaseId int,
    @SchemaId int,
    @TableId int,
    @lndexId int;

-- Create the index list table
DECLARE @IndexList TABLE
(
    DatabaseName nvarchar(128) NOT NULL,
    DatabaseId int NOT NULL,
    SchemaName nvarchar(128) NOT NULL,
    SchemaId int NOT NULL,
    TableName nvarchar(128) NOT NULL,
    TableId int NOT NULL,
    IndexName nvarchar(128),
    IndexId int NOT NULL,
    Fragmentation decimal(20, 2),
PRIMARY KEY (DatabaseId, SchemaId, TableId, IndexId) );

-- Populate index list table
INSERT INTO @IndexList
(
    DatabaseName,
    DatabaseId,
    SchemaName,
    SchemaId,
    TableName,
    TableId,
    IndexName,
    IndexId,
    Fragmentation
)
SELECT
    db_name(),
    db_id(),
    s.Name,
    s.schema_id,
```

```
      t.Name,
      t.object_id,
      i.Name,
      i.index_id,
MAX(ip.avg_fragmentation_in_percent) FROM sys.tables t INNER JOIN sys.schemas s
ON t.schema_id=s.schema_id INNER JOIN sys.indexes i
ON t.object_id=i.object_id INNER JOIN sys.dm_db_index_physical_stats (db_id(), NULL, NULL,
NULL, NULL) ip
ON ip.object_id=t.object_id AND ip.index_id=i.index_id WHERE ip.database_id=db_id()
 GROUP BY
      s.Name,
      s.schema_id,
      t.Name,
      t.object_id,
      i.Name,
      i.index_id;
-- If user specified rebuild, use a cursor to loop through all indexes
-- rebuild them
IF @ShowOrRebuild=N'rebuild'
BEGIN

-- Declare a cursor to create the dynamic SQL statements
DECLARE Index_Cursor CURSOR FAST_FORWARD
FOR SELECT SchemaName, TableName, IndexName
FROM @IndexList
WHERE Fragmentation>@MaxFrag
ORDER BY Fragmentation DESC, TableName ASC, IndexName ASC;

-- Open the cursor for reading
OPEN Index_Cursor;
-- Loop through all the tables in the database
FETCH NEXT FROM Index_Cursor
INTO @Schema, @Table, @Index;

WHILE @@FETCH_STATUS=0 BEGIN -- Create ALTER INDEX statement to rebuild inddex
SET @Sql=N'ALTER INDEX ' +
 QUOTENAME(RTRIM(@Index))+N' ON '+QUOTENAME(RTRIM(@Table))+N'.' +
 QUOTENAME(RTRIM(@Table))+N' REBUIId WITH (ONLINE=OFF); ';

PRINT @Sql;

-- Execute dynamic SQL
EXEC (@Sql);

-- Get the next index
FETCH NEXT FROM Index_Cursor
INTO @Schema, @Table, @Index;
END
```

```
-- Close and deallocate the cursor.
CLOSE Index_Cursor;
DEALLOCATE Index_Cursor;
END
-- Show results, including oId fragmentation and new fragmentation
-- after index rebuiId
SELECT
il.DatabaseName,
il.SchemaName,
il.TableName,
il.IndexName,
il.Fragmentation AS FragmentationStart,
MAX(
  CAST(ip.avg_fragmentation_in_percent AS DECIMAL(20, 2))
) AS FragmentationEnd
FROM @IndexList il
INNER JOIN sys.dm_db_index_physical_stats(@DatabaseId, NULL, NULL, NULL, NULL) ip
ON DatabaseId = ip.database_id
  AND TableId = ip.object_id
  AND IndexId = ip.index_id
GROUP BY
  il.DatabaseName,
  il.SchemaName,
  il.TableName,
  il.IndexName,
  il.Fragmentation ORDER BY
  Fragmentation DESC,
  TableName ASC,
  IndexName ASC;
  RETURN;
END
GO
-- Execute index rebuild stored procedure
EXEC dbo.RebuildIndexes N'rebuild', 30;
```

	DatabaseName	SchemaName	TableName	IndexName	FragmentationStart	FragmentationEnd
1	AdventureWorks2012	Sales	Store	PXML_Store__Demographics	98.44	98.44
2	AdventureWorks2012	Production	ProductModel	PXML_ProductModel_CatalogDescription	80.00	80.00
3	AdventureWorks2012	Purchasing	ProductVendor	PK_ProductVendor_ProductID_BusinessEntityID	80.00	80.00
4	AdventureWorks2012	dbo	DatabaseLog	PK_DatabaseLog_DatabaseLogID	75.00	75.00
5	AdventureWorks2012	Production	ProductModelProductDescriptionCulture	PK_ProductModelProductDescriptionCulture_Product...	75.00	75.00
6	AdventureWorks2012	Person	BusinessEntityContact	IX_BusinessEntityContact_ContactTypeID	66.67	66.67
7	AdventureWorks2012	Person	BusinessEntityContact	IX_BusinessEntityContact_PersonID	66.67	66.67
8	AdventureWorks2012	HumanResources	Employee	AK_Employee_LoginID	66.67	66.67
9	AdventureWorks2012	Production	ProductCostHistory	PK_ProductCostHistory_ProductID_StartDate	66.67	66.67
10	AdventureWorks2012	Production	ProductDescription	AK_ProductDescription_rowguid	66.67	66.67
11	AdventureWorks2012	Production	ProductListPriceHistory	PK_ProductListPriceHistory_ProductID_StartDate	66.67	66.67
12	AdventureWorks2012	Production	ProductReview	IX_ProductReview_ProductID_Name	66.67	66.67
13	AdventureWorks2012	Sales	SpecialOfferProduct	PK_SpecialOfferProduct_SpecialOfferID_ProductID	66.67	66.67

Figure 3-12. *The Results of a Cursor-based Index Rebuild in the AdventureWorks Database*

The dbo.RebuildIndexes procedure shown in Listing 3-17 populates a table variable with the information necessary to identify all indexes on all tables in the current database. It also uses the sys.dm_db_indexphysical_ stats catalog function to retrieve initial index fragmentation information.

```
--Populate index list table

INSERT INTO @IndexList
(
DatabaseName,
DatabaseId,
SchemaName,
SchemaId,
TableName,
TableId,
IndexName,
IndexId,
Fragmentation
)
SELECT
  db_name(),
db_id(),
s.Name,
s.schema_id,
t.Name,
t.object_id,
i.Name,
i.index_id,
MAX(ip.avg_fragmentation_in_percent)
FROM sys.tables t
INNER JOIN sys.schemas s
  ON t.schema_id=s.schema_id
INNER JOIN sys.indexes i
  ON t.object_id=i.object_id
INNER JOIN sys.dm_db_index_physical_stats (db_id(), NULL, NULL,NULL, NULL) ip
ON ip.object_id=t.object_id
   AND ip.index_id=i.index_id
WHERE ip.database_id=db_id()
 GROUP BY
   s.Name,
   s.schema_id,
   t.Name,
   t.object_id,
   i.Name,
   i.index_id;
```

If you specify a rebuild action when you call the procedure, it creates a cursor to loop through the rows of the @IndexList table, but only for indexes with a fragmentation percentage higher than the level that you specified when calling the procedure.

```
-- Declare a cursor to create the dynamic SOL statements
DECLARE Index_Cursor CURSOR FAST_FORWARD
FOR
```

```
SELECT
  SchemaName,
  TableName,
  IndexName FROM @IndexList
WHERE Fragmentation>@MaxFrag
ORDER BY
  Fragmentation DESC,
  TableName ASC,
  IndexName ASC;
```

The procedure then loops through all the indexes in the @IndexList table, creating an ALTER INDEX statement to rebuild each index. Each ALTER INDEX statement is created as dynamic SQL to be printed and executed using the SQL PRINT and EXEC statements.

```
-- Open the cursor for reading
OPEN Index_Cursor;

-- Loop through all the tables in the database
FETCH NEXT FROM Index_Cursor
INTO @Schema,@Table, @Index;

WHILE @@FETCH_STATUS=0
BEGIN
 -- Create ALTER INDEX statement to rebuild index
SET @Sql=N'ALTER INDEX ' +
 QUOTENAME(RTRIM(@Index))+N' ON '+OUOTENAME(l@Schema)+N'.' +
 OUOTENAME(RTRIM(@Table))+N' REBUILD WITH (ONLINE=OFF); ';

PRINT @Sql;

-- Execute dynamic SQL
EXEC (@Sql);

-- Get the next index
FETCH NEXT FROM Index_Cursor
INTO @Schema, @Table, @lndex;
END

-- Close and deallocate the cursor.
CLOSE Index_Cursor;
DEALLOCATE Index_Cursor;
```

The dynamic SQL statements generated by the procedure look similar to the following:

```
ALTER INDEX [IX_PurchaseOrderHeader_EmployeeID]
ON [Purchasing].[PurchaseOrderHeader] REBUILD WITH (ONLINE=OFF);
```

The balance of the code simply displays the results, including the new fragmentation percentage after the indexes are rebuilt.

NO DBCC?

You'll notice in the sample code in Listing 3-17 that we specifically avoided using database console commands (DBCCs) like DBCC DBREINDEX and DBCC SHOWCONTIG to manage index fragmentation and rebuild the indexes in the database. There's a very good reason for this—these DBCC statements, and many others, are deprecated. Microsoft is planning to do away with many common DBCC statements in favor of catalog views and enhanced T-SQL statement syntax. The DBCC DBREINDEX statement, for instance, is now being replaced by the ALTER INDEX REBUILD syntax, and DBCC SHOWCONTIG is replaced by the sys.dm_db_index_physical_stats catalog function. Keep this in mind when porting code from legacy systems and creating new code.

Another situation where we would advise developers to use cursors is when the solution required is a one-off task, a set-based solution would be very complex, and time is short. Examples include creating complex running sum-type calculations or performing complex data-scrubbing routines on a very limited timeframe. We would not advise using a cursor as a permanent production application solution without exploring all available set-based options, however. Remember that whenever you use a cursor, you override SQL Server's automatic optimizations; and the SQL Server query engine has much better and more current information to optimize operations than you will have access to at any given point in time. Also keep in mind that the tasks you consider extremely complex today will become much easier as SQL's set-based processing becomes second nature to you.

CURSORS, CURSORS EVERYWHERE

Although cursors commonly get a lot of bad press from SQL gurus, there is nothing inherently evil about them. They are just another tool in the toolkit and should be viewed as such. What is wrong, however, is the ways in which developers abuse them. Generally speaking, and perhaps as much as 90 percent of the time, cursors are absolutely not the best tool for the job when you're writing T-SQL code. Unfortunately, many SQL newbies find set-based logic difficult to grasp at first. Cursors provide a comfort zone for procedural developers because they lend themselves to procedural design patterns.

One of the worst design patterns you can adopt is the "cursors, cursors everywhere" design pattern. Believe it or not, there are people out there who have been writing SQL code for years and have never bothered learning about SQL's set-based processing. These people tend to approach every SQL problem as if it were a C# or Visual Basic problem, and their code tends to reflect it with the "cursors, cursors everywhere" design pattern. And remember, replacing cursor-based code with WHILE loops does not solve the problem. Simulating the behavior of cursors with WHILE loops doesn't solve the design flaw inherent in the cursor-based solution: row-by-row processing of data. WHILE loops might, under some circumstances, perform comparably to cursors; in many situations, however, even a cursor will outperform a WHILE loop.

Another horrible design pattern results from what are actually best practices in other procedural languages. Code reuse is not SQL's strong point. Many programmers coming from object-oriented languages that promote heavy code reuse tend to write layers and layers of SPs that call one another. These SPs often have cursors, and cursors within cursors, to feed each layer of procedures. While it does promote code reuse, this design pattern causes severe performance degradation. A commonly used term for this type of design pattern, popularized by SQL professional Jeff Moden, is "row-by-agonizing-row" (or RBAR) processing. This design pattern is high on our top ten list of ways to abuse SQL Server and will cause you far more problems than it ever solves. SQL Server 2012 offers a feature, the *table-valued parameter,* which may help increase manageability and performance of the layered SP design methodology. We'll discuss table-valued parameters in Chapter 5.

SQL Server supports syntax for both ISO standard cursors and T-SQL extended syntax cursors. The ISO standard supports the following cursor options:

- The INSENSITIVE option makes a temporary copy of the cursor result set and uses that copy to fulfill cursor requests. This means that changes to the underlying tables are not reflected when you request rows from the cursor.

- The SCROLL option allows you to use all cursor fetch options to position the cursor on any row in the cursor result set. The cursor fetch options include FIRST, LAST, NEXT, PRIOR, ABSOLUTE, and RELATIVE. If the SCROLL option is not specified, only the NEXT cursor fetch option is allowed.

- The READ ONLY option in the cursor FOR clause prevents updates to the underlying data through the cursor. In a non-read only cursor, you can update the underlying data with the WHERE CURRENT OF clause in the UPDATE and DELETE statements.

- The UPDATE OF option allows you to specify a list of updatable columns in the cursor's result set. You can specify UPDATE without the OF keyword and its associated column list to allow updates to all columns.

The T-SQL extended syntax provides many more options than the ISO syntax. In addition to supporting read-only cursors (the keyword is READONLY, however), the UPDATE OF option, the SCROLL option, and insensitive cursors (using the STATIC keyword), T-SQL extended syntax cursors support the following options:

- Cursors that are local to the current batch, procedure, or trigger in which they are created via the LOCAL keyword. Cursors that are global to the connection in which they are created can be defined using the GLOBAL keyword.

- The FORWARDONLY option, which is the opposite of the SCROLL option, allowing you to only fetch rows from the cursor using the NEXT option.

- The KEYSET option, which specifies that the number and order of rows is fixed at the time the cursor is created. Trying to fetch rows that are subsequently deleted does not succeed, and a @@FETCH_STATUS value of −2 is returned.

- The DYNAMIC option, which specifies a cursor that reflects all data changes made to the rows in its underlying result set. This type of cursor is one of the slowest, since every change to the underlying data must be reflected whenever you scroll to a new row of the result set.

- The FAST_FORWARD option, which specifies a performance-optimized combination forward-only/read-only cursor.

- The SCROLLLOCKS option, which locks underlying data rows as they are read to ensure that data modifications will succeed. The SCROLLLOCKS option is mutually exclusive with the FAST_FORWARD and STATIC options.

- The OPTIMISTIC option, which uses timestamps to determine if a row has changed since the cursor was loaded. If a row has changed, the OPTIMISTIC option will not allow the current cursor to update the same row. The OPTIMISTIC option is incompatible with the FAST_FORWARD option.

- The TYPEWARNING option, which sends a warning if a cursor will be automatically converted from the requested type to another type. This can happen, for instance, if SQL Server needs to convert a forward-only cursor to a static cursor.

▪ **Note** If you don't specify a cursor as LOCAL or GLOBAL, cursors that are created default to the setting defined by the default to local cursor database setting.

CURSOR COMPARISONS

Cursors come in several flavors, and you could spend a lot of time just trying to figure out which one you need to perform a given task. Most of the time, the cursors you'll need are forward-only/read-only cursors. These cursors are efficient because they move in only one direction and do not need to perform updates on the underlying data. Maximizing cursor efficiency by choosing the right type of cursor for the job is a quick-win strategy that you should keep in mind when you have to resort to a cursor.

Summary

In this chapter, we introduced SQL 3VL, which consists of three logical result values: true, false, and unknown. This is a key concept to understanding SQL development in general, but it can be a foreign idea to developers coming from backgrounds in other programming languages. If you're not yet familiar with the 3VL chart, we highly recommend revisiting Figure 3-1. This chart summarizes the logic that governs SQL 3VL.

We also introduced T-SQL's control-of-flow statement offerings, which allow you to branch conditionally and unconditionally within your code, loop, handle exceptions, and force delays within your code. We also covered the two flavors of CASE expression, and some of the more advanced uses of CASE, including dynamic pivot table queries and CASE-based functions like COALESCE and NULLIF.

Finally, we discussed the redheaded stepchild of SQL development, the cursor. Although cursors commonly get a bad rap, there's nothing inherently bad about them; the problem is with how people use them. We focused our discussion of cursors on some common scenarios where they might be considered the best tool for the job, including administrative and complex one-off tasks. Finally, we presented the options available for ISO-compliant cursors and T-SQL extended syntax cursors, both of which are supported by SQL Server 2012.

In the next chapter, we'll begin discussing T-SQL programmability features, starting with an in-depth look at T-SQL UDFs in all their various forms.

EXERCISES
---

1. [True/False] SQL 3VL supports the logical result values true, false, and unknown.

2. [Choose one] SQL NULL represents which of the following:

    - An unknown or missing value

    - The number 0

    - An empty (zero-length) string

    - All of the above

3. [True/False] The BEGIN and END keywords delimit a statement block and limit the scope of variables declared within that statement block, like curly braces ({ }) in C#.

4. [Fill in the blank] The _____keyword forces a WHILE loop to terminate immediately.

5. [True/False] The TRY...CATCH block can catch every possible SQL Server error.

6. [Fill in the blanks] SQL CASE expressions come in two forms, _____ and _____.

7. [Choose all that apply] T-SQL supports which of the following cursor options:

   - Read-only cursors

   - Forward-only cursors

   - Backward-only cursors

   - Write-only cursors

8. Modify the code in Listing 3-10 to generate a pivot table result set that returns the total dollar amount (TotalDue) of orders by region, instead of the count of orders by region.

CHAPTER 4

User-Defined Functions

Each new version of SQL Server features improvements to T-SQL that make development easier. SQL Server 2000 introduced (among other things) the concept of user-defined functions (UDFs). Like functions in other programming languages, T-SQL UDFs provide a convenient way for developers to define routines that accept parameters, perform actions based on those parameters, and return data to the caller. T-SQL functions come in three flavors: inline table-valued functions (TVFs), multistatement TVFs, and scalar functions. SQL Server 2012 also supports the ability to create CLR integration UDFs, which we'll talk about in Chapter 14.

Scalar Functions

Basically a scalar UDF is a function that accepts zero or more parameters and returns a single scalar value as the result. You're probably already familiar with scalar functions in mathematics, and with T-SQL's built-in scalar functions (e.g., ABS and SUBSTRING). The CREATE FUNCTION statement allows you to create custom scalar functions that behave like the built-in scalar functions. To demonstrate scalar UDFs, we'll take a trip back in time to high school geometry class. In accordance with the rules passed down from Euclid, this UDF accepts a circle's radius and returns the area of the circle using the formula $area = \pi \times r^2$. Listing 4-1 demonstrates this simple scalar UDF.

Listing 4-1. Simple Scalar UDF

```
CREATE FUNCTION dbo.CalculateCircleArea (@Radius float =1.0)
RETURNS float
WITH RETURNS NULL ON NULL INPUT
AS
BEGIN
   RETURN PI() * POWER(@Radius, 2);
END;
```

The first line of the CREATE FUNCTION statement defines the schema and name of the function using a standard SQL Server two-part name (dbo.CalculateCircleArea) and a single required parameter, the radius of the circle (@Radius). The @Radius parameter is defined as a T-SQL float type. The parameter is assigned a default value of 1.0 by the = 1.0 after the parameter declaration.

```
CREATE FUNCTION dbo.CalculateCircleArea (@Radius float =1.0)
```

The next line contains the RETURNS keyword, which specifies the data type of the result that will be returned by the UDF. In this instance, the RETURNS keyword indicates that the UDF will return a float result.

```
RETURNS float
```

The third line contains additional options following the WITH keyword. In the sample, we use the RETURNS NULL ON NULL INPUT function option for a performance improvement. The RETURNS NULL ON NULL INPUT option is a performance-enhancing option that automatically returns NULL if any of the parameters passed in are NULL. The performance enhancement occurs because SQL Server will not execute the body of the function if a NULL is passed in and this option is specified.

The AS keyword indicates the start of the function body which must be enclosed in the T-SQL BEGIN and END keywords. The sample function in Listing 4-1 is very simple, consisting of a single RETURN statement that immediately returns the value of the circle area calculation. The RETURN statement must be the last statement before the END keyword in every scalar UDF.

```
RETURN PI() * POWER(@radius, 2);
```

You can test this simple UDF with a few SELECT statements like the following. The results are shown in Figure 4-1.

```
SELECT dbo.CalculateCircleArea(10);
SELECT dbo.CalculateCircleArea(NULL);
SELECT dbo.CalculateCircleArea(2.5);
```

Figure 4-1. *The Results of the Sample Circle Area Calculations*

UDF PARAMETERS

UDF parameters operate similarly to, but slightly differently from, stored procedure (SP) parameters. It's important to be aware of the differences. For instance, if you create a UDF that accepts no parameters, you still need to include empty parentheses after the function name—both when creating and invoking the function. Some built-in functions, like the PI() function used in Listing 4-1, which represents the value of the constant π (3.14159265358979), do not take parameters. Notice that when the function is called in the UDF, it is still called with empty parentheses.

Also, when SPs are assigned default values, you can simply leave the parameter off your parameter list completely when calling the procedure. This is not an option with UDFs. To use a UDF default value, you must use the DEFAULT keyword when calling the UDF. To use the default value for the @radius parameter of the example dbo.CalculateCircleArea UDF, you would call the UDF like this:

```
SELECT dbo.CalculateCircleArea (DEFAULT);
```

Finally, SPs have no equivalent to the RETURNS NULL ON NULL INPUT option. You can simulate this functionality to some extent by checking your parameters for NULL immediately on entering the SP, though. We'll discuss SPs in greater detail in Chapter 5.

UDFs provide several creation-time options that allow you to improve performance and security, including the following:

- The ENCRYPTION option can be used to store your UDF in the database in obfuscated format. Note that this is not true encryption, but rather an easily circumvented obfuscation of your code. See the "UDF 'Encryption'" sidebar for more information.

- The SCHEMABINDING option indicates that your UDF will be bound to database objects referenced in the body of the function. With SCHEMABINDING turned on, attempts to change or drop referenced tables and other database objects results in an error. This helps to prevent inadvertent changes to tables and other database objects that can break your UDF. Additionally, the SQL Server Database Engine team has published information indicating that SCHEMABINDING can improve the performance of UDFs, even if they don't reference other database objects at all (http://blogs.msdn.com/b/sqlprogrammability/archive/2006/05/12/596424.aspx).

- The CALLED ON NULL INPUT option is the opposite of RETURNS NULL ON NULL INPUT. When CALLED ON NULL INPUT is specified, SQL Server executes the body of the function even if one or more parameters are NULL. CALLED ON NULL INPUT is a default option for all scalar-valued functions.

- The EXECUTE AS option manages caller security on UDFs. You can specify that the UDF will be executed as any of the following:

  - CALLER indicates that the UDF should be run under the security context of the user calling the function. This is the default.

  - SELF indicates that the UDF should be run under the security context of the user who created (or altered) the function.

  - OWNER indicates that the UDF should run under the security context of the owner of the UDF (or the owner of the schema containing the UDF).

  - Finally, you can specify that the UDF should run under the security context of a specific user by specifying a username.

UDF "ENCRYPTION"

Using the ENCRYPTION option on UDFs performs a simple obfuscation of your code. It actually does little more than "keep honest people honest," and in reality it tends to be more trouble than it's worth. Many a developer and DBA have spent precious time scouring the Internet for tools to decrypt their database objects because they were convinced the scripts in their source control database were out of sync with the production database. Keep in mind that those same decryption tools are available to anyone with an Internet connection and a browser. If you write commercial database scripts or perform database consulting services, your best (and really only) protection against curious DBAs and developers reverse-engineering and modifying your code is a well-written contract. Keep this in mind when deciding whether to "encrypt" your database objects.

Recursion in Scalar User-Defined Functions

Now that we've covered the basics, we think we'll hang out in math class for a few more minutes to talk about recursion. Like most procedural programming languages that allow function definitions, T-SQL allows recursion in UDFs. There's hardly a better way to demonstrate recursion than the most basic recursive algorithm around: the factorial function.

For those who put factorials out of their minds immediately after graduation, let us give a brief rundown of what they are. A factorial is the product of all natural (or counting) numbers less than or equal to n, where $n > 0$. Factorials are represented in mathematics with the *bang* notation: $n!$. As an example, $5! = 1 \times 2 \times 3 \times 4 \times 5 = 120$. The simple scalar dbo.CalculateFactorial UDF in Listing 4-2 calculates a factorial recursively for an integer parameter passed into it.

Listing 4-2. Recursive Scalar UDF

```
CREATE  FUNCTION  dbo.CalculateFactorial  (@n  int = 1)
RETURNS decimal(38, 0)
WITH  RETURNS NULL ON NULL INPUT
AS
BEGIN
      RETURN
      (CASE
         WHEN  @n  <=  0  THEN  NULL
         WHEN  @n  >  1  THEN  CAST(@n  AS  float) * dbo.CalculateFactorial (@n - 1)
         WHEN @n = 1 THEN 1
      END);
END;
```

The first few lines are similar to Listing 4-1. The function accepts a single int parameter and returns a scalar decimal value. The RETURNS NULL ON NULL INPUT option returns NULL immediately if NULL is passed in.

```
CREATE FUNCTION dbo.CalculateFactorial(@n int = 1)
RETURNS decimal(38, 0)
WITH RETURNS NULL ON NULL INPUT
```

We've decided to return a decimal result in this example because of the limitations of the int and bigint types. Specifically, the int type overflows at 13! and bigint bombs out at 21!. In order to put the UDF through its paces, we have to allow it to return results up to 32!, which I'll discuss later in this section. As in Listing 4-1, the body of this UDF is a single RETURN statement, this time with a searched CASE expression.

```
RETURN (CASE
WHEN @n <= 0 THEN NULL
WHEN @n > 1 THEN CAST(@n AS float) * dbo.CalculateFactorial (@n - 1)
WHEN @n = 1 THEN 1 END);
```

The CASE expression checks the value of the UDF parameter, @n. If @n is 0 or negative, dbo.CalculateFactorial returns NULL since the result is undefined. If @n is greater than 1, dbo.CalculateFactorial returns @n * dbo.CalculateFactorial(@n - 1), the recursive part of the UDF. This ensures that the UDF will continue calling itself recursively, multiplying the current value of @n by (@n-1)!.

Finally, when @n reaches 1, the UDF returns 1. This is the part of dbo.CalculateFactorial that actually stops the recursion. Without the check for @n = 1, you could theoretically end up in an infinite recursive loop. In practice, however, SQL Server will save you from yourself by limiting you to a maximum of 32 levels of recursion. Demonstrating the 32-level limit on recursion is why we decided it was important the UDF needed to return results up to 32!. Following are some examples of dbo.CalculateFactorial calls with various parameters and their results.

```
SELECT dbo.CalculateFactorial(NULL); -- Returns NULL
SELECT dbo.CalculateFactorial(-1);   -- Returns NULL
SELECT dbo.CalculateFactorial(0);    -- Returns NULL
SELECT dbo.CalculateFactorial(5);    -- Returns 120
SELECT dbo.CalculateFactorial(32);   -- Returns 263130836933693520000000000000000000
```

As you can see, the dbo.CalculateFactorial function easily handles the 32 levels of recursion required to calculate 32!. If you try to go beyond that limit, you'll get an error message. Executing the following code, which attempts 33 levels of recursion, does not work.

```
SELECT dbo.CalculateFactorial(33);
```

This causes SQL Server to grumble loudly with an error message similar to the following:

```
Msg 217, Level 16, State 1, Line 1
Maximum stored procedure, function, trigger, or view nesting level exceeded (limit 32).
```

MORE THAN ONE WAY TO SKIN A CAT

The 32-level recursion limit is a *hard limit*; that is, you can't programmatically change it through server or database settings. This really isn't as bad a limitation as you might think. Very rarely do you actually need to recursively call a UDF more than 32 times, and doing so could result in a severe performance penalty. There's generally more than one way to get the job done, however, and you can work around the 32-level recursion limitation in the dbo.CalculateFactorial function by rewriting it with a WHILE loop or using a recursive common table expression (CTE), as shown here:

```
CREATE FUNCTION dbo.CalculateFactorial (@n int = 1)
RETURNS float
WITH RETURNS NULL ON NULL INPUT
AS
BEGIN
    DECLARE @result float;
    SET @result = NULL;

  IF @n > 0
  BEGIN
    SET @result = 1.0;

  WITH Numbers (num)
  AS (
      SELECT 1
      UNION ALL
      SELECT num + 1
      FROM Numbers
      WHERE num < @n
      )
```

```
        SELECT @result=@result * num
        FROM Numbers;
  END;
  RETURN @result;
END;
```

This rewrite of the dbo.CalculateFactorial function averts the recursive function call limit by eliminating the recursive function calls. Instead, it pushes the recursion back into the body of the function through the use of a recursive CTE. By default, SQL Server allows up to 100 levels of recursion in a CTE (you can override this with the MAXRECURSION option), greatly expanding your factorial calculation power. With this function, you can easily find out that 33! is 8.68331761881189E+36, or even that 100! is 9.33262154439441E+157. The important idea to take away from this discussion is that while recursive function calls have hard limits on them, you can often work around those limitations using other T-SQL functionality.

Also keep in mind that although we used factorial calculation as a simple example of recursion, this method is considered naive, and there are several more-efficient methods of calculating factorials.

Please note that no cats were harmed during the writing of this book.

Procedural Code in User-Defined Functions

So far, we've talked about simple functions that demonstrate the basic points of scalar UDFs. But in all likelihood, unless we're implementing business logic for a swimming pool installation company, neither you nor us will likely need to spend much time calculating the area of a circle in T-SQL.

A common problem that you have a much greater chance of running into is name-based searching. T-SQL offers tools for exact matching, partial matching, and even limited pattern matching via the LIKE predicate. T-SQL even offers built-in phonetic matching (sound-alike matching) through the built-in SOUNDEX function.

Heavy-duty approximate matching, however, usually requires a more advanced tool, like a better phonetic matching algorithm. We'll use one of these algorithms, the New York State Identification and Intelligence System (NYSIIS) algorithm, to demonstrate procedural code in UDFs.

THE SOUNDEX ALGORITHM

The NYSIIS algorithm is an improvement on the Soundex phonetic encoding algorithm, itself nearly 90 years old. The NYSIIS algorithm converts groups of one, two, or three alphabetic characters (known as *n-grams*) in names to a phonetic ("sounds like") approximation. This makes it easier to search for names that have similar pronunciations but different spellings, such as *Smythe* and *Smith*. As mentioned in this section, SQL Server provides a built-in SOUNDEX function, but Soundex provides very poor accuracy and usually results in many false hits. NYSIIS and other modern algorithms provide much better results than Soundex.

To demonstrate procedural code in UDFs, we will implement a UDF that phonetically encodes names using NYSIIS encoding rules. The rules for NYSIIS phonetic encoding are relatively simple, with the majority of the rules requiring simple n-gram substitutions. The following is a complete list of NYSIIS encoding rules:

1. Remove all nonalphabetic characters from the name.

2. The first characters of the name are encoded according to the n-gram substitutions shown in the "Start of Name" table in Figure 4-2. In Figure 4-2, the n-grams shown on the left-hand side of the arrows are replaced with the n-grams on the right-hand side of the arrows during the encoding process.

3. The last characters of the name are encoded according to the n-gram substitutions shown in the "End of Name" table in Figure 4-2.

4. The first character of the encoded value is set to the first character of the name.

5. After the first and last n-grams are encoded, all remaining characters in the name are encoded according to the n-gram substitutions shown in the "Middle of Name" table in Figure 4-2.

6. All side-by-side duplicate characters in the encoded name are reduced to a single character. This means that *AA* is reduced to *A* and *SS* is reduced to *S.*

7. If the last character of the encoded name is *S*, it is removed.

8. If the last characters of the encoded name are *AY*, they are replaced with *Y.*

9. If the last character of the encoded name is *A*, it is removed.

10. The result is truncated to six characters maximum length.

NYSIIS Phonetic Encoding Rules

Start of Name	Middle of Name	End of Name
SCH ➤ SSS	SCH ➤ SSS	EE,IE ➤ Y
MAC ➤ MCC	EV ➤ AF	DT,ND,NT,RD,RT ➤ D
PH,PF ➤ FF	PH ➤ FF	
KN ➤ NN	KN,M ➤ N	
K ➤ C	Z ➤ S	
	Q ➤ G	
	K ➤ C	
	A,E,I,O,U ➤ A	

Special Rules

H ➤ (previous) if next or previous is non-vowel
W ➤ (previous) if previous is a vowel

Figure 4-2. NYSIIS Phonetic Encoding Rules/Character Substitutions

You could use some fairly large CASE expressions to implement these rules, but we've chosen the more flexible option of using a replacement table. This table will contain the majority of the replacement rules in just the three columns, as described here:

- Location: This column tells the UDF whether the rule should be applied to the start, end, or middle of the name.

- NGram: This column is the n-gram, or sequence of characters, that will be encoded. These n-grams correspond to the left-hand side of the arrows in Figure 4-2.

- Replacement: This column represents the replacement value for the corresponding n-gram on the same row. These character sequences correspond to the right-hand side of the arrows in Figure 4-2.

Listing 4-3 is a CREATE TABLE statement that builds the NYSIIS phonetic encoding replacement rules table.

Listing 4-3. Creating the NYSIIS Replacement Rules Table

```
-- Create the NYSIIS replacement rules table
CREATE TABLE dbo.NYSIIS_Replacements
  (Location    nvarchar(10) NOT NULL,
   NGram nvarchar(10) NOT NULL,
   Replacement nvarchar(10) NOT NULL,

   PRIMARY KEY (Location, NGram));
```

Listing 4-4 is a single INSERT statement that uses row constructors to populate all of the NYSIIS replacement rules, as shown in Figure 4-2.

Listing 4-4. INSERT Statement to Populate NYSIIS Replacement Rules Table

```
INSERT INTO NYSIIS_Replacements (Location, NGram, Replacement)
  VALUES(N'End', N'DT', N'DD'),
        (N'End', N'EE', N'YY'),
        (N'End', N'IE', N'YY'),
        (N'End', N'ND', N'DD'),
        (N'End', N'NT', N'DD'),
        (N'End', N'RD', N'DD'),
        (N'End', N'RT', N'DD'),
        (N'Mid', N'A', N'A'),
        (N'Mid', N'E', N'A'),
        (N'Mid', N'T', N'A'),
        (N'Mid', N'K', N'C'),
        (N'Mid', N'M', N'N'),
        (N'Mid', N'O', N'A'),
        (N'Mid', N'Q', N'G'),
        (N'Mid', N'U', N'A'),
        (N'Mid', N'Z', N'S'),
        (N'Mid', N'AW', N'AA'),
        (N'Mid', N'EV', N'AF'),
        (N'Mid', N'EW', N'AA'),
        (N'Mid', N'IW', N'AA'),
        (N'Mid', N'KN', N'NN'),
        (N'Mid', N'OW', N'AA'),
        (N'Mid', N'PH', N'FF'),
        (N'Mid', N'UW', N'AA'),
        (N'Mid', N'SCH', N'SSS'),
        (N'Start', N'K', N'C'),
        (N'Start', N'KN', N'NN'),
        (N'Start', N'PF', N'FF'),
        (N'Start', N'PH', N'FF'),
        (N'Start', N'MAC', N'MCC'),
        (N'Start', N'SCH', N'SSS');
GO
```

Listing 4-5 is the actual UDF that encodes a string using NYSIIS. This UDF demonstrates the complexity of the control-of-flow logic that can be implemented in a scalar UDF.

Listing 4-5. Function to Encode Strings Using NYSIIS

```
CREATE FUNCTION dbo.EncodeNYSIIS
(
    @String nvarchar(100)
)
RETURNS nvarchar(6)
WITH RETURNS NULL ON NULL INPUT
AS
BEGIN
  DECLARE @Result nvarchar(100);
  SET @Result = UPPER(@String);

-- Step 1: Remove All Nonalphabetic Characters
WITH Numbers (Num)
AS
(
  SELECT 1

UNION ALL

SELECT Num + 1
FROM Numbers
WHERE Num < LEN(@Result)
)
SELECT @Result = STUFF
(
  @Result,
  Num,
  1,
 CASE WHEN SUBSTRING(@Result, Num, 1) >= N'A'
      AND SUBSTRING(@Result, Num, 1) <= N'Z'
           THEN SUBSTRING(@Result, Num, 1)
           ELSE N'.'
 END )
FROM Numbers;

SET @Result = REPLACE(@Result, N'.', N'');

-- Step 2: Replace the Start N-gram
SELECT TOP (1) @Result = STUFF
(
  @Result,
  1,
  LEN(NGram),
  Replacement
)
FROM dbo.NYSIIS_Replacements
WHERE Location = N'Start'
  AND SUBSTRING(@Result, 1, LEN(NGram)) = NGram
ORDER BY LEN(NGram) DESC;
```

```sql
-- Step 3: Replace the End N-gram
SELECT TOP (1) @Result = STUFF
 (
    @Result,
    LEN(@Result) - LEN(NGram)+1,
    LEN(NGram),
    Replacement
 )
FROM dbo.NYSIIS_Replacements
WHERE Location = N'End'
  AND SUBSTRING(@Result, LEN(@Result) - LEN(NGram)+1, LEN(NGram)) = NGram
ORDER BY LEN(NGram) DESC;

-- Step 4: Save the First Letter of the Name
DECLARE @FirstLetter nchar(1);
SET @FirstLetter = SUBSTRING(@Result, 1, 1);

-- Step 5: Replace All Middle N-grams
DECLARE @Replacement nvarchar(10);
DECLARE @i int;
SET @i = 1;
WHILE @i <= LEN(@Result)
BEGIN
    SET @Replacement = NULL;

-- Grab the middle-of-name replacement n-gram
SELECT TOP (1) @Replacement = Replacement
FROM dbo.NYSIIS_Replacements
WHERE Location = N'Mid'
    AND SUBSTRING(@Result, @i, LEN(NGram)) = NGram
ORDER BY LEN(NGram) DESC;

SET @Replacement = COALESCE(@Replacement, SUBSTRING(@Result, @i, 1));

-- If we found a replacement, apply it
  SET @Result = STUFF(@Result, @i, LEN(@Replacement), @Replacement)

-- Move on to the next n-gram
  SET @i = @i + COALESCE(LEN(@Replacement), 1);
END;

-- Replace the first character with the first letter we saved at the start
SET @Result = STUFF(@Result, 1, 1, @FirstLetter);

-- Here we apply our special rules for the 'H' character. Special handling for 'W'
-- characters is taken care of in the replacement rules table
WITH Numbers (Num)
AS
(
  SELECT 2     -- Don't bother with the first character

  UNION ALL
```

```
    SELECT Num+1
    FROM Numbers
    WHERE Num<LEN(@Result)
)
SELECT @Result=STUFF
    (
    @Result,
    Num,
    1,
    CASE SUBSTRING(@Result, Num, 1)
        WHEN N'H' THEN
          CASE WHEN SUBSTRING(@Result, Num+1, 1)
                    NOT IN (N'A', N'E', N'I', N'O', N'U')
             OR SUBSTRING(@Result, Num - 1, 1)
              NOT IN (N'A', N'E', N'I', N'O', N'U')
             THEN SUBSTRING(@Result, Num - 1, 1)
           ELSE N'H'
    END
 ELSE SUBSTRING(@Result, Num, 1)
END
)
FROM Numbers;

-- Step 6: Reduce All Side-by-side Duplicate Characters
-- First replace the first letter of any sequence of two side-by-side
-- duplicate letters with a period
WITH Numbers (Num)
AS
(
    SELECT 1

    UNION ALL

    SELECT Num+1
    FROM Numbers
    WHERE Num<LEN(@Result)
)
SELECT @Result=STUFF
    (
    @Result,
    Num,
    1,
    CASE SUBSTRING(@Result, Num, 1)
       WHEN SUBSTRING(@Result, Num+1, 1) THEN N'.'
           ELSE SUBSTRING(@Result, Num, 1)
    END
    )
FROM Numbers;

-- Next replace all periods '.' with an empty string ''
SET @Result=REPLACE(@Result, N'.', N'');
```

```
-- Step 7: Remove Trailing 'S' Characters
WHILE RIGHT(@Result, 1)=N'S' AND LEN(@Result)>1
    SET @Result=STUFF(@Result, LEN(@Result), 1, N'');

-- Step 8: Remove Trailing 'A' Characters
WHILE RIGHT(@Result, 1)=N'A' AND LEN(@Result)>1
    SET @Result=STUFF(@Result, LEN(@Result), 1, N'');

-- Step 9: Replace Trailing 'AY' Characters with 'Y'
IF RIGHT(@Result, 2)='AY'
    SET @Result=STUFF(@Result, LEN(@Result) - 1, 1, N'');

-- Step 10: Truncate Result to 6 Characters
RETURN COALESCE(SUBSTRING(@Result, 1, 6), '');
END;
GO
```

The NYSIISReplacements table rules reflect most of the NYSIIS rules described by Robert L. Taft in his famous paper "Name Search Techniques." The start and end n-grams are replaced, and then the remaining n-gram rules are applied in a WHILE loop. The special rules for the letter *H* are applied, side-by-side duplicates are removed, special handling of certain trailing characters is performed, and the first six characters of the result are returned.

NUMBERS TABLES

In this example, we use recursive CTEs to dynamically generate virtual numbers tables in a couple of places. A *numbers table* is simply a table of numbers counting up to a specified maximum. The following recursive CTE generates a small numbers table (the numbers 1 through 100):

```
WITH Numbers (Num)
AS
(
    SELECT 1
    UNION ALL
    SELECT Num+1
    FROM Numbers
    WHERE Num<100
)

SELECT Num FROM Numbers;
```

In Listing 4-5, we used the number of characters in the name to limit the recursion of the CTEs. This speeds up the UDF overall. You can get even more performance gains by creating a permanent numbers table in your database with a clustered index/primary key on it, instead of using CTEs. A numbers table is always handy to have around, doesn't cost you very much to build or maintain, doesn't take up much storage space, and is extremely useful for converting loops and cursors to set-based code. A numbers table is by far one of the handiest and simplest tools you can add to your T-SQL toolkit.

As an example, we used the query in Listing 4-6 to phonetically encode the last names of all contacts in the AdventureWorks database using NYSIIS. Partial results are shown in Figure 4-3.

Listing 4-6. Using NYSIIS to Phonetically Encode All AdventureWorks Contacts

```
SELECT LastName,
    dbo.EncodeNYSIIS(LastName) AS NYSIIS
FROM Person.Person
GROUP BY LastName;
```

	LastName	NYSIIS
1	Abbas	AB
2	Abel	ABAL
3	Abercrombie	ABARCR
4	Abolrous	ABALR
5	Acevedo	ACAFAD
6	Achong	ACANG
7	Ackerman	ACARNA
8	Adams	ADAN
9	Adina	ADIN
10	Agbonile	AGBANI
11	Agcaoili	AGCAIL
12	Aguilar	AGAILA
13	Ahlering	ALARIN
14	Ajenstat	AJANS
15	Akers	ACAR
16	Alameda	ALANAD
17	Alan	ALAN
18	Alberts	ALBAR

Figure 4-3. *Partial Results of NYSIIS Encoding AdventureWorks Contacts*

Using the dbo.EncodeNYSIIS UDF is relatively simple. Listing 4-7 is a simple example of using the new UDF in the WHERE clause to retrieve all AdventureWorks contacts whose last name is phonetically similar to the name Liu. The results are shown in Figure 4-4.

Listing 4-7. Retrieving All Contact Phonetic Matches for Liu

```
SELECT
  BusinessEntityID,
  LastName,
  FirstName,
  MiddleName,
  dbo.EncodeNYSIIS(LastName) AS NYSIIS
FROM Person.Person
WHERE dbo.EncodeNYSIIS(LastName) = dbo.EncodeNYSIIS(N' Liu');
```

	BusinessEntityID	LastName	FirstName	MiddleName	NYSIIS
1	5520	Li	Aaron	NULL	LI
2	5264	Li	Adam	NULL	LI
3	5792	Li	Aimee	NULL	LI
4	17301	Li	Alan	M	LI
5	12470	Li	Alejandro	A	LI
6	11941	Li	Alisha	W	LI
7	4341	Li	Alvin	NULL	LI
8	20702	Li	Amy	J	LI
9	9768	Li	Arturo	NULL	LI
10	6279	Li	Austin	B	LI
11	5909	Li	Autumn	P	LI
12	11538	Li	Barbara	NULL	LI
13	6739	Li	Benjamin	H	LI
14	6938	Li	Brandon	NULL	LI
15	17989	Li	Brent	P	LI
16	5575	Li	Caleb	NULL	LI
17	6331	Li	Cameron	NULL	LI
18	4831	Li	Cara	NULL	LI

Figure 4-4. *Partial listinging of AdventureWorks Contacts with Names Phonetically Similar to Liu*

The example in Listing 4-7 is the naive method of using a UDF. The query engine must apply the UDF to every single row of the source table. In this case, the dbo.EncodeNYSIIS function is applied to the nearly 20,000 last names in the Person.Contact table, resulting in an inefficient query plan and excessive I/O. A more efficient method is to perform the NYSIIS encodings ahead of time—to pre-encode the names. The pre-encoding method is demonstrated in Listing 4-8.

Listing 4-8. Pre-encoding AdventureWorks Contact Names with NYSIIS

```
CREATE TABLE Person.ContactNYSIIS
(
    BusinessEntityID int NOT NULL,
    NYSIIS nvarchar(6) NOT NULL,
    PRIMARY KEY(NYSIIS, BusinessEntityID)
);
GO

INSERT INTO Person.ContactNYSIIS
(
    BusinessEntityID,
    NYSIIS
)
SELECT
    BusinessEntityID,
    dbo.EncodeNYSIIS(LastName)
FROM Person.Person;
GO
```

Once you have pre-encoded the data, queries are much more efficient. The query shown in Listing 4-9 uses the table created in Listing 4-8 to return the same results as Listing 4-7—just much more efficiently, since this version doesn't need to encode every row of data for comparison in the WHERE clause at query time.

Listing 4-9. Efficient NYSIIS Query Using Pre-encoded Data

```
SELECT
    cn.BusinessEntityID,
    c.LastName,
    c.FirstName,
    c.MiddleName,
    cn.NYSIIS
FROM Person.ContactNYSIIS cn
INNER JOIN Person.Person c
    ON cn.BusinessEntityID=c.BusinessEntityID
WHERE cn.NYSIIS=dbo.EncodeNYSIIS(N'Liu');
```

To keep the efficiency of the dbo.EncodeNYSIIS UDF-based searches optimized, we highly recommend pre-encoding your search data. This is especially true in production environments where performance is critical. NYSIIS (and phonetic matching in general) is an extremely useful tool for approximate name-based searches in a variety of applications, such as customer service, business reporting, and law enforcement.

Multistatement Table-Valued Functions

Multistatement TVFs are similar in style to scalar UDFs, but instead of returning a single scalar value, they return their result as a table data type. The declaration is very similar to that of a scalar UDF, with a few important differences:

- The return type following the RETURNS keyword is actually a table variable declaration, with its structure declared immediately following the table variable name.

- The RETURNS NULL ON NULL INPUT and CALLED ON NULL INPUT function options are not valid in a multistatement TVF definition.

- The RETURN statement in the body of the multistatement TVF has no values or variables following it.

Inside the body of the multistatement TVF, you can use the SQL Data Manipulation Language (DML) statements INSERT, UPDATE, MERGE, and DELETE to create and manipulate the return results in the table variable that will be returned as the result.

For the example of a multistatement TVF, we'll create another business application function. Namely, we are going to create a product pull list for AdventureWorks. This TVF will match the AdventureWorks sales orders stored in the Sales.SalesOrderDetail table against the product inventory in the Production.ProductInventory table. It will effectively create a list for AdventureWorks employees, telling them exactly which inventory bin to go to in order to fill an order. There are some business rules that need to be defined before we write this multistatement TVF:

- In some cases, the number of ordered items might be more than are available in one bin. In that case, the pull list will instruct the employee to grab the product from multiple bins.

- Any partial fills from a bin will be reported on the list.

- Any substitution work (e.g., substituting a different colored item of the same model) will be handled by a separate business process and won't be allowed on this list.

- No zero fills (ordered items for which there is no matching product in inventory) will be reported back on the list.

For purposes of this example, we'll say that there are three customers: Jill, Mike, and Dave. Each of these three customers places an order for exactly five of item number 783, the black Mountain-200 42-inch mountain bike. We'll also say that AdventureWorks has six of this particular inventory item in bin 1, shelf A, location 7, and another three of this particular item in bin 2, shelf B, location 10. Our business rules will create a pull list like the following:

- *Jill's order:* Pull five of item 783 from bin 1, shelf A, location 7; mark the order as a complete fill.

- *Mike's order:* Pull one of item 783 from bin 1, shelf A, location 7; mark the order as a partial fill.

- *Mike's order:* Pull three of item 783 from bin 2, shelf B, location 10; mark the order as a partial fill.

In this example, there are only 9 of the ordered items in inventory, while 15 total items have been ordered (3 customers multiplied by 5 items each). Because of this, Dave's order will be zero-filled—no items will be pulled from inventory to fill his order. Figure 4-5 is designed to help you visualize the sample inventory/order fill scenario we've described up to this point.

Figure 4-5. *Filling Orders from Inventory*

Since the inventory is out of item 783 at this point (there were nine items in inventory and all nine were used to fill Jill and Mike's orders), Dave's order will not even be listed on the pull list report. This function doesn't concern itself with product substitutions—for example, completing Mike's and Dave's orders with a comparable product such as item ID number 780 (the silver Mountain-200 42-inch mountain bike), if there happens to be some in stock. The business rule for substitutions states that a separate process will handle this aspect of order fulfillment.

Many developers might see this problem as an opportunity to flex their cursor-based coding muscles. If you look at the problem from a procedural point of view, it essentially calls for performing nested loops through AdventureWorks's customer orders and inventory to match them up. However, this code does not require procedural code, and the task can be completed in a set-based fashion using a numbers table, as described in the previous section. A numbers table with numbers from 0 to 30000 is adequate for this task, and the code to create the numbers table is shown in Listing 4-10.

Listing 4-10. Creating a Numbers Table

```
USE [AdventureWorks2012]
GO

IF EXISTS (SELECT * FROM sys.objects
          WHERE object_id=OBJECT_ID(N'[dbo].[Numbers]')
                AND type in (N'U'))
DROP TABLE [dbo].[Numbers];

-- Create a numbers table to allow the product pull list to be
-- created using set-based logic
CREATE TABLE dbo.Numbers (Num int NOT NULL PRIMARY KEY);
GO
```

```
-- Fill the numbers table with numbers from 0 to 30,000
WITH NumCTE (Num)
AS
(
SELECT 0

UNION ALL

SELECT Num+1
FROM NumCTE
WHERE Num< 30000
)

INSERT INTO dbo.Numbers (Num) SELECT Num FROM NumCTE
OPTION (MAXRECURSION 0);
GO
```

So, with a better understanding of order fulfillment logic and business rules, Listing 4-11 creates a multistatement TVF to return the product pull list according to the rules provided. As we mentioned, this multistatement TVF uses set-based logic (no cursors or loops) to retrieve the product pull list.

LOOK MA, NO CURSORS!

Many programming problems in business present a procedural loop-based solution on first glance. This applies to problems that you must solve in T-SQL as well. If you look at business problems with a set-based mindset, you'll often find a set-based solution. In the product pull list example, the loop-based process of comparing every row of inventory to the order detail rows is immediately apparent.

However, if you think of the inventory items and order detail items as two sets, then the problem becomes a set-based problem. In this case, the solution is a variation of the classic computer science/mathematics *bin-packing problem.* In the bin-packing problem, you are given a set of bins (in this case orders) in which to place a finite set of items (inventory items in this example). The natural bounds provided are the number of each item in inventory and the number of each item on each order detail line.

By solving this as a set-based problem in T-SQL, you allow SQL Server to optimize the performance of your code based on the most current information available. As we mentioned in Chapter 3, when you use cursors and loops, you take away SQL Server's performance optimization options and you assume the responsibility for performance optimization yourself. We chose to use set-based logic instead of cursors and loops to solve this particular problem. In reality, solving this problem with a set-based solution took only about 30 minutes of our time. A cursor or loop-based solution would have taken just as long or longer, and it wouldn't have been nearly as efficient.

Listing 4-11. Creating a Product Pull List

```
CREATE FUNCTION dbo.GetProductPullList()
RETURNS @result table
(
    SalesOrderID int NOT NULL,
    ProductID int NOT NULL,
    LocationID smallint NOT NULL,
    Shelf nvarchar(10) NOT NULL,
```

```
        Bin  tinyint  NOT  NULL,
        QuantityInBin smallint NOT NULL,
        QuantityOnOrder smallint NOT NULL,
        QuantityToPull smallint NOT NULL,
        PartialFillFlag nchar(1) NOT NULL,
        PRIMARY KEY (SalesOrderID, ProductID, LocationID, Shelf, Bin)
)
AS
BEGIN
    INSERT INTO @result
    (
        SalesOrderID,
        ProductID,
        LocationID,
        Shelf,
        Bin,
        QuantityInBin,
        QuantityOnOrder,
        QuantityToPull,
        PartialFillFlag
    )
    SELECT
        Order_Details.SalesOrderID,
        Order_Details.ProductID,
        Inventory_Details.LocationID,
        Inventory_Details.Shelf,
        Inventory_Details.Bin,
        Inventory_Details.Quantity,
        Order_Details.OrderQty,
        COUNT(*) AS PullQty,
        CASE WHEN COUNT(*)<Order_Details.OrderQty
        THEN N'Y'
        ELSE N'N'
        END AS PartialFillFlag
    FROM
    (
        SELECT ROW_NUMBER() OVER
        (
        PARTITION  BY  p.ProductID
        ORDER  BY  p.ProductID,
        p.LocationID,
        p.Shelf,
        p.Bin
        )  AS  Num,
        p.ProductID,
        p.LocationID,
        p.Shelf,
        p.Bin,
        p.Quantity
        FROM Production.ProductInventory p
        INNER JOIN dbo.Numbers n
        ON  n.Num  BETWEEN  1  AND  Quantity
```

97

```
    )  Inventory_Details
    INNER JOIN
    (
        SELECT ROW_NUMBER() OVER
        (
        PARTITION  BY  o.ProductID
        ORDER  BY  o.ProductID,
        o.SalesOrderID
        )  AS  Num,
        o.ProductID,
        o.SalesOrderID,
        o.OrderQty
        FROM Sales.SalesOrderDetail o
        INNER JOIN dbo.Numbers n
        ON  n.Num  BETWEEN  1  AND  o.OrderQty
    )  Order_Details
    ON Inventory_Details.ProductID=Order_Details.ProductID
        AND Inventory_Details.Num=Order_Details.Num
    GROUP BY
        Order_Details.SalesOrderID,
        Order_Details.ProductID,
        Inventory_Details.LocationID,
        Inventory_Details.Shelf,
        Inventory_Details.Bin,
        Inventory_Details.Quantity,
        Order_Details.OrderQty;
    RETURN;
END;
GO
```

Retrieving the product pull list involves a simple SELECT query like the following. Partial results are shown in Figure 4-6.

	SalesOrderID	ProductID	LocationID	Shelf	Bin	QuantityInBin	QuantityOnOrder	QuantityToPull	PartialFillFlag
1	43659	709	7	N/A	0	180	6	6	N
2	43659	711	7	N/A	0	216	4	4	N
3	43659	712	7	N/A	0	288	2	2	N
4	43659	714	7	N/A	0	180	3	3	N
5	43659	716	7	N/A	0	252	1	1	N
6	43659	771	7	N/A	0	49	1	1	N
7	43659	772	7	N/A	0	88	1	1	N
8	43659	773	7	N/A	0	83	2	2	N
9	43659	774	7	N/A	0	62	1	1	N
10	43659	776	7	N/A	0	78	1	1	N
11	43659	777	7	N/A	0	49	3	3	N
12	43659	778	7	N/A	0	88	1	1	N
13	43660	758	7	N/A	0	116	1	1	N
14	43660	762	7	N/A	0	75	1	1	N
15	43661	708	7	N/A	0	324	5	5	N

Figure 4-6. *AdventureWorks Product Pull List (Partial)*

```
SELECT
    SalesOrderID,
    ProductID,
    LocationID,
    Shelf,
    Bin,
    QuantityInBin,
    QuantityOnOrder,
    QuantityToPull,
    PartialFillFlag
FROM dbo.GetProductPullList();
```

One interesting aspect of the multistatement TVF is the actual CREATE FUNCTION keyword and its RETURNS clause, which define the name of the procedure, parameters passed in (if any), and the resulting set table structure.

```
CREATE FUNCTION dbo.GetProductPullList()
RETURNS @result table
(
    SalesOrderIlD int NOT NULL,
    ProductID int NOT NULL,
    LocationID smallint NOT NULL,
    Shelf nvarchar(10) NOT NULL,
    Bin tinyint NOT NULL,
    QuantityInBin smallint NOT NULL,
    QuantityOnOrder smallint NOT NULL,
    QuantityToPull smallint NOT NULL,
    PartialFillFlag nchar(1) NOT NULL,
PRIMARY KEY (SalesOrderID, ProductID, LocationID, Shelf, Bin)
)
```

You may notice that we've defined a primary key on the table result. This also serves as the clustered index for the result set. Due to limitations in table variables, you can't explicitly specify other indexes on the result set.

The body of the function begins with the INSERT INTO and SELECT clauses that follow:

```
INSERT INTO @result
(
    SalesOrderID,
    ProductID,
    LocationID,
    Shelf,
    Bin,
    QuantitylnBin,
    QuantityOnOrder,
    QuantityToPull,
    PartialFillFlag
)
SELECT
    Order_Details.SalesOrderID,
    Order_Details.ProductID,
    Inventory_Details.LocationID,
    Inventory_Details.Shelf,
    Inventory_Details.Bin,
```

```
    Inventory_Details.Quantity,
    Order_Details.OrderQty,
    COUNT(*) AS PullQty,
    CASE WHEN COUNT(*)<Order_Details.OrderQty
        THEN N'Y'
            ELSE N'N'
END AS PartialFillFlag
```

These clauses establish population of the @result table variable. The most important point to notice here is that the return results of this multistatement TVF are created by manipulating the contents of the @result table variable. When the function ends, the @result table variable is returned to the caller. Some other important facts about this portion of the multi-statement TVF are that the COUNT(*) AS PullQty aggregate function returns the total number of each item to pull from a given bin to fill a specific order detail row, and the CASE expression returns Y when an order detail item is partially filled from a single bin and N when an order detail item is completely filled from a single bin.

The source for the SELECT query is composed of two subqueries joined together. The first subquery, aliased as InventoryDetails, is shown following. This subquery returns a single row for every item in inventory with information identifying the precise location where the inventory item can be found.

```
(
    SELECT ROW_NUMBER() OVER
        (
        PARTITION  BY  p.ProductID
        ORDER  BY  p.ProductID,
        p.LocationID,
        p.Shelf,
        p.Bin
        ) AS  Num,
        p.ProductID,
        p.LocationID,
        p.Shelf,
        p.Bin,
        p.Quantity
    FROM Production.ProductInventory p
    INNER JOIN dbo.Numbers n
        ON n.Num  BETWEEN  1  AND  Quantity
) Inventory_Details
```

Considering the previous example with the customers Jill, Mike, and Dave, if there are nine black Mountain-200 42-inch mountain bikes in inventory, this query returns nine rows, one for each instance of the item in inventory, and each with a unique row number counting from 1.

The InventoryDetails subquery is inner-joined to a second subquery, identified as Order_Details, as shown following:

```
(
    SELECT ROW_NUMBER() OVER
        (
        PARTITION  BY  o.ProductID
        ORDER  BY  o.ProductID,
        o.SalesOrderID
        ) AS  Num,
        o.ProductID,
```

```
        o.SalesOrderID,
        o.OrderQty
    FROM Sales.SalesOrderDetail o
    INNER JOIN dbo.Numbers n
        ON  n.Num  BETWEEN  1  AND  o.OrderQty
)  Order_Details
```

This subquery breaks up quantities of items in all order details into individual rows. Again considering the example of Jill, Mike, and Dave, this query will break each of the order details into five rows, one for each item of each order detail. The rows are assigned unique numbers for each product. So in the example, the rows for each black Mountain-200 42-inch mountain bike that our three customers ordered will be numbered individually from 1 to 15.

The rows of both subqueries are joined based on their ProductID numbers and the unique row numbers assigned to each row of each subquery. This effectively assigns one item from the inventory to fill exactly one item in each order. Figure 4-7 is a visualization of the process that we've described here, where the inventory items and order detail items are split into separate rows and the two rowsets are joined together.

Figure 4-7. *Splitting and Joining Individual Inventory and Sales Detail Items*

The SELECT statement also requires a GROUP BY to aggregate the total number of items to be pulled from each bin to fill each order detail, as opposed to returning the raw inventory-to-order detail items on a one-to-one basis.

```
GROUP BY
    Order_Details.SalesOrderID,
    Order_Details.ProductID,
    Inventory_Details.LocationID,
    Inventory_Details.Shelf,
    Inventory_Details.Bin,
    Inventory_Details.Quantity,
    Order_Details.OrderQty;
```

Finally, the RETURN statement returns the @result table back to the caller as the multistatement TVF result. Notice that the RETURN statement in a multistatement TVF isn't followed by an expression or variable as it is in a scalar UDF:

```
RETURN;
```

The table returned by a TVF can be used just like a table in a WHERE clause or a JOIN clause of an SQL SELECT query. Listing 4-12 is a sample query that joins the example TVF to the Production.Product table to get the product names and colors for each product listed in the pull list. Figure 4-8 shows the output of the product pull list joined to the Production.Product table.

Listing 4-12. Retrieving a Product Pull List with Product Names

```
SELECT
    p.Name AS ProductName,
    p.ProductNumber,
    p.Color,
    ppl.SalesOrderID,
    ppl.ProductID,
    ppl.LocationID,
    ppl.Shelf,
    ppl.Bin,
    ppl.QuantityInBin,
    ppl.QuantityOnOrder,
    ppl.QuantityToPull,
    ppl.PartialFillFlag
FROM Production.Product p
INNER JOIN dbo.GetProductPullList() ppl
    ON p.ProductID=ppl.ProductID;
```

	ProductName	ProductNumber	Color	SalesOrderID	ProductID	LocationID	Shelf	Bin	QuantityInBin	QuantityOnOrder	QuantityToPull	PartialFillFlag
1	Mountain Bike Socks, M	SO-B909-M	White	43659	709	7	N/A	0	180	6	6	N
2	Sport-100 Helmet, Blue	HL-U509-B	Blue	43659	711	7	N/A	0	216	4	4	N
3	AWC Logo Cap	CA-1098	Multi	43659	712	7	N/A	0	288	2	2	N
4	Long-Sleeve Logo Jersey, M	LJ-0192-M	Multi	43659	714	7	N/A	0	180	3	3	N
5	Long-Sleeve Logo Jersey, XL	LJ-0192-X	Multi	43659	716	7	N/A	0	252	1	1	N
6	Mountain-100 Silver, 38	BK-M82S-38	Silver	43659	771	7	N/A	0	49	1	1	N
7	Mountain-100 Silver, 42	BK-M82S-42	Silver	43659	772	7	N/A	0	88	1	1	N
8	Mountain-100 Silver, 44	BK-M82S-44	Silver	43659	773	7	N/A	0	83	2	2	N
9	Mountain-100 Silver, 48	BK-M82S-48	Silver	43659	774	7	N/A	0	62	1	1	N
10	Mountain-100 Black, 42	BK-M82B-42	Black	43659	776	7	N/A	0	78	1	1	N
11	Mountain-100 Black, 44	BK-M82B-44	Black	43659	777	7	N/A	0	49	3	3	N
12	Mountain-100 Black, 48	BK-M82B-48	Black	43659	778	7	N/A	0	88	1	1	N
13	Road-450 Red, 52	BK-R68R-52	Red	43660	758	7	N/A	0	116	1	1	N
14	Road-650 Red, 44	BK-R50R-44	Red	43660	762	7	N/A	0	75	1	1	N
15	Sport-100 Helmet, Black	HL-U509	Black	43661	708	7	N/A	0	324	5	5	N
16	Sport-100 Helmet, Blue	HL-U509-B	Blue	43661	711	7	N/A	0	216	2	2	N
17	AWC Logo Cap	CA-1098	Multi	43661	712	7	N/A	0	288	4	4	N
18	Long-Sleeve Logo Jersey, L	LJ-0192-L	Multi	43661	715	7	N/A	0	216	4	4	N
19	Long-Sleeve Logo Jersey, XL	LJ-0192-X	Multi	43661	716	7	N/A	0	252	2	2	N
20	HL Mountain Frame - Black...	FR-M94B-38	Black	43661	747	10	N/A	0	121	2	2	N
21	Mountain-100 Silver, 44	BK-M82S-44	Silver	43661	773	7	N/A	0	83	2	2	N

Figure 4-8. Joining the Product Pull List to the Production.Product Table

Inline Table-Valued Functions

If scalar UDFs and multistatement TVFs aren't enough to get you excited about T-SQL's UDF capabilities, here comes a third form of UDF: the inline TVF. *Inline TVFs* are similar to multi-statement TVFs in that they return a tabular rowset result.

However, where a multistatement TVF can contain multiple SQL statements and control-of-flow statements in the function body, the inline function consists of only a single SELECT query. The inline TVF is literally "inlined" by SQL Server (expanded by the query optimizer as part of the SELECT statement that contains it), much like a view. In fact, because of this behavior, inline TVFs are sometimes referred to as parameterized views.

The inline TVF declaration must simply state that the result is a table via the RETURNS clause. The body of the inline TVF consists of an SQL query after a RETURN statement. Since the inline TVF returns the result of a single SELECT query, you don't need to bother with declaring a table variable or defining the return table structure. The structure of the result is implied by the SELECT query that makes up the body of the function.

The sample inline TVF we'll introduce performs a function commonly implemented by developers in T-SQL using control-of-flow statements. Many times, a developer will determine that a function or SP requires that a large or variable number of parameters be passed in to accomplish a particular goal. The ideal situation would be to pass an array as a parameter. T-SQL doesn't provide an "array" data type per se, but you can split a comma-delimited list of strings into a table to simulate an array. This gives you the flexibility of an "array" that you can use in SQL joins.

■ **Tip** SQL Server 2012 also allows table-valued parameters, which will be covered in Chapter 5 in the discussion of SPs. Because table-valued parameters have special requirements, they may not be optimal in all situations.

While you could do this using a multistatement TVF and control-of-flow statement such as a WHILE loop, you'll get better performance if you let SQL Server do the heavy lifting with a set-based solution. The sample function will accept a comma-delimited varchar(max) string and return a table with two columns, Num and Element, which are described by the following:

- The Num column contains a unique number for each element of the array, counting from 1 to the number of elements in the comma-delimited string.
- The Element column contains the substrings extracted from the comma-delimited list.

Listing 4-13 is the full code listing for the comma-separated string-splitting function. This function accepts a single parameter, which is a comma-delimited string like Ronnie,Bobbie,Ricky,Mike. The output is a table-like rowset with each comma-delimited item returned on its own row. To avoid looping and procedural constructs (which are not allowed in an inline TVF), we've used the same Numbers table created previously in Listing 4-10.

Listing 4-13. Comma-Separated String-Splitting Function

```
CREATE  FUNCTION  dbo.GetCommaSplit  (@String  nvarchar(max))
RETURNS table
AS
RETURN
(
    WITH Splitter (Num, String)
    AS
    (
        SELECT Num, SUBSTRING(@String,
        Num,
        CASE  CHARINDEX(N',',  @String,  Num)
        WHEN  O  THEN  LEN(@String)  -  Num  +  1
        ELSE CHARINDEX(N',', @String, Num) - Num
        END
        ) AS  String
    FROM  dbo.Numbers
    WHERE Num <= LEN(@String)
        AND (SUBSTRING(@String, Num - 1, 1)=N',' OR Num=0)
    )
    SELECT
        ROW_NUMBER() OVER (ORDER BY Num) AS Num,
        RTRIM(LTRIM(String)) AS Element
    FROM  Splitter
    WHERE String <> ''
);
GO
```

The inline TVF name and parameters are defined at the beginning of the CREATE FUNCTION statement. The RETURNS table clause specifies that the function returns a table. Notice that the structure of the table is not defined as it is with a multistatement TVF.

```
CREATE FUNCTION dbo.GetCommaSplit (@String varchar(max)) RETURNS table
```

The body of the inline TVF consists of a single RETURN statement followed by a SELECT query. For this example, we used a CTE called Splitter to perform the actual splitting of the comma-delimited list. The query of the CTE returns each substring from the comma-delimited list. CASE expressions are required to handle two special cases, as follows:

- the first item in the list because it is not preceded by a comma

- the last item in the list because it is not followed by a comma

```
WITH Splitter (Num, String)
AS
(
  SELECT Num, SUBSTRING(@String,
```

```
    Num,
    CASE CHARINDEX(N',', @String, Num)
        WHEN 0 THEN LEN(@String) - Num+1
        ELSE CHARINDEX(N',', @String, Num) - Num
    END
) AS String
FROM dbo.Numbers
WHERE Num <= LEN(@String)
    AND (SUBSTRING(@String, Num - 1, 1) = N',' OR Num=0)
)
```

Finally, the query selects each ROWNUMBER and Element from the CTE as the result to return to the caller. Extra space characters are stripped from the beginning and end of each string returned, and empty strings are ignored.

```
SELECT
    ROW_NUMBER() OVER (ORDER BY Num) AS Num,
    LTRIM(RTRIM(String)) AS Element
FROM Splitter
WHERE String <> ''
```

You can use this inline TVF to split up the Jackson family, as shown in Listing 4-14. The results are shown in Figure 4-9.

Listing 4-14. Splitting up the Jacksons

```
SELECT Num, Element
FROM dbo.GetCommaSplit ('Michael,Tito,Jermaine,Marlon,Rebbie,Jackie,Janet,La Toya,Randy');
```

	Num	Element
1	1	Michael
2	2	Tito
3	3	Jermaine
4	4	Marlon
5	5	Rebbie
6	6	Jackie
7	7	Janet
8	8	La Toya
9	9	Randy

Figure 4-9. *Splitting up the Jacksons*

Or, possibly more usefully, you can use it to pull descriptions for a specific set of AdventureWorks products. A usage like this is good for front-end web page displays or business reports where end users can select multiple items for which they want data returned. Listing 4-15 retrieves product information for a comma-delimited list of AdventureWorks product numbers. The results are shown in Figure 4-10.

Listing 4-15. Using the FnCommaSplit Function

```
SELECT n.Num,
    p.Name,
    p.ProductNumber,
    p.Color,
    p.Size,
    p.SizeUnitMeasureCode,
    p.StandardCost,
    p.ListPrice
FROM Production.Product p
INNER JOIN dbo.GetCommaSplit('FR-R38R-52,FR-M94S-52,FR-M94B-44,BK-M68B-38') n
    ON p.ProductNumber = n.Element;
```

	Num	Name	Product Number	Color	Size	Size Unit Measure Code	StandardCost	List Price
1	4	Mountain-200 Black, 38	BK-M68B-38	Black	38	CM	1251.9813	2294.99
2	3	HL Mountain Frame - Black, 44	FR-M94B-44	Black	44	CM	699.0928	1349.60
3	2	HL Mountain Frame - Silver, 48	FR-M94S-52	Silver	48	CM	706.811	1364.50
4	1	LL Road Frame - Red, 52	FR-R38R-52	Red	52	CM	187.1571	337.22

Figure 4-10. *Using a Comma-delimited List to Retrieve Product Information*

Restrictions on User-Defined Functions

T-SQL imposes some restrictions on UDFs. In this section, we'll discuss these restrictions and some of the reasoning behind them.

Nondeterministic Functions

T-SQL prohibits the use of nondeterministic functions inside of UDFs. A *deterministic* function is one that returns the same value every time when passed a given set of parameters (or no parameters). A *nondeterministic* function can return different results with the same set of parameters passed to it. An example of a deterministic function is ABS, the mathematical absolute value function. Every time—and no matter how many times—you call ABS(-10), the result is always 10. This is the basic idea behind determinism.

On the flip side, there are functions that do not return the same value despite the fact that you pass in the same parameters, or no parameters. Built-in functions such as RAND (without a seed value) and NEWID are nondeterministic because they return a different result every time they are called. One hack that people sometimes use to try to circumvent this restriction is creating a view that invokes the nondeterministic function and selecting from that view inside their UDFs. While this may work to some extent, it is not recommended, as it could fail to produce the desired results or cause a significant performance hit, since SQL won't be able to cache or effectively index the results of nondeterministic functions. Also, if you create a computed column that tries to reference your UDF, the nondeterministic functions you are trying to access via your view can produce unpredictable results. If you need to use nondeterministic functions in your application logic, SPs are probably the better alternative. We'll discuss SPs in Chapter 5.

NONDETERMINISTIC FUNCTIONS IN A UDF

In previous versions of SQL, there were several restrictions on the use of nondeterministic system functions in UDFs. In SQL Server 2012, these restrictions are somewhat relaxed. In SQL Server 2012, you can use the nondeterministic system functions listed in the following table in your UDFs. One thing these system functions have in common is that they don't cause side effects or change the database state when you use them.

Nondeterministic System Functions Allowed in UDFs

@@CONNECTIONS	@@PACK_RECEIVED	@@TOTAL_WRITE
@@CPU_BUSY	@@PACK_SENT	CURRENT_TIMESTAMP
@@DBTS	@@PACKET_ERRORS	GET_TRANSMISSION_STATUS
@@IDLE	@@TIMETICKS	GETDATE
@@IO_BUSY	@@TOTAL_ERRORS	GETUTCDATE
@@MAX_CONNECTIONS	@@TOTAL_READ	

If you want to build an index on a view or computed column that uses a UDF, your UDF has to be deterministic. The requirements to make a UDF deterministic include the following:

- The UDF must be declared using the WITH SCHEMABINDING option. When a UDF is schema-bound, no changes are allowed to any tables or objects that it's dependent on without dropping the UDF first.

- Any functions that you refer to in your UDF must also be deterministic. This means that if you use a nondeterministic system function—such as GETDATE—in your UDF, it will be marked nondeterministic.

- You cannot invoke extended stored procedures (XPs) inside the function. This shouldn't be a problem, since XPs are deprecated and will be removed from future versions of SQL Server.

If your UDF meets all these criteria, you can check to see if SQL Server has marked it deterministic via the OBJECTPROPERTY function, with a query like the following:

```
SELECT OBJECTPROPERTY (OBDECT_ID('dbo.GetCommaSplit'), 'IsDeterministic');
```

The OBJECTPROPERTY function will return 0 if your UDF is nondeterministic and 1 if it is deterministic.

State of the Database

One of the restrictions on UDFs is that they are not allowed to change the state of the database or cause other side effects. This prohibition on side effects in UDFs means that you can't even execute PRINT statements from within a UDF. It also means that while you can query database tables and resources, you can't execute INSERT, UPDATE, MERGE, or DELETE statements against database tables. Some other restrictions include the following:

- You can't create temporary tables within a UDF. You can, however, create and modify table variables within the body of a UDF.

- You cannot execute CREATE, ALTER, or DROP on database tables from within a UDF.

- Dynamic SQL is not allowed within a UDF, although XPs and SQLCLR functions can be called.

- A TVF can return only a single table/result set. If you need to return more than one table/result set, you might be better served by an SP.

MORE ON SIDE EFFECTS

Although XPs and SQL CLR functions can be called from a UDF, Microsoft warns against depending on results returned by XPs and SQL CLR functions that cause side effects. If your XP or SQL CLR function modifies tables, alters the database schema, accesses the file system, changes system settings, or utilizes nondeterministic resources external to the database, you might get unpredictable results from your UDF. If you need to change database state or rely on side effects in your server-side code, consider using an SQL CLR function or a regular SP instead of a UDF.

The prohibition on UDF side effects extends to the SQL Server display and error systems. This means that you cannot use the T-SQL PRINT or RAISERROR statements within a UDF. The PRINT and RAISERROR statements are useful in debugging stored procedures and T-SQL code batches, but are unavailable for use in UDFs. One workaround that we often use is to temporarily move the body of our UDF code to an SP while testing. This gives us the ability to use PRINT and RAISERROR while testing and debugging code in development environments.

Variables and table variables created within UDFs have a well-defined scope and cannot be accessed outside of the UDF. Even if you have a recursive UDF, you cannot access the variables and table variables that were previously declared and assigned values by the calling function. If you need values that were generated by a UDF, you must pass them in as parameters to another UDF call or return them to the caller in the UDF result.

Summary

In this chapter, we discussed the three types of T-SQL UDFs and provided working examples of the different types. Scalar UDFs are analogous to mathematical functions that accept zero or more parameters and return a single scalar value for a result. You can use the standard SQL statements, as well as control-of-flow statements, in a scalar UDF. Multistatement TVFs allow control-of-flow statements as well but return a table-style result set to the caller. You can use the result set returned by a multistatement TVF in WHERE and JOIN clauses. Finally, inline TVFs return table-style result sets to the caller as well; however, the body consists of a single SELECT query much like an SQL view. In fact, inline TVFs are sometimes referred to as parameterized views.

The type of UDF that you need to accomplish a given task depends on the problem you're trying to solve. For instance, if you need to calculate a single scalar value, a scalar UDF will do the job. On the other hand, if you need to perform complex calculations or manipulations and return a table, a multistatement TVF might be the correct choice.

We also discussed recursion in UDFs, including the 32-level recursion limit. Although 32 levels of recursion is the hard limit, for all practical purposes you should rarely—if ever—hit this limit. If you do find the need for recursion beyond 32 levels, you can replace recursive function calls with CTEs and other T-SQL constructs.

Finally, we talked about determinism and side effects in your UDFs. Specifically, your UDFs should not cause side effects, and there are specific criteria that must be met in order for SQL Server to mark your UDFs as deterministic. Determinism is an important aspect to UDFs if you plan on using them in indexed views or computed columns.

In the next chapter, we will look at SPs—another tool that allows procedural T-SQL code to be consolidated into server-side units.

EXERCISES

1. [Fill in the blank] SQL Server supports three types of T-SQL UDFs: _____, _____, and _____.

2. [True/False] The RETURNS NULL ON NULL INPUT option is a performance-enhancing option available for use with scalar UDFs.

3. [True/False] The ENCRYPTION option provides a secure option that prevents anyone from reverse-engineering your source code.

4. [Choose all that apply] You are not allowed to do which of the following in a multistatement TVF:

   a. Execute a PRINT statement

   b. Call RAISERROR to generate an exception

   c. Declare a table variable

   d. Create a temporary table

5. The algebraic formula for converting Fahrenheit measurements to the Celsius scale is

   $C = (F - 32.0) \times (5/9)$

   where F is the measurement in degrees Fahrenheit and C is the measurement in degrees Celsius. Write a deterministic scalar UDF that converts a measurement in degrees Fahrenheit to degrees Celsius. The UDF should accept a single float parameter and return a float result. You can use the OBJECTPROPERTY function to ensure that the UDF is deterministic.

CHAPTER 5

Stored Procedures

Stored procedures (SPs) have been a part of T-SQL from the beginning. SPs provide a means for creating server-side subroutines written in T-SQL. This chapter begins with a discussion of what SPs are and why you might want to use them, and it continues with a discussion of SP creation and usage, including examples.

Introducing Stored Procedures

SPs are saved collections of one or more T-SQL statements stored on the server as code units. They are analogous to procedures or subroutines in procedural languages like Visual Basic or C#. And just like procedures in procedural languages, SPs give you the ability to effectively extend the language of SQL Server by letting you add named custom subroutines to your databases.

An SP declaration begins with the `CREATE PROCEDURE` keywords followed by the name of the SP. Microsoft recommends against naming the SP with the prefix sp_. This prefix is used by SQL Server to name system stored procedures and is not recommended for user SPs in databases other than the master database. The name can specify a schema name and procedure name, or just a procedure name. If you don't specify a schema name when creating an SP, SQL Server will create it in the default schema for your login. It's a best practice to always specify the schema name so that your SPs are always created in the proper schema, rather than leaving it up to SQL Server. SQL Server allows you to drop groups of procedures with the same name with a single `DROP PROCEDURE` statement.

■ **Warning**   You can also define the stored procedure with the group number option during SP creation. The group number option is deprecated and will be removed from a future version of SQL Server. Don't use this option in new development, and start planning to update code that uses this option.

SPs, like the T-SQL user-defined functions (UDFs) discussed in Chapter 4, can accept and return parameter values from and to the caller. The parameters are specified in a comma-separated list following the procedure name in the `CREATE PROCEDURE` statement. Unlike UDFs, when you call an SP, you can specify the parameters in any order, and omit them altogether if you assigned a default value at creation time. You can also specify `OUTPUT` parameters, which return values back from the procedure. All of this makes SP parameters far more flexible than UDF.

Each parameter is declared as a specific type and can also be declared as `OUTPUT` or with the `VARYING` keyword (for cursor parameters only). When calling SPs, you have two choices: you can specify parameters by position or by name. If you specify an unnamed parameter list, the values are assigned based on position. If you specify named parameters in the format `@parameter = value`, they can be in any order. If your parameter specifies a default value in its declaration, you don't have to pass a value in for that parameter. Unlike UDFs, SPs don't require the `DEFAULT` keyword as a placeholder to specify default values. Just leaving a parameter out when you call the SP will apply the default value to that parameter.

Unlike UDFs, which can return results only via the RETURN statement, SPs can communicate with the caller in a variety of ways:

- The RETURN statement of the SP can return an int value to the caller. Unlike UDFs, SPs do not require a RETURN statement. If the RETURN statement is left out of the SP, 0 is returned by default if no errors were raised during execution.

- SPs don't have the same restrictions on database side effects and determinism as do UDFs. SPs can read, write, delete, and update permanent tables. In this way, the caller and SP can communicate information to one another through the use of permanent tables.

- When a temporary table is created in an SP, that temporary table is available to any SPs called by that SP. There are two types of temporary tables, local and global. The scope of the local temporary table is the current session and the global temporary table is all the sessions. The local temporary table is prefixed with # and the global temporary table is prefixed with ##. Furthermore, the temporary tables are accessible to any SPs subsequently called by those SPs. As an example, if dbo.MyProc1 creates a local temporary table named #Temp and then calls dbo.MyProc2, dbo.MyProc2 will be able to access #Temp as well. If dbo.MyProc2 then calls dbo.MyProc3, dbo.MyProc3 will also have access to the same #Temp temporary table. Global temporary tables are accessible by all users and all connections after they are created. This provides a useful method of passing an entire table of temporary results from one SP to another for further processing.

- Output parameters provide the primary method of retrieving scalar results from an SP. Parameters are specified as output parameters with the OUTPUT keyword.

- To return table-type results from an SP, the SP can return one or more result sets. Result sets are like virtual tables that can be accessed by the caller. Unlike views, updates to these result sets by applications do not change the underlying tables used to generate them. Also, unlike TVFs and inline functions that return a single table only, SPs can return multiple result sets with a single call.

SP RETURN STATEMENTS

Since the SP RETURN statement can't return tables, character data, decimal numbers, and so on, it is normally used only to return an int status or error code. This is a good convention to follow, since most developers who use your SPs will be expecting it. The normal practice, followed by most of SQL Server's system SPs, is to return a value of 0 to indicate success and a nonzero value or an error code to indicate an error or a failure.

Metadata Discovery

SQL Server 2012 introduces two new stored procedures and supporting Dynamic Management Views (DMV) to provide new capabilities to help determine metadata associated with code batches or stored procedures. This set of capabilities replaces the SET FMTONLY option, which is being deprecated. Often it is necessary to determine the format of the result set without actually executing the query and there are also scenarios where we have to ensure that the column and parameter metadata from query execution is compatible or identical with the format you specified before executing the query. For example, if you want to generate dynamic screens based on a select statement, you need make sure there are no metadata errors after query execution, so in turn you need to determine if the parameter metadata is compatible pre- and post-query execution.

The new functionality introduces metadata discovery capabilities for result set and parameters using the stored procedures sp_describe_first_result_set and sp_describe_undeclared_parameters and DMV's dm_exec_describe_first_result_set and dm_exec_describe_first_result_set_for_object.

The stored procedure sp_describe_first_result_set analyzes all possible first result sets and returns the metadata information for the first result set that is executed from the input T-SQL batch. If the stored procedure returns multiple result sets, this procedure will only return the first result set. If SQL Server is unable to determine the metadata for the first query, then an error will be raised.This procedure takes three parameters: @tsql passes the T-SQL batch, @params passes the parameters for the T-SQL batch, and @browse_information_mode determines if additional browse information for each result set is returned.

Alternatively you can use the DMV sys.dm_exec_describe_first_result_set to query against, and this DMV returns the same details as the stored procedure sp_describe_first_result_set. You can use the DMV sys.dm_exec_describe_first_result_set_for_object to analyze objects such as stored procedures or triggers in the database and return the metadata for the first possible result set and the errors associated with them. Let's say you want to analyze all the objects within the database and use the information for documentation purpose; instead of analyzing the objects one by one, you can use the DMV sys.dm_exec_describe_first_result_set_for_object with query similar to following:

```
SELECT p.name, p.schema_id, x.* FROM sys.procedures p CROSS APPLY
sys.dm_exec_describe_first_result_set_for_object(p.object_id,0) x
```

The stored procedure sp_describe_undeclared_parameters analyzes the T-SQL batch and returns the suggestion for the best parameter datatype based on least number of conversions. This feature is very useful when you have complicated calculations or expressions and you are trying to figure out the best datatype for the undeclared parameter value.

Calling Stored Procedures

You can call an SP without the EXECUTE keyword if it is the first statement in a batch. For instance, if you have an SP named MyProc with schema dbo, you can call it like this:

```
dbo.MyProc;
```

We recommend you qualify stored procedures with schema names. If a nonqualified stored procedure is called then the database engine looks for the procedure in the following order: in the sys schema, in the caller's default schema, and then in the dbo schema. On the other hand, you can invoke an SP from anywhere in a batch or from another SP with the EXECUTE statement. Calling it like the following will discard the int return value:

```
EXECUTE dbo.MyProc;
```

If you need the return value from the SP, you can use the following variation of EXECUTE to assign the return value to a predefined int variable:

```
EXECUTE @variable = dbo.MyProc;
```

Listing 5-1 is a simple SP example with the schema Person that accepts an AdventureWorks employee's ID and returns the employee's full name and e-mail address via output parameters.

Listing 5-1. *Retrieving an Employee's Name and E-mail with an SP*

```
CREATE  PROCEDURE  Person.GetEmployee  (@BusinessEntityID  int  =  199,
    @Email_Address nvarchar(50) OUTPUT,
    @Full_Name nvarchar(100) OUTPUT)
AS
BEGIN
    -- Retrieve email address and full name from HumanResources.Employee table
    SELECT @Email_Address = ea.EmailAddress,
        @Full_Name = p.FirstName + ' ' + COALESCE(p.MiddleName,'') + ' ' + p.LastName
    FROM  HumanResources.Employee  e
    INNER JOIN Person.Person p
        ON  e.BusinessEntityID  =  p.BusinessEntityID
    INNER JOIN Person.EmailAddress ea
        ON  p.BusinessEntityID  =  ea.BusinessEntityID
    WHERE e.BusinessEntityID = @BusinessEntityID;

    --  Return a code of 1 when no match is found, 0 for success
    RETURN (
        CASE
        WHEN  @Email_Address  IS  NULL  THEN  1
        ELSE 0
        END
    );
END;
GO
```

The SP in the example, `Person.GetEmployee`, accepts a business entity ID number as an input parameter and returns the corresponding employee's e-mail address and full name as output parameters. If the business entity ID number passed in is valid, the SP returns 0 as a return value; otherwise 1 is returned. Listing 5-2 shows a sample call to the `Person.GetEmployee` SP, with results shown in Figure 5-1.

Listing 5-2. *Calling the Person.GetEmployee SP*

```
-- Declare variables to hold the result
DECLARE @Email nvarchar(50),@Name nvarchar(100),@Result int;
--Call procedure to get employee information
EXECUTE @Result = Person.GetEmployee 123, @Email OUTPUT, @Name OUTPUT;
```

Display the results SELECT @Result AS Result, @Email AS Email, @Name AS [Name];

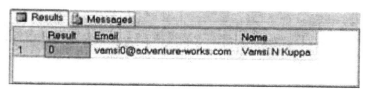

Figure 5-1. *Results of the Sample Person.GetEmployee SP Call*

The sample SP call retrieves the information for the employee with ID number 123 in variables, and displays the results in a result set via `SELECT`. Notice that the `OUTPUT` keyword in the call to the SP is required after the two output parameters.

Let's discuss another common scenario we come across, which occurs when we need to define or modify the metadata of the stored procedure or dynamic SQL or batch. For example there are cases where the column names need to be redefined to indicate the result set better, or the data type needs to be changed for certain columns.

You can write complex code using table variables or temporary tables or even use openrowset without creating a temporary table, however you will need to enable the Ad Hoc Distributed Queries feature. SQL 2012 introduces a new feature called WITH RESULT SETS to the EXECUTE statement that allows you to modify the data types or column names returned by the stored procedure. One thing to keep in mind when using WITH RESULT SETS is that the column set should match the number of columns in the SP execution. If the data type for the column returned by the query does not match the WITH RESULT SETS option, SQL Server will make an attempt to convert the data returned by the query implicitly and will raise an error if the conversion is not possible.

Listing 5-3 is a slight modification to the SP example that you saw in Listing 5-1. This stored procedure accepts an AdventureWorks employee's ID and returns the contact's id, full name, title, last updated date, and the type of contact.

Listing 5-3. Retrieving a Contact's ID, Name, Title, and DOB with an SP

```
CREATE   PROCEDURE  Person.GetContactDetails  (@ID  int)
AS
BEGIN
        SET NOCOUNT ON
    -- Retrieve Name and title for a given PersonID
        SELECT @ID, p.FirstName + ' ' + COALESCE(p.MiddleName,'') + ' ' + p.LastName, ct.[Name],
cast(p.ModifiedDate as varchar(20)), 'Vendor Contact'
        FROM [Purchasing].[Vendor] AS v
                INNER JOIN [Person].[BusinessEntityContact] bec
                ON bec.[BusinessEntityID] = v.[BusinessEntityID]
                INNER JOIN [Person].ContactType ct
                ON ct.[ContactTypeID] = bec.[ContactTypeID]
                INNER JOIN [Person].[Person] p
                ON p.[BusinessEntityID] = bec.[PersonID]
        WHERE bec.[PersonID] = @ID;
END;
GO
```

The SP in the example, Person.GetContactDetails, accepts a BusinessEntityID number as an input parameter and returns the corresponding contact's id, name, title, last updated date, and type of contact in the result set, and there is nothing fancy about any of that. However, when the result set is being returned, the output column names have to be ContactID, ContactName, Title and LastUpdatedBy, and also the data type for the column LastUpdatedBy has to be varchar. Listing 5-4 shows a sample call to Person.GetContactDetails using WITH RESULT SETS. Figure 5-2 shows the resulting output.

Listing 5-4. Calling the Person.GetContactDetails SP

```
-- Declare variables to hold the result
DECLARE @ContactID int;
SET @ContactID = 1511;
--Call procedure to get consumer information
EXEC dbo.GetContactDetails @ContactID with result sets(
```

```
(
ContactID int,--Column Name changed
ContactName varchar(200),--Column Name changed
Title varchar(50),--Column Name changed
LastUpdatedBy varchar(20),--Column Name changed and the data type has been changed from date to
varchar
TypeOfContact varchar(20)
))
```

Figure 5-2. *Results of the Sample Person.GetContactDetails SP Call*

The feature WITH RESULT SETS can be extended to Multiple Active Result Sets (MARS) as well. MARS Connection is the connection attribute that enables the applications to execute multiple batches in one connection. Let's extend the stored procedure in Listing 5-5 and see how we can use this feature with MARS.

Listing 5-5. Retrieving a Contact's ID, Name, Title, and DOB with an SP

```
ALTER   PROCEDURE   Person.GetContactDetails
AS
BEGIN
        SET NOCOUNT ON
    -- Retrieve Name and title for a given PersonID
        SELECT p.BusinessEntityID, p.FirstName + ' ' + COALESCE(p.MiddleName,'') + ' ' +
p.LastName, ct.[Name], cast(p.ModifiedDate as varchar(20)), 'Vendor Contact'
        FROM [Purchasing].[Vendor] AS v
                INNER JOIN [Person].[BusinessEntityContact] bec
                ON bec.[BusinessEntityID] = v.[BusinessEntityID]
                INNER JOIN [Person].ContactType ct
                ON ct.[ContactTypeID] = bec.[ContactTypeID]
                INNER JOIN [Person].[Person] p
                ON p.[BusinessEntityID] = bec.[PersonID];

        SELECT p.BusinessEntityID, p.FirstName + ' ' + COALESCE(p.MiddleName,'') + ' ' +
p.LastName, ct.[Name], cast(p.ModifiedDate as varchar(20)), p.Suffix, 'Store Contact'
        FROM [Sales].[Store] AS s
                INNER JOIN [Person].[BusinessEntityContact] bec
                ON bec.[BusinessEntityID] = s.[BusinessEntityID]
                INNER JOIN [Person].ContactType ct
                ON ct.[ContactTypeID] = bec.[ContactTypeID]
                INNER JOIN [Person].[Person] p
                ON p.[BusinessEntityID] = bec.[PersonID];
END;
GO
```

Listing 5-6 shows a sample call to `Person.GetContactDetails` using `WITH RESULT SETS`. Figure 5-3 shows the output. The order of the rows in the result set may vary in your system.

Listing 5-6. Calling the Modified Person.GetContactDetails SP

```
--Call procedure to get consumer information
EXEC Person.GetContactDetails  with result sets(
--Return Vendor Contact Details
(
ContactID int,--Column Name changed
ContactName varchar(200),--Column Name changed
Title varchar(50),--Column Name changed
LastUpdatedBy varchar(20),--Column Name changed and the data type has been changed from date to
varchar
TypeOfContact varchar(20)
),
--Return Store Contact Details
(
ContactID int,--Column Name changed
ContactName varchar(200),--Column Name changed
Title varchar(50),--Column Name changed
LastUpdatedBy varchar(20),--Column Name changed and the data type has been changed from date to
varchar
Suffix varchar(5),
TypeOfContact varchar(20)
)
)
```

	ContactID	ContactName	Title	LastUpdatedBy	TypeOfContact
1	1509	Julia Moseley	Assistant Sales Agent	Feb 25 2006 12:00AM	Vendor Contact
2	1517	Albert Mungin	Assistant Sales Agent	Jan 24 2006 12:00AM	Vendor Contact
3	1521	Billie Jo Murray	Assistant Sales Agent	Feb 25 2006 12:00AM	Vendor Contact
4	1527	Suzanne Nelson	Assistant Sales Agent	Mar 6 2006 12:00AM	Vendor Contact
5	1535	Lorraine Nay	Assistant Sales Agent	Feb 17 2006 12:00AM	Vendor Contact
6	1541	Amir T. Netz	Assistant Sales Agent	Feb 25 2006 12:00AM	Vendor Contact
7	1567	Fred A. Ortiz	Assistant Sales Agent	Feb 17 2006 12:00AM	Vendor Contact
8	1581	Jyothi Pai	Assistant Sales Agent	Feb 25 2006 12:00AM	Vendor Contact
9	1593	Trish E. Pederson	Assistant Sales Agent	Mar 6 2006 12:00AM	Vendor Contact

	ContactID	ContactName	Title	LastUpdatedBy	Suffix	TypeOfContact
1	291	Gustavo Achong	Owner	May 16 2009 4:33PM	NULL	Store Contact
2	293	Catherine R. Abel	Owner	May 16 2009 4:33PM	NULL	Store Contact
3	295	Kim Abercrombie	Owner	May 16 2009 4:33PM	NULL	Store Contact
4	297	Humberto Acevedo	Owner	May 16 2009 4:33PM	NULL	Store Contact
5	299	Pilar Ackerman	Owner	May 16 2009 4:33PM	NULL	Store Contact
6	301	Frances B. Adams	Owner	May 16 2009 4:33PM	NULL	Store Contact
7	303	Margaret J. Smith	Owner	May 16 2009 4:33PM	NULL	Store Contact
8	305	Carla J. Adams	Owner	May 16 2009 4:33PM	NULL	Store Contact
9	315	Robert E. Ahlering	Owner	Sep 1 2007 12:00AM	NULL	Store Contact

Figure 5-3. *Results of the Modified Person.GetContactDetails SP Call*

■ **Tip** You don't *have to* wrap the body of your SP in a BEGIN...END block as we're doing in these examples, but we personally think it makes the code more readable. It can also help when using the newest version of SSMS or third-party editors that provide collapsible code blocks, as described in Chapter 2.

As with UDFs, there are additional options you can specify when you create a procedure. The options include the following:

- The ENCRYPTION option obfuscates the SP text and helps prevent unauthorized users from accessing the obfuscated text. This option does for SPs what the UDF ENCRYPTION option does for functions.

- The RECOMPILE option prevents the SQL Server engine from caching the execution plan for the SP, forcing runtime compilation of your SP.

- The EXECUTE AS clause specifies the context that the SP will run under. You can specify CALLER, SELF, OWNER, or a specific username with the EXECUTE AS clause. These options are the same as they are for the UDF EXECUTE AS clause, described in Chapter 4.

Additionally, you can specify FOR REPLICATION to create an SP specifically for replication purposes. An SP created with the FOR REPLICATION option can't be executed on the replication subscriber. FOR REPLICATION can't be used with the RECOMPILE option, and this option is not available for contained databases either. A contained database stores all the database and application level objects within the database such as tables, functions, schemas, logins, linked sever details, etc.

Managing Stored Procedures

T-SQL provides two statements that allow you to modify and delete SPs: the ALTER PROCEDURE and DROP PROCEDURE statements, respectively. ALTER PROCEDURE allows you to modify the code for an SP without first dropping it. The syntax is the same as the CREATE PROCEDURE statement, except that the keywords ALTER PROCEDURE are used in place of CREATE PROCEDURE. ALTER PROCEDURE, like CREATE PROCEDURE, must always be the first statement in a batch. Using the CREATE, DROP and ALTER PROCEDURE statements forces SQL Server to generate a new query plan. The advantage of ALTER over CREATE or DROP is that ALTER preserves the permissions for the object whereas CREATE or DROP resets the permissions.

To delete a procedure from your database, use the DROP PROCEDURE statement. Listing 5-7 shows how to drop the procedure created in Listing 5-1.

Listing 5-7. Dropping the Person.GetEmployee SP

```
DROP PROCEDURE Person.GetEmployee;
```

You can specify multiple SPs in a single DROP PROCEDURE statement by putting the SP names in a comma-separated list. Note that you cannot specify the database or server name when dropping an SP, and you must be in the database containing the SP in order to drop it. Additionally, as with other database objects, you can grant or deny EXECUTE permissions on an SP through the GRANT and DENY statements.

Stored Procedures Best Practices

Stored procedures enable you to store batches of Transact-SQL or Managed CLR (Common Language Runtime) code centrally on the server. Stored procedures can be very efficient, and here are some of the best practices that can aid development and avoid common pitfalls that can hurt performance.

- Use the SET NOCOUNT ON statement after the AS keyword, as the first statement in the body of the procedure when you have multiple statements within your stored procedure. This turns off the DONE_IN_PROC messages that SQL Server sends back to the client after each statement in the stored procedure is executed. This also reduces the processing performed by SQL Server and the size of response sent across the network.

- Use schema names when creating or referencing the stored procedure and the database objects within the procedure. This will help SQL Server to find the objects faster and thus reduces compile lock, which will result in less processing time.

- Do not use SP_ or sys** prefixes for naming user-created database objects. They are reserved for Microsoft and have different behaviors.

- Avoid using scalar functions in SELECT statements that return many rows of data. Because the scalar function must be applied to every row, the resulting behavior is like row-based processing and degrades performance.

- Avoid the use of SELECT * and select only the columns you need. This will reduce the processing in the database server as well as network traffic.

- Use parameters when calling stored procedures to increase performance. In your stored procedures explicitly create parameters with type, size, and precision to avoid type conversions.

- Use explicit transactions by using BEGIN/END TRANSACTION and keep transactions as short as possible. The longer the transaction, the more chances you have for locking or blocking and in some cases deadlocking as well. So, keep the transactions short to reduce blocking and locking.

- Use the Transact-SQL TRY...CATCH feature for error handling inside a procedure. TRY...CATCH can encapsulate an entire block of Transact-SQL statements. If you are using TRY...CATCH with loops, place it outside the loop for better performance.This not only creates less performance overhead; it also makes error reporting more accurate with significantly less programming.

- Use NULL or NOT NULL for each column in a temporary table. The ANSI_DFLT_ON and ANSI_DFLT_OFF options control the way the Database Engine assigns the NULL or NOT NULL attributes to columns when these attributes are not specified in a CREATE TABLE or ALTER TABLE statement. If a connection executes a procedure with different settings for these options than the connection that created the procedure, the columns of the table created for the second connection can have different nullability and exhibit different behavior. If NULL or NOT NULL is explicitly stated for each column, the temporary tables are created by using the same nullability for all connections that execute the procedure.

- Use the UNION ALL operator instead of the UNION or OR operators, unless there is a specific need for distinct values. The UNION filters and removes the duplicate records, whereas the UNION ALL operator requires less processing overhead since duplicates are not filtered out of the result set.

WHY STORED PROCEDURES?

Debates have raged through the years over the utility of SQL Server SPs. SPs cache and reuse query execution plans, which provided significant performance improvements in SQL Server 6.5 and 7.0. Although SQL Server 2012 SPs offer the same execution plan caching and reuse, the luster of this benefit has faded somewhat. Query optimization, query caching, and reuse of query execution plans for parameterized queries have been in a state of constant improvement since SQL Server 2000. Query optimization has been improved even more in SQL Server 2012. SPs still offer the performance benefit of not having to send large and complex queries over the network, but the primary benefit of query execution plan caching and reuse is not as enticing as it once was.

So why use SPs? Apart from the performance benefit, which is not as big a factor in these days of highly efficient parameterized queries, SPs offer code modularization and security. Creating code modules helps reduce redundant code, eliminating potential maintenance nightmares caused by duplicate code stored in multiple locations. By using SPs, you can deny users the capability to perform direct queries against tables, but still allow them to use SPs to retrieve the relevant data from those tables. SPs also offer the advantage of centralized administration of portions of your database code. Finally, SPs can return multiple result sets with a single procedure call, such as the sp_help system SP demonstrated here (the results are shown in Figure 5-4):

```
EXECUTE dbo.sp_help;
```

Figure 5-4. *Results of the dbo.sp_help SP Call*

Using SPs, you can effectively build an application programming interface (API) for your database. You can also minimize and almost prevent SQL injection by using stored procedures with input parameters to filter and validate all the inputs. Creation and adherence to such an API can help ensure consistent access across applications and make development easier for front-end and client-side developers who need to access your database. Some third-party applications, such as certain ETL programs and database drivers, also require SPs.

What are the arguments against SPs? One major argument tends to be that they tightly couple your code to the DBMS. A code base that is tightly integrated with SQL Server 2012 will be more difficult to port over to another RDBMS (such as Oracle, DB2, or MySQL) in the future. A loosely coupled application, on the other hand, is much easier to port to different SQL DBMSs.

Portability, in turn, has its own problems. Truly portable code can result in databases and applications that are slow and inefficient. To get true portability out of any RDBMS system, you have to take great care to code everything in *plain vanilla* SQL, meaning that a lot of the platform-specific performance-enhancing functionality offered by SQL Server is off-limits.

We're not going to dive too deeply into a discussion of the pluses and minuses of SPs. In the end, the balance between portability and performance needs to be determined by your business needs and corporate IT policies on a per-project basis. Just keep these competing factors in mind when making that decision.

Stored Procedure Example

A common application of SPs is to create a layer of abstraction for various data query, aggregation, and manipulation functionality. The example SP in Listing 5-8 performs the common business reporting task of calculating a running total. The results are shown in Figure 5-5.

Listing 5-8. Procedure to Calculate and Retrieve Running Total for Sales

```
CREATE PROCEDURE Sales.GetSalesRunningTotal (@Year int)
AS
BEGIN
WITH RunningTotalCTE
AS
    (
        SELECT soh.SalesOrderNumber,
        soh.OrderDate,
        soh.TotalDue,
        (
        SELECT  SUM(soh1.TotalDue)
        FROM    Sales.SalesOrderHeader  soh1
        WHERE   soh1.SalesOrderNumber  <=  soh.SalesOrderNumber
        ) AS  RunningTotal,
        SUM(soh.TotalDue) OVER () AS GrandTotal
        FROM Sales.SalesOrderHeader soh
        WHERE DATEPART(year, soh.OrderDate) = @Year
        GROUP BY soh.SalesOrderNumber,
        soh.OrderDate,
        soh.TotalDue
    )
    SELECT rt.SalesOrderNumber,
        rt.OrderDate,
        rt.TotalDue,
        rt.RunningTotal,
        (rt.RunningTotal / rt.GrandTotal) * 100 AS PercentTotal
```

```
        FROM  RunningTotalCTE  rt
        ORDER BY rt.SalesOrderNumber;
        RETURN 0;
END;
GO


EXEC  Sales.GetSalesRunningTotal @Year = 2005;
GO
```

	SalesOrderNumber	OrderDate	TotalDue	RunningTotal	PercentTotal
1	SO43659	2005-07-01 00:00:00.000	23153.2339	23153.2339	0.18
2	SO43660	2005-07-01 00:00:00.000	1457.3288	24610.5627	0.19
3	SO43661	2005-07-01 00:00:00.000	36865.8012	61476.3639	0.48
4	SO43662	2005-07-01 00:00:00.000	32474.9324	93951.2963	0.74
5	SO43663	2005-07-01 00:00:00.000	472.3108	94423.6071	0.74
6	SO43664	2005-07-01 00:00:00.000	27510.4109	121934.018	0.96
7	SO43665	2005-07-01 00:00:00.000	16158.6961	138092.7141	1.08
8	SO43666	2005-07-01 00:00:00.000	5694.8564	143787.5705	1.13
9	SO43667	2005-07-01 00:00:00.000	6876.3649	150663.9354	1.18
10	SO43668	2005-07-01 00:00:00.000	40487.7233	191151.6587	1.50
11	SO43669	2005-07-01 00:00:00.000	807.2585	191958.9172	1.51
12	SO43670	2005-07-01 00:00:00.000	6893.2549	198852.1721	1.56
13	SO43671	2005-07-01 00:00:00.000	9153.6054	208005.7775	1.63
14	SO43672	2005-07-01 00:00:00.000	6895.41	214901.1875	1.69
15	SO43673	2005-07-01 00:00:00.000	4216.0258	219117.2133	1.72
16	SO43674	2005-07-01 00:00:00.000	2955.0542	222072.2675	1.74
17	SO43675	2005-07-01 00:00:00.000	6434.0848	228506.3523	1.80
18	SO43676	2005-07-01 00:00:00.000	15992.7446	244499.0969	1.92

Figure 5-5. *Partial Results of the Running Total Calculation for Year 2005*

The SP in Listing 5-8 accepts a single int parameter indicating the year for which the calculation should be performed:

```
CREATE PROCEDURE Sales.GetSalesRunningTotal (@Year int)
```

Inside the SP, we've used a CTE to return the relevant data for the year specified, including calculations for the running total via a simple scalar subquery and the grand total via a SUM calculation with an OVER clause:

```
WITH RunningTotalCTE
AS
(
    SELECT soh.SalesOrderNumber,
        soh.OrderDate,
        soh.TotalDue,
        (
        SELECT  SUM(soh1.TotalDue)
```

```
        FROM  Sales.SalesOrderHeader  soh1
        WHERE  soh1.SalesOrderNumber  <=  soh.SalesOrderNumber
        )  AS  RunningTotal,
        SUM(soh.TotalDue) OVER () AS GrandTotal
    FROM Sales.SalesOrderHeader soh
    WHERE DATEPART(year, soh.OrderDate) = @Year
    GROUP BY soh.SalesOrderNumber,
        soh.OrderDate,
        soh.TotalDue
)
```

The result set is returned by the CTE's outer SELECT query, and the SP finishes up with a RETURN statement that sends a return code of 0 back to the caller:

```
SELECT rt.SalesOrderNumber,
rt.OrderDate,
rt.TotalDue,
rt.RunningTotal,
(rt.RunningTotal / rt.GrandTotal) * 100 AS PercentTotal FROM RunningTotalCTE rt ORDER BY
rt.SalesOrderNumber; RETURN 0;
```

RUNNING SUMS

The *running sum*, or running total, is a very commonly used business reporting tool. A running sum calculates totals as of certain points in time (usually dollar amounts, and often calculated over days, months, quarters, or years—but not always). In Listing 5-8, the running sum is calculated per order, for each day over the course of a given year.

The running sum generated in the sample gives you a total sales amount as of the date and time when each order is placed. When the first order is placed, the running sum is equal to the amount of that order. When the second order is placed, the running sum is equal to the amount of the first order plus the amount of the second order, and so on. Another closely related and often used calculation is the *running average*, which represents a calculated point-in-time average as opposed to a point-in-time sum.

As an interesting aside, the ISO SQL standard allows you to use the OVER clause with aggregate functions like SUM and AVG. The ISO SQL standard allows the ORDER BY clause to be used with the aggregate function OVER clause, making for extremely efficient and compact running sum calculations. Unfortunately, SQL Server 2012 does not support this particular option, so you will still have to resort to subqueries and other less efficient methods of performing these calculations for now.

For the next example, assume that AdventureWorks management has decided to add a database-driven feature to its web site. The feature they want is a "recommended products list" that will appear when customers add products to their online shopping carts. Of course, the first step to implementing any solution is to clearly define the requirements. The details of the requirements-gathering process are beyond the scope of this book, so we'll work under the assumption that the AdventureWorks business analysts have done their due diligence and reported back the following business rules for this particular function:

- The recommended products list should include additional items on orders that contain the product selected by the customer. As an example, if the product selected by the customer is product ID 773 (the silver Mountain-100 44-inch bike), then items previously bought by other customers in conjunction with this bike—like product ID 712 (the AWC logo cap)—should be recommended.

- Products that are in the same category as the product the customer selected should not be recommended. As an example, if a customer has added a bicycle to an order, other bicycles should not be recommended.

- The recommended product list should never contain more than ten items.

- The default product ID should be 776, the black Mountain-100 42-inch bike.

- The recommended products should be listed in descending order of the total quantity that has been ordered. In other words, the best-selling items will be listed in the recommendations list first.

Listing 5-9 shows the SP that implements all of these business rules to return a list of recommended products based on a given product ID.

Listing 5-9. Recommended Product List SP

```
CREATE PROCEDURE Production.GetProductRecommendations (@ProductID int = 776)
AS
BEGIN
WITH RecommendedProducts
(
ProductID,
ProductSubCategoryID,
TotalQtyOrdered,
TotalDollarsOrdered
)
AS
(
SELECT
od2.ProductID,
p1.ProductSubCategoryID,
SUM(od2.OrderQty) AS TotalQtyOrdered,
SUM(od2.UnitPrice * od2.OrderQty) AS TotalDollarsOrdered
FROM Sales.SalesOrderDetail od1
INNER JOIN Sales.SalesOrderDetail od2
ON od1.SalesOrderID = od2.SalesOrderID
INNER JOIN Production.Product p1
ON od2.ProductID = p1.ProductID
WHERE od1.ProductID = @ProductID
AND od2.ProductID <> @ProductID
GROUP BY
od2.ProductID,
p1.ProductSubcategoryID
)
SELECT TOP(10) ROW_NUMBER() OVER
(
ORDER BY rp.TotalQtyOrdered DESC
) AS Rank,
```

```
rp.TotalQtyOrdered,
rp.ProductID,
rp.TotalDollarsOrdered,
p.[Name]
FROM RecommendedProducts rp
INNER JOIN Production.Product p
ON rp.ProductID = p.ProductID
WHERE rp.ProductSubcategoryID <>
(
SELECT ProductSubcategoryID
FROM Production.Product
WHERE ProductID = @ProductID
)
ORDER BY TotalQtyOrdered DESC;
END;
GO
```

The SP begins with a declaration that accepts a single parameter, @ProductID. The default @ProductID is set to 776, per the AdventureWorks management team's rules:

```
CREATE PROCEDURE Production.GetProductRecommendations (@ProductID int = 776)
```

Next, the CTE that will return the TotalQtyOrdered, ProductID, TotalDollarsOrdered, and ProductSubCategoryID for each product is defined:

```
WITH RecommendedProducts (
ProductID,
ProductSubCategorylD,
TotalQtyOrdered,
TotalDollarsOrdered )
```

In the body of the CTE, the Sales.SalesOrderDetail table is joined to itself based on SalesOrderlD. A join to the Production.Product table is also included to get each product's SubcategorylD. The point of the self-join is to grab the total quantity ordered (OrderQty) and the total dollars ordered (UnitPrice * OrderQty) for each product.

The query is designed to include only orders that contain the product passed in via @ProductID in the WHERE clause, and it also eliminates results for @ProductID itself from the final results. All of the results are grouped by ProductID and ProductSubcategorylD:

```
(
SELECT
od2.ProductID,
p1.ProductSubCategoryID,
SUM(od2.OrderQty) AS TotalQtyOrdered,
SUM(od2.UnitPrice * od2.OrderQty) AS TotalDollarsOrdered
FROM Sales.SalesOrderDetail od1
INNER JOIN Sales.SalesOrderDetail od2
ON od1.SalesOrderID = od2.SalesOrderID
INNER JOIN Production.Product p1
ON od2.ProductID = p1.ProductID
WHERE od1.ProductID = @ProductID
AND od2.ProductID <> @ProductID
```

```
GROUP BY
od2.ProductID,
p1.ProductSubcategoryID
)
```

The final part of the CTE excludes products that are in the same category as the item passed in by @ProductID. It then limits the results to the top ten and numbers the results from highest to lowest by TotalQtyOrdered. It also joins on the Production.Product table to get each product's name:

```
SELECT TOP(10) ROW_NUMBER() OVER (
ORDER BY rp.TotalQtyOrdered DESC ) AS Rank,
rp.TotalQtyOrdered,
rp.ProductID,
rp.TotalDollarsOrdered,
p.[Name]

FROM RecommendedProducts rp INNER JOIN Production.Product p
ON rp.ProductID = p.ProductID WHERE rp.ProductSubcategoryID <> (
SELECT ProductSubcategoryID FROM Production.Product WHERE ProductID = @ProductID ) ORDER BY
TotalQtyOrdered DESC;
```

Figure 5-6 shows the result set of a recommended product list for people who bought a silver Mountain-100 44-inch bike (ProductID = 773), as shown in Listing 5-10.

	Rank	TotalQtyOrde.	ProductID	TotalDollarsOrde.	Name
1	1	878	709	4881.72	Mountain Bike Socks, M
2	2	340	715	9762.4748	Long-Sleeve Logo Jersey, L
3	3	297	712	1538.3157	AWC Logo Cap
4	4	235	711	4743.8275	Sport-100 Helmet, Blue
5	5	201	708	4057.4865	Sport-100 Helmet, Black
6	6	177	707	3578.0105	Sport-100 Helmet, Red
7	7	156	716	4499.1024	Long-Sleeve Logo Jersey, XL
8	8	150	714	4326.06	Long-Sleeve Logo Jersey, M
9	9	148	748	108944.0452	HL Mountain Frame - Silver, 38
10	10	145	741	118711.50	HL Mountain Frame - Silver, 48

Figure 5-6. *Recommended Product List for ProductID 773*

Listing 5-10. Getting a Recommended Product List

```
EXECUTE Production..GetProductRecommendations 773;
```

Implementing this business logic in an SP provides a layer of abstraction that makes it easier to use from front-end applications. Front-end application programmers don't need to worry about the details of which tables need to be accessed, how they need to be joined, and so on. All your application developers need to know to utilize this logic from the front end is that they need to pass the SP a ProductID number parameter and it will return the relevant information in a well-defined result set.

The same procedure promotes code reuse, and if you have a business logic implemented with complex code in an SP, the code does not have to be written multiple times; instead you can simply call the SP to access the code. Also, if you need to change the business logic, it can be done one time, in one place. Consider what happens if the AdventureWorks management decides to make suggestions based on total dollars worth of a product ordered instead of the total quantity ordered. Simply change the ORDER BY clause from the following:

```
ORDER BY TotalQtyOrdered DESC;
```

to the following:

```
ORDER BY TotalDollarsOrdered DESC;
```

This simple change in the procedure does the trick. No additional changes to front-end code or logic are required, and no recompilation and redeployment of code to web server farms is required, since the interface to the SP remains the same.

Recursion in Stored Procedures

Like UDFs, SPs can call themselves recursively. There is an SQL Server-imposed limit of 32 levels of recursion. To demonstrate recursion, we'll solve a very old puzzle.

The Towers of Hanoi puzzle consists of three pegs and a specified number of discs of varying sizes that slide onto the pegs. The puzzle begins with the discs stacked on top of one another, from smallest to largest, all on one peg. The Towers of Hanoi puzzle start position is shown in Figure 5-7.

Figure 5-7. *The Towers of Hanoi Puzzle Start Position*

The object of the puzzle is to move all of the discs from the first tower to the third tower. The trick is that you can only move one disc at a time, and no larger disc may be stacked on top of a smaller disc at any time. You can temporarily place discs on the middle tower as necessary, and you can stack any smaller disc on top of a larger disc on any tower. The Towers of Hanoi puzzle is often used as an exercise in computer science courses to demonstrate recursion in procedural languages. This makes it a perfect candidate for a T-SQL solution to demonstrate SP recursion.

Our T-SQL implementation of the Towers of Hanoi puzzle will use five discs and display each move as the computer makes it. The complete T-SQL Towers of Hanoi puzzle solution is shown in Listing 5-11.

Listing 5-11. The Towers of Hanoi Puzzle

```
--  This stored procedure displays all the discs in the appropriate
-- towers.
CREATE   PROCEDURE   dbo.ShowTowers
AS
BEGIN

    -- Each disc is displayed like this "===3===" where the number is the disc
    -- and the width of the === signs on either side indicates the width of the
    --  disc.
-- These CTEs are designed for displaying the discs in proper order on each
-- tower.
WITH FiveNumbers(Num) -- Recursive CTE generates table with numbers 1...5
AS
(
    SELECT 1

    UNION ALL

    SELECT Num + 1
    FROM FiveNumbers
    WHERE Num < 5
),
GetTowerA (Disc)                    -- The discs for Tower A
AS
(
    SELECT COALESCE(a.Disc, -1) AS Disc
    FROM FiveNumbers f
    LEFT JOIN #TowerA a
    ON  f.Num  =         a.Disc
),
GetTowerB (Disc)                    -- The discs for Tower B
AS
(
    SELECT COALESCE(b.Disc, -1) AS Disc
    FROM FiveNumbers f
    LEFT JOIN #TowerB b
    ON  f.Num  =         b.Disc
),
GetTowerC (Disc)                    -- The discs for Tower C
AS
(
    SELECT COALESCE(c.Disc, -1) AS Disc
    FROM FiveNumbers f
    LEFT JOIN #TowerC c
    ON  f.Num  =         c.Disc
)
-- This SELECT query generates the text representation for all three towers
-- and all five discs. FULL OUTER JOIN is used to represent the towers in a
--  side-by-side format.
SELECT CASE a.Disc
        WHEN 5 THEN '  =====5===== '
        WHEN 4 THEN '   ====4==== '
```

```
            WHEN  3   THEN     '===3===      '
            WHEN  2   THEN     ' ==2==      '
            WHEN  1   THEN     '  =1=       '
            ELSE  '   |  '
            END  AS Tower_A,
            CASE b.Disc
            WHEN 5 THEN '  =====5=====  '
            WHEN 4 THEN '   ====4====  '
            WHEN  3   THEN  ' ===3===      '
            WHEN  2   THEN  '  ==2==     '
            WHEN  1   THEN  '   =1=      '
            ELSE  '   |  '
            END  AS Tower_B,
            CASE c.Disc
            WHEN 5 THEN '  =====5=====  '
            WHEN 4 THEN '   ====4====  '
            WHEN  3   THEN  ' ===3===      '
            WHEN  2   THEN  '  ==2==     '
            WHEN  1   THEN  '   =1=      '
            ELSE  '   |  '
            END AS Tower_C
        FROM  (
            SELECT ROW_NUMBER() OVER(ORDER BY Disc) AS Num,
            COALESCE(Disc, -1) AS Disc
            FROM GetTowerA
        ) a
        FULL  OUTER  JOIN  (
            SELECT ROW_NUMBER() OVER(ORDER BY Disc) AS Num,
            COALESCE(Disc,  -1)  AS  Disc
            FROM GetTowerB
        ) b
            ON  a.Num  =  b.Num
        FULL  OUTER  JOIN   (
            SELECT ROW_NUMBER() OVER(ORDER BY Disc) AS Num,
            COALESCE(Disc, -1) AS Disc
            FROM GetTowerC
        ) c
            ON  b.Num  =  c.Num
        ORDER BY a.Num;
END;
GO

--  This SP moves a single disc from the specified source tower to the
--  specified destination tower.
CREATE  PROCEDURE  dbo.MoveOneDisc  (@Source  nchar(1),
    @Dest nchar(1))
AS
BEGIN
    --  @SmallestDisc is the smallest disc on the source tower
    DECLARE @SmallestDisc int = 0;
--  IF ... ELSE conditional statement gets the smallest disc from the
--  correct source tower
```

129

```
IF  @Source = N'A'
BEGIN
    -- This gets the smallest disc from Tower   A
    SELECT @SmallestDisc = MIN(Disc)
    FROM #TowerA;

    -- Then delete it from Tower   A
    DELETE FROM #TowerA
    WHERE Disc = @SmallestDisc;
END
ELSE IF  @Source =   N'B'
BEGIN
    -- This gets the smallest disc from Tower  B
    SELECT @SmallestDisc = MIN(Disc)
    FROM #TowerB;

    -- Then delete it from Tower   B
    DELETE FROM #TowerB
    WHERE Disc = @SmallestDisc;
END
ELSE IF  @Source =   N'C'
BEGIN
    -- This gets the smallest disc from Tower   C
    SELECT @SmallestDisc = MIN(Disc)
    FROM #TowerC;

    -- Then delete it from Tower   C
    DELETE FROM #TowerC
    WHERE Disc = @SmallestDisc;
END

-- Show the disc move performed
SELECT N'Moving Disc (' + CAST(COALESCE(@SmallestDisc, 0) AS nchar(1)) +
    N') from Tower ' + @Source + N' to Tower ' + @Dest + ':' AS Description;

-- Perform the move - INSERT the disc from the source tower into the
-- destination tower
IF  @Dest = N'A'
    INSERT INTO #TowerA (Disc) VALUES (@SmallestDisc);
ELSE IF @Dest = N'B'
    INSERT INTO #TowerB (Disc) VALUES (@SmallestDisc);
ELSE IF @Dest = N'C'
    INSERT INTO #TowerC (Disc) VALUES (@SmallestDisc);
    -- Show the towers
    EXECUTE dbo.ShowTowers;
END;
GO

-- This SP moves multiple discs recursively
CREATE  PROCEDURE  dbo.MoveDiscs (@DiscNum  int,
    @MoveNum int OUTPUT,
    @Source nchar(1) = N'A',
    @Dest nchar(1) = N'C',
    @Aux nchar(1) = N'B'
)
```

130

```
AS
BEGIN
    -- If the number of discs to move is 0, the solution has been found
    IF  @DiscNum = 0
        PRINT N'Done';
    ELSE
    BEGIN
        -- If the number of discs to move is 1, go ahead and move it
        IF  @DiscNum = 1
        BEGIN

        -- Increase the move counter by 1
        SELECT  @MoveNum  += 1;

        -- And finally move one disc from source to destination
        EXEC dbo.MoveOneDisc @Source, @Dest;
        END
        ELSE
        BEGIN
        -- Determine number of discs to move from source to auxiliary tower
        DECLARE  @n  int = @DiscNum - 1;

        -- Move (@DiscNum - 1) discs from source to auxiliary tower
        EXEC  dbo.MoveDiscs  @n,  @MoveNum      OUTPUT, @Source, @Aux, @Dest;

        -- Move 1 disc from source to final destination tower
        EXEC  dbo.MoveDiscs  1,  @MoveNum OUTPUT, @Source, @Dest, @Aux;

        -- Move (@DiscNum - 1) discs from auxiliary to final destination tower
        EXEC  dbo.MoveDiscs  @n,  @MoveNum      OUTPUT, @Aux, @Dest, @Source;
        END;
    END;
END;
GO
-- This SP creates the three towers and populates Tower A with 5 discs
CREATE   PROCEDURE          dbo.SolveTowers
AS
BEGIN
    -- SET NOCOUNT ON to eliminate system messages that will clutter up
    -- the Message display
    SET  NOCOUNT  ON;

    --   Create the three towers: Tower A, Tower B, and Tower C
    CREATE TABLE #TowerA (Disc int PRIMARY KEY NOT NULL);
    CREATE TABLE #TowerB (Disc int PRIMARY KEY NOT NULL);
    CREATE TABLE #TowerC (Disc int PRIMARY KEY NOT NULL);

    -- Populate Tower A with all five discs
    INSERT INTO #TowerA (Disc)
    VALUES (1), (2), (3), (4), (5);

    --   Initialize the move number to 0
    DECLARE @MoveNum int = 0;

    -- Show the initial state of the towers
    EXECUTE dbo.ShowTowers;
```

131

```
    -- Solve the puzzle. Notice you don't need to specify the parameters
    -- with defaults
    EXECUTE dbo.MoveDiscs 5, @MoveNum OUTPUT;

    -- How many moves did it take?
    PRINT N'Solved in ' + CAST (@MoveNum AS nvarchar(10)) + N' moves.';

    -- Drop the temp tables to clean up - always a good idea.
    DROP TABLE #TowerC;
    DROP TABLE #TowerB;
    DROP TABLE #TowerA;

    -- SET NOCOUNT OFF before we exit
    SET  NOCOUNT        OFF;
END;
GO
```

To solve the puzzle, just run the following statement:

```
-- Solve the puzzle
EXECUTE dbo.SolveTowers;
```

Figure 5-8 is a screenshot of the processing as the discs are moved from tower to tower.

■ **Note**   The results of Listing 5-11 are best viewed in Results to Text mode. You can put SSMS in Results to Text mode by pressing Ctrl + T while in the Query Editor window. To switch to Results to Grid mode, press Ctrl + D.

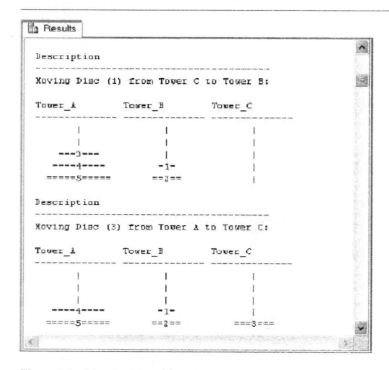

Figure 5-8. *Discs Are Moved from Tower to Tower*

The main procedure you call to solve the puzzle is dbo.SolveTowers. This SP creates three temporary tables, named #TowerA, #TowerB, and #TowerC. It then populates #TowerA with five discs and initializes the current move number to 0.

```
--  Create the three towers: Tower A, Tower B, and Tower C
CREATE TABLE #TowerA (Disc int PRIMARY KEY NOT NULL);
CREATE TABLE #TowerB (Disc int PRIMARY KEY NOT NULL);
CREATE TABLE #TowerC (Disc int PRIMARY KEY NOT NULL);

-- Populate Tower A with all five discs
INSERT INTO #TowerA (Disc)
VALUES (1), (2), (3), (4), (5);

--  Initialize the move number to 0
DECLARE @MoveNum INT = 0;
```

Since this SP is the entry point for the entire puzzle-solving program, it displays the start position of the towers and calls dbo.MoveDiscs to get the ball rolling:

```
-- Show the initial state of the towers
EXECUTE dbo.ShowTowers;
-- Solve the puzzle. Notice you don't need to specify the parameters
-- with defaults
EXECUTE dbo.MoveDiscs 5, @MoveNum OUTPUT;
```

When the puzzle is finally solved, control returns back from dbo.MoveDiscs to dbo. SolveTowers, which displays the number of steps it took to complete the puzzle and performs some cleanup work, like dropping the temporary tables.

```
-- How many moves did it take?
PRINT N'Solved in ' + CAST (@MoveNum AS nvarchar(10)) + N' moves.';
-- Drop the temp tables to clean up - always a good idea.
DROP TABLE #TowerC;
DROP TABLE #TowerB;
DROP TABLE #TowerA;
-- SET NOCOUNT OFF before we exit
SET NOCOUNT OFF;
```

■ **Tip** When an SP that created temporary tables ends, the temporary tables are automatically dropped. Because temporary tables are created in the tempdb system database, it's a good idea to get in the habit of explicitly dropping temporary tables. By explicitly dropping temporary tables, you can guarantee that they exist only as long as they are needed, which can help minimize contention in the tempdb database.

The procedure responsible for moving discs from tower to tower recursively is dbo.MoveDiscs. This procedure accepts several parameters, including the number of discs to move (@DiscNum); the number of the current move (@MoveNum); and the names of the source, destination, and auxiliary/intermediate towers. This procedure uses T-SQL procedural IF statements to determine which types of moves are required—single disc moves, recursive multiple-disc moves, or no more moves (when the solution is found). If the solution has been found, the message Done is displayed and control is subsequently passed back to the calling procedure, dbo.SolveTowers.

```
-- If the number of discs to move is 0, the solution has been found
IF @DiscNum = 0
   PRINT N'Done';
ELSE
RETURN 0;
```

If there is only one disc to move, the move counter is incremented and dbo.MoveOneDisc is called to perform the move:

```
-- If the number of discs to move is 1, go ahead and move it
IF @DiscNum = 1

BEGIN
-- Increase the move counter by 1
SELECT @MoveNum += 1;

-- And finally move one disc from source to destination
EXEC dbo.MoveOneDisc @Source, @Dest;
END
```

Finally, if there is more than one disc move required, dbo.MoveDiscs calls itself recursively until there are either one or zero discs left to move:

```
ELSE
BEGIN
-- Determine number of discs to move from source to auxiliary tower
DECLARE @n INT = @DiscNum - 1;

-- Move (@DiscNum - 1) discs from source to auxiliary tower
EXEC dbo.MoveDiscs @n, @MoveNum OUTPUT, @Source, @Aux, @Dest;

-- Move 1 disc from source to final destination tower
EXEC dbo.MoveDiscs 1, @MoveNum OUTPUT, @Source, @Dest, @Aux;

-- Move (@DiscNum - 1) discs from auxiliary to final destination tower
EXEC dbo.MoveDiscs @n, @MoveNum OUTPUT, @Aux, @Dest, @Source;
END;
```

The basis of the Towers of Hanoi puzzle is the movement of a single disc at a time from tower to tower, so the most basic procedure, dbo.MoveOneDisc, simply moves a disc from the specified source tower to the specified destination tower. Given a source and destination tower as inputs, this procedure first determines the smallest (or top) disc on the source and moves it to the destination table using simple SELECT queries. The smallest disc is then deleted from the source table.

```
-- @SmallestDisc is the smallest disc on the source tower
DECLARE @SmallestDisc int = 0;
-- IF ... ELSE conditional statement gets the smallest disc from the
-- correct source tower
IF @Source = N'A'
BEGIN
-- This gets the smallest disc from Tower A
SELECT @SmallestDisc = MIN(Disc)
FROM #TowerA;
```

```
-- Then delete it from Tower A
DELETE FROM #TowerA
WHERE Disc = @SmallestDisc;
END
```

Once the smallest disc of the source table is determined, dbo.MoveOneDisc displays the move it is about to perform, and then performs the INSERT to place the disc in the destination tower. Finally, it calls the dbo.ShowTowers procedure to show the current state of the towers and discs.

```
-- Show the disc move performed
SELECT N'Moving Disc (' + CAST(COALESCE(@SmallestDisc, 0) AS nchar(1)) + N') from Tower ' +
@Source + N' to Tower ' + @Dest + ':' AS Description;

-- Perform the move - INSERT the disc from the source tower into the
-- destination tower
IF @Dest = N'A'
INSERT INTO #TowerA (Disc) VALUES (@SmallestDisc);
ELSE IF @Dest = N'B'
INSERT INTO #TowerB (Disc) VALUES (@SmallestDisc);
ELSE IF @Dest = N'C'
INSERT INTO #TowerC (Disc) VALUES (@SmallestDisc);
-- Show the towers
EXECUTE dbo.ShowTowers;
```

The dbo.ShowTowers procedure doesn't affect processing; it's simply included as a convenience to output a reasonable representation of the towers and discs they contain at any given point during processing.

This implementation of a solver for the Towers of Hanoi puzzle demonstrates several aspects of SPs we've introduced in this chapter, including the following:

- SPs can call themselves recursively. This is demonstrated with the dbo.MoveDiscs procedure, which calls itself until the puzzle is solved.

- When default values are assigned to parameters in an SP declaration, you do not have to specify values for them when you call the procedure. This concept is demonstrated in the dbo.SolveTowers procedure, which calls the dbo.MoveDiscs procedure.

- The scope of temporary tables created in an SP includes the procedure in which they are created, as well as any SPs it calls, and any SPs they in turn call. This is demonstrated in dbo.SolveTowers, which creates three temporary tables, and then calls other procedures that access those same temporary tables. The procedures called by dbo.SolveTowers and those called by those procedures (and so on) can also access these same temporary tables.

- The dbo.MoveDiscs SP demonstrates output parameters. This procedure uses an output parameter to update the count of the total number of moves performed after each move.

Table-Valued Parameters

Beginning with SQL Server 2008, developers have the capability of passing table-valued parameters to SPs and UDFs. Prior to SQL Server 2008, the primary methods of passing multiple rows of data to an SP included the following:

- Converting your multiple rows to an intermediate format like comma-delimited or XML. If you use this method, you have to parse out the parameter into a temporary table, table variable, or subquery to extract the rows from the intermediate format. These conversions to and from intermediate format can be costly, especially when large amounts of data are involved.

- Placing rows in a permanent or temporary table and calling the procedure. This method eliminates conversions to and from the intermediate format, but is not without problems of its own. Managing multiple sets of input rows from multiple simultaneous users can introduce a lot of overhead and additional conversion code that must be managed.

- Passing lots and lots of parameters to the SP. SQL Server SPs can accept up to 2,100 parameters. Conceivably, you could pass several rows of data using thousands of parameters and ignore those parameters you don't need. One big drawback to this method, however, is that it results in complex code that can be extremely difficult to manage.

- Calling procedures multiple times with a single row of data each time. This method is probably the simplest method, resulting in code that is very easy to create and manage. The downside to this method is that querying and manipulating potentially tens of thousands of rows of data or more, one row at a time, can result in a big performance penalty.

A table-valued parameter allows you to pass rows of data to your TSQL statement or SPs and UDFs in tabular format. To create a table-valued parameter you must first create a *table type* that defines your table structure, as shown in Listing 5-12.

Listing 5-12. Creating a Table Type

```
CREATE TYPE HumanResources.LastNameTableType
AS TABLE (LastName nvarchar(50) NOT NULL PRIMARY KEY);
GO
```

The CREATE TYPE statement in Listing 5-12 creates a simple table type that represents a table with a single column named LastName, which also serves as the primary key for the table. To use table-valued parameters, you must declare your SP with parameters of the table type. The SP in Listing 5-13 accepts a single table-valued parameter of the HumanResources.LastNameTableType type from Listing 5-12. It then uses the rows in the table-valued parameter in an inner join to restrict the rows returned by the SP.

Listing 5-13. Simple Procedure Accepting a Table-valued Parameter

```
CREATE  PROCEDURE  HumanResources.GetEmployees
    (@LastNameTable HumanResources.LastNameTableType READONLY)
AS
BEGIN
    SELECT
        p.LastName,
        p.FirstName,
        p.MiddleName,
        e.NationalIDNumber,
        e.Gender,
        e.HireDate
    FROM  HumanResources.Employee  e
    INNER JOIN Person.Person p
```

```
        ON  e.BusinessEntityID  =  p.BusinessEntityID
    INNER JOIN @LastNameTable lnt
        ON p.LastName = lnt.LastName
    ORDER BY
        p.LastName,
        p.FirstName,
        p.MiddleName;
END;
GO
```

The CREATE PROCEDURE statement in Listing 5-13 declares a single table-valued parameter, @LastNameTable, of the HumanResources.LastNameTableType created in Listing 5-12.

```
CREATE PROCEDURE HumanResources.GetEmployees
(@LastNameTable HumanResources.LastNameTableType READONLY)
```

The table-valued parameter is declared READONLY, which is mandatory. Although you can query and join to the rows in a table-valued parameter just like a table variable, you cannot manipulate the rows in table-valued parameters with INSERT, UPDATE, DELETE, or MERGE statements.

The HumanResources.GetEmployees procedure performs a simple query to retrieve the names, national ID number, gender, and hire date for all employees whose last names match any of the last names passed into the SP via the @LastNameTable table-valued parameter. As you can see in Listing 5-13, the SELECT query performs an inner join against the table-valued parameter to restrict the rows returned:

```
SELECT
    p.LastName,
    p.FirstName,
    p.MiddleName,
    e.NationalIDNumber,
    e.Gender,
    e.HireDate
FROM HumanResources.Employee e
INNER JOIN Person.Person p
    ON e.BusinessEntitylD = p.BusinessEntityID
INNER JOIN @LastNameTable lnt
    ON p.LastName = Int.LastName
ORDER BY
    p.LastName,
    p.FirstName,
    p.MiddleName;
```

To call a procedure with a table-valued parameter, like the HumanResources.GetEmployees SP in Listing 5-13, you need to declare a variable of the same type as the table-valued parameter. Then you populate the variable with rows of data and pass the variable as a parameter to the procedure. Listing 5-14 demonstrates how to call the HumanResources.GetEmployees SP with a table-valued parameter. The results are shown in Figure 5-9.

Listing 5-14. Calling a Procedure with a Table-valued Parameter

```
DECLARE @LastNameList HumanResources.LastNameTableType;
INSERT INTO @LastNameList
(LastName)
VALUES
```

```
(N'Walters'),
(N'Anderson'),
(N'Chen'),
(N'Rettig'),
(N'Lugo'),
(N'Zwilling'),
(N'Johnson');

EXECUTE HumanResources.GetEmployees @LastNameList;
```

	LastName	FirstNa...	MiddleNa...	NationalIDNum...	Gen...	HireDate
1	Anderson	Nancy	A	693325305	F	1999-02-03 00:00:00.000
2	Chen	Hao	O	416679555	M	1999-03-10 00:00:00.000
3	Chen	John	Y	305522471	M	1999-03-13 00:00:00.000
4	Johnson	Barry	K	912265825	M	1998-02-07 00:00:00.000
5	Johnson	David	N	486138869	M	1999-01-03 00:00:00.000
6	Johnson	Willis	T	332040978	M	1999-01-14 00:00:00.000
7	Lugo	Jose	R	788456780	M	1999-03-14 00:00:00.000
8	Rettig	Bjorn	M	420023788	M	1999-02-09 00:00:00.000
9	Walters	Rob	NULL	112457891	M	1998-01-05 00:00:00.000
10	Zwilling	Michael	J	582347317	M	2000-03-26 00:00:00.000

Figure 5-9. *Employees Returned by the SP Call in Listing 5-14*

In addition to being read-only, the following additional restrictions apply to table-valued parameters:

- As with table variables, you cannot use a table-valued parameter as the target of an INSERT EXEC or SELECT INTO assignment statement.

- Table-valued parameters are scoped just like other parameters and local variables declared within a procedure or function. They are not visible outside of the procedure in which they are declared.

- SQL Server does not maintain column-level statistics for table-valued parameters, which can affect performance if you are passing large numbers of rows of data via table-valued parameters.

You can also pass table-valued parameters to SPs from ADO.NET clients, which we will discuss in Chapter 15.

Temporary Stored Procedures

In addition to normal SPs, T-SQL provides what are known as *temporary SPs*. Temporary SPs are created just like any other SPs; the only difference is that the name must begin with a number sign (#) for a local temporary SP and two number signs (##) for a global temporary SP.

While a normal SP remains in the database and schema it was created in until it is explicitly dropped via the DROP PROCEDURE statement, temporary SPs are dropped automatically. A local temporary SP is visible only to the current session and is dropped when the current session ends. A global temporary SP is visible to all connections and is automatically dropped when the last session using it ends.

Normally you won't use temporary SPs, as they are usually used for specialized solutions, like database drivers. Open Database Connectivity (ODBC) drivers, for instance, make use of temporary SPs to implement SQL Server connectivity functions. Temporary SPs are useful when you want the advantages of using stored procedures such as execution plan reuse and improved error handling with the advantages of ad hoc code. However, temporary stored procedures bring some other effects as well. The temporary stored procedures are often not destroyed until the connection is closed or explicitly dropped. This may cause the procedures to fill up tempdb over time and cause queries to fail. Creating temporary SPs within a transaction may also cause blocking problems since the stored procedure creation causes data page locking in several system tables for the transaction duration.

Recompilation and Caching

SQL Server has several features that work behind the scenes to optimize your SP performance. The first time you execute an SP, SQL Server compiles it into a query plan, which it then caches. This compilation process invokes a certain amount of overhead, which can be substantial for procedures that are complex or that are run very often. SQL Server uses a complex caching mechanism to store and reuse query plans on subsequent calls to the same SP, in an effort to minimize the impact of SP compilation overhead. In this section, we'll talk about managing query plan recompilation and cached query plan reuse.

Stored Procedure Statistics

SQL Server 2012 provides DMVs and *dynamic management functions (DMFs)* to expose SP query plan usage and caching information that can be useful for performance tuning and general troubleshooting. Listing 5-15 is a procedure that retrieves and displays several relevant SP statistics from a few different DMVs and DMFs.

Listing 5-15. Procedure to Retrieve SP Statistics with DMVs and DMFs

```
CREATE  PROCEDURE  dbo.GetProcStats  (@order  varchar(100)  =  'use')
AS
BEGIN
    WITH GetQueryStats
    (
        plan_handle,
        total_elapsed_time,
        total_logical_reads,
        total_logical_writes,
        total_physical_reads
    )
    AS
    (
        SELECT
        qs.plan_handle,
        SUM(qs.total_elapsed_time)  AS  total_elapsed_time,
        SUM(qs.total_logical_reads)  AS  total_logical_reads,
        SUM(qs.total_logical_writes) AS total_logical_writes,
        SUM(qs.total_physical_reads)  AS  total_physical_reads
        FROM sys.dm_exec_query_stats qs
        GROUP BY qs.plan_handle
    )
```

```
SELECT
    DB_NAME(st.dbid) AS database_name,
    OBJECT_SCHEMA_NAME(st.objectid, st.dbid) AS schema_name,
    OBJECT_NAME(st.objectid, st.dbid) AS proc_name,
    SUM(cp.usecounts) AS use_counts,
    SUM(cp.size_in_bytes) AS size_in_bytes,
    SUM(qs.total_elapsed_time) AS total_elapsed_time,
    CAST
    (
    SUM(qs.total_elapsed_time)  AS  decimal(38, 4)
    ) /  SUM(cp.usecounts)  AS  avg_elapsed_time_per_use,
    SUM(qs.total_logical_reads) AS total_logical_reads,
    CAST
    (
    SUM(qs.total_logical_reads)  AS  decimal(38, 4)
    ) /  SUM(cp.usecounts)  AS  avg_logical_reads_per_use,
    SUM(qs.total_logical_writes) AS total_logical_writes,
    CAST
    (
    SUM(qs.total_logical_writes)  AS   decimal(38, 4)
    ) /  SUM(cp.usecounts)  AS  avg_logical_writes_per_use,
    SUM(qs.total_physical_reads) AS total_physical_reads,
    CAST
    (
    SUM(qs.total_physical_reads)  AS            decimal(38, 4)
    ) /  SUM(cp.usecounts)  AS  avg_physical_reads_per_use,
    st.text
FROM  sys.dm_exec_cached_plans  cp
CROSS APPLY sys.dm_exec_sql_text(cp.plan_handle) st
INNER JOIN GetQueryStats qs
    ON  cp.plan_handle  =  qs.plan_handle
INNER JOIN sys.procedures p
    ON st.objectid = p.object_id
    WHERE p.type IN ('P', 'PC')
    GROUP BY st.dbid, st.objectid, st.text
    ORDER BY
    CASE  @order
    WHEN  'name'  THEN  OBJECT_NAME(st.objectid)
    WHEN 'size' THEN SUM(cp.size_in_bytes)
    WHEN  'read'  THEN      SUM(qs.total_logical_reads)
    WHEN  'write'  THEN  SUM(qs.total_logical_writes)
    ELSE  SUM(cp.usecounts)
    END DESC;
END;
GO
```

This procedure uses the `sys.dm_exec_cached_plans` and `sys.dm_exec_query_stats` DMVs in conjunction with the `sys.dmexecsqltext` DMF to retrieve relevant SP execution information. The `sys.procedures` catalog view is used to limit the results to only SPs (type P). Aggregation is required on most of the statistics since the DMVs and DMFs can return multiple rows, each representing individual statements within SPs. The `dbo.GetProcStats` procedure accepts a single parameter that determines how the result rows are sorted. Setting the `@order` parameter to `size` sorts the results in descending order by the `sizeinbytes` column, while `read` sorts in descending order by the `totallogicalreads` column. Other possible values include `name` and `write`—all other values sort by the default `usecounts` column in descending order.

■ **Tip**   In this SP, we used a few useful system functions: `DB_NAME` accepts the ID of a database and returns the database name; `OBDECT_SCHEMA_NAME` accepts the ID of an object and a database ID and returns the name of the schema in which the object resides; and `OBJECT_NAME` accepts the object ID and returns the name of the object itself. These are handy functions, and you can retrieve the same information via SQL Server's catalog views.

Listing 5-16 demonstrates how to call this SP. Sample results are shown in Figure 5-10.

Listing 5-16. Retrieving SP Statistics

```
EXEC dbo.GetProcStats @order = 'use';
GO
```

	database_name	schema_name	proc_name	use_counts	size_in_bytes	total_elapsed_time	avg_elapsed_time_per_use	total_logic
1	AdventureWorks	Sales	GetSalesRunningTotal	2	147456	18967722	9483861.000000	954353
2	AdventureWorks	Production	GetProductRecommendations	1	90112	135876	135876.000000	2647
3	AdventureWorks	HumanResources	GetEmployees	1	73728	42842	42842.000000	582

Figure 5-10. *Partial Results of Calling the GetProcStats Procedure*

SQL Server DMVs and DMFs can be used in this way to answer several questions about your SPs, including the following:

- Which SPs are executed the most?
- Which SPs take the longest to execute?
- Which SPs perform the most logical reads and writes?

The answers to these types of questions can help you quickly locate performance bottlenecks and focus your performance-tuning efforts where they are most needed. We will discuss the performance tuning in detail in Chapter 19, Performance Monitoring and Tuning.

Parameter Sniffing

SQL Server uses a method known as *parameter sniffing* to further optimize SP calls. During compilation or recompilation of an SP, SQL Server captures the parameters used and passes the values along to the optimizer. The optimizer then generates and caches a query plan optimized for those parameters. This can actually cause problems in some cases—for example, when your SP can return wildly varying numbers of rows based on the parameters passed in. Listing 5-17 shows a simple SP that retrieves all products from the `Production.Product` table with a Name like the `@Prefix` parameter passed into the SP.

Listing 5-17. Simple Procedure to Demonstrate Parameter Sniffing

```
CREATE  PROCEDURE  Production.GetProductsByName
    @Prefix NVARCHAR(100)
AS
BEGIN
    SELECT
        p.Name,
        p.ProductID
    FROM  Production.Product  p
    WHERE p.Name LIKE @Prefix;
END;
GO
```

Calling this SP with the @Prefix parameter set to % results in a query plan optimized to return 504 rows of data with a nonclustered index scan, as shown in Figure 5-11.

Figure 5-11. *Query Plan Optimized to Return 504 Rows*

If you run the Production.GetProductsByName procedure a second time with the @Prefix parameter set to M%, the query plan will show that the plan is still optimized to return 504 estimated rows, although only 102 rows are actually returned by the SP. Figure 5-12 shows the query plan for the second procedure call.

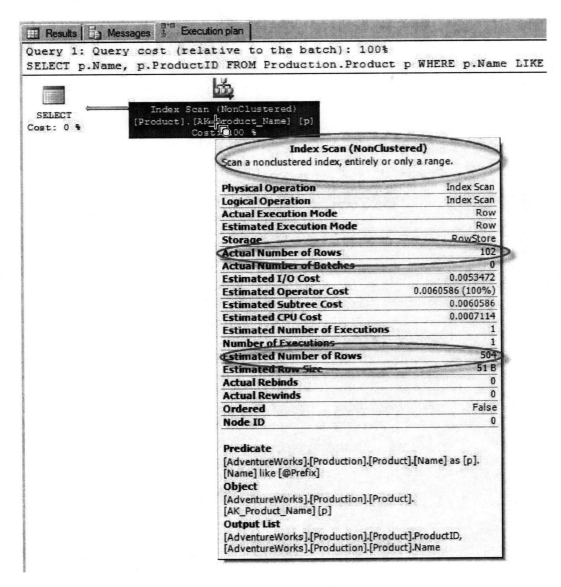

Figure 5-12. *Query Plan Optimized for the Wrong Number of Rows*

In cases where you expect widely varying numbers of rows to be returned by your SPs, you can override parameter sniffing on a per-procedure basis. Overriding parameter sniffing is simple—just declare a local variable in your SP, assign the parameter value to the variable, and use the variable in place of the parameter in your query. When you override parameter sniffing, SQL Server uses the source table data distribution statistics to estimate the number of rows to return. The theory is that the estimate will be better for a wider variety of possible parameter values. In this case, the estimate will still be considerably off for the extreme case of the 504 rows returned in this example, but it will be much closer and will therefore generate better query plans for other possible parameter values. Listing 5-18 alters the SP in Listing 5-17 to override parameter sniffing. Figure 5-13 shows the results of calling the updated SP with a @Prefix parameter of M%.

Figure 5-13. *Results of the SP with Parameter Sniffing Overridden*

Listing 5-18. Overriding Parameter Sniffing in an SP

```
ALTER PROCEDURE Production.GetProductsByName
@Prefix NVARCHAR(100)
AS
BEGIN
DECLARE @PrefixVar NVARCHAR(100) = @Prefix;
    SELECT
        p.Name,
        p.ProductID
    FROM  Production.Product  p
    WHERE p.Name LIKE @PrefixVar;
END;
GO
```

With parameter sniffing overridden, the query plan for the SP in Listing 5-18 uses the same estimated number of rows, in this case 27.0914, no matter what value you pass in the @Prefix parameter. This results in a query plan that uses a nonclustered index seek—not an index scan—which is a much better query plan for the vast majority of possible parameter values for this particular SP.

Recompilation

As we discussed previously in this chapter, SQL Server optimizes performance by caching compiled query plans while it can. The recompilation of stored procedures is performed on individual statements within stored procedures rather than entire stored procedures to avoid unnecessary recompile consuming CPU resources.

There are several reasons why the stored procedures are recompiled:

- If the object is modified between executions, each statement within the SP that references this object is recompiled.

- If sufficient data has changed in the table that is being referenced by the SP since the original query plan was generated, the SP will recompile the plan.

- Use of temporary table in the SP may cause the SP to be recompiled evey time the procedure is executed.

- If the SP was created with the recompile option, this may cause the SP to be recompiles every time the procedure is executed.

Caching the query plan eliminates the overhead associated with recompiling your query on subsequent runs, but occasionally this feature can cause performance to suffer. When you expect your SP to return widely varying numbers of rows in the result set with each call, the cached query execution plan will only be optimized for the first call. It won't be optimized for subsequent executions. In cases like this, you may decide to force recompilation with each call. Consider Listing 5-19, which is an SP that returns order header information for a given salesperson.

Listing 5-19. SP to Retrieve Orders by Salesperson

```
CREATE  PROCEDURE  Sales.GetSalesBySalesPerson (@SalesPersonId  int)
AS
BEGIN
    SELECT
        soh.SalesOrderID,
        soh.OrderDate,
        soh.TotalDue
    FROM  Sales.SalesOrderHeader  soh
    WHERE soh.SalesPersonID = @SalesPersonId;
END;
GO
```

There happens to be a nonclustered index on the SalesPersonID column of the Sales.SalesOrderHeader table, which you might expect to be considered by the optimizer. However, when this SP is executed with the EXECUTE statement in Listing 5-20, the optimizer ignores the nonclustered index, and instead performs a clustered index scan, as shown in Figure 5-14.

Listing 5-20. Retrieving Sales for Salesperson 277

```
EXECUTE Sales.GetSalesBySalesPerson 277;
```

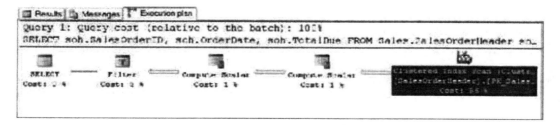

Figure 5-14. The SP Ignores the Nonclustered Index

The reason the SP ignores the nonclustered index on the SalesPersonID column is because 473 matching rows are returned by the query in the procedure. SQL Server uses a measure called *selectivity,* the ratio of qualifying rows to the total number of rows in the table, as a factor in determining which index, if any, to use. In Listing 5-20, the parameter value 277 represents low selectivity, meaning that there are a large number of rows returned relative to the number of rows in the table. SQL Server favors indexes for highly selective queries, to the point of completely ignoring indexes when the query has low selectivity.

If you subsequently call the SP with the @SalesPersonId parameter set to 285, which represents a highly selective value (only 16 rows are returned), query plan caching forces the same clustered index scan, even though it's suboptimal for a highly selective query. Fortunately, SQL Server provides options that allow you to force recompilation at the SP level or the statement level. You can force a recompilation in your SP call by adding the WITH RECOMPILE option to your EXECUTE statement, as shown in Listing 5-21.

Listing 5-21. Executing an SP with Recompilation

```
EXECUTE Sales.GetSalesBySalesPerson 285 WITH RECOMPILE;
```

The WITH RECOMPILE option of the EXECUTE statement forces a recompilation of your SP when you execute it. This option is useful if your data has significantly changed since the last SP recompilation or if the parameter value you're passing to the procedure represents an atypical value. The query plan for this SP call with the highly selective value 285 is shown in Figure 5-15.

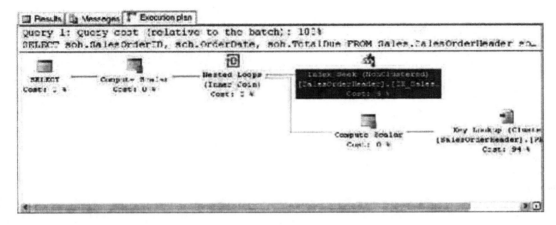

Figure 5-15. *SP Query Plan Optimized for Highly Selective Parameter Value*

You can also use the sp_recompile system SP to force an SP to recompile the next time it is run.

If you expect that the values submitted to your SP will vary a lot, and that the "one execution plan for all parameters" model will cause poor performance, you can specify statement-level recompilation by adding OPTION (RECOMPILE) to your statements. The statement-level recompilation also considers the values of local variables during the recompilation process. Listing 5-22 alters the SP created in Listing 5-20 to add statement-level recompilation to the SELECT query.

Listing 5-22. Adding Statement-Level Recompilation to the SP

```
ALTER  PROCEDURE  Sales.GetSalesBySalesPerson (@SalesPersonId  int)
AS
BEGIN
    SELECT
        soh.SalesOrderID,
        soh.OrderDate,
        soh.TotalDue
    FROM  Sales.SalesOrderHeader  soh
    WHERE soh.SalesPersonID = @SalesPersonId
    OPTION (RECOMPILE);
END;
GO
```

As an alternative, you can specify procedure-level recompilation by adding the WITH RECOMPILE option to your CREATE. PROCEDURE statement. This option is useful if you don't want SQL Server to cache the query plan for the SP. With this option in place, SQL Server recompiles the entire SP every time you run it. This can be useful for procedures containing several statements that need to be recompiled often. Keep in mind, however, that this option is less efficient than a statement-level recompile since the entire SP needs to be recompiled. Because it is less efficient than statement-level recompilation, this option should be used with care.

To extend on the Stored Procedure Statistics section, SQL Server 2012 provides details about the last time when the SP or the statements were recompiled with DMVs. This will help you identify the most recompiled

147

stored procedures and allow you to focus on resolving the recompilation issues. Listing 5-23 is a procedure that returns the stored procedures that have been recompiled.

Listing 5-23. SP to Retutn List of Stored Procedures That Have Been Recompiled

```
CREATE  PROCEDURE  dbo.GetRecompiledProcs
AS
BEGIN
    SELECT
        sql_text.text,
        stats.sql_handle,
        stats.plan_generation_num,
        stats.creation_time,
        stats.execution_count,
        sql_text.dbid,
        sql_text.objectid
    FROM sys.dm_exec_query_stats stats
        Cross apply sys.dm_exec_sql_text(sql_handle) as sql_text
    WHERE stats.plan_generation_num > 1
        and sql_text.objectid is not null --Filter adhoc queries
    ORDER BY stats.plan_generation_num desc
END;
GO
```

This procedure uses the sys.dm_exec_query_stats DMV with the sys.dm_exec_sql_text DMF to retrieve relevant SP execution information. The query returns only the stored procedures that have been recompiled by filtering the plan_generation_num, and the ad hoc queries are being filered out by removing the object_id with null values.

Listing 5-24 demonstrates how to call this SP, and partial results are shown in Figure 5-16.

Listing 5-24. Retrieving SP Statistics

```
EXEC dbo.GetRecompiledProcs;
GO
```

	text	sql_handle	plan_generation_num	creation
1	CREATE PROCEDURE [dbo].[CleanBrokenSnapshots] @...	0x03000500C80EF6438BD82A012DA0000001000000000000...	8	2012-05-
2	CREATE PROCEDURE [dbo].[CleanBrokenSnapshots] @...	0x03000500C80EF6438BD82A012DA0000001000000000000...	7	2012-05-
3	CREATE PROCEDURE [dbo].[CleanBrokenSnapshots] @...	0x03000500C80EF6438BD82A012DA0000001000000000000...	6	2012-05-
4	CREATE PROCEDURE [dbo].[CleanBrokenSnapshots] @...	0x03000500C80EF6438BD82A012DA0000001000000000000...	5	2012-05-
5	CREATE PROCEDURE [dbo].[CleanBrokenSnapshots] @...	0x03000500C80EF6438BD82A012DA0000001000000000000...	4	2012-05-
6	CREATE PROCEDURE [dbo].[CleanBrokenSnapshots] @...	0x03000500C80EF6438BD82A012DA0000001000000000000...	3	2012-05-
7	CREATE PROCEDURE [dbo].[CleanBrokenSnapshots] @...	0x03000500C80EF6438BD82A012DA0000001000000000000...	2	2012-05-

Figure 5-16. *Partial Results for Stored Procedure dbo.GetRecompiledProcs*

Summary

SPs are powerful tools for SQL Server development. They provide a flexible method of extending the power of SQL Server by allowing you to create custom server-side subroutines. While some of the performance advantages provided by SPs in older releases of SQL Server are not as pronounced in SQL Server 2012, the ability to modularize server-side code, administer your T-SQL code base in a single location, provide additional security, and ease front-end programming development still make SPs powerful development tools in any T-SQL developer's toolkit.

In this chapter, we introduced key aspects of SP development, including SP creation and management, passing scalar parameters to SPs, and retrieving result sets, output parameters, and return values from SPs. We also demonstrated some advanced topics, including the use of temporary tables to pass tabular data between SPs, writing recursive SPs, and SQL Server 2012's table-valued parameters.

Finally, we finished the chapter with a discussion of SP optimizations, including SP caching, accessing SP cache statistics through DMVs and DMFs, parameter sniffing, and recompilation options, including statement-level and procedure-level recompilation.

The samples provided in this chapter are designed to demonstrate several aspects of SP functionality in SQL Server 2012. The next chapter introduces further important aspects of T-SQL programming for SQL Server 2012: DML and DDL triggers.

EXERCISES

1. [True/False] The SP RETURN statement can return a scalar value of any data type.

2. The recursion level for SPs is 32 levels, as demonstrated by the following code sample, which errors out after reaching the maximum depth of recursion:

```
CREATE PROCEDURE dbo.FirstProc (@i int)
AS
BEGIN
PRINT @i;
SET @i += 1;
EXEC dbo.FirstProc @i; END; GO
EXEC dbo.FirstProc 1;
```

Write a second procedure and modify this one to prove that the recursion limit applies to two SPs that call each other recursively.

3. [Choose one] Table-valued parameters must be declared with which of the following modifiers:

- READWRITE

- WRITEONLY

- RECOMPILE

- READONLY

4. [Choose all that apply] You can use which of the following methods to force SQL Server to recompile an SP:

a. The sp_recompile system SP

- The WITH RECOMPILE option

- The FORCE RECOMPILE option

- The DBCC RECOMPILE_ALL_SPS command

CHAPTER 6

Triggers

SQL Server provides triggers as a means of executing T-SQL code in response to database object, database, and server events. SQL Server 2012 implements three types of triggers: classic T-SQL Data Manipulation Language (DML) triggers, which fire in response to INSERT, UPDATE, and DELETE events against tables; Data Definition Language (DDL) triggers, which fire in response to CREATE, ALTER, and DROP statements; and logon triggers, which fire in response to LOGON events. DDL triggers can also fire in response to some system SPs that perform DDL-like operations.

Triggers are a form of specialized SP, closely tied to your data and database objects. In the past, DML triggers were used to enforce various aspects of business logic, such as foreign key and other constraints on data, and other more complex business logic. Cascading declarative referential integrity (DRI) and robust check constraints in T-SQL have supplanted DML triggers in many areas, but they are still useful in their own right. In this chapter, we will discuss how triggers work, how to use them, and when they are most appropriate. We will also discuss DDL triggers and explore their use.

DML Triggers

DML triggers are composed of T-SQL code that is executed (fired) in response to an INSERT, an UPDATE, a DELETE, or a MERGE statement on a table or view. DML triggers are created via the CREATE TRIGGER statement, which allows you to specify the following details about the trigger:

- The name of the trigger, which is the identifier you can use to manage the trigger. You can specify a two-part name for a trigger (schema and trigger name), but the schema must be the same as the schema for the table on which the trigger executes.

- The table or view on which the trigger executes.

- The triggering events, which can be any combination of INSERT, UPDATE, and DELETE. The triggering events indicate the type of events that the trigger fires in response to.

- The AFTER/FOR or INSTEAD OF indicators, which determine whether the trigger is fired after the triggering statement completes or the trigger overrides the firing statement.

- Additional options like the ENCRYPTION and EXECUTE AS clauses, which allow you to obfuscate the trigger source code and specify the context that the trigger executes under, respectively.

■ **Note** DML triggers have some restrictions on their creation that you should keep in mind. For one, DML triggers cannot be defined on temporary tables. Also, DML triggers cannot be declared on table variables. Finally, only INSTEAD OF triggers can be used on views.

In addition to the CREATE TRIGGER statement, SQL Server provides an ALTER TRIGGER statement to modify the definition of a trigger, a DROP TRIGGER statement to remove an existing trigger from the database, and DISABLE TRIGGER and ENABLE TRIGGER statements to disable and enable a trigger, respectively.

Listing 6-1 shows how to disable and enable a specific trigger named HumanResources. EmployeeUpdateTrigger, or all triggers on an object, namely, the HumanResources.Employee table. It also contains an example of how to query the sys.triggers catalog view to return all the disabled triggers in the current database.

Listing 6-1. Disabling and Enabling Triggers

```
DISABLE TRIGGER HumanResources.EmployeeUpdateTrigger
ON HumanResources.Employee;

SELECT
    name,
    OBJECT_SCHEMA_NAME(parent_id) +'.'+ OBJECT_NAME(parent_id) as Parent
FROM sys.triggers
WHERE is_disabled = 1;

ENABLE TRIGGER HumanResources.EmployeeUpdateTrigger
ON HumanResources.Employee;

-- disabling and enabling all triggers on the object
DISABLE TRIGGER ALL ON HumanResources.Employee;
ENABLE TRIGGER ALL ON HumanResources.Employee;
```

Disabling triggers can greatly improve performance when you apply a batch of modifications on a table. Just make sure, of course, that the rules enforced by the trigger(s) will be checked in another way, for instance manually after the batch. Do not forget also to re-enable the trigger at the end of the process.

MULTIPLE TRIGGERS

You can create multiple triggers on the same objects. They will fire in no specific order. If you really need to, you can only specify that a trigger will be fired first or last, by using the sp_settriggerorder system stored procedure. For example:

```
EXEC sp_settriggerorder @triggername = 'MyTrigger', @order = 'first', @stmttype = 'UPDATE';
```

That sets the MyTrigger trigger to fire first on UPDATE actions. However, in our opinion, this shouldn't be used, because it adds uneccessary complexity in your database. If you really need to manage precedence between trigger actions, it is best to consolidate what you need to do in the same trigger.

When to Use DML Triggers

Way back in the day, using triggers was the best (and in some cases only) way to perform a variety of tasks, such as ensuring cascading DRI, validating data before storing it in tables, auditing changes, and enforcing complex business logic. Newer releases of SQL Server have added functionality that more closely integrates many of these functions into the core database engine. For instance, in most cases, you can use SQL Server's built-in cascading DRI to ensure referential integrity and check constraints for simple validations during insert and update operations. DML triggers are still a good choice when simple auditing tasks or validations with complex business logic are required.

■ **Note** DRI is not enforced across databases. What this means is that you cannot reference a table in a different database in a DRI/foreign key constraint. Because they can reference objects such as tables and views in other databases, triggers are still a good option when this type of referential integrity enforcement is necessary.

Listing 6-2 shows a very simple trigger that we created on the HumanResources.Employee table of the AdventureWorks database. The HumanResources.EmployeeUpdateTrigger trigger simply updates the ModifiedDate column of the HumanResources.Employee table with the current date and time whenever a row is updated.

Listing 6-2. HumanResources.EmployeeUpdateTrigger Code

```
CREATE TRIGGER HumanResources.EmployeeUpdateTrigger
ON HumanResources.Employee
AFTER UPDATE
NOT FOR REPLICATION
AS
BEGIN
    -- stop if no row was affected
    IF @@ROWCOUNT = 0 RETURN
    -- Turn off "rows affected" messages
    SET NOCOUNT ON;

    -- Make sure at least one row was affected
    -- Update ModifiedDate for all affected rows
    UPDATE HumanResources.Employee
    SET ModifiedDate = GETDATE()
    WHERE EXISTS
      (
        SELECT 1
        FROM inserted i
        WHERE i.BusinessEntityID = HumanResources.Employee.BusinessEntityID
      );
END;
```

The first part of the CREATE TRIGGER statement defines the name of the trigger and specifies that it will be created on the HumanResources.Employee table. The definition also specifies that the trigger will fire after rows are updated, and the NOT FOR REPLICATION keywords prevent replication events from firing the trigger.

```
CREATE TRIGGER HumanResources.EmployeeUpdateTrigger
ON HumanResources.Employee
AFTER UPDATE
NOT FOR REPLICATION
```

The body of the trigger starts by checking the number of rows affected by the UPDATE with the @@ROWCOUNT system function. This is an optimization that skips the body of the trigger if no rows were affected.

Whenever any trigger is fired, it is implicitly wrapped in the same transaction as the DML statement that fired it. This has big performance and concurrency implications. What it means is that whatever your trigger does, it should do it as quickly and efficiently as possible. The T-SQL statements in your trigger body can potentially create locks in your database, a situation that you want to minimize. It is not unheard of for inefficient triggers to cause blocking problems. You should also minimize the amount of work done inside the trigger and optimize the operations it has to perform. It also means that a ROLLBACK TRANSACTION statement in the trigger will roll back DML statements executed in the trigger, as well as the original DML statement that fired the trigger (and all explicit transactions in which the statement is run, for that matter).

Checking @@ROWCOUNT at the start of your trigger helps ensure that your triggers are efficient. If @@ROWCOUNT is 0, it means that no rows were affected by the original DML statement that fired the trigger. Then your trigger has no work to do, and you can skip the rest.

```
-- stop if no row was affected
IF @@ROWCOUNT = 0 RETURN
```

■ **Caution**   Checking @@ROWCOUNT must be done at the very first line. Any previous action in the trigger, even SET commands, could change the @@ROWCOUNT value.

Next, the trigger turns off the rows affected messages via the SET NOCOUNT ON statement.

```
-- Turn off "rows affected" messages
SET NOCOUNT ON;
```

■ **Note**   Using SET NOCOUNT ON is not strictly required in triggers, but it prevents superfluous rows affected messages from being generated by the trigger. Some older database drivers—and even some more recent ones, such as certain Java Database Connectivity (JDBC) drivers—can get confused by these extra messages, so it's not a bad idea to disable them in the body of your triggers. Any SET statement can be used in the body of a trigger. The statement remains in effect while the trigger executes and reverts to its former setting when the trigger completes.

The IF statement contains an UPDATE statement that sets the ModifiedDate column to the current date and time when rows in the table are updated. An important concept of trigger programming is to be sure that you account for multiple row updates. It's not safe to assume that a DML statement will update only a single row of your table, because triggers in SQL Server are set-oriented and fire only once for a statement. There is no such thing as a per-row trigger in SQL Server. In this trigger, the UPDATE statement uses the EXISTS predicate in the WHERE clause to ensure that ModifiedDate is updated for every row that was affected. It accomplished this by using the inserted virtual table, described in the "The inserted and deleted Virtual Tables" sidebar in this section.

```
-- Update ModifiedDate for all affected rows
UPDATE HumanResources.Employee
SET ModifiedDate = GETDATE()
WHERE EXISTS
(
    SELECT 1
    FROM inserted i
    WHERE i.BusinessEntityID = HumanResources.Employee.BusinessEntityID
);
```

THE INSERTED AND DELETED VIRTUAL TABLES

A DML trigger needs to know which rows were affected by the DML statement that fired it. The inserted and deleted virtual tables fulfill this need. When a trigger fires, SQL Server populates the inserted and deleted virtual tables and makes them available within the body of the trigger. These two virtual tables have the same structure as the affected table and contain the data from all affected rows.

The inserted table contains all rows inserted into the destination table by an INSERT statement. The deleted table contains all rows deleted from the destination table by a DELETE statement. For UPDATE statements, the rows are treated as a DELETE followed by an INSERT, so that the pre-UPDATE-affected rows are stored in the deleted table, while the post-UPDATE-affected rows are stored in the inserted table.

The virtual tables are read-only and cannot be modified directly. The example in Listing 6-2 uses the inserted virtual table to determine which rows were affected by the UPDATE statement that fired the trigger. The trigger updates the ModifiedDate column for every row in the HumanResources.Employee table with a matching row in the inserted table. We'll be using the inserted and deleted virtual tables in other sample code in this section.

Testing the trigger is as simple as using SELECT and UPDATE. The sample in Listing 6-3 changes the marital status of employees with BusinessEntityID numbers 1 and 2 to M (for "married").

Listing 6-3. Testing HumanResources.EmployeeUpdateTrigger

```
UPDATE HumanResources.Employee
SET MaritalStatus = 'M'
WHERE BusinessEntityID IN (1, 2);

SELECT BusinessEntityID, NationalIDNumber, MaritalStatus, ModifiedDate
FROM HumanResources.Employee
WHERE BusinessEntityID IN (1, 2);
```

The results, shown in Figure 6-1 demonstrate that the UPDATE statement fired the trigger and properly updated the ModifiedDate for the two specified rows.

	BusinessEntityID	NationalIDNumber	MaritalStatus	ModifiedDate
1	1	295847284	M	2012-04-22 13:49:42.447
2	2	245797967	M	2012-04-22 13:49:42.447

Figure 6-1. *Updated Marital Status for Two Employees*

155

> ■ **Caution**   If the `RECURSIVE_TRIGGERS` database option is turned on in the AdventureWorks database, `HumanResources.EmployeeUpdateTrigger` will error out with a message that the "nesting limit has been exceeded." This is caused by the trigger recursively firing itself after the `UPDATE` statement in the trigger is executed. Use `ALTER DATABASE AdventureWorks SET RECURSIVE_TRIGGERS OFF` to turn off recursive triggers and `ALTER DATABASE AdventureWorks SET RECURSIVE_TRIGGERS ON` to turn the option back on. The default is `OFF`. Recursive triggers will be covered later in this chapter.

Auditing with DML Triggers

Another common use for DML triggers is auditing DML actions against tables. The primary purpose of DML auditing is to maintain a record of changes to the data in your database. This might be required for a number of reasons, including regulatory compliance or to fulfill contractual obligations.

USING CHANGE DATA CAPTURE INSTEAD

Since SQL Server 2008 you can use the feature known as *Change Data Capture (CDC)*, which provides built-in auditing functionality. The CDC functionality provides another option for logging DML actions against tables. While CDC functionality is beyond the scope of this book, we recommend looking into this option before deciding which method to use when you need DML logging functionality, because it might be a more elegant and efficient way to audit data changes. One of the drawbacks with triggers is the performance impact they have on DML operations, especially because they are part of the DML transaction. CDC is much faster because it acts as a separate process that tracks the database transaction log for modifications applied to the audited tables and writes changes to internal change tables, using the same technology as transaction replication. Moreover, CDC can also automatically prune the audit tables to keep their size manageable.

CDC is available only in Enterprise Edition.

The first step to implementing DML auditing is to create a table to store your audit information. Listing 6-4 creates just such a table.

Listing 6-4. DML Audit Logging Table

```
CREATE TABLE dbo.DmlActionLog (
    EntryNum int IDENTITY(1, 1) PRIMARY KEY NOT NULL,
    SchemaName sysname NOT NULL,
    TableName sysname NOT NULL,
    ActionType nvarchar(10) NOT NULL,
    ActionXml xml NOT NULL,
    LoginName sysname NOT NULL,
    ApplicationName sysname NOT NULL,
    HostName sysname NOT NULL,
    ActionDateTime datetime2(0) NOT NULL DEFAULT (SYSDATETIME())
);
GO
```

The dbo.DmlActionLog table in Listing 6-4 will store information for each DML action performed against a table, including the name of the schema and table against which the DML action was performed, the type of DML action performed, XML-formatted snapshots of the before and after states of the rows affected, and additional information to identify who performed the DML action and when the action was performed. Once the audit logging table is created, it's time to create a trigger to log DML actions. This is shown in Listing 6-5.

Listing 6-5. DML Audit Logging Trigger

```
CREATE TRIGGER HumanResources.DepartmentChangeAudit
ON HumanResources.Department
AFTER INSERT, UPDATE, DELETE
NOT FOR REPLICATION
AS
BEGIN
    -- stop if no row was affected
    IF @@ROWCOUNT = 0 RETURN

    -- Turn off "rows affected" messages
    SET NOCOUNT ON;

    DECLARE @ActionType nvarchar(10), @ActionXml xml;

    -- Get count of inserted rows
    DECLARE @inserted_count int = (
        SELECT COUNT(*)
        FROM inserted
    );
    -- Get count of deleted rows
    DECLARE @deleted_count int = (
        SELECT COUNT(*)
        FROM deleted
    );

    -- Determine the type of DML action that fired the trigger
    SET @ActionType = CASE
        WHEN (@inserted_count > 0) AND (@deleted_count = 0) THEN N'insert'
        WHEN (@inserted_count = 0) AND (@deleted_count > 0) THEN N'delete'
        ELSE N'update'
    END;

    -- Use FOR XML AUTO to retrieve before and after snapshots of the changed
    -- data  in  XML  format
    SELECT @ActionXml = COALESCE
    (
        (
            SELECT  *
            FROM  deleted
            FOR  XML  AUTO
        ), N'<deleted/>'
    )  +  COALESCE
```

```
    (
        (
            SELECT  *
            FROM  inserted
            FOR  XML  AUTO
        ),  N'<inserted/>'
    );

    -- Insert a row for the logged action in the audit logging table
    INSERT INTO dbo.DmlActionLog
    (
        SchemaName,
        TableName,
        ActionType,
        ActionXml,
        LoginName,
        ApplicationName,
        HostName
    )
    SELECT
        OBJECT_SCHEMA_NAME(@@PROCID, DB_ID()),
        OBJECT_NAME(t.parent_id, DB_ID()),
        @ActionType,
        @ActionXml,
        SUSER_SNAME(),
        APP_NAME(),
        HOST_NAME()
    FROM sys.triggers t
    WHERE t.object_id = @@PROCID;
END;
GO
```

The trigger in Listing 6-5 is created on the HumanResources.Department table, although it is written in such a way that the body of the trigger contains no code specific to the table it's created on. This means you can easily modify the trigger to work as-is on most tables.

The HumanResources.DepartmentChangeAudit trigger definition begins with the CREATE TRIGGER statement, which names the trigger and creates it on the HumanResources.Department table. It also specifies that the trigger should fire after INSERT, UPDATE, or DELETE statements are performed against the table. Finally, the NOT FOR REPLICATION clause specifies that replication events will not cause the trigger to fire.

```
CREATE TRIGGER HumanResources.DepartmentChangeAudit
ON HumanResources.Department
AFTER INSERT, UPDATE, DELETE
NOT FOR REPLICATION
```

The trigger body begins by checking the number of rows affected by the DML statement with the @@ROWCOUNT function. The trigger skips the remainder of the statements in the body if no rows were affected.

```
-- stop if no row was affected
IF @@ROWCOUNT = 0 RETURN
```

The main body of the trigger begins with an initialization that turns off extraneous rows affected messages, declares local variables, and gets the count of rows inserted and deleted by the DML statement from the inserted and deleted virtual tables.

```
-- Turn off "rows affected" messages
SET NOCOUNT ON;

DECLARE @ActionType nvarchar(10), @ActionXml xml;

-- Get count of inserted rows
DECLARE @inserted_count int = (
    SELECT COUNT(*)
    FROM inserted
);
-- Get count of deleted rows
DECLARE @deleted_count int = (
    SELECT COUNT(*)
    FROM deleted
);
```

Since the trigger is logging the type of DML action that caused it to fire (an INSERT, a DELETE, or an UPDATE action), it must determine the type programmatically. This can be done by applying the following simple rules to the counts of rows from the inserted and deleted virtual tables:

1. If at least one row was inserted but no rows were deleted, the DML action was an insert.

2. If at least one row was deleted but no rows were inserted, the DML action was a delete.

3. If at least one row was deleted and at least one row was inserted, the DML action was an update.

These rules are applied in the form of a CASE expression, as shown in the following:

```
-- Determine the type of DML action that fired the trigger
SET @ActionType = CASE
    WHEN (@inserted_count > 0) AND (@deleted_count = 0) THEN N'insert'
    WHEN (@inserted_count = 0) AND (@deleted_count > 0) THEN N'delete'
    ELSE N'update'
END;
```

The next step in the trigger uses the SELECT statement's FOR XML AUTO clause to generate XML-formatted before and after snapshots of the affected rows. FOR XML AUTO is useful because it automatically uses the source table name as the XML element name—in this case inserted or deleted. The FOR XML AUTO clause automatically uses the names of the columns in the table as XML attributes for each element. Because the inserted and deleted virtual tables have the same column names as this affected table, you don't have to hard-code column names into the trigger. In the resulting XML, the < deleted > elements represent the before snapshot and the < inserted > elements represent the after snapshot of the affected rows.

```
-- Use FOR XML AUTO to retrieve before and after snapshots of the changed
--   data in XML format
SELECT @ActionXml = COALESCE
(
    (
        SELECT *
        FROM deleted
        FOR XML AUTO
    ), N'<deleted/>'
) + COALESCE
```

```
(
    (
        SELECT  *
        FROM  inserted
        FOR  XML  AUTO
    ),  N'<inserted/>'
);
```

■ **Tip**   The DML audit logging trigger was created to be flexible so that you could use it with minimal changes on most tables. However, there are some circumstances where it might require use of additional options or more extensive changes to work with a given table. As an example, if your table contains a `varbinary` column, you have to use the `FOR XML` clause's `BINARY BASE64` directive (`FOR XML, BINARY BASE64`).

The final step in the trigger inserts a row representing the logged action into the dbo.DmlActionLog table. Several SQL Server metadata *functions*—like @@PROCID, OBJECT_SCHEMA_NAME(), and OBJECT_NAME(), as well as the sys.triggers catalog view—are used in the INSERT statement to dynamically identify the current trigger procedure ID, and the schema and table name information. Also, functions like SUSER_SNAME(), APP_NAME(), and HOST_NAME() allow you to retrieve useful audit information on the execution context. Again, this means that almost nothing needs to be hard-coded into the trigger, making it easier to use the trigger on multiple tables with minimal changes.

```
-- Insert a row for the logged action in the audit logging table
INSERT INTO dbo.DmlActionLog
(
    SchemaName,
    TableName,
    ActionType,
    ActionXml,
    LoginName,
    ApplicationName,
    HostName
)
SELECT
    OBJECT_SCHEMA_NAME(@@PROCID, DB_ID()),
    OBJECT_NAME(t.parent_id, DB_ID()),
    @ActionType,
    @ActionXml,
    SUSER_SNAME(),
    APP_NAME(),
    HOST_NAME()
FROM sys.triggers t
WHERE t.object_id = @@PROCID;
```

■ **Tip**   SQL Server includes several metadata functions, catalog views, and dynamic management views and functions that are useful for dynamically retrieving information about databases, database objects, and the current state of the server. We will describe more of these useful T-SQL functions and views as they're encountered in later chapters.

You can easily verify the trigger with a few simple DML statements. Listing 6-6 changes the name of the AdventureWorks Information Services department to Information Technology, and then inserts and deletes a Customer Service department. The results are shown in Figure 6-2.

Listing 6-6. Testing the DML Audit Logging Trigger

```
UPDATE HumanResources.Department SET Name = N'Information Technology'
WHERE DepartmentId = 11;

INSERT INTO HumanResources.Department
(
    Name,
    GroupName
)
VALUES
(
    N'Customer Service',
    N'Sales and Marketing'
);

DELETE
FROM HumanResources.Department
WHERE Name = N'Customer Service';

SELECT
    EntryNum,
    SchemaName,
    TableName,
    ActionType,
    ActionXml,
    LoginName,
    ApplicationName,
    HostName,
    ActionDateTime
FROM dbo.DmlActionLog;
```

	EntryNum	SchemaName	TableName	ActionType	ActionXml	LoginName	ApplicationName
1	1	HumanResources	Department	update	<deleted DepartmentID="11"...	SQL2012\Administrator	Microsoft SQL Server
2	2	HumanResources	Department	insert	<deleted />inserted Departm...	SQL2012\Administrator	Microsoft SQL Server
3	3	HumanResources	Department	delete	<deleted DepartmentID="17"...	SQL2012\Administrator	Microsoft SQL Server

Figure 6-2. *Audit Logging Results*

The FOR XML AUTO-generated ActionXml column data deserves a closer look. As we mentioned earlier in this section, the FOR XML AUTO clause automatically generates element and attribute names based on the source table and source column names. The UPDATE statement in Listing 6-6 generates the ActionXml entry shown in Figure 6-3. Note that we've formatted the XML for easier reading, but we have not changed the content.

```
ActionXml1.xml*   ✕
  ⊟<deleted
        DepartmentID="11"
        Name="Information Services"
        GroupName="Executive General and Administration"
        ModifiedDate="2002-06-01T00:00:00" />

  ⊟<inserted
        DepartmentID="11"
        Name="Information Technology"
        GroupName="Executive General and Administration"
        ModifiedDate="2002-06-01T00:00:00" />
```

Figure 6-3. *The ActionXml Entry Generated by the UPDATE Statement*

SHARING DATA WITH TRIGGERS

A commonly asked question is "How do you pass parameters to triggers?" The short answer is you can't. Because they are automatically fired in response to events, SQL Server triggers provide no means to pass parameters. If you need to pass additional data to a trigger, you do have a couple of options available, however. The first option is to create a table, which the trigger can then access via SELECT queries. The advantage to this method is that the amount of data your trigger can access is effectively unlimited. A disadvantage is the additional overhead required to query the table within your trigger.

Another option, if you have small amounts of data to share with your triggers, is to use the CONTEXT_INFO function. You can assign up to 128 bytes of varbinary data to the CONTEXT_INFO for the current session through the SET CONTEXT_INFO statement. This statement accepts only a variable or constant value—no other expressions are allowed. After you've set the CONTEXT_INFO for your session, you can access it within your trigger via the CONTEXT_INFO() function. The disadvantage of this method is the small amount of data you can store in the CONTEXT_INFO. Keep these methods in mind, as you may one day find that you need to pass information into a trigger from a batch or SP.

Nested and Recursive Triggers

SQL Server supports triggers firing other triggers through the concept of nested triggers. A *nested trigger* is simply a trigger that is fired by the action of another trigger, on the same or a different table. Triggers can be nested up to 32 levels deep. We would advise against nesting triggers deeply, however, since the additional levels of nesting will affect performance. If you do have triggers nested deeply, you might want to reconsider your trigger design. Nested triggers are turned on by default, but you can turn them off with the sp_configure statement, as shown in Listing 6-7.

Listing 6-7. Turning Off Nested Triggers

```
EXEC sp_configure 'nested triggers', 0;
RECONFIGURE;
GO
```

Set the nested triggers option to 1 to turn nested triggers back on. This option affects only AFTER triggers. INSTEAD OF triggers can be nested and will execute regardless of the setting. Triggers can also be called recursively. There are two types of trigger recursion:

- *Direct recursion:* Occurs when a trigger performs an action that causes it to recursively fire itself.

- *Indirect recursion:* Occurs when a trigger fires another trigger (which can fire another trigger, etc.), which eventually fires the first trigger.

Direct and indirect recursion of triggers applies only to triggers of the same type. As an example, an INSTEAD OF trigger that causes another INSTEAD OF trigger to fire is direct recursion. Even if a different type of trigger is fired between the first and second firing of the same trigger, it is still considered direct recursion. For example, if one or more AFTER triggers are fired between the first and second firings of the same INSTEAD OF trigger, it is still considered direct recursion. Indirect recursion occurs when a trigger of the same type is called between firings of the same trigger.

You can use the ALTER DATABASE statement's SET RECURSIVE_TRIGGERS option to turn direct recursion of AFTER triggers on and off, as shown in Listing 6-8. Turning off direct recursion of INSTEAD OF triggers requires that you also set the nested triggers option to 0, as shown previously in Listing 6-7.

Listing 6-8. Turning Off Recursive AFTER Triggers

```
ALTER DATABASE AdventureWorks SET RECURSIVE_TRIGGERS OFF;
```

Actions taken with an INSTEAD OF trigger will not cause it to fire again. Instead, the INSTEAD OF trigger will perform constraint checks and fire any AFTER triggers. As an example, if an INSTEAD OF UPDATE trigger on a table is fired, and during the course of its execution performs an UPDATE statement against the table, the UPDATE will not fire the INSTEAD OF trigger again. Instead the UPDATE statement will initiate constraint check operations and fire AFTER triggers on the table.

▥ **Caution**   Nested and recursive triggers should be used with care, since nesting and recursion that's too deep will cause your triggers to throw exceptions. You can use the TRIGGER_NESTLEVEL() function to determine the current level of recursion from within a trigger.

The UPDATE() and COLUMNS_UPDATED() Functions

Triggers can take advantage of two system functions, UPDATE() and COLUMNS_UPDATED(), to tell you which columns are affected by the INSERT or UPDATE statement that fires the trigger in the first place. UPDATE() takes the name of a column as a parameter and returns true if the column is updated or inserted, and false otherwise. COLUMNS_UPDATED() returns a bit pattern indicating which columns are affected by the INSERT or UPDATE statement.

In case of an UPDATE, *affected* means that the column is present in the statement, not that the value of the column effectively changed. There is only one way to know if the value of a column really changed: by comparing the content of the deleted and inserted virtual tables. You can adapt the query example below to do that with your trigger.

```
SELECT i.ProductId, d.Color as OldColor, i.Color as NewColor
FROM deleted as d
JOIN inserted as i ON d.ProductId = i.ProductId
    AND COALESCE(d.Color, '') <> COALESCE(i.Color, '');
```

This fragment is designed to be part of a trigger that could be created on the Production.Product table. The JOIN condition associates lines from the deleted and inserted tables on the primary key column and adds a non-equi join condition (joining on difference rather than on equivalence) on the Color column, to keep only rows where the Color value was changed. The COALESCE() function allows us to take into account the possibility of a NULL being present in the previous or new value.

Getting back to the UPDATE() and COLUMNS_UPDATED() functions, the sample trigger in Listing 6-9 demonstrates the use of triggers to enforce business rules. In this example, the trigger uses the UPDATE function to determine if the Size or SizeUnitMeasureCode has been affected by an INSERT or UPDATE statement. If either of these columns is affected by an INSERT or UPDATE statement, the trigger checks to see if a recognized SizeUnitMeasureCode was used. If so, the trigger converts the Size to centimeters. The trigger recognizes several SizeUnitMeasureCode values, including centimeters (CM), millimeters (MM), and inches (IN).

Listing 6-9. Trigger to Enforce Standard Sizes

```
CREATE TRIGGER Production.ProductEnforceStandardSizes
ON Production.Product
AFTER INSERT, UPDATE
NOT FOR REPLICATION
AS
BEGIN
    -- Make sure at least one row was affected and either the Size or
    -- SizeUnitMeasureCode column was changed
    IF (@@ROWCOUNT > 0) AND (UPDATE(SizeUnitMeasureCode) OR UPDATE(Size))
    BEGIN
        -- Eliminate "rows affected" messages
        SET NOCOUNT ON;
        -- Only accept recognized units of measure or NULL
        IF EXISTS
        (
            SELECT 1
            FROM inserted
            WHERE NOT
                ( SizeUnitMeasureCode IN (N'M', N'DM', N'CM', N'MM', N'IN')
                    OR SizeUnitMeasureCode IS NULL
                )
        )
        BEGIN
            -- If the unit of measure wasn't recognized raise an error and roll back
            -- the transaction
            RAISERROR ('Invalid Size Unit Measure Code.', 10, 127);
            ROLLBACK TRANSACTION;
        END
        ELSE
        BEGIN
            -- If the unit of measure is a recognized unit of measure then set the
            -- SizeUnitMeasureCode to centimeters and perform the Size conversion
            UPDATE Production.Product
            SET SizeUnitMeasureCode = CASE
                    WHEN Production.Product.SizeUnitMeasureCode IS NULL THEN NULL ELSE N'CM'
                    END,
```

```
                  Size = CAST (
                      CAST ( CAST(i.Size AS float) *
                          CASE i.SizeUnitMeasureCode
                              WHEN N'M' THEN 100.0
                              WHEN N'DM' THEN 10.0
                              WHEN N'CM' THEN 1.0
                              WHEN N'MM' THEN 0.10
                              WHEN N'IN' THEN 2.54
                          END
                      AS int
                      ) AS nvarchar(5)
                  )
              FROM inserted i
              WHERE Production.Product.ProductID = i.ProductID
              AND i.SizeUnitMeasureCode IS NOT NULL;
          END;
      END;
END;
GO
```

The first part of the trigger definition gives the trigger its name, `Production.ProductEnforceStandardSizes`, and creates it on the `Production.Product` table. It is specified as an AFTER INSERT, UPDATE trigger and is declared as NOT FOR REPLICATION.

```
CREATE TRIGGER Production.ProductEnforceStandardSizes
ON Production.Product
AFTER INSERT, UPDATE
NOT FOR REPLICATION
```

The code in the body of the trigger immediately checks @@ROWCOUNT to make sure that at least one row was affected by the DML statement that fired the trigger, and uses the UPDATE function to ensure that the Size or SizeUnitMeasureCode columns were affected by the DML statement:

```
IF (@@ROWCOUNT > 0)
AND (UPDATE(SizeUnitMeasureCode) OR UPDATE(Size)) BEGIN
• • •
END;
```

Once the trigger has verified that at least one row was affected and the appropriate columns were modified, the trigger sets NOCOUNT ON to prevent the rows affected messages from being generated by the trigger. The IF EXISTS statement checks to make sure that valid unit-of-measure codes are used. If not, the trigger raises an error and rolls back the transaction.

```
-- Eliminate "rows affected" messages
SET NOCOUNT ON;
-- Only accept recognized units of measure or NULL
IF EXISTS
(
    SELECT 1
    FROM inserted
    WHERE NOT
        ( SizeUnitMeasureCode IN (N'M', N'DM', N'CM', N'MM', N'IN')
            OR SizeUnitMeasureCode IS NULL
        )
)
```

```
BEGIN
    -- If the unit of measure wasn't recognized raise an error and roll back
    -- the transaction
    RAISERROR ('Invalid Size Unit Measure Code.', 10, 127);
    ROLLBACK TRANSACTION;
END
```

▨ **Tip** The `ROLLBACK TRANSACTION` statement in the trigger rolls back the transaction and prevents further triggers from being fired by the current trigger. Two error messages will be received by the client: the one raised by `RAISERROR()`, and the error 3609 or 3616, warning that the transaction ended in the trigger.

If the unit-of-measure validation is passed, the `SizeUnitMeasureCode` is set to centimeters and the `Size` is converted to centimeters for each inserted or updated row.

```
BEGIN
    -- If the unit of measure is a recognized unit of measure then set the
    -- SizeUnitMeasureCode to centimeters and perform the Size conversion
    UPDATE Production.Product
        SET SizeUnitMeasureCode = CASE
            WHEN Production.Product.SizeUnitMeasureCode IS NULL THEN NULL ELSE N'CM' END,
            Size = CAST (
                CAST ( CAST(i.Size AS float) *
                    CASE i.SizeUnitMeasureCode
                        WHEN N'M' THEN 100.0
                        WHEN N'DM' THEN 10.0
                        WHEN N'CM' THEN 1.0
                        WHEN N'MM' THEN 0.10
                        WHEN N'IN' THEN 2.54
                    END
                AS int
            ) AS nvarchar(5)
        )
    FROM inserted i
    WHERE Production.Product.ProductID = i.ProductID
    AND i.SizeUnitMeasureCode IS NOT NULL;
END;
```

This trigger enforces simple business logic by ensuring that standard-size codes are used when updating the `Production.Product` table and converting the `Size` values to centimeters. To test the trigger, you can perform updates of existing rows in the `Production.Product` table. Listing 6-10 updates the sizes of the products with ProductID 680 and 780 to 600 millimeters and 22.85 inches, respectively. The results, with the `Size` values automatically converted to centimeters, are shown in Figure 6-4.

Listing 6-10. *Testing the Trigger by Adding a New Product*

```
UPDATE  Production.Product
SET Size = N'600',
    SizeUnitMeasureCode = N'MM'
WHERE  ProductId  =  680;
```

```
UPDATE  Production.Product
SET Size = N'22.85',
    SizeUnitMeasureCode = N'IN'
WHERE  ProductId  =  706;

SELECT  ProductID,
    Name,
    ProductNumber,
    Size,
    SizeUnitMeasureCode
FROM  Production.Product
WHERE  ProductID  IN  (680,  706);
```

	ProductID	Name	ProductNumber	Size	SizeUnitMeasureCode
1	680	HL Road Frame - Black, 58	FR-R92B-58	60	CM
2	706	HL Road Frame - Red, 58	FR-R92R-58	58	CM

Figure 6-4. *The Results of the Production.ProductEnforceStandardSizes Trigger Test*

While the UPDATE() function accepts a column name and returns true if the column is affected, the COLUMNS_UPDATED() function accepts no parameters and returns a varbinary value with a single bit representing each column. You can use the bitwise AND operator (&) and a bit mask to test which columns are affected. The bits are set from left to right, based on the ColumnID number of the columns from the sys.columns catalog view or the COLUMNPROPERTY() function.

■ **Caution**   The position of COLUMNS_UPDATED() is not the same as the ORDINAL_POSITION value found in the INFORMATION_SCHEMA.COLUMNS catalog view. Rely on the sys.columns.ColumnID value instead.

To create a bit mask, you must use 2^0 (1) to represent the first column, 2^1 (2) to represent the second column, and so on. Because COLUMNS_UPDATED() returns a varbinary result, the column indicator bits can be spread out over several bytes. To test columns beyond the first eight, like the Size and SizeUnitMeasureCode columns in the example code (columns 11 and 12), you can use the SUBSTRING function to return the second byte of COLUMNS_UPDATED() and test the appropriate bits with a bit mask of 12 ($12 = 2^2 + 2^3$). The sample trigger in Listing 6-9 can be modified to use the COLUMNS_UPDATED() function, as shown here:

```
IF (@@ROWCOUNT > 0) AND (SUBSTRING(COLUMNS_UPDATED(), 2, 1) & 12 <> 0x00)
```

The COLUMNS_UPDATED() function will not return correct results if the ColumnID values of the table are changed. If the table is dropped and recreated with columns in a different order, you will need to change the triggers that use COLUMNS_UPDATED() to reflect the changes. There may be specialized instances in which you'll be able to take advantage of the COLUMNS_UPDATED() functionality, but in general we would advise against using COLUMNS_UPDATED(), and instead use the UPDATE() function to determine which columns were affected by the DML statement that fired your trigger.

Triggers on Views

Although you cannot create AFTER triggers on views, SQL Server does allow you to create INSTEAD OF triggers on your views. A trigger can be useful for updating views that are otherwise nonupdatable, such as views with multiple base tables or views that contain aggregate functions. INSTEAD OF triggers on views also give you fine-grained control, since you can control which columns of the view are updatable through the trigger. The AdventureWorks database comes with a view named Sales.vSalesPerson, which is formed by joining 11 separate tables together. The INSTEAD OF trigger in Listing 6-11 allows you to update specific columns of two of the base tables used in the view by executing UPDATE statements directly against the view.

Listing 6-11. INSTEAD OF Trigger on a View

```
CREATE TRIGGER Sales.vIndividualCustomerUpdate
ON Sales.vIndividualCustomer
INSTEAD OF UPDATE
NOT FOR REPLICATION
AS
BEGIN
    -- First make sure at least one row was affected
    IF @@ROWCOUNT = 0 RETURN
    -- Turn off "rows affected" messages
    SET NOCOUNT ON;
    -- Initialize a flag to indicate update success
    DECLARE @UpdateSuccessful bit = 0;

    -- Check for updatable columns in the first table
    IF UPDATE(FirstName) OR UPDATE(MiddleName) OR UPDATE(LastName)
    BEGIN
        -- Update columns in the base table
        UPDATE Person.Person
        SET FirstName = i.FirstName,
            MiddleName = i.MiddleName,
            LastName = i.LastName
        FROM inserted i
        WHERE i.BusinessEntityID = Person.Person.BusinessEntityID;

        -- Set flag to indicate success
        SET @UpdateSuccessful = 1;
    END;
    -- If updatable columns from the second table were specified, update those
    -- columns in the base table
    IF UPDATE(EmailAddress)
    BEGIN
        -- Update columns in the base table
        UPDATE Person.EmailAddress
        SET EmailAddress = i.EmailAddress
        FROM inserted i
        WHERE i.BusinessEntityID = Person.EmailAddress.BusinessEntityID;

        -- Set flag to indicate success
        SET @UpdateSuccessful = 1;
    END;
```

```
    -- If the update was not successful, raise an error and roll back the
    -- transaction
    IF @UpdateSuccessful = 0
        RAISERROR('Must specify updatable columns.', 10, 127);
END;
GO
```

The trigger in Listing 6-11 is created as an INSTEAD OF UPDATE trigger on the Sales.vIndividualCustomer view, as shown following:

```
CREATE TRIGGER Sales.vIndividualCustomerUpdate
ON Sales.vIndividualCustomer
INSTEAD OF UPDATE
NOT FOR REPLICATION
```

As with the previous examples in this chapter, this trigger begins by checking @@ROWCOUNT to ensure that at least one row was updated:

```
-- First make sure at least one row was affected
IF @@ROWCOUNT = 0 RETURN;
```

Once the trigger verifies that one or more rows were affected by the DML statement that fired the trigger, it turns off the rows affected messages and initializes a flag to indicate success or failure of the update operation:

```
-- Turn off "rows affected" messages
SET NOCOUNT ON;
-- Initialize a flag to indicate update success
DECLARE @UpdateSuccessful bit = 0;
```

The trigger then checks to see if the columns designated as updatable were affected by the UPDATE statement. If the proper columns were affected by the UPDATE statement, the trigger performs updates on the appropriate base tables for the view. For purposes of this demonstration, the columns that are updatable by the trigger are the FirstName, MiddleName, and LastName columns from the Person.Person table, and the EmailAddress column from the Person.EmailAddress column.

```
-- Check for updatable columns in the first table
IF UPDATE(FirstName) OR UPDATE(MiddleName) OR UPDATE(LastName)
BEGIN
    -- Update columns in the base table
    UPDATE Person.Person
    SET FirstName = i.FirstName,
        MiddleName = i.MiddleName,
        LastName = i.LastName
    FROM inserted i
    WHERE i.BusinessEntityID = Person.Person.BusinessEntityID;

    -- Set flag to indicate success
    SET @UpdateSuccessful = 1;
END;

-- If updatable columns from the second table were specified, update those
-- columns in the base table
```

```
IF UPDATE(EmailAddress) BEGIN
    -- Update columns in the base table
    UPDATE Person.EmailAddress
    SET EmailAddress = i.EmailAddress
    FROM inserted i
    WHERE i.BusinessEntityID = Person.EmailAddress.BusinessEntityID;

    -- Set flag to indicate success
    SET @UpdateSuccessful = 1;
END;
```

Finally, if no updatable columns were specified by the UPDATE statement that fired the trigger, an error is raised and the transaction is rolled back:

```
-- If the update was not successful, raise an error and roll back the
-- transaction
IF @UpdateSuccessful = 1
    RAISERROR('Must specify updatable columns.', 10, 127);
```

Listing 6-12 demonstrates a simple UPDATE against the Sales.vIndividualCustomer view with the INSTEAD OF trigger from Listing 6-11 created on it. The result is shown in Figure 6-5.

Listing 6-12. Updating a View Through an INSTEAD OF Trigger

```
UPDATE Sales.vIndividualCustomer
SET FirstName = N'Dave',
    MiddleName = N'Robert',
    EmailAddress = N'dave.robinett@adventure-works.com'
WHERE BusinessEntityID = 1699;

SELECT BusinessEntityID, FirstName, MiddleName, LastName, EmailAddress
FROM Sales.vIndividualCustomer
WHERE BusinessEntityID = 1699;
```

	BusinessEntityID	FirstName	MiddleName	LastName	EmailAddress
1	1699	Dave	Robert	Robinett	dave.robinett@adventure-works.com

Figure 6-5. *The Result of the INSTEAD OF Trigger View Update*

DDL Triggers

Since SQL Server 2005, T-SQL programmers have had the ability to create DDL triggers that fire when DDL events occur within a database or on the server. In this section, we will discuss DDL triggers, the events that fire them, and the purpose. The format of the CREATE TRIGGER statement for DDL triggers is only slightly different from the DML trigger syntax, with the major difference being that you must specify the scope for the trigger, either ALL SERVER or DATABASE. The DATABASE scope causes the DDL trigger to fire if an event of a specified event type or event group occurs within the database in which the trigger was created. ALL SERVER scope causes the DDL trigger to fire if an event of the specified event type or event group occurs anywhere on the current server.

DDL triggers can only be specified as FOR or AFTER (there's no INSTEAD OF-type DDL trigger). The event types that can fire a DDL trigger are largely of the form CREATE, ALTER, DROP, GRANT, DENY, or REVOKE. Some system SPs that perform DDL functions also fire DDL triggers. The ALTER TRIGGER, DROP TRIGGER, DISABLE TRIGGER, and ENABLE TRIGGER statements all work for DDL triggers just as they do for DML triggers.

DDL triggers are useful when you want to prevent changes to your database, perform actions in response to a change in the database, or audit changes to the database. Which DDL statements can fire a DDL trigger depends on the scope of the trigger.

DDL EVENT TYPES AND EVENT GROUPS

DDL triggers can fire in response to a wide variety of event types and event groups, scoped at either the database or server level. The events that fire DDL triggers are largely DDL statements like CREATE and DROP, and DCL (Data Control Language) statements like GRANT and DENY. Event groups form a hierarchical structure of DDL events in logical groupings, like DDL_FUNCTION_EVENTS and DDL_PROCEDURE_EVENTS. Event groups allow you to fire triggers in response to a wide range of DDL events.

BOL has complete listings of all available DDL trigger event types and event groups, so we won't reproduce them fully here. Just keep in mind that you can fire triggers in response to most T-SQL DDL and DCL statements. You can also query the sys.trigger_event_types catalog view to retrieve available DDL events.

With DDL triggers, you can specify either an event type or an event group, the latter of which can encompass multiple events or other event groups. If you specify an event group, any events included within that group, or within the subgroups of that group, will fire the DDL trigger.

■ **Note** Creation of a DDL trigger with ALL SERVER scope requires CONTROL SERVER permission on the server. Creating a DDL trigger with DATABASE scope requires ALTER ANY DATABASE DDL TRIGGER permissions.

Once the DDL trigger fires, you can access metadata about the event that fired the trigger with the EVENTDATA() function. EVENTDATA() returns information such as the time, connection, object name, and type of event that fired the trigger. The results are returned as a SQL Server xml data type instance. Listing 6-13 shows a sample of the type of data returned by the EVENTDATA function.

Listing 6-13. EVENTDATA() Function Sample Data

```
<EVENT_INSTANCE><EventType>CREATE_TABLE</EventType><PostTime>2012-04-21T17:08:28.527
</PostTime><SPID>115</SPID>

<ServerName>SQL2012</ServerName><LoginName>SQL2012\Rudi</LoginName>
<UserName>dbo</UserName><DatabaseName>AdventureWorks</DatabaseName>
<SchemaName>dbo</SchemaName><ObjectName>MyTable</ObjectName>
<ObjectType>TABLE</ObjectType><TSQLCommand><SetOptions ANSI_NULLS="ON"
ANSI_NULL_DEFAULT="ON"
ANSI_PADDING="ON"
QUOTED_IDENTIFIER="ON"
ENCRYPTED="FALSE" /><CommandText>
CREATE TABLE dbo.MyTable (i int);
</CommandText>
</TSQLCommand></EVENT_INSTANCE>
```

You can use the xml data type's value() method to retrieve specific nodes from the result. The sample DDL trigger in Listing 6-14 creates a DDL trigger that fires in response to the CREATE TABLE statement in the AdventureWorks database. It logs the event data to a table named dbo.DdlActionLog.

Listing 6-14. CREATE TABLE DDL Trigger Example

```
-- Create a table to log DDL CREATE TABLE actions
CREATE TABLE dbo.DdlActionLog
(
    EntryId int NOT NULL IDENTITY(1, 1) PRIMARY KEY,
    EventType nvarchar(200) NOT NULL,
    PostTime datetime NOT NULL,
    LoginName sysname NOT NULL,
    UserName sysname NOT NULL,
    ServerName sysname NOT NULL,
    SchemaName sysname NOT NULL,
    DatabaseName sysname NOT NULL,
    ObjectName sysname NOT NULL,
    ObjectType sysname NOT NULL,
    CommandText nvarchar(max) NOT NULL
);
GO

CREATE TRIGGER AuditCreateTable
ON DATABASE
FOR CREATE_TABLE
AS
BEGIN
    -- Assign the XML event data to an xml variable
    DECLARE @eventdata xml = EVENTDATA();

    -- Shred the XML event data and insert a row in the log table
    INSERT INTO dbo.DdlActionLog
    (
        EventType,
        PostTime,
        LoginName,
        UserName,
        ServerName,
        SchemaName,
        DatabaseName,
        ObjectName,
        ObjectType,
        CommandText
    )
    SELECT
        EventNode.value(N'EventType[1]', N'nvarchar(200)'),
        EventNode.value(N'PostTime[1]', N'datetime'),
        EventNode.value(N'LoginName[1]', N'sysname'),
        EventNode.value(N'UserName[1]', N'sysname'),
        EventNode.value(N'ServerName[1]', N'sysname'),
        EventNode.value(N'SchemaName[1]', N'sysname'),
```

```
        EventNode.value(N'DatabaseName[1]', N'sysname'),
        EventNode.value(N'ObjectName[1]', N'sysname'),
        EventNode.value(N'ObjectType[1]', N'sysname'),
        EventNode.value(N'(TSQLCommand/CommandText)[1]', 'nvarchar(max)')
    FROM @eventdata.nodes('/EVENT_INSTANCE') EventTable(EventNode);
END;
GO
```

The first part of the example in Listing 6-14 creates a simple table to store the event-specific data generated by events that fire the DDL trigger:

```
-- Create a table to log DDL CREATE TABLE actions
CREATE TABLE dbo.DdlActionLog
(
    EntryId int NOT NULL IDENTITY(1, 1) PRIMARY KEY,
    EventType nvarchar(200) NOT NULL,
    PostTime datetime NOT NULL,
    LoginName sysname NOT NULL,
    UserName sysname NOT NULL,
    ServerName sysname NOT NULL,
    SchemaName sysname NOT NULL,
    DatabaseName sysname NOT NULL,
    ObjectName sysname NOT NULL,
    ObjectType sysname NOT NULL,
    CommandText nvarchar(max) NOT NULL
);
GO
```

The DDL trigger definition begins with the name, the scope (DATABASE), and the DDL action that fires the trigger. In this example, the action that fires this trigger is the CREATE TABLE event. Notice that unlike DML triggers, DDL triggers do not belong to schemas and do not have schemas specified in their names.

```
CREATE TRIGGER AuditCreateTable
ON DATABASE
FOR CREATE_TABLE
```

The body of the trigger begins by declaring an xml variable, @eventdata. This variable holds the results of the EVENTDATA() function for further processing later in the trigger.

```
-- Assign the XML event data to an xml variable
DECLARE @eventdata xml = EVENTDATA();
```

Next, the trigger uses the nodes() and value() methods of the @eventdata xml variable to shred the event data, which is then inserted into the dbo.DdlActionLog table in relational form:

```
-- Shred the XML event data and insert a row in the log table
INSERT INTO dbo.DdlActionLog
(
    EventType,
    PostTime,
    LoginName,
    UserName,
    ServerName,
    SchemaName,
    DatabaseName,
```

```
    ObjectName,
    ObjectType,
    CommandText
)
SELECT
    EventNode.value(N'EventType[1]', N'nvarchar(200)'),
    EventNode.value(N'PostTime[1]', N'datetime'),
    EventNode.value(N'LoginName[1]', N'sysname'),
    EventNode.value(N'UserName[1]', N'sysname'),
    EventNode.value(N'ServerName[1]', N'sysname'),
    EventNode.value(N'SchemaName[1]', N'sysname'),
    EventNode.value(N'DatabaseName[1]', N'sysname'),
    EventNode.value(N'ObjectName[1]', N'sysname'),
    EventNode.value(N'ObjectType[1]', N'sysname'),
    EventNode.value(N'(TSQLCommand/CommandText)[1]', 'nvarchar(max)')
FROM @eventdata.nodes('/EVENT_INSTANCE') EventTable(EventNode);
```

Listing 6-15 demonstrates the DDL trigger by performing a CREATE TABLE statement. Partial results are shown in Figure 6-6.

Listing 6-15. Testing the DDL Trigger with a CREATE TABLE Statement

```
CREATE TABLE dbo.MyTable (i int);
GO

SELECT
    EntryId,
    EventType,
    UserName,
    ObjectName,
    CommandText
FROM DdlActionLog;
```

	EntryId	EventType	UserName	ObjectName	CommandText
1	2	CREATE_TABLE	dbo	MyTable	CREATE TABLE dbo.MyTable (i int);

Figure 6-6. *DDL Audit Logging Results*

Dropping a DDL trigger is as simple as executing the DROP TRIGGER statement, as shown in Listing 6-16. Notice that the ON DATABASE clause is required in this instance. The reason is that the DDL trigger exists outside the schemas of the database, so you must tell SQL Server whether the trigger exists at the database or server scope.

Listing 6-16. Dropping a DDL Trigger

```
DROP TRIGGER AuditCreateTable
ON DATABASE;
```

Logon Triggers

SQL Server offers yet another type of trigger: the logon trigger. *Logon triggers* were first made available in SQL Server 2005 SP 2. These triggers fire in response to an SQL Server LOGON event—after authentication succeeds, but before the user session is established. You can perform tasks ranging from simple LOGON event auditing to more advanced tasks like restricting the number of simultaneous sessions for a login or denying users the ability to create sessions during certain times.

The code example for this section uses logon triggers to deny a given user the ability to log into SQL Server during a specified time period (e.g., during a resource-intensive nightly batch process). Listing 6-17 begins the logon trigger example by creating a sample login and a table that holds a logon denial schedule. The first entry in this table will be used to deny the sample login the ability to log into SQL Server between the hours of 9:00 and 11:00 PM on Saturday nights.

Listing 6-17. Creating a Test Login and Logon Denial Schedule

```
CREATE LOGIN PublicUser WITH PASSWORD = 'p@$$w0rd';
GO

USE Master;

CREATE TABLE dbo.DenyLogonSchedule (
    UserId sysname NOT NULL,
    DayOfWeek tinyint NOT NULL,
    TimeStart time NOT NULL,
    TimeEnd time NOT NULL,
    PRIMARY KEY (UserId, DayOfWeek, TimeStart, TimeEnd)
);
GO

INSERT INTO dbo.DenyLogonSchedule (
    UserId,
    DayOfWeek,
    TimeStart,
    TimeEnd
) VALUES (
    'PublicUser',
    7,
    '21:00:00',
    '23:00:00'
);
```

The logon trigger that makes use of this table to deny logons on a schedule is shown in Listing 6-18.

Listing 6-18. Sample Logon Trigger

```
USE Master;

CREATE TRIGGER DenyLogons
ON ALL SERVER
WITH EXECUTE AS 'sa'
FOR LOGON
AS
BEGIN
```

```
    IF EXISTS ( SELECT 1
        FROM Master .dbo.DenyLogonSchedule
        WHERE UserId = ORIGINAL_LOGIN()
        AND DayOfWeek = DATEPART(WeekDay, GETDATE())
        AND CAST(GETDATE() AS TIME) BETWEEN TimeStart AND TimeEnd
    ) BEGIN
        ROLLBACK TRANSACTION;
    END;
END;
```

■ **Caution**   If your logon trigger errors out, you will be unable to log into SQL Server normally. You can still connect using the Dedicated Administrator Connection (DAC), which bypasses logon triggers, however. Make sure that the table dbo.DenyLogonSchedule exists and that your logon trigger works properly before putting it in production.

The CREATE TRIGGER statement begins much like the other trigger samples we've used to this point, by specifying the name and scope (ALL SERVER). The WITH EXECUTE clause is used to specify that the logon trigger should run under the sa security context, and the FOR LOGON clause indicates that this is actually a logon trigger.

```
CREATE TRIGGER DenyLogons
ON ALL SERVER
WITH EXECUTE AS 'sa'
FOR LOGON
```

The trigger body is fairly simple. It simply checks for the existence of an entry in the AdventureWorks.dbo. DenyLogonSchedule table, indicating that the current user (retrieved with the ORIGINAL_LOGIN() function) is denied login based on the current date and time. If there is an entry indicating that the login should be denied, then the ROLLBACK TRANSACTION statement is executed, denying the login.

```
IF EXISTS ( SELECT 1
    FROM AdventureWorks.dbo.DenyLogonSchedule
    WHERE UserId = ORIGINAL_LOGIN()
    AND DayOfWeek = DATEPART(WeekDay, GETDATE())
    AND CAST(GETDATE() AS TIME) BETWEEN TimeStart AND TimeEnd
) BEGIN
    ROLLBACK TRANSACTION;
END;
```

Notice that the three-part name of the table is used in this statement, since the user attempting to log in may be connecting to a different default database. Attempting to log onto SQL Server using the PublicUser account on Saturday night between the hours indicated results in an error message like the one shown in Figure 6-7.

■ **Tip**   Logon triggers are useful for auditing and restricting logins, but because they only fire after a successful authentication, they cannot be used to log unsuccessful login attempts.

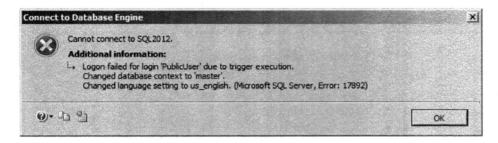

Figure 6-7. *A Logon Trigger Denying a Login*

The logon trigger also makes logon information available in XML format within the trigger via the EVENTDATA() function. An example of the logon information generated by the LOGON event is shown in Listing 6-19.

Listing 6-19. Sample Event Data Generated by a LOGON Event

```
<EVENT_INSTANCE><EventType>LOGON</EventType><PostTime>2012-04-21T23:18:33.357
</PostTime><SPID>110</SPID>
<ServerName>SQL2012</ServerName><LoginName>PublicUser</LoginName>
<LoginType>SQL Login</LoginType><SID>zgPcN6UCBE2j/HYTug0i4A==</SID><ClientHost>&lt;local
machine&gt;</ClientHost><IsPooled>0</IsPooled></EVENT_INSTANCE>
```

■ **Note**   Logon triggers to deny access to logins based on day of week, time of day, and number of sessions per login are available in the Common Criteria compliance package for SQL Server. You can download them on the SQL Server Common Criteria Certifications website: http://www.microsoft.com/sqlserver/en/us/common-criteria.aspx.

Summary

This chapter discussed triggers, including traditional DML triggers, DDL triggers, and logon triggers. As you've seen, triggers are useful tools for a variety of purposes.

DML triggers are the original form of trigger. Much of the functionality that DML triggers were used for in the past, such as enforcing referential integrity, has been supplanted by newer and more efficient T-SQL functionality over the years, like cascading DRI. DML triggers are useful for auditing DML statements and for enforcing complex business rules and logic in the database. They can also be used to implement updating for views that are normally not updatable.

In this chapter, we discussed the inserted and deleted virtual tables, which hold copies of the rows being affected by a DML statement. We also discussed the UPDATE() and COLUMNS_UPDATED() functions in DML triggers, which identify the columns that were affected by the DML statement that fired a trigger. Finally, we talked about the differences between AFTER and INSTEAD OF triggers and explained nested triggers and trigger recursion.

DDL triggers can be used to audit and restrict database object and server changes. DDL triggers can help provide protection against accidental or malicious changes to, or destruction of, database objects. In this chapter, we discussed the EVENTDATA() function and how you can use it to audit DDL actions within a database or on the server.

Logon triggers can likewise be used to audit successful logins and restrict logins for various reasons.

In the next chapter, we will discuss the native encryption functionality available in SQL Server 2012.

EXERCISES

1. [True/False] The EVENTDATA() function returns information about DDL events within DDL triggers.

2. [True/False] In a DML trigger, the inserted and deleted virtual tables are both populated with rows during an UPDATE event.

3. [Choose all that apply] Which of the following types of triggers does SQL Server 2012 support?

   - Logon triggers

   - TCL triggers

   - DDL triggers

   - Hierarchy triggers

   - DML triggers

4. [Fill in the blank] The _____ statement prevents triggers from generating extraneous rows affected messages.

5. [Choose one] The COLUMNS_UPDATED() function returns data in which of the following formats?

   - A varbinary string with bits set to represent affected columns

   - A comma-delimited varchar string with a column ID number for each affected column

   - A table consisting of column ID numbers for each affected column

   - A table consisting of all rows that were inserted by the DML operation

6. [True/False] @@ROWCOUNT, when used at the beginning of a DML trigger, reflects the number of rows affected by the DML statement that fired the trigger.

7. [True/False] You can create recursive AFTER triggers on views.

■ ■ ■

CHAPTER 7

Encryption

SQL Server 2012 supports built-in column- and database-level encryption functionality directly through T-SQL. Column-level encryption allows you to encrypt the data in your database at the column level. Back in the days of SQL Server 2000 (and before), you had to turn to third-party tools or write your own extended stored procedures (XPs) to encrypt sensitive data. Even with these tools in place, subpar implementation of various aspects of the system, such as encryption key management, could leave many systems in a vulnerable state.

SQL Server 2012's encryption model takes advantage of the Windows CryptoAPI to secure your data. With built-in encryption key management and facilities to handle encryption, decryption, and one-way hashing through T-SQL statements, SQL Server 2012 provides useful tools for efficient and secure data encryption. SQL Server 2012 also supports two encryption options: *transparent data encryption (TDE)* for supporting encryption of an entire database, and *extensible key management (EKM)* which allows you to use third-party hardware-based encryption key management and encryption acceleration.

In this chapter, we will discuss SQL Server 2012's built-in column-level encryption and decryption functionality, key management capabilities, one-way hashing functions, and TDE and EKM functionality.

The Encryption Hierarchy

SQL Server 2012 offers a layered approach to encryption key management by allowing several levels of key-encrypting keys between the top-level master key and the lowest-level data-encrypting keys. SQL Server also allows for encryption by certificates, symmetric keys, and asymmetric keys. The SQL Server 2012 encryption model is hierarchical, as shown in Figure 7-1.

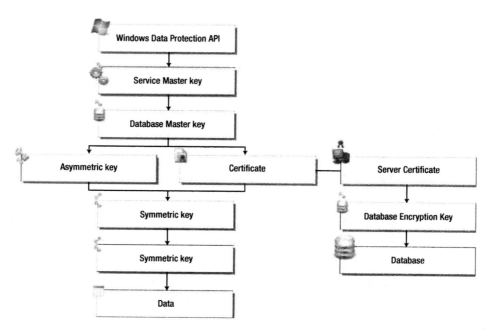

Figure 7-1. *SQL Server 2012 Encryption Hierarchy*

At the top of the SQL Server 2012 encryption hierarchy is the Windows Data Protection API (DPAPI), which is used to protect the granddaddy of all SQL Server 2012 encryption keys: the *service master key (SMK)*. The SMK is automatically generated by SQL Server the first time it is needed to encrypt another key. There is only one SMK per SQL Server instance, and it directly or indirectly secures all keys in the SQL Server encryption key hierarchy on the server.

While each SQL Server instance has only a single SMK, each database can have a *database master key (DMK)*. The DMK is encrypted by the SMK. The DMK is used to encrypt lower-level keys and certificates.

At the bottom of the SQL Server 2012 key hierarchy are the certificates, symmetric keys, and asymmetric keys used to encrypt data.

SQL Server 2012 also introduces the concept of the *server certificate,* which is a certificate created in the master database for the purpose of protecting database encryption keys. *Database encryption keys* are symmetric encryption keys created to encrypt entire databases via TDE.

Service Master Keys

As we mentioned in the previous section, the SMK is automatically generated by SQL Server the first time it is needed. Because the SMK is generated automatically and managed by SQL Server, there are only a couple of administrative tasks you need to perform for this key, namely backing it up and restoring it on a server as necessary. You will also need access to the directory where the backup file will be located. For example in Listing 7-1 you will want to create a folder named CH07 on your C drive. Listing 7-1 demonstrates the BACKUP and RESTORE SERVICE MASTER KEY statements.

Listing 7-1. BACKUP and RESTORE SMK Examples

```
-- Back up the SMK to a file
BACKUP SERVICE MASTER KEY TO FILE = 'c:\CH07\SQL2012.SMK'
ENCRYPTION BY PASSWORD = 'p@$$w0rd';

-- Restore the SMK from a file
RESTORE SERVICE MASTER KEY FROM FILE = 'c:\CH07\SQL2012.SMK'
DECRYPTION BY PASSWORD = 'p@$$w0rd';
```

The BACKUP SERVICE MASTER KEY statement allows you to back up your SMK to a file. The SMK is encrypted in the file, so the ENCRYPTION BY PASSWORD clause of this statement is mandatory

The RESTORE SERVICE MASTER KEY statement restores the SMK from a previously created backup file. The DECRYPTION BY PASSWORD clause must specify the same password used to encrypt the file when you created the backup. Backing up and restoring an SMK requires CONTROL SERVER permissions. In the scenario above, SQL Server is intelligent enough to know that the backup SMK and the SMK in the restore are the same so it doesn't need to go through an unnecessary decryption and encryption process. The data would only be encrypted again if the SMK you are trying to restore is different from the SMK you backed up.

The RESTORE SERVICE MASTER KEY statement can include the optional keyword FORCE to force the SMK to restore even if there is a data decryption failure. If you have to use the FORCE keyword, you can expect to lose data, so use this option with care and only as a last resort.

■ **Tip**   After installing SQL Server 2012, you should immediately back up your SMK and store a copy of it in a secure offsite location. If your SMK becomes corrupted or is otherwise compromised, you could lose access to all of your encrypted data if you don't have a backup of the SMK.

In addition to BACKUP and RESTORE statements, SQL Server provides the ALTER SERVICE MASTER KEY statement to allow you to change the SMK for an instance of SQL Server. When SQL Server generates the SMK, it uses the credentials of the SQL Server service account to encrypt the SMK. If you change the SQL Server service account, you can use ALTER SERVICE MASTER KEY to update it using the current service account credentials. Alternatively, you can advise SQL Server to secure the SMK using the local machine key, which is managed by the operating system. You can also use ALTER SERVICE MASTER KEY to regenerate the SMK completely.

As with the RESTORE SERVICE MASTER KEY statement, the ALTER SERVICE MASTER KEY statement allows use of the FORCE keyword. Normally, if there is a decryption error during the process of altering the SMK, SQL Server will stop the process with an error message. When FORCE is used, the SMK is regenerated even at the risk of data loss. Just like the RESTORE statement, the FORCE option should be used with care, and only as a last resort.

■ **Tip**   When you regenerate the SMK, all keys that are encrypted by it must be decrypted and reencrypted. This operation can be resource intensive and should be scheduled during off-peak time periods.

Database Master Keys

Each database can have a single DMK, which is used to encrypt certificate private keys and asymmetric key-pair private keys in the current database. The DMK is created with the CREATE MASTER KEY statement, as shown in Listing 7-2.

Listing 7-2. Creating a Master Key

```
USE AdventureWorks2012;
GO
CREATE MASTER KEY
ENCRYPTION BY PASSWORD = 'p@$$w0rd' ;
```

The CREATE MASTER KEY statement creates the DMK and uses AES to encrypt it with the supplied password. If the password you supply does not meet Windows's password complexity requirements, SQL Server will complain with an error message like the following:

```
Msg 15118, Level 16, State 1, Line 1

Password validation failed. The password does not meet Windows

policy requirements because it is not complex enough.
```

■ **Note** Versions of SQL prior to SQL 2012 used triple DES (Data Encryption Standard) for encrypting SMKs and DMKs. SQL Server 2012 uses the more advanced AES encryption. If you upgrade SQL Server from a previous version you will need to also upgrade your encryption keys. This can be accomplished by using either the ALTER SERVICE MASTER KEY or the ALTER MASTER KEY and using the REGENERATE clause.

SQL Server 2012 automatically uses the SMK to encrypt a copy of the DMK. When this feature is used, SQL Server can decrypt your DMK when needed without the need to first open the master key. When this feature is not in use, you must issue the OPEN MASTER KEY statement and supply the same password initially used to encrypt the DMK whenever you need to use it. The potential downside to encrypting your DMK with the SMK is that any member of the sysadmin server role can decrypt the DMK. You can use the ALTER MASTER KEY statement to change the method SQL Server uses to decrypt the DMK. Listing 7-3 shows how to turn off encryption by SMK for a DMK.

Listing 7-3. Turning off DMK Encryption by the SMK

```
ALTER MASTER KEY
   DROP ENCRYPTION BY SERVICE MASTER KEY;
```

When the DMK is regenerated, all the keys it protects are decrypted and reencrypted with the new DMK. The FORCE keyword is used to force SQL Server to regenerate the DMK even if there are decryption errors. As with the SMK, the FORCE keyword should be used only as a last resort. You can expect to lose data if you have to use FORCE.

You can also back up and restore a DMK with the BACKUP MASTER KEY and RESTORE MASTER KEY statements. The BACKUP MASTER KEY statement is similar in operation to the BACKUP SERVICE MASTER KEY statement. When you back up the DMK, you must specify the password that SQL Server will use to encrypt the DMK in the output file. When you restore the DMK, you must specify the same password in the DECRYPTION BY PASSWORD clause to decrypt the DMK in the output file. In addition, you must specify an encryption password that SQL Server will use to encrypt the password in the ENCRYPTION BY PASSWORD clause. Listing 7-4 demonstrates backing up and restoring a DMK.

Listing 7-4. Backing up and Restoring a DMK

```
USE AdventureWorks2012;
GO

OPEN MASTER KEY DECRYPTION BY PASSWORD = 'p@$$w0rd' ;

BACKUP MASTER KEY
   TO FILE = 'c:\CH07\AdventureWorks2012.DMK'
   ENCRYPTION BY PASSWORD = 'p@$$w0rd';

-- Restore DMK from backup
RESTORE MASTER KEY
  FROM FILE = 'c:\CH07\AdventureWorks2012.DMK'
  DECRYPTION BY PASSWORD = 'p@$$w0rd'
  ENCRYPTION BY PASSWORD = '3rt=d4uy';

CLOSE MASTER KEY;
```

The FORCE keyword is available for use with the RESTORE MASTER KEY statement, but as with other statements, it should only be used as a last resort, as it could result in unrecoverable encrypted data.

The DROP MASTER KEY statement can be used to remove a DMK from the database. DROP MASTER KEY will not remove a DMK if it is currently being used to encrypt other keys in the database. If you want to drop a DMK that is protecting other keys in the database, the protected keys must be altered to remove their encryption by the DMK first.

■ **Tip**   Always make backups of your DMKs immediately upon creation and store them in a secure location.

If you choose to disable automatic key management with the ALTER MASTER KEY statement, you will need to use the OPEN MASTER KEY and CLOSE MASTER KEY statements every time you wish to perform encryption and decryption in a database.

OPEN MASTER KEY requires you to supply the same password used to encrypt the DMK in the DECRYPTION BY PASSWORD clause. This password is used to decrypt the DMK, a required step when you are encrypting and decrypting data. When finished using the DMK, issue the CLOSE MASTER KEY statement. If your DMK is encrypted by the SMK, you do not need to use the OPEN MASTER KEY and CLOSE MASTER KEY statements; SQL Server will handle that task for you automatically.

Certificates

Certificates are asymmetric encryption key pairs with additional metadata, such as subject and expiration date, in the X.509 certificate format. Asymmetric encryption is a method of encrypting data using two separate but mathematically related keys. SQL Server 2012 uses the standard public key/private key encryption methodology. You can think of a certificate as a wrapper for an asymmetric encryption public key/private key pair. The CREATE CERTIFICATE statement can be used to either install an existing certificate or create a new certificate on SQL Server. Listing 7-5 shows how to create a new certificate on SQL Server.

Listing 7-5. Creating a Certificate on SQL Server

```
CREATE CERTIFICATE TestCertificate
  ENCRYPTION BY PASSWORD = 'p@$$wOrd'
  WITH SUBJECT = 'Adventureworks2012 Test Certificate',
  EXPIRY_DATE = '2026-10-31';
```

The CREATE CERTIFICATE statement includes several options. The only things mandatory are the SQL Server identifier for the certificate immediately following the CREATE CERTIFICATE statement (in this case TestCertificate), and the WITH SUBJECT clause, which sets the certificate subject name. If the ENCRYPTION BY PASSWORD clause is not used when you create a certificate, the certificate's private key is encrypted by the DMK. Additional options available to the CREATE CERTIFICATE statement include START_DATE and EXPIRY_DATE, which set the start and expiration dates for the certificate; and the ACTIVE FOR BEGIN DIALOG clause, which makes the certificate available for use by Service Broker dialogs.

■ **Tip** If START_DATE is not specified, the current date is used. If EXPIRY_DATE is omitted, the expiration date is set to one year after the start date.

You can also use the CREATE CERTIFICATE statement to load an existing certificate in a variety of ways, including the following:

- You can use the FROM ASSEMBLY clause to load an existing certificate from a signed assembly already loaded in the database.

- You can use the EXECUTABLE FILE clause to create a certificate from a signed DLL file.

- You can use the FILE clause to create a certificate from an existing Distinguished Encoding Rules (DER) X.509 certificate file.

- You can also use the WITH PRIVATE KEY clause with the FILE or EXECUTABLE FILE options to specify a separate file containing the certificate's private key. When you specify the WITH PRIVATE KEY clause, you can specify the optional DECRYPTION BY PASSWORD and ENCRYPTION BY PASSWORD clauses to specify the password that will be used to decrypt the private key if it is encrypted in the source file, and to secure the private key once it is loaded.

■ **Note** SQL Server generates private keys that are 1,024 bits in length. If you import a private key from an external source, it must be a multiple of 64 bits, between 384 and 3,456 bits in length.

After creating a certificate—as with DMKs and SMKs—you should immediately make a backup and store it in a secure location. Listing 7-6 demonstrates how to make a backup of a certificate.

Listing 7-6. Backing up a Certificate

```
BACKUP CERTIFICATE TestCertificate
  TO FILE = 'c:\CH07\TestCertificate.CER'
  WITH PRIVATE KEY
```

```
(
  FILE = 'c:\CH07\TestCertificate.PVK',
  ENCRYPTION BY PASSWORD = ' 7&rtOxp2',
  DECRYPTION BY PASSWORD = 'p@$$wOrd'
);
```

The BACKUP CERTIFICATE statement in Listing 7-6 backs up the TestCertificate certificate to the c:\TestCertificate.CER file and the certificate's private key to the c:\TestCertificate.PVK file. The DECRYPTION BY PASSWORD clause specifies the password to use to decrypt the certificate, and ENCRYPTION BY PASSWORD gives SQL Server the password to use when encrypting the private key in the file. There is no RESTORE statement for certificates; instead, the CREATE CERTIFICATE statement has all the options necessary to restore a certificate from a backup file by simply creating from an existing certificate using the FROM FILE clause. T-SQL also provides an ALTER CERTIFICATE statement that allows you to make changes to an existing certificate.

You can use certificates to encrypt and decrypt data directly with the certificate encryption and decryption functions, EncryptByCert, and DecryptByCert. The EncryptByCert function encrypts a given clear text message with a specified certificate. The function accepts an int certificate ID and a plain text value to encrypt. The int certificate ID can be retrieved by passing the certificate name to the CertID function. Listing 7-7 demonstrates this function. EncryptByCert returns a varbinary value up to a maximum of 432 bytes in length (the length of the result depends on the length of the key). The "Limitations of Asymmetric Encryption" sidebar describes some of the limitations of asymmetric encryption on SQL Server, including encryption by certificate.

LIMITATIONS OF ASYMMETRIC ENCRYPTION

Asymmetric encryption has certain limitations that should be noted before you attempt to encrypt data directly with certificates or asymmetric keys. The EncryptByCert function can accept a char, varchar, binary, nchar, nvarchar, or varbinary constant, column name, or variable as clear text to encrypt. Asymmetric encryption, including encryption by certificate, on SQL Server returns a varbinary result, but will not return a result longer than 432 bytes. As mentioned, the maximum length of the result depends on the length of the encryption key used. As an example, with the default private key length of 1,024 bits, you can encrypt a varchar plain text message with a maximum length of 117 characters and an nvarchar plain text message with a maximum length of 58 characters. The result in either case is a varbinary result of 128 bytes.

Microsoft recommends that you avoid using asymmetric encryption to encrypt data directly because of the size limitations, and for performance reasons. Symmetric encryption algorithms use shorter keys but operate more quickly than asymmetric encryption algorithms. The SQL Server 2012 encryption key hierarchy provides the best of both worlds, with the long key lengths of asymmetric keys protecting the shorter, more efficient symmetric keys. To maximize performance, Microsoft recommends using symmetric encryption to encrypt data and asymmetric encryption to encrypt symmetric keys.

The DecryptByCert function decrypts text previously encrypted by EncryptByCert. The DecryptByCert function accepts an int certificate ID, an encrypted varbinary cipher text message, and an optional certificate password that must match the one used when the certificate was created (if one was specified at creation time). If no certificate password is specified, the DMK is used to decrypt it. Listing 7-7 demonstrates encryption and decryption by certificate for short plain text. The results are shown in Figure 7-2. If you get an error during the CREATE MASTER KEY and the CREATE CERTIFICATE commands, then be sure to run the final DROP statements prior to creating the objects.

Listing 7-7. Sample Encryption and Decryption by Certificate

```
--      Create a DMK
CREATE  MASTER  KEY
    ENCRYPTION BY PASSWORD = 'P@55w0rd';

-- Create a certificate
CREATE  CERTIFICATE  TestCertificate
    WITH  SUBJECT  = N'Adventureworks  Test  Certificate',
    EXPIRY_DATE = '2026-10-31';

-- Create the plain text data to encrypt
DECLARE @plaintext nvarchar(58) =
    N'This is a test string to encrypt';
SELECT 'Plain  text  =  ',  @plaintext;

-- Encrypt the plain text by certificate
DECLARE @ciphertext varbinary(128) =
    EncryptByCert(Cert_ID('TestCertificate'), @plaintext);
SELECT 'Cipher text=', @ciphertext;

--  Decrypt the cipher text by certificate
DECLARE @decryptedtext nvarchar(58) =
    DecryptByCert(Cert_ID('TestCertificate'), @ciphertext);
SELECT 'Decrypted  text  =  ',  @decryptedtext;

-- Drop the test certificate
DROP  CERTIFICATE TestCertificate;

--      Drop the DMK
DROP  MASTER KEY;
```

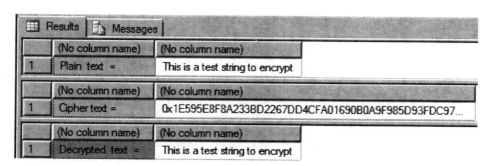

Figure 7-2. Result of Encrypting and Decrypting by Certificate

Listing 7-7 first creates a DMK and a test certificate using the CREATE MASTER KEY and CREATE CERTIFICATE statements presented previously in this chapter. It then generates an nvarchar plain text message to encrypt.

```
-- Create a DMK
CREATE MASTER KEY ENCRYPTION BY PASSWORD = 'P@55w0rd';

-- Create a certificate
CREATE CERTIFICATE TestCertificate
WITH SUBJECT = N'Adventureworks Test Certificate',
EXPIRY_DATE = '2026-10-31';

-- Create the plain text data to encrypt
DECLARE @plaintext nvarchar(58) =
N'This is a test string to encrypt';
SELECT 'Plain text = ', @plaintext;
```

The sample uses the EncryptByCert function to encrypt the plain text message. The CertID function is used to retrieve the int certificate ID for TestCertificate.

```
-- Encrypt the plain text by certificate
DECLARE @ciphertext varbinary(128) =
EncryptByCert(Cert_ID('TestCertificate'), @plaintext);
SELECT 'Cipher text = ', @ciphertext;
```

The DecryptByCert function is then used to decrypt the cipher text. Again, the CertID function is used to retrieve the TestCertificate certificate ID.

```
-- Decrypt the cipher text by certificate
DECLARE @decryptedtext nvarchar(58) =
DecryptByCert(Cert_ID('TestCertificate'), @ciphertext);
SELECT 'Decrypted text = ', @decryptedtext;
```

The balance of the code performs some cleanup, dropping the certificate and DMK:

```
-- Drop the test certificate
DROP CERTIFICATE TestCertificate;
-- Drop the DMK
DROP MASTER KEY;
```

You can also use a certificate to generate a signature for a plain text message. SignByCert accepts a certificate ID, a plain text message, and an optional certificate password. The result is a varbinary string, up to a length of 432 characters (again, the length of the result is determined by the length of the encryption key). When SignByCert is used, the slightest change in the plain text message—even a single character—will result in a completely different signature being generated for the message. This allows you to easily detect whether your plain text has been tampered with. Listing 7-8 uses the SignByCert function to create a signature for a plain text message. The results are shown in Figure 7-3.

Listing 7-8. Signing a Message with the SignByCert Function

```
-- Create a DMK
CREATE MASTER KEY ENCRYPTION BY PASSWORD = 'P@55w0rd';
-- Create a certificate
CREATE CERTIFICATE TestCertificate
WITH SUBJECT = 'Adventureworks Test Certificate',
EXPIRY_DATE = '2026-10-31';
```

```
-- Create message
DECLARE @message nvarchar(4000) = N'Four score and seven years ago our fathers brought forth on
this continent a new nation, conceived in Liberty, and dedicated to the proposition that all men
are created equal.
Now we are engaged in a great civil war, testing whether that nation, or any nation, so
conceived and so dedicated, can long endure. We are met on a great battle-field of that war. We
have come to dedicate a portion of that field, as a final resting place for those who here gave
their lives that that nation might live. It is altogether fitting and proper that we should do
this. ';
-- Sign the message by certificate
SELECT SignByCert(Cert_ID(N'TestCertificate'), @message);
-- Drop the certificate
DROP CERTIFICATE TestCertificate;
-- Drop the DMK DROP MASTER KEY;
```

Figure 7-3. *Signature Generated by SignByCert (Partial)*

Asymmetric Keys

Asymmetric keys are actually composed of a key pair: a *public key*, which is publicly accessible, and a *private key*, which is kept secret. The mathematical relationship between the public and private keys allows for encryption and decryption without revealing the private key. T-SQL includes statements for creating and managing asymmetric keys.

The CREATE ASYMMETRIC KEY statement allows you to generate an asymmetric key pair or install an existing key pair on the server, in much the same manner as when creating a certificate. Encryption key length is often used as an indicator of relative encryption strength, and when you create an asymmetric key on SQL Server, you can specify an RSA key length, as shown in Table 7-1.

Table 7-1. *Asymmetric Key Algorithms and Limits*

Algorithm	Key Length	Plain Text	Cipher Text	Signature Length
RSA_512	512 bits	53 bytes	64 bytes	64 bytes
RSA_1024	1,024 bits	117 bytes	128 bytes	128 bytes
RSA_2048	2,048 bits	245 bytes	256 bytes	256 bytes

Listing 7-9 creates an asymmetric key pair on SQL Server 2012.

Listing 7-9. Creating an Asymmetric Key Pair

```
CREATE ASYMMETRIC KEY TempAsymmetricKey WITH ALGORITHM = RSA_1024;
```

You can alter an existing asymmetric key with the ALTER ASYMMETRIC KEY statement. ALTER ASYMMETRIC KEY offers the following options for managing your asymmetric keys:

- You can use the REMOVE PRIVATE KEY clause to remove the private key from the asymmetric public key/private key pair.

- You can use the WITH PRIVATE KEY clause to change the method used to protect the private key.

- You can change the asymmetric key protection method from DMK encryption to password encryption with the ENCRYPTION BY PASSWORD option.

- You can switch from password protection for your asymmetric key to DMK protection with the DECRYPTION BY PASSWORD clause.

- You can specify both the ENCRYPTION BY PASSWORD and DECRYPTION BY PASSWORD clauses together to change the password used to encrypt the private key.

The DROP ASYMMETRIC KEY statement removes an asymmetric key from the database.

The EncryptByAsymKey and DecryptByAsymKey functions allow you to encrypt and decrypt data with an asymmetric key in the same way as EncryptByCert and DecryptByCert.

The EncryptByAsymKey function accepts an int asymmetric key ID and plain text to encrypt. The AsymKeyID function can be used to retrieve an asymmetric key ID by name. DecryptByAsymKey accepts an asymmetric key ID, encrypted cipher text to decrypt, and an optional password to decrypt the asymmetric key. If the password is specified, it must be the same password used to encrypt the asymmetric key at creation time.

▓ **Tip** The limitations for asymmetric key encryption and decryption on SQL Server are the same as those for certificate encryption and decryption.

Listing 7-10 demonstrates the use of asymmetric key encryption and decryption functions. Be sure to drop any master keys prior to running the code. The results are shown in Figure 7-4.

Listing 7-10. Encrypting and Decrypting with Asymmetric Keys

```
-- Create DMK
CREATE MASTER KEY
ENCRYPTION BY PASSWORD = 'P@55w0rd';

-- Create asymmetric key
CREATE ASYMMETRIC KEY TestAsymmetricKey WITH ALGORITHM = RSA_512;

--Assign a credit card number to encrypt
DECLARE @CreditCard nvarchar(26) = N'9000 1234 5678 9012';
SELECT @CreditCard;

--Encrypt the credit card number
DECLARE @EncryptedCreditCard varbinary(64) =
  EncryptByAsymKey(AsymKey_ID(N'TestAsymmetricKey'), @CreditCard);
  SELECT @EncryptedCreditCard;
```

```
--Decrypt the encrypted credit card number
DECLARE @DecryptedCreditCard nvarchar(26) =
  DecryptByAsymKey(AsymKey_ID(N'TestAsymmetricKey'), @EncryptedCreditCard);
SELECT @DecryptedCreditCard;

-- Drop asymmetric key
DROP ASYMMETRIC KEY TestAsymmetricKey;

--Drop DMK
DROP MASTER KEY;
```

Figure 7-4. *Asymmetric Key Encryption Results*

This example first creates a DMK and an RSA asymmetric key with a 512-bit private key length. Then it creates plain text representing a simple credit card number.

```
-- Create DMK
CREATE MASTER KEY ENCRYPTION BY PASSWORD = 'P@55w0rd';

-- Create asymmetric key
CREATE ASYMMETRIC KEY TestAsymmetricKey WITH ALGORITHM = RSA_512;

--Assign a credit card number to encrypt
DECLARE @CreditCard nvarchar(26) = N'9000 1234 5678 9012';
SELECT @CreditCard;
```

■ **Note**   You have the option to create an asymmetric key without a corresponding database master key. If you decide to do this then you must have a password assigned to the asymmetric key, otherwise; a password is optional.

The sample then encrypts the credit card number with the EncryptByAsymKey function, and decrypts it with the DecryptByAsymKey function. Both functions use the AsymKeyID function to retrieve the asymmetric key ID.

```
-- Encrypt the credit card number
DECLARE @EncryptedCreditCard varbinary(64) =
EncryptByAsymKey(AsymKey_ID(N'TestAsymmetricKey'), @CreditCard);
SELECT @EncryptedCreditCard;
```

```
-- Decrypt the encrypted credit card number
DECLARE @DecryptedCreditCard nvarchar(26) =
DecryptByAsymKey(AsymKey_ID(N'TestAsymmetricKey'), @EncryptedCreditCard);
SELECT @DecryptedCreditCard;
```

The sample finishes up with a little housekeeping, namely dropping the asymmetric key and the DMK created for the example.

```
-- Drop asymmetric key
DROP ASYMMETRIC KEY TestAsymmetricKey;
-- Drop DMK
DROP MASTER KEY;
```

Like certificates, asymmetric keys offer a function to generate digital signatures for plain text. The SignByAsymKey function accepts a string up to 8,000 bytes in length and returns a varbinary signature for the string. The length of the signature is dependent on the key length, as previously shown in Table 7-1. Listing 7-11 is a simple example of the SignByAsymKey function in action. The results are shown in Figure 7-5.

Listing 7-11. Signing a Message by Asymmetric Key

```
-- Create DMK
CREATE MASTER KEY
ENCRYPTION BY PASSWORD = 'P@55w0rd';

-- Create asymmetric key
CREATE ASYMMETRIC KEY TestAsymmetricKey WITH ALGORITHM = RSA_512;

-- Create message
DECLARE @message nvarchar(4000) = N'Alas, poor Yorick!';
SELECT @message;

-- Sign message by asymmetric key
SELECT SignByAsymKey(AsymKey_ID(N'TestAsymmetricKey'), @message);

-- Drop asymmetric key
DROP ASYMMETRIC KEY TestAsymmetricKey;

-- Drop DMK
DROP MASTER KEY;
```

Figure 7-5. Signing a Message with an Asymmetric Key

ASYMMETRIC KEY "BACKUPS"

SQL Server provides no BACKUP or RESTORE statements for asymmetric keys. For physical backups of your asymmetric keys, you should install the asymmetric keys from an external source like an assembly, an executable file, a strong-name file, or a hardware security module (HSM). You can make backups of the source files containing your asymmetric keys. As an alternative, you can use certificates instead of asymmetric keys. Keep these options in mind when you are planning to take advantage of SQL Server 2012 encryption.

Symmetric Keys

Symmetric keys are at the bottom of the SQL Server encryption key hierarchy. Symmetric encryption algorithms use trivially related keys to both encrypt and decrypt your data. *Trivially related* simply means that the algorithm can use either the same key for both encryption and decryption, or two keys that are mathematically related via a simple transformation to derive one key from the other. Symmetric keys on SQL Server 2012 are specifically designed to support SQL Server's symmetric encryption functionality. The algorithms provided by SQL Server 2012 use a single key for both encryption and decryption. In the SQL Server 2012 encryption model, symmetric keys are encrypted by certificates or asymmetric keys, and they can be used in turn to encrypt other symmetric keys or raw data. The CREATE SYMMETRIC KEY statement allows you to generate symmetric keys, as shown in Listing 7-12.

Listing 7-12. Creating a Symmetric Key

```
CREATE SYMMETRIC KEY TestSymmetricKey WITH ALGORITHM = AES_128 ENCRYPTION BY PASSWORD = 'p@55w0rd';
```

The options specified in the CREATE SYMMETRIC KEY statement in Listing 7-12 specify that the symmetric key will be created with the name TestSymmetricKey, it will be protected by the password p@55w0rd, and it will use the Advanced Encryption Standard (AES) algorithm with a 127-bit key (AES128) to encrypt data.

When creating a symmetric key you can specify any of several encryption algorithms, including the following:

- AES128, AES192, and AES256 specify the AES block encryption algorithm with a symmetric key length of 128, 192, or 256 bits, and a block size of 128 bits.

- DES specifies the DES block encryption algorithm, which has a symmetric key length of 56 bits and a block size of 64 bits.

- DESX specifies the DES-X block encryption algorithm, which was introduced as a successor to the DES algorithm. DES-X also has a symmetric key length of 56 bits (although because the algorithm includes security augmentations, the effective key length is calculated at around 118 bits) and a block size of 64 bits.

- RC2 specifies the RC2 block encryption algorithm, which has a key size of 128 bits and a block size of 64 bits.

- RC4 and RC4_128 specify the RC4 stream encryption algorithm, which has a key length of 40 or 128 bits. RC4 and RC4_128 are not recommended, as they do not generate random initialization vectors to further obfuscate the cipher text.

The CREATE SYMMETRIC KEY statement also provides additional options that allow you to specify options for symmetric key creation, including the following:

- You can specify a KEYSOURCE to designate a passphrase to be used as key material from which the symmetric key is derived. If you don't specify a KEY SOURCE, SQL Server generates the symmetric key from random key material.

- The ENCRYPTION BY clause specifies the method used to encrypt this symmetric key in the database. You can specify encryption by a certificate, password, asymmetric key, another symmetric key, or HSM.

- The PROVIDER_KEY_NAME and CREATION_DISPOSITION clauses allow you to use your symmetric key with EKM security.

- The IDENTITYVALUE clause specifies an identity phrase that is used to generate a GUID to "tag" data encrypted with the key.

■ **Caution** When a symmetric key is encrypted with a password instead of the public key of the database master key, the TRIPLE DES encryption algorithm is used. Because of this, keys that are created with a strong encryption algorithm, such as AES, are themselves secured by a weaker algorithm.

TEMPORARY SYMMETRIC KEYS

You can create temporary symmetric keys by prefixing the symmetric key name with a number sign (#). A temporary symmetric key exists only during the current session and is automatically removed when the current session ends. Temporary symmetric keys are not accessible to any sessions outside of the session they are created in. When referencing a temporary symmetric key, the number sign (#) prefix must be used. You can use the same WITH clause options described in this section to specify how the symmetric key should be created. To be honest, we don't really see much use for temporary symmetric keys at this point, although we don't want to discount them totally. After all, someone may find a use for them in the future.

SQL Server also provides the ALTER SYMMETRIC KEY and DROP SYMMETRIC KEY statements for symmetric key management. The ALTER statement allows you to add or remove encryption methods on a symmetric key. As an example, if you created a symmetric key and encrypted it by password but later wished to change it to encryption by certificate, you would issue two ALTER SYMMETRIC KEY statements—the first ALTER statement would specify the ADD ENCRYPTION BY CERTIFICATE clause, and the second would specify DROP ENCRYPTION BY PASSWORD, as shown in Listing 7-13. Again, you may need to drop the certificate and key prior to running the code.

Listing 7-13. Changing the Symmetric Key Encryption Method

```
-- Create certificate to protect symmetric key
CREATE CERTIFICATE TestCertificate
  WITH SUBJECT = 'AdventureWorks Test Certificate',
  EXPIRY_DATE = '2026-10-31';

CREATE SYMMETRIC KEY TestSymmetricKey WITH ALGORITHM = AES_128 ENCRYPTION BY PASSWORD = 'p@55w0rd';

OPEN SYMMETRIC KEY TestSymmetricKey
  DECRYPTION BY PASSWORD = 'p@55w0rd';

ALTER SYMMETRIC KEY TestSymmetricKey
  ADD ENCRYPTION BY CERTIFICATE TestCertificate;
```

```
ALTER SYMMETRIC KEY TestSymmetricKey
  DROP ENCRYPTION BY PASSWORD = 'p@55w0rd';

CLOSE SYMMETRIC KEY TestSymmetricKey;

-- Drop the symmetric key
DROP SYMMETRIC KEY TestSymmetricKey;

-- Drop the certificate
DROP CERTIFICATE TestCertificate;
```

■ **Note**   Before you alter a symmetric key, you must first open it with the OPEN SYMMETRIC KEY statement.

The DROP SYMMETRIC KEY statement allows you to remove a symmetric key from the database.

Once you create a symmetric key, you can encrypt data with the EncryptByKey and DecryptByKey functions. Listing 7-14 creates a symmetric key and encrypts 100 names with it. Partial results are shown in Figure 7-6.

Listing 7-14. Encrypting Data with a Symmetric Key

```
-- Create a temporary table to hold results
CREATE TABLE #TempNames
(
    BusinessEntityID int PRIMARY KEY,
    FirstName       nvarchar(50),
    MiddleName      nvarchar(50),
    LastName        nvarchar(50),
    EncFirstName    varbinary(200),
    EncMiddleName   varbinary(200),
    EncLastName     varbinary(200)
);

-- Create DMK
CREATE MASTER KEY
  ENCRYPTION BY PASSWORD = 'Test_P@ssw0rd';

-- Create certificate to protect symmetric key
CREATE CERTIFICATE TestCertificate
  WITH SUBJECT = 'AdventureWorks Test Certificate',
  EXPIRY_DATE = '2026-10-31';

-- Create symmetric key to encrypt data
CREATE SYMMETRIC KEY TestSymmetricKey
  WITH ALGORITHM = AES_128
  ENCRYPTION BY CERTIFICATE TestCertificate;

-- Open symmetric key
OPEN SYMMETRIC KEY TestSymmetricKey
  DECRYPTION BY CERTIFICATE TestCertificate;
```

```
-- Populate temp table with 100 encrypted names from the Person.Person table
INSERT
INTO #TempNames
(
BusinessEntityID,
EncFirstName,
EncMiddleName,
EncLastName
)
SELECT TOP(100) BusinessEntityID,
  EncryptByKey(Key_GUID(N'TestSymmetricKey'), FirstName),
  EncryptByKey(Key_GUID(N'TestSymmetricKey'), MiddleName),
  EncryptByKey(Key_GUID(N'TestSymmetricKey'), LastName)
FROM Person.Person
ORDER BY BusinessEntityID;

-- Update the temp table with decrypted names
UPDATE #TempNames
SET FirstName = DecryptByKey(EncFirstName),
  MiddleName = DecryptByKey(EncMiddleName),
  LastName = DecryptByKey(EncLastName);

-- Show the results
SELECT BusinessEntityID,
  FirstName,
  MiddleName,
  LastName,
  EncFirstName,
  EncMiddleName,
  EncLastName
FROM #TempNames;

-- Close the symmetric key
CLOSE SYMMETRIC KEY TestSymmetricKey;

-- Drop the symmetric key
DROP SYMMETRIC KEY TestSymmetricKey;

-- Drop the certificate
DROP CERTIFICATE TestCertificate;

--Drop the DMK
DROP MASTER KEY;

--Drop the temp table
DROP TABLE #TempNames;
```

	Busi...	FirstName	MiddleName	LastName	EncFirstName	EncMiddleName	EncLastName
1	1	Ken	J	Sánchez	0x00524377DAF38C468528F0E5D...	0x00524377DAF38C468528F0...	0x00524377DAF38C468528F0E5D521E79701...
2	2	Tem	Lee	Duffy	0x00524377DAF38C468528F0E5D...	0x00524377DAF38C468528F0...	0x00524377DAF38C468528F0E5D521E79701...
3	3	Roberto	NULL	Tamburello	0x00524377DAF38C468528F0E5D...	NULL	0x00524377DAF38C468528F0E5D521E79701...
4	4	Rob	NULL	Walters	0x00524377DAF38C468528F0E5D...	NULL	0x00524377DAF38C468528F0E5D521E79701...
5	5	Gail	A	Erickson	0x00524377DAF38C468528F0E5D...	0x00524377DAF38C468528F0...	0x00524377DAF38C468528F0E5D521E79701...
6	6	Jossef	H	Goldberg	0x00524377DAF38C468528F0E5D...	0x00524377DAF38C468528F0...	0x00524377DAF38C468528F0E5D521E79701...
7	7	Dylan	A	Miller	0x00524377DAF38C468528F0E5D...	0x00524377DAF38C468528F0...	0x00524377DAF38C468528F0E5D521E79701...
8	8	Diane	L	Margheim	0x00524377DAF38C468528F0E5D...	0x00524377DAF38C468528F0...	0x00524377DAF38C468528F0E5D521E79701...
9	9	Gigi	N	Matthew	0x00524377DAF38C468528F0E5D...	0x00524377DAF38C468528F0...	0x00524377DAF38C468528F0E5D521E79701...
10	10	Michael	NULL	Raheem	0x00524377DAF38C468528F0E5D...	NULL	0x00524377DAF38C468528F0E5D521E79701...
11	11	Ovidiu	V	Cracium	0x00524377DAF38C468528F0E5D...	0x00524377DAF38C468528F0...	0x00524377DAF38C468528F0E5D521E79701...
12	12	Thierry	B	D'Hers	0x00524377DAF38C468528F0E5D...	0x00524377DAF38C468528F0...	0x00524377DAF38C468528F0E5D521E79701...
13	13	Janice	M	Galvin	0x00524377DAF38C468528F0E5D...	0x00524377DAF38C468528F0...	0x00524377DAF38C468528F0E5D521E79701...

Figure 7-6. *Symmetric Key Encryption Results (Partial)*

Listing 7-14 first creates a temporary table to hold the encryption and decryption results:

```
-- Create a temporary table to hold results
CREATE TABLE #TempNames
(
BusinessEntityID  int PRIMARY KEY,
FirstName             nvarchar(50),
MiddleName            nvarchar(50),
LastName              nvarchar(50),
EncFirstName          varbinary(200),
EncMiddleName         varbinary(200),
EncLastName       varbinary(200)
);
```

Then a DMK is created to protect the certificate that will be created next. The certificate that's created is then used to encrypt the symmetric key.

```
-- Create DMK
CREATE MASTER KEY
  ENCRYPTION BY PASSWORD = 'Test_P@ssw0rd';

-- Create certificate to protect symmetric key
CREATE CERTIFICATE TestCertificate
  WITH SUBJECT = 'AdventureWorks Test Certificate',
  EXPIRY_DATE = '2026-10-31';

-- Create symmetric key to encrypt data
CREATE SYMMETRIC KEY TestSymmetricKey
  WITH ALGORITHM = AES_128
  ENCRYPTION BY CERTIFICATE TestCertificate;
```

In order to encrypt data with the symmetric key the sample must first execute the OPEN SYMMETRIC KEY statement to open the symmetric key. The DECRYPTION BY clause specifies the method to use to decrypt the symmetric key for use. In this example, the key is protected by certificate, so DECRYPTION BY CERTIFICATE is used. You can specify decryption by certificate, asymmetric key, symmetric key, or password. If the DMK was used to encrypt the certificate or asymmetric key, leave off the WITH PASSWORD clause.

```
-- Open symmetric key
OPEN SYMMETRIC KEY TestSymmetricKey
  DECRYPTION BY CERTIFICATE TestCertificate;
```

The next step is to use the EncryptByKey function to encrypt the data. In this example, the FirstName, MiddleName, and LastName for 100 rows from the Person.Person table are encrypted with EncryptByKey. The EncryptByKey function accepts a clear text char, varchar, binary, varbinary, nchar, or nvarchar constant, column, or T-SQL variable with a maximum length of 8,000 bytes. The result returned is the encrypted data in varbinary format with a maximum length of 8,000 bytes. In addition to clear text, EncryptByKey accepts a GUID identifying the symmetric key you wish to encrypt the clear text with. The KeyGUID function returns a symmetric key's GUID by name.

```
-- Populate temp table with 100 encrypted names from the Person.Person table
INSERT
INTO #TempNames
(
    BusinessEntityID,
EncFirstName,
EncMiddleName,
EncLastName
)

SELECT TOP(100) BusinessEntityID,
    EncryptByKey(Key_GUID(N'TestSymmetricKey'), FirstName),
    EncryptByKey(Key_GUID(N'TestSymmetricKey'), MiddleName),
    EncryptByKey(Key_GUID(N'TestSymmetricKey'), LastName)
FROM Person.Person
ORDER BY BusinessEntityID;
```

The sample code then uses the DecryptByKey function to decrypt the previously encrypted cipher text in the temporary table. SQL Server stores the GUID of the symmetric key used to encrypt the data with the encrypted data, so you don't need to supply the symmetric key GUID to DecryptByKey. In the sample code, the varbinary encrypted cipher text is all that's passed to the EncryptByKey function.

```
-- Update the temp table with decrypted names
UPDATE #TempNames
SET FirstName = DecryptByKey(EncFirstName),
    MiddleName = DecryptByKey(EncMiddleName),
    LastName = DecryptByKey(EncLastName);
```

Finally, the results are shown and the symmetric key is closed with the CLOSE SYMMETRIC KEY statement:

```
-- Show the results
SELECT BusinessEntityID,
 FirstName,
 MiddleName,
 LastName,
 EncFirstName,
 EncMiddleName,
 EncLastName
FROM #TempNames;
```

```
-- Close the symmetric key
CLOSE SYMMETRIC KEY TestSymmetricKey;
```

The balance of the code drops the symmetric key, the certificate, the master key, and the temporary table:

```
-- Drop the symmetric key
DROP SYMMETRIC KEY TestSymmetricKey;

-- Drop the certificate
DROP CERTIFICATE TestCertificate;

-- Drop the DMK
DROP MASTER KEY;

-- Drop the temp table
DROP TABLE #TempNames;
```

■ **Note** You can close a single symmetric key by name or use the CLOSE ALL SYMMETRIC KEYS statement to close all open symmetric keys. Opening and closing symmetric keys affects only the current session on the server. All open symmetric keys available to the current session are automatically closed when the current session ends.

SALT AND AUTHENTICATORS

The *initialization vector (IV)*, or *salt*, is an important aspect of encryption security. The IV is a block of bits that further obfuscates the result of an encryption. The idea is that the IV will help prevent the same data from generating the same cipher text if it is encrypted more than once by the same key and algorithm. SQL Server does not allow you to specify an IV when encrypting data with a symmetric key, however. Instead SQL Server generates a random IV automatically when you encrypt data with block ciphers like AES and DES. The obfuscation provided by the IV helps eliminate patterns from your encrypted datapatterns that cryptanalysts can use to their advantage when attempting to hack your encrypted data. The downside to SQL Server's randomly generated IVs is that they make indexing an encrypted column a true exercise in futility.

In addition to random IV generation, SQL Server's EncryptByKey and DecryptByKey functions provide another tool to help eliminate patterns in encrypted data. Both functions provide two options parameters: an add_authenticator flag and an authenticator value. If the add_authenticator flag is set to 1, SQL Server will derive an authenticator from the authenticator value passed in. The authenticator is then used to obfuscate your encrypted data further, preventing patterns that can reveal information to hackers through correlation analysis attacks. If you supply an authenticator value during encryption, the same authenticator value must be supplied during decryption.

When SQL Server encrypts your data with a symmetric key, it automatically adds metadata to the encrypted result, as well as padding, making the encrypted result larger (sometimes significantly larger) than the unencrypted plain text. The format for the encrypted result with metadata follows the following format:

- The first 16 bytes of the encrypted result represent the GUID of the symmetric key used to encrypt the data.
- The next 4 bytes represent a version number, currently hard-coded as 0x01000000.

- The next 8 bytes for DES encryption (16 bytes for AES encryption) represent the randomly generated IV.

- If an authenticator was used, the next 8 bytes contain header information with an additional 20-byte SHA1 hash of the authenticator, making the header information 28 bytes in length.

- The last part of the encrypted data is the actual padded data itself. For DES algorithms, the length of this encrypted data will be a multiple of 8 bytes. For AES algorithms, the length will be a multiple of 16 bytes.

In addition to DecryptByKey, SQL Server 2012 provides DecryptByKeyAutoCert and DecryptByKeyAutoAsymKey functions. Both functions combine the functionality of the OPEN SYMMETRIC KEY statement with the DecryptByKey function, meaning that you don't need to issue an OPEN SYMMETRIC KEY to decrypt your cipher text. The DecryptByKeyAutoAsymKey function automatically opens an asymmetric key protecting a symmetric key, while DecryptByKeyAutoCert automatically opens a certificate protecting a symmetric key. If a password is used to encrypt your asymmetric key or certificate, that same password must be passed to these functions. If the asymmetric key is encrypted with the DMK, you pass NULL as the password. You can also specify an authenticator with these functions if one was used during encryption. Decryption of data in bulk using these functions might cause a pretty severe performance penalty over using the OPEN SYMMETRIC KEY statement and the DecryptByKey function.

Encryption without Keys

SQL Server 2012 provides additional functions for encryption and decryption without keys, and for one-way hashing which is the concept of inputing a value into the function to get a hash value but not being able to use the hash value to reproduce the input. These functions are named EncryptByPassPhrase, DecryptByPassPhrase, and HashBytes, respectively.

The EncryptByPassPhrase function accepts a *passphrase* and clear text to encrypt. The passphrase is simply a plain text phrase from which SQL Server can derive an encryption key. The idea behind the passphrase is that users are more likely to remember a simple phrase than a complex encryption key. The function derives a temporary encryption key from the passphrase and uses it to encrypt the plain text. You can also pass an optional authenticator value to EncryptByPassPhrase if you wish. EncryptByPassPhrase always uses the triple DES algorithm to encrypt the clear text passed in.

DecryptByPassPhrase decrypts cipher text that was previously encrypted with EncryptByPassPhrase. To decrypt using this function, you must supply the same passphrase and authenticator options that you used when encrypting the clear text.

Hashing Data

The HashBytes function performs a one-way hash on the data passed to it and returns the hash value generated. HashBytes accepts two parameters: a hash algorithm name and the data to hash. The return value is a fixed-length varbinary hash value, which is analogous to a fingerprint for any given data. Table 7-2 lists the SQL Server-supported hash algorithms.

Table 7-2. *SQL Server-Supported Hash Algorithms*

Algorithm	Hash Length
MD2, MD4, MD5	128 bits (16 bytes)
SHA, SHA1	160 bits (20 bytes)

■ **Caution** For highly secure applications, the MD2, MD4, and MD5 series of hashes should be avoided. Cryptanalysts have produced *meaningful hash collisions* with these algorithms over the past few years that have revealed vulnerabilities to hacker attacks. A *hash collision* is a string of bytes that produces a hash value that is identical to another string of bytes. A *meaningful hash* collision is one that can be produced with meaningful (or apparently meaningful) strings of bytes. Generating a hash collision by modifying the content of a certificate would be an example of a meaningful, and dangerous, hash collision.

Listing 7-15 demonstrates the EncryptByPassPhrase, DecryptByPassPhrase, and HashBytes functions. The results are shown in Figure 7-7.

Listing 7-15. Encryption and Decryption by Passphrase and Byte Hashing

```
DECLARE @cleartext nvarchar(256);
DECLARE @encrypted varbinary(512);
DECLARE @decrypted nvarchar(256);

SELECT  @cleartext = N'To be,  or  not  to  be:  that  is  the  question:  '  +
    N'Whether ''tis nobler in the mind to suffer ' +
    N'The slings and arrows of outrageous fortune, ' +
    N'Or  to  take  arms  against  a  sea  of  troubles';

SELECT @encrypted = EncryptByPassPhrase(N'Shakespeare''s Donkey', @cleartext);

SELECT  @decrypted  =  CAST
(
    DecryptByPassPhrase(N'Shakespeare''s Donkey', @encrypted)
        AS  nvarchar(128)
);

SELECT  @cleartext  AS  ClearText;
SELECT  @encrypted  AS  Encrypted;
SELECT  @decrypted  AS  Decrypted;
SELECT  HashBytes  ('SHA1',  @ClearText)  AS  Hashed;
```

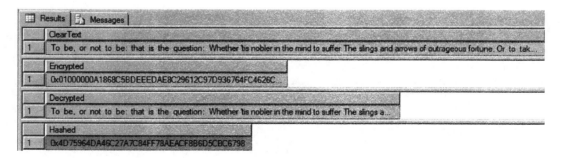

Figure 7-7. *Results of Encryption by Passphrase and Hashing*

Extensible Key Management

SQL Server 2012 contains a feature added in SQL 2008 known as EKM, which allows you to encrypt your SQL Server asymmetric keys (and symmetric keys) with keys generated and stored on a third-party HSM. To use EKM, you must first turn on the EKM provider enabled option with spconfigure, as shown in Listing 7-16.

▧ **Note**   EKM is available only on the Enterprise, Developer, and Evaluation editions of SQL Server 2012, and it requires a third-party HSM and supporting software.

Listing 7-16. Enabling EKM Providers

```
sp_configure 'show advanced', 1;
GO
RECONFIGURE;
GO
sp_configure 'EKM provider enabled', 1;
GO
RECONFIGURE;
GO
```

Once you have enabled EKM providers and have an HSM available, you must register a cryptographic provider with SQL Server. The cryptographic provider references a vendor-supplied DLL file installed on the server. Listing 7-17 gives an example of registering a cryptographic provider with SQL Server.

Listing 7-17. Registering a Cryptographic Provider

```
CREATE CRYPTOGRAPHIC PROVIDER Eagle_EKM_Provider
FROM FILE = 'c:\Program Files\Eagle_EKM\SQLEKM.DLL';
 GO
```

Once your EKM provider is registered with SQL Server, creating an asymmetric key that is encrypted by an existing key on the HSM is simply a matter of specifying the EKM provider, the CREATIONDISPOSITION option, and the name of the key on the EKM device via the PROVIDER_KEY_NAME option. Listing 7-18 gives an example.

Listing 7-18. Creating an Asymmetric Key with HSM Protection

```
CREATE ASYMMETRIC KEY AsymKeyEKMProtected
  FROM PROVIDER Eagle_EKM_Provider
  WITH PROVIDER_KEY_NAME = 'EKM_Key_1',
    CREATION_DISPOSITION = OPEN_EXISTING;
GO
```

EKM is designed to support enterprise-level encryption key management by providing additional encryption key security. It provides this additional security by physically separating the encryption keys from the data they encrypt. In addition to external storage of encryption keys, HSM vendors can also provide hardware-based bulk encryption and decryption functionality and external support for additional encryption options beyond what is supported natively by SQL Server 2012. Some of the additional options provided by HSM vendors include key aging and key rotation functionality.

Transparent Data Encryption

Up to this point, we've talked about the column-level encryption functionality available in SQL Server 2012. These functions are specifically designed to encrypt data stored in the columns of your database tables. SQL Server 2012 provides a method of encryption, TDE, which allows you to encrypt your entire database at once.

TDE automatically encrypts every page in your database and decrypts pages as required when you access them. This feature allows you to secure an entire database without worrying about all those little details that pop up when encrypting at the column level. TDE does not require extra storage space, and it allows the query optimizer to generate far more efficient query plans than it can when you search on encrypted columns. As an added bonus, TDE is easy to implement and allows you to secure the data in your databases with no changes to middle-tier or front-end code.

The first step to implement TDE in your database is to create a *server certificate* (see Listing 7-19). A server certificate is simply a certificate created in the master database for the purpose of encrypting databases with TDE.

Listing 7-19. Creating a Server Certificate

```
CREATE CERTIFICATE ServerCert
  WITH SUBJECT = 'Server Certificate for TDE',
  EXPIRY_DATE = '2022-12-31';
GO
```

■ **Tip** Remember to back up your server certificate immediately after you create it!

Once you've created a server certificate, you can create a database encryption key in the database to be encrypted (see Listing 7-20). The database encryption key is created with the CREATE DATABASE ENCRYPTION KEY statement. Using this statement, you can create a key using one of the four different algorithms listed in Table 7-3.

Table 7-3. *Database Encryption Key Algorithms*

Algorithm	Description
AES_128	AES, 127-bit key
AES_192	AES, 192-bit key
AES_256	AES, 256-bit key
TRIPLE_DES_3KEY	Three-key triple-DES, ~112-bit effective key

Listing 7-20. Creating a Database Encryption Key and Securing the Database

```
USE AdventureWorks2012;
GO

CREATE DATABASE ENCRYPTION KEY
  WITH ALGORITHM = AES_128
  ENCRYPTION BY SERVER CERTIFICATE ServerCert;
GO
```

```
ALTER DATABASE AdventureWorks2012
SET ENCRYPTION ON;

GO
```

The obvious question at this point is, since TDE is so simple and secure, why not use it all the time? Well, the simplicity and security of TDE comes at a cost. When you encrypt a database with TDE, SQL Server also encrypts the database log file and the `tempdb` database. This is done to prevent leaked data that a hacker with the right tools might be able to access. Because `tempdb` is encrypted, the performance of every database on the same server takes a hit. Also, SQL Server incurs additional CPU overhead since it has to decrypt noncached data pages that are accessed by queries.

Summary

Back in the days of SQL Server 2000, database encryption functionality could be achieved only through third-party tools or by creating your own encryption and decryption functions. SQL Server 2012 continues the tradition of T-SQL column-level encryption and decryption functionality introduced in SQL Server 2005. The tight integration of Windows DPAPI encryption functionality with native T-SQL statements and functions makes database encryption easier and more secure than ever.

SQL Server 2012 also introduces new functionality, including TDE for quickly and easily encrypting entire databases transparently, and EKM for providing access to third-party HSMs to implement enterprise-level security solutions and bulk encryption functionality.

In this chapter, we discussed the SQL Server hierarchical encryption model, which defines the relationship between SMKs, DMKs, certificates, asymmetric keys, and symmetric keys. SQL Server provides a variety of T-SQL statements to create and manage encryption keys and certificates, which we demonstrated in code samples throughout the chapter. SQL Server also provides several functions for generating one-way hashes, generating data signatures, and encrypting data by certificate, asymmetric key, symmetric key, and passphrase.

In the next chapter, we'll cover the topics of SQL windowing functions and common table expressions (CTEs).

EXERCISES

1. [True/False] Symmetric keys can be used to encrypt other symmetric keys or data.

2. [Choose all that apply] SQL Server provides native support for which of the following built-in encryption algorithms?

    a. DES

    b. AES

    c. Loki

    d. Blowfish

    e. RC4

3. [True/False] SQL Server 2012 T-SQL includes a BACKUP ASYMMETRIC KEY statement.

4. [Fill in the blank] You must set the _____ option to turn on EKM for your server.

5. [True/False] TDE automatically encrypts the `tempdb`, `model`, and `master` databases.

6. [True/False] SQL Server automatically generates random initialization vectors when you use symmetric encryption.

CHAPTER 8

Common Table Expressions and Windowing Functions

SQL Server 2012 continues support for the extremely useful common table expression (CTE), first introduced in SQL Server 2005. CTEs can simplify your queries to make them more readable and maintainable. SQL Server also supports self-referential CTEs, which make for very powerful recursive queries.

In addition, SQL Server supports windowing functions, which allow you to partition your results and apply numbering and ranking values to the rows in the result set partitions. This chapter begins with a discussion of the power and benefits of CTEs and finishes with a discussion of SQL Server windowing functions.

Common Table Expressions

CTEs are a powerful addition to SQL Server. A CTE is more like temporary table that generates a named result set that exists only during the life of a single query or DML statement or until they are explicitly dropped. A CTE is built in the same code line as the SELECT statement or the DML statement that uses it, whereas creating and using a temporary table is usually a two-step process. CTEs offer several benefits over derived tables and views, including the following:

- CTEs are transient, existing only for the life of a single query or DML statement. This means that you don't have create them as permanent database objects like views.

- A single CTE can be referenced multiple times by name in a single query or DML statement, making your code more manageable. Derived tables have to be rewritten in their entirety every place they are referenced.

- CTEs can be used to enable grouping by columns that are derived from a scalar subset or a function that is not deterministic.

- CTEs can be self-referencing, providing a powerful recursion mechanism.

- Queries referencing a CTE can be used to define a cursor.

CTEs can range in complexity from extremely simple to highly elaborate constructs. All CTEs begin with the WITH keyword followed by the name of the CTE and a list of the columns it returns. This is followed by the AS keyword and the body of the CTE which is the associated query or DML statement with semicolon as terminator for multistatement batch. Listing 8-1 is a very simple example of a CTE designed to show the basic syntax.

Listing 8-1. Simple CTE

```
WITH GetNamesCTE (
BusinessEntityID,
FirstName,
MiddleName,
LastName )
AS (
SELECT
BusinessEntityID, FirstName, MiddleName, LastName
FROM Person.Person ) SELECT
BusinessEntityID,
FirstName,
MiddleName,
LastName FROM GetNamesCTE
;
```

In Listing 8-1, the CTE is defined with the name GetNamesCTE and returns columns named BusinessEntityID, FirstName, MiddleName, and LastName. The CTE body consists of a simple SELECT statement from the AdventureWorks 2012 Person.Person table. The CTE has an associated SELECT statement immediately following it. The SELECT statement references the CTE in its FROM clause.

WITH OVERLOADED

The WITH keyword is *overloaded* in SQL Server, meaning that it's used in many different ways for many different purposes in T-SQL. It's used to specify additional options in DDL CREATE statements, to add table hints to queries and DML statements, and to declare XML namespaces when used in the WITH XMLNAMESPACES clause, just to name a few. Now it's also used as the keyword that indicates the beginning of a CTE definition. Because of this, whenever a CTE is not the first statement in a batch, the statement preceding it must end with a semicolon. This is one reason why we strongly recommend using the statement-terminating semicolon throughout your code.

Simple CTEs have some restrictions on their definition and declaration:

- A CTE must be followed by single INSERT, DELETE, UPDATE or SELECT statement.

- All columns returned by a CTE must have a unique name. If all of the columns returned by the query in the CTE body have unique names, you can leave the column list out of the CTE declaration.

- A CTE can reference other previously defined CTEs in the same WITH clause, but cannot reference CTEs defined after the current CTE (known as *a forward reference*).

- You cannot use the following keywords, clauses, and options within a CTE: COMPUTE, COMPUTE BY, FOR BROWSE, INTO, and OPTION (query hint). Also, you cannot use ORDER BY unless you specify the TOP clause.

- Multiple CTEs can be defined in a nonrecursive CTE and all the definitions must be combined by one these set operators: UNION ALL, UNION, INTERSECT or EXCEPT

- As we mentioned in the "WITH Overloaded" sidebar, when a CTE is not the first statement in a batch, the preceding statement must end with a semicolon statement terminator.

Keep these restrictions in mind when you create CTEs.

Multiple Common Table Expressions

You can define multiple CTEs for a single query or DML statement by separating your CTE definitions with commas. The main reason for doing this is to simplify your code to make it easier to read and manage. CTEs provide a means of visually splitting your code into smaller functional blocks, making it easier to develop and debug. Listing 8-2 demonstrates a query with multiple CTEs, with the second CTE referencing the first. Results are shown in Figure 8-1.

Listing 8-2. Multiple CTEs

```
WITH GetNamesCTE (
BusinessEntityID,
FirstName,
MiddleName,
LastName )
AS (
SELECT
BusinessEntityID, FirstName, MiddleName, LastName
FROM Person.Person ),
GetContactCTE (
BusinessEntityID,
FirstName,

MiddleName, LastName, Email, HomePhoneNumber
)
AS ( SELECT gn.BusinessEntityID, gn.FirstName, gn.MiddleName, gn.LastName, ea.EmailAddress,
pp.PhoneNumber FROM GetNamesCTE gn LEFT JOIN Person.EmailAddress ea
ON gn.BusinessEntityID = ea.BusinessEntityID LEFT JOIN Person.PersonPhone pp ON
gn.BusinessEntityID = pp.BusinessEntityID AND pp.PhoneNumberTypeID = 2 )
SELECT BusinessEntityID, FirstName, MiddleName, LastName, Email,
HomePhoneNumber FROM GetContactCTE;
```

	BusinessEntityID	FirstName	MiddleName	LastName	Email	HomePhoneNumber
135	7458	Ana	R	Alexander	ana17@adventure-works.com	1 (11) 500 555-0181
136	7678	Angela	NULL	Alexander	angela21@adventure-works.com	NULL
137	7161	Angelica	NULL	Alexander	angelica18@adventure-works.com	214-555-0150
138	3683	Anna	NULL	Alexander	anna44@adventure-works.com	150-555-0156
139	13220	Antonio	NULL	Alexander	antonio19@adventure-works.com	NULL
140	7719	Arianna	NULL	Alexander	arianna17@adventure-works.com	140-555-0167
141	12597	Ashley	J	Alexander	ashley46@adventure-works.com	NULL
142	6266	Austin	NULL	Alexander	austin15@adventure-works.com	1 (11) 500 555-0140
143	6726	Benjamin	A	Alexander	benjamin20@adventure-works.com	240-555-0151
144	6919	Brandon	NULL	Alexander	brandon16@adventure-works.com	780-555-0152
145	19276	Brianna	NULL	Alexander	brianna64@adventure-works.com	242-555-0137
146	7210	Brittany	NULL	Alexander	brittany17@adventure-works.com	804-555-0125
147	5561	Caleb	NULL	Alexander	caleb15@adventure-works.com	670-555-0141
148	6315	Cameron	NULL	Alexander	cameron14@adventure-works.com	399-555-0196
149	6800	Caroline	NULL	Alexander	caroline20@adventure-works.com	NULL

Figure 8-1. *Partial results of a query with multiple CTEs*

CTE READABILITY BENEFITS

You can use CTEs to make your queries more readable than equivalent query designs that utilize nested subqueries. To demonstrate, the following query uses nested subqueries to return the same result as the CTE-based query in Listing 8-2.

```
SELECT
    gn.BusinessEntityID,
    gn.FirstName,
    gn.MiddleName,
    gn.LastName,
    gn.EmailAddress,
    gn.HomePhoneNumber
FROM
(
    SELECT
        p.BusinessEntityID,
        p.FirstName,
        p.MiddleName,
        p.LastName,
        ea.EmailAddress,
        ea.HomePhoneNumber

    FROM Person.Person p
    LEFT JOIN
    (
        SELECT
        ea.BusinessEntityID,
        ea.EmailAddress,
        pp.HomePhoneNumber
        FROM Person.EmailAddress ea
        LEFT JOIN
        (
        SELECT
        pp.BusinessEntityID,
        pp.PhoneNumber  AS  HomePhoneNumber,
        pp.PhoneNumberTypeID
        FROM  Person.PersonPhone  pp
        ) pp
        ON  ea.BusinessEntityID  =  pp.BusinessEntityID
        AND pp.PhoneNumberTypeID = 2
    ) ea
    ON  p.BusinessEntityID  =  ea.BusinessEntityID
) gn
```

The CTE-based version of the above query as shown in Listing 8-2 simplifies the code, encapsulates the query logic and is much easier to read and understand than the nested subquery version, which makes it easier to debug and maintain in the long term.

The sample in Listing 8-2 contains two CTEs, named GetNamesCTE and GetContactCTE. The GetNamesCTE is borrowed from Listing 8-1; it simply retrieves the names from the Person.Person table.

```
WITH GetNamesCTE ( BusinessEntityID, FirstName, MiddleName, LastName )
AS ( SELECT
BusinessEntityID, FirstName, MiddleName, LastName FROM Person.Person )
```

The second CTE, GetContactCTE, joins the results of GetNamesCTE to the Person.EmailAddress table and the Person.PersonPhone tables:

```
GetContactCTE (BusinessEntityID, FirstName, MiddleName, LastName, Email,
HomePhoneNumber )
AS ( SELECT gn. BusinessEntityID, gn.FirstName, gn.MiddleName, gn.LastName, ea.EmailAddress,
pp.PhoneNumber FROM GetNamesCTE gn LEFT JOIN Person.EmailAddress ea
ON gn. BusinessEntityID = ea. BusinessEntityID LEFT JOIN Person.PersonPhone pp ON gn.
BusinessEntityID = pp. BusinessEntityID AND pp.PhoneNumberTypeID = 2 )
```

Notice that the WITH keyword is only used once at the beginning of the entire statement. The second CTE declaration is separated from the first by a comma, and does not accept the WITH keyword. Finally, notice how simple and readable the SELECT query associated with the CTEs becomes when the joins are moved into CTEs.

```
SELECT
BusinessEntityID,
FirstName,
MiddleName,
LastName,
EmailAddress,
HomePhoneNumber FROM GetContactCTE;
```

■ **Tip** You can reference a CTE from within the body of another CTE or from the associated query or DML statement. Both types of CTE references are shown in Listing 8-2—the GetNamesCTE is referenced by the GetContactCTE and the GetContactCTE is referenced in the query associated with the CTEs.

Recursive Common Table Expressions

A recursive CTE is the one where the initial CTE is executed repeatedly to return the subset of the data until the complete resultset is returened. CTEs can reference themselves in the body of the CTE, is a powerful feature for querying hierarchical data stored in the adjacency list model. Recursive CTEs are similar to nonrecursive CTEs, except that the body of the CTE consists of multiple sets of queries that generate result sets with multiple rows unioned together with the UNION ALL set operator. At least one of the queries in the body of the recursive CTE must not reference the CTE; this query is known as the *anchor query*. Recursive CTEs also contain one or more *recursive queries* that reference the CTE. These recursive queries are unioned together with the anchor query (or queries) in the body of the CTE. Recursive CTEs require a top-level UNION ALL operator to union the recursive and nonrecursive queries together. Multiple anchor queries may be unioned together with INTERSECT, EXCEPT, or UNION operators, while multiple recursive queries can be unioned together with UNION ALL. The recursion stops when there are no rows returned from the previous query. Listing 8-3 is a simple recursive CTE that retrieves a result set consisting of the numbers 1 through 10.

Listing 8-3. Simple Recursive CTE

```
WITH Numbers (n) AS ( SELECT 1 AS n
UNION ALL
```

```
SELECT n + 1 FROM Numbers WHERE n < 10 )
```

```
SELECT n FROM Numbers;
```

The CTE in Listing 8-3 begins with a declaration that defines the CTE name and the column returned:

```
WITH Numbers (n)
```

The CTE body contains a single anchor query that returns a single row with the number 1 in the n column:

```
SELECT 1 AS n
```

The anchor query is unioned together with the recursive query by the UNION ALL set operator. The recursive query contains a self-reference to the Numbers CTE, adding 1 to the n column with each recursive reference. The WHERE clause limits the resultset to the first 10 numbers.

```
SELECT n + 1 FROM Numbers WHERE n < 10
```

Recursive CTEs have a maximum recursion level of 100 by default. This means that the recursive query in the CTE body can only call itself 100 times. You can use the MAXRECURSION option to increase the maximum recursion level of CTEs on an individual basis. Listing 8-4 modifies the CTE in Listing 8-3 to return the numbers 1 to 1000. The modified query uses the MAXRECURSION option to increase the maximum recursion level. Without the MAXRECURSION option, this CTE would error out after the first 100 levels of recursion.

Listing 8-4. Recursive CTE with MAXRECURSION Option

```
WITH Numbers (n) AS ( SELECT 0 AS n
UNION ALL
SELECT n + 1
FROM Numbers
WHERE n < 1000 )
SELECT n FROM Numbers OPTION (MAXRECURSION 1000);
```

The MAXRECURSION value specified must be between 0 and 32767. SQL Server throws an exception if the MAXRECURSION limit is surpassed. A MAXRECURSION value of 0 indicates that no limit should be placed on recursion for the CTE. Be careful with this option—if you don't properly limit the results in the query with a WHERE clause, you can easily end up in an infinite loop.

■ **Tip** Creating a permanent table of counting numbers can be more efficient than using a recursive CTE to generate numbers, particularly if you plan to execute the CTEs that generate numbers often.

Recursive CTEs are useful for querying data stored in a hierarchical adjacency list format. The adjacency list provides a model for storing hierarchical data in relational databases. In the adjacency list model, each row of the table contains a pointer to its parent in the hierarchy. The Production.BillOfMaterials table in the AdventureWorks database is a practical example of the adjacency list model. This table contains two important columns, ComponentID and ProductAssemblyID that reflect the hierarchical structure. The ComponentID is a unique number identifying every component that AdventureWorks uses to manufacture their products. The ProductAssemblyID is a parent component created from one or more AdventureWorks product components. Figure 8-2 demonstrates the relationship between components and product assemblies in the AdventureWorks database.

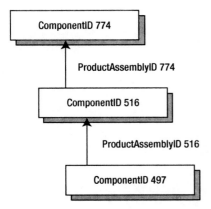

Figure 8-2. *Component/product assembly relationship*

The recursive CTE shown in Listing 8-5 retrieves the complete AdventureWorks hierarchical bill of materials (BOM) for a specified component. The component used in the example is the AdventureWorks silver Mountain-100 48-inch bike, ComponentID 774. Partial results are shown in Figure 8-3.

Listing 8-5. Recursive BOM CTE

```
DECLARE @ComponentID int = 774;

WITH  BillOfMaterialsCTE
(
    BillOfMaterialsID,
    ProductAssemblyID,
    ComponentID,
    Quantity,
    Level
)
AS
(
        SELECT
        bom.BillOfMaterialsID,
        bom.ProductAssemblyID,
        bom.ComponentID,
        bom.PerAssemblyQty  AS  Quantity,
        0  AS  Level
        FROM Production.BillOfMaterials bom
        WHERE bom.ComponentID = @ComponentID

        UNION ALL

        SELECT
        bom.BillOfMaterialsID,
        bom.ProductAssemblyID,
        bom.ComponentID,
        bom.PerAssemblyQty,
        Level + 1
        FROM Production.BillOfMaterials bom
```

```
        INNER JOIN BillOfMaterialsCTE bomcte
        ON  bom.ProductAssemblyID  =  bomcte.ComponentID
        WHERE bom.EndDate IS NULL
)
SELECT
    bomcte.ProductAssemblyID,
    p.ProductID,
    p.ProductNumber,
    p.Name,
    p.Color,
    bomcte.Quantity,
    bomcte.Level
FROM  BillOfMaterialsCTE bomcte
INNER  JOIN  Production.Product  p
    ON bomcte.ComponentID = p.ProductID
order by bomcte.Level;
```

	ProductAssemblyID	ProductID	ProductNumber	Name	Color	Quantity	Level
1	NULL	774	BK-M82S-48	Mountain-100 Silver, 48	Silver	1.00	0
2	774	518	SA-M687	HL Mountain Seat Assembly	NULL	1.00	1
3	774	741	FR-M94S-52	HL Mountain Frame - Silver, 48	Silver	1.00	1
4	774	807	HS-3479	HL Headset	NULL	1.00	1
5	774	810	HB-M918	HL Mountain Handlebars	NULL	1.00	1
6	774	817	FW-M928	HL Mountain Front Wheel	Black	1.00	1
7	774	825	RW-M928	HL Mountain Rear Wheel	Black	1.00	1
8	774	894	RD-2308	Rear Derailleur	Silver	1.00	1
9	774	907	RB-9231	Rear Brakes	Silver	1.00	1
10	774	937	PD-M562	HL Mountain Pedal	Silv...	1.00	1
11	774	945	FD-2342	Front Derailleur	Silver	1.00	1
12	774	948	FB-9873	Front Brakes	Silver	1.00	1
13	774	951	CS-9183	HL Crankset	Black	1.00	1
14	774	952	CH-0234	Chain	Silver	1.00	1
15	774	998	BB-8108	HL Bottom Bracket	NULL	1.00	1
16	998	3	BE-2349	BB Ball Bearing	NULL	10.00	2
17	998	526	SH-9312	HL Shell	NULL	1.00	2

Figure 8-3. *Partial results of the recursive BOM CTE*

Like the previous CTE examples, Listing 8-3 begins with the CTE name and column list declaration.

```
WITH BillOfMaterialsCTE
(
BillOfMaterialsID, ProductAssemblyID, Components, Quantity, Level )
```

The anchor query simply retrieves the row from the table where the ComponentID matches the specified ID. This is the top-level component in the BOM, set to 774 in the example. Notice that the CTE can reference T-SQL variables like @ComponentID in the example.

```
SELECT
bom.BillOfMaterialsID,
bom.ProductAssemblyID,
```

```
bom.Components,
bom.PerAssemblyQty AS Quantity,
0 AS Level FROM Production.BillOfMaterials bom WHERE bom.ComponentID = @ComponentID
```

The recursive query retrieves successive levels of the BOM from the CTE where the ProductAssemblyID of each row matches the ComponentID of the higher-level rows. That is to say, the recursive query of the CTE retrieves lower-level rows in the hierarchy that match the hierarchical relationship previously illustrated in Figure 8-2.

```
SELECT
bom.BillOfMaterialsID,
bom.ProductAssemblyID,
bom.ComponentID,
bom.PerAssemblyQty,
Level + 1 FROM Production.BillOfMaterials bom INNER JOIN BillOfMaterialsCTE bomcte
ON bom.ProductAssemblyID = bomcte.ComponentID WHERE bom.EndDate IS NULL
```

The CTE has a SELECT statement associated with it that joins the results to the Production. Product table to retrieve product-specific information like the name and color of the component:

```
SELECT
bomcte.ProductAssemblyID,
p.ProductID,
p.ProductNumber,
p.Name,
p.Color,
bomcte.Quantity,
bomcte.Level FROM BillOfMaterialsCTE bomcte INNER JOIN Production.Product p
ON bomcte.ComponentID = p.ProductID;
```

The restrictions on simple CTEs that I described earlier in this chapter also apply to recursive CTEs. In addition, the following restrictions apply specifically to recursive CTEs:

- Recursive CTEs must have at least one anchor query and at least one recursive query specified in the body of the CTE. All anchor queries must appear before any recursive queries.

- All anchor queries must be unioned with the set operators UNION, UNION ALL, INTERSECT, or EXCEPT. When using multiple anchor queries and recursive queries, the last anchor query and the first recursive query must be unioned together with the UNION ALL operator. Additionally, all recursive queries must be unioned together with UNION ALL.

- The data types of all columns in the anchor queries and recursive queries must match.

- The from clause of the recursive member should refer to the CTE name only once.

- The recursive queries cannot contain the following operators and keywords: GROUP BY, HAVING, LEFT JOIN, RIGHT JOIN, OUTER JOIN, and SELECT DISTINCT. Recursive queries also cannot contain aggregate functions (like SUM and MAX), windowing functions, sub-queries, or hints on the recursive CTE reference.

Window Functions

SQL Server 2012 supports windowing functions that partition results and can apply numbering, ranking, and aggregate functions to each partition. The key to windowing functions is the OVER clause, which allows you to define the partitions, and in some cases the ordering of rows in the partition, for your data. In this section, we'll discuss SQL Server 2012 windowing functions and the numbering, ranking, and aggregate functions that support the OVER clause.

ROW_NUMBER Function

The ROW_NUMBER function takes the OVER clause with an ORDER BY clause and an optional PARTITION BY clause. Listing 8-6 retrieves names from the Person.Person table. The OVER clause is used to partition the rows by LastName and order the rows in each partition by LastName, FirstName, and MiddleName. The ROW_NUMBER function is used to assign a number to each row.

Listing 8-6. ROW_NUMBER with Partitioning

```
SELECT
    ROW_NUMBER() OVER
    (
        PARTITION BY
        LastName
        ORDER BY
        LastName,
        FirstName,
        MiddleName
    ) AS  Number,
    LastName,
    FirstName,
    MiddleName
FROM Person.Person;
```

The partition created in Listing 8-6 acts as a window that slides over your result set (hence the name "windowing function"). The ORDER BY clause orders the rows of each partition by LastName, FirstName, and MiddleName. SQL Server applies the ROW_NUMBER function to each partition. The net result is that the ROWNUMBER function numbers all rows in the result set, restarting the numbering at 1 every time it encounters a new LastName, as shown in Figure 8-4.

■ **Note**   When PARTITION BY is used, it must appear before ORDER BY inside of the OVER clause.

	Number	LastName	FirstName	MiddleName
1	1	Abbas	Syed	E
2	1	Abel	Catherine	R.
3	1	Abercrombie	Kim	NULL
4	2	Abercrombie	Kim	NULL
5	3	Abercrombie	Kim	B
6	1	Abolrous	Hazem	E
7	2	Abolrous	Sam	NULL
8	1	Acevedo	Humberto	NULL
9	1	Achong	Gustavo	NULL
10	1	Ackerman	Pilar	NULL
11	2	Ackerman	Pilar	G
12	1	Adams	Aaron	B
13	2	Adams	Adam	NULL
14	3	Adams	Alex	C
15	4	Adams	Alexandra	J

Figure 8-4. Using ROW_NUMBER to number rows in partitions

The ROW_NUMBER function can also be used without the PARTITION BY clause, in which case the entire result set is treated as one partition. Treating the entire result set as a single patition can be useful in some cases, but it is more common to partition.

Query Paging with OFFSET/FETCH

SQL Server gives you various options for paging through result sets. The traditional way of paginating is to use the TOP operator to select the TOP n number of rows returned by the query. SQL Server 2005 introduced ROW_NUMBER, which you can use to achieve the same functionality, but in a slightly different manner. SQL Server 2012 takes things to their logical conclusion and introduces new keywords in the SELECT statement specifically in support of query pagination.

SQL Server 2012's OFFSET keyword provides support for much easier pagination. It essentially allows you to specify from which row you want to start returning the data. FETCH then allows you to return a specified number of rows in the resultset. If you combine both OFFSET and FETCH, along with the ORDER BY clause, you can return any part of the data from within the resultset that you like, paging through the data as desired.

Listing 8-7 shows the approach to pagination using OFFSET and FETCH. The stored procedure uses the OFFSET and FETCH clause to retrieve the rows from the Person.Person table in the Adventureworks database based on input parameter values specified in the procedure call. The procedure determines how the pagination is determined by input parameters, @RowsPerPage and @StartPageNum. @RowsPerPage determines how many rows should be included in the resultset per page and @StartPageNum determines which page should the result set be returned for. OFFSET specifies the number of rows to skip from the beginning of the possible query result. FETCH specifies the number of rows to return in each query page.

Listing 8-7. OFFSET/FETCH Example

```
CREATE  PROCEDURE  Person.GetContacts
        @StartPageNum int,
        @RowsPerPage int
```

```
AS
        SELECT
                LastName,
                FirstName,
                MiddleName
        FROM Person.Person
        ORDER BY
                LastName,
                FirstName,
                MiddleName
        OFFSET (@StartPageNum - 1) * @RowsPerPage ROWS
        FETCH NEXT @RowsPerPage ROWS ONLY;
GO
```

The sample procedure call that uses the OFFSET/FETCH clause EXEC Person.GetContacts 16,10 passes an @RowsPerPage parameter value of 10 and an @StartPageNum parameter value of 16 to the procedure and returns the ten rows for the 16th page, as shown in Figure 8-5. The OFFSET keyword in the above select statement skips the rows before the page number specified in the input parameters @StartPageNum and @RowsPerPage. In this example, we are skipping 150 rows and we are starting to return the results from 151st row. FETCH keyword returns the number of rows specified by the @RowsPerPage parameter, which is 10 rows. The query plan is shown in Figure 8-6.

	LastName	FirstName	MiddleName
1	Alexander	Cassidy	NULL
2	Alexander	Chloe	NULL
3	Alexander	Christian	C
4	Alexander	Connor	G
5	Alexander	Dakota	NULL
6	Alexander	Dalton	NULL
7	Alexander	David	NULL
8	Alexander	Destiny	NULL
9	Alexander	Devin	NULL
10	Alexander	Dylan	NULL

Figure 8-5. *Using OFFSET and FETCH to implement client-side paging*

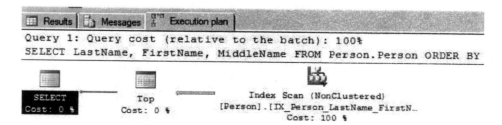

Figure 8-6. *Query plan for the client-side paging implemetnation using OFFSET and FETCH*

The query in Listing 8-7 is a much more readable and elegant solution for query pagination, than using the Top clause or ROW_NUMBER function with CTEs. The only exception would be if you are using OFFSET/FETCH and want to retrieve ROW_NUMBER, you would have to add ROW_NUMBER function to your query. Thus the OFFSET/FETCH clause provides a much cleaner way to implement ad-hoc pagination.

There are some restrictions though. Keep the following in mind when using OFFSET and FETCH:

- OFFSET and FETCH must be used with an ORDER BY clause.

- FETCH cannot be used without OFFSET; however OFFSET can be used without FETCH.

- Number of rows specified using OFFSET clause must be greater than or equal to 0.

- Number of rows specified by FETCH clause must be greater than or equal to 1.

- Queries that use OFFSET and FETCH cannot use the TOP operator.

- The OFFSET/FETCH values must be constants, or they must be parameters having integer values

- OFFSET and FETCH is not supported with OVER clause.

- OFFSET/FETCH is not supported with indexed views or the views WITH CHECK OPTION

In general, if operating under SQL Server 2012, the combination of OFFSET and FETCH provides for the cleanest appoach to paginating through query results.

The RANK and DENSE_RANK Functions

The RANK and DENSE_RANK functions are SQL Server's ranking functions. They both assign a numeric rank value to each row in a partition, however the difference lies in how ties are dealt with. For example:

- If you have three values 7, 7, and 9, then RANK wil assign ranks as 1, 1, and 3. That's because the two 7s are tied for first place, whereas the 9 is third in the list. RANK does not respect the earlier tie when computing the rank for the value 9.

- But DENSE_RANK will assign rans 1, 1, and 2. That's because DENSE_RANK lumps both 7s together in rank 1, and does not count them separately when computing the rank for the value 9.

There's no right or wrong way to rank your data absent any business requirements. SQL Server provides for two options and you can choose the one that fits your business need.

Suppose you want to figure out AdventureWorks best one-day sales dates for the calendar year 2006. This scenario might be phrased with a business question like "What were the best one-day sales days in 2006?" RANK can easily give you that information, as shown in Listing 8-8. Partial results are shown in Figure 8-7.

Listing 8-8. Ranking AdventureWorks Daily Sales Totals

```
WITH TotalSalesBySalesDate
(
    DailySales,
    OrderDate
)
AS
(
    SELECT
        SUM(soh.SubTotal) AS DailySales,
        soh.OrderDate
```

```
        FROM  Sales.SalesOrderHeader  soh
        WHERE soh.OrderDate >= '20060101'
            AND soh.OrderDate < '20070101'
        GROUP BY soh.OrderDate
)
SELECT
    RANK() OVER
    (
        ORDER BY
        DailySales  DESC
    ) AS  Ranking,
    DailySales,
    OrderDate
FROM  TotalSalesBySalesDate
ORDER  BY  Ranking;
```

	Ranking	DailySales	OrderDate
1	1	3617451.9232	2006-08-01 00:00:00.000
2	2	3064632.131	2006-11-01 00:00:00.000
3	3	2888213.6087	2006-09-01 00:00:00.000
4	4	2408187.2542	2006-07-01 00:00:00.000
5	5	2306297.6081	2006-05-01 00:00:00.000
6	6	2205251.3127	2006-12-01 00:00:00.000
7	7	1919379.3786	2006-02-01 00:00:00.000
8	8	1815297.7111	2006-10-01 00:00:00.000
9	9	1473667.5818	2006-03-01 00:00:00.000
10	10	1016116.847	2006-06-01 00:00:00.000

Figure 8-7. *Ranking AdventureWorks daily sales totals*

Listing 8-8 is a CTE that returns two columns, DailySales and OrderDate. The DailySales is the sum of all sales grouped by OrderDate. The results are limited by the WHERE clause to include only sales in the 2006 sales year.

```
WITH  TotalSalesBySalesDate
(
    DailySales,
    OrderDate
)
AS
(
    SELECT
        SUM(soh.SubTotal) AS DailySales,
        soh.OrderDate
    FROM  Sales.SalesOrderHeader  soh
    WHERE soh.OrderDate >= '20060101'
        AND soh.OrderDate < '20070101'
    GROUP BY soh.OrderDate
)
```

The RANK function is used with the OVER clause to apply ranking values to the rows returned by the CTE in descending order (highest to lowest) by the DailySales column:

```
SELECT
RANK() OVER ( ORDER BY
DailySales DESC ) AS Ranking, DailySales, OrderDate

FROM TotalSalesBySalesDate ORDER BY Ranking;
```

Like the ROW_NUMBER function, RANK can accept the PARTITION BY clause in the OVER clause. Listing 8-9 builds on the previous example and uses the PARTITION BY clause to rank the daily sales for each month. This type of query can answer a business question like "What were AdventureWorks's best one-day sales days for each month of 2005?" Partial results are shown in Figure 8-8.

Listing 8-9. Determining the daily sales rankings partitioned by month

```
WITH TotalSalesBySalesDatePartitioned
(
    DailySales,
    OrderMonth,
    OrderDate
)
AS
(
    SELECT
        SUM(soh.SubTotal) AS DailySales,
        DATENAME(MONTH, soh.OrderDate) AS OrderMonth,
        soh.OrderDate
    FROM  Sales.SalesOrderHeader  soh
    WHERE soh.OrderDate >= '20050101'
        AND soh.OrderDate < '20060101'
    GROUP BY soh.OrderDate
)
SELECT
    RANK() OVER
    (
        PARTITION BY
        OrderMonth
        ORDER BY
        DailySales  DESC
    ) AS  Ranking,
    DailySales,
    OrderMonth,
    OrderDate
FROM TotalSalesBySalesDatePartitioned
ORDER BY DATEPART(mm,OrderDate),
    Ranking;
```

	Ranking	DailySales	OrderMonth	OrderDate
1	1	503805.9169	July	2005-07-01 00:00:00.000
2	2	38241.29	July	2005-07-22 00:00:00.000
3	3	28041.32	July	2005-07-27 00:00:00.000
4	4	25568.7082	July	2005-07-19 00:00:00.000
5	5	25047.89	July	2005-07-14 00:00:00.000
6	6	20909.78	July	2005-07-09 00:00:00.000
7	7	19785.3646	July	2005-07-28 00:00:00.000
8	8	17688.07	July	2005-07-29 00:00:00.000
9	9	17534.79	July	2005-07-26 00:00:00.000
10	10	15012.1782	July	2005-07-03 00:00:00.000
11	10	15012.1782	July	2005-07-05 00:00:00.000
12	10	15012.1782	July	2005-07-31 00:00:00.000
13	10	15012.1782	July	2005-07-23 00:00:00.000
14	14	14402.3382	July	2005-07-30 00:00:00.000
15	15	14313.08	July	2005-07-16 00:00:00.000

Figure 8-8. *Partial results of daily sales rankings, partitioned by month*

The query in Listing 8-9, like the previous example shown in Listing 8-8, begins with a CTE to calculate one-day sales totals for the year and the results are shown in Figure 8-9. The main differences between this CTE and the previous example are that Listing 8-9 returns an additional OrderMonth column and the results are limited to the year 2005. Here is that CTE:

	Ranking	DailySales	OrderMonth	OrderDate
68	7	19785.3646	July	2005-07-28 00:00:00.000
69	8	17688.07	July	2005-07-29 00:00:00.000
70	9	17534.79	July	2005-07-26 00:00:00.000
71	10	15012.1782	July	2005-07-03 00:00:00.000
72	10	15012.1782	July	2005-07-23 00:00:00.000
73	10	15012.1782	July	2005-07-05 00:00:00.000
74	10	15012.1782	July	2005-07-31 00:00:00.000
75	14	14402.3382	July	2005-07-30 00:00:00.000
76	15	14313.08	July	2005-07-16 00:00:00.000

Figure 8-9. *The RANK function skips a value in the case of a tie*

```
WITH TotalSalesBySalesDatePartitioned
(
    DailySales,
    OrderMonth,
    OrderDate
)
AS
(
    SELECT
        SUM(soh.SubTotal) AS DailySales,
        DATENAME(MONTH, soh.OrderDate) AS OrderMonth,
        soh.OrderDate
    FROM   Sales.SalesOrderHeader  soh
    WHERE soh.OrderDate >= '20050101'
        AND soh.OrderDate < '20060101'
    GROUP BY soh.OrderDate
)
```

The SELECT query associated with the CTE uses the RANK function to assign rankings to the results. The PARTITION BY clause is used to partition the results by OrderMonth so that the rankings restart at 1 for each new month. For example:

```
SELECT
RANK() OVER
(
PARTITION BY OrderMonth

        ORDER BY
        DailySales  DESC
    )  AS  Ranking,
    DailySales,
    OrderMonth,
    OrderDate
FROM TotalSalesBySalesDatePartitioned
ORDER BY DATEPART(mm,OrderDate),
    Ranking;
```

When the RANK function encounters two equal DailySales amounts in the same partition, it assigns the same rank number to both and skips the next number in the ranking. As shown in Figure 8-9, the DailySales total for four days in July 2005 was \$15012.1782, resulting in the RANK function assigning all four days a Ranking value of 10. The RANK function then skips the Ranking value from 11 through 13 and assigns the next row a Ranking of 14.

DENSE_RANK, like RANK, assigns duplicate values the same rank, but with one important difference: it does not skip the next ranking in the list. Listing 8-10 modifies Listing 8-9 to use the RANK and DENSE_RANK functions. As you can see in Figure 8-10, DENSE_RANK still assigns the same Ranking to both rows in the result, but it doesn't skip the next Ranking value whereas RANK skips the next ranking value.

Listing 8-10. Using DENSE_RANK to Rank Best Daily Sales Per Month

```
WITH TotalSalesBySalesDatePartitioned
(
    DailySales,
    OrderMonth,
```

221

```
        OrderDate
)
AS
(
    SELECT
        SUM(soh.SubTotal) AS DailySales,
        DATENAME(MONTH, soh.OrderDate) AS OrderMonth,
        soh.OrderDate
    FROM  Sales.SalesOrderHeader  soh
    WHERE soh.OrderDate >= '20050101'
        AND soh.OrderDate < '20060101'
    GROUP BY soh.OrderDate
)
SELECT
 RANK() OVER
    (
        PARTITION BY
        OrderMonth
        ORDER BY
        DailySales  DESC
    )  AS  Ranking,
    DENSE_RANK() OVER
    (
        PARTITION BY
        OrderMonth
        ORDER BY
        DailySales  DESC
    )  AS  Dense_Ranking,
    DailySales,
    OrderMonth,
    OrderDate
FROM TotalSalesBySalesDatePartitioned
ORDER BY DATEPART(mm,OrderDate),
    Ranking;
```

	Ranking	Dense_Ranking	DailySales	OrderMonth	OrderDate
8	8	8	17688.07	July	2005-07-29 00:00:00.000
9	9	9	17534.79	July	2005-07-26 00:00:00.000
10	10	10	15012.1782	July	2005-07-03 00:00:00.000
11	10	10	15012.1782	July	2005-07-05 00:00:00.000
12	10	10	15012.1782	July	2005-07-31 00:00:00.000
13	10	10	15012.1782	July	2005-07-23 00:00:00.000
14	14	11	14402.3382	July	2005-07-30 00:00:00.000
15	15	12	14313.08	July	2005-07-16 00:00:00.000
16	15	12	14313.08	July	2005-07-06 00:00:00.000

Figure 8-10. DENSE_RANK does not skip ranking values after a tie

The NTILE Function

NTILE is another ranking function that fulfills a slightly different need. This function divides your result set into approximate n-tiles. An *n-tile* can be a quartile (1/4th, or 25 percent slices), a quintile (1/5th, or 20 percent slices), a percentile (1/100th, or 1 percent slices), or just about any other fractional slice you can imagine. The reason NTILE divides result sets into *approximate* n-tiles is that the number of rows returned might not be evenly divisible into the required number of groups. A table with 27 rows, for instance, is not evenly divisible into quar-tiles or quintiles. When you query a table with the NTILE function and the number of rows is not evenly divisible by the specified number of groups, NTILE creates groups of two different sizes. The larger groups will all be one row larger than the smaller groups, and the larger groups are numbered first. In the example of 27 rows divided into quintiles (1/5th), the first two groups will have six rows each, and the last three groups will have five rows each.

Like the ROW_NUMBER function, you can include both PARTITION BY and ORDER BY in the OVER clause. NTILE requires an additional parameter that specifies how many groups it should divide your results into.

NTILE is useful for answering business questions like "Which salespeople comprised the top 4 percent of the sales force in July 2005? and What were their sales totals?" Listing 8-11 uses NTILE to divide the AdventureWorks salespeople into four groups, each one representing 4 percent of the total sales force. The ORDER BY clause is used to specify that rows are assigned to the groups in order of their total sales. The results are shown in Figure 8-11.

Listing 8-11. Using NTILE to Group and Rank Salespeople

```
WITH SalesTotalBySalesPerson
(
SalesPersonID, SalesTotal
)
AS
(
SELECT
soh.SalesPersonID, SUM(soh.SubTotal) AS SalesTotal
FROM Sales.SalesOrderHeader soh
WHERE DATEPART(YEAR, soh.OrderDate) = 2005
        AND DATEPART(MONTH, soh.OrderDate) = 7
GROUP BY soh.SalesPersonID ) SELECT
NTILE(4) OVER
( ORDER BY
st.SalesTotal DESC
) AS Tile,
p.LastName,
p.FirstName,
p.MiddleName,
st.SalesPersonID,
st.SalesTotal FROM SalesTotalBySalesPerson st INNER JOIN Person.Person p
ON st.SalesPersonID = p.BusinessEntityID ;
```

	Tile	LastName	FirstName	MiddleName	SalesPersonID	SalesTotal
1	1	Saraiva	José	Edvaldo	282	106251.7277
2	1	Reiter	Tsvi	Michael	279	104419.3291
3	1	Campbell	David	R	283	69472.9963
4	2	Blythe	Michael	G	275	63762.9228
5	2	Ito	Shu	K	281	59708.3208
6	3	Carson	Jillian	NULL	277	46695.5564
7	3	Ansman-Wolfe	Pamela	O	280	24432.6088
8	4	Vargas	Garrett	R	278	9109.1683
9	4	Mitchell	Linda	C	276	5475.9485

Figure 8-11. AdventureWorks salespeople grouped and ranked by NTILE

The code begins with a simple CTE that returns the SalesPersonID and sum of the order SubTotal values from the Sales.SalesOrderHeader table. The CTE limits its results to the sales that occurred for the month of July in the year 2005. Here is the CTE:

```
WITH SalesTotalBySalesPerson (
SalesPersonID,
SalesTotal )
AS (
SELECT
son.SalesPersonID,
SUM(soh.SubTotal) AS SalesTotal
FROM Sales.SalesOrderHeader soh
WHERE DATEPART(YEAR, soh.OrderDate) = 2005
        AND DATEPART(MONTH, soh.OrderDate) = 7
GROUP BY soh.SalesPersonID )
```

The SELECT query associated with this CTE uses NTILE(4) to group the AdventureWorks salespeople into four groups of approximately 4 percent each. The OVER clause specifies that the groups should be assigned based on the SalesTotal in descending order. The entire SELECT query is:

```
SELECT
NTILE(4) OVER
( ORDER BY
st.SalesTotal DESC
) AS Tile,
p.LastName,
p.FirstName,
p.MiddleName,
st.SalesPersonID,
st.SalesTotal FROM SalesTotalBySalesPerson st INNER JOIN Person.Person p
ON st.SalesPersonID = p.BusinessEntityID ;
```

Aggregate Functions, Analytic Functions, and the OVER Clause

As previously discussed, the numbering and ranking functions (ROW_NUMBER, RANK, etc.) all work with the OVER clause to define the order and partitioning of their input rows via the ORDER BY and PARTITION BY clauses. The

OVER clause also provides windowing functionality to T-SQL aggregate functions such as SUM, COUNT, and SQL CLR user-defined aggregates.

Window functions help us with common business questions like those involving running totals or sliding averages. For instance, you can apply the OVER clause to the Purchasing.PurchaseOrderDetail table in the AdventureWorks database to retrieve the SUM of the dollar values of products ordered in the form of a running total. You can further restrict the resultset in which you want to perform the aggregation by partitioning the resultset by PurchaseOrderId essentially generating the running-total separately for each purchase order. An example query is shown in Listing 8-13. Partial results are shown in Figure 8-12.

Listing 8-13. Using the OVER Clause with SUM

```
SELECT
        PurchaseOrderID,
        ProductID,
        OrderQty,
        UnitPrice,
        LineTotal,
        SUM(LineTotal)
        OVER (PARTITION BY PurchaseOrderID
                ORDER BY ProductId
                RANGE BETWEEN UNBOUNDED PRECEDING AND CURRENT ROW)
                        AS CumulativeOrderOty
FROM Purchasing.PurchaseOrderDetail;
```

	PurchaseOrderID	ProductID	OrderQty	UnitPrice	LineTotal	CumulativeOrderOty
1	1	1	4	50.26	201.04	201.04
2	2	359	3	45.12	135.36	135.36
3	2	360	3	45.5805	136.7415	272.1015
4	3	530	550	16.086	8847.30	8847.30
5	4	4	3	57.0255	171.0765	171.0765
6	5	512	550	37.086	20397.30	20397.30
7	6	513	550	26.5965	14628.075	14628.075
8	7	317	550	27.0585	14882.175	14882.175
9	7	318	550	33.579	18468.45	33350.625
10	7	319	550	46.0635	25334.925	58685.55
11	8	403	3	47.4705	142.4115	142.4115
12	8	404	3	45.3705	136.1115	278.523
13	8	405	3	49.644	148.932	427.455
14	8	406	3	45.3705	136.1115	563.5665
15	8	407	3	43.2705	129.8115	693.378
16	9	422	3	47.523	142.569	142.569
17	9	423	3	45.423	136.269	278.838
18	9	424	3	49.6965	149.0895	427.9275
19	9	425	3	45.423	136.269	564.1965
20	9	426	3	43.323	129.969	694.1655
21	10	320	3	47.4705	142.4115	142.4115

Figure 8-12. Partial results from query generating a running SUM

Notice the following new clause in Listing 8-13: RANGE BETWEEN UNBOUNDED PRECEDING AND CURRENT ROW

This is known as a *framing clause*. In this case, it specifies that each sum will include all values from the first row in the partition through to the current row. A framing clause like this makes sense only when there is order to the rows, and that is the reason for the ORDER BY ProductId clause. It is the framing clause in combination with the ORDER BY clause that together generates the running sum that you see in Figure 8-12.

■ **Tip** Other framing clauses are possible. The RANGE BETWEEN UNBOUNDED PRECEDING AND CURRENT ROW in Listing 8-13 will be the default if no framing clause is specified. Keep that point in mind, as it is common for query writers to be confounded by unexpected results due to not knowing that a default framing clause is being applied.

Let's look at an example to see how the default framing clause can affect the query results. For example, let's say you want to calculate and return the total sales amount by PurchaseOrder with each line item. Based on how the framing is defined you can get very different results since total can mean grand total or running total. Let's modify the query in Listing 8-13 and specify the framing clause RANGE BETWEEN UNBOUNDED PRECEDING AND UNBOUNDED FOLLOWING along with the default framing clause and review the results. The modified query is shown in Listing 8-14 and results are shown in Figure 8-13.

Listing 8-14. Query results due to default framing specification

```
SELECT
        PurchaseOrderID,
        ProductID,
        OrderQty,
        UnitPrice,
        LineTotal,
        SUM(LineTotal)
OVER (PARTITION BY PurchaseOrderID
ORDER BY ProductId
)
AS TotalSalesDefaultFraming,
        SUM(LineTotal)
OVER (PARTITION BY PurchaseOrderID
ORDER BY ProductId RANGE BETWEEN UNBOUNDED PRECEDING
        AND UNBOUNDED FOLLOWING
)
AS TotalSalesDefinedFraming
FROM Purchasing.PurchaseOrderDetail
ORDER BY PurchaseOrderID;
```

Figure 8-13. *Partial results from the query with different windowing specifications*

In the above Figure 8-13 you can see that the Total Sales in the last 2 columns differ significantly. The column 6, `TotalSalesDefaultFraming` lists the total cumulative sales meaning since the framing is not specified for that column, the default framing `RANGE BETWEEN UNBOUNDED PRECEDING AND CURRENT ROW` is extended to this column, which means that the aggreagte is calculated only till the current row. However for column7, `TotalSalesDefinedFraming` the framing clause `RANGE BETWEEN UNBOUNDED PRECEDING AND UNBOUNDED FOLLOWING` is specified meaning the framing is extended for all the rows within the partition and hence the Total for the sales across the entire PurchaseOrder is calculated. Given the objective is to calculate and return the total sales amount for the purchase order with each line item, not specifying the framing clause yields running total. So, with the above example you can see that it is important to specify proper framing clause to achieve the desired result sets.

Now, let's look at another example in Listing 8-15, one that modifies Listing 8-13 to return the two-day average of the total amount. In this case, we are again applying the `OVER` clause to the `Purchasing.PurchaseOrderDetail` table in the AdventureWorks database, but this time to retrieve the two-day average of the total dollr amount of products ordered. Results are sorted by by `DueDate`.

Notice the different framing clause in this query: `ROWS BETWEEN 1 PRECEDING AND CURRENT ROW`

Rows are sorted by date. For each row, the two-day average considers the current row and the row from the day previous. Partial results are shown in Figure 8-14.

Listing 8-15. Using the OVER Clause define frame sizes to return two-day, moving average

```
SELECT
        PurchaseOrderID,
        ProductID,
        Duedate,
        LineTotal,
        Avg(LineTotal)
        OVER (ORDER BY Duedate
                ROWS BETWEEN 1 PRECEDING AND CURRENT ROW)
                AS [2DayAvg]
FROM Purchasing.PurchaseOrderDetail
ORDER BY Duedate;
```

	PurchaseOrderID	ProductID	Duedate	Line Total	2DayAvg
1	1	1	2005-05-31 00:00:00.000	201.04	201.04
2	2	359	2005-05-31 00:00:00.000	135.36	168.20
3	2	360	2005-05-31 00:00:00.000	136.7415	136.0507
4	3	530	2005-05-31 00:00:00.000	8847.30	4492.0207
5	4	4	2005-05-31 00:00:00.000	171.0765	4509.1882
6	5	512	2005-06-14 00:00:00.000	20397.30	10284.1882
7	6	513	2005-06-14 00:00:00.000	14628.075	17512.6875
8	7	317	2005-06-14 00:00:00.000	14882.175	14755.125
9	7	318	2005-06-14 00:00:00.000	18468.45	16675.3125
10	7	319	2005-06-14 00:00:00.000	25334.925	21901.6875
11	8	403	2005-06-14 00:00:00.000	142.4115	12738.6682
12	8	404	2005-06-14 00:00:00.000	136.1115	139.2615
13	8	405	2005-06-14 00:00:00.000	148.932	142.5217
14	8	406	2005-06-14 00:00:00.000	136.1115	142.5217
15	8	407	2005-06-14 00:00:00.000	129.8115	132.9615
16	9	422	2006-01-28 00:00:00.000	142.569	136.1902
17	9	423	2006-01-28 00:00:00.000	136.269	139.419

Figure 8-14. *Partial results from a query returning a two-day, moving average*

Let's review one last scenario in which you want to calculate the running total of sales by ProductID to provide information to management on which products are selling quickly. For this example, let's modify the query from Listing 8-15 further to define multiple windows by partitioning the resultset by ProductId. You see the resulting query in Lisitng 8-16.

You'll be able to see how the frame expands as the calculation is done within the frame. Once the ProductId changes, the frame is reset and the calculation is restarted. Figure 8-15 shows partial result set.

Listing 8-16. Defining frames from within the OVER clause to calcualte running total

```
SELECT
        PurchaseOrderID,
        ProductID,
        OrderQty,
        UnitPrice,
        LineTotal,
        SUM(LineTotal) OVER (PARTITION BY ProductId ORDER BY DueDate
          RANGE BETWEEN UNBOUNDED PRECEDING AND CURRENT ROW) AS  CumulativeTotal,
        ROW_NUMBER() OVER (PARTITION BY ProductId ORDER BY DueDate ) AS  No
FROM Purchasing.PurchaseOrderDetail
ORDER BY ProductId, DueDate;
```

	PurchaseOrderID	ProductID	OrderQty	UnitPrice	LineTotal	CumulativeTotal	No
46	3536	1	3	50.2635	150.7905	6986.6125	46
47	3615	1	3	50.2635	150.7905	7137.403	47
48	3694	1	3	50.2635	150.7905	7288.1935	48
49	3773	1	3	50.2635	150.7905	7438.984	49
50	3852	1	3	50.2635	150.7905	7589.7745	50
51	3931	1	3	50.2635	150.7905	7740.565	51
52	79	2	3	41.916	125.748	125.748	1
53	158	2	3	41.916	125.748	251.496	2
54	237	2	3	41.916	125.748	377.244	3
55	316	2	3	41.916	125.748	502.992	4
56	395	2	3	41.916	125.748	628.74	5

Figure 8-15. Partial results showing a running total by product ID

You can also see in the query from Listing 8-16 that you are not just limited to use one aggregate function in the SELECT statement. You can specify multiple aggregate functions in the same query.

Framing can be defined by either ROWS or RANGE with lower boundary and upper boundary. If you define only the lower boundary, then the upper boundary will be set to the current row. When you define the framing with ROWS you can specify the boundary with a number or scalar expression that returns an integer. If you do not define the boundary for framing, then the default value of RANGE BETWEEN UNBOUNDED PRECEDING AND CURRENT ROW is assumed.

Analytic Function Examples

SQL Server 2012 introduces several helpful, analytical functions. Some of the more useful of these are described in the subsections to follow. Some are statistics oriented. Others are useful for reporting scenarios in which you need to access values across rows in a result set.

CUME_DIST and PERCENT_RANK

CUME_DIST and PERCENT_RANK are two new analytical functions that have been introduced in SQL Server 2012. Suppose you want to figure out AdventureWorks Company's best, average and worst salespeople perform in comparision to each other and especially interested in the data for the sales person Jillian Carson, whom you know exist in the table by pre-querying the data. This scenario might be phrased with a business question like "How does sales person Jillian Carson rank when compared to the total sales percentile for all the sales people?" CUME_DIST can easily give you that information, as shown in Listing 8-17. Query results are shown in Figure 8-16.

Listing 8-17. Using the CUME_DIST function

```
SELECT
        round(SUM(TotalDue),1) AS Sales,
        LastName,
        FirstName,
        SalesPersonId,
        CUME_DIST() OVER (ORDER BY round(SUM(TotalDue),1)) as CUME_DIST
```

```
FROM
        Sales.SalesOrderHeader soh
                JOIN Sales.vSalesPerson sp
                ON soh.SalesPersonID = sp.BusinessEntityID
GROUP BY SalesPersonID,LastName,FirstName;
```

	Sales	LastName	FirstName	SalesPersonId	CUME_DIST
1	195528.80	Abbas	Syed	285	0.0588235294117647
2	826417.50	Alberts	Amy	287	0.117647058823529
3	1235934.40	Jiang	Stephen	274	0.176470588235294
4	1606441.40	Tsoflias	Lynn	286	0.235294117647059
5	2062393.10	Valdez	Rachel	288	0.294117647058824
6	2608116.40	Mensa-Annan	Tete	284	0.352941176470588
7	3748246.10	Ansman-Wolfe	Pamela	280	0.411764705882353
8	4069422.20	Vargas	Garrett	278	0.470588235294118
9	4207894.60	Campbell	David	283	0.529411764705882
10	5087977.20	Varkey Chudukatil	Ranjit	290	0.588235294117647
11	6683536.70	Saraiva	José	282	0.647058823529412
12	7259567.90	Ito	Shu	281	0.705882352941177
13	8086073.70	Reiter	Tsvi	279	0.764705882352941
14	9585124.90	Pak	Jae	289	0.823529411764706
15	10475367.10	Blythe	Michael	275	0.882352941176471
16	11342385.90	Carson	Jillian	277	0.941176470588235
17	11695019.10	Mitchell	Linda	276	1

Figure 8-16. *Results of CUME_DIST calculation*

The query in Listing 8-17 rounds the TotalDue for the Sales Amount just to improve the query value readability. Since CUME_DIST returns the position of the row, the column results has to be formatted to return the percentage by multiplying by 100. The result in Figure 8-16 show that 94.11 % of the total salespeople have total sales less than or equal to salesperson Jillian Carson which is represented by the Cumulative distribution value of 0.9411.

If you slightly rephrase the question to "In what percentile is the total sales for sales person Jillian Carson?" PERCENT_RANK can answer that question. Listing 8-18 is a modified version Listing 8-17's query, now including a call to PERCENT_RANK. Partial results are shown in Figure 8-17.

Listing 8-18. Using the PERCENT_RANK function

```
SELECT
        round(SUM(TotalDue),1) AS Sales,
        LastName,
        FirstName,
        SalesPersonId,
        CUME_DIST() OVER (ORDER BY round(SUM(TotalDue),1)) as CUME_DIST
        ,PERCENT_RANK() OVER (ORDER BY round(SUM(TotalDue),1)) as PERCENT_RANK
```

```
FROM
        Sales.SalesOrderHeader soh
                JOIN Sales.vSalesPerson sp
                ON soh.SalesPersonID = sp.BusinessEntityID
GROUP BY SalesPersonID,LastName,FirstName;
```

	Sales	LastName	FirstName	SalesPersonId	CUME_DIST	PERCENT_RANK
1	195528.80	Abbas	Syed	285	0.0588235294117647	0
2	826417.50	Alberts	Amy	287	0.117647058823529	0.0625
3	1235934.40	Jiang	Stephen	274	0.176470588235294	0.125
4	1606441.40	Tsoflias	Lynn	286	0.235294117647059	0.1875
5	2062393.10	Valdez	Rachel	288	0.294117647058824	0.25
6	2608116.40	Mensa-Annan	Tete	284	0.352941176470588	0.3125
7	3748246.10	Ansman-Wolfe	Pamela	280	0.411764705882353	0.375
8	4069422.20	Vargas	Garrett	278	0.470588235294118	0.4375
9	4207894.60	Campbell	David	283	0.529411764705882	0.5
10	5087977.20	Varkey Chudukatil	Ranjit	290	0.588235294117647	0.5625
11	6683536.70	Saraiva	José	282	0.647058823529412	0.625
12	7259567.90	Ito	Shu	281	0.705882352941177	0.6875
13	8086073.70	Reiter	Tsvi	279	0.764705882352941	0.75
14	9585124.90	Pak	Jae	289	0.823529411764706	0.8125
15	10475367.10	Blythe	Michael	275	0.882352941176471	0.875
16	11342385.90	Carson	Jillian	277	0.941176470588235	0.9375
17	11695019.10	Mitchell	Linda	276	1	1

Figure 8-17. Results of CUME_DIST and PERCENT_RANK calculation for salesperson

The PERCENT_RANK function returns the percentage of the total sales within all the sales order in AdventureWorks. As you can see in the results, there are 17 unique values and the first value starts at 0 and the last value ends at 1 while other rows have the values based on the number of rows -1. From the above example, you can see that the salesperson Jillian Carson is at 93.75% percentile of the overall sales in AdventureWorks, which is represented by a percent rank value of 0.9375.

■ **Note**   You can apply the PARTITION BY clause to the CUME_DIST and PERCENT_RANK functions to define the window in which you apply those calculations.

PERCENTILE_CONT and PERCENTILE_DISC

PERCENTILE_CONT and PERCENTILE_DISC are new distribution functions that are essentially the inverse of the CUME_DIST and PERCENT_RANK functions.

Suppose you want to figure out AdventureWorks company's 40th percentile sales total for all the accounts, it can be phrased with the business question "What is the 40th percentile for all the sales for all the accounts". PERCENTILE_CONT and PERCENTILE_DISC requires the WITHIN GROUP clause to sepcify the ordering and the columns for the calcualtion. PERCENTILE_CONT interpolates over all the values in the window, so the result will be a calculated value whereas PERCENTILE_DISC returns the value of the actual column. Both the functions PERCENTILE_CONT and PERCENTILE_DISC requires the percentile as the argument which is a value ranges between 0.0 to 1.0. The following example in Listing 8-19 returns the answer for the business question to calcualte the sales total for the 40th percentile partitioned by account number. Hence the example uses the PERCENTILE_CONT and PERCENTILE_DISC function with the median value of 0.4 as the percentile to compute, meaning 40th percentile value. Query results are shown in Figure 8-18.

Listing 8-19. Using PERCENTILE_CONT AND PERCENTILE_DISC

```
SELECT
        round(SUM(TotalDue),1) AS Sales,
        LastName,
        FirstName,
        SalesPersonId,
        AccountNumber,
        PERCENTILE_CONT(0.4) WITHIN GROUP (ORDER BY round(SUM(TotalDue),1))
                        OVER(PARTITION BY AccountNumber ) AS PERCENTILE_CONT,
        PERCENTILE_DISC(0.4) WITHIN GROUP(ORDER BY round(SUM(TotalDue),1))
                OVER(PARTITION BY AccountNumber ) AS PERCENTILE_DISC
FROM
        Sales.SalesOrderHeader soh
                JOIN Sales.vSalesPerson sp
                ON soh.SalesPersonID = sp.BusinessEntityID
GROUP BY AccountNumber,SalesPersonID,LastName,FirstName
```

	Sales	LastName	FirstName	SalesPersonId	AccountNumber	PERCENTILE_CONT	PERCENTILE_DISC
1	95924.00	Ansman-Wolfe	Pamela	280	10-4020-000001	95924	95924.00
2	28310.00	Campbell	David	283	10-4020-000002	28310	28310.00
3	176830.40	Carson	Jillian	277	10-4020-000003	198391.28	176830.40
4	230732.60	Blythe	Michael	275	10-4020-000003	198391.28	176830.40
5	222309.60	Carson	Jillian	277	10-4020-000004	308720.28	222309.60
6	438336.30	Blythe	Michael	275	10-4020-000004	308720.28	222309.60
7	97031.20	Ito	Shu	281	10-4020-000005	97031.2	97031.20
8	3023.30	Mitchell	Linda	276	10-4020-000006	3023.3	3023.30
9	3302.50	Jiang	Stephen	274	10-4020-000007	4166.78	3302.50
10	5463.20	Mitchell	Linda	276	10-4020-000007	4166.78	3302.50
11	25064.60	Reiter	Tsvi	279	10-4020-000008	25064.6	25064.60

Figure 8-18. Results from the PERCENTILE_CONT AND PERCENTILE_DISC functions

You can see from the above Figure 8-18 that lists the 40th percentile for the AdventureWorks sales total and the PERCENTILE_CONT value and PERCENTILE_DISC values differ based on the account number. For account number 10-4020-000003, regardless of the salesperson, the PERCENTILE_CONT listed as 198391.28 which is an interpolated value regardless of it exists in the data set or not whereas PERCENTILE_DISC listed as 176830.40 is the value from the actual column. Whereas for the account number 10-4020-000004 the PERCENTILE_CONT listed as 308720.28 and PERCENTILE_DISC listed as 222309.60.

LAG and LEAD functions

LAG and LEAD are new offset functions that enable you to perform calculations based on the specified row that is before or after the current row. These functions provide a method to access more than one row at a time without having to create a self join. LAG provides access to row preceding the current row, whereas LEAD provides access to the row that is after the current row.

LAG helps us answer business questions such as "For all my active products that has not been discontinued, what is the current and the previous production cost?" Listing 8-20 provides a sample query that calculates the current production cost and the last production cost for all active products using the LAG function. Partial results are shown in Figure 8-19.

Listing 8-20. Using the LAG function

```
WITH ProductCostHistory AS
(SELECT
ProductID,
LAG(StandardCost) OVER (PARTITION BY ProductID ORDER BY ProductID) AS PreviousProductCost,
StandardCost AS CurrentProductCost,
Startdate,Enddate
FROM  Production.ProductCostHistory
)
SELECT
ProductID,
PreviousProductCost,
CurrentProductCost,
StartDate,
EndDate
FROM ProductCostHistory
WHERE Enddate IS NULL
```

	ProductID	PreviousProductCost	CurrentProductCost	StartDate	EndDate
1	707	13.8782	13.0863	2007-07-01 00:00:00.000	NULL
2	708	13.8782	13.0863	2007-07-01 00:00:00.000	NULL
3	711	13.8782	13.0863	2007-07-01 00:00:00.000	NULL
4	712	5.2297	6.9223	2007-07-01 00:00:00.000	NULL
5	713	29.0807	38.4923	2007-07-01 00:00:00.000	NULL
6	714	29.0807	38.4923	2007-07-01 00:00:00.000	NULL
7	715	29.0807	38.4923	2007-07-01 00:00:00.000	NULL
8	716	29.0807	38.4923	2007-07-01 00:00:00.000	NULL
9	717	722.2568	868.6342	2007-07-01 00:00:00.000	NULL
10	718	722.2568	868.6342	2007-07-01 00:00:00.000	NULL
11	719	722.2568	868.6342	2007-07-01 00:00:00.000	NULL
12	720	722.2568	868.6342	2007-07-01 00:00:00.000	NULL
13	721	722.2568	868.6342	2007-07-01 00:00:00.000	NULL
14	722	170.1428	204.6251	2007-07-01 00:00:00.000	NULL
15	723	170.1428	204.6251	2007-07-01 00:00:00.000	NULL
16	724	170.1428	204.6251	2007-07-01 00:00:00.000	NULL
17	736	170.1428	204.6251	2007-07-01 00:00:00.000	NULL
18	737	170.1428	204.6251	2007-07-01 00:00:00.000	NULL
19	738	170.1428	204.6251	2007-07-01 00:00:00.000	NULL
20	739	660.9142	747.2002	2007-07-01 00:00:00.000	NULL

Figure 8-19. *Results of production cost history comparision using the LAG fucntion*

233

In the above example, you can see that Listing 8-20 uses the LAG function within a CTE to calculate the production cost difference between the current production cost and the previous product production cost by partitioning the data set by ProductID:

```
SELECT
ProductID,
LAG(StandardCost) OVER (PARTITION BY ProductID ORDER BY ProductID) AS PreviousProductCost,
StandardCost AS CurrentProductCost,
Startdate,Enddate
FROM  Production.ProductCostHistory
```

The SELECT query associated with the CTE returns the rows that are the latest production cost from the dataset with EndDate being null in the call:

```
SELECT
ProductID,
PreviousProductCost,
CurrentProductCost,
StartDate,
EndDate
FROM ProductCostHistory
WHERE Enddate IS NULL
```

Opposite to LAG, LEAD helps us answer business questions such as "How does each months sales compare with the sales for the following month for all the salespeople of AdventureWorks over the year 2007?" Listing 8-21 provides a sample query that lists the next month's total sales relative to the current month's sales for year 2007 using the LEAD function. Partial results are shown in Figure 8-20.

Listing 8-21. Using the LEAD function

```
Select
        LastName,
        SalesPersonID,
        Sum(SubTotal) CurrentMonthSales,
        DateNAME(Month,OrderDate) Month,
        DateName(Year,OrderDate) Year,
        LEAD(Sum(SubTotal),1) OVER (ORDER BY SalesPersonID, OrderDate) TotalSalesNextMonth
  FROM
        Sales.SalesOrderHeader soh
                JOIN Sales.vSalesPerson sp
                ON soh.SalesPersonID = sp.BusinessEntityID
WHERE DateName(Year,OrderDate)  = 2007
  GROUP BY
                FirstName, LastName, SalesPersonID,OrderDate
ORDER BY SalesPersonID,OrderDate;
```

	LastName	SalesPersonID	CurrentMonthSales	Month	Year	TotalSalesNextMonth
162	Pak	289	388950.7724	October	2007	230046.2238
163	Pak	289	230046.2238	November	2007	509599.3448
164	Pak	289	509599.3448	December	2007	34516.2132
165	Varkey ...	290	34516.2132	January	2007	113442.2926
166	Varkey ...	290	113442.2926	February	2007	59856.0271
167	Varkey ...	290	59856.0271	March	2007	56935.0391
168	Varkey ...	290	56935.0391	April	2007	188133.5582
169	Varkey ...	290	188133.5582	May	2007	87056.0785
170	Varkey ...	290	87056.0785	June	2007	55465.4076
171	Varkey ...	290	55465.4076	July	2007	686874.3293
172	Varkey ...	290	686874.3293	August	2007	196850.7723
173	Varkey ...	290	196850.7723	September	2007	53834.4018
174	Varkey ...	290	53834.4018	October	2007	614268.4004
175	Varkey ...	290	614268.4004	November	2007	139467.2278
176	Varkey ...	290	139467.2278	December	2007	NULL

Figure 8-20. *Results of employee's sales performance comparision for year 2007 using the LEAD fucntion*

The above Figure 8-20 lists the results of the sales performance of the AdventureWorks sales team for year 2007. The query returns the next month's sales total for the sales person compared to the previous months for the year 2007. You can also see that the last row returns null for the next month's sales meaning, there is no LEAD for the last row.

FIRST_VALUE and LAST_VALUE

FIRST_VALUE and LAST_VALUE are the offset functions that return the first and last values in the window defined using the OVER clause. FIRST_VALUE returns the first value of the window, and LAST_VALUE returns the last value in the window.

These functions help us answer questions like "What are the beginning and ending sales order totals for any given month for the sales person?" Listing 8-22 provides a sample query that answers the question just posed. Partial query results are shown in Figure 8-21.

Listing 8-22. Using FIRST_VALUE and LAST_VALUE

```
SELECT DISTINCT
        LastName,
        SalesPersonID,
        datename(year,OrderDate) OrderYear,
        datename(month, OrderDate) OrderMonth,
        FIRST_VALUE(SubTotal) OVER (PARTITION BY SalesPersonID, OrderDate ORDER BY
SalesPersonID ) FirstSalesAmount,
        LAST_VALUE(SubTotal) OVER (PARTITION BY SalesPersonID, OrderDate ORDER BY
SalesPersonID) LastSalesAmount,
OrderDate
 FROM
        Sales.SalesOrderHeader soh
                JOIN Sales.vSalesPerson sp
                ON soh.SalesPersonID = sp.BusinessEntityID
ORDER BY OrderDate;
```

	LastName	SalesPersonID	OrderYear	OrderMonth	FirstSalesAmount	LastSalesAmount	OrderDate
1	Blythe	275	2005	July	6122.082	20541.4072	2005-07-01 00:00:00.000
2	Mitchell	276	2005	July	419.4589	5056.4896	2005-07-01 00:00:00.000
3	Carson	277	2005	July	6107.082	874.794	2005-07-01 00:00:00.000
4	Vargas	278	2005	July	7793.1108	1316.0575	2005-07-01 00:00:00.000
5	Reiter	279	2005	July	20565.6206	419.4589	2005-07-01 00:00:00.000
6	Ansman-Wolfe	280	2005	July	24432.6088	24432.6088	2005-07-01 00:00:00.000
7	Ito	281	2005	July	9799.9243	38510.8973	2005-07-01 00:00:00.000
8	Saraiva	282	2005	July	32726.4786	2624.382	2005-07-01 00:00:00.000
9	Campbell	283	2005	July	14352.7713	3463.2998	2005-07-01 00:00:00.000
10	Jiang	274	2005	August	20544.7015	20544.7015	2005-08-01 00:00:00.000
11	Blythe	275	2005	August	32940.1556	4049.988	2005-08-01 00:00:00.000
12	Mitchell	276	2005	August	3911.5991	39450.7884	2005-08-01 00:00:00.000
13	Carson	277	2005	August	1718.8983	36724.0974	2005-08-01 00:00:00.000
14	Vargas	278	2005	August	919.5201	50948.9161	2005-08-01 00:00:00.000
15	Reiter	279	2005	August	8580.0739	19411.9336	2005-08-01 00:00:00.000
16	Ansman-Wolfe	280	2005	August	10993.3942	19734.8665	2005-08-01 00:00:00.000

Figure 8-21. *Results showing the first and last sales amount*

In this example, we return the first and last sales amounts for the sales person by month and year. You can see from the Figure 8-21 that in some cases, the FirstSalesAmount and LastSalesAmount are the same, which means that there was only one sale in those months. In the months where there has been more than one sale, the amount of First Sales Order and Last Sales Order is listed.

Summary

CTEs are powerful SQL Server features that come in two varieties: recursive and nonrecursive. Nonrecursive CTEs allow you to write expressive T-SQL code that is easier to code, debug, and manage than complex queries that make extensive use of derived tables. Recursive CTEs simplify queries of hierarchical data and allow for easily generating result sets consisting of sequential numbers, which are very useful in themselves.

SQL Server's support for windowing functions and the OVER clause makes calculating aggregates with window framing and ordering, simple. SQL Server supports several windowing functions, including the following:

- ROW_NUMBER: This function numbers the rows of a result set sequentially, beginning with 1.

- RANK *and* DENSE_RANK: These functions rank a result set, applying the same rank value in the case of a tie.

- NTILE: This function groups a result set into a user-specified number of groups.

- CUME_DIST, PERCENTILE_CONT, PERCENT_RANK *and* PERCENTILE_DISC: These functions provide analytical capabilities within T-SQL and enables cumulative distribution value calcuilations.

- LAG *and* LEAD: These offset functions return access to the rows at a given offset value.

- FIRST_VALUE *and* LAST_VALUE: These offset functions return the first and last row for a given window defined by the partition sub-clause.

You can also use the OVER clause to apply windowing functionality to built-in aggregate functions and SQL CLR user-defined aggregates.

Both CTEs and windowing functions provide useful functionality and extend the syntax of T-SQL, allowing you to write more powerful code than ever in a simpler syntax than was possible without them.

EXERCISES

1. [True/false] When a CTE is not the first statement in a batch, the statement preceding it must end with a semicolon statement terminator.

2. [Choose all that apply] A recursive CTE requires which of the following:

    a.   The WITH keyword

    b.   An anchor query

    c.   The EXPRESSION keyword

    d.   A recursive query

3. [Fill in the blank] The MAXRECURSION option can accept a value between 0 and _____.

4. [Choose one] SQL Server supports which of the following windowing functions:

    a.   ROW_NUMBER

    b.   RANK

    c.   DENSE_RANK

    d.   NTILE

    e.   All of the above

5. [True/false] You can use ORDER BY in the OVER clause when used with aggregate functions.

6. [True/false] When PARTITION BY and ORDER BY are both used in the OVER clause, PARTITION BY must appear first.

7. [Fill in the blank] The names of all columns returned by a CTE must be_____.

8. [Fill in the blank] The default framing clause is _____.

9. [True/False] If Order By is not specified for the functions that do not require in OVER clause, the window frame is defined for the entire partition

10. [True/False] Checksum can be used with Over clause

CHAPTER 9

Data Types and Advanced Data Types

Transact-SQL is a strongly-typed language. Columns and variables must have a valid data type, and the type is a constraint of the column. In this chapter, we will not cover all data types comprehensively. We will skip the obvious part and concentrate on specific information and on more complex and sophisticated data types that were introduced in SQL Server over time.

Basic Data Types

Basic data types like integer or varchar are pretty much self-explanatory. Some of these types have interesting and important-to-know properties or behavior, and even the most used, like varchar, are worth a look.

Characters

Many tools, like the Microsoft Access Upsizing Wizard, generate tables in SQL Server using some default choices. For all character strings, they create nvarchar columns by default. The n stands for UNICODE, the double-bytes representation of a character, with enough room to fit all worldwide language signs (also called logograms in linguistics), like traditional and simplified Chinese, Arabic, and Farsi. nvarchar must be used when the column has to store non-European languages, but as they induce an obvious overhead, you should avoid creating unneeded nvarchar or nchar columns.

The real size of the data in bytes is returned by the DATALENGTH() function, while the LEN() string function, designed to hide internal storage specifics from the T-SQL developer, will return the number of characters. We test the different values returned by these functions in Listing 9-1. The results are shown in Figure 9-1.

Listing 9-1. Unicode Handling

```
DECLARE
    @string VARCHAR(50) = 'hello earth',
    @nstring NVARCHAR(50) = 'hello earth';

SELECT
    DATALENGTH(@string) as DatalengthString,
    DATALENGTH(@nstring) as DatalengthNString,
    LEN(@string) as lenString,
    LEN(@nstring) as lenNString;
```

239

	DatalengthString	DatalengthNString	lenString	lenNString
1	11	22	11	11

Figure 9-1. *The Results of LEN() and DATALENGTH()*

You can see the the nvarchar storage of our 'hello earth' is 22 bytes. Imagine a 100 million-row table: having such a column with an average of 11-character strings, the storage needed to accomodate the extra bytes would be 1.1 GB.

■ **Note** To represent a T-SQL identifier, like a login name or a table name, you can use the special sysname type, which corresponds to nvarchar(128).

The Max Data Types

In the heady days of SQL Server 2000, large object (LOB) data storage and manipulation required use of the old style text, ntext, and image data types. These types have been deprecated and were replaced with easier-to-use types in SQL Server 2005, namely the varchar(max), nvarchar(max), and varbinary(max) types.

Like the older types, each of these new data types can hold over 2.1 billion bytes of character or binary data, but they handle data in a much more efficient way. The old text or image types required a dedicated type of allocation that created a b-tree structure for each value inserted, regardless of its size. This of course had a significant performance impact when retrieving the columns' content, because the storage engine had to follow pointers to this complex allocation structure for each and every row being read, even if its value was a few bytes long. The (n)varchar(max) or varbinary(max) are more clever types that are handled differently depending on the size of the value. The storage engine creates the LOB structure only if the data inserted cannot be kept in the 8 KB page.

Also, unlike the legacy LOB types, the max data types operate similarly to the standard varchar, nvarchar, and varbinary data types. Standard string manipulation functions such as LEN() and CHARINDEX(), which didn't work well with the older LOB data types, work as expected with the new max data types. The new data types also eliminate the need for awkward solutions involving the TEXTPTR, READTEXT, and WRITETEXT statements to manipulate LOB data.

■ **Note** The varchar(max), nvarchar(max), and varbinary(max) data types are complete replacements for the SQL Server 2000 text, ntext, and image data types. The text, ntext, and image data types and their support functions will be removed in a future version of SQL Server. Because they are deprecated, Microsoft recommends you avoid these older data types for new development.

The new max data types support a .WRITE clause extension to the UPDATE statement to perform optimized minimally logged updates and appends to varchar(max), varbinary(max), and nvarchar(max) types. You can use the .WRITE clause by appending it to the end of the column name in your UPDATE statement. The example in Listing 9-2 compares performance of the .WRITE clause to a simple string concatenation when updating a column. The results of this simple comparison are shown in Figure 9-2.

Listing 9-2. Comparison of .WRITE Clause and String Append

```
-- Turn off messages that can affect performance
SET NOCOUNT ON;
-- Create and initially populate a test table
CREATE TABLE #test (
    Id int NOT NULL PRIMARY KEY,
    String varchar(max) NOT NULL
);

INSERT INTO #test (
    Id,
    String
) VALUES (
    1,
    ''
), (
    2,
    ''
);
-- Initialize variables and get start time
DECLARE @i int = 1;
DECLARE @quote varchar(50) = 'Four score and seven years ago…';
DECLARE @start_time datetime2(7) = SYSDATETIME();
-- Loop 2500 times and use .WRITE to append to a varchar(max) column
WHILE @i < 2500
BEGIN
    UPDATE #test
    SET string.WRITE(@quote, LEN(string), LEN(@quote))
    WHERE Id = 1;

    SET @i += 1;
END;

SELECT '.WRITE Clause', DATEDIFF(ms, @start_time, SYSDATETIME()), 'ms';

-- Reset variables and get new start time
SET @i  = 1;
SET @start_time = SYSDATETIME();

-- Loop 2500 times and use string append to a varchar(max) column
WHILE @i < 2500
BEGIN
    UPDATE #test
    SET string += @quote
    WHERE Id = 2;

    SET @i += 1;
END;

SELECT 'Append Method', DATEDIFF(ms, @start_time, SYSDATETIME()), 'ms';
```

241

```
SELECT
    Id,
    String,
    LEN(String)
FROM #test;

DROP TABLE #test;
```

Figure 9-2. *Testing the .WRITE Clause against Simple String Concatenation*

As you can see in this example, the .WRITE clause is appreciably more efficient than a simple string concatenation when updating a max data type column. Note that these times were achieved on one of our development machines, and your results may vary significantly depending on your specific configuration. You can expect the .WRITE method to perform more efficiently than simple string concatenation when updating max data type columns, however.

You should note the following about the .WRITE clause:

- The second .WRITE parameter, @offset, is a zero-based bigint and cannot be negative. The first character of the target string is at offset 0.

- If the @offset parameter is NULL, the expression is appended to the end of the target string. @length is ignored in this case.

- If the third parameter, @length, is NULL, SQL Server truncates anything past the end of the string expression (the first .WRITE parameter) after the target string is updated. The @length parameter is a bigint and cannot be negative.

Numerics

There are two types of numeric: exact and approximate. Integer and decimal are exact numbers. It is worth knowing that any exact numeric can be used as an auto-incremented IDENTITY column. Most of the time of course, a 32-bit int is chosen as an auto-incremented surrogate key.

■ **Note** We call surrogate key a technical, non-natural unique key, in other words a column storing values created inside the database, and having no meaning outside of it. Most of the time in SQL Server it is an IDENTITY (auto-incremented) number, of a `uniqueidentifier` (a Globally Unique Identifier, or GUID) that we will see later in this chapter.

Because there is no unsigned numeric in SQL Server, the range of values that can be generated by the IDENTITY property is from –2,147,483,648 to +2,147,483,647. Indeed, as the IDENTITY property takes a seed and an increment as parameters, nothing prevents you from declaring it as in Listing 9-3:

Listing 9-3. *Use the Full Range of 32-bit Integer for IDENTITY Columns*

```
CREATE TABLE dbo.bigtable (
    bigtableId int identity(-2147483648,1) NOT NULL
);

INSERT INTO dbo.bigtable DEFAULT VALUES;
INSERT INTO dbo.bigtable DEFAULT VALUES;

SELECT * FROM dbo.bigtable;
```

The seed parameter of the `bigtableId` column IDENTITY property is set as the lowest possible int value, instead of the most commonly seen IDENTITY(1,1) declaration. The results follow in Figure 9-3.

Figure 9-3. *The First Two IDENTITY Values Inserted*

This allows for twice the range of available values in your key and might save you from choosing a `bigint` (64-bit integer) to accommodate values for a table in which you expect to have more than 2 billion rows but less than 4 billion rows. Once again, on a 100-million row table, it will save about 400 MB, and probably much more than that because there are strong chances that the key value will be used in indexes and foreign keys.

■ **Note** Some are reluctant to use this tip because it creates keys with negative numbers. Theoretically, a surrogate key is precisely meaningless by nature and should not be seen by the end user. It is merely there to provide a unique value to identify and reference a row. Sometimes, when these surrogate keys are shown to users, they start to acquire a life of their own, a purpose. For example, people start to talk about customer 3425 instead of using her name—hence the difficulty with negative values.

We talked about exact numeric types. A word of caution about approximate types: do not use approximate numeric types for anything other than scientific purpose. A column defined as float or real stores floating-point values as defined by the IEEE Standard for Floating-Point Arithmetic (IEEE 754), and any result of an operation on float or real will be approximate. Think about the number pi: you always give a non-precise representation of pi, and you will never get the precise value of pi because you need to round or truncate it at some decimal. To store the precise decimal values that most of us manipulate in business applications—amounts, measurements, etc.— you need to use either money or decimal which are fixed data types.

The bit data type is mostly used to store Boolean values. It can be 0, 1, or NULL, and it consumes one byte of storage, but with an optimization: if you create up to 8-bit columns in your table, they will share the same byte. So bit columns take very little space. SQL Server recognizes also the string values 'TRUE' and 'FALSE' when they are applied to a bit, and they will be converted to 1 and 0, respectively.

Date and Time Data Types

The date and time types were enriched in SQL Server 2008 by the distinct date and time types, and the more precise datetime2 and datetimeoffset. Before that, only datetime and smalldatetime were available. Table 9-1 summarizes the differences between all SQL Server 2012 date and time data types before we delve more into details.

Table 9-1. *SQL Server 2012 Date and Time Data Type Comparison*

Data Type	Components	Range	Precision
datetime	Date and time	1753-01-01 to 9999-12-31	Fixed, three fractional second digits, 3.33 ms.
smalldatetime	Date and time	1900-01-01 to 2079-06-06	Fixed, one minute.
date	Date	0001-01-01 to 9999-12-31	Fixed, one day.
time	Time	00:00:00 to 23:59:59	User-defined, one to seven fractional second digits, 100 ns.
datetime2	Date and time	0001-01-01 to 9999-12-31	User-defined, one to seven fractional second digits, 100 ns.
datetimeoffset	Date, time, and offset	0001-01-019999-12-31	User-defined, one to seven fractional second digits, 100 ns, offset range of -14:00 to +14:00.

The date data type allows solving a very common problem we had until SQL server 2008. How can we express date without having to take time into account? Before date, it was tricky to do a straight comparison as shown in Listing 9-4.

Listing 9-4. Date Comparison

```
SELECT *
FROM Person.StateProvince
WHERE ModifiedDate = '2008-03-11';
```

Because the ModifiedDate column data type is datetime, SQL Server converts implictly the '2008-03-11' value to the full '2008-03-11 00:00:00.000' datetime representation before carrying out the comparison. If the

ModifiedDate time part is not '00:00:00.000', no line will be returned, which is the case in our example. With datetime-like data types, we are forced to do things as shown in Listing 9-5.

Listing 9-5. Date Comparison Executed Correctly

```
SELECT *
FROM Person.StateProvince
WHERE ModifiedDate BETWEEN '2008-03-11' AND '2008-03-12';
-- or
SELECT *
FROM Person.StateProvince
WHERE CONVERT(CHAR(10), ModifiedDate, 126) = '2008-03-11';
```

But both tricks are unsatisfactory. The first one has a flaw: because the BETWEEN operator is inclusive, lines with ModifiedDate set at '2008-03-12 00:00:00.000' would be included. To be safe, we should have written the query as in Listing 9-6.

Listing 9-6. Correcting the Date Comparison

```
SELECT *
FROM Production.Product
WHERE ModifiedDate BETWEEN '2008-03-11' AND '2008-03-11 23:59:59.997';
-- or
SELECT *
FROM Person.StateProvince
WHERE ModifiedDate >= '2008-03-11' AND ModifiedDate < '2008-03-12';
```

The second example, in Listing 9-5, has a performance implication, because it makes the condition non-sargable.

■ **Note** We say that a predicate is sargable (from Search ARGument–able) when it can take advantage of an index seek. Here, no index on the ModifiedDate column can be used for a seek operation if its value is altered in the query, and thus does not match what was indexed in the first place.

So, the best choice we had was to enforce, maybe by trigger, that every value entered in the column had its time part stripped off or written with '00:00:00.000,' but that time part was still taking up storage space for nothing. Now, the date type, costing 3 bytes, stores a date with one day accuracy.

Listing 9-7 shows a simple usage of the date data type, demonstrating that the DATEDIFF() function works with the date type just as it does with the datetime data type.

Listing 9-7. Sample Date Data Type Usage

```
-- August 19, 14 C.E.
DECLARE @d1 date = '0014-08-19';

-- February 26, 1983
DECLARE @d2 date = '1983-02-26';
SELECT @d1  AS Date1, @d2 AS Date2, DATEDIFF(YEAR, @d1,  @d2) AS YearsDifference;
```

The results of this simple example are shown in Figure 9-4.

Figure 9-4. *The Results of the Date Data Type Example*

In contrast to the date data type, the time data type lets you store time-only data. The range for the time data type is defined on a 24-hour clock, from 00:00:00.0000000 through 23:59:59.9999999, with a user-definable fractional second precision of up to seven digits. The default precision, if you don't specify one, is seven digits of fractional second precision. Listing 9-8 demonstrates the time data type in action.

Listing 9-8. Demonstrating Time Data Type Usage

```
-- 6:25:19.1 AM
DECLARE @start_time time(1) = '06:25:19.1'; -- 1 digit fractional precision
-- 6:25:19.1234567 PM
DECLARE @end_time time = '18:25:19.1234567'; -- default fractional precision
SELECT @start_time AS start_time, @end_time AS end_time,
DATEADD(HOUR, 6, @start_time) AS StartTimePlus, DATEDIFF(HOUR, @start_time, @end_time) AS
 EndStartDiff;
```

In Listing 9-8, two data type instances are created. The @start_time variable is explicitly declared with a fractional second precision of one digit. You can specify a fractional second precision of one to seven digits with 100-nanosecond (ns) accuracy; the fixed fractional precision of the classic datetime data type is three digits with 3.33-millisecond (ms) accuracy. The default fractional precision for the time data type, if no precision is specified, is seven digits. The @end_time variable in the listing is declared with the default precision. As with the date and datetime data types, the DATEDIFF() and DATEADD() functions also work with the time data type. The results of Listing 9-8 are shown in Figure 9-5.

	start_time	end_time	StartTimePlus	EndStartDiff
1	06:25:19.1	18:25:19.1234567	12:25:19.1	12

Figure 9-5. *The Results of the Time Data Type Example*

The cleverly named datetime2 data type is an extension to the standard datetime data type. The datetime2 data type combines the benefits of the date and time data types, giving you the wider date range of the date data type and the greater fractional-second precision of the time data type. Listing 9-9 demonstrates simple declaration and usage of datetime2 variables.

Listing 9-9. Declaring and Querying Datetime2 Variables

```
DECLARE @start_dt2 datetime2 = '1972-07-06 T07:13:28.8230234',
        @end_dt2   datetime2 = '2009-12-14 T03:14:13.2349832';
SELECT @start_dt2 AS start_dt2, @end_dt2 AS end_dt2;
```

The results of Listing 9-9 are shown in Figure 9-6.

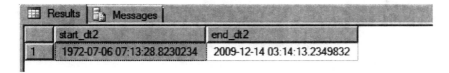

Figure 9-6. *Declaring and Selecting Datetime2 data Type Variables*

The datetimeoffset data type builds on datetime2 by adding the ability to store offsets relative to the International Telecommunication Union (ITU) standard for Coordinated Universal Time (UTC) with your date and time data. When creating a datetimeoffset instance, you can specify an offset that complies with the ISO 8601 standard, which is in turn based on UTC. Basically, the offset must be specified in the range –14:00 to +14:00. The Z offset identifier is shorthand for the offset designated "zulu," or +00:00. Listing 9-10 shows the datetimeoffset data type in action.

Listing 9-10. Datetimeoffset Data Type Sample

```
DECLARE @start_dto datetimeoffset = '1492-10-12 T13:29:59.9999999-05:00';
SELECT @start_dto AS start_to, DATEPART(YEAR, @start_dto) AS start_year;
```

The results of Listing 9-10 are shown in Figure 9-7.

Figure 9-7. *The Result of the Datetimeoffset Sample*

A sampling of possible offsets is shown in Table 9-2. Note that this list is not exhaustive, but demonstrates some common offsets.

Table 9-2. *Common Standard Time Zones*

Time Zone Offset	Name	Locations
−10:00	Hawaii-Aleutian Standard	Alaska (Aleutian Islands), Hawaii
−08:00	Pacific Standard	US West Coast; Los Angeles, CA
−05:00	Eastern Standard	US East Coast; New York, NY
−04:00	Atlantic Standard	Bermuda
+00:00	Coordinated Universal	Dublin, Lisbon, London
+01:00	Central European	Paris, Berlin, Madrid, Rome
+03:00	Baghdad	Kuwait, Riyadh
+06:00	Indian Standard	India
+09:00	Japan Standard	Japan

UTC AND MILITARY TIME

Some people see the acronym *UTC* and think that it stands for "Universal Time Coordination" or "Universal Time Code." Unfortunately, the world is not so simple. When the ITU standardized Coordinated Universal Time, it was decided that it should have the same acronym in every language. Of course, international agreement could not be reached, with the English-speaking countries demanding the acronym *CUT* and French-speaking countries demanding that *TUC (temps universel coordonné)* be used. In the final compromise, the nonsensical *UTC* was adopted as the international standard.

You may notice that we use "military time," or the 24-hour clock, when representing time in the code samples throughout this book. There's a very good reason for that—the 24-hour clock is an ISO international standard. The ISO 8601 standard indicates that time should be represented in computers using the 24-hour clock to prevent ambiguity.

The 24-hour clock begins at 00:00:00, which is midnight or 12 AM. Noon, or 12 PM, is represented as 12:00:00. One second before midnight is 23:59:59, or 11:59:59 PM. In order to convert the 24-hour clock to AM/PM time, simply look at the hours. If the hours are less than 12, then the time is AM. If the hours are equal to 12, you are in the noon hour, which is PM. If the hours are greater than 12, subtract 12 and add PM to your time.

So, with all these types at your disposal, which do you choose? As a rule, avoid datetime: it doesn't align with the SQL Standard, takes generally more space and has lower precision than the other types. It costs 8 bytes, ranges from 1753 through 9999, and rounds the time to 3 milliseconds. For example, let's try the code in Listing 9-11.

Listing 9-11. Demonstration of Datetime Rounding

```
SELECT CAST('2011-12-31 T23:59:59.999' as datetime) as WhatTimeIsIt;
```

You can see the result in Figure 9-8.

Figure 9-8. *The Results of the Datetime Rounding Sample*

The 999 milliseconds were rounded to the next value, and 998 would have been rounded to 997. For most usages this is not an issue, but `datetime2` does not have this drawback, or at least you have control over it by defining the precision.

Date and Time Functions

One of the difficulties of T-SQL is the handling of dates in the code. Internally, the `date` and `time` data types are stored in a numeric representation, but of course, they have to be made human-readable in a string format. The format is important for input or output, but it has nothing to do with storage, and it is a common misconception to consider that a date is stored in a particular format. The output is managed by the client. For example, in SSMS, dates are always returned in the ODBC API ts (timestamp) format (yyyy-mm-dd hh:mm:ss.. . .), regardless of the computer's regional settings. If you want to force a particular format in T-SQL, you will need to use a conversion function. The `CONVERT()` function is a legacy function that returns a formatted string from a date and time data type or vice-versa, while the `FORMAT()` function, new in SQL Server 2012, uses the more common .NET format strings and an optional culture to return a formatted `nvarchar` value. We demonstrate usage of these two functions in Listing 9-12.

Listing 9-12. CONVERT() and FORMAT() Usage Sample

```
DECLARE @dt2 datetime2 = '2011-12-31 T23:59:59';

SELECT  FORMAT(@dt2, 'F', 'en-US') as with_format,
        CONVERT(varchar(50), @dt2, 109) as with_convert;
```

The results are shown in Figure 9-9.

Figure 9-9. *The Results of the Datetime2 Formatting Sample*

Of course, data input must also be done using a string representation that can be understood by SQL Server as a date. This depends on the language settings of the session. Each session has a language environment that is the default language of the login, unless a `SET LANGUAGE` command changed it at some time. You can retrieve the language of the current session with one of the two ways shown in Listing 9-13.

Listing 9-13. How to Check the Current Language of the Session

```
SELECT language
FROM sys.dm_exec_sessions
WHERE session_id = @@SPID;
-- or
SELECT @@LANGUAGE;
```

Formatting your date strings for input with a language dependent format is risky, because anyone running the code under another language environment would get an error, as shown in Listing 9-14.

Listing 9-14. Language Dependent Date String Representations

```
DECLARE @lang sysname;

SET @lang = @@LANGUAGE

SELECT CAST('12/31/2012' as datetime2); --this works

SET LANGUAGE 'spanish';

SELECT
    CASE WHEN TRY_CAST('12/31/2012' as datetime2) IS NULL
    THEN 'Cast failed'
    ELSE 'Cast succeeded'
END AS Result;

SET LANGUAGE @lang;
```

The second CAST() attempt, using the TRY_CAST() to prevent an exception from being raised, will return 'Cast failed' because 'MM/dd/yyyy' is not recognized as a valid date format in Spanish. If we would have used CAST() instead of TRY_CAST(), we would have received a conversion error in the Spanish language, and the last SET LANGUAGE command wouldn't have been executed, due to the preceding exception.

You have two options to prevent this. First, you can use the SET DATEFORMAT instruction that sets the order of the month, day, and year date parts for interpreting date character strings, as shown in Listing 9-15.

Listing 9-15. Usage of SET DATEFORMAT

```
SET DATEFORMAT mdy;
SET LANGUAGE 'spanish';
SELECT CAST('12/31/2012' as datetime2); --this works now
```

Or you can decide—this is a better option—to stick with a language-neutral format that will be recognized regardless of what the language environment is. You can do that by making sure you always have your date strings formatted in an ISO 8601 standard variant. In ISO 8601, date and time values are organized from the most to the least significant, starting with the year. The two most common ones are yyyy-MM-ddTHH:mm:ss (note the T character to separate date and time) and yyyyMMdd HH:mm:ss. In a .NET client code, you could generate those formats with the .NET format strings, as shown in the pseudo-code examples of Listing 9-16.

Listing 9-16. Samples of ISO 8601 Date Formatting in .NET Pseudo-code

```
DateTime.Now.Format( "s" );
DateTime.Now.ToString ( "s", System.Globalization.CultureInfo.InvariantCulture );
```

The first line calls the Format() method of the the DateTime .NET type, and the second line uses the ToString() method of .NET objects, that can take a format string and a culture as parameters when applied to a DateTime.

With more complete and precise date and time data types comes also a wide range of built-in date- and time-related functions. You might already know the GETDATE() and CURRENT_TIMESTAMP functions. Since SQL Server 2008, you have had more functions for returning the current date and time of the server.

The SYSDATETIME() function returns the system date and time, as reported by the server's local operating system, as a datetime2 value without time offset information. The value returned by GETDATE(), CURRENT_TIMESTAMP and SYSDATETIME() is the date and time reported by Windows on the computer where your SQL Server instance is installed.

The SYSUTCDATETIME() function returns the system date and time information converted to UTC as a datetime2 value. As with the SYSDATETIME() function, the value returned does not contain additional time offset information.

The SYSDATETIMEOFFSET() function returns the system date and time as a datetimeoffset value, including the time offset information. Listing 9-17 uses these functions to display the current system date and time in various formats. The results are shown in Figure 9-10.

Listing 9-17. Using the Date and Time Functions

```
SELECT SYSDATETIME() AS [SYSDATETIME];
SELECT SYSUTCDATETIME() AS [SYSUTCDATETIME];
SELECT SYSDATETIMEOFFSET() AS [SYSDATETIMEOFFSET];
```

Figure 9-10. The Current System Date and Time in a Variety of Formats

The TODATETIMEOFFSET() function allows you to add time offset information to date and time data without time offset information. You can use TODATETIMEOFFSET to add time offset information to a date, time, datetime, datetime2, or datetimeoffset value. The result returned by the function is a datetimeoffset value with time offset information added. Listing 9-18 demonstrates by adding time offset information to a datetime value. The results are shown in Figure 9-11.

Listing 9-18. Adding an Offset to a Datetime Value

```
DECLARE @current datetime = CURRENT_TIMESTAMP;
SELECT @current AS [No_Offset];
SELECT TODATETIMEOFFSET(@current, '-04:00') AS [With_Offset];
```

251

Figure 9-11. *Converting a Datetime Value to a Datetimeoffset*

The SWITCHOFFSET() function adjusts a given datetimeoffset value to another given time offset. This is useful when you need to convert a date and time to another time offset. In Listing 9-19, we use the SWITCHOFFSET() function to convert a datetimeoffset value in Los Angeles to several other regional time offsets. The values are calculated for Daylight Saving Time. The results are shown in Figure 9-12.

■ **Tip** You can use the Z time offset in datetimeoffset literals as an abbreviation for UTC (+00:00 offset). You cannot, however, specify Z as the time offset parameter with the TODATETIMEOFFSET and SWITCHOFFSET functions.

Listing 9-19. Converting a Datetimeoffset to Several Time Offsets

```
DECLARE @current datetimeoffset = '2012-05-04 19:30:00-07:00';
SELECT 'Los Angeles' AS [Location], @current AS [Current Time]
UNION ALL
SELECT 'New York', SWITCHOFFSET(@current, '-04:00')
UNION ALL
SELECT 'Bermuda', SWITCHOFFSET(@current, '-03:00')
UNION ALL
SELECT 'London', SWITCHOFFSET(@current, '+01:00');
```

	Location	Current Time
1	Los Angeles	2012-05-04 19:30:00.0000000 -07:00
2	New York	2012-05-04 22:30:00.0000000 -04:00
3	Bermuda	2012-05-04 23:30:00.0000000 -03:00
4	London	2012-05-05 03:30:00.0000000 +01:00

Figure 9-12. *Date and Time Information in Several Different Time Offsets*

TIME ZONES AND OFFSETS

Time offsets are not the same thing as time zones. A time offset is relatively easy to calculate—it's simply a plus or minus offset in hours and minutes from the UTC offset (+00:00), as defined by the ISO 8601 standard. A time zone, however, is an identifier for a specific location or region and is defined by regional laws and regulations. Time zones can have very complex sets of rules that include such oddities as Daylight Saving Time (DST). SQL Server uses time offsets in calculations, not time zones. If you want to perform date and time calculations involving actual time zones, you will have to write custom code. Just keep in mind that time zone calculations are fairly involved, especially since calculations like DST can change over time. Case in point—the start and end dates for DST were changed to extend DST in the United States beginning in 2007.

The Uniqueidentifier Data Type

In Windows, you see a lot of GUIDs (Globally Unique IDentifiers) in the registry and as a way to provide code and modules (like COM objects) with unique identifiers. GUIDs are 16-byte values generally represented as 32-character hexadecimal strings, and can be stored in SQL Server in the uniqueidentifier data type. uniqueidentifier could be used to create unique keys across tables, servers or data centers. To create a new GUID and store it in a uniqueidentifier column, you use the NEWID() function, as demonstrated in Listing 9-20. The results are shown in Figure 9-13.

Listing 9-20. Using Uniqueidentifier

```
CREATE TABLE dbo.Document (
    DocumentId uniqueidentifier NOT NULL PRIMARY KEY DEFAULT (NEWID())
);

INSERT INTO dbo.Document DEFAULT VALUES;
INSERT INTO dbo.Document DEFAULT VALUES;
INSERT INTO dbo.Document DEFAULT VALUES;

SELECT * FROM dbo.Document;
```

	DocumentId
1	8BEAD517-5068-4CF7-B768-10322C13728A
2	9BDC122F-148A-42C2-9DA8-75718EEE8DE2
3	05A8D779-A15D-4CCE-A317-AFD6AABE990E

Figure 9-13. Results Generated by the Newid() Function

Each time the NEWID() function is called, it generates a new value using an algorithm based on a pseudo-random generator. The risk of two generated numbers being the same is statistically negligible: hence the global uniqueness it offers.

However, usage of `uniqueidentifier` columns should be carefully considered, because it bears significant consequences. We have already talked about the importance of data type size, and especially key size. Choosing a `uniqueidentifier` over an `int` as a primary key creates an overhead of 12 bytes per row that impacts the size of the table, of the primary key index, of all other indexes if the primary key is defined as clustered (as it is by default), and of all tables that have a foreign key associated to it, and finally on all indexes on these foreign keys. Needless to say, it could considerably increase the size of your database.

There is another problem with `uniqueidentifier` values, because of their inherent randomness. If your primary key is clustered, the physical order of the table depends upon the value of the key, and at each insert or update, SQL Server must place the new or modified lines at the right place, in the right data pages. GUID random values will cause page splits that will noticeably decrease performances and generate table fragmentation.

To address this last issue, SQL Server 2008 introduced the `NEWSEQUENTIALID()` function to use as a default constraint with an `uniqueidentifier` primary key. `NEWSEQUENTIALID()` generates sequential GUIDs in increasing order. Its usage is shown in Listing 9-21. Results are shown in Figure 9-14; notice that the GUID digits are displayed in groups in reverse order. In the results, the first byte of each GUID represents the sequentially increasing values generated by `NEWSEQUENTIALID()` with each row inserted.

Listing 9-21. Generating Sequential GUIDs

```
CREATE TABLE #TestSeqID (
    ID uniqueidentifier DEFAULT NEWSEQUENTIALID() PRIMARY KEY NOT NULL,
    Num int NOT NULL
);

INSERT INTO #TestSeqID (Num)
VALUES (1), (2), (3);

SELECT ID, Num
FROM #TestSeqID;

DROP TABLE #TestSeqID;
```

	ID	Num
1	4CDDEF6B-F395-E111-897E-080027D3B4E2	1
2	4DDDEF6B-F395-E111-897E-080027D3B4E2	2
3	4EDDEF6B-F395-E111-897E-080027D3B4E2	3

Figure 9-14. *Results Generated by the NEWSEQUENTIALID Function*

The Hierarchyid Data Type

The `hierarchyid` data type offers a new twist on an old model for representing hierarchical data in the database. This data type introduced in SQL Server 2008 offers built-in support for representing your hierarchical data using one of the simplest models available: materialized paths.

REPRESENTING HIERARCHICAL DATA

The representation of hierarchical data in relational databases has long been an area of interest for SQL developers. The most common model of representing hierarchical data with SQL Server is the *adjacency list* model. In this model, each row of a table maintains a reference to its parent row. The following illustration demonstrates how the adjacency list model works in an SQL table.

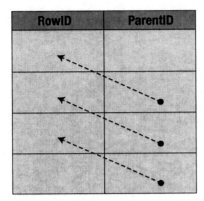

The AdventureWorks sample database makes use of the adjacency list model in its `Production.BillOfMaterials` table, where every component references its parent assembly.

The *materialized path* model requires that you store the actual hierarchical path from the root node to the current node. The hierarchical path is similar to a modern file system path, where each folder or directory represents a node in the path. The `hierarchyid` data type supports generation and indexing of materialized paths for hierarchical data modeling. The following illustration shows how the materialized path might look in SQL.

It is a relatively simple matter to represent adjacency list model data using materialized paths, as you'll see later in this section in the discussion on converting AdventureWorks adjacency list data to the materialized path model using the `hierarchyid` data type.

Another model for representing hierarchical data is the *nested sets* model. In this model, every row in the table is considered a set that may contain or be contained by another set. Each row is assigned a pair of numbers defining the lower and upper bounds for the set. The following illustration shows a logical representation of the nested sets model, with the lower and upper bounds for each set shown to the set's left and right. Notice that the sets in the figure are contained within one another logically, in a structure from which this model derives its name.

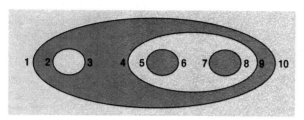

In this section, we'll use the AdventureWorks Production.BillOfMaterials table extensively to demonstrate the adjacency list model, the materialized path model, and the hierarchyid data type. Technically speaking, a bill of materials (BOM), or "parts explosion," is a *directed acyclic graph*. A directed acyclic graph is essentially a generalized tree structure in which some subtrees may be shared by different parts of the tree. Think of a cake recipe, represented as a tree, in which "sugar" can be used multiple times (once in the "cake mix" subtree, once in the "frosting" subtree, and so on). This book is not about graph theory, though, so we'll pass on the technical details and get to the BOM at hand. Although *directed acyclic graph* is the technical term for a true BOM, we'll be representing the AdventureWorks BOMs as materialized path hierarchies using the hierarchyid data type, so you'll see the term *hierarchy* used a lot in this section.

In order to understand the AdventureWorks BOM hierarchies, it's important to understand the relationship between product assemblies and components. Basically, a *product* assembly is composed of one or more *components*. An assembly can become a component for use in other assemblies, defining the recursive relationship. All components with a product assembly of NULL are top-level components, or "root nodes," of each hierarchy. If a hierarchyid data type column is declared a primary key, it can contain only a single hierarchyid root node.

The hierarchyid data type stores hierarchy information as an optimized materialized path, which is a very efficient way to store hierarchical information. We will go though a complete example of its use.

Hierarchyid Example

In this example, we will convert the AdventureWorks BOMs to materialized path form using the hierarchyid data type. The first step, shown in Listing 9-22, is to create the table that will contain the hierarchyid BOMs. To differentiate it from the Production.BillOfMaterials table, we have called this table Production.HierBillOfMaterials.

Listing 9-22. Creating the Hierarchyid Bill of Materials Table

```
CREATE TABLE Production.HierBillOfMaterials
(
    BomNode hierarchyid NOT NULL PRIMARY KEY NONCLUSTERED,
    ProductAssemblyID int NULL,
    ComponentID int NULL,
    UnitMeasureCode nchar(3) NULL,
    PerAssemblyQty decimal(8, 2) NULL,
    BomLevel AS BomNode.GetLevel()
);
```

The `Production.HierBillOfMaterials` table consists of the `BomNode` `hierarchyid` column, which will contain the hierarchical path information for each component. The `ProductAssemblyID`, `ComponentID`, `UnitMeasureCode`, and `PerAssemblyQty` are all pulled from the source tables. `BomLevel` is a calculated column that contains the current level of each `BomNode`. The next step is to convert the adjacency list BOMs to `hierarchyid` form, which will be used to populate the `Production.HierBillOfMaterials` table. This is demonstrated in Listing 9-23.

Listing 9-23. Converting AdventureWorks BOMs to hierarchyid Form

```
;WITH BomChildren
(
    ProductAssemblyID,
    ComponentID
)
AS
(
    SELECT
        b1.ProductAssemblyID,
        b1.ComponentID
    FROM Production.BillOfMaterials b1
    GROUP BY
        b1.ProductAssemblyID,
        b1.ComponentID
),
BomPaths
(
    Path,
    ComponentID,
    ProductAssemblyID
)
AS
(
    SELECT
        hierarchyid::GetRoot() AS Path,
        NULL,
        NULL
    UNION ALL

    SELECT
        CAST
        ('/' + CAST (bc.ComponentId AS varchar(30)) + '/' AS hierarchyid) AS Path,
        bc.ComponentID,
        bc.ProductAssemblyID
    FROM BomChildren AS bc
    WHERE bc.ProductAssemblyID IS NULL

    UNION ALL

    SELECT
        CAST
        (bp.path.ToString() +
            CAST(bc.ComponentID AS varchar(30))+'/' AS hierarchyid) AS Path,
```

```
            bc.ComponentID,
            bc.ProductAssemblyID
    FROM  BomChildren  AS  bc
    INNER JOIN BomPaths AS bp
        ON bc.ProductAssemblyID = bp.ComponentID
)
INSERT INTO Production.HierBillOfMaterials
(
    BomNode,
    ProductAssemblyID,
    ComponentID,
    UnitMeasureCode,
    PerAssemblyQty
)
SELECT
    bp.Path,
    bp.ProductAssemblyID,
    bp.ComponentID,
    bom.UnitMeasureCode,
    bom.PerAssemblyQty
FROM BomPaths AS bp
LEFT OUTER JOIN Production.BillOfMaterials bom
    ON  bp.ComponentID = bom.ComponentID
        AND COALESCE(bp.ProductAssemblyID, -1) = COALESCE(bom.ProductAssemblyID, -1)
WHERE bom.EndDate IS NULL
GROUP BY
    bp.path,
    bp.ProductAssemblyID,
    bp.ComponentID,
    bom.UnitMeasureCode,
    bom.PerAssemblyQty;
```

This statement is a little more complex than the average hierarchyid data example you'll probably run into, since most people currently out there are demonstrating conversion of the simple, single-hierarchy AdventureWorks organizational chart. The AdventureWorks Production.BillOfMaterials table actually contains several individual hierarchies.

We will go through the code step by step here to show you exactly what's going on in this statement. The first part of the statement is a common table expression (CTE) called BomChildren. It returns all ProductAssemblyIDs and ComponentIDs from the Production.BillOfMaterials table.

```
;WITH  BomChildren
(
    ProductAssemblyID,
    ComponentID
)
AS
(
    SELECT
        b1.ProductAssemblyID,
        b1.ComponentID
    FROM  Production.BillOfMaterials  b1
```

```
GROUP BY
    b1.ProductAssemblyID,
    b1.ComponentID
),
```

While the organizational chart represents a simple top-down hierarchy with a single root node, the BOM is actually composed of dozens of separate hierarchies with no single hierarchyid root node. BomPaths is a recursive CTE that returns the current hierarchyid, ComponentID, and ProductAssemblyID for each row.

```
BomPaths
(
    Path,
    ComponentID,
    ProductAssemblyID
)
```

The anchor query for the CTE is in two parts. The first part returns the root node for the entire hierarchy. In this case, the root just represents a logical grouping of all the BOM's top-level assemblies; it does not represent another product that can be created by mashing together every product in the AdventureWorks catalog.

```
SELECT
    hierarchyid::GetRoot(),
    NULL,
    NULL
```

The second part of the anchor query returns the hierarchyid path to the top-level assemblies. Each top-level assembly has its ComponentId appended to the root path, represented by a leading forward slash (/).

```
SELECT
    CAST
    ('/' + CAST (bc.ComponentId AS varchar(30)) + '/' AS hierarchyid) AS Path,
    bc.ComponentID,
    bc.ProductAssemblyID
FROM BomChildren AS bc
WHERE bc.ProductAssemblyID IS NULL
```

The recursive part of the CTE recursively appends forward slash-separated ComponentId values to the path to represent each component in any given assembly:

```
SELECT
    CAST
    (bp.path.ToString() +
        CAST(bc.ComponentID AS varchar(30))+'/' AS hierarchyid) AS Path,
    bc.ComponentID,
    bc.ProductAssemblyID
FROM BomChildren AS bc
INNER JOIN BomPaths AS bp
    ON bc.ProductAssemblyID = bp.ComponentID
)
```

The next part of the statement inserts the results of the recursive BomPaths CTE into the Production. HierBillOfMaterials table. The results of the recursive CTE are joined to the Production.BillOfMaterials table for a couple of reasons:

- to ensure that only components currently in use are put into the hierarchy by making sure that the EndDate is NULL for each component

- to retrieve the UnitMeasureCode and PerAssemblyQty columns for each component

We use a LEFT OUTER JOIN in this statement instead of an INNER JOIN because of the inclusion of the hierarchyid root node, which has no matching row in the Production.BillOfMaterials table. If you had opted not to include the hierarchyid root node, you could turn this join back into an INNER JOIN.

```
INSERT INTO Production.HierBillOfMaterials
(
    BomNode,
    ProductAssemblyID,
    ComponentID,
    UnitMeasureCode,
    PerAssemblyQty
)
SELECT
    bp.Path,
    bp.ProductAssemblyID,
    bp.ComponentID,
    bom.UnitMeasureCode,
    bom.PerAssemblyQty
FROM BomPaths AS bp
LEFT OUTER JOIN Production.BillOfMaterials bom
    ON   bp.ComponentID = bom.ComponentID
         AND COALESCE(bp.ProductAssemblyID, -1) = COALESCE(bom.ProductAssemblyID, -1)
WHERE bom.EndDate IS NULL
GROUP BY
    bp.path,
    bp.ProductAssemblyID,
    bp.ComponentID,
    bom.UnitMeasureCode,
    bom.PerAssemblyQty;
```

The simple query in Listing 9-24 shows the BOM after conversion to materialized path form with the hierarchyid data type, and ordered by the hierarchyid column to demonstrate that the hierarchy is reflected from the hierarchyid content itself. Partial results are shown in Figure 9-15.

Listing 9-24. Viewing the Hierarchyid BOMs

```
SELECT
    BomNode,
    BomNode.ToString(),
    ProductAssemblyID,
    ComponentID,
    UnitMeasureCode,
    PerAssemblyQty,
    BomLevel
FROM Production.HierBillOfMaterialsORDER BY BomNode;
```

	BomNode	(No column name)	ProductAssemblyID	ComponentID	UnitMeasureCode	PerAssemblyQty	BomLevel
1	0x	/	NULL	NULL	NULL	NULL	0
2	0xEA2EC0	/749/	NULL	749	EA	1.00	1
3	0xEA2EF999F0	/749/519/	749	519	EA	1.00	2
4	0xEA2EF999FE644C	/749/519/497/	519	497	EA	4.00	3
5	0xEA2EF999FE6844	/749/519/528/	519	528	EA	1.00	3
6	0xEA2EF999FE6854	/749/519/530/	519	530	EA	1.00	3
7	0xEA2EF999FEC84C	/749/519/913/	519	913	EA	1.00	3
8	0xEA2EFA3BB0	/749/717/	749	717	EA	1.00	2
9	0xEA2EFA3BBE2E64	/749/717/324/	717	324	EA	2.00	3
10	0xEA2EFA3BBE2E67989D	/749/717/324/486/	324	486	EA	1.00	4
11	0xEA2EFA3BBE2E6C	/749/717/325/	717	325	EA	2.00	3
12	0xEA2EFA3BBE2E74	/749/717/326/	717	326	EA	1.00	3

Figure 9-15. *Partial Results of the hierarchical BOM Conversion*

As you can see, the hierarchyid column, BomNode, represents the hierarchy as a compact path in a variable-length binary format. Converting the BomNode column to string format with the ToString() method results in a forward slash-separated path reminiscent of a file path. The BomLevel column uses the GetLevel() method to retrieve the level of each node in the hierarchy. The hierarchyid root node has a BomLevel of 0. The top-level assemblies are on level 1, and their children are on levels 2 and below.

Hierarchyid Methods

The hierarchyid data type includes several methods for querying and manipulating hierarchical data. The IsDescendantOf() method, for instance, can be used to retrieve all descendants of a given node. The example in Listing 9-25 retrieves the descendant nodes of product assembly 749. The results are shown in Figure 9-16.

Listing 9-25. Retrieving Descendant Nodes of Assembly 749

```
DECLARE @CurrentNode hierarchyid;

SELECT @CurrentNode = BomNode
FROM Production.HierBillOfMaterials
WHERE ProductAssemblyID = 749;

SELECT
    BomNode,
    BomNode.ToString(),
    ProductAssemblyID,
    ComponentID,
    UnitMeasureCode,
    PerAssemblyQty,
    BomLevel
FROM Production.HierBillOfMaterials
WHERE @CurrentNode.IsDescendantOf(BomNode) = 1;
```

	BomNode	(No column name)	ProductAssemblyID	ComponentID	UnitMeasureCode	PerAssemblyQty	BomLevel
1	0x	/	NULL	NULL	NULL	NULL	0
2	0xEA2EC0	/749/	NULL	749	EA	1.00	1
3	0xEA2EFB8990	/749/996/	749	996	EA	1.00	2

Figure 9-16. *Descendant Nodes of Assembly 749*

Table 9-3 is a quick summary of the hierarchyid data type methods.

Table 9-3. *hierarchyid Data Type Methods*

Method	Description
GetAncestor(n)	Retrieves the nth ancestor of the hierarchyid node instance.
GetDescendant(n)	Retrieves the nth descendant of the hierarchyid node instance.
GetLevel()	Gets the level of the hierarchyid node instance in the hierarchy.
GetRoot()	Gets the hierarchyid instance root node; GetRoot() is a static method.
IsDescendantOf(node)	Returns 1 if a specified node is a descendant of the hierarchyid instance node.
Parse(string)	Converts the given canonical string, in forward slash-separated format, to a hierarchyid path.
GetReparentedValue (old_root, new_root)	Returns a node reparented from old_root to new_root.
ToString()	Converts a hierarchyid instance to a canonical forward slash-separated string representation.

Spatial Data Types

Since version 2008, SQL Server includes two data types for storing, querying, and manipulating spatial data. The geometry data type is designed to represent flat-earth, or Euclidean, spatial data per the Open Geospatial Consortium (OGC) standard. The geography data type supports round-earth, or ellipsoidal, spatial data. Figure 9-17 shows a simple two-dimensional flat geometry for a small area, with a point plotted at location (2, 1).

Figure 9-17. Flat Spatial Representation

The spatial data types store representations of spatial data using instance types. There are 12 instance types, all derived from the Geography Markup Language (GML) abstract Geometry type. Of those 12 instance types, only 7 are concrete types that can be instantiated; the other 5 serve as abstract base types from which other types derive. Figure 9-18 shows the spatial instance type hierarchy with the XML-based GML top-level elements.

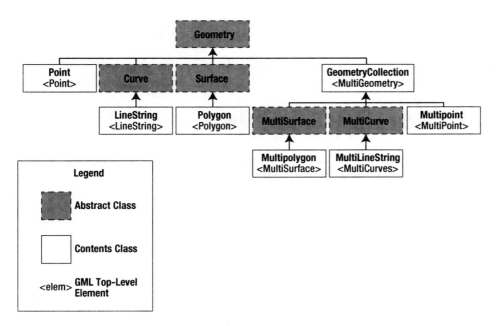

Figure 9-18. Spatial Instance Type Hierarchy

The available spatial instance types include the following:

- `Point`: This object represents a zero-dimensional object representing a single location. The `Point` requires, at a minimum, a two-dimensional (x, y) coordinate pair, but it may also have an elevation coordinate (z) and an additional user-defined measure. The `Point` object has no area or length.

- `MultiPoint`: This type represents a collection of multiple points. It has no area or length.

- `LineString`: This is a one-dimensional object representing one or more connected line segments. Each segment is defined by a start point and an endpoint, and all segments are connected in such a way that the endpoint of one line segment is the start point for the next line segment. The `LineString` has length, but no area.

- `MultiLineString`: This is a one-dimensional object composed of multiple `LineString` objects. The `LineString` objects in a `MultiLineString` do not necessarily have to be connected to one another. The `MultiLineString` has no area, but it has an associated length, which is the sum of the lengths of all `LineString` objects in the `MultiLineString`.

- `Polygon`: This is a two-dimensional object defined by a sequence of connected points. The `Polygon` object must have a single exterior bounding ring, which defines the interior region of the `Polygon` object. In addition, the `Polygon` may have interior bounding rings, which exclude portions of the area inside the interior bounding ring from the `Polygon`'s area. `Polygon` objects have a length, which is the length of the exterior bounding ring, and an area, which is the area defined by the exterior bounding ring minus the areas defined by any interior bounding rings.

- `MultiPolygon`: This is a collection of `Polygon` objects. Like the `Polygon`, the `MultiPolygon` has both length and area.

- `GeometryCollection`: This is the base class for the "multi" types (e.g. `MultiPoint`, `MultiLine`, and `MultiPolygon`). This class can be instantiated and can contain a collection of any spatial objects.

You can populate spatial data using Well-Known Text (WKT) strings or GML-formatted data. WKT strings are passed into the geometry and geography data types' `STGeomFromText()` static method and related static methods. Spatial data types can be populated from GML-formatted data with the `GeomFromGml()` static method. Listing 9-26 shows how to populate a spatial data type with a `Polygon` instance via a WKT-formatted string. The coordinates in the WKT `Polygon` are the borders of the state of Wyoming, chosen for its simplicity. The result of the SELECT in the SSMS spatial data pane is shown in Figure 9-19.

Listing 9-26. Representing Wyoming as a Geometry Object

```
DECLARE @Wyoming geometry;
SET @Wyoming = geometry::STGeomFromText ('POLYGON (
( -104.053108 41.698246, -104.054993 41.564247,
-104.053505 41.388107, -104.051201 41.003227,
-104.933968 40.994305, -105.278259 40.996365,
-106.202896 41.000111, -106.328545 41.001316,
-106.864838 40.998489, -107.303436 41.000168,
-107.918037 41.00341, -109.047638 40.998474,
-110.001457 40.997646, -110.062477 40.99794,
-111.050285 40.996635, -111.050911 41.25848,
-111.050323 41.578648, -111.047951 41.996265,
-111.046028 42.503323, -111.048447 43.019962,
```

```
-111.04673 43.284813, -111.045998 43.515606,
-111.049629 43.982632, -111.050789 44.473396,
-111.050842 44.664562, -111.05265 44.995766,
-110.428894 44.992348, -110.392006 44.998688,
-109.994789 45.002853, -109.798653 44.99958,
-108.624573 44.997643, -108.258568 45.00016,
-107.893715 44.999813, -106.258644 44.996174,
-106.020576 44.997227, -105.084465 44.999832,
-105.04126 45.001091, -104.059349 44.997349,
-104.058975 44.574368, -104.060547 44.181843,
-104.059242 44.145844, -104.05899 43.852928,
-104.057426 43.503738, -104.05867 43.47916,
-104.05571 43.003094, -104.055725 42.614704,
-104.053009 41.999851, -104.053108 41.698246) )', 0);
SELECT @Wyoming as Wyoming;
```

Figure 9-19. *The Wyoming Polygon*

Listing 9-26 demonstrates a couple of interesting items. The first point is that the coordinates are given in latitude-longitude order, not in (x, y).

(X, Y) OR (LATITUDE, LONGITUDE)?

Coordinates in spatial data are generally represented using (x, y) coordinate pairs. However, we often say "latitude-longitude" when we refer to coordinates. The problem is that latitude is the y axis, while longitude is the x axis. The Well-Known Text format we'll discuss later in this section represents spatial data using (x, y) coordinate pair ordering for the geometry and geography data types. But the GML syntax expresses coordinates the other way around, with latitude before longitude. You need to be aware of this difference when entering coordinates.

The second point is that the final coordinate pair, (−104.053108, 41.698246), is the same as the first coordinate pair. This is a requirement for Polygon objects.

You can populate a geography instance similarly using WKT or GML. Listing 9-27 populates a geography instance with the border coordinates for the state of Wyoming using GML. The result will be the same as shown previously in Figure 9-19.

Listing 9-27. Using GML to Represent Wyoming as a Geography Object

```
DECLARE @Wyoming geography;
SET @Wyoming = geography::GeomFromGml (' < Polygon
    xmlns = "http://www.opengis.net/gml">
    <exterior>
        <LinearRing>
        <posList>
        41.698246   -104.053108   41.999851        -104.053009
        43.003094   -104.05571    43.503738        -104.057426
        44.145844   -104.059242   44.574368        -104.058975
        45.001091   -105.04126    44.997227        -106.020576
        44.999813   -107.893715   44.997643        -108.624573
        45.002853   -109.994789   44.992348        -110.428894
        44.664562   -111.050842   43.982632        -111.049629
        43.284813   -111.04673    42.503323        -111.046028
        41.578648   -111.050323   40.996635        -111.050285
        40.997646   -110.001457   41.00341         -107.918037
        40.998489   -106.864838   41.000111        -106.202896
        40.994305   -104.933968   41.388107        -104.053505
        41.698246   -104.053108
        </posList>
        </LinearRing>
    </exterior>
</Polygon>', 4269);
```

Like the geometry data type, the geography data type has some interesting features. The first thing to notice is that the coordinates are given in latitude-longitude order, because of the GML format. Another thing to notice is that in GML format, there are no comma separators between coordinate pairs. All coordinates are separated by whitespace characters. GML also requires you to declare the GML namespace http://www.opengis.net/gml.

The coordinate pairs in Listing 9-27 are also listed in reverse order from the geometry instance in Listing 9-26. This is required because the geography data type represents ellipsoidal spatial data. Ellipsoidal data in SQL Server has a couple of restrictions on it: an object must all fit in one hemisphere and it must be expressed with a counterclockwise orientation. These limitations do not apply to the geometry data type. These limitations are discussed further in the Hemisphere and Orientation sidebar in this section.

The final thing to notice is that when you create a geometry instance, you must specify a spatial reference identifier (SRID). The SRID used here is 4269, which is the GCS North American Datum 1983 (NAD 83). A datum is an associated ellipsoid model of Earth on which the coordinate data is based. We used SRID 4269 because the coordinates used in the example are borrowed from the US Census Bureau's TIGER/Line data, which is in turn based on NAD 83. As you can see, using the geography data type is slightly more involved than using the geometry data type, but it can provide more accurate results and additional functionality for Earth-based geographic information systems (GISs).

HEMISPHERE AND ORIENTATION

In SQL Server 2008, the geography data type required spatial objects to be contained in a single hemisphere—they couldn't cross the equator. That was mostly for performance reasons. In SQL Server 2012, you can create geography instances larger than a single hemisphere by using the new object type named FULLGLOBE.

You need also to specifiy the right ring orientation. So why is ring orientation so important, and what is the "right" ring orientation? To answer these questions, you have to ask yet another question: "What is the inside of a Polygon?" You might instinctively say that the inside of a Polygon is the smallest area enclosed by the coordinates you supply. But you could end up in a situation where your Polygon should be the larger area enclosed by your coordinates. If you created a border around the North Pole, for instance, is your Polygon the area within the border or is it the rest of the Earth minus the North Pole? Your answer to this question determines what the "inside" of the Polygon really is.

The next step is to tell SQL Server where the inside of the Polygon lies. SQL Server's geography instance makes you define your coordinates in counterclockwise order, so the inside of the Polygon is everything that falls on the left-hand side of the lines connecting the coordinates. In the following illustration, the image on the left side is an invalid orientation because the coordinates are defined in a clockwise order. The image on the right side is a valid orientation because its coordinates are defined in a counterclockwise order. If you follow the direction of the arrows on the image, you'll notice that the area on the left-hand side of the arrows is the area "inside" the Polygon. This eliminates any ambiguity from your Polygon definitions.

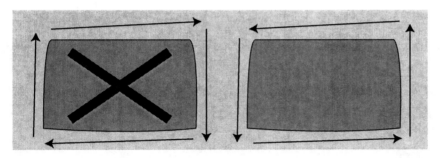

Keep these restrictions in mind if you decide to use the geography data type in addition to, or instead of, the geometry data type.

Polygon and MultiPolygon are two of the more interesting and complex spatial objects you can create. We like to use the state of Utah as a real-world example of a Polygon object for a couple of reasons. First, the exterior bounding ring for the state is very simple, composed of relatively straight lines. Second, the Great Salt Lake within the state can be used as a highly visible example of an interior bounding ring. Figure 9-20 shows the state of Utah.

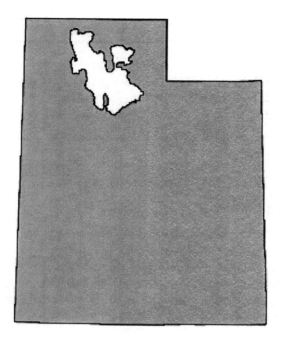

Figure 9-20. *The state of Utah with the Great Salt Lake as an Interior Bounding Ring*

The state of Michigan provides an excellent example of a MultiPolygon object. Michigan is composed of two distinct peninsulas, known as the Upper Peninsula and Lower Peninsula, respectively. The two peninsulas are separated by the Straits of Mackinac, which join Lake Michigan to Lake Huron. Figure 9-21 shows the Michigan MultiPolygon.

Figure 9-21. *Michigan as a MultiPolygon*

MICHIGAN AND THE GREAT LAKES

Michigan's two peninsulas are separated by the Straits of Mackinac, which is a five-mile-wide channel that joins two of the Great Lakes, Lake Michigan and Lake Huron. Although these two bodies of water are historically referred to as separate lakes, hydrologists consider them to be one contiguous body of water. Hydrology experts sometimes refer to the lakes as a single entity, Lake Michigan-Huron. On the other hand, it makes sense to consider the two lakes as separate from a political point of view, since Lake Michigan is wholly within the borders of the United States, while the border between the United States and Canada divides Lake Huron. For the purposes of this section, the most important fact is that the lakes separate Michigan into two peninsulas, making it a good example of a `MultiPolygon`.

Through the use of the spatial instance types, you can create spatial objects that cover the entire range from very simple to extremely complex. Once you've created spatial objects, you can use the geometry and geography data type methods on them or create spatial indexes on spatial data type columns to increase calculation efficiency. Listing 9-28 uses the geography data type instance created in Listing 9-22 and the `STIntersects()` method to report whether the town of Laramie and the Statue of Liberty are located within the borders of Wyoming. The results are shown in Figure 9-22.

Listing 9-28. Are the Statue of Liberty and Laramie in Wyoming?

```
DECLARE @Wyoming geography,
    @StatueOfLiberty geography,
    @Laramie geography;

SET  @Wyoming = geography::GeomFromGml (' < Polygon
    xmlns = "http://www.opengis.net/gml">
    <exterior>
        <LinearRing>
        <posList>
        41.698246  -104.053108  41.999851    -104.053009
        43.003094  -104.05571   43.503738    -104.057426
        44.145844  -104.059242  44.574368    -104.058975
        45.001091  -105.04126   44.997227    -106.020576
        44.999813  -107.893715  44.997643    -108.624573
        45.002853  -109.994789  44.992348    -110.428894
        44.664562  -111.050842  43.982632    -111.049629
        43.284813  -111.04673   42.503323    -111.046028
        41.578648  -111.050323  40.996635    -111.050285
        40.997646  -110.001457  41.00341     -107.918037
        40.998489  -106.864838  41.000111    -106.202896
        40.994305  -104.933968  41.388107    -104.053505
        41.698246  -104.053108
        </posList>
        </LinearRing>
    </exterior>
</Polygon>', 4269);

SET @StatueOfLiberty = geography::GeomFromGml(' < Point
    xmlns = "http://www.opengis.net/gml">
```

```
    <pos>
        40.689124 -74.044483
    </pos>
    </Point>', 4269);

SET @Laramie = geography::GeomFromGml('< Point
    xmlns = "http://www.opengis.net/gml">
    <pos>
        41.312928 -105.587253
    </pos>
    </Point>', 4269);

SELECT 'Is the Statue of Liberty in Wyoming?',
    CASE @Wyoming.STIntersects(@StatueOfLiberty)
        WHEN 0 THEN 'No'
        ELSE 'Yes'
    END AS Answer
UNION
SELECT 'Is Laramie in Wyoming?',
    CASE @Wyoming.STIntersects(@Laramie)
        WHEN 0 THEN 'No'
        ELSE 'Yes'
    END;
```

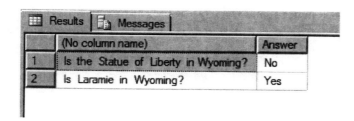

(No column name)	Answer
1 Is the Statue of Liberty in Wyoming?	No
2 Is Laramie in Wyoming?	Yes

Figure 9-22. *The Results of the STIntersection() Method Example*

SQL Server also allows you to create spatial indexes that optimize spatial data calculations. Spatial indexes are created by decomposing your spatial data into a b-tree-based grid hierarchy four levels deep. Each level represents a further subdivision of the cells above it in the hierarchy. Figure 9-23 shows a simple example of a decomposed spatial grid hierarchy.

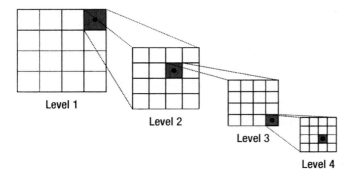

Figure 9-23. *Decomposing Space for Spatial Indexing*

The CREATE SPATIAL INDEX statement allows you to create spatial indexes on spatial data type columns. Listing 9-29 is an example of a CREATE SPATIAL INDEX statement.

Listing 9-29. Creating a Spatial Index

```
CREATE SPATIAL INDEX SIX_Location ON MyTable (SpatialColumn);
```

Spatial indexing is one of the biggest benefits of storing spatial data inside the database. As one astute developer pointed out, "Without spatial indexing, you may as well store your spatial data in flat files."

■ **Note** *Pro Spatial with SQL Server 2012*, by Alastair Aitchison (Apress, 2012), is a fully dedicated book about SQL Server Spatial, a feature much more complex that what we present here.

FILESTREAM Support

SQL Server is optimized for dealing with highly structured relational data, but SQL developers have long had to deal with heterogeneous unstructured data. The varbinary(max) LOB (Large Object) data type provides a useful method of storing arbitrary binary data directly in database tables; however, it still has some limitations, including the following:

- There is a hard 2.1 GB limit on the size of binary data that can be stored in a varbinary(max) column, which can be an issue if the documents you need to store are larger.

- Storing and managing large varbinary(max) data in SQL Server can have a negative impact on performance, owing largely to the fact that the SQL Server engine must maintain proper locking and isolation levels to ensure data integrity in the database.

Many developers and administrators have come up with clever solutions to work around this problem. Most of these solutions are focused on storing LOB data as files in the file system and storing file paths pointing to those files in the database. This introduces additional complexities to the system since you must maintain the links between database entries and physical files in the file system. You also must manage LOB data stored in the file system using external tools, outside of the scope of database transactions. Finally, this type of solution can double the amount of work required to properly secure your data, since you must manage security in the database and separately in the file system.

SQL Server provides a third option: integrated FILESTREAM support. SQL Server can store FILESTREAM-enabled varbinary(max) data as files in the file system. SQL Server can manage the contents of the FILESTREAM containers on the file system for you and control access to the files, while the NT File System (NTFS) provides efficient file streaming and file system transaction support. This combination of SQL Server and NTFS functionality provides several advantages when dealing with LOB data, including increased efficiency, manageability, and concurrency. Microsoft provides some general guidelines for use of FILESTREAM over regular LOB data types, including the following:

- When the average size of your LOBs is greater than 1 MB

- When you have to store any LOBs that are larger than 2.1 GB

- When fast-read access is a priority

- When you want to access LOB data from middle-tier code

■ **Tip** For smaller and limited LOB data, storing the data directly in the database might make more sense than using FILESTREAM.

Enabling FILESTREAM Support

The first step to using FILESTREAM functionality in SQL Server is enabling it. You can enable FILESTREAM support through the SQL Server Configuration Manager. You can set FILESTREAM access in the SQL Server service Properties ➤ FILESTREAM page. Once you've enabled FILESTREAM support, you can set the level of access for the SQL Server instance with sp_configure and then restart the SQL Server service. Listing 9-30 enables FILESTREAM support on the SQL Server instance for the maximum allowable access.

Listing 9-30. Enabling FILESTREAM Support on the Server

```
EXEC sp_configure 'filestream access level', 2;
RECONFIGURE;
```

The configuration value defines the access level for FILESTREAM support. The levels supported are listed in Table 9-4.

Table 9-4. *FILESTREAM Access Levels*

Configuration Value	Description
0	Disabled (default)
1	Access via T-SQL only
2	Access via T-SQL and file system

You can use the query in Listing 9-31 to see the FILESTREAM configuration information at any time. Sample results from our local server are shown in Figure 9-24.

Listing 9-31. Viewing FILESTREAM Configuration Information

```
SELECT
    SERVERPROPERTY('ServerName') AS ServerName,
    SERVERPROPERTY('FilestreamSharename') AS ShareName,
    CASE SERVERPROPERTY('FilestreamEffectiveLevel')
        WHEN 0 THEN 'Disabled'
        WHEN 1 THEN 'T-SQL Access Only'
        WHEN 2 THEN 'Local T-SOL/File System Access Only'
        WHEN 3 THEN 'Local T-SOL/File System and Remote File System Access'
    END AS Effective_Level,
    CASE SERVERPROPERTY('FilestreamConfiguredLevel')
        WHEN 0 THEN 'Disabled'
        WHEN 1 THEN 'T-SQL Access Only'
        WHEN 2 THEN 'Local T-SOL/File System Access Only'
        WHEN 3 THEN 'Local T-SOL/File System and Remote File System Access'
    END AS Configured_Level;
```

	ServerName	ShareName	Effective_Level	Configured_Level
1	SQL2012	MSSQLSERVER	Local T-SOL/File System and Remote File System A...	Local T-SOL/File System and Remote File System A...

Figure 9-24. *Viewing FILESTREAM Configuration Information*

Creating FILESTREAM Filegroups

Once you've enabled FILESTREAM support on your SQL Server instance, you have to create an SQL Server filegroup with the CONTAINS FILESTREAM option. This filegroup is where SQL Server will store FILESTREAM LOB files. As AdventureWorks 2012 is shipped without a FILESTREAM filegroup, we need to add it manually. Listing 9-32 shows the final generated CREATE DATABASE statement as if we had created the database from scratch. The FILEGROUP clause of the statement that creates the FILESTREAM filegroup is shown in bold.

Listing 9-32. CREATE DATABASE for AdventureWorks Database

```
CREATE DATABASE [AdventureWorks]
 CONTAINMENT = NONE
 ON  PRIMARY
( NAME = N'AdventureWorks2012_Data', FILENAME =
N'C:\sqldata\MSSQL11.MSSQLSERVER\MSSQL\DATA\ AdventureWorks2012_Data.mdf', SIZE = 226304 KB ,
MAXSIZE = UNLIMITED, FILEGROWTH = 16384 KB ),
FILEGROUP [FILESTREAM1] CONTAINS FILESTREAM  DEFAULT
( NAME = N'AdventureWordsFS', FILENAME =
N'C:\sqldata\MSSQL11.MSSQLSERVER\MSSQL\DATA\AdventureWordsFS' , MAXSIZE=UNLIMITED)
 LOG ON
( NAME = N'AdventureWorks2012_Log', FILENAME =
N'C:\sqldata\MSSQL11.MSSQLSERVER\MSSQL\DATA\AdventureWorks2012_log.ldf' , SIZE = 5696 KB ,
MAXSIZE = UNLIMITED, FILEGROWTH = 10 %);
```

To create this FILESTREAM filegroup on an already existing database, we used the ALTER DATABASE statement as shown in Listing 9-33.

Listing 9-33. Adding a FILESTREAM Filegroup to an Existing Database

```
ALTER DATABASE AdventureWorks
ADD FILEGROUP FILESTREAM1 CONTAINS FILESTREAM;
GO
ALTER DATABASE AdventureWorks
ADD FILE
(
NAME = N' AdventureWordsFS',
FILENAME = N' C:\sqldata\MSSQL11.MSSQLSERVER\MSSQL\DATA\AdventureWordsFS' )
TO FILEGROUP FILESTREAM1;
```

You can see that the file created is in fact not a file, but a directory where the files will be stored by SQL Server.

FILESTREAM-Enabling Tables

Once you've enabled FILESTREAM on the server instance and created a FILESTREAM filegroup, you're ready to create FILESTREAM-enabled tables. FILESTREAM storage is accessed by creating a varbinary(max) column in a table with the FILESTREAM attribute. The FILESTREAM-enabled table must also have a uniqueidentifier column with a ROWGUIDCOL attribute and a unique constraint on it. The Production.Document table in the AdventureWorks sample database is ready for FILESTREAM. In fact, its Document column was declared as a varbinary(max) with the FILESTREAM attribute in AdventureWorks 2008, but this dependency was removed in AdventureWorks 2012. Now, the Document column is still a varbinary(max), and the rowguid column is declared as a uniqueidentifier with the ROWGUIDCOL attribute. To convert it to a FILESTREAM-enabled table, we create a new table named Production.DocumentFS and import the lines from Production.Document into that new table. Let's see how it works in Listing 9-34. The Document and rowguid columns are shown in bold.

Listing 9-34. Production.Document FILESTREAM-Enabled Table

```
CREATE TABLE Production.DocumentFS (
    DocumentNode      hierarchyid NOT NULL PRIMARY KEY,
    DocumentLevel     AS (DocumentNode.GetLevel()),
    Title             nvarchar(50) NOT NULL,
    Owner             int NOT NULL,
    FolderFlag        bit NOT NULL,
    FileName          nvarchar(400) NOT NULL,
    FileExtension     nvarchar(8) NOT NULL,
    Revision          nchar(5) NOT NULL,
    ChangeNumber      int NOT NULL,
    Status            tinyint NOT NULL,
    DocumentSummary   nvarchar(max) NULL,
    Document          varbinary(max) FILESTREAM NULL,
    rowguid           uniqueidentifier ROWGUIDCOL NOT NULL UNIQUE,
    ModifiedDate      datetime NOT NULL
);
GO

INSERT INTO Production.DocumentFS
    (DocumentNode, Title, Owner, FolderFlag, FileName, FileExtension, Revision, ChangeNumber,
Status, DocumentSummary, Document, rowguid, ModifiedDate)
```

```
SELECT
    DocumentNode, Title, Owner, FolderFlag, FileName, FileExtension, Revision, ChangeNumber,
Status, DocumentSummary, Document, rowguid, ModifiedDate
FROM Production.Document;
```

When the table is created, we insert the content of Production.Document into it. Now, we can open Windows Explorer and go to the location of the FILESTREAM directory. The content of the directory is shown in Figure 9-25. The file names appear as a jumble of grouped digits that don't offer up much information about the LOB files' contents, because SQL Server manages the file names internally.

Figure 9-25. *LOB Files Stored in the FILESTREAM Filegroup*

■ **Caution**   SQL Server also creates a file named filestream.hdr. This file is used by SQL Server to manage FILESTREAM data. Do not open or modify this file.

Accessing FILESTREAM Data

You can access and manipulate your FILESTREAM-enabled varbinary(max) columns using standard SQL Server SELECT queries and DML statements like INSERT and DELETE. Listing 9-35 demonstrates querying the varbinary(max) column of the Production.DocumentFS table. The results are shown in Figure 9-26.

Listing 9-35. *Querying a FILESTREAM-Enabled Table*

```
SELECT
    d.Title,
    d.Document.PathName() AS LOB_Path,
    d.Document AS LOB_Data
FROM Production.DocumentFS d
WHERE d.Document IS NOT NULL;
```

Figure 9-26. *Results of Querying the FILESTREAM-enabled Table*

A property called PathName() is exposed on FILESTREAM-enabled varbinary(max) columns to retrieve the full path to the file containing the LOB data. The query in Listing 9-35 uses PathName() to retrieve the LOB path along with the LOB data. As you can see from this example, SQL Server abstracts away the NTFS interaction to a large degree, allowing you to query and manipulate FILESTREAM data as if it were relational data stored directly in the database.

■ **Tip**   In most cases, it's not a good idea to retrieve all LOB data from a FILESTREAM-enabled table in a single query as in this example. For large tables with large LOBs, this can cause severe performance problems and make client applications unresponsive. In this case, however, the LOB data being queried is actually very small in size, and there are few rows in the table.

SQL Server 2008 and 2012 provide support for the OpenSqlFilestream API for accessing and manipulating FILESTREAM data in client applications. A full description of the OpenSqlFilestream API is beyond the scope of this book, but *Accelerated SQL Server 2008,* by Rob Walters et al. (Apress, 2008), provides a description of the OpenSqlFilestream API with source code for a detailed client application.

FileTable Support

SQL Server 2012 improved greatly the FILESTREAM type by introducing filetables. As we have seen, to use FILESTREAM we need to manage the content only through SQL Server, by T-SQL or with the OpenSqlFilestream API. It is unfortunate, because we have access to a directory on our file system, which cannot be managed simply and publishes cryptic file names. In short, we have a great functionality that could be more flexible and user-friendly. Filetable brings that to the table. It makes the Windows filesystem namespace compatible with SQL Server tables. With it, you can create a table in SQL Server that merely reflects the content of a directory and its subdirectories, and you can manage its content at the file system level, out of SQL Server, with regular tools like the Windows Explorer, or by file I/O APIs in your client application. All changes made to the file system will be immediately reflected in the filetable. In fact, the file system as we see it in the share does not exist *per se*; it is a kind of mirage created by SQL Server. Files or directories will be internally handled by SQL Server and filestream objects, and if you try to access the real directory with Windows Explorer, it will be as jumbled as any other FILESTREAM directory.

To be able to use filetables, you first need to have activated the filestream support at the instance level as we have seen in the previous section. The filestream_access_level option needs to be set to 2 to accept file I/O streaming access. In addition, the FILESTREAM property of the database must be set to accept non-transacted access. We will see how to do that in our example. We have downloaded a zip package from the http:// openclipart.org/ web site, containing the entire collection of free cliparts. It represents almost 27,000 image files at this time. We will add them in a filetable. First, in Listing 9-36, we create a dedicated database with a FILESTREAM filegroup that will store our filetable. The FILESTREAM filegroup creation is shown in bold.

Listing 9-36. Creating a Database with a FILESTREAM Filegroup

```
CREATE DATABASE cliparts
CONTAINMENT = NONE
ON  PRIMARY
( NAME = N'cliparts', FILENAME = N'C:\sqldata\MSSQL11.MSSQLSERVER\MSSQL\DATA\cliparts.mdf' ,
SIZE = 5120 KB , FILEGROWTH = 1024 KB ),
FILEGROUP [filestreamFG1] CONTAINS FILESTREAM
( NAME = N'filestream1', FILENAME=N'C:\sqldata\MSSQL11.MSSQLSERVER\MSSQL\DATA\filestream1' )
LOG ON
( NAME = N'cliparts_log', FILENAME = N'C:\sqldata\MSSQL11.MSSQLSERVER\MSSQL\DATA\cliparts_log.ldf',
SIZE = 1024 KB , FILEGROWTH = 10 %);
GO

ALTER DATABASE [cliparts] SET FILESTREAM( NON_TRANSACTED_ACCESS = FULL, DIRECTORY_NAME =
N'cliparts' );
```

▓ **Note**   As filetables are stored in a FILESTREAM filegroup, filetables are included in database backups, unless you perform filegroup backups and you exclude the FILESTREAM filegroup.

In the last line of Listing 9-36, we set the filestream option to NON_TRANSACTED_ACCESS = FULL, which will ensure that files will be writable from the share outside of SQL Server. We also specify the directory name 'cliparts.' It will be shown as a sub-directory in the FILESTREAM share.

The path where a filetable will be found on the share depends on the directory set at the database level, plus a sub-directory set when the table is created. In Listing 9-37, we create the filetable and a directory by inserting a line in the filetable.

Listing 9-37. Creating the Filetable

```
USE [cliparts];
GO

CREATE TABLE dbo.OpenClipartsLibrary AS FILETABLE
WITH
    (
        FILETABLE_DIRECTORY = 'OpenClipartsLibrary'
    );
GO

INSERT INTO dbo.OpenClipartsLibrary (name,is_directory)
VALUES ('import_20120501',1);
```

To create a filetable, we simple create a table AS FILETABLE. We specify with the option FILETABLE_ DIRECTORY = 'OpenClipartsLibrary' in which directory in the share the content of the table will be found.

▓ **Note**   The directory of a filetable can be changed later with an ALTER TABLE.

As you can see, the table structure is not part of the CREATE TABLE statement. A filetable schema is fixed. We describe the filetable columns in Table 9-5.

Table 9-5. *Filetable Structure*

Column	Type	Description
stream_id	uniqueindetifier	The unique id of the line, being a file (a FILESTREAM document) or a directory. There is a UNIQUE constraint on it.
file_stream	varbinary(max)	The FILESTREAM column containing the file. NULL if it is a directory.
name	nvarchar(255)	Contains the name of the file or directory.
path_locator	hierarchyid	The position of the file or directory in the directory's hierarchy. The primary key of the table.
parent_path_locator	hierarchyid	The path_locator of the parent (ie., the directory containing the file or directory). A calculated column.
file_type	nvarchar(255)	The type (extension) of the file. A calculated column. NULL if it is a directory.
cached_file_size	bigint	The size of the file in bytes. A calculated column. NULL if it is a directory.
creation_time	datetimeoffset(7)	The date and time of creation. It is set by default at the current date and time when the object is created.
last_write_time	datetimeoffset(7)	The date and time of the last modification of the file or directory. Can be set manually like creation_time.
last_access_time	datetimeoffset(7)	The date and time when the file was last accessed. Can be set manually like creation_time.
is_directory	bit	1 if it is a directory. Calculated.
is_offline	bit	1 if the extended NTFS attribute Offline is set on the file. That would mean that the file is not physically in the directory but stored remotely.
is_hidden	bit	1 if the file has the hidden attribute.
is_readonly	bit	1 if the file has the read-only attribute.
is_archive	bit	1 if the file has the archive bit set.
is_system	bit	1 if the file has the system attribute.
is_temporary	bit	1 if the file has the temporary attribute.

To retrieve the filetables in our database, we can query the `sys.filetables` catalog view. We also can find them in SSMS Object Explorer, in the Tables | FileTables node, as shown in Figure 9-27.

Object Explorer   ▾ � ×

Connect ▾ 🔌 🔌 ■ ▽ 🔄 🔳

- ⊟ 🔷 SQL2012 (SQL Server 11.0.2100 - SQL2012\Administrator)
  - ⊟ 📁 Databases
    - ⊞ 📁 System Databases
    - ⊞ 📁 Database Snapshots
    - ⊞ 📄 AdventureWorks
    - ⊟ 📄 cliparts
      - ⊞ 📁 Database Diagrams
      - ⊟ 📁 Tables
        - ⊞ 📁 System Tables
        - ⊟ 📁 FileTables
          - ⊞ 📊 dbo.OpenClipartsLibrary
      - ⊞ 📁 Views
      - ⊞ 📁 Synonyms
      - ⊞ 📁 Programmability
      - ⊞ 📁 Service Broker
      - ⊞ 📁 Storage
      - ⊞ 📁 Security

Figure 9-27. *Filetables in SSMS*

You can see the share itself in Windows Explorer by going to Network, choosing your server name and entering the share name you set in the SQL Server Configuration Manager. You can also right-click on the filetable in the SSMS Object Explorer—as we see in Figure 9-27—and click on "Explore FileTable Directory," which will open a Windows Explorer window directly on the filetable directory. You need to access it through the network share, and not directly through the local directory, because the local directory will only show you FILESTREAM GUID names, while the network share, managed by SQL Server, will show you a virtual directory hierarchy that looks like a regular hierarchy of directores and files. This is logical anyway, as clients are not supposed to access directly local server directories. For our example, we did that and copied the full unzipped cliparts directory and subdirectories. When the copy was finished, a COUNT(*) from dbo.OpenClipartsLibrary returned 27,890 lines.

To manage files and directories, you can do it by issuing T-SQL statements against the filetable, directly in the share with Windows tools, or programmatically with Windows I/O APIs. As an example of how to do it also by T-SQL, Listing 9-38 creates a new directory under the OpenClipartsLibrary root directory.

Listing 9-38. Inserting a Directory in the Filetable

```
INSERT INTO dbo.OpenClipartsLibrary (name, is_directory)
VALUES ('directory01',1);
```

Setting the is_directory column to 1 is all you have to do to create a directory. You can also modifiy the file or directory properties by Windows I/O APIs or by T-SQL queries against the table. In Listing 9-39, we insert a subdirectory or the newly created directory01 and set a creation date as different from the current date and time.

Listing 9-39. Inserting a Subdirectory

```
INSERT INTO dbo.OpenClipartsLibrary
    (name, is_directory, creation_time, path_locator)
```

```
SELECT
    'directory02',1, dateadd(year, -1, sysdatetime()), path_locator.GetDescendant(NULL, NULL)
FROM dbo.OpenClipartsLibrary
WHERE name = 'directory01'
AND   is_directory = 1
AND   parent_path_locator IS NULL;
```

The code in Listing 9-39 creates a directory named directory02 as a subdirectory of directory01 by setting the path_locator of the created directory with the GetDescendant() hierarchyId method of the directory01 path_locator column. GetDescendant(NULL, NULL) returns the least descendant node of the current hierarchyId value. To be sure that directory01 is the one we created at the root level, we check that its parent_path_locator is NULL. We also set manually the creation_date to be one year ago.

In Figure 9-28, we verify with Windows Explorer that the directory was effectively created. Once again, you need to do it through the network share.

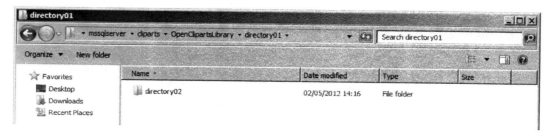

Figure 9-28. *The Newly Created Directory02 Directory*

▨ **Note** You cannot change a file to be a directory or vice versa. A check constraint on the filetable enforces that is_directory cannot be set to 1 when the file_stream column is not NULL.

Whenever you add, move or delete a file on the share, or by T-SQL statements against the filetable, it will be immediately reflected at both places. SQL Server intercepts all I/O operations on the share and converts them into DML actions on the filetable. File system rules like name limitations are enforced by constraints on the filetable, and trying to create invalid files or folders (with names containing / ? < > \ : * | ") in the filetable will result in a constraint violation.

There is however an important difference between managing the filetable content by T-SQL or at the Windows level. The DML statements against a filetable can be part of a transaction and rolled back, while creating, modifying, moving, or deleting files and folders by the means of the Windows I/O APIs cannot be part of a transaction. That's the reason why we enabled non_transacted_access support in our database. If you want to enable transactional modification of a file in a filetable outside of T-SQL context, you can use the OpenSqlFileStream API in your client code, which we discussed previously.

Filetable Functions

You can use dedicated functions, FILESTREAM related functions, and hierarchyid functions to manipulate files and folders in a filetable.

The FileTableRootPath() function returns the database share directory if called without argument, or the filetable share directory if called with the name of a filetable provided in a nvarchar argument, as shown in Listing 9-40. The results are shown in Figure 9-29.

Listing 9-40. Using FileTableRootPath()

```
USE cliparts;

SELECT FileTableRootPath();
SELECT FileTableRootPath('dbo.OpenClipartsLibrary');
```

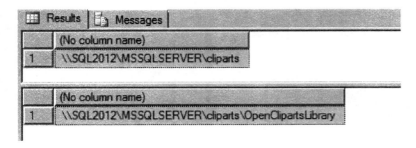

Figure 9-29. The Results of FileTableRootPath()

The function takes a second optional parameter, @option, which is useful to return the full path in NETBIOS format or with the full domain name (FDN) of the server. The @option possible values are detailed in Table 9-6.

Table 9-6. FileTableRootPath @options

@option value	Description
0	Returns the path in NETBIOS format; this is the default value. A NETBIOS computer name has a maximum of 16 characters in uppercase.
1	Returns the path without conversion.
2	Returns the path with the full domain name (FDN) of the machine.

To get the path of a specific file or folder in the filetable, the GetFileNamespacePath() function comes in handy. It is called as a method of the file_stream column, and takes two optional parameters, the first, @is_full_path, allows the path returned to be relative (0) or absolute (1). Calling GetFileNamespacePath(1) will produce full paths and saves you from concatenating the result of FileTableRootPath() with the relative path. The second option, @option, has the same values as the @option parameter of the FileTableRootPath() function. We demonstrate the usage of GetFileNamespacePath() in Listing 9-41.

Listing 9-41. Using GetFileNamespacePath().

```
SELECT file_stream.GetFileNamespacePath(1) as path
FROM dbo.OpenClipartsLibrary
WHERE is_directory = 1
ORDER BY path_locator.GetLevel(), path;
```

The statement in Listing 9-41 returns all the directories of absolute paths ordered by their level in the directories' hierarchy and their name. The GetLevel() hierarchyid function applied to the path_locator column allows you to return the current level of the item in the file system relative to the filetable root.

As we can see, hierarchyid functions are interesting ways to move through the hierarchy. An example is given in Listing 9-42 that returns a directory and the name of its parent directory. A partial result is shown in Figure 9-30.

Listing 9-42. Using hierarchyid Functions

```
SELECT l1.name, l1.path_locator.GetLevel(), l2.name as parent_directory
FROM dbo.OpenClipartsLibrary l1
JOIN dbo.OpenClipartsLibrary l2 ON l1.path_locator.GetAncestor(1) = l2.path_locator
WHERE l1.is_directory = 1;
```

	name	Level	parent_directory
1	_TylzaeL_	2	import_20120501
2	00Inkscape	2	import_20120501
3	1in9ui5t	2	import_20120501
4	43ad5web	2	import_20120501
5	a_sanyal59	2	import_20120501
6	aaha	2	import_20120501
7	zeratul	2	import_20120501
8	zerothis	2	import_20120501
9	zesarvictoria	2	import_20120501
10	zlatkodesign	2	import_20120501
11	Ztyx	2	import_20120501
12	yyycatch	2	import_20120501

Figure 9-30. *The Results of Using hierarchyid Functions*

By using the GetAncestor() hierarchyid function on the path_locator in the JOIN clause, we retrieve the parent path_locator and display its name. An easier way to do that is to use directly the parent_path_locator computed column that maintains a foreign key relationship with the path_locator column in the same table. The query in Listing 9-43 returns exactly the same result as the query in Listing 9-42.

Listing 9-43. Using Parent_path_locator Column

```
SELECT l1.name, l1.path_locator.GetLevel(), l2.name as parent_directory
FROM dbo.OpenClipartsLibrary l1
JOIN dbo.OpenClipartsLibrary l2 ON l1.parent_path_locator = l2.path_locator
WHERE l1.is_directory = 1;
```

Thanks to the recursive relationship between parent_path_locator and path_locator, we can travel down the directory's path with a recursive Common Table Expression (CTE), as follows in Listing 9-44.

Listing 9-44. *Using a CTE to Travel Down the Directories' Hierarchy*

```
;WITH mycte AS (
    SELECT name, path_locator.GetLevel() as Level, path_locator
    FROM dbo.OpenClipartsLibrary
    WHERE name = 'Yason'
    AND is_directory = 1

    UNION ALL

    SELECT l1.name, l1.path_locator.GetLevel() as Level, l1.path_locator
    FROM dbo.OpenClipartsLibrary l1
    JOIN mycte l2 ON l1.parent_path_locator = l2.path_locator
    WHERE l1.is_directory = 1
)
SELECT name, Level
FROM mycte
ORDER BY level, name;
```

Of course, as the path_locator column is a hierarchyid, we might as well express it as in Listing 9-45.

Listing 9-45. *Using hierarchyid Functions to Travel Down the Directory's Hierarchy*

```
SELECT l1.name, l1.path_locator.GetLevel() as Level
FROM dbo.OpenClipartsLibrary l1
JOIN dbo.OpenClipartsLibrary l2 ON l1.path_locator.IsDescendantOf(l2.path_locator) = 1 OR
l1.path_locator = l2.path_locator
WHERE l1.is_directory = 1
AND l2.is_directory = 1
AND l2.name = 'Yason'
ORDER BY level, name;
```

In Listing 9-45, we use the IsDescendantOf() function to retrieve all descendent directories of the directory named Yason. We have copied a few directories in Yason, and the queries in Listings 9-44 and 9-45 return exactly the same result shown in Figure 9-31.

	name	Level
1	Yason	2
2	yamazaki	3
3	yeKcim	3
4	yish	3
5	yman	3

Figure 9-31. *The Results of the Queries in Listings 9-44 and 9-45*

Finally, the GetPathLocator() function returns a path_locator value for a file system full path. The example in Listing 9-46 retrieves the path_locator of the Yason directory, and uses it to find the matching line in the OpenClipartsLibrary table. The result is shown in Figure 9-32.

Listing 9-46. Using the GetPathLocator() function.

```
DECLARE @path_locator hierarchyid

SET @path_locator = GetPathLocator('\\Sql2012\mssqlserver\cliparts\OpenClipartsLibrary\
import_20120501\Yason');

SELECT *
FROM dbo.OpenClipartsLibrary
WHERE path_locator = @path_locator;
```

Figure 9-32. *The Line Found Using the GetPathLocator() Function*

Triggers on Filetables

Filetables can have triggers like any other tables. Because making changes in the filetable share at the Windows level results in SQL Server calls behind the scene, a trigger will also receive these events.

▪ **Note**   But replication and related features (including transactional replication, merge replication, change data capture, and change tracking) are not supported with FileTables. You can see a FileTable Compatibility list with SQL Server features at this address: http://msdn.microsoft.com/en-us/library/gg492086.aspx.

We will demonstrate that with the audit table and the trigger created in Listing 9-47.

Listing 9-47. Creating an Audit Table and a Trigger on the OpenClipartsLibrary Table

```
CREATE TABLE dbo.cliparts_log (
    path nvarchar(4000) not null,
    deletion_date datetime2(0),
    deletion_user sysname,
    is_directory bit
)
GO

CREATE TRIGGER OpenClipartsLibrary_logTrigger
ON [dbo].[OpenClipartsLibrary]
AFTER DELETE
```

CHAPTER 9CHAPTER 9 ▪ DATA TYPES AND ADVANCED DATA TYPES

```
AS BEGIN
    IF @@ROWCOUNT = 0 RETURN;
    SET NOCOUNT ON;

    INSERT INTO dbo.cliparts_log (path, deletion_date, deletion_user, is_directory)
    SELECT name, SYSDATETIME(), SUSER_SNAME(),is_directory
    FROM deleted
END;
```

First, we create an audit table named cliparts_log. We want to keep track of file and directory deletions. We want to keep the date and time of deletion and name of the account that deleted the item. To record deletion into the table, we create a trigger named OpenClipartsLibrary_logTrigger that will fire for every DELETE statement against the OpenClipartsLibrary table.

To test it, we go to the filetable share with Windows Explorer and delete the \\Sql2012\mssqlserver\cliparts\OpenClipartsLibrary\import_20120501\acspike directory. It contains two files. What gets written in the table is shown in Figure 9-33.

	path	deletion_date	deletion_user	is_directory
1	acspike_male_user_icon.png	2012-05-02 17:32:25	SQL2012\Administrator	0
2	acspike_male_user_icon.svg	2012-05-02 17:32:25	SQL2012\Administrator	0
3	acspike	2012-05-02 17:32:25	SQL2012\Administrator	1

Figure 9-33. The Content of the Cliparts_log Table after the Directory's Deletion

Summary

In this chapter, we first discussed some details to know about basic data types. Mastering how basic data types work allows you to understand the impact they have on the storage, and therefore on the performance, of your database. For instance, the nvarchar data type stores UNICODE values and consumes twice the space of the same varchar content. If used lightly, it can blow up the size of your database file. The varchar(max) and varbinary(max) types replace the legacy text and image data types. They allow an easy and more performant handling on Large Objects (LOB) inside the database. We then spent some time on the date and time data types. They have been improved in SQL Server 2008 with new types that are more precise and compact.

We also covered more advanced data types, like uniqueidentifier, which stored a 16-byte globally unique identifier, and hierarchyid, a .NET-based data type that can be used in a hierarchical table to represent a tree structure, as well as the spatial geometry and geography data types.

Finally, we explored the FILESTREAM type. With FILESTREAM, you can keep binary documents inside a database more efficiently. Through SQL Server, the document will be stored in the NTFS file system and can be retrieved directly with I/O APIs. Transactional coherence is maintained on the files as if they were inside the database file. The new filetable feature improves upon FILESTREAM by offering special database tables storing FILESTREAM documents and folder definitions that can be accessed simply on the filesystem with a network share managed by SQL Server

285

EXERCISES

1. [True/False] Storing character strings with European language accents (é,à, ö, for instance) requires you to use a UNICODE encoding.

2. [Choose all that apply] Which of the following LOB data types are deprecated?

    a. image

    b. varchar(max)

    c. text

    d. ntext

    e. All of the above

3. [True/False] The new date data type stores time offset information.

4. What model does the hierarchyid data type use to represent hierarchical data in the database?

5. [Choose one] Which of the following is true of Polygon spatial objects when created in geography data type instances?

    a. They must have a clockwise orientation.

    b. They must have a counterclockwise orientation.

    c. Orientation does not matter.

    d. They cannot cross up to two hemispheres.

6. [Choose one] Which of the following functions adjusts a given datetimeoffset value to another specified time offset?

    e. TODATETIMEOFFSET

    f. SWITCHOFFSET

    g. CHANGEOFFSET

    h. CALCULATEOFFSET

7. [True/False] The FILESTREAM functionality in SQL Server 2012 uses NTFS to provide streaming LOB data support.

8. What is the name of the filetable column that allows you to retrieve the path of the file or directory on the filetable network share?DATA TYPES AND ADVANCED DATA TYPES

■ ■ ■

CHAPTER 10

Full-Text Search

Full-text search (FTS) is a powerful SQL Server feature allowing for advanced searches using multiple languages to find information in documents as well as document properties. FTS is tightly integrated with SQL Server 2012 and can be easily managed with SQL Server Management Studio (SSMS) and monitored with standard dynamic management views. FTS broadens the scope of what is thought of as a T-SQL search by providing meaningful results from sometimes seemingly unstructured textual data. SQL Server 2012 also introduces statistical semantics which allow for searching on document meaning as opposed to simply searching content. Based on word distributions and other factors, statistical semantics allows you to find documents with similar contents.

FTS Architecture

As mentioned earlier, the FTS architecture is tightly integrated with the SQL Server database engine. In fact, FTS consists of two main components: the sqlserver process (sqlserver.exe) and the filter daemon host (fdhost.exe). The filter daemon is responsible for retrieving the text data from the tables and applying word breaks as well as determining the type of text is being retrieved. The filter daemon host applies different rules based on whether the document is a Word document, an Excel file, or even XML. Information is passed between the SQL Server process and the filter daemon host. Because the fdhost process has the responsibility to directly access and filter the data, the process requires a separate security account. This keeps the entire FTS process much more secure than in previous implementations.

The SQL Server process is primarily responsible for maintaining full-text indexes, controlling query optimization, and maintaining the stoplist and theasaures objects. A stoplist is a list of non-essentials words which should be ignored in most linguistic searches. A thesaurus is something you fill out in order to extend the reach of searches to find matches that FTS may not have been able to suggest on its own. Figure 10-1 shows how these architectural components are put to together.

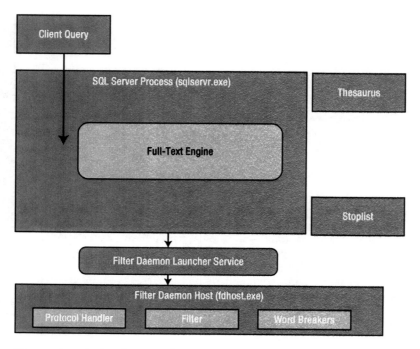

Figure 10-1. *FTS architecture (simplified)*

Here is a quick summary of some of the beneficial features of FTS:

- The full-text engine is hosted in the SQL Server process, eliminating much of the overhead associated with interservice communications.

- Integration with the SQL Server process to better predict query performance through the use of new query operators.

- Full-text indexes are maintained by the SQL Server process for better optimization.

- Ability to create customized stoplists of words to ignore during FTS, and the ability to create a thesaurus for more efficient and accurate searching.

- Dynamic management views and functions that provide greater transparency in understanding how FTS queries are processed and executed.

Creating Full-Text Catalogs and Indexes

The first step to take advantage of SQL Server FTS is to create full-text catalogs and full-text indexes. A full-text catalog can contain one or more full-text indexes, and each full-text index can only be assigned to one full-text catalog. You can create full-text catalogs and full-text indexes in SSMS using GUI (graphical user interface) wizards or T-SQL statements.

Creating Full-Text Catalogs

You can access the GUI full-text catalog wizard by right-clicking Full Text Catalogs in the SSMS Object Explorer. The New Full-Text Catalog option on the pop-up context menu starts the wizard (see Figure 10-2).

Figure 10-2. *New Full-Text Catalog Context Menu Option*

After selecting New Full-Text Catalog, SSMS presents the wizard's New Full-Text Catalog window. This window allows you to define the name of your full-text catalog, the full-text catalog's owner, an accent sensitivity setting, and whether or not this full-text catalog is designated as the default for a database. The New Full-Text Catalog window is shown in Figure 10-3.

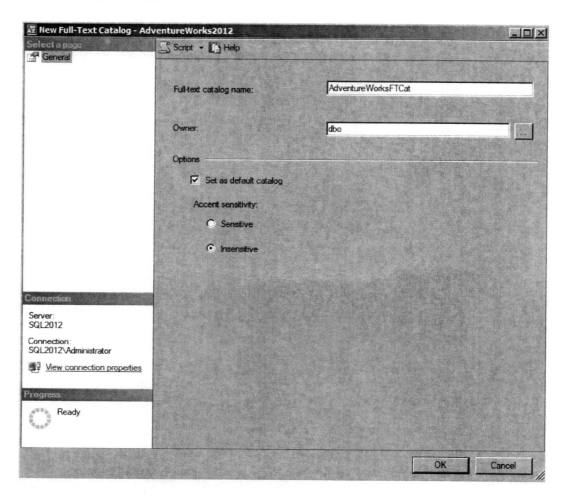

Figure 10-3. *New Full-Text Catalog Window*

For this sample full-text catalog, we chose the following options:

- The full-text catalog is named AdventureWorksFTCat, and dbo is designated as the owner.

- The first created full-text catalog is designated the default full-text catalog for the database. When a new full-text index is created you will have a choice to create it in the default catalog or in any additional non-default catalogs.

- The accent sensitivity is set to Insensitive, meaning that words with accent marks are treated as equivalent to those without accent marks (e.g., for search purposes, *resumé* is the same as *resume*).

You can also create and manage full-text catalogs using T-SQL statements. Listing 10-1 shows how to create the same full-text catalog that we created previously in this section with the SSMS wizard.

Listing 10-1. Creating a Full-Text Catalog with T-SQL

```
CREATE FULLTEXT CATALOG AdventureWorksFTCat
  WITH ACCENT_SENSITIVITY=OFF
  AS DEFAULT
  AUTHORIZATION dbo;
```

Once you've created your full-text catalog, the next step is to build full-text indexes. We describe full-text index creation in the next section. Maximum performance full-text catalogs, particularly those you anticipate will become very large, should be created on filegroups that are located on their own physical drives. This is also useful for administrative functions such as performing filegroup backups and restores independent of data and log files.

Creating Full-Text Indexes

As with full-text catalogs, you have two options for creating full-text indexes—you can use the GUI wizard in SSMS, or you can use T-SQL statements. Once you've created a full-text catalog, as described in the previous section, it's time to define your full-text indexes. Begin by right-clicking a table; the example in Figure 10-4 uses the Production.ProductModel table, in the SSMS Object Explorer to pull up the table context menu. From the context menu, choose the Full-Text Index ➤ Define Full-Text Index option, shown in Figure 10-4.

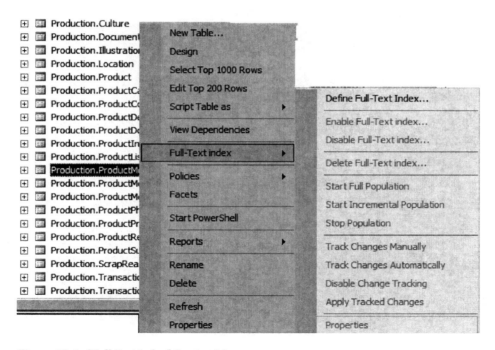

Figure 10-4. "Full-Text Index" Context Menu

The full-text index wizard shows a splash screen the first time you access it. You can choose to turn off the splash screen or just ignore it. On the next screen, shown in Figure 10-5, the wizard allows you to select a single-column unique index on the table. Every full-text index requires a single-column unique index that allows the full-text index to reference individual rows in the table. If you don't have a single-column unique index defined on the table you're trying to create a full-text index on, the wizard will display an error message as soon as you try to run it. In this example, we've chosen to use the table's integer primary key for the full-text index.

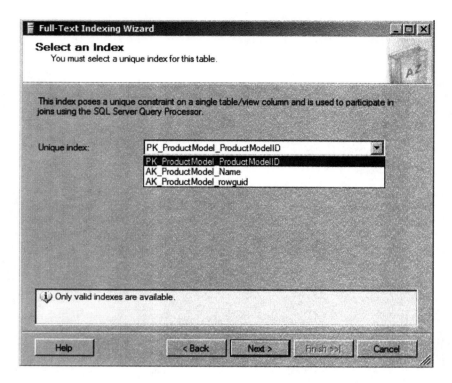

Figure 10-5. *Selecting a Single-column Unique Index*

■ **Tip** It's recommended that you specify a single-column unique index defined on an integer column when creating a full-text index. This will help maximize performance and minimize full-text index storage requirements.

After you select a unique index, you'll choose the columns that will provide the searchable content for the full-text index. You can specify char, nchar, varchar, nvarchar, xml, varbinary, varbinary(max), and image columns in this step. In Figure 10-6, the nvarchar and xml data type columns of the table are selected to participate in the full-text index. We've also selected English as the word-breaker language for each of these columns. The word-breaker language specification determines the language used for word-breaking and stemming. SQL Server 2012 currently recognizes over 50 different languages.

Figure 10-6. *Selecting Columns to Participate in Full-text Searches*

■ **Note** The *type column* is the name of a column indicating the document type (e.g., Microsoft Word, Excel, PowerPoint, Adobe PDF, and others) when you full-text index documents stored in varbinary(max) or image columns. Be aware that some document types require installation and configuration of additional IFilter components. More information about full-text and the new filetable feature is available on Microsoft TechNet at http://social. technet.microsoft.com/wiki/contents/articles/9809.store-and-index-documents-in-sql-server-2012- an-end-to-end-walkthrough.aspx.

After you've selected the columns that will participate in full-text searches against a table, you must select the change-tracking option. *Change tracking* determines whether SQL Server maintains a change log for the full-text indexed columns, and how the log is used to update the full-text index. Figure 10-7 shows the change-tracking options available through the wizard.

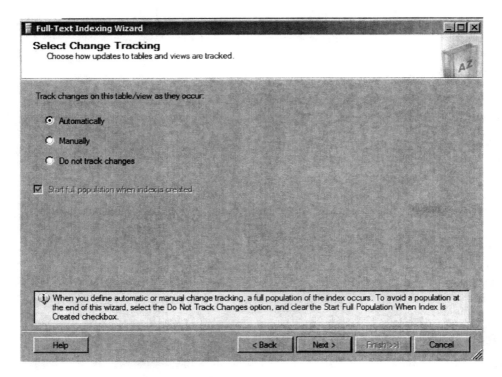

Figure 10-7. *Selecting a Change-tracking Option*

The change-tracking options available through the wizard include the following:

- *Automatically:* SQL Server updates the full-text index automatically when data is modified in the columns that participate in the full-text index. This is the default option.

- *Manually:* The change-tracking log is either used to update the full-text index via SQL Agent on a scheduled basis, or through manual intervention. This option is useful when automatic full-text index updates could slow down your server during business hours.

- *Do not track changes:* SQL Server does not track changes. Updating the full-text index requires you to issue an ALTER FULLTEXT INDEX statement with the START FULL or INCREMENTAL POPULATION clause to populate the entire full-text index.

■ **Tip**   Keep in mind that *automatic* updates to the full-text index are not necessarily *immediate* updates. When automatic change tracking is specified, there may be some lag time between changes in the table data and updates to the full-text index.

The next step in the wizard allows you to assign your full-text index to a full-text catalog. You can choose a preexisting full-text catalog, like the AdventureWorksFTCat shown in Figure 10-8, or you can create a new full-text catalog. You can also choose a filegroup and full-text stoplist for the full-text index in this step.

Figure 10-8. *Assigning a Full-text Index to a Catalog*

The final steps of the wizard allow you to create a full-text index population schedule and review your previous wizard selections. Since automatic population is used in the example, no schedule is necessary.

■ **Note**   It is possible you may receive an error on the population schedule screen when using SQL Server 2012 Express Advanced Services. This might be due to a bug in the application. You can ignore the error and continue. Express Advanced Services does support population schedules so you can avoid the error by manually creating the schedule and bypassing the GUI. It also may be possible to create the schedule through the GUI later by selecing the index properties. For more, go to http://connect.microsoft.com/SQLServer/feedback/details/740181/management-studio-does-not-fully-manage-full-text-in-sql-server-express.

In the review window of the wizard, shown in Figure 10-9, you can look at the choices you've made in each step of the wizard and go back to previous steps to make changes if necessary. Once you click the Finish button, the full-text index is created in your database.

Figure 10-9. Review Wizard Selections

The SSMS full-text index wizard is very thorough, but you can also create and manage full-text indexes using T-SQL statements. Listing 10-2 shows the T-SQL statements required to create and enable a full-text index with the same options previously selected in the SSMS wizard example.

Listing 10-2. Creating a Full-Text Index with T-SQL Statements

```
CREATE FULLTEXT INDEX
ON Production.ProductModel
(
  CatalogDescription LANGUAGE English,
  Instructions LANGUAGE English,
  Name LANGUAGE English
  )
KEY INDEX PK_ProductModel_ProductModelID
ON
(
  AdventureWorksFTCat
)
WITH
(
CHANGE_TRACKING AUTO
);
GO
```

```
ALTER FULLTEXT INDEX
ON Production.ProductModel ENABLE;
GO
```

The `CREATE FULLTEXT INDEX` statement builds the full-text index on the Production.ProductModel table with the specified options. In this example, the CatalogDescription, Instructions, and Name columns are all participating in the full-text index. The `LANGUAGE` clause specifies that the English language word breaker will be used to index the columns. A word breaker is a naturally occurring break between words based on a language's lexicon. Setting the word breaker language to English helps FTS understand how the sentences are structured in order to better search on individual words. The `KEY INDEX` clause specifies the primary key of the table, PK_ProductModel_ProductModelID, as the single-column unique index for the table. Finally, the `CHANGE TRACKING AUTO` option turns on automatic change tracking for the full-text index.

The `ALTER FULLTEXT INDEX` statement in the listing enables the full-text index and starts a full population. `ALTER FULLTEXT INDEX` is a flexible statement that can be used to add columns to, or remove columns from, a full-text index. You can also use it to enable or disable a full-text index, set the change-tracking options, start or stop a full-text index population, or change full-text index stoplist settings.

■ **Note** *Stoplists* are lists of words that are considered unimportant for purposes of FTS. These words are known as *stopwords*. Stopwords are language dependent, with the English system stoplist containing words like *a, an, and,* and *the* (and many others). SQL Server 2012 provides a system stoplist and allows you to create your own custom stoplists. We will discuss stoplists later in this chapter.

Full-Text Querying

After you create a full-text catalog and a full-text index, you can take advantage of FTS with SQL Server's FTS predicates and functions. SQL Server provides four ways to query a full-text index. The `FREETEXT` and `CONTAINS` predicates retrieve rows from a table that match a given FTS criteria, in much the same way that the `EXISTS` predicate returns rows that meet given criteria. The `FREETEXTTABLE` and `CONTAINSTABLE` functions return rowsets with two columns: a key column, which is a row identifier (the unique index value specified when the full-text index was created) and a rank column, which is a relevance rating.

The FREETEXT Predicate

The `FREETEXT` predicate offers the simplest method of using FTS to search character-based columns of a full-text index. `FREETEXT` searches for words that match inflectional forms and thesaurus expansions and replacements. The `FREETEXT` predicate accepts a column name or list of columns, a free-text search string, and an optional language identifier (a locale ID, or LCID). Because it is a predicate, `FREETEXT` can be used in the `WHERE` clause of a `SELECT` query or DML statement. All rows for which the `FREETEXT` predicate returns true (a match) are returned. Listing 10-3 shows a simple `FREETEXT` query that uses the full-text index created on the Production.ProductModel table in the previous section. The results are shown in Figure 10-10. The wildcard character (*) passed as a parameter to the `FREETEXT` predicate indicates that all columns participating in the full-text index should be searched for a match. The second `FREETEXT` parameter is the word you want to match.

Listing 10-3. Simple FREETEXT Full-Text Query

```
SELECT
    ProductModelID,
    Name,
    CatalogDescription,
    Instructions
FROM Production.ProductModel
WHERE FREETEXT(*, N'sock');
```

	ProductModelID	Name	CatalogDescription	Instructions
1	18	Mountain Bike Socks	NULL	NULL
2	24	Racing Socks	NULL	NULL

Figure 10-10. *Using FREETEXT to Find Socks*

The FREETEXT predicate automatically stems words to find inflectional forms. The query in Listing 10-3 returns rows that contain an inflectional form of the word *sock*—in this case, FTS finds two rows that contain the plural form of the word, *socks*. Notice that if you were to replace the word "socks" with "sox" you receive the same result set. This is because FREETEXT also performs FTS thesaurus expansions and replacements automatically, if a thesaurus file is available.

The integration of FTS with the SQL Server query engine results in a more efficient FTS experience. In SQL Server 2012, FTS can take advantage of optimized operators like the Table Valued Function [FulltextMatch] operator shown in Figure 10-11. The query plan shown is generated by the query in Listing 10-3.

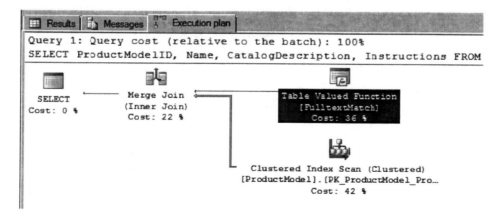

Figure 10-11. *FREETEXT Query Execution Plan*

FTS PERFORMANCE OPTIMIZATION

In previous releases of SQL Server, the FTS functionality was provided via an independent service known as MSFTESQL (Microsoft Full-Text Engine for SQL Server). Because it was completely separate from the SQL Server query engine, the MSFTESQL service could not take advantage of T-SQL operators to optimize performance. As an example, consider the following variation on the query in Listing 10-3:

```
SELECT
  ProductModelID,
  Name,
  CatalogDescription,
  Instructions
FROM Production.ProductModel
WHERE FREETEXT(*, N'sock')
AND ProductModelID < 100;
```

Imagine for a moment that the `Production.ProductModel` table has 1,000,000 rows that match the `FREETEXT` predicate. Versions of SQL Server prior to SQL Server 2008 were incapable of using the additional T-SQL `ProductModelID < 100` predicate in the `WHERE` clause to limit the rows accessed by the FTS service. The MSFTESQL service had to return all 1,000,000 rows from the `FREETEXT` predicate and then narrow them down. Beginning with SQL 2008 and continuing in SQL Server 2012, the FTS engine can work in tandem with the SQL Server query engine to optimize the query plan and limit the number of rows touched by the `FREETEXT` predicate.

■ **Tip** You'll see heavy use of the phrase *inflectional forms* throughout this section. Inflectional forms of words include verb conjugations like *go, goes, going, gone*, and *went*. Inflectional forms also include plural and singular noun variants of words, like *bike* and *bikes*. Searching for any word with FREETEXT automatically results in matches of all supported inflectional forms.

Listing 10-4 demonstrates a FREETEXT query that retrieves all rows that contain inflectional forms of the word *ride* in the CatalogDescription column. Another word for this process is called *stemming*. Inflectional forms that are matched in this query include the plural noun *riders* and the verb *riding*. In this FREETEXT query, the CatalogDescription column name is identified by name to restrict the search to a single column, and the LANGUAGE specifier is used to indicate LCID 1033, which is US English. The results are shown in Figure 10-12.

Listing 10-4. FREETEXT Query with Automatic Word Stemming

```
SELECT
  ProductModelID,
  Name,
  CatalogDescription,
  Instructions
FROM Production.ProductModel
WHERE FREETEXT(CatalogDescription, N'weld', LANGUAGE 1033);
```

	ProductModelID	Name	CatalogDescription	Instructions
1	19	Mountain-100	<?xml-stylesheet href="ProductDescription.xsl" t...	NULL
2	25	Road-150	<?xml-stylesheet href="ProductDescription.xsl" t...	NULL

Figure 10-12. Automatic Stemming with FREETEXT

You can't see the words that matched in the xml type CatalogDescription (there's not enough space on the page to reproduce the entire result). Rest assured that FREETEXT has located valid matches in the row. For the first match the XML has the text "The heat treated welded aluminum," while the second match has the text "it is welded and heat treated."

The CONTAINS Predicate

In addition to the FREETEXT predicate, SQL Server 2012 supports the CONTAINS predicate. CONTAINS allows more advanced full-text query options than the FREETEXT predicate. Just like FREETEXT, the CONTAINS predicate accepts a column name or list of columns, a search condition, and an optional language identifier as parameters. The CONTAINS predicate can search for simple strings like FREETEXT, but it also allows sophisticated search conditions that include word or phrase prefixes, words that are in close proximity to other words, inflectional word forms, thesaurus synonyms, and combinations of search criteria.

The simplest CONTAINS predicates are basic word searches, similar to FREETEXT. Unlike FREETEXT, however, the CONTAINS predicate does not automatically search for inflectional forms of words or thesaurus expansions and replacements. Listing 10-5 modifies Listing 10-4 to demonstrate a simple CONTAINS query. The results are shown in Figure 10-13. As you can see, a couple of rows that do not contain an exact match for the word *weld* are eliminated from the results.

Listing 10-5. Simple CONTAINS Query

```
SELECT
  ProductModelID ,
  Name,
  CatalogDescription,
  Instructions
FROM Production.ProductModel
WHERE CONTAINS (*, N'weld');
```

	ProductModelID	Name	CatalogDescription	Instructions
1	7	HL Touring Frame	NULL	<root xmlns="http://schemas.microsoft.com/sqlser...
2	10	LL Touring Frame	NULL	<root xmlns="http://schemas.microsoft.com/sqlser...
3	47	LL Touring Handlebars	NULL	<root xmlns="http://schemas.microsoft.com/sqlser...
4	48	HL Touring Handlebars	NULL	<root xmlns="http://schemas.microsoft.com/sqlser...

Figure 10-13. Results of the Simple CONTAINS Query

To use inflectional forms or thesaurus expansions and replacements with CONTAINS, use the FORMSOF generation term in your search condition. Listing 10-6 performs a CONTAINS search on the Name and CatalogDescription columns of the Production.ProductModel table. The results, which include matches for inflectional forms of the word *sport,* like *sports* and *sporting,* are shown in Figure 10-14.

Listing 10-6. Sample CONTAINS Query with FORMSOF Inflectional Generation Term

```
SELECT
  ProductModelID ,
  Name,
  CatalogDescription
FROM Production.ProductModel
WHERE CONTAINS
(
  (
    Name,
    CatalogDescription
  ),
  N'FORMSOF(INFLECTIONAL, sport)'
);
```

	ProductModelID	Name	CatalogDescription
1	13	Men's Sports Shorts	NULL
2	28	Road-450	<?xml-stylesheet href="ProductDescription.xsl" t...
3	33	Sport-100	NULL

Figure 10-14. *Results of the CONTAINS Query with Inflectional FORMSOF Term*

The CONTAINS predicate also allows you to combine simple search terms like these with the AND (&), AND NOT (&!), and OR (|) Boolean operators. Listing 10-7 demonstrates combining two search terms in a CONTAINS predicate. The results of this sample query, which retrieves all rows containing inflectional forms of the word *sport* (like *sports*) or the word *tube* in the Name or CatalogDescription columns, are shown in Figure 10-15.

Listing 10-7. Compound CONTAINS Search Term

```
SELECT
  ProductModelID ,
  Name,
  CatalogDescription
FROM Production.ProductModel
WHERE CONTAINS
(
  (
    Name,
    CatalogDescription
),
N'"tube" | FORMSOF (INFLECTIONAL, sport)'
);
```

	ProductModelID	Name	CatalogDescription
1	13	Men's Sports Shorts	NULL
2	19	Mountain-100	<?xml-stylesheet href="ProductDescription.xsl" t...
3	28	Road-450	<?xml-stylesheet href="ProductDescription.xsl" t...
4	33	Sport-100	NULL
5	34	Touring-1000	<?xml-stylesheet href="ProductDescription.xsl" t...
6	92	Mountain Tire Tube	NULL
7	93	Road Tire Tube	NULL
8	94	Touring Tire Tube	NULL

Figure 10-15. *Results of the CONTAINS Query with a Compound Search Term*

Listing 10-7 uses FORMSOF to return matches for inflectional forms. You can also use the FORMSOF (THESAURUS, ...) format to return matches for expansions and replacements of words, as defined in your language-specific thesaurus files.

CONTAINS also supports prefix searches using the wildcard asterisk (*) character. Place the search word or phrase, immediately followed by the wildcard character, in double quotes to specify a prefix search. Listing 10-8 demonstrates a simple prefix search to retrieve all rows that have a word starting with the prefix *bot* in the Name column. The results are shown in Figure 10-16.

Listing 10-8. CONTAINS Prefix Search

```
SELECT
  ProductModelID ,
  Name
FROM Production.ProductModel
WHERE CONTAINS (Name, N'"bot*"');
```

	ProductModelID	Name
1	95	LL Bottom Bracket
2	96	ML Bottom Bracket
3	97	HL Bottom Bracket
4	111	Water Bottle
5	112	Mountain Bottle Cage
6	113	Road Bottle Cage

Figure 10-16. *Results of the CONTAINS Prefix Search*

The CONTAINS predicate also supports the NEAR (~) keyword for proximity searches. NEAR will return matches for words that are close to one another in the source columns. Listing 10-9 demonstrates a NEAR proximity search that looks for instances of the word *aluminum* that occur in close proximity to the word *jig* in the Instructions column. The results are shown in Figure 10-17. This example is considered a generic proximity search.

Listing 10-9. CONTAINS Proximity Search

```
SELECT
  ProductModelID ,
  Name
FROM Production.ProductModel
WHERE CONTAINS (Instructions, N'aluminum NEAR jig');
```

	ProductModelID	Name
1	7	HL Touring Frame
2	10	LL Touring Frame
3	47	LL Touring Handlebars
4	48	HL Touring Handlebars

Figure 10-17. CONTAINS Proximity Query Results

■ **Tip** Avoid using generic proximity searches. These will be deprecated in future versions of SQL Server. Instead, use the custom proximity searches discussed later in this chapter.

SQL Server 2012 introduces a custom proximity search for the NEAR clause. It allows you to easily search for words within a customizable distance from one another. It also allows you to define the order of the phrases in your search. The distance is determined by the number of non-searchable words between the words included in your search. If we take the example in Listing 10-9 and convert it to a custom proximity search, we find that in order to get the same results we have to include a distance of three. This means that a maximum of three words exist between the words aluminum and jig. Listing 10-10 shows the revised code.

Listing 10-10. CONTAINS Custom Search

```
SELECT
  ProductModelID ,
  Name
FROM Production.ProductModel
WHERE CONTAINS(Instructions, 'NEAR((aluminum,jig), 3)');
```

Listing 10-10 gives you the same results as Figure 10-17. A distance of two will give you no results but any other number above three gives you the same results as the original. Keep in mind the distance between the words also includes stopwords. Remember stopwords are words usually not included in searches. Keep in mind too that the custom proximity clause is not limited to only two search words. You could have also included words like "bike," "weld," and "frame"—for example, NEAR((bike, weld, frame), 3). You can even include phrases like "bike riding" or "welding frame." Whatever you choose, the distance is still based on the distance between the first and last word listed in the condition.

By default the custom proximity search will ignore the order of the search words. In the example above, jig could be within a distance of three either before or after the word aluminum. If you want to control the order of the search words then you need add the TRUE clause in the NEAR statement. Listing 10-11 shows two examples. The first has jig before aluminum and the second has aluminum before jig. Notice that only the second example returns values.

Listing 10-11. Custom Search with TRUE Clause

```
SELECT
  ProductModelID ,
  Name
FROM Production.ProductModel
WHERE CONTAINS(Instructions, 'NEAR((jig, aluminum),3, TRUE)');

SELECT
  ProductModelID ,
  Name
FROM Production.ProductModel
WHERE CONTAINS(Instructions, 'NEAR((aluminum, jig),3, TRUE)');
```

The custom proximity search also allows for search conditions which combine multiple grouping of words using expressions like AND, OR, and AND NOT. The added flexibility of the SQL Server 2012 custom proximity search adds advanced features not available in the generic search. Going forward, all searches should be done using the custom properties.

The FREETEXTTABLE and CONTAINSTABLE Functions

SQL Server provides TVF-based counterparts to the FREETEXT and CONTAINS predicates, known as FREETEXTTABLE and CONTAINSTABLE. These functions operate like the similarly named predicates, but both functions return result sets consisting of a table with two columns, named KEY and RANK. The KEY column contains the key index values relating back to the unique index of matching rows in the source table, and the RANK column contains relevance rankings.

The FREETEXTTABLE function accepts the name of the table to search, a single column name or column list, a search string, and an optional language identifier just like the FREETEXT predicate. FREETEXTTABLE can also take an additional "top *n* by rank" parameter to limit the rows returned to a specific number of the highest-ranked rows. The results of FREETEXTTABLE are useful for joining back to the source table via the KEY column of the results. Listing 10-12 demonstrates a simple FREETEXTTABLE query that locates rows where the word *aluminum* appears in the Instructions column of the Production.ProductModel table. The results are joined back to the source table to return the ProductModelID and Name, as shown in Figure 10-18.

Listing 10-12. FREETEXTTABLE Results Joined to Source Table

```
SELECT
  ftt.[KEY],
  ftt.[RANK],
  pm.ProductModelID ,
  pm.Name FROM FREETEXTTABLE
(
  Production.ProductModel,
  Instructions,
  N'aluminum'
) ftt
INNER JOIN Production.ProductModel pm
  ON ftt.[KEY]=pm.ProductModelID;
```

	KEY	RANK	ProductModelID	Name
1	7	567	7	HL Touring Frame
2	10	567	10	LL Touring Frame
3	47	636	47	LL Touring Handlebars
4	48	636	48	HL Touring Handlebars

Figure 10-18. *Results of the FREETEXTTABLE Query*

The CONTAINSTABLE function offers the advanced search capabilities of the CONTAINS predicate in a function form. The CONTAINSTABLE function accepts the name of the source table, a single column name or list of columns, and a CONTAINS-style search condition. Like FREETEXTTABLE, the CONTAINSTABLE function also accepts an optional language identifier and "top *n* by rank" parameter. Listing 10-13 demonstrates the CONTAINSTABLE function in a simple keyword search that retrieves KEY and RANK values for all rows containing inflectional forms of the word *tours*. The results are shown in Figure 10-19.

Listing 10-13. Simple CONTAINSTABLE Query

```
SELECT
  [KEY],
  [RANK]
FROM CONTAINSTABLE (
Production.ProductModel,
[Name],
N'FORMSOF(INFLECTIONAL, tours)'
);
```

	KEY	RANK
1	7	64
2	10	64
3	34	64
4	35	64
5	36	64
6	43	64
7	44	64
8	47	64
9	48	64
10	53	64
11	65	64
12	66	64
13	67	64
14	91	64
15	94	64
16	120	64

Figure 10-19. *Results of the CONTAINSTABLE Query with Inflectional Forms*

CONTAINSTABLE supports all of the options supported by the CONTAINS predicate, including the ISABOUT term, which allows you to assign weights to the matched words it locates. With ISABOUT, you assign a weight value between 0.0 and 1.0 to each search word. CONTAINSTABLE applies the weight to the relevance rankings returned in the RANK column. Listing 10-14 shows two CONTAINSTABLE queries. The first query returns all products with the words *aluminum* or *polish* in their XML Instructions column. The second query uses ISABOUT to assign each of these words a weight between 0.0 and 1.0, which is then applied to the result RANK for each row. The results, shown in Figure 10-20, demonstrate how ISABOUT weights can rearrange the rankings of your CONTAINSTABLE query results.

Listing 10-14. ISABOUT in a CONTAINSTABLE Query

```
SELECT
  ct.[RANK],
  ct.[KEY],
  pm.[Name]
FROM CONTAINSTABLE
(
  Production.ProductModel,
  Instructions,
  N'aluminum OR polish'
) ct
INNER JOIN Production.ProductModel pm
  ON ct.[KEY]=pm.ProductModelID
ORDER BY ct.[RANK] DESC;

  SELECT
  ct.[RANK],
  ct.[KEY],
  pm.[Name] FROM CONTAINSTABLE
(
  Production.ProductModel,
  Instructions,
N'ISABOUT(aluminum WEIGHT(1.0 ), polish WEIGHT(0.1))'
) ct
INNER JOIN Production.ProductModel pm
  ON ct.[KEY]=pm.ProductModelID
ORDER BY ct.[RANK] DESC;
```

	RANK	KEY	Name
1	24	7	HL Touring Frame
2	24	10	LL Touring Frame
3	19	47	LL Touring Handlebars
4	19	48	HL Touring Handlebars

	RANK	KEY	Name
1	19	47	LL Touring Handlebars
2	19	48	HL Touring Handlebars
3	18	7	HL Touring Frame
4	18	10	LL Touring Frame

Figure 10-20. *Changing Result Set Rankings with ISABOUT*

Thesauruses and Stoplists

The FREETEXT predicate and FREETEXTTABLE function automatically perform word stemming for inflectional forms and thesaurus expansions and replacements. The CONTAINS predicate and CONTAINSTABLE function require you to explicitly specify that you want inflectional forms and thesaurus expansions and replacements with the FORMSOF term. While inflectional forms include verb conjugations and plural forms of words, thesaurus functionality is based on user-managed XML files that define word replacement and expansion patterns.

Each language-specific thesaurus is located in an XML file in the FTData directory of your SQL Server installation. If you installed SQL Server with the default settings then the directory would be located in the path C:\Program Files\Microsoft SQL Server\MSSQL11.MSSQLSERVER\MSSQL\FTData\. The thesaurus files are named using the format *tsnnn*.xml, where *nnn* is a three-letter code representing a specific language. The file name tsenu.xml, for instance, is the US English thesaurus. To demonstrate the FTS thesaurus capabilities, we'll begin by creating a new full-text index on the Production.Product table using the code in Listing 10-15.

Listing 10-15. Creating a Full-Text Index

```
CREATE  FULLTEXT  INDEX  ON  Production.Product
(
    Name  LANGUAGE  English,
    Color LANGUAGE English
)
KEY  INDEX PK_Product_ProductID
ON  (AdventureWorksFTCat)
WITH
(
    CHANGE_TRACKING AUTO,
    STOPLIST = SYSTEM
);
GO

ALTER FULLTEXT INDEX ON Production.Product
ENABLE;
GO
```

You can edit the thesaurus XML files with a simple text editor or a more advanced XML editor. For this example, we opened the tsenu.xml thesaurus file in Notepad, made the appropriate changes, and saved the file back to the MSSQLFTData directory. The contents of the tsenu.xml file, after our edits, are shown in Listing 10-16.

Listing 10-16. Tsenu.xml US English XML Thesaurus File

```
<XML  ID="Microsoft  Search  Thesaurus">
    <thesaurus xmlns="x-schema:tsSchema.xml">
        <diacritics_sensitive>0</diacritics_sensitive>
        <expansion>
        <sub>thin</sub>
        <sub>flat</sub>
        </expansion>
        <replacement>
        <pat>sapphire</pat>
        <pat>indigo</pat>
        <pat>navy</pat>
```

```
        <sub>blue</sub>
      </replacement>
  </thesaurus>
</XML>
```

After editing the XML thesaurus file, you can use the `sys.spfulltextloadthesaurusfile` stored procedure (SP) to reload the thesaurus file. This procedure accepts an integer LCID parameter, as shown in Listing 10-17. The LCID used in the listing is 1033, which specifies US English.

■ **Note** Starting in SQL Server 2008, reloading a thesaurus in SQL Server did not require an SQL Server service restart.

Listing 10-17. Reloading US English XML Thesaurus

```
EXEC sys.sp_fulltext_load_thesaurus_file 1033;
GO
```

The `diacritics_sensitive` element of the thesaurus file indicates whether accent marks are replaced during expansion and replacement. For instance, if `diacritics_sensitive` is set to 0, the words *cafe* and *café* are considered equivalent for purposes of the thesaurus. If `diacritics_sensitive` is set to 1, however, these two words would be considered different.

The `expansion` element indicates substitutions that should be applied during the full-text query. The word being searched is expanded to match the other words in the expansion set. In the example, if the user queries for the word *thin*, the search is automatically expanded to include matches for the word *flat*, and vice versa. An expansion set can include as many substitutions as you care to define, and the thesaurus can contain as many expansion sets as you need. The sample `FREETEXT` query in Listing 10-18 shows the expansion sets in action, with partial results shown in Figure 10-21.

Listing 10-18. FREETEXT Query with Thesaurus Expansion Sets

```
SELECT
  ProductID,
  Name
FROM Production.Product
WHERE FREETEXT(*, N'flat');
```

	ProductID	Name
1	341	Flat Washer 1
2	342	Flat Washer 6
3	343	Flat Washer 2
4	344	Flat Washer 9
5	345	Flat Washer 4
6	346	Flat Washer 3
7	347	Flat Washer 8
8	348	Flat Washer 5
9	349	Flat Washer 7
10	359	Thin-Jam Hex Nut 9
11	360	Thin-Jam Hex Nut 10
12	361	Thin-Jam Hex Nut 1
13	362	Thin-Jam Hex Nut 2
14	363	Thin-Jam Hex Nut 15
15	364	Thin-Jam Hex Nut 16

Figure 10-21. *Partial Results of the Full-text Query with Expansion Sets*

The replacement section of the thesaurus file indicates replacements for words that are used in a full-text query. In the example, we've defined patterns like navy, sapphire, and indigo, which will be replaced with the word blue. The result is that a full-text query for these replacement patterns will be converted internally to a search for blue. Listing 10-19 shows a FREETEXT query that uses the replacement patterns defined in the thesaurus. You can use any of the replacement patterns defined in the thesaurus file in the full-text query to get the same result. Figure 10-22 shows the results.

Listing 10-19. FREETEXT Query with Thesaurus Replacement Patterns

```
SELECT
  ProductID,
  Name,
  Color
FROM Production.Product
WHERE FREETEXT(*, N'navy');
```

Previous versions of FTS had system-defined lists of noise words, which provided a way to essentially ignore commonly occurring words that don't help the search. Commonly cited noise words included those like the, a, an, and others. The noise word implementation in previous versions stored the noise words in files in the file system.

	ProductID	Name	Color
1	495	Paint - Blue	NULL
2	711	Sport-100 Helmet, Blue	Blue
3	864	Classic Vest, S	Blue
4	865	Classic Vest, M	Blue
5	866	Classic Vest, L	Blue
6	890	HL Touring Frame - Blue, 46	Blue
7	891	HL Touring Frame - Blue, 50	Blue
8	892	HL Touring Frame - Blue, 54	Blue
9	893	HL Touring Frame - Blue, 60	Blue
10	895	LL Touring Frame - Blue, 50	Blue
11	896	LL Touring Frame - Blue, 54	Blue
12	897	LL Touring Frame - Blue, 58	Blue
13	898	LL Touring Frame - Blue, 62	Blue

Figure 10-22. *Partial Results of the Full-text Query with Replacement Sets*

SQL Server 2012 implements the classic noise words, known in FTS as stopwords. Stopwords are managed inside the SQL Server database using structures known as stoplists. You can use the system-supplied stoplists or create and manage your own language-specific stoplists with the CREATE FULLTEXT STOPLIST, ALTER FULLTEXT STOPLIST, and DROP FULLTEXT STOPLIST statements. The statement in Listing 10-20 creates a stoplist based on the system stoplist.

Listing 10-20. Creating a Full-Text Stoplist

```
CREATE FULLTEXT STOPLIST AWStoplist
FROM SYSTEM STOPLIST;
GO
```

Stoplists are more flexible than the old noise word lists since you can easily use T-SQL statements to add words to your stoplists. Consider AdventureWorks product model searches where the word *instructions* appears in several of the XML documents in the Instructions column. You can add the word *instructions* to the previously created stoplist with the ALTER FULLTEXT STOPLIST statement, and then associate the stoplist with the full-text index on the Production.ProductModel table via the ALTER FULLTEXT INDEX statement, as shown in Listing 10-21. This will effectively ignore the word *instructions* during full-text searches on this column.

Listing 10-21. Adding the Word "Instructions" to the Stoplist

```
ALTER FULLTEXT STOPLIST AWStoplist
ADD N'instructions' LANGUAGE English;
GO


ALTER FULLTEXT INDEX ON Production.ProductModel
SET STOPLIST AWStoplist;
GO
```

After application of the newly created stoplist, a full-text query against the Production.ProductModel table for the word *instructions,* as shown in Listing 10-22, will return no results.

Listing 10-22. Full-Text Query with Newly Created Stoplist

```
SELECT
  ProductModelID,
  Name
FROM Production.ProductModel
WHERE FREETEXT(*, N'instructions');
```

Stored Procedures and Dynamic Management Views and Functions

SQL Server 2012 provides access to many of the legacy FTS SPs available in previous releases of SQL Server. Most of these procedures have been deprecated, however, and have been replaced by fully integrated T-SQL statements and dynamic management views and functions.

SQL Server 2012 FTS uses the sys.sp_fulltext_load_thesaurus_file procedure that we introduced earlier in this chapter to load an XML thesaurus file. Another procedure is the sys.sp_fulltext_resetfdhostaccount procedure that updates the Windows username and password that SQL Server uses to start the filter daemon service.

A big issue for developers who used FTS in SQL Server 2005 and earlier was the lack of transparency. Basically everything that FTS did was well hidden from view, and developers and administrators had to troubleshoot FTS issues in the dark. SQL Server 2008 introduced some catalog views and dynamic management functions that made FTS more transparent, and this continues to be the case in SQL Server 2012.

If you're experiencing FTS query performance issues, the sys.fulltext_index_fragments catalog view can provide insight. This catalog view reports full-text index fragments and their status. You can use the information in this catalog view to decide if it's time to reorganize your full-text index.

The sys.fulltext_stoplists and sys.fulltext_stopwords catalog views let you see the user-defined stopwords and stoplists defined in the current database. The information returned by these catalog views is useful for troubleshooting issues with certain words being ignored (or not being ignored) in full-text queries. The sys.fulltext_system_stopwords catalog view returns a row for every stopword in the system stoplist, which is useful information to have if you want to use the system stoplist as the basis for your own stoplists.

The sys.dm_fts_parser function is a useful tool for troubleshooting full-text queries. This function accepts a full-text query string, an LCID, a stoplist ID, and an accent sensitivity setting. The result returned by the function shows the results produced by the word breaker and stemmer for any given full-text query. This information is very useful if you need to troubleshoot or just want to better understand exactly how the word breaker and stemmer affect your queries. Listing 10-23 is a simple demonstration of stemming the word *had* with the sys.dm_fts_parser function. Results are shown in Figure 10-23.

Listing 10-23. Using Sys.dm_fts_parser to See Word Breaking and Stemming

```
SELECT
  keyword,
  group_id,
  phrase_id,
  occurrence,
  special_term,
  display_term,
  expansion_type,
```

```
    source_term
FROM sys.dm_fts_parser
(
    N'FORMSOF(FREETEXT,had)',
    1033,
    NULL,
    0
);
```

	keyword	group_id	phrase_id	occurrence	special_term	display_term	expansion_type	source_term
1	0x006800610073	1	0	1	Exact Match	has	2	had
2	0x0068006100760065	1	0	1	Exact Match	have	2	had
3	0x00680061007600650027330073	1	0	1	Exact Match	have's	2	had
4	0x00680061007600650073	1	0	1	Exact Match	haves	2	had
5	0x0068006100760065007300027	1	0	1	Exact Match	haves'	2	had
6	0x0068006100760069006E0067	1	0	1	Exact Match	having	2	had
7	0x006800610064	1	0	1	Exact Match	had	0	had

Figure 10-23. *Results of Word-breaking and Stemming the Word "Had"*

Statistical Semantics

When you created the index (see Figure 10-6) you had the option to select statistical semantics. Statistical semantics is new in SQL Server 2012 and it dramatically changes what it means to search documents. Everything discussed up to now was focused on searching words within a document. If you needed to find all the words similar to "weld," you could find them by using FTS functions against text data stored in the SQL Server engine. But what if you wanted to find all the documents stored in your SQL Server database that were related to finance or a particular law case? Or, let's say, you needed to search through hundreds of resumes to determine which ones best fit a particular job application. This is where statistical semantics becomes helpful. Statistical semantics is used to search for the meaning of documents and not just their content.

The statistical semantic feature requires FTS but is installed as a separate feature. The install file is located on the SQL Server install disk. The 64bit version is located at . . . \x64\Setup and the file name is SemanticLanguageDatabase.msi. The install wizard is straight-forward. The wizard extracts the semantic database files to a directory. The default directory is C:\Program Files\Microsoft Semantic Language Database. You will then want to copy or move these database files to another location, preferably the same location as your other database files, and then attach the database. Once the database is attached, run the command in Listing 10-24.

Listing 10-24. Initializing the Statistical Semantics Database

```
EXEC sp_fulltext_semantic_register_language_statistics_db @dbname=N'semanticsdb';
```

Once initialized, you can verify the database is ready by running the code in Listing 10-25. Figure 10-24 shows the results.

Listing 10-25. Verifying Active Statistical Semantics Database

```
SELECT * FROM sys.fulltext_semantic_language_statistics_database
```

	database_id	register_date	registered_by	version
1	9	2012-07-14 18:21:38.980	1	11.0.1153.1.1

Figure 10-24. *Results of Querying the Semantics Database*

From here you can now go back to the properties of the Production.ProductModel FTS index we created earlier in the chapter and checkmark the Statistical Semantics column as shown in Figure 10-25.

Figure 10-25. *Enabling Statistical Semantics on Table Columns*

Now that statistical semantics is installed we can do things like search for key phrases or find related documents. To find a key phrase we use the TVF `semantickeyphrasetable`. Searching for key phrases on the Production.ProductModel name column yields the results we see in Figure 10-26. Run the code in Listing 10-26 to get the results.

Listing 10-26. Using the Semantickeyphrasetable Function

```
SELECT TOP(10) KEYP_TBL.keyphrase
FROM SEMANTICKEYPHRASETABLE
    (
    Production.ProductModel,
        Name
    ) AS KEYP_TBL
ORDER BY KEYP_TBL.score DESC;
GO
```

	keyphrase
1	derailleur
2	derailleur
3	panniers
4	short-sleeve
5	taillight
6	weatherproof
7	long-sleeve
8	hydration
9	bib
10	handlebars

Figure 10-26. *Results from Semantickeyphrasetable Function*

Semantic searching offers some interesting possibilities and broadens the scope of traditional FTS. If you include the SQL Server 2012 FileTable feature then the possibilities widen even further. FileTable allows documents stored on a file system to be integrated and managed through SQL Server. Semantic searching can be performed against these and any other document managed by the SQL Server engine.

Summary

FTS functionality is highly integrated with SQL Server, providing more efficient full-text queries than ever before. Full-text indexes and stoplists are stored in the database, making FTS more manageable, flexible, and scalable.

SQL Server provides the powerful `FREETEXT` and `CONTAINS` predicates, and `FREETEXTTABLE` and `CONTAINSTABLE` functions, to perform full-text searches. SQL Server also supports thesaurus and stoplist functionality to help customize FTS as well as the new `CONTAIN` custom search and statistical semantics. SQL Server 2012 also provides dynamic management views and functions to make FTS more transparent and easier to troubleshoot than was the case in previous versions of SQL Server.

EXERCISES

1. [True/False] Stoplists and full-text indexes are stored in the database.

2. [Choose one] You can create a full-text index with which of the following methods:

    a. Using a wizard in SSMS

    b. Using the T-SQL CREATE FULLTEXT INDEX statement

    c. Both (a) and (b)

    d. None of the above

3. [Fill in the blanks] The FREETEXT predicate automatically performs word stemming and thesaurus _____ and _____.

4. [Fill in the blank] Stoplists contain stopwords, which are words that are _____ during full-text querying.

5. [True/False] The sys.dm_fts_parser dynamic management function shows the results produced by word breaking and stemming.

CHAPTER 11

XML

SQL Server 2012 continues the standard for XML integration included with the SQL Server 2008 release. SQL Server 2012 XML still offers tight integration with T-SQL through the xml data type, support for the World Wide Web Consortium (W3C) XQuery and XML Schema recommendations.

SQL Server 2012's tight XML integration and the xml data type provide streamlined methods of performing several XML-related tasks that used to require clunky code to interface with COM objects and other tools external to the SQL Server engine. This chapter discusses the xml data type and the XML tools built into T-SQL to take advantage of this functionality.

Legacy XML

T-SQL support for XML was introduced with the release of SQL Server 2000 via the FOR XML clause of the SELECT statement, the OPENXML rowset provider, and the sp_xml_preparedocument and sp_xml_removedocument system SPs. In this section, we'll discuss the legacy OPENXML, sp_xml_preparedocument, and sp_xml_removedocument functionality. Though these tools still exist in SQL Server 2012 and can be used for backward-compatibility scripts, they are awkward and kludgy to use.

OPENXML

OPENXML is a legacy XML function that provides a rowset view of XML data. The process of converting XML data to relational form is known as *shredding*. OPENXML is technically a *rowset provider*, which means its contents can be queried and accessed like a table. The legacy SQL Server XML functionality requires the sp_xml_preparedocument and sp_xml_removedocument system SPs to parse text into an XML document and clean up afterward. These procedures are used in conjunction with the OPENXML function to move XML data from its textual representation into a parsed internal representation of an XML document, and from there into a tabular format.

This method is rather clunky compared to the newer methods first introduced by SQL Server 2005, but you might need it if you're writing code that needs to be backward compatible. The OPENXML method has certain disadvantages based on its heritage, some of which are listed here:

- OPENXML relies on COM to invoke the Microsoft XML Core Services Library (MSXML) to perform XML manipulation and shredding.

- When it is invoked, MSXML assigns one-eighth of SQL Server's total memory to the task of parsing and manipulating XML data.

- If you fail to call spxmlremovedocument after preparing an XML document with the spxmlpreparedocument procedure, it won't be removed from memory until the SQL Server service is restarted.

■ **Tip** We strongly recommend using xml data type methods like nodes(), value(), and query() to shred your
XML data instead of using OPENXML. We'll discuss these xml data type methods later in this chapter, in the section
titled "The XML Data Type Methods."

The sample query in Listing 11-1 is a simple demonstration of using OPENXML to shred XML data. The partial
results of this query are shown in Figure 11-1.

Listing 11-1. Simple OPENXML Query

```
DECLARE @docHandle int;

DECLARE @xmlDocument nvarchar(max) = N'<Customers>
    <Customer CustomerID="1234" ContactName="Larry" CompanyName="APress">
        <Orders>
            <Order   CustomerID="1234"     OrderDate="2006-04-25T13:22:18"/>
            <Order   CustomerID="1234"     OrderDate="2006-05-10T12:35:49"/>
        </Orders>
    </Customer>
    <Customer CustomerID="4567" ContactName="Bill" CompanyName="Microsoft">
        <Orders>
            <Order   CustomerID="4567"     OrderDate="2006-03-12T18:32:39"/>
            <Order   CustomerID="4567"     OrderDate="2006-05-11T17:56:12"/>
        </Orders>
    </Customer>
</Customers>';

EXECUTE sp_xml_preparedocument @docHandle OUTPUT, @xmlDocument;

SELECT
        Id,
        ParentId,
        NodeType,
        LocalName,
        Prefix,
        NameSpaceUri,
        DataType,
        Prev,
        [Text]
FROM  OPENXML(@docHandle, N'/Customers/Customer');

EXECUTE sp_xml_removedocument @docHandle;
GO
```

	Id	ParentId	NodeType	LocalName	Prefix	NameSpaceUri	DataType	Prev	Text
1	2	0	1	Customer	NULL	NULL	NULL	NULL	NULL
2	3	2	2	CustomerID	NULL	NULL	NULL	NULL	NULL
3	24	3	3	#text	NULL	NULL	NULL	NULL	1234
4	4	2	2	ContactName	NULL	NULL	NULL	NULL	NULL
5	25	4	3	#text	NULL	NULL	NULL	NULL	Larry
6	5	2	2	CompanyName	NULL	NULL	NULL	NULL	NULL
7	26	5	3	#text	NULL	NULL	NULL	NULL	APress
8	6	2	1	Orders	NULL	NULL	NULL	NULL	NULL
9	7	6	1	Order	NULL	NULL	NULL	NULL	NULL
10	8	7	2	CustomerID	NULL	NULL	NULL	NULL	NULL
11	27	8	3	#text	NULL	NULL	NULL	NULL	1234
12	9	7	2	OrderDate	NULL	NULL	NULL	NULL	NULL
13	28	9	3	#text	NULL	NULL	NULL	NULL	2006-04-25T13:22:18
14	10	6	1	Order	NULL	NULL	NULL	7	NULL

Figure 11-1. *Results of the OPENXML Query*

The first step in using OPENXML is to call the sp_xml_preparedocument SP to convert an XML-formatted string into an XML document:

```
DECLARE @docHandle int;

DECLARE @xmlDocument nvarchar(max) = N'<Customers>
    <Customer CustomerID="1234" ContactName="Larry" CompanyName="APress">
        <Orders>
            <Order   CustomerID="1234"    OrderDate="2006-04-25T13:22:18"/>
            <Order   CustomerID="1234"    OrderDate="2006-05-10T12:35:49"/>
        </Orders>
    </Customer>
    <Customer CustomerID="4567" ContactName="Bill" CompanyName="Microsoft">
        <Orders>
            <Order   CustomerID="4567"    OrderDate="2006-03-12T18:32:39"/>
            <Order   CustomerID="4567"    OrderDate="2006-05-11T17:56:12"/>
        </Orders>
    </Customer>
</Customers>';

EXECUTE sp_xml_preparedocument @docHandle OUTPUT, @xmlDocument;
```

The sp_xml_preparedocument procedure invokes MSXML to parse your XML document into an internal Document Object Model (DOM) tree representation of the nodes. The sp_xml_preparedocument procedure accepts up to three parameters, as follows:

- The first parameter, called hdoc, is an output parameter that returns an int handle to the XML document created by the SP.

- The second parameter is the original XML document. This parameter is known as xmltext and can be a char, nchar, varchar, nvarchar, text, ntext, or xml data type. If NULL is passed in or the xmltext parameter is omitted, an empty XML document is created. The default for this parameter is NULL.

- A third optional parameter, xpathnamespaces, specifies the namespace declarations used in OPENXML XPath expressions. Like xmltext, the xpath_namespaces parameter can be a char, nchar, varchar, nvarchar, text, ntext, or xml data type. The default xpath_namespaces value is < root xmlns:mp = "urn:schemas-microsoft-com: xml-metaprop" > .

The OPENXML rowset provider shreds the internal DOM representation of the XML document into relational format. The result of the rowset provider can be queried like a table or view, as shown following:

```
SELECT
    Id,
    ParentId,
    NodeType,
    LocalName,
    Prefix,
    NameSpaceUri,
    DataType,
    Prev,
    [Text]
FROM OPENXML(@docHandle, N'/Customers/Customer');
```

The OPENXML rowset provider accepts up to three parameters:

- The first parameter, hdoc, is the int document handle returned by the call to the sp_xml_preparedocument procedure.

- The second parameter, known as rowpattern, is an nvarchar XPath query pattern that determines which nodes of the XML document are returned as rows.

- The third parameter is an optional flags parameter. This tinyint value specifies the type of mapping to be used between the XML data and the relational rowset. If specified, flags can be a combination of the values listed in Table 11-1.

Table 11-1. *OPENXML Flags Parameter Options*

Value	Name	Description
0	DEFAULT	A flags value of 0 tells OPENXML to default to attribute-centric mapping. This is the default value if the flags parameter is not specified.
1	XML_ATTRIBUTES	A flags value of 1 indicates that OPENXML should use attribute-centric mapping.
2	XML_ELEMENTS	A flags value of 2 indicates that OPENXML should use element-centric mapping.
3	XML_ATTRIBUTES | XML_ELEMENTS	Combining the XML_ATTRIBUTES flag value with the XML_ELEMENTS flag value (logical OR) indicates that attribute-centric mapping should be applied first, and element-centric mapping should be applied to all columns not yet dealt with.
8		A flags value of 8 indicates that the consumed data should not be copied to the overflow property @mp:xmltext. This value can be combined (logical OR) with any of the other flags values.

The internal XML document generated by sp_xml_preparedocument is cached and will continue to take up SQL Server memory until it is explicitly removed with the sp_xml_removedocument procedure. The sp_xml_removedocument procedure accepts a single parameter, the int document handle initially generated by sp_xml_preparedocument:

```
EXECUTE sp_xml_removedocument @docHandle;
```

■ **Caution**   Always call sp_xml_removedocument to free up memory used by XML documents created with sp_xml_createdocument. Any XML documents created with sp_xml_createdocument remain in memory until sp_xml_removedocument is called or the SQL Server service is restarted. Microsoft advises that not freeing up memory with sp_xml_removedocument could cause your server to run out of memory.

OPENXML Result Formats

The sample in Listing 11-1 returns a table in *edge table format,* which is the default OPENXML rowset format. According to BOL, "Edge tables represent the fine-grained XML document structure . . . in a single table" (http://msdn2.microsoft.com/en-us/library/ ms186918(SQL.11).aspx). The columns returned by the edge table format are shown in Table 11-2.

Table 11-2. *Edge Table Format*

Column Name	Data Type	Description
id	bigint	The unique ID of the document node. The root element ID is 0.
parentid	bigint	The identifier of the parent of the node. If the node is a top-level node, the parentid is NULL.
nodetype	int	The column that indicates the type of the node. It can be 1 for an element node, 2 for an attribute node, or 3 for a text node.
localname	nvarchar	The local name of the element or attribute, or NULL if the DOM object does not have a name.
prefix	nvarchar	The namespace prefix of the node.
namespaceuri	nvarchar	The namespace URI of the node, or NULL if there's no namespace.
datatype	nvarchar	The data type of the element or attribute row, which is inferred from the inline DTD or inline schema.
prev	bigint	The XML ID of the previous sibling element, or NULL if there is no direct previous sibling.
text	ntext	The attribute value or element content.

OPENXML supports an optional WITH clause to specify a user-defined format for the returned rowset. The WITH clause lets you specify the name of an existing table or a schema declaration to define the rowset format. By adding a WITH clause to the OPENXML query in Listing 11-1, you can specify an explicit schema for the resulting rowset. This technique is demonstrated in Listing 11-2, with results shown in Figure 11-2. The differences between Listings 11-2 and 11-1 are shown in bold.

Listing 11-2. OPENXML and WITH Clause, Explicit Schema

```
DECLARE @docHandle int;

DECLARE @xmlDocument nvarchar(max)=N'<Customers>
    <Customer CustomerID="1234" ContactName="Larry" CompanyName="APress">
        <Orders>
            <Order  CustomerID="1234"    OrderDate="2006-04-25T13:22:18"/>
            <Order  CustomerID="1234"    OrderDate="2006-05-10T12:35:49"/>
        </Orders>
    </Customer>
    <Customer CustomerID="4567" ContactName="Bill" CompanyName="Microsoft">
        <Orders>
            <Order  CustomerID="4567"    OrderDate="2006-03-12T18:32:39"/>
            <Order  CustomerID="4567"    OrderDate="2006-05-11T17:56:12"/>
        </Orders>
    </Customer>
</Customers>';
EXECUTE sp_xml_preparedocument @docHandle OUTPUT, @xmlDocument;

SELECT
    CustomerID,
        CustomerName,
        CompanyName,
        OrderDate
FROM  OPENXML(@docHandle, N'/Customers/Customer/Orders/Order')
WITH
(
        CustomerID nchar(4) N'../../@CustomerID',
        CustomerName nvarchar(50) N'../../@ContactName',
        CompanyName nvarchar(50) N'../../@CompanyName',
        OrderDate datetime
);

EXECUTE sp_xml_removedocument @docHandle;
GO
```

	CustomerID	CustomerName	CompanyName	OrderDate
1	1234	Larry	APress	2006-04-25 13:22:18.000
2	1234	Larry	APress	2006-05-10 12:35:49.000
3	4567	Bill	Microsoft	2006-03-12 18:32:39.000
4	4567	Bill	Microsoft	2006-05-11 17:56:12.000

Figure 11-2. *Results of OPENXML with an Explicit Schema Declaration*

The OPENXML WITH clause can also use the schema from an existing table to format the relational result set. This is demonstrated in Listing 11-3. The differences between Listing 11-3 and 11-2 are shown in bold.

Listing 11-3. OPENXML with WITH Clause, Existing Table Schema

```
DECLARE @docHandle int;

DECLARE @xmlDocument nvarchar(max) = N'<Customers>
    <Customer CustomerID="1234" ContactName="Larry" CompanyName="APress">
        <Orders>
            <Order   CustomerID="1234"       OrderDate="2006-04-25T13:22:18"/>
            <Order   CustomerID="1234"       OrderDate="2006-05-10T12:35:49"/>
        </Orders>
    </Customer>
    <Customer CustomerID="4567" ContactName="Bill" CompanyName="Microsoft">
        <Orders>
            <Order   CustomerID="4567"       OrderDate="2006-03-12T18:32:39"/>
            <Order   CustomerID="4567"       OrderDate="2006-05-11T17:56:12"/>
        </Orders>
    </Customer>
</Customers>';

EXECUTE sp_xml_preparedocument @docHandle OUTPUT, @xmlDocument;

CREATE TABLE #CustomerInfo
(
    CustomerID nchar(4) NOT NULL,
    ContactName nvarchar(50) NOT NULL,
    CompanyName nvarchar(50) NOT NULL
);

CREATE   TABLE   #OrderInfo
(
    CustomerID nchar(4) NOT NULL,
    OrderDate datetime NOT NULL
);

INSERT   INTO   #CustomerInfo
(
    CustomerID,
    ContactName,
    CompanyName
)
SELECT
    CustomerID,
    ContactName,
    CompanyName
FROM  OPENXML(@docHandle, N'/Customers/Customer')
WITH #CustomerInfo;

INSERT   INTO   #OrderInfo
(
    CustomerID,
    OrderDate
)
```

```
SELECT
    CustomerID,
    OrderDate
FROM OPENXML(@docHandle, N'//Order')
WITH  #OrderInfo;
SELECT
    c.CustomerID,
    c.ContactName,
    c.CompanyName,
    o.OrderDate
FROM #CustomerInfo c
INNER  JOIN  #OrderInfo  o
    ON  c.CustomerID = o.CustomerID;

DROP  TABLE #OrderInfo;
DROP  TABLE #CustomerInfo;

EXECUTE sp_xml_removedocument @docHandle;
GO
```

The WITH clause used by each OPENXML query in Listing 11-3 specifies a table name. OPENXML uses the table's schema to define the relational format of the result returned.

FOR XML Clause

SQL Server 2000 introduced the FOR XML clause for use with the SELECT statement to efficiently convert relational data to XML format. The FOR XML clause is highly flexible and provides a wide range of options that give you fine-grained control over your XML result.

FOR XML RAW

The FOR XML clause appears at the end of the SELECT statement and can specify one of five different modes and several mode-specific options. The first FOR XML mode is RAW mode, which returns data in XML format with each row represented as a node with attributes representing the columns. FOR XML RAW is useful for ad hoc FOR XML queries while debugging and testing. The FOR XML RAW clause allows you to specify the element name for each row returned in parentheses immediately following the RAW keyword (if you leave it off, the default name, row, is used). The query in Listing 11-4 demonstrates FOR XML RAW, with results shown in Figure 11-3.

Listing 11-4. Sample FOR XML RAW Query

```
USE AdventureWorks2012;
GO

SELECT
    ProductID,
    Name,
    ProductNumber
FROM Production.Product
WHERE ProductID IN (770, 903)
FOR XML RAW;
```

```
XML_F52E2B61-18A1...-00805F49916B1.xml*   X
⊟<row ProductID="770"
       Name="Road-650 Black, 52"
       ProductNumber="BK-R50B-52" />
⊟<row ProductID="903"
       Name="LL Touring Frame - Blue, 44"
       ProductNumber="FR-T67U-44" />
```

Figure 11-3. *Results of the FOR XML RAW Query*

The FOR XML clause modes support several additional options to control the resulting output. The options supported by all FOR XML modes are shown in Figure 11-4.

	XMLDATA*	XMLSCHEMA	ELEMENTS XSINIL	ELEMENTS ABSENT	BINARY BASE64	TYPE	ROOT	('ElementName')
FOR XML AUTO	●	●	●	●	●	●	●	
FOR XML RAW	●	●	●	●	●	●	●	●
FOR XML PATH			●	●	●	●	●	●
FOR XML EXPLICIT	●				●	●	●	

FOR XML Clause Options

*The XMLDATA option is deprecated. Use XMLSCHEMA instead.

Figure 11-4. *FOR XML Clause Options*

The options supported by FOR XML RAW mode include the following:

- The TYPE option specifies that the result should be returned as an xml data type instance. This is particularly useful when you use FOR XML in nested subqueries. By default, without the TYPE option, all FOR XML modes return XML data as a character string.

- The ROOT option adds a single top-level root element to the XML result. Using the ROOT option guarantees a well-formed XML (single root element) result.

- The ELEMENTS option specifies that column data should be returned as subelements instead of attributes in the XML result. The ELEMENTS option can have the following additional options:

  - XSINIL specifies that columns with SQL nulls are included in the result with an xsi:nil attribute set to true.

  - ABSENT specifies that no elements are created for SQL nulls. ABSENT is the default action for handling nulls.

325

- The BINARY BASE64 option specifies that binary data returned by the query should be represented in Base64-encoded form in the XML result. If your result contains any binary data, the BINARY BASE64 option is required.

- XMLSCHEMA returns an inline XML schema definition (the W3C XML Schema Recommendation is available at www.w3.org/XML/Schema).

- XMLDATA appends an *XML-Data Reduced (XDR)* schema to the beginning of your XML result. This option is deprecated and should not be used for future development. If you currently use this option, Microsoft recommends changing your code to use the XMLSCHEMA option instead.

As we discuss the other FOR XML modes, we will point out the options supported by each.

FOR XML AUTO

For a query against a single table, the AUTO keyword retrieves data in a format similar to RAW mode, but the XML node name is the name of the table and not the generic label row. For queries that join multiple tables, however, each XML element is named for the tables from which the SELECT list columns are retrieved. The order of the column names in the SELECT list determine the XML element nesting in the result. The FOR XML AUTO clause is called similarly to the FOR XML RAW clause, as shown in Listing 11-5. The results are shown in Figure 11-5.

Listing 11-5. FOR XML AUTO Query on a Single Table

```
USE AdventureWorks2012;
GO

SELECT
    ProductID,
    Name,
    ProductNumber
FROM Production.Product
WHERE ProductID IN (770, 903)
FOR XML AUTO;
```

```
XML_F52E2B61-18A1...-00805F49916B2.xml*  X

<Production.Product
    ProductID="770"
    Name="Road-650 Black, 52"
    ProductNumber="BK-R50B-52" />
<Production.Product
    ProductID="903"
    Name="LL Touring Frame - Blue, 44"
    ProductNumber="FR-T67U-44" />
```

Figure 11-5. *Results of the FOR XML AUTO Single-table Query*

Listing 11-6 demonstrates using FOR XML AUTO in a SELECT query that joins two tables. The results are shown in Figure 11-6.

Listing 11-6. FOR XML AUTO Query with a Join

```
SELECT
  Product.ProductID,
  Product.Name,
  Product.ProductNumber,
  Inventory.Quantity
FROM Production.Product Product
INNER JOIN Production.ProductInventory Inventory
ON Product.ProductID = Inventory.ProductID
WHERE Product.ProductID IN (770, 3)
FOR XML AUTO;
```

```
XML_F52E2B61-18A1...-00805F49916B9.xml  ×

<Product ProductID="3" Name="BB Ball Bearing" ProductNumber="BE-2349">
    <Inventory Quantity="585" />
    <Inventory Quantity="443" />
    <Inventory Quantity="324" />
</Product>
<Product ProductID="770" Name="Road-650 Black, 52" ProductNumber="BK-R50B-52">
    <Inventory Quantity="104" />
    <Inventory Quantity="123" />
</Product>
```

Figure 11-6. *Results of the FOR XML AUTO Query with a Join*

The FOR XML AUTO statement can be further refined by adding the ELEMENTS option. Just as with the FOR XML RAW clause, the ELEMENTS option transforms the XML column attributes into subelements, as demonstrated in Listing 11-7, with results shown in Figure 11-7.

Listing 11-7. FOR XML AUTO Query with ELEMENTS Option

```
SELECT
  ProductID,
  Name,
  ProductNumber
FROM Production.Product
WHERE ProductID = 770
FOR XML AUTO, ELEMENTS;
```

```
XML_F52E2B61-18A1...-00805F49916B4.xml

<Production.Product>
    <ProductID>770</ProductID>
    <Name>Road-650 Black, 52</Name>
    <ProductNumber>BK-R50B-52</ProductNumber>
</Production.Product>
```

Figure 11-7. *Results of the FOR XML AUTO Query with the ELEMENTS Option*

The FOR XML AUTO clause can accept almost all of the same options as the FOR XML RAW clause. The only option that you can use with FOR XML RAW that's not available to FOR XML AUTO is the user-defined ElementName option, since AUTO mode generates row names based on the names of tables in the query.

FOR XML EXPLICIT

The FOR XML EXPLICIT clause is flexible but complex. This clause allows you to specify the exact hierarchy of XML elements and attributes in your XML result. This structure is specified in the SELECT statement itself using a special ElementName!TagNumber!AttributeName!Directive notation.

■ **Tip**   The FOR XML PATH clause, described in the next section, also allows you to explicitly define your XML result structure. The FOR XML PATH clause accepts XPath-style syntax to define the structure and node names, however, and is much easier to use than FOR XML EXPLICIT. As a general recommendation, we would advise using FOR XML PATH instead of FOR XML EXPLICIT for new development and converting old FOR XML EXPLICIT queries to FOR XML PATH when possible.

In order to get FOR XML EXPLICIT to convert your relational data to XML format, there's a strict requirement on the results of the SELECT query—it must return data in *universal table* format that includes a Tag column defining the level of the current tag and a Parent column with the parent level for the current tag. The remaining columns in the query are the actual data columns. Listing 11-8 demonstrates a FOR XML EXPLICIT query that returns information about a product, including all of its inventory quantities, as a nested XML result. The results are shown in Figure 11-8.

Listing 11-8. FOR XML EXPLICIT Query

```
SELECT
        1 AS Tag,
        NULL AS Parent,
        ProductID AS [Products!1!ProductID!element],
        Name AS [Products!1!ProductName],
        ProductNumber AS [Products!1!ProductNumber],
        NULL AS [Products!2!Quantity]
        FROM Production.Product
        WHERE ProductID IN (770, 3)

UNION ALL

SELECT
  2 AS Tag,
  1 AS Parent,
  NULL,
  NULL,
  NULL,
  Quantity
FROM Production.ProductInventory
WHERE ProductID IN (770, 3)
  FOR XML EXPLICIT;
```

```
XML_F52E2B61-18A1...00805F499168 10.xml  ✕
```
```
⊟<Products ProductName="BB Ball Bearing" ProductNumber="BE-2349">
    <ProductID>3</ProductID>
  </Products>
⊟<Products ProductName="Road-650 Black, 52" ProductNumber="BK-R50B-52">
    <ProductID>770</ProductID>
    <Products Quantity="585" />
    <Products Quantity="443" />
    <Products Quantity="324" />
    <Products Quantity="104" />
    <Products Quantity="123" />
  </Products>
```

Figure 11-8. *Results of the FOR XML EXPLICIT Query*

The FOR XML EXPLICIT query in Listing 11-8 defines the top-level elements with Tag = 1 and Parent = NULL. The next level is defined with Tag = 2 and Parent = 1, referencing back to the top level. Additional levels can be added by using the UNION keyword with additional queries that increment the Tag and Parent references for each additional level.

Each column of the query must be named with the ElementName!TagNumber!AttributeName!Directive format that we mentioned previously. As specified by this format, ElementName is the name of the XML element, in this case Products. TagNumber is the level of the element, which is 1 for top-level elements. AttributeName is the name of the attribute if you want the data in the column to be returned as an XML attribute. If you want the item to be returned as an XML element, use AttributeName to specify the name of the attribute, and set the Directive value to element. The Directive values that can be specified include the following:

- The hide directive value, which is useful when you want to retrieve values for sorting purposes but do not want the specified node included in the resulting XML.

- The element directive value, which generates an XML element instead of an attribute.

- The elementxsinil directive value, which generates an element for SQL null column values.

- The xml directive value, which generates an element instead of an attribute, but does not encode entity values.

- The cdata directive value, which wraps the data in a CDATA section and does not encode entities.

- The xmltext directive value, which wraps the column content in a single tag integrated with the document.

- The id, idref, and idrefs directive values, which allow you to create internal document links.

The additional options that the FOR XML EXPLICIT clause supports are BINARY BASE64, TYPE, ROOT, and XMLDATA. These options operate the same as they do in the FOR XML RAW and FOR XML AUTO clauses.

FOR XML PATH

The FOR XML PATH clause was first introduced in SQL Server 2005. It provides another way to convert relational data to XML format with a specific structure, but is much easier to use than the FOR XML EXPLICIT clause.

Like FOR XML EXPLICIT, the FOR XML PATH clause makes you define the structure of the XML result. But the FOR XML PATH clause allows you to use a subset of the well-documented and much more intuitive XPath syntax to define your XML structure.

The FOR XML PATH clause uses column names to define the structure, as with FOR XML EXPLICIT. In keeping with the XML standard, column names in the SELECT statement with a FOR XML PATH clause are case sensitive. For instance, a column named Inventory is different from a column named INVENTORY. Any columns that do not have names are *inlined,* with their content inserted as XML content for xml data type columns or as a text node for other data types. This is useful for including the results of nameless computed columns or scalar subqueries in your XML result.

FOR XML PATH uses XPath-style path expressions to define the structure and names of nodes in the XML result. Because path expressions can contain special characters like the forward slash (/) and at sign (@), you will usually want to use quoted column aliases as shown in Listing 11-9. The results of this sample FOR XML PATH query are shown in Figure 11-9.

Listing 11-9. FOR XML PATH Query

```
SELECT
        p.ProductID AS "Product/@ID",
        p.Name AS "Product/Name",
        p.ProductNumber AS "Product/Number",
        i.Quantity AS "Product/Quantity"
FROM Production.Product p
        INNER JOIN Production.ProductInventory i
        ON p.ProductID = i.ProductID
        WHERE p.ProductID = 770
FOR XML PATH;
```

```
XML_F52E2B61-18A1...-00805F49916B2.xml  X
⊟<row>
⊟    <Product ID="770">
        <Name>Road-650 Black, 52</Name>
        <Number>BK-R50B-52</Number>
        <Quantity>104</Quantity>
     </Product>
  </row>
⊟<row>
⊟    <Product ID="770">
        <Name>Road-650 Black, 52</Name>
        <Number>BK-R50B-52</Number>
        <Quantity>123</Quantity>
     </Product>
  </row>
```

Figure 11-9. *Results of the FOR XML PATH Query*

The FOR XML PATH clause imposes some rules on column naming, since the column names define not only the names of the XML nodes generated, but also the structure of the XML result. You can also use XPath node tests in your FOR XML PATH clauses. These rules and node tests are summarized in Table 11-3.

Table 11-3. *FOR XML PATH Column-naming Conventions*

Column Name	Result
text()	The string value of the column is added as a text node.
comment()	The string value of the column is added as an XML comment.
node()	The string value of the column is inserted inline under the current element.
*	This is the same as node().
data()	The string value of the column is inserted as an atomic value. Spaces are inserted between atomic values in the resulting XML.
processing-instruction(name)	The string value of the column is inserted as an XML-processing instruction named name.
@name	The string value of the column is inserted as an attribute of the current element.
Name	The string value of the column is inserted as a subelement of the current element.
elem/name	The string value of the column is inserted as a subelement of the specified element hierarchy, under the element specified by elem.
elem/@name	The string value of the column is inserted as an attribute of the last element in the specified hierarchy, under the element specified by elem.

The FOR XML PATH clause supports the BINARY BASE64, TYPE, ROOT, and ELEMENTS options, and the user-defined ElementName options. The additional FOR XML PATH options operate the same as they do for the FOR XML AUTO and FOR XML RAW clauses.

The xml Data Type

SQL Server's legacy XML functionality can be cumbersome and clunky to use at times. Fortunately, SQL Server 2012 provides much tighter XML integration with its xml data type. The xml data type can be used anywhere that other SQL Server data types are used, including variable declarations, column declarations, SP parameters, and UDF parameters and return types. The T-SQL xml data type provides built-in methods that allow you to query and modify XML nodes. When you declare instances of the xml data type, you can create them as untyped (which is the default), or you can associate them with XML schemas to create typed xml instances. This section discusses both typed and untyped xml in T-SQL.

The xml data type can hold complete XML documents or XML fragments. An XML document must follow all the rules for well-formed XML, including the following:

- Well-formed XML must have at least one element.

- Every well-formed XML document has a single top-level, or root, element.

- Well-formed XML requires properly nested elements (tags cannot overlap).

- All tags must be properly closed in a well-formed XML document.

- Attribute values must be quoted in a well-formed XML document.

- Special characters in element content must be properly *entitized,* or converted to XML entities such as & for the ampersand character.

An XML fragment must conform to all the rules for well-formed XML, except that it may have more than one top-level element. The stored internal representation of an XML document or fragment stored in an xml variable or column maxes out at around 2.1 GB of storage.

Untyped xml

Untyped xml variables and columns are created by following them with the keyword xml in the declaration, as shown in Listing 11-10.

Listing 11-10. Untyped xml Variable and Column Declarations

```
DECLARE @x XML;
CREATE TABLE XmlPurchaseOrders
(
    PoNum int NOT NULL PRIMARY KEY,
    XmlPurchaseOrder xml );
```

Populating an xml variable or column with an XML document or fragment requires a simple assignment statement. You can implicitly or explicitly convert char, varchar, nchar, nvarchar, varbinary, text, and ntext data to xml. There are some rules to consider when converting from these types to xml:

- The XML parser always treats nvarchar, nchar, and nvarchar(max) data as a two-byte Unicode-encoded XML document or fragment.

- SQL Server treats char, varchar, and nvarchar(max) data as a single-byte-encoded XML document or fragment. The code page of the source string, variable, or column is used for encoding by default.

- The content of varbinary data is passed directly to the XML parser, which accepts it as a stream. If the varbinary XML data is Unicode encoded, the byte-order mark/encoding information must be included in the varbinary data. If no byte-order mark/encoding information is included, the default of UTF-8 is used.

■ **Note** The binary data type can also be implicitly or explicitly converted to xml, but it must be the exact length of the data it contains. The extra padding applied to binary variables and columns when the data they contain is too short can cause errors in the XML-parsing process. Use the varbinary data type when you need to convert binary data to XML.

Listing 11-11 demonstrates implicit conversion from nvarchar to the xml data type. The CAST or CONVERT functions can be used when an explicit conversion is needed.

Listing 11-11. Populating an Untyped xml Variable

```
DECLARE @x xml = N'<?xml version="1.0" ?>
        <Address>
                <Latitude>47.642737</Latitude>
                <Longitude>-122.130395</Longitude>
                <Street>ONE MICROSOFT WAY</Street>
                <City>REDMOND</City>
```

```
            <State>WA</State>
            <Zip>98052</Zip>
            <Country>US</Country>
        </Address>';

SELECT @x;
```

Typed xml

To create a typed xml variable or column in SQL Server 2012, you must first create an XML schema collection with the CREATE XML SCHEMA COLLECTION statement. The CREATE XML SCHEMA COLLECTION statement allows you to specify a SQL Server name for your schema collection and an XML schema to add. Listing 11-12 shows how to create an XML schema collection.

Listing 11-12. Creating a Typed xml Variable

```
CREATE XML SCHEMA COLLECTION AddressSchemaCollection
    AS N'<?xml version="1.0" encoding="utf-16" ?>
    <xsd:schema xmlns:xsd="http://www.w3.org/2001/XMLSchema">
        <xsd:element name="Address">
                <xsd:complexType>
                        <xsd:sequence>
                            <xsd:element name="Latitude" type="xsd:decimal" />
                            <xsd:element name="Longitude" type="xsd:decimal" />
                            <xsd:element name="Street" type="xsd:string" />
                        <xsd:element name="City" type="xsd:string" />
                            <xsd:element name="State" type="xsd:string" />
                            <xsd:element name="Zip" type="xsd:string" />
                            <xsd:element name="Country" type="xsd:string" />
                        </xsd:sequence>
                </xsd:complexType>
        </xsd:element>
    </xsd:schema>';
GO
DECLARE @x XML (CONTENT AddressSchemaCollection);

SELECT @x =   N'<?xml version="1.0" ?>
        <Address>
                <Latitude>47.642737</Latitude>
                <Longitude>-122.130395</Longitude>
                <Street>ONE  MICROSOFT  WAY</Street>
                <City>REDMOND</City>
                <State>WA</State>
                <Zip>98052</Zip>
                <Country>US</Country>
        </Address>';

SELECT @x;

DROP  XML SCHEMA COLLECTION AddressSchemaCollection;
GO
```

The first step in creating a typed xml instance is to create an XML schema collection, as we did in Listing 11-12:

```
CREATE  XML  SCHEMA  COLLECTION  AddressSchemaCollection
     AS  N'<?xml  version="1.0"  encoding="utf-16"  ?>
     <xsd:schema xmlns:xsd="http://www.w3.org/2001/XMLSchema">
          <xsd:element name="Address">
               <xsd:complexType>
                    <xsd:sequence>
                         <xsd:element  name="Latitude"  type="xsd:decimal" />
                         <xsd:element  name="Longitude" type="xsd:decimal" />
                         <xsd:element  name="Street"    type="xsd:string" />
                         <xsd:element  name="City"      type="xsd:string" />
                         <xsd:element  name="State"     type="xsd:string" />
                         <xsd:element  name="Zip"       type="xsd:string" />
                         <xsd:element  name="Country"   type="xsd:string" />
                    </xsd:sequence>
               </xsd:complexType>
          </xsd:element>
     </xsd:schema>';
```

▒ **Tip** The World Wide Web Consortium (W3C) maintains the standards related to XML schemas. The official XML Schema recommendations are available at www.w3.org/TR/xmlschema-1/ and www.w3.org/TR/xmlschema-2/. These W3C recommendations are an excellent starting point for creating your own XML schemas.

The next step is to declare the variable as xml type, but with an XML schema collection specification included:

```
DECLARE @x XML (CONTENT AddressSchemaCollection);
```

In the example, we used the CONTENT keyword before the schema collection name in the xml variable declaration. SQL Server offers two keywords, DOCUMENT and CONTENT, that represent *facets* you can use to constrain typed xml instances. Using the DOCUMENT facet in your typed xml variable or column declaration constrains your typed XML data so that it must contain only one top-level root element. The CONTENT facet allows zero or more top-level elements. CONTENT is the default if neither is specified explicitly.

The next step in the example is the assignment of XML content to the typed xml variable. During the assignment, SQL Server validates the XML content against the XML schema collection.

```
SELECT @x =  N'<?xml version="1.0" ?>
     <Address>
          <Latitude>47.642737</Latitude>
          <Longitude>-122.130395</Longitude>
          <Street>ONE  MICROSOFT  WAY</Street>
          <City>REDMOND</City>
          <State>WA</State>
          <Zip>98052</Zip>
          <Country>US</Country>
     </Address>';

SELECT @x;
```

The DROP XML SCHEMA COLLECTION statement in the listing removes the XML schema collection from SQL Server.

```
DROP XML SCHEMA COLLECTION AddressSchemaCollection;
```

You can also add new XML schemas and XML schema components to XML schema collections with the ALTER XML SCHEMA COLLECTION statement.

The xml Data Type Methods

The xml data type has several methods for querying and modifying xml data. The built-in xml data type methods are summarized in Table 11-4.

This section introduces each of these xml data type methods.

Table 11-4. *xml Data Type Methods*

Method	Result
query(xquery)	Performs an XQuery query against an xml instance. The result returned is an untyped xml instance.
value(xquery, sql_type)	Performs an XQuery query against an xml instance and returns a scalar value of the specified SQL Server data type.
exist(xquery)	Performs an XQuery query against an xml instance and returns one of the following bit values: 1 if the xquery expression returns a nonempty result, 0 if the xquery expression returns an empty result, NULL if the xml instance is NULL
modify(xml_dml)	Performs an XML Data Modification Language (XML DML) statement to modify an xml instance.
nodes(xquery) as table_name(column_name)	Performs an XQuery query against an xml instance and returns matching nodes as an SQL result set. The table_name and column_name specify aliases for the virtual table and column to hold the nodes returned. These aliases are mandatory for the nodes() method.

The query Method

The xml data type query() method accepts an XQuery query string as its only parameter. This method returns all nodes matching the XQuery as a single untyped xml instance. Conveniently enough, Microsoft provides sample typed xml data in the Resume column of the HumanResources.JobCandidate table. Though all of its xml is well formed with a single root element, the Resume column is faceted with the default of CONTENT.

Listing 11-13 shows how to use the query() method to retrieve names from the resumes in the HumanResources.JobCandidate table.

Listing 11-13. Using the Query Method on the HumanResources.JobCandidate Resume XML

```
SELECT Resume.query(N'declare namespace ns =
    "http://schemas.microsoft.com/sqlserver/2004/07/adventure-works/Resume";
    /ns:Resume/ns:Name') AS [NameXML]
FROM HumanResources.JobCandidate;
```

The first thing to notice is the namespace declaration inside the XQuery query via the declare namespace statement. This is done because the Resume column's xml data declares a namespace. In fact, the namespace declaration used in the XQuery is exactly the same as the declaration used in the xml data. The declaration section of the XQuery looks like this:

```
declare namespace ns =
"http://schemas.microsoft.com/sqlserver/2004/07/adventure-works/Resume";
```

The actual query portion of the XQuery query is a simple path expression:

```
/ns:Resume/ns:Name
```

A sample of the results of Listing 11-13 are shown in Figure 11-10 (reformatted for easy reading).

```
NameXML 1.xml*  X
<ns:Name xmlns:ns="http://schemas.microsoft.com/sqlserver/2004/07/adventure-works/Resume">
    <ns:Name.Prefix />
    <ns:Name.First>Shai</ns:Name.First>
    <ns:Name.Middle />
    <ns:Name.Last>Bassli</ns:Name.Last>
    <ns:Name.Suffix />
</ns:Name>
<ns:Name xmlns:ns="http://schemas.microsoft.com/sqlserver/2004/07/adventure-works/Resume">
    <ns:Name.Prefix>Mr.</ns:Name.Prefix>
    <ns:Name.First>Max</ns:Name.First>
    <ns:Name.Middle />
    <ns:Name.Last>Benson</ns:Name.Last>
    <ns:Name.Suffix />
</ns:Name>
<ns:Name xmlns:ns="http://schemas.microsoft.com/sqlserver/2004/07/adventure-works/Resume">
    <ns:Name.Prefix>Mr.</ns:Name.Prefix>
    <ns:Name.First>Krishna</ns:Name.First>
    <ns:Name.Middle />
    <ns:Name.Last>Sunkammurali</ns:Name.Last>
    <ns:Name.Suffix />
</ns:Name>
```

Figure 11-10. Retrieving Job Candidate Names with the Query Method (Partial Results)

■ **Tip** SQL Server 2012 implements a subset of the W3C XQuery recommendation. Chapter 12 discusses SQL Server's XPath and XQuery implementations in detail. If you're just getting started with XQuery, additional resources include the W3C recommendation available at http://www.w3.org/standards/techs/xquery#w3c_all/, and on BOL at http://msdn.microsoft.com/en-us/library/ms189075.aspx.

The value Method

The xml data type's value() method performs an XQuery query against an xml instance and returns a scalar result. The scalar result of value() is automatically cast to the T-SQL data type specified in the call to value(). The sample code in Listing 11-14 uses the value() method to retrieve all last names from AdventureWorks job applicant resumes. The results are shown in Figure 11-11.

Listing 11-14. xml Data Type Value Method Sample

```
SELECT Resume.value (N'declare namespace ns =
    "http://schemas.microsoft.com/sqlserver/2004/07/adventure-works/Resume";
    (/ns:Resume/ns:Name/ns:Name.Last)[1]',
    'nvarchar(100)') AS [LastName]
FROM HumanResources.JobCandidate;
```

Figure 11-11. *Using the Value Method to Retrieve Job Candidate Last Names*

Like the query() method described previously, the value() method sample XQuery query begins by declaring a namespace:

```
declare namespace ns =
    "http://schemas.microsoft.com/sqlserver/2004/07/adventure-works/Resume";
```

The actual query portion of the XQuery query is a simple path expression:

```
(/ns:Resume/ns:Name/ns:Name.Last)[1]
```

Because value() returns a scalar value, the query is enclosed in parentheses with an XQuery numeric predicate [1] following it to force the return of a singleton atomic value. The second parameter passed into value() is the T-SQL data type that value() will cast the result to, in this case nvarchar. The value() method cannot cast its result to a SQL CLR user-defined type or an xml, image, text, ntext, or sql_variant data type.

The exist Method

The xml data type provides the exist() method for determining if an XML node exists in an xml instance, or if an existing XML node value meets a specific set of criteria. The example in Listing 11-15 uses the exist() method in a query to return all AdventureWorks job candidates that reported a bachelor's degree level of education. The results are shown in Figure 11-12.

Listing 11-15. *xml Data Type Exist Method Example*

```
SELECT Resume.value (N'declare namespace ns =
  "http://schemas.microsoft.com/sqlserver/2004/07/adventure-works/Resume";
  (/ns:Resume/ns:Name/ns:Name.Last) [1]',
  'nvarchar(100)') AS [BachelorsCandidate]
FROM HumanResources.JobCandidate
WHERE Resume.exist (N'declare namespace ns =
  "http://schemas.microsoft.com/sqlserver/2004/07/adventure-works/Resume";
  /ns:Resume/ns:Education/ns:Edu.Level [ . = "Bachelor" ]') = 1;
```

	BachelorsCandidate
1	Bassli
2	Benson
3	Sunkammurali
4	Jiang

Figure 11-12. *Using the Exist Method to Retrieve Bachelor's Degree Job Candidates*

The first part of the query borrows from the value() method example in Listing 11-13 to retrieve matching job candidate names:

```
SELECT Resume.value (N'declare namespace ns =
"http://schemas.microsoft.com/sqlserver/2004/07/adventure-works/Resume";
(/ns:Resume/ns:Name/ns:Name.Last) [1]',
'nvarchar(100)') AS [BachelorsCandidate] FROM HumanResources.JobCandidate
```

The exist() method in the WHERE clause specifies the xml match criteria. Like the previous sample queries, the exist() method XQuery query begins by declaring a namespace:

```
declare namespace ns =
"http://schemas.microsoft.com/sqlserver/2004/07/adventure-works/Resume";
```

The query itself compares the Edu.Level node text to the string Bachelor:

```
/ns:Resume/ns:Education/ns:Edu.Level [ . = "Bachelor" ]
```

If there is a match, the query returns a result and the exist() method returns 1. If there is no match, there will be no nodes returned by the XQuery query, and the exist() method will return 0. If the xml is NULL, exist() returns NULL. The query limits the results to only matching resumes by returning only those where exist() returns 1.

The nodes Method

The nodes() method of the xml data type retrieves XML content in relational format—a process known as shredding. The nodes() method returns a rowset composed of the xml nodes that match a given XQuery

expression. Listing 11-16 retrieves product names and IDs for those products with the *word Alloy* in the
Material node of their CatalogDescription column. The table queried is Production.ProductModel.
Notice that the CROSS APPLY operator is used to perform the nodes() method on all rows of the
Production.ProductModel table.

Listing 11-16. xml Data Type Nodes Example

```
SELECT
        ProductModelID,
        Name,
        Specs.query('.') AS Result
FROM Production.ProductModel
CROSS APPLY CatalogDescription.nodes('declare namespace ns =
"http://schemas.microsoft.com/sqlserver/2004/07/adventure-works/ProductModelDescription";
/ns:ProductDescription/ns:Specifications/Material/text()
  [ contains ( . , "Alloy" ) ]')
AS NodeTable(Specs);
```

The first part of the SELECT query retrieves the product model ID, the product name, and the results of the
nodes() method via the query() method:

```
SELECT
  ProductModelId,
  Name,
  Specs.query('.') AS Result
FROM Production.ProductModel
```

One restriction of the nodes() method is that the relational results generated cannot be retrieved directly.
They can only be accessed via the exist(), nodes(), query(), and value() methods of the xml data type, or
checked with the IS NULL and IS NOT NULL operators.

The CROSS APPLY operator is used with the nodes() method to generate the final result set. The XQuery
query used in the nodes() method begins by declaring a namespace:

```
CROSS APPLY CatalogDescription.nodes('declare namespace ns =
"http://schemas.microsoft.com/sqlserver/2004/07/adventure-works/ProductModelDescription";
```

The query portion is a path expression that retrieves XML nodes in which a Material node's text contains
the word *Alloy:*

```
/ns:ProductDescription/ns:Specifications/Material/text() [ contains ( . , "Alloy" ) ]')
```

Notice that the nodes() method requires you to provide aliases for both the virtual table returned and
the column that will contain the result rows. In this instance, we chose to alias the virtual table with the name
NodeTable and the column with the name Specs.

```
AS NodeTable(Specs);
```

The modify Method

The xml data type modify() method can be used to modify the content of an xml variable or column.
The modify() method allows you to insert, delete, or update xml content. The main restrictions on the modify()
method is that it must be used in a variable SET statement or in the SET clause of an UPDATE statement.

The example in Listing 11-17 demonstrates the modify() method on an untyped xml variable. The results are shown in Figure 11-13.

■ **Tip** Although the SELECT and SET statements are similar in their functionality when applied to variables, the modify() method of the xml data type will not work in SELECT statements—even SELECT statements that assign values to variables. Use the SET statement as demonstrated in Listing 11-17 to use the modify() method on an xml variable.

Listing 11-17. xml Data Type Modify Method Example

```
DECLARE @x xml = N'<?xml version="1.0" ?>
<Address>
  <Street>1 MICROSOFT WAY</Street>
  <City>REDMOND</City>
  <State>WA</State>
  <Zip>98052</Zip>
  <Country>US</Country>
  <Website>http://www.microsoft.com</Website>
</Address>';

SELECT @x;

SET @x.modify ('insert
(
  <CompanyName>Microsoft Corporation</CompanyName>,
  <Url>http://msdn.microsoft.com</Url>,
  <UrlDescription>Microsoft Developer Network</UrlDescription>
)
into (/Address)[1] ');

SET @x.modify('replace value of
  (/Address/Street/text())[1]
  with "ONE MICROSOFT WAY"
');

SET @x.modify('
delete /Address/Website
');

SELECT @x;
```

```
  --BEFORE
<Address>
    <Street>1 MICROSOFT WAY</Street>
    <City>REDMOND</City>
    <State>WA</State>
    <Zip>98052</Zip>
    <Country>US</Country>
    <Website>http://www.microsoft.com</Website>
  </Address>

  --AFTER
  <Address>
      <Street>ONE MICROSOFT WAY</Street>
      <City>REDMOND</City>
      <State>WA</State>
      <Zip>98052</Zip>
      <Country>US</Country>
      <CompanyName>Microsoft Corporation</CompanyName>
      <Url>http://msdn.microsoft.com</Url>
      <UrlDescription>Microsoft Developer Network</UrlDescription>
  </Address>
```

Figure 11-13. *Before-and-after Results of the Modify Method*

The sample begins by creating an xml variable and assigning XML content to it:

```
DECLARE @x xml = N'<?xml version="1.0" ?><Address>
        <Street>1 MICROSOFT WAY</Street>
        <City>REDMOND</City>
        <State>WA</State>
        <Zip>98052</Zip>
        <Country>US</Country>
        <Website>http://www.microsoft.com</Website> </Address>';
SELECT @x;
```

The XML DML insert statement inserts three new nodes into the xml variable, right below the top-level Address node:

```
SET @x.modify ('insert
(
  <CompanyName>Microsoft Corporation</CompanyName>,
  <Url>http://msdn.microsoft.com</Url>,
  <UrlDescription>Microsoft Developer's Network</UrlDescription>
)
into (/Address)[1] ');
```

The replace value of statement specified in the next modify() method updates the content of the Street node with the street address our good friends at Microsoft prefer: ONE MICROSOFT WAY, instead of 1 MICROSOFT WAY.

```
SET @x.modify('replace value of (/Address/Street/text())[1]
  with "ONE MICROSOFT WAY"
');
```

Finally, the XML DML method delete statement is used to remove the old <Website> tag from the xml variable's content:

```
SET @x.modifyC
    delete /Address/Website
');

SELECT @x;
```

XML Indexes

SQL Server provides XML indexes to increase the efficiency of querying xml data type columns. XML indexes come in two flavors:

- *Primary XML index:* An XML column can have a single primary XML index declared on it. The primary XML index is different from the standard relational indexes most of us are used to. Rather, it is a persisted preshredded representation of your XML data. Basically, the XML data stored in a column with a primary XML index is converted to relational form and stored in the database. By persisting an xml data type column in relational form, you eliminate the implicit shredding that occurs with every query or manipulation of your XML data. In order to create a primary XML index on a table's xml column, a clustered index must be in place on the primary key columns for the table.

- *Secondary XML index:* Secondary XML indexes can also be created on a table's xml column. Secondary XML indexes are nonclustered relational indexes created on primary XML indexes. In order to create secondary XML indexes on an xml column, a primary XML index must already exist on that column. You can declare any of three different types of secondary XML index on your primary XML indexes:

  - The PATH index is a secondary XML index optimized for XPath and XQuery path expressions that rely heavily on path and node values. The PATH index creates an index on path and node values on the columns of the primary XML index. The path and node values are used as key columns for efficient path seek operations.

  - The VALUE index is optimized for queries by value where the path is not necessarily known. This type of index is the inverse of the PATH index, with the primary XML index node values indexed before the node paths.

  - The PROPERTY index is optimized for queries that retrieve data from other columns of a table based on the value of nodes or paths in the xml data type column. This type of secondary index is created on the primary key of the base table, node paths, and node values of the primary XML index.

Consider the example XQuery FLWOR (for, let, where, order by, return) expression in Listing 11-18 that retrieves the last, first, and middle names of all job applicants in the HumanResources.JobCandidate table with an education level of Bachelor. The results of this query are shown in Figure 11-14.

Listing 11-18. Retrieving Job Candidates with Bachelor's Degrees

```
SELECT Resume.query('declare namespace ns =
  "http://schemas.microsoft.com/sqlserver/2004/07/adventure-works/Resume";
for $m in /ns:Resume
where $m/ns:Education/ns:Edu.Level[. = "Bachelor" ]
return < Name>
    {
      data(($m/ns:Name/ns:Name.Last)[1]),
      data(($m/ns:Name/ns:Name.First)[1]),
      data(($m/ns:Name/ns:Name.Middle)[1])
    } </Name > ')
FROM HumanResources.JobCandidate;
GO
```

	Results
	(No column name)
1	<Name>Bassli Shai </Name>
2	<Name>Benson Max </Name>
3	<Name>Sunkammurali Krishna </Name>
4	<Name>Jiang Stephen Y </Name>

Figure 11-14. *Retrieving Candidate Names with a FLWOR Expression*

We'll describe FLWOR expressions in greater detail, with examples, in Chapter 12. For the purposes of this discussion, however, the results are not as important as what's going on under the hood. This FLWOR expression is returning the last, first, and middle names of all candidates for which the Edu.Level node contains the value Bachelor. As shown in Figure 11-15, the execution cost of this query is 41.2849. Although the subtree cost is an arbitrary number, it represents the total cost in relationship to the batch. In this case the number is large enough in relationship to the batch to warrant investigation.

SELECT

Cached plan size	152 KB
Degree of Parallelism	0
Estimated Operator Cost	0 (0%)
Estimated Subtree Cost	41.2849
Memory Grant	1024
Estimated Number of Rows	13

Statement

```
SELECT Resume.query('declare namespace
ns =

"http://schemas.microsoft.com/sqlserver/2
004/07/adventure-works/Resume";
for $m in /ns:Resume
where $m/ns:Education/ns:Edu.Level[. =
"Bachelor" ]
return <Name>
  {
    data(($m/ns:Name/ns:Name.Last)[1]),
    data(($m/ns:Name/ns:Name.First)[1]),
    data(($m/ns:Name/ns:Name.Middle)
[1])
  } </Name>')
FROM HumanResources.JobCandidate;
```

Figure 11-15. *The Execution Cost of the Query*

By far the most expensive part of this query is contained in a step called *Table Valued Function [XML Reader with XPath Filter]*. This is the main operator SQL Server uses to shred XML data on the fly whenever you query XML data. In this query plan, it is invoked two times at a cost of 13.052 each, and three more times at a cost of 4.89054 each, accounting for over 98 percent of the query plan cost (see Figure 11-16).

Table Valued Function

Table valued function.

Physical Operation	Table Valued Function
Logical Operation	Table Valued Function
Actual Execution Mode	Row
Estimated Execution Mode	Row
Actual Number of Rows	16
Actual Number of Batches	0
Estimated I/O Cost	0
Estimated Operator Cost	13.052 (32%)
Estimated Subtree Cost	13.052
Estimated CPU Cost	1.004
Estimated Number of Executions	13
Number of Executions	13
Estimated Number of Rows	200
Estimated Row Size	39 B
Actual Rebinds	13
Actual Rewinds	0
Node ID	20

Object
[XML Reader with XPath filter]
Output List
[XML Reader with XPath filter].id, [XML Reader with XPath filter].value

Figure 11-16. *Table Valued Function [XML Reader with XPath Filter] Cost*

Adding XML indexes to this column of the HumanResources.JobCandidate table significantly improves XQuery query performance by eliminating on-the-fly XML shredding. Listing 11-19 adds a primary and secondary XML index to the Resume column.

Listing 11-19. Adding XML Indexes to the Resume Column

```
CREATE PRIMARY XML INDEX PXML_JobCandidate
ON HumanResources.JobCandidate (Resume);
GO

CREATE XML INDEX IXML_Education
ON HumanResources.JobCandidate (Resume)
USING XML INDEX PXML_JobCandidate
FOR PATH;
GO
```

With the primary and secondary XML indexes in place, the query execution cost drops significantly from 41.2849 to 0.278555, as shown in Figure 11-17.

SELECT

Cached plan size	184 KB
Degree of Parallelism	0
Estimated Operator Cost	0 (0%)
Estimated Subtree Cost	0.278555
Estimated Number of Rows	13

Statement

SELECT Resume.query('declare namespace ns =

"http://schemas.microsoft.com/sqlserver/2004/07/adventure-works/Resume";
for $m in /ns:Resume
where $m/ns:Education/ns:Edu.Level[. = "Bachelor"]
return <Name>
  {
    data(($m/ns:Name/ns:Name.Last)[1]),
    data(($m/ns:Name/ns:Name.First)[1]),
    data(($m/ns:Name/ns:Name.Middle)[1])
  } </Name>')
FROM HumanResources.JobCandidate;

Figure 11-17. *The Query Execution Cost with XML Indexes*

The greater efficiency is brought about by the *XML Reader with XPath Filter* step being replaced with efficient index seek operators on both clustered and nonclustered indexes. The primary XML index eliminates the need to shred XML data at query time and the secondary XML index provides additional performance enhancement by providing a nonclustered index that can be used to efficiently fulfill the FLWOR expression where clause.

The CREATE PRIMARY XML INDEX statement in the example creates a primary XML index on the Resume column of the HumanResources.JobCandidate table. The primary XML index provides a significant performance increase by itself, since it eliminates on-the-fly XML shredding at query time.

```
CREATE PRIMARY XML INDEX PXML_JobCandidate ON HumanResources.JobCandidate (Resume);
```

The primary XML index is a prerequisite for creating the secondary XML index that will provide additional performance enhancement for XQuery queries that specify both a path and a predicate based on node content. The CREATE XML INDEX statement in the example creates the secondary XML PATH index.

```
CREATE XML INDEX IXML_Education ON HumanResources.JobCandidate (Resume) USING XML INDEX
PXML_JobCandidate FOR PATH;
```

The USING XML INDEX clause of the CREATE XML INDEX statement specifies the name of the primary XML index on which to build the secondary XML index. The FOR clause determines the type of secondary XML index that will be created. You can specify a VALUE, PATH, or PROPERTY type as described previously.

The optional WITH clause of both of the XML index creation statements allows you to specify a variety of XML index creation options, as shown in Table 11-5.

Table 11-5. *XML Index Creation Options*

Option	Description
PAD_INDEX	This option specifies whether index padding is on or off. The default is OFF.
FILLFACTOR	This option indicates how full the leaf level index pages should be made during XML index creation or rebuild. Values of 0 and 100 are equivalent. The FILLFACTOR option is used in conjunction with the PAD_INDEX option.
SORT_IN_TEMPDB	This option specifies that intermediate sort results should be stored in tempdb. By default, SORT_IN_TEMPDB is set to OFF and intermediate sort results are stored in the local database.
STATISTICS_NORECOMPUTE	This option indicates whether distribution statistics are automatically recomputed. The default is OFF.
DROP_EXISTING	This option specifies that the preexisting XML index of the same name should be dropped before creating the index. The default is OFF.
ALLOW_ROW_LOCKS	This option allows SQL Server to use row locks when accessing the XML index. The default is ON.
ALLOW_PAGE_LOCKS	This option allows SQL Server to use page locks when accessing the XML index. The default is ON.
MAXDOP	This option determines the maximum degree of parallelism SQL Server can use during the XML index creation operation. MAXDOP can be one of the following values: 0: Uses up to the maximum number of processors available. 1: Uses only one processor; no parallel processing. 2 through 64: Restricts the number of processors used for parallel processing to the number specified or less.

XSL Transformations

One of the powerful features available to SQL Server 2012 is its ability to execute .NET Framework-based code via the SQL Common Language Runtime (SQL CLR). You can use standard .NET Framework classes to access XML-based functionality that is not supported directly within T-SQL. One useful feature that can be accessed via CLR Integration is the W3C *Extensible Stylesheet Language Transformations (XSLT)*. As defined by the W3C, XSLT is a language designed for the sole purpose of "transforming XML documents into other XML documents." SQL Server 2012 provides access to XSL transformations via a combination of the built-in xml data type and the .NET Framework XslCompiledTransform class.

■ **Tip**   The XSLT 1.0 standard is available at www.w3.org/TR/xslt.

You can access XSLT from SQL Server to perform server-side transformations of your relational data into other XML formats. I've chosen to use XHTML as the output format for this example, although some would argue that generating XHTML output is best done away from SQL Server, in the middle tier or presentation layer. Arguments can also be made for performing XSL transformations close to the data, for efficiency reasons. I'd like to put those arguments aside for the moment, and focus on the main purpose of this example, demonstrating that additional XML functionality is available to SQL Server via SQL CLR. Listing 11-20 demonstrates the first step in the process of performing server-side XSL transformations using FOR XML to convert relational data to an xml variable.

Listing 11-20. Using FOR XML to Convert Relational Data to Populate an xml Variable

```
DECLARE @xml xml =
(
    SELECT
        p.ProductNumber AS "@Id",
        p.Name AS "Name",
        p.Color AS "Color",
        p.ListPrice AS "ListPrice",
        p.SizeUnitMeasureCode AS "Size/@UOM",
        p.Size AS "Size",
        p.WeightUnitMeasureCode AS "Weight/@UOM",
        p.Weight AS "Weight",
        (
        SELECT  COALESCE(SUM(i.Quantity),  0)
        FROM  Production.ProductInventory  i
        WHERE  i.ProductID  =  p.ProductID
        )  AS  "QuantityOnHand"
    FROM  Production.Product  p
    WHERE p.FinishedGoodsFlag = 1
    ORDER BY p.Name
    FOR  XML  PATH  ('Product'),
        ROOT ('Products')
);

SELECT @xml;
```

The resulting xml document looks like Figure 11-18.

```
<Products>
  <Product Id="ST-1401">
    <Name>All-Purpose Bike Stand</Name>
    <ListPrice>159.0000</ListPrice>
    <QuantityOnHand>144</QuantityOnHand>
  </Product>
  <Product Id="CA-1098">
    <Name>AWC Logo Cap</Name>
    <Color>Multi</Color>
    <ListPrice>8.9900</ListPrice>
    <QuantityOnHand>288</QuantityOnHand>
  </Product>
  <Product Id="CL-9009">
    <Name>Bike Wash - Dissolver</Name>
    <ListPrice>7.9500</ListPrice>
    <QuantityOnHand>36</QuantityOnHand>
  </Product>
  <Product Id="LO-C100">
    <Name>Cable Lock</Name>
    <ListPrice>25.0000</ListPrice>
    <QuantityOnHand>252</QuantityOnHand>
  </Product>
```

Figure 11-18. *Partial Results of the FOR XML Product Query*

The next step is to create the XSLT style sheet to specify the transformation and assign it to an xml data type variable. Listing 11-21 demonstrates a simple XSLT style sheet to convert XML data to HTML.

Listing 11-21. XSLT Style Sheet to Convert Data to HTML

```
DECLARE @xslt xml=N'<?xml version="1.0" encoding="utf-16"?>
<xsl:stylesheet version="1.0"
        xmlns:xsl="http://www.w3.org/1999/XSL/Transform">
<xsl:template match="/Products">
<html>
        <head>
            <title>AdventureWorks Product Listing Report</title>
            <style type="text/css">
        tr.row-heading {
            background-color: 000099;
            color: ffffff;
            font-family: tahoma, arial, helvetica, sans-serif;
            font-size: 12px;
        }
        tr.row-light {
            background-color: ffffff;
            font-family: tahoma, arial, helvetica, sans-serif;
            font-size: 12px;
        }
        tr.row-dark {
            background-color: 00ffff;
            font-family: tahoma, arial, helvetica, sans-serif;
            font-size: 12px;
        }
        td.col-right {
            text-align: right;
        }
            </style>
</head>
<body>
    <table>
      <tr class="row-heading">
        <th>ID</th>
        <th>Product Name</th>
        <th>On Hand</th>
        <th>List Price</th>
        <th>Color</th>
        <th>Size</th>
        <th>Weight</th>
      </tr>
      <xsl:for-each select="Product">
            <xsl:element name="tr">
              <xsl:choose>
                <xsl:when test="position() mod 2=0">
                    <xsl:attribute name="class">row-light</xsl:attribute>
                </xsl:when>
```

```
                    <xsl:otherwise>
                        <xsl:attribute  name = "class" > row-dark</xsl:attribute>
                     </xsl:otherwise>
                    </xsl:choose>
                    <td><xsl:value-of select = "@Id"/></td>
                    <td><xsl:value-of select = "Name"/></td>
                    <td  class = "col-right">
                        <xsl:value-of select = "QuantityOnHand"/>
                    </td>
                    <td  class = "col-right" ><xsl:value-of select = "ListPrice"/></td>
                    <td><xsl:value-of select = "Color"/></td>
                    <td  class = "col-right">            <xsl:value-of  select = "Size"/>
                        <xsl:value-of  select = "Size/@UOM"/>
                    </td>
                    <td  class = "col-right">
                        <xsl:value-of  select = "Weight"/>
                        <xsl:value-of  select = "Weight/@UOM"/>
             </td>
          </xsl:element>
       </xsl:for-each>
        </table>
      </body>
    </html>
  </xsl:template>
</xsl:stylesheet > ';
```

■ **Tip** We won't dive into the details of XSLT style sheet creation in this book, but information can be found at the official W3C XSLT 1.0 standard site, at http://www.w3.org/TR/xslt20/. The book *Pro SQL Server 2008 XML* (Apress, 2008) also offers a detailed discussion of XSLT on SQL Server.

The final step is to create an SQL CLR SP that accepts the raw XML data and the XSLT style sheet, performs the XSL transformation, and writes the results to an HTML file. The SQL CLR SP code is shown in Listing 11-22.

Listing 11-22. SQL CLR SP for XSL Transformations

```
using System.Data.SqlTypes;
using System.Xml;
using System.Xml.Xsl;

namespace Apress.Samples
{
        public partial class XSLT
        {
                [Microsoft.SqlServer.Server.SqlProcedure]
                public static void XmlToHtml
                        (
                        SqlXml RawXml,
                        SqlXml XslStyleSheet,
                        SqlString OutputPage
                        )
```

```
            {
            // Create and load the XslCompiledTransform object
            XslCompiledTransform xslt = new XslCompiledTransform();
            XmlDocument xmldoc1 = new XmlDocument();
            xmldoc1.LoadXml(XslStyleSheet.Value);
            xslt.Load(xmldoc1);

            // Create and load the Raw XML document
            XmlDocument xml = new XmlDocument();
            xml.LoadXml(RawXml.Value);

            // Create the XmlTextWriter for output to HTML document
            XmlTextWriter htmlout = new XmlTextWriter
            (
            OutputPage.Value,
            System.Text.Encoding.Unicode
            );

    // Perform the transformation
    xslt.Transform
    (
            xml,
            htmlout
    );

            // Close the XmlTextWriter
            htmlout.Close();
        }
    }
};
```

SQL CLR SECURITY SETTINGS

There are a few administrative details you need to take care of before you deploy SQL CLR code to SQL Server. The first thing to do is set the database to trustworthy mode with the ALTER DATABASE statement, as shown following:

```
ALTER DATABASE AdventureWorks2012 SET TRUSTWORTHY ON;
```

A better alternative to setting your database to trustworthy mode is to sign your assemblies with a certificate. While signing SQL CLR assemblies is beyond the scope of this book, authors Robin Dewson and Julian Skinner cover this topic in their book *Pro SQL Server 2005 Assemblies* (Apress, 2005). The book covers SQL 2005 but the topics are still relevant and applicable to SQL Server 2012.

For the example in Listing 11-22, which accesses the local file system, you also need to set the CLR assembly permission level to External. You can do this through Visual Studio, as shown in the following illustration, or you can use WITH PERMISSION_SET clause of the CREATE ASSEMBLY or ALTER ASSEMBLY statements in T-SQL.

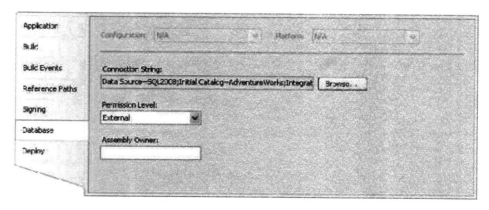

For SQL CLR code that doesn't require access to external resources or unmanaged code, a permission level of Safe is adequate. For SQL CLR assemblies that need access to external resources like hard drives or network resources, External permissions are the minimum required. Unsafe permissions are required for assemblies that access unsafe or unmanaged code. Always assign the minimum required permissions when deploying SQL CLR assemblies to SQL Server.

Finally, make sure the SQL Server service account has permissions to any required external resources. For this example, the service account needs permissions to write to the c:\Documents and Settings\ All Users\Documents directory.

After you have deployed the SQL CLR assembly to SQL Server and set the appropriate permissions, you can call the XmlToHtml procedure to perform the XSL transformation, as shown in Listing 11-23. The resulting HTML file is shown in Figure 11-19.

Listing 11-23. Performing a SQL CLR XSL Transformation

```
EXECUTE XmlToHtml @xml,
    gxslt,
    'c:\Documents and SettingsXAll Users\Documents\adventureworks-inventory.html';
```

Figure 11-19. *Results of the XML-to-HTML Transformation*

Summary

In this chapter, we discussed SQL Server 2012's integrated XML functionality. We began with a discussion of legacy XML functionality carried forward, and in some cases improved upon, from the days of SQL Server 2005. This legacy functionality includes the flexible FOR XML clause and the OPENXML rowset provider.

We then discussed the powerful xml data type and its many methods:

- The query() method allows you to retrieve XML nodes using XQuery queries.

- The value() method lets you retrieve singleton atomic values using XQuery path expressions to locate nodes.

- The exist() method determines whether a specific node exists in your XML data.

- The modify() method allows you to use XML DML to modify your XML data directly.

- The nodes() method makes shredding XML data simple.

We also presented SQL Server's primary and secondary XML indexes, which are designed to optimize XML query performance. Finally, we touched on SQL Server's SQL CLR integration and demonstrated how to use it to access .NET Framework XML functionality not directly available through the T-SQL language.

In the next chapter, we will continue the discussion of SQL Server XML by introducing XPath and XQuery support, including a more detailed discussion of the options, functions, operators, and expressions available for querying and manipulating XML on SQL Server.

EXERCISES

1. [Choose all that apply] SQL Server's FOR XML clause supports which of the following modes:

   a. FOR XML RAW

   b. FOR XML PATH

   c. FOR XML AUTO

   d. FOR XML EXPLICIT

   e. FOR XML RECURSIVE

2. [Fill in the blank] By default, the OPENXML rowset provider returns data in _____ table format.

3. [True/False] The xml data type query() method returns its results as an untyped xml data type instance.

4. [Choose one] A SQL Server primary XML index performs which of the following functions:

   a. It creates a nonclustered index on your xml data type column or variable.

   b. It creates a clustered index on your xml data type column or variable.

   c. It stores your xml data type columns in a preshredded relational format.

   d. It stores your xml data type columns using an inverse index format.

5. [True/False] When you perform XQuery queries against an xml data type column with no primary XML index defined on it, SQL Server automatically shreds your XML data to relational format.

6. [True/False] You can access additional XML functionality on SQL Server through the .NET Framework via SQL Server's SQL CLR integration.

■ ■ ■

CHAPTER 12

XQuery and XPath

As we described in Chapter 11, SQL Server 2012 continues the high level of XML integration begun in SQL Server 2005. As part of that integration, SQL Server's xml data type provides built-in functionality for shredding XML data into relational format, querying XML nodes and singleton atomic values via XQuery, and modifying XML data via XML Data Modification Language (XML DML). This chapter focuses on how to get the most out of SQL Server's implementation of the powerful and flexible XPath and XQuery standards.

The XML data model represents a departure from the relational model SQL Server developers know so well. XML is not a replacement for the relational model, but it does nicely complement relational data. XML is very useful for sharing data with a wide variety of web services and message systems including MSMQ and disparate systems, and highly structured XML data from remote data sources is often shredded to relational format for easy storage and querying. The SQL Server 2012 xml data type and XML-specific query and conversion tools represent a marriage of some of the best features of relational database and XML technologies.

■ **Note** This chapter is not meant to be a comprehensive guide to XPath and XQuery, but rather an introduction to SQL Server's XPath and XQuery implementations, which are both subsets of the W3C XPath 2.0 and XQuery 1.0 recommendations. In addition to the discussion in this chapter, Appendix B provides a reference to the XQuery Data Model (XDM) type system as implemented by SQL Server.

XPath and FOR XML PATH

The FOR XML PATH clause of the SELECT statement uses XPath 2.0-style path expressions to specify the structure of the XML result. Listing 12-1 demonstrates a simple FOR XML PATH query that returns the names and e-mail addresses of people in the AdventureWorks database. Partial results are shown in Figure 12-1, which you can display by clicking on the XML within the column.

Listing 12-1. Retrieving Names and E-mail Addresses with FOR XML PATH

```
SELECT
        p.BusinessEntityID AS "Person/ID",
        p.FirstName AS "Person/Name/First",
        p.MiddleName AS "Person/Name/Middle",
        p.LastName AS "Person/Name/Last",
        e.EmailAddress AS "Person/Email"
FROM Person.Person p INNER JOIN Person.EmailAddress e
ON p.BusinessEntityID = e.BusinessEntityID
FOR XML PATH, ROOT('PersonEmailAddress');
```

```
XML_F52E2B61-18A1...-00805F49916B1.xml  X

  <row>
    <Person>
      <ID>285</ID>
      <Name>
        <First>Syed</First>
        <Middle>E</Middle>
        <Last>Abbas</Last>
      </Name>
      <Email>syed0@adventure-works.com</Email>
    </Person>
  </row>
  <row>
    <Person>
      <ID>2357</ID>
      <Name>
        <First>Sam</First>
        <Last>Abolrous</Last>
      </Name>
      <Email>sam1@adventure-works.com</Email>
    </Person>
  </row>
  <row>

100 %
```

Figure 12-1. *Partial Results of Retrieving Names and E-mail Addresses with FOR XML PATH*

Because they are used specifically to define the structure of an XML result, FOR XML PATH XPath expressions are somewhat limited in their functionality. Specifically, you cannot use features that contain certain filter criteria or use absolute paths. Briefly, here are the restrictions:

- A FOR XML PATH XPath expression may not begin or end with the /step operator, and it may not begin with, end with, or contain //.

- FOR XML PATH XPath expressions cannot specify axis specifiers such as child:: or parent::.

- The . (context node) and .. (context node parent) axis specifiers are not allowed.

- The functions defined in Part 4 of the XPath specification, Core Function Library, are not allowed.

- Predicates, which are used to filter result sets, are not allowed. [position()=4] is an example of a predicate.

Basically, the FOR XML PATH XPath subset allows you to specify the structure of the resulting XML relative to the implicit root node. This means that advanced functionality of XPath expressions above and beyond defining a simple relative path expression is not allowed. In general, XPath 2.0 features that can be used to locate specific nodes, return sets of nodes, or filter result sets are not allowed with FOR XML PATH.

By default, FOR XML PATH uses the name row for the root node of each row it converts to XML format. The results of FOR XML PATH also default to an *element-centric* format, meaning that results are defined in terms of element nodes.

In Listing 12-1, we've aliased the column names using the XPath expressions that define the structure of the XML result. Because the XPath expressions often contain characters that are not allowed in SQL identifiers, you will probably want to use quoted identifiers.

```
SELECT p.BusinessEntityID AS "Person/ID", p.FirstName AS "Person/Name/First", p.MiddleName AS
"Person/Name/Middle", p.LastName AS "Person/Name/Last", e.EmailAddress AS "Person/Email"
```

XPath expressions are defined as a path separated by *step operators*. The step operator (/) indicates that a node is a child of the preceding node. For instance, the XPath expression Person/ID in the example indicates that a node named ID will be created as a child of the node named Person in a hierarchical XML structure.

XPath Attributes

Alternatively, you can define a relational column as an attribute of a node. Listing 12-2 modifies Listing 12-1 slightly to demonstrates this. We've shown the differences between the two listings in bold print. Partial results are shown in Figure 12-2, reformatted slightly for easier reading.

Listing 12-2. FOR XML PATH Creating XML Attributes

```
SELECT p.BusinessEntityID  AS "Person/@ID",
                e.EmailAddress AS "Person/@Email",
                p.FirstName AS "Person/Name/First",
                p.MiddleName AS "Person/Name/Middle",
                p.LastName AS "Person/Name/Last"
FROM Person.Person p INNER JOIN Person.EmailAddress e
ON p.BusinessEntityID=e.BusinessEntityID FOR XML PATH;
```

Figure 12-2. *Creating Attributes with FOR XML PATH*

The bold portion of the SELECT statement in Listing 12-2 generates XML attributes of the ID and Email nodes by preceding their names in the XPath expression with the @ symbol. The result is that ID and Email become attributes of the Person element in the result:

```
p.BusinessEntityID AS "Person/@ID", e.EmailAddress AS "Person/@Email",
```

Columns without Names and Wildcards

Some of the other XPath expression features you can use with FOR XML PATH include columns without names and wildcard expressions, which are turned into inline content. The sample in Listing 12-3 demonstrates this.

Listing 12-3. Using Columns without Names and Wildcards with FOR XML PATH

```
SELECT p.BusinessEntityID AS "*", ',' + e.EmailAddress,
p.FirstName AS "Person/Name/First",
p.MiddleName AS "Person/Name/Middle",
p.LastName AS "Person/Name/Last" FROM Person.Person p INNER JOIN Person.EmailAddress e
ON p.BusinessEntityID=e.BusinessEntityID FOR XML PATH;
```

In this example, the XPath expression for BusinessEntityID is the wildcard character *. The second column is defined as ',' + EmailAddress and the column is not given a name. Both of these columns are turned into inline content immediately below the row element, as shown in Figure 12-3. This is particularly useful functionality when creating lists within your XML data, or when your XML data conforms to a schema that looks for combined, concatenated, or list data in XML text nodes.

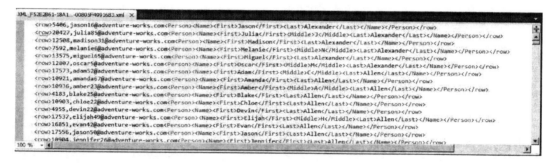

Figure 12-3. *Columns without Names and Wildcard Expressions in FOR XML PATH*

Element Grouping

As you saw in the previous examples, FOR XML PATH groups together nodes that have the same parent elements. For instance, the First, Middle, and Last elements are all children of the Name element. They are grouped together in all of the examples because of this. However, as shown in Listing 12-4, this is not the case when these elements are separated by an element with a different parent element.

Listing 12-4. Two Elements with a Common Parent Element Separated

```
SELECT p.BusinessEntityID AS "@ID",
               e.EmailAddress AS "@EmailAddress",
               p.FirstName AS "Person/Name/First",
               pp.PhoneNumber AS "Phone/BusinessPhone",
               p.MiddleName AS "Person/Name/Middle",
               p.LastName AS "Person/Name/Last"
FROM Person.Person p
INNER JOIN Person.EmailAddress e
       ON p.BusinessEntityID = e.BusinessEntityID
INNER JOIN  Person.PersonPhone pp
       ON p.BusinessEntityID = pp.BusinessEntityID
     AND pp.PhoneNumberTypeID = 3 FOR XML PATH;
```

The results of this query include a new Phone element as a direct child of the Person element. Because this new element is positioned between the Person/Name/First and Person/Name/Middle elements, FOR XML PATH creates two separate Person/Name elements: one to encapsulate the First element, and another to encapsulate the Middle and Last elements, as shown in Figure 12-4.

Figure 12-4. Breaking Element Grouping with FOR XML PATH

The data Function

The FOR XML PATH XPath expression provides support for a function called data(). If the column name is specified as data(), the value is treated as an atomic value in the generated XML. If the next item generated is also an atomic value, FOR XML PATH appends a space to the end of the data returned. This is useful for using subqueries to create lists of items, as in Listing 12-5, which demonstrates use of the data() function.

Listing 12-5. *The FOR XML PATH XPath data Node Test*

```
SELECT DISTINCT soh.SalesPersonID AS "SalesPerson/@ID", (
       SELECT soh2.SalesOrderID AS "data()"
       FROM Sales.SalesOrderHeader soh2
       WHERE soh2.SalesPersonID = soh.SalesPersonID FOR XML PATH ('') ) AS
"SalesPerson/@Orders",
       p.FirstName AS "SalesPerson/Name/First",
       p.MiddleName AS "SalesPerson/Name/Middle",
       p.LastName AS "SalesPerson/Name/Last",
       e.EmailAddress AS "SalesPerson/Email"
       FROM Sales.SalesOrderHeader soh
       INNER JOIN Person.Person p
              ON p.BusinessEntityID = soh.SalesPersonID
       INNER JOIN Person.EmailAddress e
              ON p.BusinessEntityID = e.BusinessEntityID
       WHERE soh.SalesPersonID IS NOT NULL FOR XML PATH;
```

This sample retrieves all SalesPerson ID numbers from the Sales.SalesOrderHeader table (eliminating NULLs for simplicity) and retrieves their names in the main query. The subquery uses the data() function to retrieve a list of each salesperson's sales order numbers and places them in a space-separated list in the Orders attribute of the SalesPerson element. A sample of the results is shown in Figure 12-5.

Figure 12-5. *Creating Lists with the data Node Test*

NODE TESTS AND FUNCTIONS

The SQL Server 2012 FOR XML PATH expression provides access to both the text() function and the data() node test. In terms of FOR XML PATH, the text() function returns the data in the text node as inline text with no separator. The data() node test returns the data in the XML text node as a space-separated concatenated list.

In XQuery expressions, the data() node test, the text() function, and the related string() function all return slightly different results. The following code snippet demonstrates their differences:

```
DECLARE @x xml;
SET @x = N'<a>123<b>456</b><c>789</c></a><a>987<b>654</b><c>321</c></a>';
SELECT @x.query('/a/text()');
SELECT @x.query('data(/a)');
SELECT @x.query('string(/a[1])');
```

The text() function in this example returns the concatenated text nodes of the <a> elements; in this example, it returns 123987.

The data() node test returns the concatenated XML text nodes of the <a> elements and all their child elements. In this example, data() returns 123456789 987654321, the concatenation of the <a> elements and the <b> and <c> subelements they contain. The data() node test puts a space separator between the <a> elements during the concatenation.

The string() function is similar to the data() node test in that it concatenates the data contained in the specified element and all child elements. The string() function requires a singleton node instance, which is why we specified string(/a[i]) in the example. The result of the string() function used in the example is 123456789. We'll discuss the text() and string() functions in greater detail later in this chapter.

XPath and NULL

In all of the previous examples, FOR XML PATH maps SQL NULL to a missing element or attribute. Consider the results of Listing 12-1 for Kim Abercrombie, shown in Figure 12-6. Because her MiddleName in the table is NULL, the Name/Middle element is missing from the results.

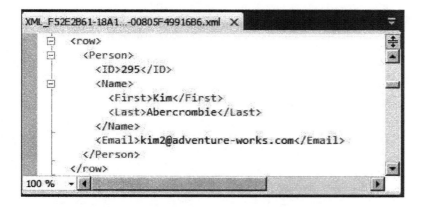

Figure 12-6. NULL Middle Name Eliminated from the FOR XML PATH Results

If you want SQL NULL-valued elements and attributes to appear in the final results, use the `ELEMENTS XSINIL` option of the FOR XML clause, as shown in Listing 12-6.

Listing 12-6. FOR XML with the ELEMENTS XSINIL Option

```
SELECT
p.BusinessEntityID AS "Person/ID",
p.FirstName AS "Person/Name/First",
p.MiddleName AS "Person/Name/Middle",
p.LastName AS "Person/Name/Last",
e.EmailAddress AS "Person/Email" FROM Person.Person p INNER JOIN Person.EmailAddress e
ON p.BusinessEntityID=e.BusinessEntityID FOR XML PATH,
ELEMENTS XSINIL;
```

With the `ELEMENTS XSINIL` option, Kim's results now look like the results shown in Figure 12-7. The `FOR XML PATH` clause adds a reference to the `xsi` namespace, and elements containing SQL NULL are included but marked with the `xsi:nil = "true"` attribute.

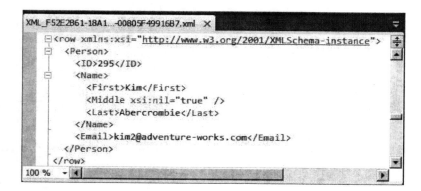

```
XML_F52E2B61-18A1...-00805F49916B7.xml  ✕

<row xmlns:xsi="http://www.w3.org/2001/XMLSchema-instance">
  <Person>
    <ID>295</ID>
    <Name>
      <First>Kim</First>
      <Middle xsi:nil="true" />
      <Last>Abercrombie</Last>
    </Name>
    <Email>kim2@adventure-works.com</Email>
  </Person>
</row>

100 %
```

Figure 12-7. NULL Marked with the xsi:nil Attribute

The WITH XMLNAMESPACES Clause

Namespace support is provided for FOR XML clauses and other XML functions by the WITH XMLNAMESPACES clause. The WITH XMLNAMESPACES clause is added to the front of your SELECT queries to specify XML namespaces to be used by FOR XML clauses or xml data type methods. Listing 12-7 demonstrates the use of the WITH XMLNAMESPACES clause with FOR XML PATH.

Listing 12-7. Using WITH XMLNAMESPACES to Specify Namespaces

```
WITH XMLNAMESPACES('http://www.apress.com/xml/sampleSqlXmlNameSpace' as ns)
SELECT
p.BusinessEntityID AS "ns:Person/ID",
p.FirstName AS "ns:Person/Name/First",
p.MiddleName AS "ns:Person/Name/Middle",
p.LastName AS "ns:Person/Name/Last",
e.EmailAddress AS "ns:Person/Email"
FROM Person.Person p
```

```
INNER JOIN Person.EmailAddress e
ON p.BusinessEntityID = e.BusinessEntityID
FOR XML PATH;
```

The WITH XMLNAMESPACES clause in this example declares a namespace called ns with the URI
http://www.apress.com/xml/sampleSqlXmlNameSpace. The FOR XML PATH clause adds this namespace
prefix to the Person element, as indicated in the XPath expressions used to define the structure of the result.
A sample of the results is shown in Figure 12-8.

```
XML_F52E2B61-...05F-4991689.xml
    <row xmlns:ns="http://www.apress.com/xml/sampleSqlXmlNameSpace">
      <ns:Person>
        <ID>285</ID>
        <Name>
          <First>Syed</First>
          <Middle>E</Middle>
          <Last>Abbas</Last>
        </Name>
        <Email>syed0@adventure-works.com</Email>
      </ns:Person>
    </row>
```

Figure 12-8. *Adding an XML Namespace to the FOR XML PATH Results*

Node Tests

In addition to the previous options, the FOR XML PATH XPath implementation supports four node tests, including
the following:

- The text() node test turns the string value of a column into a text node.

- The comment() node test turns the string value of a column into an XML comment.

- The node() node test turns the string value of a column into inline XML content; it is the
  same as using the wildcard * as the name.

- The processing-instruction(name) node test turns the string value of a column into an
  XML-processing instruction with the specified name.

Listing 12-8 demonstrates use of XPath node tests as column names in a FOR XML PATH query. The results
are shown in Figure 12-9.

Listing 12-8. FOR XML PATH Using XPath Node Tests

```
SELECT
p.NameStyle AS "processing-instruction(nameStyle)",
p.BusinessEntityID AS "Person/@ID",
p.ModifiedDate AS "comment()",
pp.PhoneNumber AS "text()",
FirstName AS "Person/Name/First",
MiddleName AS "Person/Name/Middle",
LastName AS "Person/Name/Last",
EmailAddress AS "Person/Email"
```

```
FROM Person.Person p
INNER JOIN Person.EmailAddress e
ON p.BusinessEntityID=e.BusinessEntityID
INNER JOIN Person.PersonPhone pp
ON p.BusinessEntityID=pp.BusinessEntityID
FOR XML PATH;
```

```
XML_F52E2B61~...F49916B10.xml*
<row>
   <?nameStyle 0?>
   <Person ID="1" />
   <!--1999-02-08T00:00:00-->
   697-555-0142
   <Person>
      <Name>
         <First>Ken</First>
         <Middle>J</Middle>
         <Last>Sánchez</Last>
      </Name>
      <Email>ken0@adventure-works.com</Email>
   </Person>
</row>
```

Figure 12-9. *Using Node Tests with FOR XML PATH*

In this example, the NameStyle column value is turned into an XML-processing instruction called nameStyle, the ModifiedDate column is turned into an XML comment, and the contact PhoneNumber is turned into a text node for each person in the AdventureWorks database.

XQuery and the xml Data Type

XQuery represents the most advanced standardized XML querying language to date. Designed as an extension to the W3C XPath 2.0 standard, XQuery is a case-sensitive, declarative, functional language with a rich type system based on the XDM. The SQL Server 2012 xml data type supports querying of XML data using a subset of XQuery via the query() method. Before diving into the details of the SQL Server implementation, we are going to start this section with a discussion of XQuery basics.

Expressions and Sequences

XQuery introduces several advances on the concepts introduced by XPath and other previous XML query tools and languages. Two of the most important concepts in XQuery are *expressions* and *sequences*. A sequence is an ordered collection of items—either nodes or atomic values. The word *ordered,* as it applies to sequences, does not necessarily mean numeric or alphabetic order. Sequences are generally in *document order* (the order in which their contents appear in the raw XML document or data) by default, unless you specify a different ordering. The roughly analogous XPath 1.0 structure was known as a *node set,* a name that implies ordering was unimportant. Unlike the relational model, however, the order of nodes is extremely important to XML. In XML, the ordering of nodes and content provides additional context and can be just as important as the data itself. The XQuery sequence was defined to ensure that the importance of proper ordering is recognized. There are also some other differences that we will cover later in this section.

Sequences can be returned by XQuery expressions or created by enclosing one of the following in parentheses:

- Lists of items separated by the comma operator (,)
- Range expressions
- Filter expressions

■ **Tip** Range expressions and the range expression keyword to are not supported in SQL Server 2012 XQuery. If you are converting an XQuery with range expressions like (1 to 10), you will have to modify it to run on SQL Server 2012.

A sequence created as a list of items separated by the comma operator might look like the following:

```
(1, 2, 3, 4, (5, 6), 7, 8, (), 9, 10)
```

The comma operator evaluates each of the items in the sequence and concatenates the result. Sequences cannot be nested, so any sequences within sequences are "flattened out." Also, the empty sequence (a sequence containing no items, denoted by empty parentheses: ()) is eliminated. Evaluation of the previous sample sequence results in the following sequence of ten items:

```
(1, 2, 3, 4, 5, 6, 7, 8, 9, 10)
```

Notice that the nested sequence (5, 6) has been flattened out, and the empty sequence () is removed during evaluation.

■ **Tip** SQL Server 2012 XQuery does not support the W3C-specified sequence operators union, intersect, and except. If you are porting XQuery code that uses these operators, it will have to be modified to run on SQL Server 2008.

Another method of generating a sequence is with a filter expression. *A filter expression* is a primary expression followed by zero or more predicates. An example of a filter expression to generate a sequence might look like the following:

```
(//Coordinates/*/text())
```

An important property of sequences is that a sequence of one item is indistinguishable from a singleton atomic value. So the sequence (1.0) is equivalent to the singleton atomic value 1.0.

Sequences come in three flavors: empty sequences, homogeneous sequences, and heterogeneous sequences. *Empty sequences* are sequences that contain no items. As mentioned before, the empty sequence is annotated with a set of empty parentheses: ().

Homogeneous sequences are sequences of one or more items of the same or compatible types. The examples already given are all examples of homogenous sequences.

Heterogeneous sequences are sequences of two or more items of incompatible types, or singleton atomic types and nodes. The following is an example of a heterogeneous sequence:

```
("Harry", 299792458, xs:date("2006-12-29Z"))
```

SQL Server does not allow heterogeneous sequences that mix nodes with singleton atomic values. Trying to declare the following sequence results in an error:

```
(<tag/>, "you are it!")
```

■ **Note**   *Singleton atomic values* are defined as values that are in the value space of the atomic types. The *value space* is the complete set of values that can be expressed with a given type. For instance, the complete value space for the xs:boolean type is true and false. Singleton atomic values are indivisible for purposes of the XDM standard (although you can extract portions of their content in some situations). Values that fall into this space are decimals, integers, dates, strings, and other primitive data types.

Primary expressions are the building blocks of XQuery. An expression in XQuery evaluates to a singleton atomic value or a sequence. Primary expressions can be any of several different items, including the following:

- *Literals:* These include string and numeric data type literals. String literals can be enclosed in either single or double quotes and may contain the XML-defined entity references >, <, &, ", and ', or Unicode character references such as &#x20AC, which represents the euro symbol (€).

- *Variable references:* These are XML-qualified names (QNames) preceded by a $ sign. A variable reference is defined by its local name. Note that SQL Server 2012 does not support variable references with namespace URI prefixes, which are allowed under the W3C recommendation. An example of a variable reference is $count.

- *Parenthesized expressions:* These are expressions enclosed in parentheses. Parenthesized expressions are often used to force a specific order of operator evaluation. For instance, in the expression (3 + 4) * 2, the parentheses force the addition to be performed before the multiplication.

- *Context item expressions:* These are expressions that evaluate to the context item. The context item is the node or atomic value currently being referenced by the XQuery query engine.

- *Function calls:* These are composed of a QName followed by a list of arguments in parentheses. Function calls can reference built-in functions. SQL Server 2012 does not support XQuery user-defined functions.

The query Method

The query() method can be used to query and retrieve XML nodes from xml variables or xml-typed columns in tables, as demonstrated in Listing 12-9, with partial results shown in Figure 12-10.

Listing 12-9. Retrieving Job Candidates with the query Method

```
SELECT Resume.query
(
N'//*:Name.First,
//*:Name.Middle,
//*:Name.Last,
//*:Edu.Level'
)
FROM HumanResources.JobCandidate;
```

Figure 12-10. Sample Job Candidate Returned by the query Method

The simple XQuery query retrieves all first names, middle names, last names, and education levels for all AdventureWorks job candidates. The XQuery path expressions in the example demonstrate some key XQuery concepts, including the following:

- The first item of note is the // axis at the beginning of each path expression. This axis notation is defined as shorthand for the descendant-or-self::node(), which we'll describe in more detail in the next section. This particular axis retrieves all nodes with a name matching the location step, regardless of where it occurs in the XML being queried.

- In the example, the four node tests specified are Name.First, Name.Middle, Name.Last, and Edu.Level. All nodes with the names that match the node tests are returned no matter where they occur in the XML.

- The * namespace qualifier is a wildcard that matches any namespace occurring in the XML. Each node in the result node sequence includes an xmlns namespace declaration.

- This XQuery query is composed of four different paths denoting the four different node sequences to be returned. They are separated from one another by commas.

Location Paths

The *location path* determines which nodes should be accessed by XQuery. Following a location path from left to right is generally analogous to moving down and to the right in your XML node tree (there are exceptions, of course, which we discuss in the section on axis specifiers). If the first character of the path expression is a single forward slash (/), then the path expression is an absolute location path, meaning that it starts at the root of the XML. Listing 12-10 demonstrates the use of an XQuery absolute location path. The results are shown in Figure 12-11.

■ **Tip** The left-hand forward slash actually stands for a conceptual root node that encompasses your XML input. The conceptual root node doesn't actually exist, and can neither be viewed in your XML input nor accessed or manipulated directly. It's this conceptual root node that allows XQuery to properly process XML fragments that are not well formed (i.e., XML with multiple root nodes) as input. Using a path expression that consists of only a single forward slash returns every node below the conceptual root node in your XML document or fragment.

Listing 12-10. *Querying with an Absolute Location Path*

```
DECLARE @x xml=N'<?xml version="1.0"?>
<Geocode>
<Info ID="1">
<Coordinates Resolution="High">
<Latitude>37.859609</Latitude>
<Longitude>-122.291673</Longitude>
</Coordinates>
<Location Type="Business">
<Name>APress, Inc.</Name>
</Location>
</Info>
<Info ID="2">
<Coordinates Resolution="High">
<Latitude>37.423268</Latitude>
<Longitude>-122.086345</Longitude>
</Coordinates>
<Location Type="Business">
<Name>Google, Inc.</Name>
</Location>
</Info>
</Geocode>';
SELECT @x.query(N'/Geocode/Info/Coordinates');
```

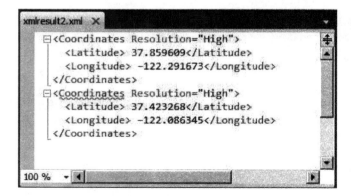

Figure 12-11. *Absolute Location Path Query Result*

Listing 12-10 defines an xml variable and populates it with an XML document containing geocoding data for a couple of businesses. We've used an absolute location path in the query to retrieve a node sequence of the latitude and longitude coordinates for the entire XML document.

A relative location path indicates a path relative to the current context node. The *context node* is the current node being accessed by the XQuery engine at a given point when the query is executed. The context node changes during execution of the query. Relative location paths are specified by excluding the leading forward slash, as in the following modification to Listing 12-10:

```
SELECT @x.query(N'Geocode/Info/Coordinates');
```

And, as previously mentioned, using a double forward slash (//) in the lead position returns nodes that match the node test anywhere they occur in the document. The following modification to Listing 12-10 demonstrates this:

```
SELECT @x.query(N'//Coordinates');
```

In addition, the wildcard character (*) can be used to match any node by name. The following example retrieves the root node, all of the nodes on the next level, and all Coordinates nodes below that:

```
SELECT @x.query(N'//*/*/Coordinates');
```

Because the XML document in the example is a simple one, all the variations of Listing 12-10 return the same result. For more complex XML documents or fragments, the results of different relative location paths could return completely different results.

Node Tests

The *node tests* in the previous example are simple *name node tests*. For a name node test to return a match, the nodes must have the same names as those specified in the node tests. In addition to name node tests, SQL Server 2012 XQuery supports four node *kind* tests, as listed in Table 12-1.

Table 12-1. *Supported Node Tests*

Node Kind Test	Description
comment()	Returns true for a comment node only.
node()	Returns true for any kind of node.
processing-instruction("*name*")	Returns true for a processing instruction node. The *name* parameter is an optional string literal. If it is included, only processing instruction nodes with that name are returned; if not included, all processing instructions are returned.
text()	Returns true for a text node only.

■ **Tip** Keep in mind that XQuery, like XML, is case sensitive. This means your node tests and other identifiers must all be of the proper case. The identifier PersonalID, for instance, does not match personalid in XML or XQuery. Also note that your database collation case sensitivity settings do not affect XQuery queries.

Listing 12-11 demonstrates use of the processing-instruction() node test to retrieve the processing instruction from the root level of a document for one product model. The results are shown in Figure 12-12.

Listing 12-11. Sample Processing-instruction Node Test

```
SELECT CatalogDescription.query(N'/processing-instruction()') AS Processing_Instr
FROM Production.ProductModel
WHERE ProductModelID = 19;
```

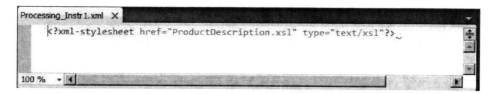

Figure 12-12. *Results of the Processing-instruction Node Test Query*

The sample can be modified to retrieve all XML comments from the source by using the comment() node test, as in Listing 12-12. The results are shown in Figure 12-13.

Listing 12-12. Sample comment Node Test

```
SELECT CatalogDescription.query(N'//comment()') AS Comments
FROM Production.ProductModel
WHERE ProductModelID = 19;
```

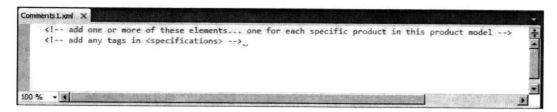

Figure 12-13. *Results of the comment Node Test Query*

Listing 12-13 demonstrates use of another node test, node(), to retrieve the specifications for product model 19. Results are shown in Figure 12-14.

Listing 12-13. Sample node Node Test

```
SELECT CatalogDescription.query(N'//*:Specifications/node()') AS Specifications
FROM Production.ProductModel
WHERE ProductModelID = 19;
```

```
Specifications1.xml*
    These are the product specifications.
    <Material>Almuminum Alloy</Material>
    <Color>Available in most colors</Color>
    <ProductLine>Mountain bike</ProductLine>
    <Style>Unisex</Style>
    <RiderExperience>Advanced to Professional riders</RiderExperience>
```

Figure 12-14. *Results of the node Node Test Query*

SQL Server 2012 XQuery does not support other node kind tests specified in the XQuery recommendation. Specifically, the schema-element(), schema-attribute(), and document-node() kind tests are not implemented. SQL Server 2012 also doesn't provide support for *type tests,* which are node tests that let you query nodes based on their associated type information.

Namespaces

You might notice that the first node of the result shown in Figure 12-14 is not enclosed in XML tags. This node is a text node located in the Specifications node being queried. You might also notice that the * namespace wildcard mentioned previously is used in this query. This is because namespaces are declared in the XML of the CatalogDescription column. Specifically the root node declaration looks like this:

```
<pl:ProductDescription xmlns:pl="http://schemas.microsoft.com/sqlserver/2004➙ 07/adventure-
works/ProductModelDescription" xmlns:wm="http://schemas.microsoft.com/sqlserver/2004/07/➙
adventure-works/ProductModelWarrAndMain" xmlns:wf="http://www.adventure-works.com/
schemas/OtherFeatures" xmlns:html="http://www.w3.org/1999/xhtml" ProductModelID="19"
ProductModelName="Mountain 100">
```

The Specifications node of the XML document is declared with the pi namespace in the document. Not using a namespace in the query at all, as shown in Listing 12-14, results in an empty sequence being returned (no matching nodes).

Listing 12-14. Querying CatalogDescription with No Namespaces

```
SELECT CatalogDescription.query(N'//Specifications/node()') AS Specifications
FROM Production.ProductModel
WHERE ProductModelID=19;
```

In addition to the wildcard namespace specifier, you can use the XQuery prolog to define namespaces for use in your query. Listing 12-15 shows how the previous example can be modified to include the p1 namespace with a namespace declaration in the prolog.

Listing 12-15. Prolog Namespace Declaration

```
SELECT CatalogDescription.query
(
N'declare namespace
p1="http://schemas.microsoft.com/sqlserver/2004/07/adventure-works/ProductModelDescription";
//p1:Specifications/node()'
)
```

```
FROM Production.ProductModel
WHERE ProductModelID = 19;
```

The keywords declare namespace allow you to declare specific namespaces that will be used in the query. You can also use the declare default element namespace keywords to declare a default namespace, as in Listing 12-16.

Listing 12-16. Prolog Default Namespace Declaration

```
SELECT CatalogDescription.query
(
N'declare default element namespace
"http://schemas.microsoft.com/sqlserver/2004/07/adventure-works/ProductModelDescription";
//Specifications/node()'
)
FROM Production.ProductModel
WHERE ProductModelID = 19;
```

Declaring a default namespace with the declare default element namespace keywords allows you to eliminate namespace prefixes in your location paths (for steps that fall within the scope of the default namespace, of course). Listings 12-15 and 12-16 both generate the same result as the query in Listing 12-13.

■ **Tip** You can also use the T-SQL WITH XMLNAMESPACES clause, described previously in this chapter, to declare namespaces for use by xml data type methods.

SQL Server defines an assortment of predeclared namespaces that can be used in your queries. With the exception of the xml namespace, you can redeclare these namespaces in your queries using the URIs of your choice. The predeclared namespaces are listed in Table 12-2.

Table 12-2. *SQL Server Predeclared XQuery Namespaces*

Namespace	URI	Description
fn	http://www.w3.org/2005/ xpath-functions	XQuery 1.0, XPath 2.0, XSLT 2.0 functions and operators namespace.
sqltypes	http://schemas.microsoft.com/ sqlserver/2004/sqltypes	This namespace provides SQL Server 2005 to base type mapping.
xdt	http://www.w3.org/2005/ xpath-datatypes/	XQuery 1.0/XPath 2.0 data types namespace.
xml	http://www.w3.org/XML/ 1998/namespace	Default XML namespace.
xs	http://www.w3.org/2001/XMLSchema	XML schema namespace.
xsi	http://www.w3.org/2001/	XML schema instance namespace; XMLSchema-instance.

■ **Tip** The W3C-specified local functions namespace, `local` (`http://www.w3.org/2005/xquery-local-functions`), is not predeclared in SQL Server. SQL Server 2012 does not support XQuery user-defined functions.

Another useful namespace is `http://www.w3.org/2005/xqt-errors`, which is the namespace for XPath and XQuery function and operator error codes. In the XQuery documentation, this URI is bound to the namespace `err`, though this is not considered normative.

Axis Specifiers

Axis specifiers define the direction of movement of a location path step relative to the current context node. The XQuery standard defines several axis specifiers, which can be defined as *forward axes* or *reverse axes*. SQL Server 2012 supports a subset of these axis specifiers, as listed in Table 12-3.

Table 12-3. *SQL 2012 Supported Axis Specifiers*

Axis Name	Direction	Description
`child::`	Forward	Retrieves the children of the current context node.
`descendant::`	Forward	Retrieves all descendents of the current context node, recursive style. This includes children of the current node, children of the children, and so on.
`self::`	Forward	Contains just the current context node.
`descendant-or-self::`	Forward	Contains the context node and children of the current context node.
`attribute::`	Forward	Returns the specified attribute(s) of the current context node. This axis specifier may be abbreviated using an at sign (@).
`parent::`	Reverse	Returns the parent of the current context node. This axis specifier may be abbreviated as two periods (..).

In addition, the *context-item expression,* indicated by a single period (.), returns the current context item (which can be either a node or an atomic value). The current context item is the current node or atomic value being processed by the XQuery engine at any given point during query execution.

■ **Note** The following axes, defined as *optional axes* by the XQuery 1.0 specification, are not supported by SQL Server 2012: `following-sibling::`, `following::`, `ancestor::`, `preceding-sibling::`, `preceding::`, `ancestor-or-self::`, and the deprecated `namespace::`. If you are porting XQuery queries from other sources, they may have to be modified to avoid these axis specifiers.

In all of the examples so far, the axis has been omitted, and the default axis of `child::` is assumed by XQuery in each step. Because `child::` is the default axis, the two queries in Listing 12-17 are equivalent.

Listing 12-17. *Query with and Without Default Axes*

```
SELECT CatalogDescription.query(N'//*:Specifications/node()') AS Specifications
FROM Production.ProductModel
WHERE ProductModelID = 19;
SELECT CatalogDescription.query(N'//child::*:Specifications/child::node()')
AS Specifications
FROM Production.ProductModel
WHERE ProductModelID = 19;
```

Listing 12-18 demonstrates the use of the parent:: axis to retrieve Coordinates nodes from the sample XML.

Listing 12-18. *Sample Using the parent:: Axis*

```
DECLARE @x xml = N'<?xml version = "1.0"?>
<Geocode>
<Info ID = "1">
<Coordinates Resolution = "High">
<Latitude > 37.859609</Latitude>
<Longitude > -122.291673</Longitude>
</Coordinates>
<Location Type = "Business">
<Name > APress, Inc.</Name>
</Location>
</Info>
<Info ID = "2">
<Coordinates Resolution = "High">
<Latitude > 37.423268</Latitude>
<Longitude > -122.086345</Longitude>
</Coordinates>
<Location Type = "Business">
<Name > Google, Inc.</Name>
</Location>
</Info>
</Geocode >';
SELECT @x.query(N'//Location/parent::node()/Coordinates');
```

This particular query locates all Location nodes, then uses the parent:: axis to retrieve their parent nodes (Info nodes), and finally returns the Coordinates nodes, which are children of the Info nodes. The end result is shown in Figure 12-15.

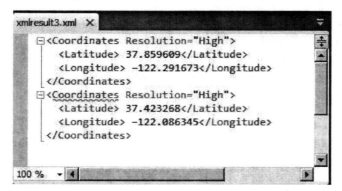

Figure 12-15. *Retrieving Coordinates Nodes with the parent:: Axis*

Dynamic XML Construction

The XQuery 1.0 recommendation is based on XPath 2.0, which is in turn based largely on XPath 1.0. The XPath 1.0 recommendation was designed to consolidate many of the best features of both the W3C XSLT and XPointer recommendations. One of the benefits of XQuery's lineage is its ability to query XML and dynamically construct well-formed XML documents from the results. Consider the example in Listing 12-19, which uses an XQuery *direct constructor* to create an XML document. Figure 12-16 shows the results.

Listing 12-19. XQuery Dynamic XML Construction

```
DECLARE @x xml = N'<?xml version = "1.0"?>
<Geocode>
        <Info ID = "1">
        <Location Type = "Business">
        <Name > APress,  Inc.</Name>
        </Location>
        </Info>
        <Info ID = "2">
        <Location Type = "Business">
        <Name > Google,  Inc.</Name>
        </Location>
        </Info>
</Geocode>';
SELECT  @x.query(N'<Companies>
        {
        //Info/Location/Name
        }
</Companies>');
```

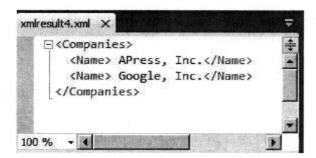

Figure 12-16. *Dynamic Construction of XML with XQuery*

The direct constructor in the XQuery example looks like this:
```
<Companies>
{
//Info/Location/Name
}
</Companies>
```

The < Companies > and < /Companies > opening and closing tags in the direct constructor act as the root tag for the XML result. The opening and closing tags contain the *content expression,* which consists of the location path used to retrieve the nodes. The content expression is wrapped in curly braces between the < Companies > and < /Companies > tags:

```
{
//Info/Location/Name
}
```

■ **Tip** If you need to output curly braces in your constructed XML result, you can escape them by doubling them up in your query using {{ and }}.

You can also use the element, attribute, and text computed constructors to build your XML result, as demonstrated in Listing 12-20, with the result shown in Figure 12-17.

Listing 12-20. Element and Attribute Dynamic Constructors

```
SELECT CatalogDescription.query
(
N'declare namespace
p1 = "http://schemas.microsoft.com/sqlserver/2004/07/adventure-works/ProductModelDescription";
//p1:Specifications/node()'
)
FROM Production.ProductModel
WHERE ProductModelID = 19;

DECLARE @x xml = N'<?xml version = "1.0"?>
<Geocode>
<Info ID = "1">
<Location Type = "Business">
<Name > APress, Inc.</Name>
<Address>
<Street > 2560 Ninth St, Ste 219</Street>
<City > Berkeley</City>
<State > CA</State>
<Zip > 94710-2500</Zip>
<Country > US</Country>
</Address>
</Location>
</Info>
</Geocode > ';
SELECT @x.query
(
N'element Companies
{
element FirstCompany
{
attribute CompanyID
{
(//Info/@ID)[1]
},
(//Info/Location/Name)[1]
}
}'
);
```

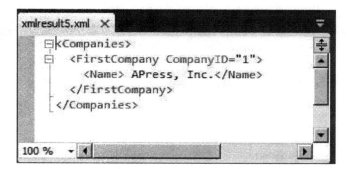

Figure 12-17. *Results of the XQuery Computed Element Construction*

The element Companies computed element constructor creates the root Companies node. The FirstCompany node is constructed as a child node using another element constructor:

```
element Companies
{
element FirstCompany
{
...
}
}
```

The content expressions of the FirstCompany elements are where the real action takes place:

```
element FirstCompany
{
attribute CompanyID
{
(//Info/@ID)[1]
},
(//Info/Location/Name)[1]
}
```

The CompanyID dynamic attribute constructor retrieves the ID attribute from the first Info node. The predicate [1] in the path ensures that only the first //Info/@ID is returned. This path location could also be written like this:

```
//Info[1]/@ID
```

The second path location retrieves the first Name node for the first Location node of the first Info node. Again, the [1] predicate ensures that only the first matching node is returned. The path is equivalent to the following:

```
//Info[1]/Location[1]/Name[1]
```

To retrieve the second node, change the predicate to [2], and so on.

■ **Tip** By definition, a predicate that evaluates to a numeric singleton value (such as the integer constant 1) is referred to as a *numeric predicate*. The effective Boolean value is `true` only when the context position is equal to the numeric predicate expression. When the numeric predicate is 3, for instance, the predicate truth value is `true` only for the third context position. This is a handy way to limit the results of an XQuery query to a single specific node.

XQuery Comments

XQuery comments (not to be confused with *XML comment nodes*) are used to document your queries inline. You can include them in XQuery expressions by enclosing them with the `(:` and `:)` symbols (just like the smiley face emoticon). Comments can be used in your XQuery expressions anywhere ignorable whitespace is allowed, and they can be nested. XQuery comments have no effect on query processing. The following example modifies the query in Listing 12-19 to include XQuery comments:

```
SELECT @x.query ( N'<Companies>(: This is the root node :) {
//Info/Location/Name (: Retrieves all company names (: ALL of them :) :) } </Companies>' );
```

You will see XQuery comments used in some of the examples later in this chapter.

Data Types

XQuery maintains the string value and typed value for all nodes in the referenced XML. XQuery defines the string value of an element node as the concatenated string values of the element node and all its child element nodes. The type of a node is defined in the XML schema collection associated with the xml variable or column. As an example, the built-in AdventureWorks Production.ManuInstructionsSchemaCollection XML schema collection defines the LocationID attribute of the Location element as an xsd:integer:

```
<xsd:attribute name = "LocationID" type = "xsd:integer" use = "required" />
```

Every instance of this attribute in the XML of the Instructions column of the Production.ProductModel table must conform to the requirements of this data type. Typed data can also be manipulated according to the functions and operators defined for this type. For untyped XML, the typed data is defined as xdt:untypedAtomic. A listing of XDM data types available to SQL Server via XQuery is given in Appendix B.

Predicates

An XQuery *predicate* is an expression that evaluates to one of the xs:boolean values true or false. In XQuery, predicates are used to filter the results of a node sequence, discarding nodes that don't meet the specified criteria from the results. Predicates limit the results by converting the result of the predicate expression into an xs:boolean value, referred to as the *predicate truth value*. The predicate truth value is determined for each item of the input sequence according to the following rules:

1. If the type of the expression is numeric, the predicate truth value is true if the value of the predicate expression is equal to the context position; otherwise for a numeric predicate, the predicate truth value is false.

2. If the type of the expression is a string, the predicate is false if the length of the expression is 0. For a string type expression with a length greater than 0, the predicate truth value is true.

3. If the type of the expression is xs:boolean, the predicate truth value is the value of the expression.

4. If the expression results in an empty sequence, the predicate truth value is `false`.

5. If the value of the predicate expression is a node sequence, the predicate truth value is `true` if the sequence contains at least one node; otherwise it is `false`.

Queries that include a predicate return only nodes in a sequence for which the predicate truth value evaluates to `true`. Predicates are composed of expressions, conveniently referred to as *predicate expressions,* enclosed in square brackets ([ ]). You can specify multiple predicates in a path, and they are evaluated in order of occurrence from left to right.

■ **Note** The XQuery specification says that multiple predicates are evaluated from left to right, but it also gives some wiggle room for vendors to perform predicate evaluations in other orders, allowing them to take advantage of vendor-specific features such as indexes and other optimizations. You don't have to worry too much about the internal evaluation order of predicates, though. No matter what order predicates are actually evaluated in, the end results have to be the same as if the predicates were evaluated left to right.

Value Comparison Operators

As we mentioned, the basic function of predicates is to filter results. Results are filtered by specified comparisons, and XQuery offers a rich set of comparison operators. These operators fall into three main categories: value comparison operators, general comparison operators, and node comparison operators. Value comparison operators compare singleton atomic values only. Trying to compare sequences with value comparison operators results in an error. The value comparison operators are listed in Table 12-4.

Table 12-4. *Value Comparison Operators*

Operator	Description
Eq	Equal
Ne	Not equal
lt	Less than
le	Less than or equal to
gt	Greater than
ge	Greater than or equal to

Value comparisons follow a specific set of rules:

1. The operands on the left and right sides of the operator are atomized.

2. If either atomized operand is an empty sequence, the result is an empty sequence.

3. If either atomized operand is a sequence with a length greater than 1, an error is raised.

4. If either atomized operand is of type `xs:untypedAtomic`, it is cast to `xs:string`.

5. If the operands have compatible types, they are compared using the appropriate operator. If the comparison of the two operands using the chosen operator evaluates to true, the result is true; otherwise the result is false. If the operands have incompatible types, an error is thrown.

Consider the value comparison examples in Listing 12-21, with results shown in Figure 12-18.

Listing 12-21. Value Comparison Examples

```
DECLARE @x xml=N'<?xml version="1.0" ?>
<Animal>
Cat
</Animal>';
SELECT @x.query(N'9 eq 9.0 (: 9 is equal to 9.0 :)');
SELECT @x.query(N'4 gt 3 (: 4 is greater than 3 :)');
SELECT @x.query(N'(/Animal/text())[1] lt "Dog" (: Cat is less than Dog :)') ;
```

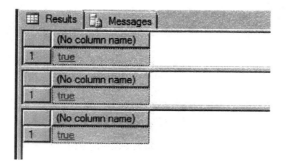

Figure 12-18. Results of the XQuery Value Comparisons

Listing 12-22 attempts to compare two values of incompatible types, namely an xs:decimal type value and an xs:string value. The result is the error message shown in the results following.

Listing 12-22. Incompatible Type Value Comparison

```
DECLARE @x xml=N'';
SELECT @x.query(N'3.141592 eq "Pi"') ;

Msg 2234, Level 16, State 1, Line 2
XQuery [query()]: The operator "eq" cannot be applied to "xs:decimal" and "xs:string" operands.
```

General Comparison Operators

General comparisons are existential comparisons that work on operand sequences of any length. *Existential* simply means that if one atomized value from the first operand sequence fulfills a value comparison with at least one atomized value from the second operand sequence, the result is true. The general comparison operators will look familiar to programmers who are versed in other computer languages, particularly C-style languages. The general comparison operators are listed in Table 12-5.

Table 12-5. *General Comparison Operators*

Operator	Description
=	Equal
!=	Not equal
<	Less than
>	Greater than
<=	Less than or equal to
>=	Greater than or equal to

Listing 12-23 demonstrates comparisons using general comparisons on XQuery sequences. The results are shown in Figure 12-19.

Listing 12-23. General Comparison Examples

```
DECLARE @x xml = '';
SELECT @x.query('(3.141592, 1) = (2, 3.141592) (: true :) ');
SELECT @x.query('(1.0, 2.0, 3.0) = 1 (: true :) ');
SELECT @x.query('("Joe", "Harold") < "Adam" (: false :) ');
SELECT @x.query('xs:date("1999-01-01") < xs:date("2006-01-01") (: true :)');
```

Figure 12-19. *General XQuery Comparison Results*

Here's how the general comparison operators work. The first query compares the sequences (3.141592, 1) and (2, 3.141592) using the = operator. The comparison atomizes the two operand sequences and compares them using the rules for the equivalent value comparison operators. Since the atomic value 3.141592 exists in both sequences, the equality test result is true.

The second example compares the sequence (1.0, 2.0, 3.0) to the atomic value 1. The atomic values 1.0 and 1 are compatible types and are equal, so the equality test result is true. The third query returns false because neither of the atomic values Doe or Harold are lexically less than the atomic value Adam.

The final example compares two xs:date values. Since the date 1999-01-01 is less than the date 2006-01-01, the result is true.

XQUERY DATE FORMAT

The XQuery implementation in SQL Server 2005 had a special requirement concerning `xs:date`, `xs:time`, `xs:dateTime`, and derived types. According to a subset of the ISO 8601 standard that SQL Server 2005 uses, date and time values had to include a mandatory time offset specifier. SQL Server 2012 does not strictly enforce this rule. When you leave the time offset information off an XQuery date or time value, SQL Server 2012 defaults to the zero meridian (*Z* specifier).

SQL Server 2012 also differs from SQL Server 2005 in how it handles time offset information. In SQL Server 2005, all dates were automatically *normalized* to coordinated universal time (UTC). SQL Server 2012 stores the time offset information you indicate when specifying a date or time value. If a time zone is provided, it must follow the date or time value, and can be either of the following:

- The capital letter Z, which stands for the *zero meridian*, or UTC. The zero meridian runs through Greenwich, England.

- An offset from the zero meridian in the format [+/−]hh:mm. For instance, the US Eastern Time zone would be indicated as −05:00.

Here are a few sample ISO 8601 formatted dates and times acceptable to SQL Server, with descriptions:

- *1999-05-16:* May 16,1999, no time, UTC

- *09:15:00-05:00:* No date, 9:15 AM, US and Canada Eastern time

- *2003-12-25T20:00:00-08:00:* December 25, 2003, 8:00 PM, US and Canada Pacific time

- *2004-07-06T23:59:59.987+01:00:* July 6, 2004,11:59:59.987 PM (.987 is fractional seconds), Central European time

Unlike the homogenous sequences in Listing 12-23, a heterogeneous sequence is one that combines nodes and atomic values, or atomic values of incompatible types (such as `xs:string` and `xs:decimal`). Trying to perform a general comparison with a heterogeneous sequence causes an error in SQL Server, as demonstrated by Listing 12-24.

Listing 12-24. General Comparison with Heterogeneous Sequence

```
DECLARE @x xml = '';
SELECT @x.query('(xs:date("2006-10-09"), 6.02E23) > xs:date("2007-01-01")');
```

The error generated by Listing 12-24 looks like the following:

```
Msg 9311, Level 16, State 1, Line 3

XOuery [queryQ]: Heterogeneous sequences are not allowed in V, found

'xs:date' and 'xs:double'.
```

SQL Server also disallows heterogeneous sequences that mix nodes and atomic values, as demonstrated by Listing 12-25.

Listing 12-25. Mixing Nodes and Atomic Values in Sequences

```
DECLARE @x xml = '';
SELECT @x.query('(1, <myNode>Testing</myNode>)');
```

Trying to mix and match nodes and atomic values in a sequence like this results in an error message indicating that you tried to create a sequence consisting of atomic values and nodes, similar to the following:

```
Msg 2210, Level 16, State 1, Line 3
XQuery [queryQ]: Heterogeneous sequences are not allowed: found
'xs:integer' and 'element(myl\lode,xdt:untyped)'
```

Node Comparisons

The third type of comparison that XQuery allows is a *node comparison*. Node comparisons allow you to compare XML nodes in document order. The node comparison operators are listed in Table 12-6.

Table 12-6. *Node Comparison Operators*

Operator	Description
is	Node identity equality
<<	Left node precedes right node
>>	Left node follows right node

The is operator compares two nodes to each other and returns true if the left node is the same node as the right node. Note that this is not a test of the equality of node content but rather of the actual nodes themselves based on an internally generated node ID. Consider the sample node comparisons in Listing 12-26 with results shown in Figure 12-20.

Listing 12-26. Node Comparison Samples

```
DECLARE @x xml=N'<?xml version="1.0"?>
<Root>
<NodeA>Test Node</NodeA>
<NodeA>Test Node</NodeA>
<NodeB>Test Node</NodeB>
</Root>';
SELECT @x.query('((/Root/NodeA)[1] is (//NodeA)[1]) (: true :)');
SELECT @x.query('((/Root/NodeA)[1] is (/Root/NodeA)[2]) (: false :)');
SELECT @x.query('((/Root/NodeA)[2] is (/Root/NodeB)[1]) (: true :)');
```

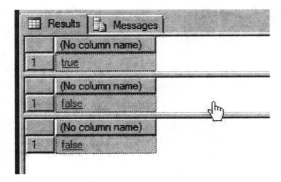

Figure 12-20. *Results of the XQuery Node Comparisons*

The first query uses the is operator to compare (/Root/NodeA)[1] to itself. The [1] numeric predicate at the end of the path ensures that only a single node is returned for comparison. The right-hand and left-hand expressions must both evaluate to a singleton or empty sequence. The result of this comparison is true only because (/Root/NodeA)[1] is the same node returned by the (//NodeA)[1] path on the right-hand side of the operator.

The second query compares (/Root/NodeA)[1] with (/Root/NodeA)[2]. Even though the two nodes have the same name and content, they are in fact different nodes. Because they are different nodes, the is operator returns false.

The final query retrieves the second NodeA node with the path (/Root/NodeA)[2]. Then it uses the « operator to determine if this node precedes the NodeB node from the path (/Root/NodeB)[1]. Since the second NodeA precedes NodeB in document order, the result of this comparison is true.

A node comparison results in an xs:boolean value or evaluates to an empty sequence if one of the operands results in an empty sequence. This is demonstrated in Listing 12-27.

Listing 12-27. Node Comparison That Evaluates to an Empty Sequence

```
DECLARE @x xml=N'<?xml version="1.0"?>
<Root>
<NodeA>Test Node</NodeA>
</Root>';
SELECT @x.query('((/Root/NodeA)[1] is (/Root/NodeZ)[1]) (: empty sequence :)');
```

The result of the node comparison is an empty sequence because the right-hand path expression evaluates to an empty sequence (because no node named NodeZ exists in the XML document).

Conditional Expressions (if ... then ... else)

As shown in the previous examples, XQuery returns xs:boolean values or empty sequences as the result of comparisons. XQuery also provides support for the conditional if...then...else expression. The if...then...else construct returns an expression based on the xs:boolean value of another expression. The format for the XQuery conditional expression is shown in the following:

```
if (test-expression) then then-expression else else-expression
```

In this syntax, test-expression represents the conditional expression that is evaluated, the result of which will determine the returned result. When evaluating test-expression, XQuery applies the following rules:

1. If test-expression results in an empty sequence, the result is false.

2. If test-expression results in an xs:boolean value, the result is the xs:boolean value of the expression.

3. If test-expression results in a sequence of one or more nodes, the result is true.

4. If these steps fail, a static error is raised.

If *test-expression* evaluates to true, *then-expression* is returned. If *test-expression* evaluates to false, *else-expression* is returned.

The XQuery conditional is a declarative expression. Unlike the C# if...else statement and Visual Basic's If...Then...Else construct, XQuery's conditional if...then...else doesn't represent a branch in procedural logic or a change in program flow. It acts like a function that accepts a conditional expression as input and returns an expression as a result. In this respect, XQuery's if...then...else has more in common with the SQL CASE expression and the C# ?: operator than the if statement in procedural languages. In the XQuery if...then...else, syntax parentheses are required around test-expression, and the else clause is mandatory.

Arithmetic Expressions

XQuery arithmetic expressions provide support for the usual suspects—standard mathematical operators found in most modern programming languages, including the following:

- Multiplication (*)
- Division (div)
- Addition (+)
- Subtraction (–)
- Modulo (mod)

INTEGER DIVISION IN XQUERY

SQL Server 2012 XQuery does not support the idiv integer division operator. Fortunately, the W3C XQuery recommendation defines the idiv operator as equivalent to the following div expression:

```
($argl div $arg2) cast as xs:integer?
```

If you need to convert XQuery code that uses idiv to SQL Server, you can use the div and cast operators as shown to duplicate idiv functionality.

XQuery also supports the unary plus (+) and unary minus (–) operators. Because the forward slash character is used as a path separator in XQuery, the division operator is specified using the keyword div. The modulo operator, mod, returns the remainder of division.

Of the supported operators, unary plus and unary minus have the highest precedence. Multiplication, division, and modulo are next. Binary addition and subtraction have the lowest precedence. Parentheses can be used to force the evaluation order of mathematical operations.

XQuery Functions

XQuery provides several built-in functions defined in the XQuery Functions and Operators specification (sometimes referred to as F&O), which is available at www.w3.org/TR/ xquery-operators/. Built-in XQuery functions are in the predeclared namespace fn.

■ **Tip** The fn namespace does not have to be specified when calling a built-in function. Some people leave it off to improve readability of their code.

We've listed the XQuery functions that SQL Server 2012 supports in Table 12-7.

Table 12-7. *Supported Built-in XQuery Functions*

Function	Description
fn:avg(x)	Returns the average of the sequence of numbers x. For example, fn:avg((10, 20, 30, 40, 50)) returns 30.
fn:ceiling(n)	Returns the smallest number without a fractional part that is not less than n. For example, fn:ceiling(1.1) returns 2.
fn:concat(s_1, s_2, ...)	Concatenates zero or more strings and returns the concatenated string as a result. For example, fn:concat("hi", ",", "how are you?") returns "hi, how are you?".
fn:contains(s_1, s_2,)	Returns true if the string s_1 contains the string s_2. For example, fn:contains("fish", "is") returns true.
fn:count(x)	Returns the number of items in the sequence x. For example, fn:count((1, 2, 4, 8, 16)) returns 5.
fn:data(a)	Returns the typed value of each item specified by the argument a. For example, fn:data((3.141592, "hello")) returns "3.141592 hello".
fn:distinct-values(x)	Returns the sequence x with duplicate values removed. For example, fn:distinct-values((1, 2, 3, 4, 5, 4, 5)) returns "1 2 3 4 5".
fn:empty(i)	Returns true if i is an empty sequence; returns false otherwise. For example, fn:empty((1, 2, 3)) returns false.
fn:expanded-QName(u, l)	Returns an xs:QName. The arguments u and l represent the xs:QName's namespace URI and local name, respectively.
fn:false()	Returns the xs:boolean value false. For example, fn:false() returns false.
fn:floor(n)	Returns the largest number without a fractional part that is not greater than n. For example, fn:floor(1.1) returns 1.
fn:id(x)	Returns the sequence of element nodes with ID values that match one or more of the IDREF values supplied in x. The parameter x is treated as a whitespace-separated sequence of tokens.
fn:last()	Returns the index number of the last item in the sequence being processed. The first index in the sequence has an index of 1.
fn:local-name(n)	Returns the local name, without the namespace URI, of the specified node n.
fn:local-name-from-QName(q)	Returns the local name part of the xs:QName argument q. The value returned is an xs:NCName.
fn:max(x)	Returns the item with the highest value from the sequence x. For example, fn:max((1.0, 2.5, 9.3, 0.3, -4.2)) returns 9.3.
fn:min(x)	Returns the item with the lowest value from the sequence x. For example, fn:min(("x", "q", "u", "e", "r", "y")) returns "e".

(continued)

Table 12-7. (*continued*)

Function	Description
fn:namespace-uri(*n*)	Returns the namespace URI of the specified node *n*.
fn:namespace-uri-from-QName(*q*)	Returns the namespace URI part of the xs:QName argument *q*. The value returned is an xs:NCName.
fn:not(*b*)	Returns true if the effective Boolean value of *b* is false; returns false if the effective Boolean value is true. For example, fn:not(xs:boolean("true")) returns false.
fn:number(*n*)	Returns the numeric value of the node indicated by *n*. For example, fn:number("/Root/NodeA[1]").
fn:position()	Returns the index number of the context item in the sequence currently being processed.
fn:round(*n*)	Returns the number closest to *n* that does not have a fractional part. For example, fn:round(10.5) returns 11.
fn:string(*a*)	Returns the value of the argument *a*, expressed as an xs:string. For example, fn:string(3.141592) returns "3.141592".
fn:string-length(*s*)	Returns the length of the string *s*. For example, fn:string- length("abcdefghij") returns 10.
fn:substring(*s*, *m*, *n*)	Returns *n* characters from the string *s*, beginning at position *m*. If *n* is not specified, all characters from position *m* to the end of the string are returned. The first character in the string is position 1. For example, fn:substring("Money", 2, 3) returns "one".
fn:sum(*x*)	Returns the sum of the sequence of numbers in *x*. For example, fn:sum((1, 4, 9, 16, 25)) returns 55.
fn:true()	Returns the xs:boolean value true. For example, fn:true() returns true.

In addition, two functions from the sql: namespace are supported. The sql:column function allows you to expose and bind SQL Server relational column data in XQuery queries. This function accepts the name of an SQL column and exposes its values to your XQuery expressions. Listing 12-28 demonstrates the sql:column function.

Listing 12-28. The sql:column Function

```
DECLARE @x xml=N'';
SELECT @x.query(N'<Name>
<ID>
{
sql:column("p.BusinessEntityID")
}
</ID>
<FullName>
{
sql:column("p.FirstName"),
```

```
sql:column("p.MiddleName"),
sql:column("p.LastName")
}
</FullName>
</Name>')
FROM Person.Person p
WHERE p.BusinessEntityID <= 5
ORDER BY p.BusinessEntityID;
```

The result of this example, shown in Figure 12-21, is a set of XML documents containing the BusinessEntityID and full name of the first five contacts from the Person.Person table.

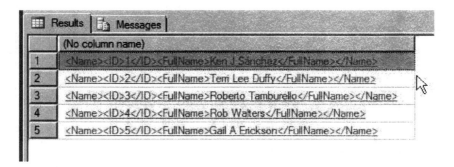

Figure 12-21. *Results of the sql:column Function Query*

The `sql variable` function goes another step, allowing you to expose T-SQL variables to XQuery. This function accepts the name of a T-SQL variable and allows you to access its value in your XQuery expressions. Listing 12-29 is an example that combines the `sql:column` and `sql:variable` functions in a single XQuery query.

Listing 12-29. XQuery sql:column and sql:variable Functions Example

```
/* 10 % discount */
DECLARE @discount NUMERIC(3, 2);
SELECT @discount = 0.10;
DECLARE @x xml;
SELECT @x = '';
SELECT @x.query('<Product>
<Model-ID>{ sql:column("ProductModelID") }</Model-ID>
<Name>{ sql:column("Name") }</Name>
<Price>{ sql:column("ListPrice") } </Price>
<DiscountPrice>
{ sql:column("ListPrice") -
(sql:column("ListPrice") * sql:variable("@discount") ) }
</DiscountPrice>
</Product>
')
FROM Production.Product p
WHERE ProductModelID = 30;
```

The XQuery generates XML documents using the `sql:column` function to retrieve the `ListPrice` from the `Production.Product` table. It also uses the `sql:variable` function to calculate a discount price for the items retrieved. Figure 12-22 shows partial results of this query (formatted for easier reading):

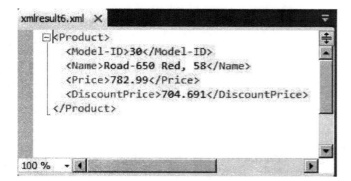

Figure 12-22. *Partial Results of the Query with the sql:column and sql:variable Functions*

Constructors and Casting

The XDM provides constructor functions to dynamically create instances of several supported types. The constructor functions are all in the format `xs:TYP(value)`, where `TYP` is the XDM type name. Most of the XDM data types have constructor functions; however, the following types do not have constructors in SQL Server XQuery: `xs:yearMonthDuration`, `xs:dayTimeDuration`, `xs: OName`, `xs:NMTOKEN`, and `xs:NOTATION`.

The following are examples of XQuery constructor functions:

```
xs:boolean("1")         (: returns true :)
xs:integer(1234)        (: returns 1234 :)
xs:float(9.8723E+3)     (: returns 9872.3 :)
xs:NCName("my-id")      (: returns the NCName "my-id" :)
```

Numeric types can be implicitly cast to their base types (or other numeric types) by XQuery to ensure proper results of calculations. The process of implicit casting is known as *type promotion*. For instance, in the following sample expression, the `xs:integer` type value is promoted to an `xs:decimal` to complete the calculation:

```
xs:integer(100)+xs:decimal(100.99)
```

■ **Note**   Only numeric types can be implicitly cast. String and other types cannot be implicitly cast by XQuery.

Explicit casting is performed using the `cast as` keywords. Examples of explicit casting include the following:

```
xs:string("98d3f4") cast as xs:hexBinary? (: 98d3f4 :)
100 cast as xs:double?  (: 1.0E+2 :)
"0" cast as xs:boolean? (: true :)
```

The ? after the target data type is the *optional occurrence indicator.* It is used to indicate that an empty sequence is allowed. SQL Server XQuery requires the ? after the `cast as` expression. SQL Server BOL provides a detailed description of the XQuery type casting rules at http://msdn.microsoft.com/en-us/library/ms191231.aspx.

The `instance of` Boolean operator allows you to determine the type of a singleton value. This operator takes a singleton value on its left side and a type on its right. The `xs:boolean` value `true` is returned if the atomic value represents an instance of the specified type. The following examples demonstrate the `instance of` operator:

```
10 instance of xs:integer (: returns true :) 100 instance of xs:decimal (: returns true :)
"hello" instance of xs:bytes  (: returns false :)
```

The `?` optional occurrence indicator can be appended after the data type to indicate that the empty sequence is allowable (though it is not mandatory, as with the `cast as` operator), as in this example:

```
9.8273 instance of xs:double? (: returns true :)
```

FLWOR Expressions

FLWOR expressions provide a way to iterate over a sequence and bind intermediate results to variables. *FLWOR* is an acronym for the keywords that define this type of expression: `for`, `let`, `where`, `order by`, and `return`. This section discusses XQuery's powerful FLWOR expressions.

The for and return Keywords

The `for` and `return` keywords have long been a part of XPath, though in not nearly so powerful a form as the XQuery FLWOR expression. The `for` keyword specifies that a variable is iteratively bound to the results of the specified path expression. The result of this iterative binding process is known as a *tuple stream*. The XQuery `for` expression is roughly analogous to the T-SQL SELECT statement. The `for` keyword must, at a minimum, have a matching `return` clause after it. The sample in Listing 12-30 demonstrates a basic `for` expression.

Listing 12-30. Basic XQuery for . . . return Expression

```
SELECT CatalogDescription.query(N'declare namespace ns =
"http://schemas.microsoft.com/sqlserver/2004/07/adventure-works/ProductModelDescription";
for $spec in //ns:ProductDescription/ns:Specifications/*
return fn:string($spec)') AS Description FROM Production.ProductModel WHERE ProductModelID=19;
```

The `for` clause iterates through all elements returned by the path expression. It then binds the elements to the `$spec` variable. The tuple stream that is bound to `$spec` consists of the following nodes in document order:

```
$spec=<Material>Almuminum Alloy</Material>
$spec=<Color>Available in most colors</Color>
$spec=<ProductLine>Mountain bike</ProductLine>
$spec=<Style>Unisex</Style>
$spec=<RiderExperience>Advanced to Professional riders</RiderExperience>
```

The `return` clause applies the `fn:string` function to the `$spec` variable to return the string value of each node as it is bound. The results look like the following:

```
Almuminum Alloy Available in most colors Mountain bike Unisex Advanced to Professional riders
```

The sample can be modified to return an XML result, using the techniques described previously in the "Dynamic XML Construction" section. Listing 12-31 demonstrates with results shown in Figure 12-23.

Listing 12-31. *XQuery for ... return Expression with XML Result*

```
SELECT CatalogDescription.query (

N'declare namespace ns =
"http://schemas.microsoft.com/sqlserver/2004/07/adventure-works/ProductModelDescription";
for $spec in //ns:ProductDescription/ns:Specifications/* return <detail>{
$spec/text() } </detail>' ) AS Description
FROM Production.ProductModel WHERE ProductModelID = 19;
```

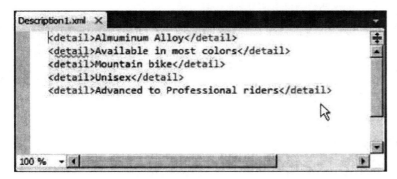

Figure 12-23. *Results of the for ... return Expression with XML Construction*

XQuery allows you to bind multiple variables in the `for` clause. When you bind multiple variables, the result is the Cartesian product of all possible values of the variables. SQL Server programmers will recognize the Cartesian product as being equivalent to the SQL `CROSS JOIN` operator. Listing 12-32 modifies the previous example further to generate the Cartesian product of the `Specifications` and `Warranty` child node text.

Listing 12-32. *XQuery Cartesian Product with for Expression*

```
SELECT CatalogDescription.query(N'declare namespace ns =
"http://schemas.microsoft.com/sqlserver/2004/07/adventure-works/ProductModelDescription";
for $spec in //ns:ProductDescription/ns:Specifications/*,
$feat in //ns:ProductDescription/*:Features/*:Warranty/node()
return <detail>
{
$spec/text()
} +
{
fn:string($feat/.)
}
</detail>'
) AS Description
FROM Production.ProductModel
WHERE ProductModelID = 19;
```

The `$spec` variable is bound to the same nodes shown previously. A second variable binding, for the variable `$feat`, is added to the `for` clause in this example. Specifically, this second variable is bound to the child nodes of the `Warranty` element, as shown following:

```
<pl:WarrantyPeriod>3 years</pl:WarrantyPeriod><pl:Description>parts and labor</pl:Description
```

The Cartesian product of the text nodes of these two tuple streams consists of ten possible combinations. The final result of the XQuery expression is shown in Figure 12-24 (formatted for easier reading).

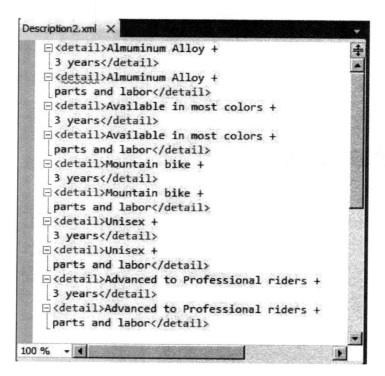

Figure 12-24. *Cartesian Product XQuery*

A bound variable can be used immediately after it is bound, even in the same for clause. Listing 12-33 demonstrates this.

Listing 12-33. Using a Bound Variable in the for Clause

```
SELECT CatalogDescription.query
(
N'declare namespace ns =
"http://schemas.microsoft.com/sqlserver/2004/07/adventure-works/ProductModelDescription";
for $spec in //ns:ProductDescription/ns:Specifications,
$color in $spec/Color
return<color>
{
$color/text()
}
</color>'
) AS Color
FROM Production.ProductModel
WHERE ProductModelID=19;
```

In this example, the $spec variable is bound to the Specifications node. It is then used in the same for clause to bind a value to the variable $color. The result is shown in Figure 12-25.

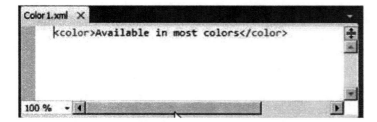

Figure 12-25. *Binding a Variable to Another Bound Variable in the for Clause*

The where Keyword

The where keyword specifies an optional clause to filter tuples generated by the for clause. The expression in the where clause is evaluated for each tuple, and those for which the effective Boolean value evaluates to false are discarded from the final result. Listing 12-34 demonstrates use of the where clause to limit the results to only those tuples that contain the letter *A*. The results are shown in Figure 12-26.

Listing 12-34. where Clause Demonstration

```
SELECT CatalogDescription.query
(
N'declare namespace ns =
"http://schemas.microsoft.com/sqlserver/2004/07/adventure-works/ProductModelDescription";
for $spec in //ns:ProductDescription/ns:Specifications/*
where $spec[ contains( . , "A" ) ]
return < detail>
{
$spec/text()
}
</detail>'
) AS Detail
FROM Production.ProductModel
WHERE ProductModelID = 19;
```

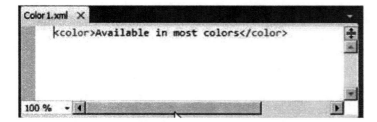

```
<detail>Almuminum Alloy</detail>
<detail>Available in most colors</detail>
<detail>Advanced to Professional riders</detail>
```

Figure 12-26. *Results of a FLWOR Expression with the where Clause*

The functions and operators described previously in this chapter (such as the contains function used in the example) can be used in the where clause expression to limit results as required by your application.

The order by Keywords

The order by clause is an optional clause of the FLWOR statement. The order by clause reorders the tuple stream generated by the for clause, using criteria that you specify. The order by criteria consists of one or more ordering specifications that are made up of an expression and an optional order modifier. Ordering specifications are evaluated from left to right.

The optional order modifier is either ascending or descending to indicate the direction of ordering. The default is ascending, as shown in Listing 12-35. The sample uses the order by clause to sort the results in descending (reverse) order. The results are shown in Figure 12-27.

Listing 12-35. order by Clause

```
SELECT CatalogDescription.query(N'declare namespace ns =
"http://schemas.microsoft.com/sqlserver/2004/07/adventure-works/ProductModelDescription";
for $spec in //ns:ProductDescription/ns:Specifications/*
order by $spec/. descending
return< detail >{ $spec/text() } </detail>') AS Detail
FROM Production.ProductModel
WHERE ProductModelID = 19;
```

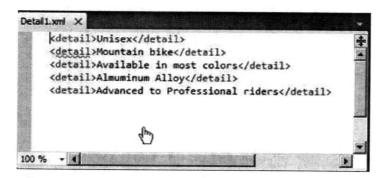

Figure 12-27. *Results of a FLWOR Expression with the order by Clause*

The let Keyword

SQL Server 2012 adds support for the FLWOR expression let clause. The let clause allows you to bind tuple streams to variables inside the body of the FLWOR expression. You can use the let clause to name repeating expressions. SQL Server XQuery inserts the expression assigned to the bound variable everywhere the variable is referenced in the FLWOR expression. Listing 12-36 demonstrates the let clause in a FLWOR expression, with results shown in Figure 12-28.

Listing 12-36. let Clause

```
SELECT CatalogDescription.query
(
N'declare namespace ns =
"http://schemas.microsoft.com/sqlserver/2004/07/adventure-works/ProductModelDescription";
for $spec in //ns:ProductDescription/ns:Specifications/*
let $val := $spec/text()
order by fn:string($val[1]) ascending
return< spec>
{
$val
}
</spec>'
) AS Detail
FROM Production.ProductModel
WHERE ProductModelID = 19;
```

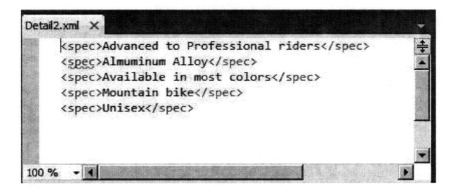

Figure 12-28. Results of a FLWOR Expression with the let Clause

UTF-16 Support

When SQL Server stores unicode data types with nchar and nvarchar it stores using UCS-2 encoding (UCS – Universal Character Set), meaning it counts every 2-byte character as single character. In recent years the charater limit was increased to 31 bits, and it would be difficult to store these characters given the fact that we only have 2 bytes per character. This led to the problem of SQL Server not handling some of the characters properly. In the previous versions of SQL Server, even though SQLXML supports UTF-16, the string functions only supported for UCS-2 unicode values. This means that even though the data can be stored and retrieved without losing the property, some of the string operations such as string length or substring functions provided wrong results since they don't recognize surrogate pairs.

Let's review this with an example, and in our case, let's say we have to store UTF-16 encoding such as musical symbol drum cleff-1 as a part of a name in our database. Drum-cleff-1 is represented by surrogate values 0xD834 and 0xDD25. Let's say we calculate the length of the string to see if SQL Server checks for surrogate pairs. Listing 12-37 demonstrates the creation of the sample row for our usage and Listing 12-38 uses the row that was created using Listing 12-37 to demonstrate UTF-16 encoding handling in SQL Server. Results for Listing 12-38 are shown in Figure 12-29.

Listing 12-37. Create Record to Demonstrate UTF-16

```
declare @BusinessEntityId int
INSERT INTO Person.BusinessEntity(rowguid, ModifiedDate)
VALUES (NEWID(),CURRENT_TIMESTAMP)
SET @BusinessEntityId=SCOPE_IDENTITY()
INSERT INTO [Person].[Person]
           ([BusinessEntityID]
           ,[PersonType]
           ,[NameStyle]
           ,[Title]
           ,[FirstName]
           ,[MiddleName]
           ,[LastName]
           ,[Suffix]
           ,[EmailPromotion]
           ,[AdditionalContactInfo]
           ,[Demographics]
           ,[rowguid]
           ,[ModifiedDate])
     VALUES
```

```
(@BusinessEntityId,
'EM',
0,
NULL,
N'T'+nchar(0xD834)+nchar(0xDD25),
'J',
'Kim',
NULL,
0,
NULL,
'<IndividualSurvey xmlns="http://schemas.microsoft.com/sqlserver/2004/07/
adventure-works/IndividualSurvey"><TotalPurchaseYTD>0</TotalPurchaseYTD></IndividualSurvey>',
NEWID(),
CURRENT_TIMESTAMP)
```

Listing 12-38. SQL Server to Check for Presence of Surrogates

```
SELECT
p.NameStyle AS "processing-instruction(nameStyle)",
p.BusinessEntityID AS "Person/@ID",
p.ModifiedDate AS "comment()",
FirstName AS "Person/Name/First",
Len(FirstName) AS "Person/FirstName/Length",
MiddleName AS "Person/Name/Middle",
LastName AS "Person/Name/Last"
FROM Person.Person p
WHERE BusinessEntityID=20778
FOR XML PATH;
```

```
<row>
    <?nameStyle 0?>
    <Person ID="20778" />
    <!--2012-08-04T02:48:40.307-->
    <Person>
        <Name>
            <First>T◻</First>
        </Name>
        <FirstName>
            <Length>3</Length>
        </FirstName>
        <Name>
            <Middle>J</Middle>
            <Last>Kim</Last>
        </Name>
    </Person>
</row>
```

Figure 12-29. *Results of SQL Server UTF-16 Surrogate Pair*

From Figure 12-29, you can see that the query returns the column length to be 3 whereas the length should be 2 because length function calculates the number of characters and we have 2 characters in our string. Since the surrogate pair is not recognized, the number of characters is listed as 3 instead of 2.

To mitigate the above issue, in SQL Server 2012 there is full support for UTF-16/UCS-4, meaning the Xquery handles the surrogate pairs properly and returns the correct results for string operations and the operators such as =,==,<,>= and LIKE. Note that some of the string operators may already be surrogate aware. However since some of the applications are already developed and being used based on the older behavior, SQL Server 2012 added a new set of flags to the collation names to indicate that the collation is UTF-16 aware. The _SC (Supplementary Characters) flag will be appended to the version 100 collation names and it be applicable for nchar, nvarchar, and sql_variant data types.

Let's modify the code snippet we have from Listing 12-38 and add the _SC collation to the query to see how SQL Server calculates the column length properly. In this example let's include the supplementary characters collation so that SQL Server is UTF-16 aware. The modified code snippet is shown in Listing 12-39 and results are shown in Figure 12-30.

Listing 12-39. Surroage Pair with UTF-16 and _SC collation

```
SELECT
p.NameStyle AS "processing-instruction(nameStyle)",
p.BusinessEntityID AS "Person/@ID",
p.ModifiedDate AS "comment()",
FirstName AS "Person/Name/First",
Len(FirstName COLLATE Latin1_General_100_CS_AS_SC) AS "Person/FirstName/Length",
MiddleName AS "Person/Name/Middle",
LastName AS "Person/Name/Last"
FROM Person.Person p
WHERE BusinessEntityID = 20778
FOR XML PATH;
```

```
⊟<row>
    <?nameStyle 0?>
    <Person ID="20778" />
    <!--2012-08-04T02:48:40.307-->
⊟   <Person>
⊟     <Name>
         <First>T⊠</First>
      </Name>
⊟     <FirstName>
         <Length>2</Length>
      </FirstName>
⊟     <Name>
         <Middle>J</Middle>
         <Last>Kim</Last>
      </Name>
    </Person>
 </row>
```

Figure 12-30. *Results of SQL Server UTF-16 Surrogate Pair with _SC collation*

Figure 12-30 demonstrates that by using supplementary characters collation, SQL Server now is UTF-16 aware, and it calculates the column length as it should: we see the proper value of 2 for the column length.

To maintain backward compatibility SQL Server is surrogate pair aware only when the compatibility mode is set to SQL11 or higher. If the compatability mode is set to SQL10 or lower, the fn:string-length and fn:substring will not be surrogate aware and the older behavior will continue.

Summary

This chapter has expanded the discussion of SQL Server XML functionality that we began in Chapter 11. In particular, we focused on the SQL Server implementations of XPath and XQuery. We provided a more detailed discussion of the SQL Server FOR XML PATH clause XPath implementation, including XPath expression syntax, axis specifiers, and supported node tests. We also discussed SQL Server support for XML namespaces via the WITH XMLNAMESPACES clause.

We used the majority of this chapter to detail SQL Server support for XQuery, which provides a powerful set of expression types, functions, operators, and support for the rich XDM data type system. SQL Server support for XQuery has improved with the release of SQL Server 2012, including new options like the FLWOR expression let clause, support for date and time literals without specifying explicit time offsets, and UTF-16 support and Supplementary Characters collation.

The next chapter discusses SQL Server 2012 catalog views and dynamic management views and functions that provide a way to look under the hood of your databases and server instances.

EXERCISES

1. [True/False] The FOR XML PATH clause supports a subset of the W3C XPath recommendation.

2. [Choose one] Which of the following symbols is used in XQuery and XPath as an axis specifier to identify XML attributes:

   - An at sign (@)
   - An exclamation point (!)
   - A period (.)
   - Two periods (..)

3. [Fill in the blanks] The context item, indicated by a single period (.) in XPath and XQuery, specifies the current _____ or scalar _____ being accessed at any given point in time during query execution.

4. [Choose all that apply] You can declare namespaces for XQuery expressions in SQL Server using which of the following methods:

   a. The T-SQL WITH XMLNAMESPACES clause
   - The XQuery declare default element namespace statement
   - The T-SQL CREATE XML NAMESPACE statement
   - The XQuery declare namespace statement

5. [Fill in the blanks] In XQuery, you can dynamically construct XML via _____ constructors or _____ constructors.

6. [True/False] SQL Server 2012 supports the for, let, where, order by, and return clauses of XQuery FLWOR expressions.

7. [Fill in the blanks] _SC collation enables SQL Server to be _____.

8. [Choose all that apply] SQL Server supports the following types of XQuery comparison operators:

   a. Array comparison operators
   b. General comparison operators
   c. Node comparison operators
   d. Value comparison operators

CHAPTER 13

■ ■ ■

Catalog Views and Dynamic Management Views

SQL Server has always offered access to metadata describing your databases, tables, views, and other database objects. Prior to the introduction of catalog views in SQL Server 2005, the primary methods of accessing this metadata included system tables, system SPs, INFORMATION_SCHEMA views, and SQL Distributed Management Objects (SQL-DMO). Catalog views provide access to a richer set of detailed information than any one of these options provided in previous SQL Server releases. SQL Server even includes catalog views that allow you to access server-wide configuration metadata.

■ **Note**   *Metadata* is simply data that describes data. SQL Server 2012 databases are largely "self-describing." The data describing the objects, structures, and relationships that comprise a database are stored within the database itself. This data describing the database structure and objects is what we refer to as metadata.

SQL Server 2012 also provides dynamic management views (DMVs) and dynamic management functions (DMFs) that allow you to access server state information. The SQL Server DMVs and DMFs provide a relational tabular view of internal SQL Server data structures that would be otherwise inaccessible. Examples of metadata that can be accessed include information about the state of internal memory structures, the contents of caches and buffers, and statuses of processes and components. You can use the information returned by DMVs and DMFs to diagnose server problems, monitor server health, and tune performance. In this chapter, we will discuss catalog views, DMVs, and DMFs.

Catalog Views

Catalog views provide insight into database objects and server-wide configuration options in much the same way that system tables, system SPs, and INFORMATION_SCHEMA views did in previous releases of SQL Server. Catalog views offer advantages over these older methods of accessing database and server metadata, including the following:

- Catalog views, unlike system SPs, can be used in queries with results joined to other catalog views or tables. You can also limit the results returned by catalog views with a WHERE clause.

- Catalog views offer SQL Server-specific information not available through the INFORMATION_SCHEMA views. The reason is that although INFORMATION_SCHEMA views are still included in SQL Server to comply with the ISO standard, they may not be regularly updated. So it is advisable to use catalog views to access the metadata instead of the system SPs or INFORMATION_SCHEMA views.

- Catalog views provide richer information than system tables and simplify the data access from the system tables regardless of the schema changes of the underlying system tables. There are also more catalog views available than legacy system tables since some catalog views inherit rows from other catalog views.

Many catalog views follow an inheritance model in which some catalog views are defined as extensions to other catalog views. The sys.tables catalog view, for instance, inherits columns from the sys.objects catalog view. Some catalog views, such as sys.allcolumns, are defined as the union of two other catalog views. In this example, the sys.allcolumns catalog view is defined as the union of the sys.columns and sys.systemcolumns catalog views.

SQL Server supplies a wide range of catalog views that return metadata about all different types of database objects and server configuration options, SQL CLR assemblies, XML schema collections, the SQL Server resource governor, change tracking, and more. Rather than give a complete list of all the available catalog views, we will use this section to provide some usage examples and descriptions of the functionality available through catalog views.

■ **Tip** BOL details the complete list of available catalog views (there are over 100 of them) at http://msdn.microsoft.com/en-us/library/ms174365.aspx.

Table and Column Metadata

Way back in the pre-SQL Server Integration Services (SSIS) days, we spent a good deal of our time creating custom ETL (extract, transform, and load) solutions. One of the problems we faced was the quirky nature of the various bulk copy APIs available. Unlike SQL Server DML statements like INSERT, which specify columns to populate by name, the available bulk copy APIs require you to specify columns to populate by their ordinal position. This can lead to all kinds of problems if the table structure changes (e.g., if new columns are added, columns are removed, or the order of existing columns is changed). One way to deal with this type of disconnect is to create your own column name-to-ordinal position-mapping function. You can use catalog views to access exactly this type of functionality. In Listing 13-1, we join the sys.schemas, sys.tables, sys.columns, and sys.types catalog views to return column-level metadata about the AdventureWorks Person.Address table. The results are shown in Figure 13-1.

Listing 13-1. Retrieving Column-level Metadata with Catalog Views

```
SELECT
s.name AS schema_name,
t.name AS table_name,
t.type_desc AS table_type,
c.name AS column_name,
c.column_id,
ty.name AS data_type_name,
c.max_Length,
c.precision,
c.scale,
c.is_nullable FROM sys.schemas s INNER JOIN sys.tables t
```

```
ON s.schema_id = t.schema_id INNER JOIN sys.columns c
ON t.object_id = c.object_id INNER JOIN sys.types ty
ON c.system_type_id = ty.system_type_id AND c.user_type_id = ty.user_type_id WHERE
s.name = 'Person'
AND t.name = 'Address';
```

	schema_name	table_name	table_type	column_name	column_id	data_type_name	max_Length	precision	scale	is_nullable
1	Person	Address	USER_TABLE	AddressID	1	int	4	10	0	0
2	Person	Address	USER_TABLE	AddressLine1	2	nvarchar	120	0	0	0
3	Person	Address	USER_TABLE	AddressLine2	3	nvarchar	120	0	0	1
4	Person	Address	USER_TABLE	City	4	nvarchar	60	0	0	0
5	Person	Address	USER_TABLE	StateProvinceID	5	int	4	10	0	0
6	Person	Address	USER_TABLE	PostalCode	6	nvarchar	30	0	0	0
7	Person	Address	USER_TABLE	SpatialLocation	7	geography	-1	0	0	1
8	Person	Address	USER_TABLE	rowguid	8	uniqueidentifier	16	0	0	0
9	Person	Address	USER_TABLE	ModifiedDate	9	datetime	8	23	3	0

Figure 13-1. *Retrieving Column-level Metadata*

This type of metadata is also useful for administrative applications or dynamic queries that need to run against several different tables for which you don't necessarily know the structure in advance.

Whether it is for administrative applications, bulk loading, or dynamic queries that need to run against several different tables, SQL Server catalog views can provide structure and attribute information for database objects. SQL Server 2012 provides several methods of retrieving metadata.

Querying Permissions

Another administrative task that can be performed through catalog views is querying and scripting database object permissions. Listing 13-2 begins this demonstration by creating a couple of new users named jack and jill in the AdventureWorks database. The jill user is assigned permissions to human resources-related objects, while jack is assigned permissions to production objects.

Listing 13-2. Creating the Jack and Jill Users

```
CREATE USER jill WITHOUT LOGIN;
CREATE USER jack WITHOUT LOGIN;
GRANT SELECT, INSERT
ON Schema::HumanResources TO jill;
GRANT SELECT
ON dbo.ufnGetContactInformation TO jill;
GRANT EXECUTE
ON HumanResources.uspUpdateEmployeeLogin TO jill;
DENY SELECT
ON Schema::Sales TO jill;
DENY SELECT
ON HumanResources.Shift (ModifiedDate) TO jill;
GRANT SELECT, UPDATE, INSERT, DELETE
ON Schema::Production TO jack WITH GRANT OPTION;
```

We have granted and denied permissions to these users on a wide selection of objects for demonstration purposes. The query in Listing 13-3 is a modified version of an example first published by SQL Server MVP Louis Davidson. The code uses the `sys.databasepermissions`, `sys.databaseprincipals`, and `sys.objects` catalog views to query the permissions granted and denied to database principals within the database. The results are shown in Figure 13-2.

Listing 13-3. Querying Permissions on AdventureWorks Objects

```
WITH Permissions (
permission,
type,
obj_name,
db_principal,
grant_type,
schema_name ) AS
(
    SELECT dp.permission_name,
        CASE dp.class_desc
        WHEN 'OBJECT_OR_COLUMN' THEN
        CASE
        WHEN  minor_id  >  0  THEN  'COLUMN'
        ELSE  o.type_desc
        END
        ELSE dp.class_desc
        END,
        CASE dp.class_desc
        WHEN  'SCHEMA'  THEN  SCHEMA_NAME(dp.major_id)
        WHEN 'OBJECT_OR_COLUMN' THEN
        CASE
        WHEN  dp.minor_id  =  0  THEN object_name(dp.major_id)
        ELSE
        (
        SELECT object_name(o.object_id) + '.' + c.name
        FROM sys.columns c
        WHERE  c.object_id  =  dp.major_id
        AND  c.column_id  =  dp.minor_id
        )
        END
        ELSE '**UNKNOWN**'
        END,
        dpr.name,
        dp.state_desc,
        SCHEMA_NAME(o.schema_id)
    FROM  sys.database_permissions  dp
    INNER JOIN sys.database_principals dpr
        ON  dp.grantee_principal_id  =  dpr.principal_id
    LEFT  JOIN  sys.objects  o
        ON o.object_id = dp.major_id
    WHERE dp.major_id > 0
)
```

```
SELECT
    p.permission,
    CASE type
        WHEN 'SCHEMA' THEN 'Schema::' + obj_name
        ELSE schema_name + '.' + obj_name
    END  AS  name,
    p.type,
    p.db_principal,
    p.grant_type
FROM Permissions p
ORDER  BY
    p.db_principal,
    p.permission;
GO
```

permission	name	type	db_principal	grant_type
1	DELETE	Schema::Production	SCHEMA	jack	GRANT_WITH_GRANT_OPTION
2	INSERT	Schema::Production	SCHEMA	jack	GRANT_WITH_GRANT_OPTION
3	SELECT	Schema::Production	SCHEMA	jack	GRANT_WITH_GRANT_OPTION
4	UPDATE	Schema::Production	SCHEMA	jack	GRANT_WITH_GRANT_OPTION
5	EXECUTE	HumanResources.uspUpdateEmployeeLogin	SQL_STORED_PROCEDURE	jill	GRANT
6	INSERT	Schema::HumanResources	SCHEMA	jill	GRANT
7	SELECT	Schema::HumanResources	SCHEMA	jill	GRANT
8	SELECT	HumanResources.Shift.ModifiedDate	COLUMN	jill	DENY
9	SELECT	dbo.ufnGetContactInformation	SQL_TABLE_VALUED_FUNCTION	jill	GRANT
10	SELECT	Schema::Sales	SCHEMA	jill	DENY

Figure 13-2. *Results of the Permissions Query*

As you can see in Figure 13-2, the query retrieves the explicit permissions granted and denied to the jack and jill database principals. These permissions are shown for each object along with information about the objects themselves. This simple example can be expanded to perform additional tasks, such as scripting object permissions.

■ **Tip** *Explicit permissions* are permissions explicitly granted or denied through T-SQL GRANT, DENY, and REVOKE statements. The effective permissions of a principal are a combination of the principal's explicit permissions, permissions inherited from the roles or groups to which the principal belongs, and permissions implied by other permissions. You can use the sys.fn_my_permissions system function to view your effective permissions.

Dynamic Management Views and Functions

In addition to catalog views, SQL Server 2012 provides 177 DMVs and DMFs that give you access to internal server state information. DMVs and DMFs are designed specifically for the benefit of database administrators (DBAs), but they can provide developers with extremely useful insights into the internal workings of SQL Server as well. Having access to this server state information can enhance the server management and administration experience, and help to identify potential problems and performance issues (for which developers are increasingly sharing responsibility).

SQL Server provides DMVs and DMFs that are scoped at the database level and at the server level. All DMVs and DMFs are in the sys schema, and their names all start with dm*. There are several categories of DMVs and DMFs, with most being grouped together using standard name prefixes. We have listed some of the most commonly used categories in Table 13-1.

Table 13-1. *Commonly Used DMV and DMF Categories*

Names	Description
sys.dm_cdc_*	Contains information about Change Data Capture (CDC) transactions and log sessions.
sys.dm_exec_*	Returns information related to user code execution.
sys.dm_fts_*	Retrieves information about integrated Full-Text Search (iFTS) functionality.
sys.dm_os_*	Displays low-level details such as locks, memory usage, and scheduling.
sys.dm_tran_*	Provides information about current transactions and lock resources.
sys.dm_io_*	Allows you to monitor network and disk I/O.
sys.dm_db_*	Returns information about databases and database-level objects.

We gave an example of DMV and DMF usage in Chapter 5 with an SP that extracts information from the SQL Server query plan cache. In this section, we will explore more uses for DMVs and DMFs.

Index Metadata

SQL Server metadata is useful for performing tedious administrative tasks, like identifying potential performance issues, updating statistics, and rebuilding indexes. Creating a customized procedure to perform these tasks gives you the ability to create scripts that are flexible and target the maintenance tasks being performed, which is not an option available with the standard maintenance plan. Listing 13-4 uses catalog views to identify all tables in the AdventureWorks database with clustered or nonclustered indexes defined on them. The procedure then generates T-SQL ALTER INDEX statements to rebuild all the indexes defined on these tables and also updates the statistics and recompiles stored procedures and triggers. We have kept this example fairly simple, although it can be used as a basis for more complex index-rebuilding procedures that make decisions based on various scenarios like rebuilding indexes for all the databases in the server and that also consider factors such as LOB to reindex the objects. Figure 13-3 shows the ALTER INDEX statements created by the procedure.

Listing 13-4. Stored Procedure to Rebuild Table Indexes

```
CREATE PROCEDURE dbo.RebuildIndexes
        @db sysname = 'Adventureworks',
        @online bit = 1,
        @maxfrag int = 10,
        @rebuildthreshold int = 30,
        @WeekdayRebuildOffline int = 1
AS
BEGIN;
        SET NOCOUNT ON;
        DECLARE
                @objectid int,
                @indexid int,
```

```
        @indextype nvarchar(60),
        @schemaname nvarchar(130),
        @objectname nvarchar(130),
        @indexname nvarchar(130),
        @frag float,
        @sqlcommand nvarchar(4000);

-- Select tables and indexes from the
-- sys.dm_db_index_physical_stats function based on the threhold defined
SELECT
        object_id AS objectid,
        index_id AS indexid,
        index_type_desc AS indextype,
        avg_fragmentation_in_percent AS frag
INTO
        #reindexobjects
FROM
        sys.dm_db_index_physical_stats(DB_ID(@db), NULL, NULL, NULL, 'LIMITED')
WHERE
        avg_fragmentation_in_percent > @maxfrag
        AND index_id > 0

-- Declare the cursor for the list of objects to be processed.
DECLARE objects CURSOR FOR
        SELECT o.* FROM #reindexobjects o
        INNER JOIN sys.indexes i ON i.object_id = o.objectid
        WHERE i.is_disabled = 0 AND i.is_hypothetical = 0;

-- Open the cursor.
OPEN objects;

WHILE (1 = 1)
BEGIN;
        FETCH NEXT FROM objects INTO @objectid, @indexid, @indextype, @frag;
        IF @@FETCH_STATUS < 0 BREAK;
        SELECT @objectname = QUOTENAME(o.name), @schemaname = QUOTENAME(s.name)
        FROM sys.objects AS o
        JOIN sys.schemas AS s ON s.schema_id = o.schema_id
        WHERE o.object_id = @objectid;

        SELECT @indexname = QUOTENAME(name)
        FROM sys.indexes
        WHERE object_id = @objectid AND index_id = @indexid;

        SET @sqlcommand = N'ALTER INDEX ' + @indexname + N' ON ' +
                            @schemaname + N'.' + @objectname;

        IF @frag > @rebuildthreshold
        BEGIN;
                SET @sqlcommand = @sqlcommand + N' REBUILD';
```

```
                         IF (DATEPART(WEEKDAY, GETDATE()) <> @WeekdayRebuildOffline)
                 AND ((@indextype Like 'HEAP') OR (@indextype like '%CLUSTERED%'))
                         SET @sqlcommand = @sqlcommand + N' WITH (ONLINE = ON)';
                 END;
                 ELSE
                         SET @sqlcommand = @sqlcommand + N' REORGANIZE';
                 PRINT N'Executing: ' + @sqlcommand;
                 EXEC (@sqlcommand) ;
         END;

         -- Close and deallocate the cursor.
         CLOSE objects;
         DEALLOCATE objects;

         --  UPDATE STATISTICS & SP_RECOMPILE
         DECLARE tablelist CURSOR FOR
                 SELECT distinct OBJECT_NAME(o.objectid) FROM #reindexobjects o;

         -- Open the cursor.
         OPEN tablelist;

         FETCH NEXT FROM tablelist INTO @objectname;

         -- Loop through the partitions.
         WHILE @@FETCH_STATUS = 0
         BEGIN;
                 --Update Statistics
                 SET @sqlcommand = ' UPDATE STATISTICS ' + @objectname;
                 PRINT N'Executing: ' + @sqlcommand;
                 EXEC (@sqlcommand) ;

                 --Recompile Stored Procedures and Triggers
                 SET @sqlcommand = ' EXEC sp_recompile ' + @objectname;
                 PRINT N'Executing: ' + @sqlcommand;
                 EXEC (@sqlcommand) ;
                 FETCH NEXT FROM tablelist INTO @objectname;
         END;

         CLOSE tablelist;
         DEALLOCATE tablelist;
         DROP TABLE #reindexobjects;
END;
GO
```

```
Executing: ALTER INDEX [PK_DatabaseLog_DatabaseLogID] ON [dbo].[DatabaseLog] REORGANIZE
Executing: ALTER INDEX [PK_DatabaseLog_DatabaseLogID] ON [dbo].[DatabaseLog] REORGANIZE
Executing: ALTER INDEX [PK_ProductInventory_ProductID_LocationID] ON [Production].[ProductInventory] REORGANIZE
Executing: ALTER INDEX [PK_SpecialOfferProduct_SpecialOfferID_ProductID] ON [Sales].[SpecialOfferProduct] REBUILD WITH (ONLINE = ON)
Executing: ALTER INDEX [PK_SpecialOfferProduct_SpecialOfferID_ProductID] ON [Sales].[SpecialOfferProduct] REBUILD WITH (ONLINE = ON)
Executing: ALTER INDEX [PK_SpecialOfferProduct_SpecialOfferID_ProductID] ON [Sales].[SpecialOfferProduct] REBUILD WITH (ONLINE = ON)
Executing: ALTER INDEX [PXML_ProductModel_CatalogDescription] ON [Production].[ProductModel] REBUILD
Executing: ALTER INDEX [PXML_ProductModel_CatalogDescription] ON [Production].[ProductModel] REBUILD
Executing: ALTER INDEX [PXML_ProductModel_CatalogDescription] ON [Production].[ProductModel] REBUILD
Executing: ALTER INDEX [PXML_ProductModel_CatalogDescription] ON [Production].[ProductModel] REBUILD
Executing: ALTER INDEX [PXML_ProductModel_Instructions] ON [Production].[ProductModel] REBUILD
Executing: ALTER INDEX [PXML_ProductModel_Instructions] ON [Production].[ProductModel] REBUILD
Executing: ALTER INDEX [PXML_ProductModel_Instructions] ON [Production].[ProductModel] REBUILD
Executing: ALTER INDEX [PXML_ProductModel_Instructions] ON [Production].[ProductModel] REBUILD
Executing: ALTER INDEX [PK_StateProvince_StateProvinceID] ON [Person].[StateProvince] REBUILD WITH (ONLINE = ON)
Executing: ALTER INDEX [PK_StateProvince_StateProvinceID] ON [Person].[StateProvince] REBUILD WITH (ONLINE = ON)
Executing: ALTER INDEX [PK_StateProvince_StateProvinceID] ON [Person].[StateProvince] REBUILD WITH (ONLINE = ON)
Executing: ALTER INDEX [PK_StateProvince_StateProvinceID] ON [Person].[StateProvince] REBUILD WITH (ONLINE = ON)
Executing: ALTER INDEX [PK_ProductModelProductDescriptionCulture_ProductModelID_ProductDescriptionID_CultureID] ON [Production].[Produc
Executing: ALTER INDEX [AK_BillOfMaterials_ProductAssemblyID_ComponentID_StartDate] ON [Production].[BillOfMaterials] REORGANIZE
Executing: ALTER INDEX [AK_BillOfMaterials_ProductAssemblyID_ComponentID_StartDate] ON [Production].[BillOfMaterials] REORGANIZE
```

Figure 13-3. *ALTER INDEX Statements to Rebuild Indexes on AdventureWorks Tables*

The procedure in Listing 13-4 uses the DMV sys.dm_db_index_physical_stats to retrieve a list of all tables in the database that have index defined on them based on the thresholds defined for the fragmentation:

```
SELECT
        object_id AS objectid,
        index_id AS indexid,
        index_type_desc AS indextype,
        avg_fragmentation_in_percent AS frag
INTO
        #reindexobjects
FROM
        sys.dm_db_index_physical_stats(DB_ID(@db), NULL, NULL, NULL, 'LIMITED')
WHERE
        avg_fragmentation_in_percent > @maxfrag
        AND index_id > 0
```

The procedure then uses the cursor to loop through the active indexes. Depending on the index rebuild thresholds, the procedure determines whether the index has to be rebuilt or reorganized. The procedure also takes into consideration if the process can be performed online or offline based on the day of the week. For example, you may consider rebuilding the index offline during weekends when the database is not too active. The procedure then executes ALTER INDEX statements for each index:

```
DECLARE objects CURSOR FOR
        SELECT o.* FROM #reindexobjects o
        INNER JOIN sys.indexes i ON i.object_id = o.objectid
        WHERE i.is_disabled = 0 AND i.is_hypothetical = 0;

-- Open the cursor.
OPEN objects;

WHILE (1 = 1)
BEGIN;
        FETCH NEXT FROM objects INTO @objectid, @indexid, @indextype, @frag;
        IF @@FETCH_STATUS < 0 BREAK;
        SELECT @objectname = QUOTENAME(o.name), @schemaname = QUOTENAME(s.name)
```

```
            FROM sys.objects AS o
            JOIN sys.schemas AS s ON s.schema_id = o.schema_id
            WHERE o.object_id = @objectid;

            SELECT @indexname = QUOTENAME(name)
            FROM sys.indexes
            WHERE object_id = @objectid AND index_id = @indexid;

            SET @sqlcommand = N'ALTER INDEX ' + @indexname + N' ON ' +
                                            @schemaname + N'.' + @objectname;

            IF @frag > @rebuildthreshold
            BEGIN;
                    SET @sqlcommand = @sqlcommand + N' REBUILD';

                    IF (DATEPART(WEEKDAY, GETDATE()) <> @WeekdayRebuildOffline)
                            AND ((@indextype Like 'HEAP') OR (@indextype like '%CLUSTERED%'))
                    SET @sqlcommand = @sqlcommand + N' WITH (ONLINE = ON)';
            END;
            ELSE
                    SET @sqlcommand = @sqlcommand + N' REORGANIZE';
            PRINT N'Executing: ' + @sqlcommand;
            EXEC (@sqlcommand) ;
END;

-- Close and deallocate the cursor.
CLOSE objects;
DEALLOCATE objects;
```

The procedure then uses the cursor to loop through the objects, updates the statistics, and then recompiles the stored procedures and triggers:

```
DECLARE tablelist CURSOR FOR
        SELECT distinct OBJECT_NAME(o.objectid) FROM #reindexobjects o;

-- Open the cursor.
OPEN tablelist;

FETCH NEXT FROM tablelist INTO @objectname;

-- Loop through the partitions.
WHILE @@FETCH_STATUS = 0
BEGIN;
        --Update Statistics
        SET @sqlcommand = ' UPDATE STATISTICS ' + @objectname;
        PRINT N'Executing: ' + @sqlcommand;
        EXEC (@sqlcommand) ;

        --Recompile Stored Procedures and Triggers
        SET @sqlcommand = ' EXEC sp_recompile ' + @objectname;
        PRINT N'Executing: ' + @sqlcommand;
```

```
        EXEC (@sqlcommand) ;
        FETCH NEXT FROM tablelist INTO @objectname;
END;

CLOSE tablelist;
DEALLOCATE tablelist;
```

The procedure then cleans up the temporary objects that were created:

```
DROP TABLE #reindexobjects;
```

Session Information

The sys.dm_exec_sessions DMV returns one row per session on the server. The information returned is similar to that returned by the sp_who2 system SP. You can use this DMV to retrieve information that includes the database id, session id, login name, client program name, CPU time and memory usage, transaction isolation level, and session settings like ANSI_NULLS and ANSI_PADDING. Listing 13-5 is a simple query against the sys.dm_exec_sessions DMV. Partial results are shown in Figure 13-4.

Listing 13-5. Retrieving Session Information

```
SELECT
        db_name(database_id) dbname,
        session_id,
        host_name,
        program_name,
        client_interface_name,
        login_name,
        cpu_time,
        CASE WHEN ansi_nulls = 0 THEN 'OFF' ELSE 'ON' END ansi_nulls,
        CASE WHEN ansi_padding = 0 THEN 'OFF' ELSE 'ON' END ansi_padding
 FROM sys.dm_exec_sessions;
```

	dbname	session_id	host_name	program_name	client_interface_name	login_name	cpu_time	ansi_nulls	ansi_padding
35	master	51	SQL2012	Microsoft SQ...	.Net SqlClient Data P...	sqluser01	0	ON	ON
36	master	52	SQL2012	Microsoft SQ...	.Net SqlClient Data P...	sqluser01	0	ON	ON
37	Repor...	53	SQL2012	Report Server	.Net SqlClient Data P...	NT SERV...	0	ON	ON
38	Repor...	54	SQL2012	Report Server	.Net SqlClient Data P...	NT SERV...	0	ON	ON
39	master	55	SQL2012	Microsoft SQ...	.Net SqlClient Data P...	sqluser01	0	ON	ON
40	Repor...	56	SQL2012	Report Server	.Net SqlClient Data P...	NT SERV...	0	ON	ON
41	master	57	SQL2012	Microsoft SQ...	.Net SqlClient Data P...	sqluser01	0	ON	ON
42	master	58	SQL2012	Microsoft SQ...	.Net SqlClient Data P...	sqluser01	0	ON	ON
43	master	59	SQL2012	Microsoft SQ...	.Net SqlClient Data P...	sqluser01	0	ON	ON
44	master	60	SQL2012	Microsoft SQ...	.Net SqlClient Data P...	sqluser01	30	ON	ON
45	master	61	SQL2012	Microsoft SQ...	.Net SqlClient Data P...	sqluser01	0	ON	ON
46	master	62	SQL2012	Microsoft SQ...	.Net SqlClient Data P...	sqluser01	0	ON	ON

Figure 13-4. *Retrieving Session Information with sys.dm_exec_sessions*

You can also use sys.dm_exec_sessions to retrieve summarized information about sessions. Listing 13-6 presents summary information for every current session on the server. The results are shown in Figure 13-5.

Listing 13-6. Retrieving Summarized Session Information

```
SELECT
        login_name,
        SUM(cpu_time) AS tot_cpu_time,
        SUM(memory_usage) AS tot_memory_usage,
        AVG(total_elapsed_time) AS avg_elapsed_time,
        SUM(reads) AS tot_reads,
        SUM(writes) AS tot_writes,
        SUM(logical_reads) AS tot_logical_reads,
        COUNT(session_id) as tot_sessions
FROM sys.dm_exec_sessions WHERE session_id > 50
GROUP BY login_name;
```

	login_name	tot_cpu_time	tot_memory_usage	avg_elapsed_time	tot_reads	tot_writes	tot_logical_reads	tot_sessions
1	NT SERVICE\ReportServer$SQL2012	0	4	0	0	0	14	2
2	sqluser01	36288	12	23164	11914	21727	188065	7

Figure 13-5. *Summary Session Information*

Connection Information

In addition to session information, you can retrieve connection information via the sys.dm_exec_connections DMV. The sys.dm_exec_connections DMV returns connection information for every session with a sessionid greater than 50 (50 and below are used exclusively by the server). Listing 13-7 uses the DMV to retrieve connection information; the results are shown in Figure 13-6. Notice that this DMV also returns client network address, port, and authentication scheme information with no fuss.

Listing 13-7. Retrieving Connection Information

```
SELECT
        Session_id,
        client_net_address,
        auth_scheme,
        net_transport,
        client_tcp_port,
        local_tcp_port,
        connection_id
FROM sys.dm_exec_connections;
```

	session_id	client_net_address	auth_scheme	net_transport	client_tcp_port	local_tcp_port	connection_id
1	51	192.168.1.13	SQL	TCP	59238	53906	D598D7DC-D0A3-4707-BCFD-030518A98908
2	52	192.168.1.13	SQL	TCP	57084	53906	C42E4F70-DE13-496E-A7E3-E372DC3DE54F
3	53	192.168.1.13	SQL	TCP	57336	53906	755666E1-1507-4C60-9011-8C1653237EA2
4	54	192.168.1.13	SQL	TCP	59469	53906	7F2B5CB6-4D35-4ABA-9C81-C93DFB018916
5	55	<local machine>	NTLM	Shared memory	NULL	NULL	6EED30DE-19A9-4555-B946-B67B0AADE1C5
6	56	192.168.1.13	SQL	TCP	53841	53906	9B8C66BE-F4A5-469A-A8D9-D8D12D890710
7	57	<local machine>	NTLM	Shared memory	NULL	NULL	E4490733-602D-44AE-878F-CDCE76C5B893
8	59	192.168.1.13	SQL	TCP	59243	53906	01B8011D-C2A3-4150-B794-ACD2CF3FE199
9	60	192.168.1.13	SQL	TCP	59290	53906	AAE03F98-6C65-4CA9-828E-474CB06D2B22

Figure 13-6. *Connection Information Retrieved via DMV*

Currently Executing SQL

The sys.dm_exec_requests DMV allows you to see all currently executing requests on SQL Server. When you combine the DMV sys.dm_exec_requests with sys.dm_exec_sessions, you can get information on the SQL statements that are executing at that point of time and whether the session is being blocked or not. You can also get additional information of any existing blocking which are active. You can use these DMV's to return the details on currently executing SQL, as shown in Listing 13-8. Partial results are shown in Figure 13-7.

■ **Tip** The sys.dm_exec_requests DMV can be used to retrieve additional information for currently executing requests like request CPU time, reads, writes, and the amount of granted memory, among others. The information returned is similar to what is returned by the sys.dm_exec_sessions DMV we described previously in this section, but on a per-request basis instead of a per-session basis.

Listing 13-8. Querying Currently Executing SQL Statements

```
SELECT
        s.session_id,
        r.request_id,
        r.blocking_session_id,
        DB_NAME(r.database_id) as database_name,
        r.[user_id],
        r.status AS request_status,
        s.status AS session_status,
        s.login_time,
        s.is_user_process,
        ISNULL (s.[host_name], '') AS [host_name],
        ISNULL (s.[program_name], '') AS [program_name],
        ISNULL (s.login_name, '') AS login_name,
        ISNULL (r.wait_type, '')  AS wait_type,
        ISNULL (r.last_wait_type, '') AS last_wait_type,
        ISNULL (r.wait_resource, '')  AS wait_resource,
        r.transaction_id,
        r.open_transaction_count,
        r.cpu_time AS request_cpu_time,
        r.logical_reads AS request_logical_reads,
        r.reads AS request_reads,
```

```
        r.writes AS request_writes,
        r.total_elapsed_time AS request_total_elapsed_time,
        r.start_time AS request_start_time,
        r.wait_time AS request_wait_time,
        s.memory_usage,
        s.cpu_time AS session_cpu_time,
        s.total_elapsed_time AS session_total_elapsed_time,
        s.last_request_start_time AS session_last_request_start_time,
        s.last_request_end_time AS session_last_request_end_time,
        r.command,
        r.sql_handle
FROM sys.dm_exec_sessions s
        LEFT OUTER MERGE JOIN sys.dm_exec_requests r
        ON s.session_id = r.session_id
WHERE r.session_id <> @@SPID AND
    ((r.session_id IS NOT NULL AND (s.is_user_process = 1 OR
        r.status NOT IN ('background', 'sleeping'))) OR
    (s.session_id IN (SELECT DISTINCT blocking_session_id
FROM sys.dm_exec_requests WHERE blocking_session_id ! = 0)))
OPTION (FORCE ORDER);
```

session_id	request_id	blocking_session_id	database_name	user_id	request_status	session_status	login_time	is_user_process	host_name	program_name
1	66	0	0	AdventureWorks	1	suspended	running	2012-07-09 04:14:23.660	1	SQL2012	Microsoft SQL Server Management
2	67	0	65	AdventureWorks	1	suspended	running	2012-07-09 18:18:29.137	1	SQL2012	Microsoft SQL Server Management

Figure 13-7. *Currently Executing SQL Statements*

The procedure in Listing 13-8 uses `sys.dm_exec_sessions` to retrieve the session details, and `sys.dm_exec_requests` to retrieve the request statistics. The field `session_id` returns the id for the current session that is being executed and the `blocking_session_id` returns the head blocker. If the query is not being blocked, the `blocking_session_id` will be 0.

The query filter then returns all active sessions. If there is blocking for any certain sessions, it will also return the head blocker even if the session is inactive.

```
    ((r.session_id IS NOT NULL AND (s.is_user_process = 1 OR r.status NOT IN ('background',
'sleeping'))) OR
    (s.session_id IN (SELECT DISTINCT blocking_session_id FROM sys.dm_exec_requests WHERE
blocking_session_id != 0)))
```

The query hint `OPTION (FORCE ORDER)` has been added to suppress the warning messages.

As you can see in the results shown in Figure 13-7, there were two active sessions in our SQL Server 2012 instance when we were running this query. Session id 67 is being blocked by session id 65 and `request_wait_time` field returns the wait time for session id 67 that is currently blocked in milliseconds. You can review the columns `wait_type` and `wait_resource` to understand what the session is waiting on and resolve the blocking issue. If you have more active sessions in your server, the query will report them all.

Most Expensive Queries

The `sys.dm_exec_query_stats` DMV allows you to see the aggregated performance statistics for the cached query plans. This DMV contains one row for each query plan and for stored procedures containing multiple statements will have more than one row. We can use this DMV in conjunction with `sys.dm_exec_sql_text` which shows the sql statement text based on the SQL handle and `sys.dm_exec_query_plan` DMV which shows the showplan in an XML format to retrieve the most expensive queries for the cached query plans in the server as shown in Listing 13-9. Partial results are shown in Figure 13-8. You can use the columns min_rows, max_rows, total_rows and last_rows to analyze the row statistics for the query plan since it has been last compiled. For example, if you have a long running query, and you are trying to analyze the cause for the query slowness, this information will help you to understand the maximum number of rows and average number of rows returned by the query over time and tune the query.

Listing 13-9. Querying Most Expensive Queries

```
SELECT
        DB_Name(qp.dbid) AS [DB],
        qp.dbid AS [DBID],
        qt.text,
        SUBSTRING(qt.TEXT,
        (qs.statement_start_offset/2) + 1,
                ((CASE qs.statement_end_offset
                        WHEN -1
                                THEN DATALENGTH(qt.TEXT)
                                ELSE qs.statement_end_offset
                        END - qs.statement_start_offset)/2) + 1) AS stmt_text,
        qs.execution_count,
        qs.total_rows,
        qs.min_rows,
        qs.max_rows,
        qs.last_rows,
        qs.total_logical_reads/qs.execution_count AS avg_logical_reads,
        qs.total_physical_reads/qs.execution_count AS avg_physical_reads,
        qs.total_logical_writes/qs.execution_count AS avg_writes,
        (qs.total_worker_time/1000)/qs.execution_count AS avg_CPU_Time_ms,
        qs.total_elapsed_time/qs.execution_count/1000 AS avg_elapsed_time_ms,
        qs.last_execution_time,
        qp.query_plan AS [Plan]
FROM sys.dm_exec_query_stats qs
        CROSS APPLY sys.dm_exec_sql_text(qs.sql_handle) qt
                CROSS APPLY sys.dm_exec_query_plan(qs.plan_handle) qp
ORDER BY
execution_count DESC, qs.total_logical_reads desc, total_rows desc;
```

Figure 13-8. *Most Expensive Queries*

You can use the DMV sys.dm_exec_query_stats and sys.dm_exec_sql_text to view the queries that are blocked in the server as shown in Listing 13-10. Partial results are shown in Figure 13-9.

Listing 13-10. Querying Most Blocked Queries

```sql
SELECT TOP 50
        (total_elapsed_time - total_worker_time) / qs.execution_count AS average_time_blocked,
        total_elapsed_time - total_worker_time AS total_time_blocked,
        qs.execution_count,
        qt.text blocked_query,
        DB_NAME(qt.dbid) dbname
FROM sys.dm_exec_query_stats qs
CROSS APPLY sys.dm_exec_sql_text(qs.sql_handle) qt
ORDER BY average_time_blocked DESC;
```

	average_time_blocked	total_time_blocked	execution_count	blocked_query	dbname
1	27473428307	27473428307	1	begin tran select * from production.product	NULL
2	2059109419	2059109419	1	SELECT * FROM Sales.SalesOrderDetail sod INNER JOI...	NULL
3	385547097	385547097	1	begin tran select * from production.product	NULL
4	376854960	376854960	1	create procedure select_product AS select * from producti...	AdventureWorks
5	5173840	10347681	2	SELECT * FROM Sales.SalesOrderDetail sod INNER JO...	NULL
6	628700	628700	1	SELECT DB_Name(qp.dbid) AS [DB], qt.text, SUBSTRI...	NULL
7	437365	874731	2	create procedure sys.sp_updatestats @resample char(8)='...	NULL
8	395732	395732	1	SELECT DB_Name(qp.dbid) AS [DB], qt.text, SUBSTRI...	NULL
9	331527	331527	1	SELECT DB_Name(qp.dbid) AS [DB], qt.text, SUBSTRI...	NULL
10	191252	191252	1	begin tran select * from production.product	NULL
11	123674	2720833	22	create procedure sys.sp_updatestats @resample char(8)='...	NULL
12	98655	2170428	22	create procedure sys.sp_updatestats @resample char(8)='...	NULL
13	48444	48444	1	select * from production.product	NULL
14	32058	1442613	45	create procedure sys.sp_updatestats @resample char(8)='...	NULL
15	5732	126108	22	create procedure sys.sp_updatestats @resample char(8)='...	NULL
16	15	93	6	select r.session_id, r.request_id, s.cpu_time, s.memory_u...	NULL
17	5	17	3	create procedure sys.sp_who2 — 1995/11/03 10:16 @t...	NULL
18	1	1	1	CREATE PROCEDURE [dbo].[AnnounceOrGetKey] @Mac...	ReportServer$SQL2012

Figure 13-9. Most Blocked Queries

As you can see in Figure 13-9 the dbname field lists the database name for some queries and does not return the database name for other queries. The reason is, sql_handle identifies only the text that is being submitted to the server. As only the text is being submitted to the server, potentially the query text can be generic enough that it can be submitted to multiple databases and in this case, the sql_handle cannot identify the database name. However, if a stored procedure resides in a database the database name can be identified and retrieved. In the above Figure 13-9, if you look at the rows 1 and 4, both queries reference the same select statement but the difference is that row 4 uses a stored procedure whereas row 1 uses a batch sql query. So, you can see that the database name was retrieved for row 4 which uses the stored procedure, while for row 1 it was not.

Tempdb Space

The tempdb system database holds a position of prominence for DBAs. The tempdb database constitutes a global server-wide resource shared by all sessions, connections, and databases for temporary storage on a single SQL Server instance. An improperly managed tempdb can bring a SQL Server instance to its knees. Listing 13-11 demonstrates a simple usage of sys.dm_db_file_space_usage to report free and used space in tempdb. The database_id for the system database tempdb is 2. The results are shown in Figure 13-10.

Listing 13-11. Querying Free and Used Space in Tempdb

```
SELECT
        db_name(database_id) AS Database_Name,
        SUM(unallocated_extent_page_count) AS free_pages,
        SUM(unallocated_extent_page_count) * 8.0 AS free_KB,
        SUM(user_object_reserved_page_count) AS user_object_pages,
        SUM(user_object_reserved_page_count) * 8.0 AS user_object_pages,
        SUM(internal_object_reserved_page_count) AS internal_object_pages,
        SUM(internal_object_reserved_page_count) * 8.0 AS internal_object_KB
FROM sys.dm_db_file_space_usage
WHERE database_id = 2
GROUP BY database_id;
```

database_name	free_pages	free_KB	user_object_pages	user_object_pages	internal_object_pages	internal_object_KB
1	tempdb	6568	52544.0	112	896.0	24	192.0

Figure 13-10. *Free and Used Space in Tempdb*

Tempdb can run out of space for various reasons, such as the objects created in the tempdb have not been dropped or the application is performing sort operations that take up the entire space allocated for the tempdb. When troubleshooting the tempdb space usage, it is important to understand the space allocation for the objects that currently reside in the tempdb. In addition to the sys.dm_db_file_space_usage DMV, SQL Server 2012 provides the sys.dm_db_partition_stats DMV that returns detailed information allocations per table. This DMV returns results based on the execution database context. The DMV returns the details on how much space has been reserved for the in-row, LOB data and variable length data in addition to the row-overflow data and how much has been used and the row count. If the table is not partitioned, then the partition number is returned as 1. Listing 13-12 demonstrates simple usage of sys.dm_db_partition_stats to report the user objects in tempdb and the details of the rowcount, reserved pages, used pages and the index type. Figure 13-11 returns partial result sets for the query.

Listing 13-12. Querying User Object Allocations in Tempdb

```
SELECT object_name(o.object_id) AS Object,
        CASE
                WHEN index_id = 0 then 'heap'
                WHEN index_id = 1 then 'clustered index'
                WHEN index_id > 1 then 'nonclustered index'
        END AS IndexType,
        SUM(reserved_page_count) AS ReservedPages,
        SUM(used_page_count) AS UsedPages,
        SUM(case when (index_id < 2) then row_count else 0 end) AS Rows
FROM sys.dm_db_partition_stats p JOIN sys.objects o ON p.object_id = o.object_id
WHERE type_desc = 'USER_TABLE'
GROUP BY o.object_id,index_id
ORDER BY sum(used_page_count) DESC;
```

	Object	IndexType	ReservedPages	UsedPages	Rows
1	#SalesOrderDetail	heap	1498	1496	121317
2	#Product	heap	16	14	504
3	#B8B161C1	heap	2	2	0
4	#B9A585FA	heap	0	0	0
5	#BF5E5F50	heap	0	0	0
6	#A59E8D4D	clustered index	0	0	0
7	#AD3FAF15	clustered index	0	0	0
8	#B01C1BC0	clustered index	0	0	0
9	#B5D4F516	clustered index	0	0	0
10	#AF27F787	heap	0	0	0
11	#1	heap	0	0	0
12	#B2046432	heap	0	0	0
13	#B7BD3D88	heap	0	0	0
14	#A0528389	heap	0	0	0
15	#A146A7C2	heap	0	0	0

Figure 13-11. *User Object Allocations in Tempdb*

In addition to this, we can use the DMV's sys.dm_db_session_space_usage and
sys.dm_db_task_space_usage to return details about the tempdb space usage based on specific session or task
to further narrow down the specific offender that consumes most tempdb space. Listing 13-13 demonstrates
simple usage of sys.dm_db_session_space_usage and sys.dm_db_task_space_usage DMVs to return the
session_id and the request associated with the session and return the object page allocation. Figure 13-12
returns a partial result set.

Listing 13-13. Querying User Object Allocations in Tempdb per Session

```
SELECT s.session_id, request_id,
       SUM(s.internal_objects_alloc_page_count+
              t.internal_objects_alloc_page_count)*8.0 AS internal_obj_pages_kb,
       SUM(s.user_objects_alloc_page_count) as user_obj_pages
FROM sys.dm_db_session_space_usage s JOIN sys.dm_db_task_space_usage t
       ON s.session_id = t.session_id
GROUP BY s.session_id, request_id;
```

	session_id	request_id	internal_obj_pages_kb	user_obj_pages
29	15	0	0.0	0
30	3	0	0.0	0
31	20	0	0.0	0
32	17	0	0.0	0
33	5	0	0.0	0
34	62	0	0.0	0
35	19	0	0.0	0
36	10	0	0.0	0
37	67	0	3712.0	0
38	24	0	0.0	0
39	12	0	0.0	0

Figure 13-12. *User Object Allocations in Tempdb with Session Data*

Server Resources

The sys.dm_os* DMVs and functions allow you to query detailed information about your server and resources. This is useful for retrieving server restart time or machine and configuration details such as whether you are using hyper threading. The DMV sys.dm_os_sys_info returns details about the server resources and also returns information on whether the SQL Server instance is physical or virtual and also details of the virtualization environment. The column virtual_machine_type_desc can be None, Hypervisor, or Other. None means the server is physical, and Hypervisor means the instance is running inside the hypervisor. Listing 13-14 retrieves server configuration information, including the number of logical CPUs on the server, the ratio of logical to physical CPUs, and physical and virtual memory available to the server, last server restart time and the hyper threading ratio. The results are shown in Figure 13-13.

Listing 13-14. Retrieving Low-level Configuration Information

```
SELECT
        cpu_count AS logical_CPUs,
        hyperthread_ratio,
        physical_memory_kb / 1048576.00 AS physical_MB,
        virtual_memory_kb / 1048576.00 AS virtual_MB,
        sqlserver_start_time,
        virtual_machine_type_desc
FROM sys.dm_os_sys_info;
```

	logical_CPUs	hyperthread_ratio	physical_MB	virtual_MB	sqlserver_start_time	virtual_machine_type_desc
1	8	8	15.9290771484	8191.9998779296	2012-07-01 00:13:54.260	NONE

Figure 13-13. *Server Configuration Details*

Another useful DMV to return the volume information is sys.dm_os_volume_stats. This DMV returns the volume information for the mount points as well, and you can check to see if the volume attribute is read-only or get the space utilization before performing a bulk operation. Checking the volume attribute would come in handy when you work with the Scalable Shared Database (SSD). SSD will enable you to attach a read-only volume to multiple SQL Server instances to help scale out the database. Listing 13-15 demonstrates a simple query that lists the volume information for all the databases including the database name, file name, and the volume id and mount points along with the space used. Partial results are shown in Figure 13-14.

Listing 13-15. Return Volume Information for All Databases

```
SELECT
        DB_NAME(f.database_id) AS DBName,
        f.name AS FileName,
        volume_mount_point,
        volume_id,
        logical_volume_name,
        total_bytes,
        available_bytes,
        CAST(CAST(available_bytes AS FLOAT)/ CAST(total_bytes AS FLOAT) AS DECIMAL(18,1))
* 100 AS [Space Used %],
        v.is_read_only
FROM sys.master_files  f
        CROSS APPLY sys.dm_os_volume_stats(f.database_id, f.file_id) v
ORDER BY f.database_id DESC;
```

Figure 13-14. Return Volume Information for All Databases

When the SQL Server process creates a dump file or mini dumps, you have to browse through the SQL Server error logs to locate the dump file and start investigating the issue. To facilitate your locating of the dump file, SQL Server 2012 introduces a DMV called sys.dm_server_memory_dumps. This DMV stores all the SQL Server dumps so that you can easily locate the dump file path along with the name size and the creation date. Listing 13-16 demonstrates the query that will list the details of the SQL dumps, and results are shown in Figure 13-15. In Figure 13-15, you can see that we have 2 SQL mini dumps in our server with the path to the dumps and the creation time to make it simple to locate the dump files. You can also correlate the dumps to the application log files to determine the code that caused the dump.

Listing 13-16. List SQL Server Dumps

```
select * from sys.dm_server_memory_dumps
```

Figure 13-15. *Return SQL Server Dump Details*

Another useful DMV is the `sys.dm_server_registry`, which lists all SQL Server registry settings. For example if you are calling CLR procedures in the code and you want to check and see if the trace flag 6527 is not enabled for the SQL Server instance so that you can make sure SQL Server will generate memory dump on the first occurrence of an out-of-memory exception, this DMV makes it easier for you to perform that check. Listing 13-17 demonstrates the query usage and Figure 13-16 shows partial result set.

Listing 13-17. List SQL Server Instance Registry Settings

```
select * from sys.dm_server_registry
```

Figure 13-16. *Return SQL Server Instance Registry Keys and Values*

Unused Indexes

Another important aspect to managing a database is determining which indexes are used and which ones aren't because indexes consume storage space and the query optimizer uses them to efficiently access the data as well. If an index is not being used, then the storage space that is being consumed by that index is an overhead. SQL Server provides the `sys.dm_db_index_usage_stats` DMV to report which indexes have been used since the SQL Server service was last started. When a query accesses the indexes the objective is to seek. If the index has a high number of user_scans, then it is a candidate for tuning so that the index can be seeked. If the index has a high number of updates and little or no seeks, lookups, or scans, then we can safely assume that the index is not being used, and hence it can be removed. Listing 13-18 demonstrates a simple query that lists all indexes that have not been used since the service was last restarted for AdventureWorks database. Partial results are shown in Figure 13-17.

Listing 13-18. Listing Unused Indexes

```
USE AdventureWorks;
SELECT
        DB_NAME() AS DatabaseName,
        OBJECT_SCHEMA_NAME(i.object_id, s.database_id) AS SchemaName,
        OBJECT_NAME(i.object_id) AS TableName,
        i.name AS IndexName,
```

```
            user_updates,
            user_seeks,
            user_scans,
            user_lookups,
            system_updates,
            last_user_seek,
            last_user_update
FROM sys.indexes i
        LEFT JOIN sys.dm_db_index_usage_stats s ON s.object_id = i.object_id AND
i.index_id = s.index_id
WHERE s.database_id = DB_ID()
ORDER BY last_user_update DESC;
```

Figure 13-17. *Indexes That Have Not Been Used Recently*

As you can see in Figure 13-17, the query returns index usage details of the table and the corresponding index. user_scans returns number of times the index has been scanned. user_seeks returns the number of times the index has been seeked. user_lookups returns the number of times the index has been used in bookmark lookups. user_updates returns number of times the index has been updated, and system_updates returns number of times the index was updated by the system. From the above Figure 13-17, you can see that the indexes AK_Product_Name and IX_vProductAndDescription have user_updates, but no user_seeks/scans/lookups which means that these indexes have not been used since the last system restart. While the indexes listed by this query have not been used since the last restart, that's no guarantee that they will not be used in the future. Instead of deleting the index based on the queries, if you gather index usage information like this on a regular basis, you can develop a picture of index usage patterns. You can use this information to optimize existing indexes and redesign or drop irrelevant indexes.

Wait Stats

Finally, let's look at one of the DMVs that will help you quickly narrow down the performance issue you are dealing with, whether it involves IO, CPU, network, locking, or memory issues. The DMV is sys.dm_os_wait_stats, and this DMV is helpful to understand why SQL Server is waiting for the resource since the server has been restarted. For example, your application team might notice a performance issue and they may conclude that multiple processes are blocking each other; however the real issue could be the delay associated with the log cache being flushed to the disk. Listing 13-19 shows the query to list the top 20 waits since the time the server has been restarted or the statistics has been cleared. Partial results have been shown in Figure 13-18.

Listing 13-19. List Top 20 Wait Types for the SQL Server Instance

```
SELECT TOP 20
 wait_type,
 wait_time_ms / 1000 wait_time_secs,
 CONVERT(DECIMAL(12,2), wait_time_ms * 100.0
                 / SUM(wait_time_ms) OVER()) Per_waiting
FROM sys.dm_os_wait_stats
ORDER BY wait_time_ms DESC;
```

	wait_type	wait_time_secs	Per_waiting
1	FT_IFTS_SCHEDULER_IDLE_WAIT	3124291	22.85
2	SQLTRACE_INCREMENTAL_FLUSH_SLEEP	1050835	7.68
3	LOGMGR_QUEUE	1050824	7.68
4	DIRTY_PAGE_POLL	1050820	7.68
5	REQUEST_FOR_DEADLOCK_SEARCH	1050809	7.68
6	HADR_FILESTREAM_IOMGR_IOCOMPLETION	1050793	7.68
7	XE_TIMER_EVENT	1050784	7.68
8	LAZYWRITER_SLEEP	1050734	7.68
9	CHECKPOINT_QUEUE	1038432	7.59
10	XE_DISPATCHER_WAIT	1024516	7.49
11	BROKER_TO_FLUSH	563389	4.12
12	SLEEP_TASK	492562	3.60
13	BROKER_TASK_STOP	61528	0.45
14	PREEMPTIVE_DEBUG	12877	0.09
15	CLR_AUTO_EVENT	114	0.00
16	LCK_M_X	77	0.00
17	SLEEP_SYSTEMTASK	45	0.00
18	CHKPT	45	0.00
19	SLEEP_MASTERDBREADY	45	0.00

Figure 13-18. Top 20 Wait Types for the SQL Server Instance

INFORMATION_SCHEMA Views

INFORMATION_SCHEMA views provide yet another method of retrieving metadata in SQL Server 2012. Defined by the SQL-92 standard, INFORMATION_SCHEMA views provide the advantage of being cross-platform compatible with other SQL-92-compliant database platforms. One of the major disadvantages is that they leave out a lot of platform-specific metadata like detailed SQL CLR assembly information. Also, unlike some of the catalog views that are server wide, all INFORMATION_SCHEMA views are database specific. The INFORMATION_SCHEMA views are listed in Table 13-2.

Table 13-2. INFORMATION_SCHEMA Views List

Name	Description
CHECK_CONSTRAINTS	Returns a row of descriptive information for each check constraint in the current database.
COLUMN_DOMAIN_USAGE	Returns a row of metadata for each column in the current database that has an alias data type.
COLUMN_PRIVILEGES	Returns a row of information for each column in the current database with a privilege that has been granted by, or granted to, the current user of the database.
COLUMNS	Returns descriptive information for each column that can be accessed by the current user in the current database.
CONSTRAINT_COLUMN_USAGE	Returns one row of metadata for each column in the current database that has a constraint defined on it, on each table-type object for which the current user has permissions.
CONSTRAINT_TABLE_USAGE	Returns one row of information for each table in the current database that has a constraint defined on it for which the current user has permissions.
DOMAIN_CONSTRAINTS	Returns a row of descriptive information for each alias data type in the current database that the current user can access and that has a rule bound to it.
DOMAINS	Returns a row of descriptive metadata for each alias data type in the current database that the current user can access.
KEY_COLUMN_USAGE	Returns a row of metadata for each column that is constrained by a key for which the current user has permissions in the current database.
PARAMETERS	Returns a row of descriptive information for each parameter for all user-defined functions (UDFs) and SPs that can be accessed by the current user in the current database. For UDFs, the results also contain a row with return value information.
REFERENTIAL_CONSTRAINTS	Returns a row of metadata for each FOREIGN KEY constraint defined in the current database, on objects for which the current user has permissions.
ROUTINE_COLUMNS	Returns a row of descriptive information for each column returned by table-valued functions (TVFs) defined in the current database. This INFORMATION_SCHEMA view only returns information about TVFs for which the current user has access.
ROUTINES	Returns a row of metadata for each SP and function in the current database that is accessible to the current user.
SCHEMATA	Returns a row of information for each schema defined in the current database.
TABLE_CONSTRAINTS	Returns a row of metadata for each table constraint in the current database on table-type objects for which the current user has permissions.
TABLE_PRIVILEGES	Returns a row of descriptive metadata for each table privilege that is either granted by, or granted to, the current user in the current database.
TABLES	Returns a row of metadata for each table in the current database for which the current user has permissions.
VIEW_COLUMN_USAGE	Returns a row of information for each column in the current database that is used in a view definition, on objects for which the current user has permissions.
VIEW_TABLE_USAGE	Returns a row of information for each table that the current user has permissions for in the current database. The tables returned are those for which the current user has permissions.
VIEWS	Returns a row of metadata for each view that can be accessed by the current user in the current database.

■ **Note**   Some of the changes in SQL Server 2012 can break backward compatibility with SQL Server 2008, 2005, or 2000 INFORMATION_SCHEMA views and applications that rely on them. Also note that SQL Server 6.5 and earlier do not implement INFORMATION_SCHEMA views. Check BOL for specific change information if your application uses INFORMATION_SCHEMA and requires backward compatibility.

Retrieving column information with the INFORMATION_SCHEMA.COLUMNS view is similar to using the sys.columns catalog view. Listing 13-20 demonstrates this, with results shown in Figure 13-19.

Listing 13-20. Retrieving Column Data with INFORMATION_SCHEMA.COLUMNS

```
SELECT
c.COLUMN_NAME,
c.ORDINAL_POSITION FROM
INFORMATION_SCHEMA.COLUMNS c WHERE c.TABLE_SCHEMA = 'Person'
AND c.TABLE_NAME = 'Person' ORDER BY c.ORDINAL_POSITION;
```

	COLUMN_NAME	ORDINAL_POSITION
1	BusinessEntityID	1
2	PersonType	2
3	NameStyle	3
4	Title	4
5	FirstName	5
6	MiddleName	6
7	LastName	7
8	Suffix	8
9	EmailPromotion	9
10	AdditionalContactInfo	10
11	Demographics	11
12	rowguid	12
13	ModifiedDate	13

Figure 13-19. *Column Metadata Retrieved via INFORMATION_SCHEMA*

INFORMATION_SCHEMA views are useful for applications that require cross-platform or high levels of ISO compatibility. Because they are ISO compliant, INFORMATION_SCHEMA views do not report a lot of platform-specific metadata. The ISO standard has also not kept up with the demand for access to server-wide metadata, so there is no standard server-scoped equivalent to INFORMATION_SCHEMA.

Summary

In this chapter, we discussed catalog views, which allow you to query database and server-wide metadata. Catalog views allow you to retrieve comprehensive information about databases, database objects, and configuration information. We provided some scenarios for catalog view usage and gave code examples to demonstrate their utility.

We also introduced DMVs and DMFs, which provide an amazing level of detailed insight into the inner workings of SQL Server. SQL Server 2012 supports the DMVs and DMFs introduced in SQL Server 2005 and introduces several more to support for SQL Server functionality like CDC and iFTS. While DMVs and DMFs are targeted to fulfill the needs of DBAs, the information they provide can be valuable to developers who are troubleshooting performance problems or other issues.

Finally, we briefly discussed the ISO standard INFORMATION_SCHEMA metadata views. The INFORMATION_SCHEMA views provide less detail than catalog views and are scoped at the database level only, but they do provide the advantage of cross-platform portability when that is a requirement. Because they have to conform to the ISO SQL standard, however, they leave out a lot of useful platform-specific metadata.

In the next chapter, we will discuss CLR integration and the improvements that Server 2012 provides over the previous release.

EXERCISES

1. [Fill in the blank] "Metadata" is defined as "data that describes _____."

2. [Fill in the blank] _____ provide insight into database objects and server-wide configuration options.

3. [Choose one] Many catalog views are defined using what model:

   a. European model

   b. Inheritance model

   c. First In, First Out model

   d. Procedural model

4. [True/False] Dynamic management views and functions provide access to internal SQL Server data structures that would be otherwise inaccessible.

5. [Choose all that apply] The advantages provided by INFORMATION_SCHEMA views include:

   a. ISO SQL standard compatibility

   b. Access to server-scoped metadata

   c. Cross-platform compatibility

   d. Operating system configuration metadata

CHAPTER 14

CLR Integration Programming

One of the most prominent enhancements to SQL Server 2005 was the introduction of the integrated SQL Common Language Runtime, that was named SQL CLR at that time. What is now called CLR integration is an SQL Server-specific version of the .NET Common Language Runtime, which allows you to run .NET managed code in the database. CLR integration programming is a broad subject that could easily fill an entire book, and in fact it does—*Pro SQL Server 2005 Assemblies,* by Robin Dewson and Julian Skinner (Apress, 2005), is an excellent resource for in-depth coverage of CLR integration programming. In this chapter, we'll discuss the methods used to extend SQL Server functionality in the past, and explain the basics of the CLR integration programming model in SQL Server 2012.

The Old Way

In versions of SQL Server prior to the 2005 release, developers could extend SQL Server functionality by writing extended stored procedures (XPs). Writing high-quality XPs required a strong knowledge of the Open Data Services (ODS) library and the poorly documented C-style Extended Stored Procedure API. Anyone who attempted the old style of XP programming can tell you it was a complex undertaking, in which a single misstep could easily result in memory leaks and corruption of the SQL Server process space. Additionally, the threading model used by XPs required SQL Server to rely on the operating system to control threading within the XP. This could lead to many issues, such as unresponsiveness of XP code.

Caution XPs have been deprecated since SQL Server 2005. Use CLR integration instead of XPs for SQL Server 2012 development.

Earlier SQL Server releases also allowed you to create OLE Automation server objects via the spOACreate SP. Creating OLE Automation servers can be complex and awkward as well. OLE Automation servers created with spOACreate can result in memory leaks and in some instances corruption of the SQL Server process space.

Another option in previous versions of SQL Server was to code all business logic exclusively in physically separate business objects. While this method is preferred by many developers and administrators, it can result in extra network traffic and a less robust security model than can be achieved through tight integration with the SQL Server security model.

The CLR Integration Way

The CLR integration programming model provides several advantages over older methods of extending SQL Server functionality via XPs, OLE Automation, or external business objects. These advantages include the following:

- A managed code base that runs on the CLR integration .NET Framework is managed by the SQL Server Operating System (SQL OS). This means that SQL Server can properly manage threading, memory usage, and other resources accessed via CLR integration code.

- Tight integration of the CLR into SQL Server means that SQL Server can provide a robust security model for running code, and maintain stricter control over database objects and external resources accessed by CLR code.

- CLR integration is more thoroughly documented in more places than the Extended Stored Procedure API ever was (or presumably ever will be).

- CLR integration does not tie you to the C language-based Extended Stored Procedure API. In theory, the .NET programming model does not tie you to any one specific language (although you cannot use dynamic languages like IronPython in CLR integration).

- CLR integration allows access to the familiar .NET namespaces, data types, and managed objects, easing development.

- CLR integration introduces SQL Server-specific namespaces that allow direct access to the underlying SQL Server databases and resources, which can be used to limit or reduce network traffic generated by using external business objects.

There's a misperception expressed by some that CLR integration is a replacement for T-SQL altogether. CLR integration is not a replacement for T-SQL, but rather a supplement that works hand in hand with T-SQL to make SQL Server 2012 more powerful than ever. So when should you use CLR code in your database? There are no hard and fast rules concerning this, but here are some general guidelines:

- Existing custom XPs on older versions of SQL Server are excellent candidates for conversion to SQL Server CLR integration assemblies—that is, if the functionality provided isn't already part of SQL Server 2012 T-SQL (e.g., encryption).

- Code that accesses external server resources, such as calls to xpcmdshell, are also excellent candidates for conversion to more secure and robust CLR assemblies.

- T-SQL code that performs lots of complex calculations and string manipulations can make strong candidates for conversion to CLR integration assemblies.

- Highly procedural code with lots of processing steps might be considered for conversion.

- External business objects that pull a lot of data across the wire and perform a lot of processing on that data might be considered for conversion. You might first consider these business objects for conversion to T-SQL SPs, especially if they don't perform a lot of processing on the data in question.

On the flip side, here are some general guidelines for items that should not be converted to CLR integration assemblies:

- External business objects that pull relatively little data across the wire, or that pull a lot of data across the wire but perform little processing on that data, are good candidates for conversion to T-SQL SPs instead of CLR assemblies.

- T-SQL code and SPs that do not perform many complex calculations or string manipulations generally won't benefit from conversion to CLR assemblies.

- T-SQL can be expected to always be faster than CLR integration for set-based operations on data stored in the database.

- You might not be able to integrate CLR assemblies into databases that are hosted on an ISP's (Internet Service Provider's) server, if the ISP didn't allow CLR integration at the database server level. This is mainly for security reasons and because there can be less control of the code within an assembly.

- CLR integration is not supported on the SQL Azure platform.

As with T-SQL SPs, the decision on whether and to what extent CLR integration will be used in your databases depends on your needs, including organizational policies and procedures. The recommendations we have presented here are guidelines of instances that can make good business cases for conversion of existing code and creation of new code.

CLR Integration Assemblies

CLR integration exposes .NET managed code to SQL Server via *assemblies*. An assembly is a compiled .NET managed code library that can be registered with SQL Server using the CREATE ASSEMBLY statement. Publicly accessible members of classes within the assemblies are then referenced in the appropriate CREATE statements, which we will describe later in this chapter. Creating a CLR integration assembly requires:

1. Designing and programminxg .NET classes that publicly expose the appropriate members.

2. Compiling the .NET classes into managed code DLL manifest files containing the assembly.

3. Registering the assemblies with SQL Server via the CREATE ASSEMBLY statement.

4. Registering the appropriate assembly members via the appropriate CREATE FUNCTION, CREATE PROCEDURE, CREATE TYPE, CREATE TRIGGER, or CREATE AGGREGATE statements.

CLR integration provides additional SQL Server-specific namespaces, classes, and attributes to facilitate development of assemblies. Visual Studio 2010 and Visual Studio 11 (in beta at the time of this writing) also include an SQL Server project type that assists in quickly creating assemblies. Also, to maximize your SQL Server development possibilities with Visual Studio, install the SQL Server Data Tools (SSDT) from the Microsoft Data Developer Center website (http://msdn.microsoft.com/en-us/data/tools.aspx) which provide an integrated environment for database developers inside Visual Studio by allowing you to create and manage database objects and data and to execute T-SQL queries directly.

Perform the following steps to create a new assembly using Visual Studio 2010:

1. Select File ➤ New ➤ Project from the menu.

2. Go to Database ➤ SQL Server in the Installed Templates list and select either Visual Basic CLR Database Project or Visual C# CLR Database Project, as shown in Figure 14-1. Make sure you target the .NET Framework 4 as it is the version of the SQL Server 2012 CLR Integration.

Figure 14-1. *Visual Studio 2010 New Project Dialog Box*

3. You will be prompted with a dialog to select a database connection for the project, as shown in Figure 14-2. You may be prompted to turn on CLR integration debugging for the connection. This is required if you want to test your assemblies in debug mode, which involves remote debugging handled by remote debugging components on the SQL Server communicating with the Visual Studio host. You might need to take extra steps to configure your firewall for it to work. Refer to *Set Up Remote Debugging* in the Visual Studio online help (http://msdn.microsoft.com/en-us/library/bt727f1t.aspx).

Figure 14-2. *The Add Database Reference Dialog Box*

4. Next, highlight the project name in the Solution Explorer and right-click. Then choose a type of CLR integration item to add to the solution (User-Defined Function, Stored Procedure, etc.), as shown in Figure 14-3.

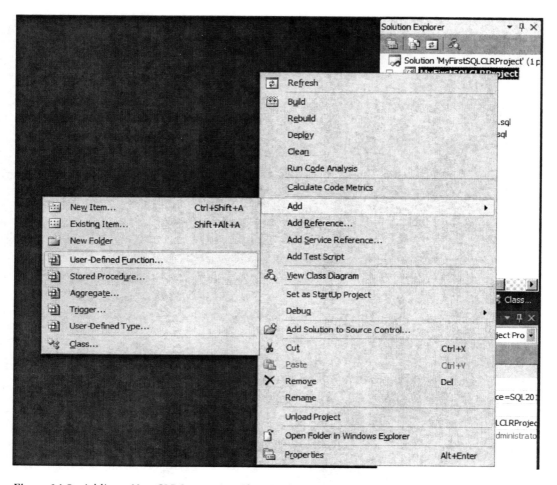

Figure 14-3. *Adding a New CLR Integration Class to Your Project*

5. Visual Studio will show you an "Add New Item" dialog box in which you can change
    the name of the item, and then automatically generate a template for the item
    you select in the language of your choice, complete with the appropriate Imports
    statements in VB.NET or using in C#.

In addition to the standard .NET namespaces and classes, CLR integration implements some SQL Server-
specific namespaces and classes to simplify interfacing your code with SQL Server. Some of the most commonly
used namespaces include the following:

-   The System namespace, which includes the base .NET data types and the Object base
    class from which all .NET classes inherit.

-   The System.Data namespace, which contains the DataSet class and other classes for
    ADO.NET data management.

-   The System.Data.SqlClient namespace, which contains the SQL Server-specific
    ADO.NET data provider.

- The System.Data.SqlTypes namespace, which contains SQL Server data types. This is important because (unlike the standard .NET data types) these types can be set to SQL NULL and are defined to conform to the same operator rules, behaviors, precision, and scale as their SQL Server type counterparts.

- The Microsoft.SqlServer.Server namespace, which contains the SqlContext and SqlPipe classes that allow assemblies to communicate with SQL Server.

Once the assembly is created and compiled, it is registered with SQL Server via the CREATE ASSEMBLY statement. Listing 14-1 demonstrates a CREATE ASSEMBLY statement that registers a CLR integration assembly with SQL Server from an external DLL file. The DLL file used in the example is not supplied in precompiled form in the sample downloads for this book, but you can compile it yourself from the code we will introduce in Listing 14-2. Source code is included in the sample downloads available on the Apress web site. As CLR integration is not enabled by default, we also need to enable it at the server level. Here, we do it using the sp_configure system stored procedure prior to running the CREATE ASSEMBLY statement. CREATE ASSEMBLY would succeed even if CLR integration is disabled; an error would be raised by SQL Server only when a CLR integration code module would be called by a user later on. The RECONFIGURE statement applies the configuration change immediately.

Listing 14-1. Registering a CLR Integration Assembly with SQL Server

```
EXEC sp_configure 'CLR Enabled';
RECONFIGURE;

CREATE ASSEMBLY ApressExamples
AUTHORIZATION dbo
FROM N'C:\MyApplication\Apress.Examples.DLL'
WITH PERMISSION_SET = SAFE;
GO
```

The CREATE ASSEMBLY statement in the example specifies an assembly name of EmailUDF. This name must be a valid SQL Server identifier, and it must be unique within the database. You will use this assembly name when referencing the assembly in other statements.

The AUTHORIZATION clause specifies the owner of the assembly, in this case dbo. If you leave out the AUTHORIZATION clause, it defaults to the current user.

The FROM clause in this example specifies the full path to the external DLL file. Alternatively, you can specify a varbinary value instead of character file name. If you use a varbinary value, SQL Server uses it, as it is a long binary string representing the compiled assembly code, and no external file needs to be specified.

Finally, the WITH PERMISSION_SET clause grants a set of Code Access Security (CAS) permissions to the assembly. Valid permission sets include the following:

- The SAFE permission set is the most restrictive, preventing the assembly from accessing system resources outside of SQL Server. SAFE is the default.

- EXTERNAL_ACCESS allows assemblies to access some external resources, such as files, network, the registry, and environment variables.

- UNSAFE permission allows assemblies unlimited access to external resources, including the ability to execute unmanaged code.

After the assembly is installed, you can use variations of the T-SQL database object creation statements (e.g., CREATE FUNCTION, CREATE PROCEDURE) to access the methods exposed by the assembly classes. We will demonstrate these statements individually in the following sections.

User-Defined Functions

CLR integration UDFs that return scalar values are similar to standard .NET functions. The primary differences with standard .NET functions are that the SqlFunction attribute must be applied to the main function of CLR integration functions if you are using Visual Studio to deploy your function or if you need to set additional attribute values like IsDeterministic and DataAccess. Listing 14-2 demonstrates a scalar UDF that accepts an input string value and a regular expression pattern and returns a bit value indicating a match (1) or no match (0). The UDF is named EmailMatch() and is declared as a method of the UDFExample class, inside the Apress.Example namespace that we will use for all our examples in this chapter.

Listing 14-2. Regular Expression Match UDF

```
using System.Data.SqlTypes;
using System.Text.RegularExpressions;

namespace Apress.Examples
{
    public static class UDFExample
    {
        private static readonly Regex email_pattern = new Regex
        (
        // Everything before the @ sign (the "local part")
        "^[a-z0-9!#$%&'*+/=?^_'{|}~-]+(?:\\.[a-z0-9!#$%&'*+/=?^_'{|}~-]+)*" +

        // Subdomains after the @ sign
        "@(?:[a-z0-9](?:[a-z0-9-]*[a-z0-9])?\\.)+" +

        // Top-level domains
        "(?:[a-z]{2}|com|org|net|gov|mil|biz|info|mobi|name|aero|jobs|museum)\\b$"
        );
        [Microsoft.SqlServer.Server.SqlFunction
        (
        IsDeterministic = true
        )]
        public static SqlBoolean EmailMatch(SqlString input)
        {
            SqlBoolean result = new SqlBoolean();
            if (input.IsNull)
                result = SqlBoolean.Null;
            else
                result = (email_pattern.IsMatch(input.Value.ToLower()) == true)
                ? SqlBoolean.True : SqlBoolean.False;
            return result;
        }
    }
}
```

The first part of the listing specifies the required namespaces to import. This UDF uses the System.Data.SqlTypes and System.Text.RegularExpressions namespaces.

```
using System.Data.SqlTypes;
using System.Text.RegularExpressions;
```

The UDFExample class and the EmailMatch function it exposes are both declared static. CLR integration functions need to be declared as static. A static function is shared between all instances of the class. Here, the class itself is also static, so it cannot be instantiated; this allows the class to be loaded faster and its memory to be shared between SQL Server sessions. The function is decorated with the Microsoft.SqlServer.Server. SqlFunction attribute with the IsDeterministic property set to true to indicate the function is a deterministic CLR integration method. The function body is relatively simple. It accepts an SqlString input string value. If the input string is NULL, the function returns NULL; otherwise the function uses the .NET Regex.IsMatch function to perform a regular expression match. If the result is a match, the function returns a bit value of 1; otherwise it returns 0.

```
public static class UDFExample
{
    private static readonly Regex email_pattern = new Regex
    (
    // Everything   before   the   @   sign   (the   "local   part")
    "^[a-z0-9!#$%&'*+/=?^_'{|}~-]+(?:\\.[a-z0-9!#$%&'*+/=?^_'{|}~-]+)*" +

    // Subdomains   after   the   @   sign
    "@(?:[a-z0-9](?:[a-z0-9-]*[a-z0-9])?\\.)+" +

    // Top-level domains
    "(?:[a-z]{2}|com|org|net|gov|mil|biz|info|mobi|name|aero|jobs|museum)\\b$"
    );

    [Microsoft.SqlServer.Server.SqlFunction
    (
    IsDeterministic   =   true
    )]
    public static SqlBoolean EmailMatch(SqlString input)
    {
        SqlBoolean result = new SqlBoolean();
        if (input.IsNull)
            result = SqlBoolean.Null;
        else
            result = (email_pattern.IsMatch(input.Value.ToLower()) == true)
            ? SqlBoolean.True : SqlBoolean.False;
        return result;
    }
}
```

The regular expression pattern used in Listing 14-2 was created by Jan Goyvaerts of Regular-Expressions.info (www.regular-expressions.info). Jan's regular expression validates e-mail addresses according to RFC 2822, the standard for e-mail address formats. While not perfect, Jan estimates that this regular expression matches over 99 percent of "e-mail addresses in actual use today." Performing this type of e-mail address validation using only T-SQL statements would be cumbersome, complex, and inefficient.

■ **Tip** It's considered good practice to use the SQL Server data types for parameters and return values to CLR Integration methods (SqlString, SqlBoolean, SqlInt32, etc.). Standard .NET data types have no concept of SQL NULL and will error out if NULL is passed in as a parameter, calculated within the function, or returned from the function.

After the assembly is installed via the CREATE ASSEMBLY statement we wrote in Listing 14-1, the function is created with the CREATE FUNCTION statement using the EXTERNAL NAME clause, as shown in Listing 14-3.

Listing 14-3. Creating CLR UDF from Assembly Method

```
CREATE FUNCTION dbo.EmailMatch (@input nvarchar(4000))
RETURNS bit
WITH EXECUTE AS CALLER
AS
EXTERNAL NAME ApressExamples.[Apress.Examples.UDFExample].EmailMatch
GO
```

After this, the CLR function can be called like any other T-SQL UDF, as shown in Listing 14-4. The results are shown in Figure 14-4.

Listing 14-4. Validating E-mail Addresses with Regular Expressions

```
SELECT
    'nospam-123@yahoo.com' AS Email,
    dbo.EmailMatch (N'nospam-123@yahoo.com') AS Valid
UNION
SELECT
    '123@456789',
    dbo.EmailMatch('123@456789')
UNION
    SELECT 'BillyG@HOTMAIL.COM',
    dbo.EmailMatch('BillyG@HOTMAIL.COM');
```

	Email	Valid
1	123@456789	0
2	BillyG@HOTMAIL.COM	1
3	nospam-123@yahoo.com	1

Figure 14-4. Results of E-mail Address Validation with Regular Expressions

■ **Tip** Normally you can automate the process of compiling your assembly, registering it with SQL Server, and installing the CLR Integration UDF with Visual Studio's Build ➤ Deploy option. You can also test the CLR Integration UDF with the Visual Studio Debug ➤ Start Debugging option. With Visual Studio 2010 this does not work, as it does not recognize SQL Server 2012, wich was released after Visual Studio. In Visual Studio 11, available in beta at the time of this writing, you should be able to deploy the assembly with Visual Studio. This is just a detail; it is straightforward to copy the assembly on the server and register it manually with CREATE ASSEMBLY as shown in Listing 14-1.

As we mentioned previously, CLR UDFs also allow tabular results to be returned to the caller. This example demonstrates another situation in which CLR integration can be a useful supplement to T-SQL functionality—accessing external resources such as the file system, network resources, or even the Internet. Listing 14-5 uses a CLR function to retrieve the Yahoo Top News Stories RSS feed and return the results as a table. Table-valued CLR UDFs are a little more complex than scalar functions. The following code could be added to the sqme Visual Studio project that we created for the first CLR function example. Here we create another class named YahooRSS.

Listing 14-5. Retrieving Yahoo RSS Feed Top News Stories

```
using System;
using System.Collections;
using System.Data.SqlTypes;
using Microsoft.SqlServer.Server;
using System.Xml;

namespace Apress.Examples {
    public partial class YahooRSS {

        [Microsoft.SqlServer.Server.SqlFunction (
            IsDeterministic = false,
            DataAccess = DataAccessKind.None,
            TableDefinition = "title nvarchar(256),"
            + "link nvarchar(256), "
            + "pubdate datetime, "
            + "description nvarchar(max)",
            FillRowMethodName = "GetRow" )
        ]
        public static IEnumerable GetYahooNews() {
            XmlTextReader xmlsource =
                new XmlTextReader("http://rss.news.yahoo.com/rss/topstories");
            XmlDocument newsxml = new XmlDocument();
            newsxml.Load(xmlsource);
            xmlsource.Close();
            return newsxml.SelectNodes("//rss/channel/item");
        }

        private static void GetRow (
            Object o,
            out SqlString title,
            out SqlString link,
            out SqlDateTime pubdate,
            out SqlString description )
        {
            XmlElement element = (XmlElement)o;
            title = element.SelectSingleNode("./title").InnerText;
            link = element.SelectSingleNode("./link").InnerText;
            pubdate = DateTime.Parse(element.SelectSingleNode("./pubDate").InnerText);
            description = element.SelectSingleNode("./description").InnerText;
        }
    }
}
```

Before we step through the source listing, we need to address security since this function accesses the Internet. Because the function needs to access an external resource, it requires EXTERNAL_ACCESS permissions. In order to deploy a non-SAFE assembly, one of two sets of conditions must be met:

- The database must be marked TRUSTWORTHY and the user installing the assembly must have EXTERNAL ACCESS ASSEMBLY or UNSAFE ASSEMBLY permission; or

- The assembly must be signed with an asymmetric key or certificate associated with a login that has proper permissions.

To meet the first set of requirements:

1. Execute the ALTER DATABASE AdventureWorks SET TRUSTWORTHY ON; statement.

2. In Visual Studio, select Project ➤ Properties ➤ Database and change the permission level to EXTERNAL_ACCESS.

3. If you manually import the assembly into SQL Server, specify the EXTERNAL_ACCESS permission set when issuing the CREATE ASSEMBLY statement as shown in Listing 14-6.

Listing 14-6. CREATE ASSEMBLY with EXTERNAL_ACCESS Permission Set

```
CREATE ASSEMBLY ApressExample
AUTHORIZATION dbo
FROM N'C:\MyApplication\Apress.Example.DLL'
WITH PERMISSION_SET = EXTERNAL_ACCESS;
```

As mentioned previously, signing assemblies is beyond the scope of this book. Additional information on signing assemblies can be found in this MSDN Data Access Technologies blog entry: http://blogs.msdn.com/b/dataaccesstechnologies/archive/2011/10/29/deploying-sql-clr-assembly-using-asymmetric-key.aspx.

The code listing begins with the using statements. This function requires the addition of the System.Xml namespace in order to parse the RSS feed, and the System.Collections namespace to allow the collection to be searched amongst other functionality specific to collections.

```
using System;
using System.Collections;
using System.Data.SqlTypes;
using Microsoft.SqlServer.Server;
using System.Xml;
```

The primary public function again requires that the SqlFunction attribute be declared. This time there are several additional attributes that need to be declared with it:

```
[Microsoft.SqlServer.Server.SqlFunction (
    IsDeterministic = false,
    DataAccess = DataAccessKind.None,
    TableDefinition = "title nvarchar(256),"
    + "link nvarchar(256), "
    + "pubdate datetime, "
    + "description nvarchar(max)",
    FillRowMethodName = "GetRow" )
]
```

```
public static IEnumerable GetYahooNews()
{
    XmlTextReader xmlsource =
        new XmlTextReader("http://rss.news.yahoo.com/rss/topstories");
    XmlDocument newsxml = new XmlDocument();
    newsxml.Load(xmlsource);
    xmlsource.Close();
    return newsxml.SelectNodes("//rss/channel/item");
}
```

We specifically set the IsDeterministic attribute to false this time to indicate that the contents of an RSS feed can change between calls, making this UDF nondeterministic. Since the function does not read data from system tables using the in-process data provider, the DataAccess attribute is set to DataAccessKind.None. This CLR TVF also sets the additional TableDefinition attribute defining the structure of the result set for Visual Studio. It also needs the FillRowMethodName attribute to designate the fill-row method. *The fill-row method* is a user method that converts each element of an IEnumerable object into an SQL Server result set row.

The public function is declared to return an IEnumerable result. This particular function opens an XmlTextReader that retrieves the Yahoo Top News Stories RSS feed and stores it in an XmlDocument. The function then uses the SelectNodes method to retrieve news story summaries from the RSS feed. The SelectNodes method, used to return results from the function, generates an XmlNodeList. The XmlNodeList class implements the IEnumerable interface. This is important since the fill-row method is fired once for each object returned by the IEnumerable collection returned (in this case the XmlNodeList).

The GetRow method is declared as a C# void function, which means that no value will be returned by the function; the method communicates with SQL Server via its out parameters. The first parameter is an Object passed by value—in this case an XmlElement. The remaining parameters correspond to the columns of the result set. The GetRow method casts the first parameter to an XmlElement (the parameter cannot be directly an XmlElement because the fill-row method signature must have an Object as first parameter). It then uses the SelectSingleNode method and InnerText property to retrieve the proper text from individual child nodes of the XmlElement, assigning each to the proper columns of the result set along the way.

```
private static void GetRow (
    Object o,
    out SqlString title,
    out SqlString link,
    out SqlDateTime pubdate,
    out SqlString description )
{
    XmlElement element = (XmlElement)o;
    title = element.SelectSingleNode("./title").InnerText;
    link = element.SelectSingleNode("./link").InnerText;
    pubdate = DateTime.Parse(element.SelectSingleNode("./pubDate").InnerText);
    description = element.SelectSingleNode("./description").InnerText;
}
```

The CLR TVF can be called with a SELECT query, as shown in Listing 14-7. The results are shown in Figure 14-5.

Listing 14-7. Querying a CLR Integration TVF

```
CREATE FUNCTION dbo.GetYahooNews()
RETURNS TABLE(title nvarchar(256), link nvarchar(256), pubdate datetime, description
nvarchar(max))
AS EXTERNAL NAME ApressExamples.[Apress.Examples.YahooRSS].GetYahooNews
GO

SELECT
    title,
    link,
    pubdate,
    description
FROM dbo.GetYahooNews();
```

Figure 14-5. Retrieving the Yahoo RSS Feed with the GetYahooNews() Function

Stored Procedures

CLR integration SPs provide an alternative to extend SQL Server functionality when T-SQL SPs just won't do. Of course, like other CLR integration functionality, there is a certain amount of overhead involved with CLR SPs, and you can expect them to be less efficient than comparable T-SQL code for set-based operations. On the other hand, if you need to access .NET functionality or external resources, or if you have code that is computationally intensive, CLR integration SPs can provide an excellent alternative to straight T-SQL code.

Listing 14-8 shows how to use CLR integration to retrieve operating system environment variables and return them as a recordset via an SP. In the Apress.Examples namespace, we create a SampleProc class.

Listing 14-8. Retrieving Environment Variables with a CLR Stored Procedure

```
using System;
using System.Collections;
using System.Data;

using System.Data.SqlClient;
using System.Data.SqlTypes;
using Microsoft.SqlServer.Server;
namespace Apress.Examples
```

```
{
    public partial class SampleProc
    {
        [Microsoft.SqlServer.Server.SqlProcedure()]
        public static void GetEnvironmentVars()
        {
            try
            {
                SortedList environment_list = new SortedList();
                foreach (DictionaryEntry de in Environment.GetEnvironmentVariables())
                {
                    environment_list[de.Key] = de.Value;
                }

                SqlDataRecord record = new SqlDataRecord (
                    new SqlMetaData("VarName", SqlDbType.NVarChar, 1024),
                    new SqlMetaData("VarValue", SqlDbType.NVarChar, 4000)
                );
                SqlContext.Pipe.SendResultsStart(record);
                foreach (DictionaryEntry de in environment_list)
                {
                    record.SetValue(0, de.Key);
                    record.SetValue(1, de.Value);
                    SqlContext.Pipe.SendResultsRow(record);
                }

                SqlContext.Pipe.SendResultsEnd();
            }
            catch (Exception ex)
            {
                SqlContext.Pipe.Send(ex.Message);
            }
        }
    }
};
```

As with the previous CLR integration examples, appropriate namespaces are imported at the top:

```
using System;
using System.Collections;
using System.Data;
using System.Data.SqlClient;
using System.Data.SqlTypes;
using Microsoft.SqlServer.Server;
```

The GetEnvironmentVars() method is declared as a public void function. The SqlProcedure() attribute is applied to the function in this code to indicate to Visual Studio that this is a CLR SP. The body of the SP is wrapped in a try . . . catch block to capture any .NET exceptions, which are returned to SQL Server. If an exception occurs in the .NET code, it's sent back to SQL Server via the SqlContext.Pipe.Send method.

```
    public partial class SampleProc
    {
        [Microsoft.SqlServer.Server.SqlProcedure()]
        public static void GetEnvironmentVars()
        {
            try
            {
                ...
            }
            catch (Exception ex)
            {
                SqlContext.Pipe.Send(ex.Message);
            }
        }
    }
};
```

THROWING READABLE EXCEPTIONS

When you need to raise an exception in a CLR SP, you have two options. For code readability reasons, I've chosen the simpler option of just allowing exceptions to bubble up through the call stack. This results in .NET Framework exceptions being returned to SQL Server. The .NET Framework exceptions return a lot of extra information, like call stack data, however.

If you want to raise a nice, simple SQL Server-style error without all the extra .NET Framework exception information, you can use a method introduced in the book *Pro SQL Server 2005*, by Thomas Rizzo et al. (Apress, 2005). This second method involves using the ExecuteAndSend() method of the SqlContext.Pipe to execute a T-SQL RAISERROR statement. This method is shown in the following C# code snippet:

```
try {
    SqlContext.Pipe.ExecuteAndSend("RAISERROR ('This is a T-SQL Error', 16, 1);");
}
catch
{
    // do nothing
}
```

The ExecuteAndSend() method call executes the RAISERROR statement on the current context connection. The try...catch block surrounding the call prevents the .NET exception generated by the RAISERROR to be handled by .NET and reported as a new error. Keep this method in mind if you want to raise SQL Server-style errors instead of returning the verbose .NET Framework exception information to SQL Server.

As the procedure begins, all of the environment variable names and their values are copied from the .NET Hashtable returned by the Environment.GetEnvironmentVariables() functions to a .NET SortedList. In this procedure, we chose to use the SortedList to ensure that the results are returned in order by key. I added the SortedList just for display purposes, but it's not required. Greater efficiency can be gained by iterating the HashTable directly without a SortedList.

```
SortedList environment_list = new SortedList();
foreach (DictionaryEntry de in Environment.GetEnvironmentVariables())
{
    environment_list[de.Key] = de.Value;
}
```

The procedure uses the SqlContext.Pipe to return results to SQL Server as a result set. The first step to using the SqlContext.Pipe to send results back is to set up an SqlRecord with the structure that you wish the result set to take. For this example, the result set consists of two nvarchar columns: VarName, which contains the environment variable names; and VarValue, which contains their corresponding values.

```
SqlDataRecord record = new SqlDataRecord (
    new SqlMetaData("VarName", SqlDbType.NVarChar, 1024),
    new SqlMetaData("VarValue", SqlDbType.NVarChar, 4000)
);
```

Next, the function calls the SendResultsStart() method with the SqlDataRecord to initialize the result set:

```
SqlContext.Pipe.SendResultsStart(record);
```

Then it's a simple matter of looping through the SortedList of environment variable key/value pairs and sending them to the server via the SendResultsRow() method:

```
foreach (DictionaryEntry de in environment_list) {
    record.SetValue(0, de.Key);
    record.SetValue(1, de.Value);
    SqlContext.Pipe.SendResultsRow(record);
}
```

The SetValue() method is called for each column of the SqlRecord to properly set the results, and then SendResultsRow() is called for each row. After all results have been sent to the client, the SendResultsEnd() method of the SqlContext.Pipe is called to complete the result set and return the SqlContext.Pipe to its initial state.

```
SqlContext.Pipe.SendResultsEnd();
```

The GetEnvironmentVars CLR SP can be called using the T-SQL EXEC statement, shown in Listing 14-9. The results are shown in Figure 14-6.

Listing 14-9. Executing the GetEnvironmentVars CLR Procedure

```
CREATE PROCEDURE dbo.GetEnvironmentVars
AS EXTERNAL NAME ApressExamples.[Apress.Examples.SampleProc].GetEnvironmentVars;
GO

EXEC dbo.GetEnvironmentVars;
```

	VarName	VarValue
1	ALLUSERSPROFILE	C:\ProgramData
2	APPDATA	C:\Users\MSSQLSERVER\AppData\Roaming
3	CommonProgramFiles	C:\Program Files\Common Files
4	CommonProgramFiles(x86)	C:\Program Files (x86)\Common Files
5	CommonProgramW6432	C:\Program Files\Common Files
6	COMPLUS_MDA	InvalidVariant;RaceOnRCWCleanup;InvalidFunctionP...
7	COMPUTERNAME	SQL2012
8	ComSpec	C:\Windows\system32\cmd.exe
9	FP_NO_HOST_CHECK	NO
10	LOCALAPPDATA	C:\Users\MSSQLSERVER\AppData\Local
11	NUMBER_OF_PROCESSORS	1
12	OS	Windows_NT

Figure 14-6. *Retrieving Environment Variables with CLR*

User-Defined Aggregates

User-defined aggregates (UDAs) are an exciting addition to SQL Server's functionality. UDAs are similar to the built-in SQL aggregate functions (SUM, AVG, etc.) in that they can act on entire sets of data at once, as opposed to one item at a time. An SQL CLR UDA has access to .NET functionality and can operate on numeric, character, date/time, or even user-defined data types. A basic UDA has four required methods:

- The UDA calls its Init() method when the SQL Server engine prepares to aggregate. The code in this method can reset member variables to their start state, initialize buffers, and perform other initialization functions.

- The Accumulate() method is called as each row is processed, allowing you to aggregate the data passed in. The Accumulate() method might increment a counter, add a row's value to a running total, or possibly perform other more complex processing on a row's data.

- The Merge() method is invoked when SQL Server decides to use parallel processing to complete an aggregate. If the query engine decides to use parallel processing, it will create multiple instances of your UDA and call the Merge() method to join the results into a single aggregation.

- The Terminate() method is the final method of the UDA. It is called after all rows have been processed and any aggregates created in parallel have been merged. The Terminate() method returns the final result of the aggregation to the query engine.

■ **Tip** In SQL Server 2005, there was a serialization limit of 8,000 bytes for an instance of a SQL CLR UDA, making certain tasks harder to perform using a UDA. For instance, creating an array, hash table, or other structure to hold intermediate results during an aggregation (like aggregates that calculate statistical mode or median) could cause a UDA to very quickly run up against the 8,000-byte limit and throw an exception for large datasets. SQL Server 2008 and 2012 do not have this limitation.

Creating a Simple UDA

The sample UDA in Listing 14-10 determines the statistical range for a set of numbers. The statistical range for a given set of numbers is the difference between the minimum and maximum values for the set. The UDA determines the minimum and maximum values of the set of numbers passed in and returns the difference.

Listing 14-10. Sample Statistical Range UDA

```
using System;
using System.Data;
using System.Data.SqlClient;
using System.Data.SqlTypes;
using Microsoft.SqlServer.Server;

namespace Apress.Examples {
    [Serializable]
    [Microsoft.SqlServer.Server.SqlUserDefinedAggregate(Format.Native)]

    public struct Range
    {
        SqlDouble min, max;

        public void Init() {
            min = SqlDouble.Null;
            max = SqlDouble.Null;
        }

        public void Accumulate(SqlDouble value)
        {
            if (!value.IsNull) {
                if (min.IsNull || value < min)
                {
                    min = value;
                }

                if (max.IsNull || value > max)
                {
                    max = value;
                }
            }
        }

        public void Merge(Range group)
        {
            if (min.IsNull || (!group.min.IsNull && group.min < min))
            {
                min = group.min;
            }
            if (max.IsNull || (!group.max.IsNull && group.max > max))
            {
                max = group.max;
            }
        }
```

```
        public SqlDouble Terminate() {
            SqlDouble result = SqlDouble.Null;
            if (!min.IsNull && !max.IsNull)
            {
                result = max - min;
            }

            return result;
        }
    }
}
```

This UDA begins, like the previous CLR integration assemblies, by importing the proper namespaces:

```
using System;
using System.Data;
using System.Data.SqlClient;
using System.Data.SqlTypes;
using Microsoft.SqlServer.Server;
```

Next, the code declares the struct that represents the UDA. The attributes Serializable and SqlUserDefinedAggregate are applied to the struct. We used the Format.Native serialization format for this UDA. Because this is a simple UDA, Format.Native will provide the best performance and will be the easiest to implement. More complex UDAs that use reference types require Format.UserDefined serialization and must implement the IBinarySerialize interface.

```
[Serializable]
[Microsoft.SqlServer.Server.SqlUserDefinedAggregate(Format.Native)]
public struct Range
{
}
```

The struct declares two member variables, min and max, which will hold the minimum and maximum values encountered during the aggregation process:

```
SqlDouble min, max;
```

The mandatory Init() method in the aggregate body initializes the min and max member variables to SqlDouble.Null:

```
public void Init() {
    min = SqlDouble.Null;
    max = SqlDouble.Null;
}
```

The Accumulate() method accepts a SqlDouble parameter. This method first checks that the value is not NULL (NULL is ignored during aggregation). Then it checks to see if the value passed in is less than the min variable (or if min is NULL), and if so, assigns the parameter value to min. The method also checks max and updates it if the parameter value is greater than max (or if max is NULL). In this way, the min and max values are determined on the fly as the query engine feeds values into the Accumulate() method.

```
public void Accumulate(SqlDouble value)
    {
        if (!value.IsNull) {
            if (min.IsNull || value < min)
            {
                min = value;
            }

            if (max.IsNull || value > max)
            {
                max = value;
            }
        }
    }
```

The Merge() method merges a Range structure that was created in parallel with the current structure. The method accepts a Range structure and compares its min and max variables to those of the current Range structure. It then adjusts the current structure's min and max variables based on the Range structure passed into the method, effectively merging the two results.

```
public void Merge(Range group)
{
    if (min.IsNull || (!group.min.IsNull && group.min < min))
    {
        min = group.min;
    }
    if (max.IsNull || (!group.max.IsNull && group.max > max))
    {
        max = group.max;
    }
}
```

The final method of the UDA is the Terminate() function, which returns an SqlDouble result. This function checks for min or max results that are NULL. The UDA returns NULL if either min or max is NULL. If neither min nor max is NULL, the result is the difference between the max and min values.

```
public SqlDouble Terminate() {
    SqlDouble result = SqlDouble.Null;
    if (!min.IsNull && !max.IsNull)
    {
        result = max - min;
    }

    return result;
}
```

■ **Note** The Terminate() method must return the same data type that the Accumulate() method accepts. If these data types do not match, an error will occur. Also, as mentioned previously, it is best practice to use the SQL Server-specific data types, since the standard .NET types will choke on NULL.

Listing 14-11 is a simple test of this UDA. The test determines the statistical range of unit prices that customers have paid for AdventureWorks products. Information like this, on a per-product or per-model basis, can be paired with additional information to help the AdventureWorks sales teams set optimal price points for their products. The results are shown in Figure 14-7.

Listing 14-11. Retrieving Statistical Ranges with UDA

```
CREATE AGGREGATE Range (@value float) RETURNS float
EXTERNAL NAME ApressExamples.[Apress.Examples.Range];
GO

SELECT
    ProductID,
    dbo.Range(UnitPrice) AS UnitPriceRange
FROM Sales.SalesOrderDetail
WHERE UnitPrice > 0
GROUP BY ProductID;
```

	ProductID	UnitPriceRange
1	707	19.2445
2	708	19.2445
3	709	0.95
4	710	0
5	711	19.2445
6	712	4.6679
7	713	0
8	714	22.4955
9	715	25.9563
10	716	22.111
11	717	100.8241
12	718	100.8241

Figure 14-7. Results of the Range Aggregate Applied to Unit Prices

■ **Caution**   This UDA is an example. It will be faster to use regular T-SQL aggregation functions for this type of calculation, especially if you have a large number of rows to process.

Creating an Advanced UDA

You can create more advanced CLR aggregates that use reference data types and user-defined serialization. When creating a UDA that uses reference (nonvalue) data types such as ArrayLists, SortedLists, and Objects, CLR integration imposes the additional restriction that you cannot mark the UDA for Format.Native serialization. Instead these aggregates have to be marked for Format.UserDefined serialization, which means that the UDA must implement the IBinarySerialize interface, including both the Read and Write methods. Basically, you have to tell SQL Server how to serialize your data when using reference types. There is a performance impact associated with Format.UserDefined serialization as opposed to Format.Native.

Listing 14-12 is a UDA that calculates the statistical median of a set of numbers. The statistical median is the middle number of an ordered group of numbers. If there is an even number of numbers in the set, the statistical median is the average (mean) of the middle two numbers in the set.

Listing 14-12. UDA to Calculate Statistical Median

```
using System;
using System.Collections.Generic;
using System.Data;
using System.Data.SqlTypes;
using System.Runtime.InteropServices;
using Microsoft.SqlServer.Server;

namespace Apress.Examples {
    [Serializable]
    [Microsoft.SqlServer.Server.SqlUserDefinedAggregate (
        Format.UserDefined,
        IsNullIfEmpty = true,
        MaxByteSize = -1 )]
    [StructLayout(LayoutKind.Sequential)]

    public struct Median : IBinarySerialize
    {
        List<double> temp; // List of numbers

        public void Init()
        {
            // Create new list of double numbers
            this.temp = new List<double> ();
        }

        public void Accumulate(SqlDouble number)
        {
            if (!number.IsNull) // Skip over NULLs
            {
                this.temp.Add(number.Value); // If number is not NULL, add it to list
            }
        }

        public void Merge(Median group)
        {
            // Merge two sets of numbers
            this.temp.InsertRange(this.temp.Count, group.temp);
        }

        public SqlDouble Terminate() {
            SqlDouble result = SqlDouble.Null; // Default result to NULL
            this.temp.Sort(); // Sort list of numbers
```

447

```
        int first, second; // Indexes to middle two numbers

        if (this.temp.Count % 2 == 1)
        {
            // If there is an odd number of values get the middle number twice
            first = this.temp.Count / 2;
            second = first;
        }
        else
        {
            // If there is an even number of values get the middle two numbers
            first = this.temp.Count / 2-1;
            second = first + 1;
        }

        if (this.temp.Count > 0) // If there are numbers, calculate median
        {
            // Calculate median as average of middle number(s)
            result = (SqlDouble)( this.temp[first] + this.temp[second] ) / 2.0;
        }

        return result;
    }

    #region IBinarySerialize Members

    // Custom serialization read method
    public void Read(System.IO.BinaryReader r)
    {
        // Create a new list of double values
        this.temp = new List<double> ();

        // Get the number of values that were serialized
        int j = r.ReadInt32();

        // Loop and add each serialized value to the list
        for (int i = 0; i < j; i++)
        {
            this.temp.Add(r.ReadDouble());
        }
    }

    // Custom serialization write method
    public void Write(System.IO.BinaryWriter w)
    {
        // Write the number of values in the list
        w.Write(this.temp.Count);

        // Write out each value in the list
        foreach (double d in this.temp)
```

```
        {
            w.Write(d);
        }
    }

    #endregion
}
}
```

This UDA begins, like the other CLR integration examples, with namespace imports. We've added the `System.Collections.Generic` namespace this time so we can use the .NET `List<T>` strongly typed list.

```
using System;
using System.Collections.Generic;
using System.Data;
using System.Data.SqlTypes;
using System.Runtime.InteropServices;
using Microsoft.SqlServer.Server;
```

The `Median` structure in the example is declared with the `Serializable` attribute to indicate that it can be serialized, and the `StructLayout` attribute with the `LayoutKind.Sequential` property to force the structure to be serialized in sequential fashion for a UDA that has a `Format` different from `Native`. The `SqlUserDefinedAggregate` attribute declares three properties, as follows:

- The `Format.UserDefined` property indicates that the UDA will implement serialization methods through the `IBinarySerialize` interface. This is required since the `List<T>` reference type is being used in the UDA.

- The `IsNullIfEmpty` property is set to `true`, indicating that `NULL` will be returned if no rows are passed to the UDA.

- The `MaxByteSize` property is set to –1 so that the UDA can be serialized if it is greater than 8,000 bytes. (The 8,000-byte serialization limit was a strict limit in SQL Server 2005 that prevented serialization of large objects, like large `ArrayList` objects, in the UDA.)

Because `Format.UserDefined` was specified on the `Median` structure, it must implement the `IBinarySerialize` interface. Inside the body of the struct, we've defined a `List<double>` named `temp` that will hold an intermediate temporary list of numbers passed into the UDA.

```
[Serializable]
[Microsoft.SqlServer.Server.SqlUserDefinedAggregate (
    Format.UserDefined,
    IsNullIfEmpty = true,
    MaxByteSize = -1 )]
[StructLayout(LayoutKind.Sequential)]
public struct Median : IBinarySerialize
{
    List<double> temp; // List of numbers
    ...
}
```

The Read() and Write() methods of the IBinarySerialize interface are used to deserialize and serialize the list, respectively:

```
#region IBinarySerialize Members

// Custom serialization read method
public void Read(System.IO.BinaryReader r)
{
    // Create a new list of double values
    this.temp = new List<double>();

    // Get the number of values that were serialized
    int j = r.ReadInt32();

    // Loop and add each serialized value to the list
    for (int i = 0; i < j; i++)
    {
        this.temp.Add(r.ReadDouble());
    }
}

// Custom serialization write method
public void Write(System.IO.BinaryWriter w)
{
    // Write the number of values in the list
    w.Write(this.temp.Count);

    // Write out each value in the list
    foreach (double d in this.temp)
    {
        w.Write(d);
    }
}

#endregion
```

The Init method of the UDA initializes the temp list by creating a new List<double> instance:

```
public void Init() {
    // Create new list of double numbers
    this.temp = new List<double>();
}
```

The Accumulate() method accepts a SqlDouble number and adds all non-NULL values to the temp list. Although you can include NULLs in your aggregate results, keep in mind that T-SQL developers are used to the NULL handling of built-in aggregate functions like SUM and AVG. In particular, developers are used to their aggregate functions discarding NULL. This is the main reason we eliminate NULL in this UDA.

```
public void Accumulate(SqlDouble number)
{
    if (!number.IsNull) // Skip over NULLs
    {
        this.temp.Add(number.Value); // If number is not NULL, add it to list
    }
}
```

The Merge() method in the example merges two lists of numbers if SQL Server decides to calculate the aggregate in parallel. If so, the server will pass a list of numbers into the Merge() method. This list of numbers must then be appended to the current list. For efficiency, we use the InsertRange() method of List<T> to combine the lists.

```
public void Merge(Median group)
{
    // Merge two sets of numbers
    this.temp.InsertRange(this.temp.Count, group.temp);
}
```

The Terminate() method of the UDA sorts the list of values and then determines the indexes of the middle numbers. If there is an odd number of values in the list, there is only a single middle number; if there is an even number of values in the list, the median is the average of the middle two numbers. If the list contains no values (which can occur if every value passed to the aggregate is NULL), the result is NULL; otherwise the Terminate() method calculates and returns the median.

```
public SqlDouble Terminate() {
    SqlDouble result = SqlDouble.Null; // Default result to NULL
    this.temp.Sort(); // Sort list of numbers

    int first, second; // Indexes to middle two numbers

    if (this.temp.Count % 2 == 1)
    {
        // If there is an odd number of values get the middle number twice
        first = this.temp.Count / 2;
        second = first;
    }
    else
    {
        // If there is an even number of values get the middle two numbers
        first = this.temp.Count / 2-1;
        second = first + 1;
    }

    if (this.temp.Count > 0) // If there are numbers, calculate median
    {
        // Calculate median as average of middle number(s)
        result = (SqlDouble)( this.temp[first] + this.temp[second] ) / 2.0;
    }

    return result;
}
```

Listing 14-13 demonstrates the use of this UDA to calculate the median UnitPrice from the Sales.SalesOrderDetail table on a per-product basis. The results are shown in Figure 14-8.

Listing 14-13. Calculating Median Unit Price with a UDA

```
CREATE AGGREGATE dbo.Median (@value float) RETURNS float
EXTERNAL NAME ApressExamples.[Apress.Examples.Median];
GO

SELECT
    ProductID,
    dbo.Median(UnitPrice) AS MedianUnitPrice
FROM Sales.SalesOrderDetail
GROUP BY ProductID;
```

	ProductID	Median Unit Price
1	707	34.99
2	708	34.99
3	709	5.7
4	710	5.7
5	711	34.99
6	712	8.99
7	713	49.99
8	714	29.994
9	715	29.994
10	716	29.994
11	717	780.8182
12	718	780.8182

Figure 14-8. *Median Unit Price for Each Product*

CLR Integration User-Defined Types

SQL Server 2000 had built-in support for user-defined data types, but they were limited in scope and functionality. The old-style user-defined data types had the following restrictions and capabilities:

- They had to be derived from built-in data types.
- Their format and/or range could only be restricted through T-SQL rules.
- They could be assigned a default value.
- They could be declared as NULL or NOT NULL.

SQL Server 2012 provides support for old-style user-defined data types and rules, presumably for backward compatibility with existing applications. The AdventureWorks database contains examples of old-style user-defined data types, like the dbo.Phone data type, which is an alias for the varchar(25) data type.

■ **Caution** Rules (CHECK constraints that can be applied to user-defined data types) have been deprecated since SQL Server 2005 and will be removed from a future version. T-SQL user-defined data types are now often referred to as alias types.

SQL Server 2012 supports a far more flexible solution to your custom data type needs in the form of CLR user-defined types. *CLR integration user-defined types* allow you to access the power of the .NET Framework to meet your custom data type needs. Common examples of CLR UDTs include mathematical concepts like points, vectors, complex numbers, and other types not built into the SQL Server type system. In fact, CLR UDTs are so powerful that Microsoft has begun including some as standard in SQL Server. These CLR UDTs include the spatial data types geography and geometry, and the hierarchyid data type.

CLR UDTs are useful for implementing data types that require special handling and that implement their own special methods and functions. Complex numbers, which are a superset of real numbers, are one example. Complex numbers are represented with a "real" part and an "imaginary" part in the format "$a+bi$," where a is a real number representing the real part of the value, b is a real number representing the imaginary part, and the literal letter i after the imaginary part stands for the imaginary number i, which is the square root of -1. Complex numbers are often used in math, science, and engineering to solve difficult abstract problems. Some examples of complex numbers include $101.9+3.7i$, $98+12i$, $-19i$, and $12+0i$ (which can also be represented as 12). Because their format is different from real numbers and calculations with them require special functionality, complex numbers are a good candidate for CLR. The example in Listing 14-14 implements a complex number CLR UDT.

■ **Note** To keep the example simple, only a partial implementation is reproduced here. The sample download file includes the full version of this CLR UDT that includes basic operators as well as additional documentation and implementations of many more mathematical operators and trigonometric functions.

Listing 14-14. Complex Numbers UDT

```
using System;
using System.Data.SqlTypes;
using Microsoft.SqlServer.Server;
using System.Text.RegularExpressions;

namespace Apress.Examples
{
    [Serializable]
    [Microsoft.SqlServer.Server.SqlUserDefinedType
      (
        Format.Native,
        IsByteOrdered = true
      )]
    public struct Complex : INullable
    {

        #region "Complex Number UDT Fields/Components"

        private bool m_Null;
        public Double real;
```

```
    public Double imaginary;

    #endregion

    #region "Complex Number Parsing, Constructor, and Methods/Properties"

    private static readonly Regex rx = new Regex(
        "^(?<Imaginary>[+-]?([0-9]+|[0-9]*\\.[0-9]+))[i|I]$|" +
        "^(?<Real>[+-]?([0-9]+|[0-9]*\\.[0-9]+))$|" +
        "^(?<Real>[+-]?([0-9]+|[0-9]*\\.[0-9]+))" +
        "(?<Imaginary>[+-]?([0-9]+|[0-9]*\\.[0-9]+))[i|I]$");

    public static Complex Parse(SqlString s)
    {
        Complex u = new Complex();
        if (s.IsNull)
            u = Null;
        else
        {
            MatchCollection m = rx.Matches(s.Value);
            if (m.Count == 0)
                throw (new FormatException("Invalid Complex Number Format."));
            String real_str = m[0].Groups["Real"].Value;
            String imaginary_str = m[0].Groups["Imaginary"].Value;
            if (real_str == "" && imaginary_str == "")
                throw (new FormatException("Invalid Complex Number Format."));
            if (real_str == "")
                u.real = 0.0;
            else
                u.real = Convert.ToDouble(real_str);
            if (imaginary_str == "")
                u.imaginary = 0.0;
            else
                u.imaginary = Convert.ToDouble(imaginary_str);
        }
        return u;
    }

    public override String ToString()
    {
        String sign = "";
        if (this.imaginary >= 0.0)
            sign = "+";
        return this.real.ToString() + sign + this.imaginary.ToString() + "i";
    }

    public bool IsNull
    {
        get
        {
            return m_Null;
        }
    }
```

```csharp
public static Complex Null
{
    get
    {
        Complex h = new Complex();
        h.m_Null = true;
        return h;
    }
}

public Complex(Double r, Double i)
{
    this.real = r;
    this.imaginary = i;
    this.m_Null = false;
}

#endregion

#region "Complex Number Basic Operators"

// Complex number addition
public static Complex operator +(Complex n1, Complex n2)
{
    Complex u;
    if (n1.IsNull || n2.IsNull)
        u = Null;
    else
        u = new Complex(n1.real + n2.real, n1.imaginary + n2.imaginary);
    return u;
}

#endregion

#region "Exposed Mathematical Basic Operator Methods"

// Add complex number n2 to n1
public static Complex CAdd(Complex n1, Complex n2)
{
    return n1 + n2;
}

// Subtract complex number n2 from n1
public static Complex Sub(Complex n1, Complex n2)
{
    return n1 - n2;
}

#endregion

// other complex operations are available in the source code
    }
}
```

The code begins with the required namespace imports and the namespace declaration for the sample:

```
using System;
using System.Data.SqlTypes;
using Microsoft.SqlServer.Server;
using System.Text.RegularExpressions;
```

Next is the declaration of the structure that represents an instance of the UDT. The Serializable, Format.Native, and IsByteOrdered = true attributes and attribute properties are all set on the UDT. In addition, all CLR UDTs must implement the INullable interface. INullable requires that the IsNull and Null properties be defined. The CLR UDT attributes are detailed in Table 14-1.

```
[Serializable]
[Microsoft.SqlServer.Server.SqlUserDefinedType
  (
    Format.Native,
    IsByteOrdered = true
  )]
public struct Complex : INullable
{
    ...
}
```

Table 14-1 shows a few of the common attributes that are used in CLR integration UDT definitions.

Table 14-1. *Common CLR UDT Attributes*

Attribute	Property	Value	Description
Serializable	n/a	n/a	Indicates that the UDT can be serialized and deserialized.
SqlUserDefinedType	Format.Native	n/a	Specifies that the UDT uses native format for serialization. The native format is the most efficient format for serialization/deserialization, but it imposes some limitations. You can only expose .NET value data types (Char, Integer, etc.) as the fields. You cannot expose reference data types (Strings, Arrays, etc.).
SqlUserDefinedType	Format. UserDefined	n/a	Specifies that the UDT uses a user-defined format for serialization. When this is specified, your UDT must implement the IBinarySerialize interface, and you are responsible for supplying the Write() and Read() methods that serialize and deserialize your UDT.
SqlUserDefinedType	IsByteOrdered	true/ false	Allows comparisons and sorting of UDT values based on their binary representation. This is also required if you intend to create indexes on columns defined as a CLR UDT type.
SqlUserDefinedType	IsFixedLength	true/ false	Should be set to true if the serialized instance of your UDT is a fixed length.
SqlUserDefinedType	MaxByteSize	<= 8000 or –1	The maximum size of your serialized UDT instances in bytes. This value must be between 1 and 8,000; or it can be –1 for a maximum size of 2.1 GB.

The public and private fields are declared inside the body of the Complex structure. The real and imaginary public fields represent the real and imaginary parts of the complex number, respectively. The m_Null field is a bool value that is set to true if the current instance of the complex type is NULL, and is set to false otherwise.

```
#region "Complex Number UDT Fields/Components"

private bool m_Null;
public Double real;
public Double imaginary;

#endregion
```

The first method declared in the UDT is the Parse method (required by all UDTs), which takes a string value from SQL Server and parses it into a complex number. The Parse method uses a .NET regular expression to simplify parsing a bit.

```
private static readonly Regex rx = new Regex(
    "^(?<Imaginary>[+-]?([0-9]+|[0-9]*\\.[0-9]+))[i|I]$|" +
    "^(?<Real>[+-]?([0-9]+|[0-9]*\\.[0-9]+))$|" +
    "^(?<Real>[+-]?([0-9]+|[0-9]*\\.[0-9]+))" +
    "(?<Imaginary>[+-]?([0-9]+|[0-9]*\\.[0-9]+))[i|I]$");

public static Complex Parse(SqlString s)
{
    Complex u = new Complex();
    if (s.IsNull)
        u = Null;
    else
    {
        MatchCollection m = rx.Matches(s.Value);
        if (m.Count == 0)
            throw (new FormatException("Invalid Complex Number Format."));
        String real_str = m[0].Groups["Real"].Value;
        String imaginary_str = m[0].Groups["Imaginary"].Value;
        if (real_str == "" && imaginary_str == "")
            throw (new FormatException("Invalid Complex Number Format."));
        if (real_str == "")
            u.real = 0.0;
        else
            u.real = Convert.ToDouble(real_str);
        if (imaginary_str == "")
            u.imaginary = 0.0;
        else
            u.imaginary = Convert.ToDouble(imaginary_str);
    }
    return u;
}
```

The regular expression (a.k.a. regex) uses *named groups* to parse the input string into Real and/or Imaginary named groups. If the regex is successful, at least one (if not both) of these named groups will be populated. If unsuccessful, both named groups will be empty and an exception of type FormatException will be thrown. If

457

at least one of the named groups is properly set, the string representations are converted to Double type and assigned to the appropriate UDT fields. Table 14-2 shows some sample input strings and the values assigned to the UDT fields when they are parsed.

Table 14-2. *Complex Number Parsing Samples*

Complex Number	Real	Imaginary	m_Null
100+11i	100.0	11.0	false
99.9	99.9	0.0	false
3.7-9.8i	3.7	−9.8	false
2.1i	0.0	2.1	false
−9-8.2i	−9.0	−8.2	false
NULL			true

The ToString() method is required for all UDTs as well. This method converts the internal UDT data to its string representation. In the case of complex numbers, ToString() needs to perform the following steps:

1. Convert the real part to a string.

2. Append a plus sign (+) if the imaginary part is 0 or positive.

3. Append the imaginary part.

4. Append the letter i to indicate that it does in fact represent a complex number.

Notice that if the imaginary part is negative, no sign is appended between the real and imaginary parts, since the sign is already included in the imaginary part:

```
public override String ToString()
    {
        String sign = "";
        if (this.imaginary >= 0.0)
            sign = "+";
        return this.real.ToString() + sign + this.imaginary.ToString() + "i";
    }
```

The IsNull and Null properties are both required by all UDTs. IsNull is a bool property that indicates whether a UDT instance is NULL or not. The Null property returns a NULL instance of the UDT type. One thing you need to be aware of any time you invoke a UDT (or any CLR integration object) from T-SQL is SQL NULL. For purposes of the Complex UDT, we take a cue from T-SQL and return a NULL result any time a NULL is passed in as a parameter to any UDT method. So a Complex value plus NULL returns NULL, as does a Complex value divided by NULL, and so on. You will notice a lot of code in the complete Complex UDT listing that is specifically designed to deal with NULL.

```
public bool IsNull
{
    get
    {
        return m_Null;
    }
}

public static Complex Null
{
    get
    {
        Complex h = new Complex();
        h.m_Null = true;
        return h;
    }
}
```

This particular UDT includes a constructor function that accepts two Double type values and creates a UDT instance from them:

```
public Complex(Double r, Double i)
{
    this.real = r;
    this.imaginary = i;
    this.m_Null = false;
}
```

■ **Tip**   For a UDT designed as a.NET structure, a constructor method is not required. In fact, a default constructor (that takes no parameters) is not even allowed. To keep later code simple, we added a constructor method to this example.

In the next region, we defined a few useful complex number constants and exposed them as static properties of the Complex UDT:

```
#region "Useful Complex Number Constants"

// The property "i" is the Complex number 0 + 1i. Defined here because
// it is useful in some calculations

public static Complex i
{
    get
    {
        return new Complex(0, 1);
    }
}

...

#endregion
```

To keep this listing short but highlight the important points, the sample UDT shows only the addition operator for complex numbers. The UDT overrides the + operator. Redefining operators makes it easier to write and debug additional UDT methods. These overridden .NET math operators are not available to T-SQL code, so the standard T-SQL math operators will not work on the UDT.

```
// Complex number addition

public static Complex operator +(Complex n1, Complex n2)
{
    Complex u;
    if (n1.IsNull || n2.IsNull)
        u = Null;
    else
        u = new Complex(n1.real + n2.real, n1.imaginary + n2.imaginary);
    return u;
}
```

Performing mathematical operations on UDT values from T-SQL must be done via explicitly exposed methods of the UDT. These methods in the Complex UDT are CAdd and Div, for complex number addition and division, respectively. Note that we chose CAdd (which stands for "complex number add") as a method name to avoid conflicts with the T-SQL reserved word ADD. We won't go too deeply into the inner workings of complex numbers, but we chose to implement the basic operators in this listing because some (like complex number addition) are straightforward operations, while others (like division) are a bit more complicated. The math operator methods are declared as static, so they can be invoked on the UDT data type itself from SQL Server instead of on an instance of the UDT.

```
#region "Exposed Mathematical Basic Operator Methods"

// Add complex number n2 to n1
public static Complex CAdd(Complex n1, Complex n2)
{
    return n1 + n2;
}

// Subtract complex number n2 from n1
public static Complex Sub(Complex n1, Complex n2)
{
    return n1 - n2;
}

#endregion
```

■ **Note** Static methods of a UDT (declared with the static keyword in C# or the Shared keyword in Visual Basic) are invoked from SQL Server using a format like this:

```
Complex::CAdd(@n1, @n2)
```

Nonshared, or instance methods of a UDT are invoked from SQL Server using a format similar to this:

```
@>n1.CAdd(@n2)
```

The style of method you use (shared or instance) is a determination you'll need to make on a case-by-case basis.

Listing 14-15 demonstrates how the Complex UDT can be used, and the results are shown in Figure 14-9.

Listing 14-15. Complex Number UDT Demonstration

```
CREATE TYPE dbo.Complex
EXTERNAL NAME ApressExamples.[Apress.Examples.Complex];
GO

DECLARE @c complex = '+100-10i',
  @d complex = '5i';
SELECT 'ADD: '+ @c.ToString()+' , '+ @d.ToString() AS Op,
  complex::CAdd(@c, @d).ToString() AS Result
UNION
SELECT 'DIV: '+ @c.ToString() +' , '+ @d.ToString(),
  complex::Div(@c, @d).ToString()
UNION
SELECT 'SUB: '+ @c.ToString() +' , '+ @d.ToString(),
  complex::Sub(@c, @d).ToString()
UNION
SELECT 'MULT: '+ @c.ToString() +' , '+ @d.ToString(),
  complex::Mult(@c, @d).ToString()
UNION
SELECT 'PI: ',
  complex::Pi.ToString();
```

	Op	Result
1	ADD: 100-10i , 0+5i	100-5i
2	DIV: 100-10i , 0+5i	-2-20i
3	MULT: 100-10i , 0+5i	50+500i
4	PI:	3.14159265358979+0i
5	SUB: 100-10i , 0+5i	100-15i

Figure 14-9. Performing Operations with the Complex UDT

In addition to the basic operations, the Complex class can be easily extended to support several more advanced complex number operators and functions. The code sample download file contains a full listing of an expanded Complex UDT, including all the basic math operators, as well as logarithmic and exponential functions (Log(), Power(), etc.) and trigonometric and hyperbolic functions (Sin(), Cos(), Tanh(), etc.) for complex numbers.

Triggers

Finally, you can also create .NET triggers. This is logical; after all, triggers are just a specialized type of stored procedures. There are few examples of really interesting .NET triggers. Most of what you want to do in a trigger can be done with regular T-SQL code. When SQL Server 2005 was released, we saw an example of a .NET trigger on a location table that calls a web service to find the coordinates of a city and adds them to a coordinates column. This could at first sound like a cool idea, but if you remember that a trigger is fired inside the scope of the DML statement's transaction, you can guess that the latency added to every insert and update on the table might be a problem. Usually, we try to keep the trigger impact as light as possible. Listing 14-16 presents an example of a .NET trigger based on our previous regular expression UDF. It tests an e-mail inserted or modified on the AdventureWorks Person.EmailAddress table, and rolls back the transaction if it does not match the pattern of a correct e-mail address. Let's see it in action.

Listing 14-16. Trigger to Validate an E-mail Address

```
using System;
using System.Data;
using System.Data.SqlClient;
using Microsoft.SqlServer.Server;
using System.Text.RegularExpressions;
using System.Transactions;

namespace Apress.Examples
{
    public partial class Triggers
    {
        private static readonly Regex email_pattern = new Regex
        (
            // Everything before the @ sign (the "local part")
            "^[a-z0-9!#$%&'*+/=?^_'{|}~-]+(?:\\.[a-z0-9!#$%&'*+/=?^_'{|}~-]+)*" +

            // Subdomains after the @ sign
            "@(?:[a-z0-9](?:[a-z0-9-]*[a-z0-9])?\\.)+" +

            // Top-level domains
            "(?:[a-z]{2}|com|org|net|gov|mil|biz|info|mobi|name|aero|jobs|museum)\\b$"
        );

        [Microsoft.SqlServer.Server.SqlTrigger(
            Name = "EmailAddressTrigger",
            Target = "[Person].[EmailAddress]",
            Event = "FOR INSERT, UPDATE")]
        public static void EmailAddressTrigger()
        {
            SqlTriggerContext tContext = SqlContext.TriggerContext;

            // Retrieve the connection that the trigger is using.
            using (SqlConnection cn
                = new SqlConnection(@"context connection=true"))
            {
                SqlCommand cmd;
                SqlDataReader r;

                cn.Open();

                cmd = new SqlCommand(@"SELECT EmailAddress FROM INSERTED", cn);
                r = cmd.ExecuteReader();
```

```
            try
            {
                while (r.Read())
                {
                    if (!email_pattern.IsMatch(r.GetString(0).ToLower()))
                        Transaction.Current.Rollback();
                }
            }
            catch (SqlException ex)
            {
                // Catch the expected exception.
            }
            finally
            {
                r.Close();
                cn.Close();
            }
        }
    }
}
}
```

As we now are used to, we first declare our .NET namespaces. To manage the transaction, we have to declare the System.Transactions namespace. In your Visual Studio project, it might not be recognized. You need to right-click on the project in the Solution Explorer and select "add reference." Then, go to the SQL Server tab, and check "System.Transactions for framework 4.0.0.0."

Then, like in our previous UDF, we declare the Regex object. The trigger body follows. In the function's decoration, we name the trigger, and we declare for which target table it is intended. We also specify at what events it will fire.

```
[Microsoft.SqlServer.Server.SqlTrigger(
    Name = "EmailAddressTrigger",
    Target = "[Person].[EmailAddress]",
    Event = "FOR INSERT, UPDATE")]
public static void EmailAddressTrigger()
{ ...
```

Then, we declare an instance of the SqlTriggerContext class. This class exposes a few properties that give information about the trigger's context, like what columns are updated, what the action is that fired the trigger, and in case of a DDL trigger, it also gives access to the EventData XML structure containing all the execution details.

```
        SqlTriggerContext tContext = SqlContext.TriggerContext;
```

The next line opens the so-called context connection to SQL Server. There is only one way to access the content of a table: with a T-SQL SELECT statement. Even a .NET code executed inside SQL Server cannot escape from this rule. To be able to retrieve the e-mails that have been inserted or updated, we need to open a connection to SQL Server and query the inserted virtual table. For that, we use a special type of connection available inside CLR integration named the context connection, which is designed to be faster than a regular network or local connection. Then we use a data reader to retrieve the e-mails in the EmailAddress column. We loop through the results and apply the regular expression pattern to each address. If it doesn't match, we roll back the transaction by using the Transaction.Current.Rollback() method. We need to protect the rollback by a try ... catch block, because it will throw an ambiguous exception, stating that "Transaction is not allowed to roll back inside a user defined routine, trigger or aggregate because the transaction is not started in that CLR level." This can be safely ignored. Another error will be raised even if the try ... catch block is there, and it must be dealt with at the T-SQL level. We will see that in our example later on.

```
using (SqlConnection cn
    = new SqlConnection(@"context connection = true"))
{
    SqlCommand cmd;
    SqlDataReader r;

    cn.Open();

    cmd = new SqlCommand(@"SELECT EmailAddress FROM INSERTED", cn);
    r = cmd.ExecuteReader();
    try
    {
        while (r.Read())
        {
            if (!email_pattern.IsMatch(r.GetString(0).ToLower()))
                Transaction.Current.Rollback();
        }
    }
    catch (SqlException ex)
    {
        // Catch the expected exception.
    }
    finally
    {
        r.Close();
        cn.Close();
    }
}
}
}
```

Now that the trigger is written, let's try it out. When the assembly is compiled and added to the AdventureWorks database using CREATE ASSEMBLY, we can add the trigger to the Person.EmailAddress table, as shown in Listing 14-17.

Listing 14-17. Creation of the CLR Trigger to Validate an E-mail Address

```
CREATE TRIGGER atr_Person_EmailAddress_ValidateEmail
ON Person.EmailAddress
AFTER INSERT, UPDATE
AS EXTERNAL NAME ApressExamples.[Apress.Examples.Triggers].EmailAddressTrigger;
```

We now try to update a line to an obviously invalid e-mail address in Listing 14-18. The result is shown in Figure 14-10.

```
Msg 3991, Level 16, State 1, Procedure atr_Person_EmailAddress_ValidateEmail, Line 1
The context transaction which was active before entering user defined routine, trigger or aggregate
"atr_Person_EmailAddress_ValidateEmail" has been ended inside of it, which is not allowed.
Change application logic to enforce strict transaction nesting.
The statement has been terminated.
```

Figure 14-10. *Result of the Trigger's Action*

Listing 14-18. Setting an Invalid E-mail Address

```
UPDATE Person.EmailAddress
SET EmailAddress = 'pro%sql@apress@com'
WHERE EmailAddress = 'dylan0@adventure-works.com';
```

As you can see, the trigger worked and rolled back the UPDATE attempt, but the error message generated for the CLR code is not very user-friendly. We need to catch the exception in our T-SQL statement. A modified UPDATE dealing with that is shown in Listing 14-19.

Listing 14-19. UPDATE Statement Modified to Handle the Error

```
BEGIN TRY
    UPDATE Person.EmailAddress
    SET EmailAddress = 'pro%sql@apress@com'
    WHERE EmailAddress = 'dylan0@adventure-works.com';
END TRY
BEGIN CATCH
    IF ERROR_NUMBER() = 3991
        RAISERROR('invalid email address', 16, 10)
END CATCH
```

This CLR trigger is an example, and it might not be the best solution to our e-mail checking needs, for two reasons: firstly because we need to handle the CLR error in our calling code, which forces us to enclose every statement modifying the EmailAddress inside a try ... catch block, and secondly because of performance considerations. Our CLR code loops through a DataReader and checks it line per line. A set-oriented T-SQL trigger like the one shown in Listing 14-20 will certainly be faster, especially if there are many rows affected by the INSERT or UPDATE statement.

Listing 14-20. T-SQL Trigger to Validate an E-mail Address

```
CREATE TRIGGER atr_Person_EmailAddress_ValidateEmail
ON Person.EmailAddress
AFTER INSERT, UPDATE
AS BEGIN
    IF @@ROWCOUNT = 0 RETURN

    IF EXISTS (SELECT * FROM inserted WHERE dbo.EmailMatch(EmailAddress) = 0)
    BEGIN
        RAISERROR('an email is invalid', 16, 10)
        ROLLBACK TRANSACTION
    END

END;
```

Summary

SQL Server 2005 introduced SQL CLR integration, allowing you to create UDFs, UDAs, SPs, UDTs, and triggers in managed .NET code. SQL Server 2008 improved on CLR integration by allowing UDTs and UDAs to have a maximum size of 2.1 GB, which is still the case in SQL Server 2012.

In this chapter, we talked about CLR integration usage considerations, and scenarios when CLR integration code might be considered a good alternative to strict T-SQL. We also discussed assemblies and security, including the SAFE, EXTERNAL_ACCESS, and UNSAFE permission sets that can be applied on a per-assembly basis.

Finally, we provided several examples of CLR integration code that cover a wide range of possible uses, including the following:

- CLR integration can be invaluable when access to external resources is required from the server.

- CLR integration can be useful when non-table specific aggregations are required.

- CLR integration simplifies complex data validations that would be complex and difficult to perform in T-SQL.

- CLR integration allows you to supplement SQL Server's data typing system with your own specialized data types that define their own built-in methods and properties.

This chapter has served as an introduction to CLR integration programming. For in-depth CLR integration programming information, I highly recommend *Pro SQL Server 2005 Assemblies*, by Robin Dewson and Julian Skinner (Apress, 2005). Though written for SQL Server 2005, much of the information it contains is still relevant to SQL Server 2012. In the next chapter, we will introduce client-side .NET connectivity to SQL Server 2012.

EXERCISES

1. [Choose all that apply] SQL Server 2012 provides support for which of the following CLR integration objects:

   - UDFs

   - UDAs

   - UDTs

   - SPs

   - Triggers

   - User-defined catalogs

2. [True/False] SQL Server 2012 limits CLR integration UDAs and UDTs to a maximum size of 8000 bytes.

3. [Choose one] SAFE permissions allow your CLR integration code to

   a. Write to the file system

   - Access network resources

   - Read the computer's registry

- Execute managed .NET code

  - All of the above

4. [True/False] CLR integration UDAs and UDTs must be defined with the Serializable attribute.

5. [Fill in the blank] A CLR integration UDA that is declared as Format.UserDefined must implement the _____ interface.

6. [Choose all that apply] A CLR integration UDA must implement which of the following methods?

   a. Init

   - Aggregate

   - Terminate

   - Merge

   - Accumulate

CHAPTER 15

■ ■ ■

.NET Client Programming

Which is more important, an efficient database or a well-designed client application that connects to the database? In our estimation, they are both equally important. After all, your database can be very well designed and extremely efficient, but that won't matter to the end user if the client application he or she uses to connect to your database is slow and unresponsive. While this book focuses on SQL Server server-side development functionality, we've decided to take a moment to introduce some of the tools available to create efficient SQL Server client applications. The .NET Framework, in particular, offers several options to make SQL Server 2012 client connectivity simple and efficient. In this chapter, we will discuss using ADO.NET, and the .NET SqlClient as a basis for building your own easy-to-use, cutting-edge SQL Server client applications, and we will venture into modern ORM trends with LINQ to SQL and Entity Framework.

ADO.NET

The System.Data.* namespaces consist of classes and enumerations that comprise the ADO.NET architecture, the .NET Framework's primary tool for database access. You can use the classes in the System.Data.* namespaces to connect to your databases and access them in real time, or in a disconnected fashion via the DataSet, DataTable, and DataAdapter classes. The following are some of the more commonly used namespaces for SQL Server data access, some of which we saw in Chapter 14 when we had a look at SQL Server .NET Integration:

- The System.Data namespace provides access to classes that implement the ADO.NET architecture, such as DataSet and DataTable.

- The System.Data.Common namespace provides access to classes that are shared by .NET Framework data access providers, such as the DbProviderFactory class.

- The primary namespace for native SQL Server connectivity is System.Data.SqlClient. This namespace includes classes that provide optimized access to SQL Server (version 7.0 and higher) via SQL Server Native Client. The classes in this namespace are designed specifically to take advantage of SQL Server-specific features and won't work with other data sources.

- The System.Data.Odbc namespace provides managed access to old-fashioned ODBC drivers. ODBC was developed in the early 1990s as a one-size-fits-all standard for connecting to a wide array of varied data sources. Because of its mission of standardizing data access across a wide variety of data sources, ODBC provides a generally "plain vanilla" interface that sometimes does not take advantage of SQL Server or other database management system (DBMS) platform-specific features. This means that ODBC is not as efficient as the SQL client, but it provides a useful option for connecting to a wide variety of data sources such as Excel spreadsheets or other DBMSs.

- Microsoft also provides the System.Data.OleDb namespaces, which can connect to a variety of data sources, including SQL Server. It is an option for applications that need to access data on multiple platforms, such as both SQL Server and Microsoft Access. OLEDB has been recently deprecated by Microsoft in favor of the more standard ODBC, even thoughOLEDB was created after ODBC.

- The System.Data.SqlTypes namespace provides .NET classes representing native, nullable SQL Server data types. These .NET SQL Server-specific data types for the most part use the same internal representation as the equivalent SQL Server native data types, helping to reduce precision loss problems. Using these types can also help speed up SQL Server connectivity, since it helps eliminate implicit conversions. And these data types, unlike the standard .NET value types, have built-in NULL-handling capability. Table 15-1 lists the .NET SqlTypes types and their corresponding native T-SQL data types.

Table 15-1. *System.Data.SqlTypes Conversions*

System.Data.SqlTypes Class	Native T-SQL Data Type
SqlBinary	binary, image, timestamp, varbinary
SqlBoolean	bit
SqlByte	tinyint
SqlDateTime	datetime, smalldatetime
SqlDecimal	decimal, numeric
SqlDouble	float
SqlGuid	uniqueidentifier
SqlInt16	smallint
SqlInt32	int
SqlInt64	bigint
SqlMoney	money, smallmoney
SqlSingle	real
SqlString	char, nchar, ntext, nvarchar, text, varchar
SqlXml	xml

■ **Note** At the time of this writing, there are no .NET SqlTypes types corresponding to the SQL Server data types introduced in SQL Server 2008 (e.g., date, time, datetimeoffset, and datetime2).

The .NET SQL Client

The .NET native SQL client (SQLNCLI) is the most efficient way to connect to SQL Server from a client application. With the possible exceptions of upgrading legacy code or designing code that must access non-SQL Server data sources, the native SQL client is the client connectivity method of choice. The main classes for establishing a connection, sending SQL commands, and retrieving results with SqlClient are listed in Table 15-2.

Table 15-2. *Commonly Used Native SQL Client Classes*

System.Data.SqlClient Class	Description
SqlCommand	The SqlCommand object represents an SQL statement or SP to execute.
SqlCommandBuilder	The SqlCommandBuilder automatically generates single-table commands to reconcile changes made to an ADO.NET DataSet.
SqlConnection	The SqlConnection establishes a connection to SQL Server.
SqlConnectionStringBuilder	The SqlConnectionStringBuilder builds connection strings for use by SqlConnection objects.
SqlDataAdapter	The SqlDataAdapter wraps a set of SqlCommand objects and a SqlConnection that can be used to fill an ADO.NET DataSet and update a SQL Server database.
SqlDataReader	The SqlDataReader provides methods to read a forward-only stream of rows from a SQL Server database.
SqlException	The SqlException class provides access to SQL Server-specific exceptions. This class can be used to capture an SQL Server error or warning.
SqlParameter	The SqlParameter represents a parameter to an SqlCommand.
SqlParameterCollection	The SqlParameter collection is a collection of SqlParameter objects associated with an SqlCommand.
SqlTransaction	The SqlTransaction class enables an SQL Server transaction to be initiated and managed from a client.

Connected Data Access

Listing 15-1 demonstrates SqlClient data access via a SqlDataReader instance. This is the type of access you might use in an ASP.NET page to quickly retrieve values for a drop-down list, for example. This sample is written to run as a C# console application. The SQL Server connection string defined in the sqlconnection variable should be modified to suit your local SQL Server environment and security.

Listing 15-1. SqlDataReader Sample

```
using System;
using System.Data.SqlClient;

namespace Apress.Examples
{
    class Listing15_1
    {
        static void Main(string[] args)
        {
            string sqlconnection=@"DATA SOURCE = SQL2012;" +
                "INITIAL CATALOG=AdventureWorks;" +
                "INTEGRATED SECURITY=SSPI;";
```

```
                    string sqlcommand = "SELECT " +
                        "   DepartmentId, " +
                        "   Name, " +
                        "   GroupName " +
                        " FROM HumanResources.Department " +
                        " ORDER BY DepartmentId";

                    try
                    {
                        connection = new SqlConnection(sqlconnection);
                        connection.Open();
                        command = new SqlCommand(sqlcommand, connection);
                        datareader = command.ExecuteReader();

                        while (datareader.Read())
                        {
                            Console.WriteLine
                                (
                                  "{0}\t{1}\t{2}",
                                  datareader["DepartmentId"].ToString(),
                                  datareader["Name"].ToString(),
                                  datareader["GroupName"].ToString()
                                );
                        }
                    }
                    catch (SqlException ex)
                    {
                        Console.WriteLine(ex.Message);
                    }
                    finally
                    {
                        connection.Close();
                    }
                    Console.Write("Press a Key to Continue...");
                    Console.ReadKey();
            }
        }
}
```

This example is a very simple console application that retrieves the list of departments from the HumanResources.Department table of the AdventureWorks database and writes the data to the display. The example begins by importing the System and System.Data.SqlClient namespaces. Though not required, importing the namespaces saves some keystrokes and helps make code more readable by eliminating the need to prefix the classes and enumerations used with their associated namespaces.

```
using System;
using System.Data.SqlClient;
```

The body of the class defines the SQL Server connection string and the T-SQL command that will retrieve the department data. The DATA_SOURCE connection string option is set at our server named SQL2012; change it accordingly to match your own server name. When defining the connection string, we prefix the string with the

@ sign, to create a verbatim string literal. This is useful because a verbatim string literal will not interpret peical characters like \. Without that, if you declare a named instance as data source, like YOUR_SERVER\SQL2012, you would have to escape it like this: YOUR_SERVER\\SQL2012. With a verbatim string literal, the \ does not need to be escaped.

```
string sqlconnection=@"DATA SOURCE=SQL2012;" +
            "INITIAL CATALOG=AdventureWorks;" +
            "INTEGRATED SECURITY=SSPI;";

        string sqlcommand="SELECT " +
        "    DepartmentId, " +
        "    Name, " +
        "    GroupName " +
        " FROM HumanResources.Department " +
        " ORDER BY DepartmentId";

        SqlConnection connection = null;
```

The SqlConnection connection string is composed of a series of key/value pairs separated by semicolons, as shown in the following:

```
DATA SOURCE=SQL2012;INITIAL CATALOG=AdventureWorks;INTEGRATED SECURITY=SSPI;
```

Some of the commonly used SqlConnection connection string keys are listed in Table 15-3.

Table 15-3. *SqlConnection Connection String Keys*

Connection String Keys	Description
AttachDBFileName	This is the name of the full path to an attachable primary database file (MDF file).
Connection Timeout	This is the length of time (in seconds) to wait for a server connection before stopping the attempt.
Data Source	This is the name or IP address of an SQL Server instance to connect to. Use the server\instance format for named instances. A port number can be added to the end of the name or network address by appending the port number with a comma.
Encrypt	This indicates that SSL encryption will be used to communicate with SQL Server.
Initial Catalog	This is the name of the database to connect to once a server connection is established.
Integrated Security	When set to true, yes, or sspi, Windows integrated security is used to connect. When false or no, SQL Server security is used.
MultipleActiveResultSets	When true, a connection can enable Multiple Active Result Sets (MARS). When false, all result sets from a batch must be processed before any other batch can be executed on the connection.
Password	This is the password for the SQL Server account used to log in. Using integrated security is recommended over SQL Server account security.

(continued)

473

Table 15-3. (*continued*)

Connection String Keys	Description
Persist Security Info	When set to false or no, sensitive security information (like a password) is not returned as part of the connection if the connection has been opened. The recommended setting is false.
User ID	This is the SQL Server account user ID used to log in. Integrated security is recommended over SQL Server account security.

■ **Note** The http://www.connectionstrings.com/ website is a handy reference of connection strings for all major database servers.

The next section of code is enclosed in a try...catch block because of the possibility that a database connection or other error might occur. If an error does occur, control is passed to the catch block and the error message is displayed. The try...catch block includes the finally block, which cleans up the database connection whether an exception is thrown or not.

```
try
{
    ...
}
catch  (SqlException ex)
{
    Console.WriteLine(ex.Message);
}
finally
{
    connection.Close();
}
```

When connecting to SQL Server from a client application, it's a very good idea to code defensively with try...catch blocks. Defensive coding simply means trying to anticipate the problems that might occur and making sure that your code handles them. Following this practice in database client applications can save you a lot of headaches down the road. Some of the possible errors you might encounter in SQL Server client applications include problems connecting to SQL Server, trying to access tables and other database objects that have been changed or no longer exist, and returning NULL when you expect other values.

Within the example's try...catch block, the SqlConnection is instantiated and opened using the connection string defined previously. Then a SqlCommand is created on the open connection and executed with the ExecuteReader method. The ExecuteReader() method returns a SqlDataReader instance, which allows you to retrieve result set rows in an efficient forward-only fashion. In this example, we use the SqlDataReader in a while loop to quickly retrieve all rows and display them on the console.

```
try
{
    connection = new SqlConnection(sqlconnection);
    connection.Open();
    command = new SqlCommand(sqlcommand, connection);
    datareader = command.ExecuteReader();
```

```
    while (datareader.Read())
    {
        Console.WriteLine
        (
            "{0}\t{1}\t{2}",
            datareader["DepartmentId"].ToString(),
            datareader["Name"].ToString(),
            datareader["GroupName"].ToString()
        );
    }
}
```

The results of the simple client utility from Listing 15-1 are shown in Figure 15-1.

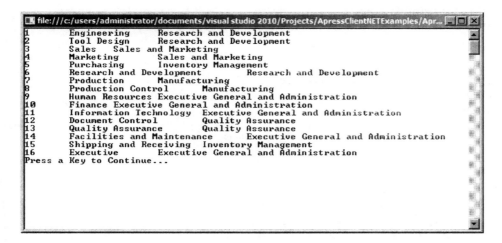

Figure 15-1. *Querying the Database Table and Iterating the Result Set*

Disconnected Datasets

The example in Listing 15-1 demonstrated the forward-only read-only SqlDataReader, which provides an efficient interface for data retrieval but is far less flexible than ADO.NET disconnected datasets. A disconnected dataset is an in-memory cache of a dataset. It provides flexibility because you do not need a constant connection to the database in order to query and manipulate the data. Listing 15-2 demonstrates how to use the SqlDataAdapter to fill a DataSet and print the results. The differences between Listing 15-2 and Listing 15-1 are shown in bold.

Listing 15-2. Using SqlDataReader to Fill a DataSet

```
using System;
using System.Data;
using System.Data.SqlClient;

namespace Apress.Examples
{
    class Listing15_2
```

```csharp
{
    static void Main(string[] args)
    {
        string sqlconnection = @"DATA SOURCE = SQL2012;" +
            "INITIAL CATALOG=AdventureWorks;" +
            "INTEGRATED SECURITY=SSPI;";

        string sqlcommand = "SELECT " +
            "   DepartmentId, " +
            "   Name, " +
            "   GroupName " +
            " FROM HumanResources.Department " +
            " ORDER BY DepartmentId";

        SqlDataAdapter adapter = null;
        DataSet dataset = null;

        try
        {
            adapter = new SqlDataAdapter(sqlcommand, sqlconnection);
            dataset = new DataSet();
            adapter.Fill(dataset);

            foreach (DataRow row in dataset.Tables[0].Rows)
            {
                Console.WriteLine
                    (
                      "{0}\t{1}\t{2}",
                      row["DepartmentId"].ToString(),
                      row["Name"].ToString(),
                      row["GroupName"].ToString()
                    );
            }
        }
        catch (SqlException ex)
        {
            Console.WriteLine(ex.Message);
        }
        finally
        {
            if (dataset != null)
            dataset.Dispose();
            if (adapter != null)
            adapter.Dispose();
        }
        Console.Write("Press a Key to Continue...");
        Console.ReadKey();
    }
}
}
```

The second version of the application, in Listing 15-2, generates the same results as Listing 15-1. The first difference is that this sample imports the System.Data namespace, because the DataSet class is a member of System.Data. Again, this is not required, but it does save wear and tear on your fingers by eliminating the need to prefix System.Data classes and enumerations with the namespace.

```
using System;
using System.Data;
using System.Data.SqlClient;
```

The SQL connection string and query string definitions are the same in both examples. Listing 15-2 departs from Listing 15-1 by declaring a SqlDataAdapter and a DataSet instead of a SqlConnection, SqlCommand, and SqlDataReader.

```
SqlDataAdapter adapter = null;
DataSet dataset = null;
```

The code to retrieve the data creates a new SqlDataAdapter and DataSet, and then populates the DataSet via the Fill() method of the SqlDataAdapter.

```
adapter = new SqlDataAdapter(sqlcommand, sqlconnection);
dataset = new DataSet();
adapter.Fill(dataset);
```

The main loop iterates through each DataRow in the single table returned by the DataSet and writes the results to the console:

```
foreach (DataRow row in dataset.Tables[0].Rows)
{
    Console.WriteLine
    (
        "{0}\t{1}\t{2}",
        row["DepartmentId"].ToString(),
        row["Name"].ToString(),
        row["GroupName"].ToString()
    );
}
```

The balance of the code handles exceptions, performs cleanup by disposing of the DataSet and SqlDataAdapter, and waits for a key press before exiting:

```
if (dataset != null)
    dataset.Dispose();
if (adapter != null)
    adapter.Dispose();
```

Parameterized Queries

ADO.NET provides a safe method for passing parameters to an SP or SQL statement, known as *parameterization*. The "classic" Visual Basic 6/VBScript method of concatenating parameter values directly into a long SQL query string is inefficient and potentially unsafe (see the "SQL Injection and Performance" sidebar later in this chapter for more information). A concatenated string query might look like this:

```
string  sqlstatement  =  "SELECT  "  +
    "      BusinessEntityID, "  +
    "      LastName, "  +
    "      FirstName, "  +
    "      MiddleName "  +
```

```
"FROM Person.Person " +
"WHERE LastName = N'" + name + "';";
```

The value of the name variable can contain additional SQL statements, leaving SQL Server wide open to SQL injection attacks. Let's imagine the name variable we use here comes directly from a text box where the user can enter the name. An attacker could enter some special characters in order to tamper with the generated query, as in the following:

```
string name = "';
DELETE FROM Person.Person; --";
```

This value for the name variable results in the following dangerous SQL statements being executed on the server:

```
SELECT
    BusinessEntityID,
    LastName,
    FirstName,
    MiddleName
FROM Person.Person
WHERE   LastName  =  N'';
DELETE  FROM  Person.Person;  -- ';
```

Parameterized queries avoid SQL injection by sending the parameter values to the server separately from the SQL statement. Listing 15-3 demonstrates a simple parameterized query. (The results are shown in Figure 15-2.)

Listing 15-3. Parameterized SQL Query

```
using System;
using System.Data;
using System.Data.SqlClient;

namespace Apress.Examples
{
    class Listing15_3
    {
        static void Main(string[] args)
        {

            string name = "SMITH";
            string sqlconnection = @"SERVER = SQL2012; " +
                "INITIAL CATALOG = AdventureWorks; " +
                "INTEGRATED SECURITY = SSPI;";

            string sqlcommand = "SELECT " +
                "  BusinessEntityID, " +
                "  FirstName, " +
                "  MiddleName, " +
                "  LastName " +
                "FROM Person.Person " +
                "WHERE LastName = @name";

            SqlConnection connection = null;
            SqlCommand command = null;
            SqlDataReader datareader = null;
```

```
try
{
    connection = new SqlConnection(sqlconnection);
    connection.Open();
    command = new SqlCommand(sqlcommand, connection);
    command.Parameters.Add("@name", SqlDbType.NVarChar, 50).Value = name;
    datareader = command.ExecuteReader();
    while (datareader.Read())
    {
        Console.WriteLine
            (
            "{0}\t{1}\t{2}\t{3}",
            datareader["BusinessEntityID"].ToString(),
            datareader["LastName"].ToString(),
            datareader["FirstName"].ToString(),
            datareader["MiddleName"].ToString()
            );
    }
}
catch (Exception ex)
{
    Console.WriteLine(ex.Message);
}
finally
{
    connection.Close();
}
Console.WriteLine("Press any key...");
Console.ReadKey();
        }
    }
}
```

Figure 15-2. Results of the Parameterized Query

Listing 15-3 retrieves and prints the contact information for all people in the AdventureWorks
Person.Person table whose last name is Smith. The sample begins by importing the appropriate namespaces.
The System.Data namespace is referenced here because it contains the SqlDbType enumeration that is used to
declare parameter data types.

```
using System;
using System.Data;
using System.Data.SqlClient;
```

The program begins by declaring a variable to hold the parameter value, the SqlClient connection string,
a parameterized SQL SELECT statement, and the SqlConnection, SqlCommand, and SqlDataReader objects.

```
string name = "SMITH";
string sqlconnection = @"SERVER = SQL2012; " +
    "INITIAL CATALOG = AdventureWorks; " +
    "INTEGRATED SECURITY = SSPI;";

string sqlcommand = "SELECT " +
    "  BusinessEntityID, " +
    "  FirstName, " +
    "  MiddleName, " +
    "  LastName " +
    "FROM Person.Person " +
    "WHERE LastName = @name";

SqlConnection connection = null;
SqlCommand command = null;
SqlDataReader datareader = null;
```

As with the previous examples, try...catch is used to capture run-time exceptions. The parameterized
SQL SELECT statement contains a reference to an SQL Server parameter named @name. Next, and a connection is
established to the AdventureWorks database:

```
connection = new SqlConnection(sqlconnection);
connection.Open();
```

An SqlCommand is created using the previously defined query string, and a value is assigned to the @name
parameter. Every SqlCommand exposes a SqlParameterCollection property called Parameters. The Add method
of the Parameters collection allows you to add parameters to the SqlCommand. In this sample, the parameter
added is named @name; it is an nvarchar type parameter, and its length is 50. The parameters in the Parameters
collection are passed along to SQL Server with the SQL statement when the ExecuteReader(), ExecuteScalar(),
ExecuteNonQuery(), or ExecuteXmlReader() method of the SqlCommand is called. The addition of a Parameter
object to the SqlCommand is critical; this is the portion of the code that inhibits SQL injection attacks.

```
command = new SqlCommand(sqlcommand, connection);
command.Parameters.Add("@name", SqlDbType.NVarChar, 50).Value = name;
```

In this instance, the ExecuteReader() method is called to return the results via SqlDataReader instance, and
a while loop is used to iterate over and display the results.

```
datareader = command.ExecuteReader();
while (datareader.Read())
{
    Console.WriteLine
    (
        "{0}\t{1}\t{2}\t{3}",
```

```
        datareader["BusinessEntityID"].ToString(),
        datareader["LastName"].ToString(),
        datareader["FirstName"].ToString(),
        datareader["MiddleName"].ToString()
    );
}
```

SQL INJECTION AND PERFORMANCE

SQL developers and DBAs have long known of the potential security risks that SQL injection attacks can pose. We often hear about exploits based on SQL injections. As an example, in 2011 hackers claimed in a press release to have stolen personal information of 1 million users on the Sony Pictures website by a single SQL injection attack. So if developers and DBAs have known all about the evils of SQL injection for years, why are so many databases getting compromised?

The problem is not that people don't know what SQL injection is. Most DBAs and developers instinctively shudder at the sound of those two little words. Instead it appears that many developers either don't know how, or are just not motivated, to properly code to defend against this vicious attack. A lot of injection-susceptible code was written on the Visual Basic 6 and classic ASP platforms, where query parameterization was a bit of a hassle. A lot of programmers have carried their bad coding habits over to .NET, despite the fact that query parameterization with SqlClient is easier than ever.

As an added benefit, when you properly parameterize your queries, you can get a performance boost. When SQL Server receives a parameterized query, it automatically caches the query plan generated by the optimizer. On subsequent executions of the same parameterized query, SQL Server can use the cached query plan. Concatenated string queries without parameterization generally cannot take advantage of cached query plan reuse, so SQL Server must regenerate the query plan every time the query is executed. Keep these benefits in mind when developing SQL Server client code.

Additionally, using stored procedures instead of ad-hoc queries built in the client code solves almost all SQL injection threats and allows the best possible query plan reuse, unless you create dynamic SQL inside the procedure, with the EXECUTE() command.

Nonquery, Scalar, and XML Querying

The examples covered so far in this chapter have all been SQL SELECT queries that return rows. SQL statements that do not return result sets are classified by .NET as nonqueries. Examples of nonqueries include UPDATE, INSERT, and DELETE statements, as well as DDL statements like CREATE INDEX and ALTER TABLE. The .NET Framework provides the ExecuteNonQuery() method of the SqlCommand class to execute statements such as these. Listing 15-4 is a code snippet that shows how to execute a nonquery using the ExecuteNonQuery() method of the SqlCommand.

Listing 15-4. Executing a Nonquery

```
SqlCommand command = new SqlCommand
    (
    "CREATE TABLE #temp " +
    " ( " +
    "    Id INT NOT NULL PRIMARY KEY, " +
```

```
"    Name NVARCHAR(50) " +
"  );", connection
  );
command.ExecuteNonQuery();
```

The example creates a temporary table named #temp with two columns. Because the statement is a DDL statement that returns no result set, the ExecuteNonQuery() method is used. In addition to queries that return no result sets, some queries return a result set consisting of a single row and a single column. For these queries, .NET provides a shortcut method of retrieving the value. The ExecuteScalar() method retrieves the single value returned as a scalar value as a .NET Object. Using this method, you can avoid the hassle of creating a SqlDataReader instance and iterating it to retrieve a single value. Listing 15-5 is a code snippet that demonstrates the ExecuteScalar() method.

Listing 15-5. Using ExecuteScalar to Retrieve a Row Count

```
SqlCommand command = new SqlCommand
  (
    "SELECT COUNT(*) " +
    "FROM Person.Person;", sqlconnection
  );
Object count = command.ExecuteScalar();
```

If you call ExecuteScalar() on a SqlCommand that returns more than one row or column, only the first row of the first column is retrieved. Your best bet is to make sure you only call ExecuteScalar() on queries that return a single scalar value (one row, one column) to avoid possible confusion and problems down the road.

■ **Tip**   You may find that using the ExecuteNonQuery() method with scalar OUTPUT parameters is more efficient than the ExecuteScalar() method for servers under heavy workload.

An additional method of retrieving results in .NET is the ExecuteXmlReader() method. This method of the SqlCommand object uses an XmlReader to retrieve XML results, such as those generated by a SELECT query with the FOR XML clause. Listing 15-6 demonstrates a modified version of the code in Listing 15-3 that uses the ExecuteXmlReader() method. Differences between this listing and Listing 15-3 are in bold.

Listing 15-6. Reading XML Data with ExecuteXmlReader

```
using System;
using System.Data;
using System.Data.SqlClient;
using System.Xml;

namespace Apress.Examples
{
    class Listing15_6
    {
        static void Main(string[] args)
        {
            string name = "SMITH";
            string sqlconnection = @"SERVER=SQL2012; " +
                "INITIAL CATALOG=AdventureWorks; " +
                "INTEGRATED SECURITY=SSPI;";
```

```csharp
        string sqlcommand = "SELECT " +
            " BusinessEntityID, " +
            " FirstName, " +
            " COALESCE(MiddleName, '') AS MiddleName, " +
            " LastName " +
            "FROM Person.Person " +
            "WHERE LastName = @name " +
            "FOR XML AUTO;";

        SqlConnection connection = null;
        SqlCommand command = null;
        XmlReader xmlreader = null;

        try
        {
            connection = new SqlConnection(sqlconnection);
            connection.Open();
            command = new SqlCommand(sqlcommand, connection);
            SqlParameter par = command.Parameters.Add("@name", SqlDbType.NVarChar,
                50);
            par.Value = name;
            xmlreader = command.ExecuteXmlReader();
            while (xmlreader.Read())
            {
                Console.WriteLine
                (
                    "{0}\t{1}\t{2}\t{3}",
                    xmlreader["BusinessEntityID"].ToString(),
                    xmlreader["LastName"].ToString(),
                    xmlreader["FirstName"].ToString(),
                    xmlreader["MiddleName"].ToString()
                );
            }
        }
        catch (Exception ex)
        {
            Console.WriteLine(ex.Message);
        }
        finally
        {
            if (xmlreader != null)
                xmlreader.Close();
            if (command != null)
                command.Dispose();
            if (connection != null)
                connection.Dispose();
        }
        Console.WriteLine("Press any key...");
        Console.ReadKey();
    }
  }
}
```

The first difference between this listing and Listing 15-3 is the addition of the System.Xml namespace, since the XmlReader class is being used:

```
using System;
using System.Data;
using System.Data.SqlClient;
using System.Xml;
```

The SQL SELECT statement is also slightly different. For one thing, the COALESCE() function is used on the MiddleName column to replace NULL middle names with empty strings. The FOR XML clause leaves NULL attributes out of the generated XML by default. Missing attributes would generate exceptions when trying to display the results. The FOR XML AUTO clause was used in the SELECT query to inform SQL Server that it needs to generate an XML result.

```
string sqlcommand = "SELECT " +
  "  BusinessEntityID, " +
  "  FirstName, " +
  "  COALESCE(MiddleName, '') AS MiddleName, " +
  "  LastName " +
  "FROM Person.Person " +
  "WHERE LastName = @name " +
  "FOR XML AUTO;";
```

Inside the try...catch block, we've used the ExecuteXmlReader() method instead of the ExecuteReader() method. The loop that displays the results is very similar to Listing 15-3 as well. The main difference in this listing is that an XmlReader is used in place of a SqlDataReader.

```
xmlreader = command.ExecuteXmlReader();
while (xmlreader.Read())
{
    Console.WriteLine
    (
        "{0}\t{1}\t{2}\t{3}",
        xmlreader["BusinessEntityID"].ToString(),
        xmlreader["LastName"].ToString(),
        xmlreader["FirstName"].ToString(),
        xmlreader["MiddleName"].ToString()
    );
}
```

The remaining code in the sample performs exception handling and proper cleanup, as do the other example listings.

SqlBulkCopy

SQL Server provides tools, such as SQL Server Integration Services (SSIS) and the Bulk Copy Program (BCP), to help populate your databases from external data sources. Some applications can benefit built-in .NET bulk load functionality. The .NET Framework (versions 2.0 and higher) SqlClient implements the SqlBulkCopy class to make efficient bulk loading easy. SqlBulkCopy can be used to load data from a database table, an XML table, a flat file, or any other type of data source you choose. The SqlBulkCopy example in Listing 15-7 loads US Postal Service ZIP code data from a tab-delimited flat file into a SQL Server table. A sample of the source text file is shown in Table 15-4.

Table 15-4. *Sample Tab-Delimited ZIP Code Data*

ZIP Code	Latitude	Longitude	City	State
99546	54.2402	−176.7874	ADAK	AK
99551	60.3147	−163.1189	AKIACHAK	AK
99552	60.3147	−163.1189	AKIAK	AK
99553	55.4306	−162.5581	AKUTAN	AK
99554	62.1172	−163.2376	ALAKANUK	AK
99555	58.9621	−163.1189	ALEKNAGIK	AK

The complete sample ZIP code file is included with the downloadable source code for this book. The target table is built with the CREATE TABLE statement in Listing 15-7. You need to execute this statement to create the target table in the AdventureWorks database (or another target database if you choose).

Listing 15-7. Creating the ZipCodes Target Table

```
CREATE   TABLE   dbo.ZipCodes
(
    ZIP  CHAR(5)  NOT  NULL  PRIMARY  KEY,
    Latitude NUMERIC(8, 4) NOT NULL,
    Longitude NUMERIC(8, 4) NOT NULL,
    City NVARCHAR(50) NOT NULL,
    State CHAR(2) NOT NULL
)
GO
```

The code presented in Listing 15-8 uses the SqlBulkCopy class to bulk copy the data from the flat file into the destination table.

Listing 15-8. SqlBulkCopy Class Example

```
using System;
using System.Data;
using System.Data.SqlClient;
using System.Data.SqlTypes;
using System.Diagnostics;
using System.IO;
using System.Globalization;

namespace Apress.Example
{
    class Listing15_8
    {
        static string sqlconnection = "DATA SOURCE = SQL2012; " +
          "INITIAL CATALOG = AdventureWorks; " +
          "INTEGRATED SECURITY = SSPI;";

        static string sourcefile = "c:\\ZIPCodes.txt";
```

```
        static DataTable loadtable = null;

        static void Main(string[] args)
        {
            Stopwatch clock = new Stopwatch();
            clock.Start();
            int rowcount = DoImport();
            clock.Stop();
            Console.WriteLine("{0} Rows Imported in {1} Seconds.",
              rowcount, (clock.ElapsedMilliseconds / 1000.0));
            Console.WriteLine("Press a Key...");
            Console.ReadKey();
        }

        static int DoImport()
        {
            using (SqlBulkCopy bulkcopier = new SqlBulkCopy(sqlconnection))
            {
                bulkcopier.DestinationTableName = "dbo.ZIPCodes";
                try
                {
                    LoadSourceFile();
                    bulkcopier.WriteToServer(loadtable);
                }
                catch (SqlException ex)
                {
                    Console.WriteLine(ex.Message);
                }
            }
            return loadtable.Rows.Count;
        }

        static void LoadSourceFile()
        {
            loadtable = new DataTable();
            DataColumn loadcolumn = new DataColumn();
            DataRow loadrow = null;

            loadcolumn.DataType = typeof(SqlString);
            loadcolumn.ColumnName = "ZIP";
            loadcolumn.Unique = true;
            loadtable.Columns.Add(loadcolumn);

            loadcolumn = new DataColumn();
            loadcolumn.DataType = typeof(SqlDecimal);
            loadcolumn.ColumnName = "Latitude";
            loadcolumn.Unique = false;
            loadtable.Columns.Add(loadcolumn);

            loadcolumn = new DataColumn();
            loadcolumn.DataType = typeof(SqlDecimal);
```

```
        loadcolumn.ColumnName = "Longitude";
        loadcolumn.Unique = false;
        loadtable.Columns.Add(loadcolumn);

        loadcolumn = new DataColumn();
        loadcolumn.DataType = typeof(SqlString);
        loadcolumn.ColumnName = "City";
        loadcolumn.Unique = false;
        loadtable.Columns.Add(loadcolumn);

        loadcolumn = new DataColumn();
        loadcolumn.DataType = typeof(SqlString);
        loadcolumn.ColumnName = "State";
        loadcolumn.Unique = false;
        loadtable.Columns.Add(loadcolumn);

        using (StreamReader stream = new StreamReader(sourcefile))
        {
            string record = stream.ReadLine();
            while (record != null)
            {
                string[] cols = record.Split('\t');
                loadrow = loadtable.NewRow();
                loadrow["ZIP"] = cols[0];
                loadrow["Latitude"] = decimal.Parse(cols[1], CultureInfo.InvariantCulture);
                loadrow["Longitude"] = decimal.Parse(cols[2], CultureInfo.InvariantCulture);
                loadrow["City"] = cols[3];
                loadrow["State"] = cols[4];
                loadtable.Rows.Add(loadrow);
                record = stream.ReadLine();
            }
        }
    }
  }
}
```

The code begins by importing required namespaces, declaring the Apress.Example namespace, and declaring the module name. The System.IO namespace is imported for the StreamReader, and the System.Diagnostics namespace is imported for the Stopwatch class so that the program can report the import time. The System.Globalization namespace will give us access to the CultureInfo class to allow a safe conversion of our decimal columns.

```
using System;
using System.Data;
using System.Data.SqlClient;
using System.Diagnostics;
using System.IO;
using System.Globalization;
```

The class defines a SQL connection string, the source file name, and a DataTable:

```
static string sqlconnection = @"DATA SOURCE = SQL2012; " +
    "INITIAL CATALOG = AdventureWorks; " +
    "INTEGRATED SECURITY = SSPI;";
```

```
static string sourcefile="c:\\ZIPCodes.txt";
```

```
static DataTable loadtable=null;
```

The class contains three functions: Main(), DoImport(), and LoadSourceFile(). The Main() function begins by starting a Stopwatch to time the import process. Then it invokes the DoImport() function that performs the actual import and reports back the number of rows. Finally, the Stopwatch is stopped and the number of rows imported and number of seconds elapsed are displayed.

```
static void Main(string[] args)
{
    Stopwatch clock=new Stopwatch();
    clock.Start();
    int rowcount=DoImport();
    clock.Stop();
    Console.WriteLine("{0} Rows Imported in {1} Seconds.",
        rowcount, (clock.ElapsedMilliseconds / 1000.0));
    Console.WriteLine("Press a Key...");
    Console.ReadKey();
}
```

The second function, DoImport(), initializes an instance of the SqlBulkCopy class. It then calls the LoadSourceFile() function to populate the DataTable with data from the source flat file. The populated DataTable is passed into the WriteToServer() method of the SqlBulkCopy object. This method performs a bulk copy of all the rows in the DataTable to the destination table. The DoImport() function ends by returning the number of rows loaded into the DataTable.

```
static int DoImport()
{
    using (SqlBulkCopy bulkcopier=new SqlBulkCopy(sqlconnection))
    {
        bulkcopier.DestinationTableName="dbo.ZIPCodes";
        try
        {
            LoadSourceFile();
            bulkcopier.WriteToServer(loadtable);
        }
        catch (SqlException ex)
        {
            Console.WriteLine(ex.Message);
        }
    }
    return loadtable.Rows.Count;
}
```

The third and final function, LoadSourceFile(), initializes the structure of the DataTable and loads the source file data into it:

```
        static void LoadSourceFile()
        {
            loadtable=new DataTable();
            DataColumn loadcolumn=new DataColumn();
            DataRow loadrow=null;
```

```
        loadcolumn.DataType = typeof(SqlString);
        loadcolumn.ColumnName = "ZIP";
        loadcolumn.Unique = true;
        loadtable.Columns.Add(loadcolumn);

        loadcolumn = new DataColumn();
        loadcolumn.DataType = typeof(SqlDecimal);
        loadcolumn.ColumnName = "Latitude";
        loadcolumn.Unique = false;
        loadtable.Columns.Add(loadcolumn);

        loadcolumn = new DataColumn();
        loadcolumn.DataType = typeof(SqlDecimal);
        loadcolumn.ColumnName = "Longitude";
        loadcolumn.Unique = false;
        loadtable.Columns.Add(loadcolumn);

        loadcolumn = new DataColumn();
        loadcolumn.DataType = typeof(SqlString);
        loadcolumn.ColumnName = "City";
        loadcolumn.Unique = false;
        loadtable.Columns.Add(loadcolumn);

        loadcolumn = new DataColumn();
        loadcolumn.DataType = typeof(SqlString);
        loadcolumn.ColumnName = "State";
        loadcolumn.Unique = false;
        loadtable.Columns.Add(loadcolumn);

        using (StreamReader stream = new StreamReader(sourcefile))
        {
            string record = stream.ReadLine();
            while (record != null)
            {
                string[] cols = record.Split('\t');
                loadrow = loadtable.NewRow();
                loadrow["ZIP"] = cols[0];
                loadrow["Latitude"] = decimal.Parse(cols[1], CultureInfo.InvariantCulture);
                loadrow["Longitude"] = decimal.Parse(cols[2], CultureInfo.InvariantCulture);
                loadrow["City"] = cols[3];
                loadrow["State"] = cols[4];
                loadtable.Rows.Add(loadrow);
                record = stream.ReadLine();
            }
        }
    }
  }
}
```

We do an explicit conversion for Latitude and Longitude, from the strings extracted from the file to decimals. We use the decimal.Parse() method to ensure that the conversion will understand the . (dot) as decimal separator even if the code is run on a machine configured with a culture where the decimal separator is not a dot, like in French.

After it completes, Listing 15-8 reports the number of rows bulk loaded and the amount of time required, as shown in Figure 15-3.

Figure 15-3. *Report of Bulk Copy Rows Imported and Time Required*

You can perform a simple SELECT statement like the one shown in Listing 15-9 to verify that the destination table was properly populated. Partial results are shown in Figure 15-4.

Listing 15-9. Verifying Bulk Copy Results

```
SELECT
    ZIP,
    Latitude,
    Longitude,
    City,
State FROM dbo.ZipCodes;
```

	ZIP	Latitude	Longitude	City	State
1	00501	40.9223	-72.6371	HOLTSVILLE	NY
2	00544	40.9223	-72.6371	HOLTSVILLE	NY
3	01001	42.1405	-72.7887	AGAWAM	MA
4	01002	42.3671	-72.4646	AMHERST	MA
5	01003	42.3696	-72.6360	AMHERST	MA
6	01004	42.3845	-72.5132	AMHERST	MA
7	01005	42.3292	-72.1395	BARRE	MA
8	01007	42.2803	-72.4021	BELCHERTOWN	MA
9	01008	42.1778	-72.9584	BLANDFORD	MA
10	01009	42.2061	-72.3405	BONDSVILLE	MA
11	01010	42.1086	-72.2045	BRIMFIELD	MA
12	01011	42.2943	-72.9528	CHESTER	MA

Figure 15-4. *ZIP Codes Bulk Loaded into the Database*

Multiple Active Result Sets

Prior to SQL Server 2005, client-side applications were limited to one open result set per connection to SQL Server. The workaround was to fully process or cancel all open result sets on a single connection before retrieving a new result set, or to open multiple connections, each with its own single open result.

SQL Server 2012, like SQL Server 2005, allows you to use MARS (Multiple Active Result Sets) functionality. MARS allows you to process multiple open result sets over a single connection. Listing 15-10 demonstrates how to use MARS to perform the following tasks over a single connection:

1. Open a result set and begin reading it.

2. Stop reading the result set after a few rows.

3. Open a second result set and read it to completion.

4. Resume reading the first result set.

Listing 15-10. Opening Two Result Sets over a Single Connection

```
using System;
using System.Data;
using System.Data.SqlClient;

namespace Apress.Examples
{
    class MARS
    {
        static string sqlconnection=@"SERVER=SQL2012; " +
            "INITIAL CATALOG=AdventureWorks; " +
            "INTEGRATED SECURITY=SSPI; " +
            "MULTIPLEACTIVERESULTSETS=true; ";

        static string sqlcommand1="SELECT " +
            " DepartmentID, " +
            " Name, " +
            " GroupName " +
            "FROM HumanResources.Department; ";

        static string sqlcommand2="SELECT " +
            " ShiftID, " +
            " Name, " +
            " StartTime, " +
            " EndTime " +
            "FROM HumanResources.Shift; ";

        static SqlConnection connection=null;
        static SqlCommand command1=null;
        static SqlCommand command2=null;
        static SqlDataReader datareader1=null;
        static SqlDataReader datareader2=null;
```

```csharp
static void Main(string[] args)
{
    try
    {
        connection = new SqlConnection(sqlconnection);
        connection.Open();
        command1 = new SqlCommand(sqlcommand1, connection);
        command2 = new SqlCommand(sqlcommand2, connection);
        datareader1 = command1.ExecuteReader();
        datareader2 = command2.ExecuteReader();
        int i = 0;

        Console.WriteLine("===========");
        Console.WriteLine("Departments");
        Console.WriteLine("===========");
        while (datareader1.Read() && i++ < 3)
        {
            Console.WriteLine
            (
              "{0}\t{1}\t{2}",
              datareader1["DepartmentID"].ToString(),
              datareader1["Name"].ToString(),
              datareader1["GroupName"].ToString()
            );
        }

        Console.WriteLine("======");
        Console.WriteLine("Shifts");
        Console.WriteLine("======");
        while (datareader2.Read())
        {
            Console.WriteLine
            (
              "{0}\t{1}\t{2}\t{3}",
              datareader2["ShiftID"].ToString(),
              datareader2["Name"].ToString(),
              datareader2["StartTime"].ToString(),
              datareader2["EndTime"].ToString()
            );
        }

        Console.WriteLine("======================");
        Console.WriteLine("Departments, Continued");
        Console.WriteLine("======================");
        while (datareader1.Read())
        {
            Console.WriteLine
            (
              "{0}\t{1}\t{2}",
              datareader1["DepartmentID"].ToString(),
              datareader1["Name"].ToString(),
```

492

```
                datareader1["GroupName"].ToString()
            );
        }
    }
    catch (SqlException ex)
    {
        Console.WriteLine(ex.Message);
    }
    finally
    {
        if (datareader1 !=null)
            datareader1.Dispose();
        if (datareader2 !=null)
            datareader2.Dispose();
        if (command1 !=null)
            command1.Dispose();
        if (command2 !=null)
            command2.Dispose();
        if (connection !=null)
            connection.Dispose();
    }
    Console.WriteLine("Press a key to end...");
    Console.ReadKey();
        }
    }
}
```

Listing 15-10 begins by importing the necessary namespaces:

```
using System;
using System.Data;
using System.Data.SqlClient;
```

The class begins by declaring an SQL connection string and two SQL query strings. It also declares an SqlConnection, two SqlCommand objects, and two SqlDataReader objects. The connection is then opened, and two SqlCommands are created on the single connection to retrieve the two result sets:

```
static string sqlconnection = @"SERVER = SQL2012; " +
   "INITIAL CATALOG = AdventureWorks; " +
   "INTEGRATED SECURITY = SSPI; " +
   "MULTIPLEACTIVERESULTSETS = true; ";

static string sqlcommand1 = "SELECT " +
   "  DepartmentID, " +
   "  Name, " +
   "  GroupName " +
   "FROM HumanResources.Department; ";

static string sqlcommand2 = "SELECT " +
   "  ShiftID, " +
   "  Name, " +
   "  StartTime, " +
   "  EndTime " +
   "FROM HumanResources.Shift; ";
```

```
static SqlConnection connection=null;
static SqlCommand command1=null;
static SqlCommand command2=null;
static SqlDataReader datareader1=null;
static SqlDataReader datareader2=null;
```

The key to enabling MARS is the MULTIPLEACTIVERESULTSETS = true key/value pair in the connection string. The Main function creates and opens the SqlConnection, the SqlCommand objects, and the SqlDataReader objects required to create two active result sets over one connection.

```
connection=new SqlConnection(sqlconnection);
connection.Open();
command1=new SqlCommand(sqlcommand1, connection);
command2=new SqlCommand(sqlcommand2, connection);
datareader1=command1.ExecuteReader();
datareader2=command2.ExecuteReader();
```

The balance of the code loops through the result sets displaying the data on the console. The code interrupts the first result set after three rows are consumed, consumes the second result set in its entirety, and then finishes up the first result set, all over a single connection. The results are shown in Figure 15-5.

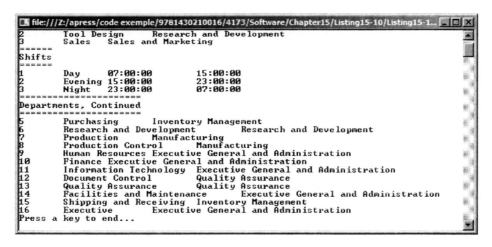

Figure 15-5. *Results of Iterating Two Active Result Sets over One Connection*

Removing the MULTIPLEACTIVERESULTSETS = true option from the connection string, as shown in the code snippet in Listing 15-11, results in the invalid operation exception in Figure 15-6 being thrown.

Listing 15-11. SQL Connection String without MARS Enabled

```
static string sqlconnection="SERVER=SQL_2012; " + "INITIAL CATALOG=AdventureWorks; " + "
INTEGRATED SECURITY=SSPI; ";
```

```
static void Main(string[] args)
{
    try
    {
        connection = new SqlConnection(sqlconnection);
        connection.Open();
        command1 = new SqlCommand(sqlcommand1, connection);
        command2 = new SqlCommand(sqlcommand2, connection);
        datareader1 = command1.ExecuteReader();
        datareader2 = command2.ExecuteReader();
        int i = 0;

        Console.WriteLine("===========");
        Console.WriteLine("Departments");
        Console.WriteLine("===========");
        while (datareader1.Read() && i++ < 3)
        {
            Console.WriteLine
            (
                "{0}\t{1}\t{2}",
```

InvalidOperationException was unhandled ✕

There is already an open DataReader associated with this Command which must be closed first.

Troubleshooting tips:

Get general help for this exception.

Search for more Help Online...

Actions:

View Detail...

Copy exception detail to the clipboard

	Value	
mand1	{System.Data.SqlClient.SqlCommand}	
mand2	{System.Data.SqlClient.SqlCommand}	
reader1	{System.Data.SqlClient.SqlDataReader}	System.[
reader2	null	System.[

Figure 15-6. *Trying to Open Two Result Sets on One Connection without MARS*

LINQ to SQL

Language Integrated Query (LINQ) is a set of technologies built into Visual Studio and the .NET Framework that allows you to query data from any data source. LINQ ships with standard libraries that support querying SQL databases, XML, and objects. Additional LINQ-enabled data providers have already been created to query Amazon.com, NHibernate, and LDAP, among others. LINQ to SQL encapsulates LINQ's built-in support for SQL database querying.

LINQ to SQL provides two things; first a basic object/relational mapping (O/RM) implementation for the .NET Framework. LINQ to SQL allows you to create .NET classes that model your database, allowing you to query and manipulate data using object-oriented methodologies. Also, LINQ offers a query language derieved from SQL, but more integrated into .NET language. Instead of enclosing queries into strings that you send to the server, you write them with the LINQ syntax. As objects are recognized through the O/RM mapping, the syntax is recognized directly like any other .NET language construct. It helps to decrease the so-called object/relational impedance mismatch between object-oriented languages and SQL (in other words, the impossibility of gracefully integrating one language into the other). In this section, we'll introduce LINQ to SQL. For an in-depth introduction, we recommend the book *LINQ for Visual C# 2008,* by Fabio Claudio Ferracchiati (Apress, 2008).

■ **Tip** In addition to Fabio's *LINQ for Visual C#* books, Apress publishes several books on LINQ. You can view the list at www.apress.com/book/search?searchterm=linq&act=search. The MSDN website (http://msdn.microsoft.com) also has several LINQ resources available.

Using the Designer

Visual Studio includes a LINQ to SQL designer that makes mapping database schema to a .NET representation a relatively painless process. The LINQ to SQL designer can be accessed from within Visual Studio by adding a new LINQ to SQL Classes item to your .NET project, as shown in Figure 15-7. Note that there is some importance placed on the file name you choose, as the .NET data contextclass (which is the main LINQ to SQL class, as we will see) created will be based on the name you choose (without the .dbml extension). In this case, we chose the name AdventureWorks.dbml.

Figure 15-7. *Adding a LINQ to SQL Classes Item to a Project*

Once the LINQ to SQL Classes item has been added, you need to create a Microsoft SQL Server SqlClient connection that points to your server and database. You can add a data connection through the Visual Studio Server Explorer, as shown in Figure 15-8.

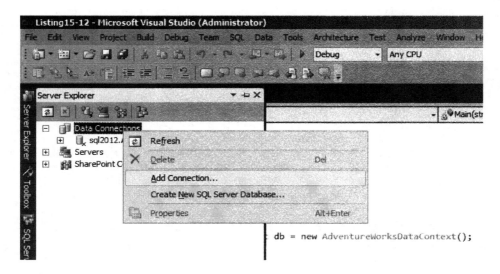

Figure 15-8. *Adding a Connection through the Server Explorer*

Once you've added the connection to your database, the Server Explorer displays the tables and other objects contained within the database. You can select tables and SPs and drag them from the Server Explorer onto the O/RM designer surface. Figure 15-9 shows the selection of two tables, Person.Person and Person.EmailAddress, in the Server Explorer.

Figure 15-9. *Viewing and Selecting Tables in the Server Explorer*

Once the tables have been dragged onto the O/RM designer surface, Visual Studio provides a visual representation of the classes it created to model the database and the relationships between them. Figure 15-10 shows the designer surface with the Person.Person and Person.EmailAddress tables added to it.

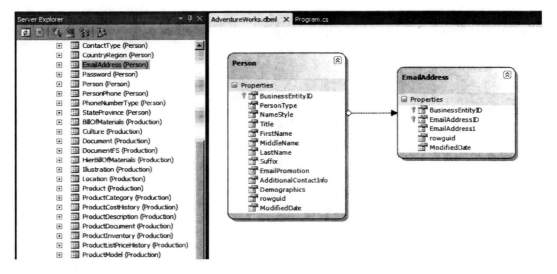

Figure 15-10. *O/RM Designer Surface with Tables Added to It*

Querying with LINQ to SQL

Once you've created your LINQ to SQL O/RM classes with the designer, it's time to write queries. LINQ not only allows you to query any data source including SQL; it is also integrated directly into Visual Basic and C# via dedicated keywords. These new LINQ-specific keywords include from, select, where, and others that will seem eerily familiar to SQL developers. These keywords, combined with some other features, provide a powerful mechanism for performing declarative queries directly in your procedural code.

Basic LINQ to SQL Querying

Our first LINQ to SQL query example, in Listing 15-12, queries the Persons property of the AdventureWorksDataContext class.

Listing 15-12. *Querying Persons with LINQ to SQL*

```
using System;
using System.Linq;

namespace Apress.Examples
{
    class Listing15_12
    {
        static void Main(string[] args)
        {
            AdventureWorksDataContext db = new AdventureWorksDataContext();
            db.Log = Console.Out;

            var query = from p in db.Persons
                        select p;
```

```
        foreach (Person p in query)
        {
            Console.WriteLine
              (
                "{0}\t{1}\t{2}",
                p.FirstName,
                p.MiddleName,
                p.LastName
              );
        }
        Console.WriteLine("Press a key to continue...");
        Console.ReadKey();
      }
    }
}
```

The first thing to notice about this example is the namespace declarations. Since we are using LINQ to SQL, we have to import the System.Linq namespace. This namespace provides access to the LINQ IQueryable interface, providing objects that can be enumerated in a foreach loop, like IEnumerable.

```
using System;
using System.Linq;
```

The Main() method of the program begins by creating an instance of the AdventureWorksDataContext, which we will query against. Notice that we've set the Log property of the AdventureWorksDataContext instance to Console.Out. This will display the actual SQL query that LINQ to SQL generates on the console.

```
AdventureWorksDataContext db = new AdventureWorksDataContext();
db.Log = Console.Out;
```

After the AdventureWorksDataContext class is instantiated, querying with the new C# keywords is as simple as assigning a query to a variable. For this example, we've taken advantage of the .NET *anonymous types* feature. Anonymous types allow you to declare variables without an explicit type through use of the var keyword. When you declare a variable using anonymous types, the compiler automatically infers the type at compile time. This is an important distinction from Object and variant data types, which represent general-purpose types that are determined at runtime. The query is simple, using the from...in clause to indicate the source of the data and the select keyword to return objects. As you can see, the LINQ to SQL syntax has a different order than the SQL syntax. The select keyword is coming at the end of the statement.

```
var query = from p in db.Persons
            select p;
```

The final part of this example uses a foreach loop to iterate over all the Person objects returned by the query and prints the names to the display. Partial results of this query are shown in Figure 15-11.

```
foreach (Person p in query)
{
    Console.WriteLine
    (
        "{0}\t{1}\t{2}",
        p.FirstName,
        p.MiddleName,
        p.LastName
    );
}
```

Figure 15-11. *Querying Persons with LINQ to SQL*

As we mentioned previously, you can use the Log attribute of your data context class to output the SQL code generated by LINQ to SQL. This is useful for debugging or just finding out more about how LINQ to SQL works internally. The SQL query generated by Listing 15-12 is shown in Listing 15–13 (reformatted for readability).

Listing 15-13. *LINQ to SQL-Generated SQL Query*

```
SELECT [t0].[BusinessEntityID], [t0].[PersonType], [t0].[NameStyle], [t0].[Title],
[t0].[FirstName], [t0].[MiddleName], [t0].[LastName], [t0].[Suffix], [t0].[EmailPromotion],
[t0].[AdditionalContactInfo], [t0].[Demographics], [t0].[rowguid], [t0].[ModifiedDate]
FROM [Person].[Person] AS [t0]
```

LINQ to SQL provides several clauses in addition to from and select. Table 15-5 is a summary of some commonly used LINQ to SQL query operators. We will continue the discussion of LINQ to SQL query operators in the sections that follow.

Table 15-5. *Useful LINQ Standard Query Operators*

Function	Keyword	Description
Restriction	where	The restriction operator restricts/filters the results returned by a query, returning only the items that match the where predicate condition. You can think of this as equivalent to the WHERE clause in SQL.
Projection	select	The projection operator is used to define/restrict the attributes that should be returned in the result collection. The select keyword approximates the SQL SELECT clause.
Join	join	The join operator performs an inner join of two sequences based on matching keys from both sequences. This is equivalent to the SQL INNER JOIN clause.
Join	join...into	The join operator can accept an into clause to perform a left outer join. This form of the join keyword is equivalent to the SQL LEFT OUTER JOIN clause.

(continued)

Table 15-5. (*continued*)

Function	Keyword	Description
Ordering	orderby	The orderby keyword accepts a comma-separated list of keys to sort your query results. Each key can be followed by the ascending or descending keyword. The ascending keyword is the default. This is equivalent to the SQL ORDER BY clause.
Grouping	group	The group keyword allows you to group your results by a specified set of key values. You can use the group...into syntax if you want to perform additional query operations on the grouped results. The behavior of this keyword approximates the SQL GROUP BY clause.
Subexpressions	let	The let keyword in a query allows you to store subexpressions in a variable during the query. You can use the variable in subsequent query clauses. SQL doesn't have an equivalent for this statement, although subqueries can approximate the behavior in some instances. The best equivalent for this keyword is the XQuery FLWOR expression let clause.

The where Clause

The where clause allows you to restrict the results returned by the query as shown in Listing 15-14. Replacing the query in Listing 15-12 with this query restricts the Person objects returned to only those with the letters *smi* in their last names.

Listing 15-14. Querying Persons with "smi" in Their Last Names

```
var query = from p in db.Persons
            where p.LastName.Contains("SMI")
            select p;
```

The SQL code generated by this LINQ to SQL query is slightly different from the previous SQL query as shown in Listing 15-15.

Listing 15-15. LINQ to SQL-Generated SQL Query with WHERE Clause

```
exec sp_executesql N'SELECT [t0].[BusinessEntityID], [t0].[PersonType], [t0].[NameStyle],
[t0].[Title], [t0].[FirstName], [t0].[MiddleName], [t0].[LastName], [t0].[Suffix],
[t0].[EmailPromotion], [t0].[AdditionalContactInfo], [t0].[Demographics], [t0].[rowguid],
[t0].[ModifiedDate]
FROM [Person].[Person] AS [t0]
WHERE [t0].[LastName] LIKE @p0',N'@p0 nvarchar(5)',@p0=N'%SMI%'
```

One interesting aspect to this query is that LINQ to SQL converts the Contains method of the Person object's LastName property to a SQL LIKE predicate. This is important because it means that LINQ to SQL is smart enough to realize that it doesn't have to retrieve an entire table, instantiate objects for every row of the table, and then use .NET methods to limit the results on the client. This can be a significant performance enhancement over the alternative. Furthermore, it uses sp_executesql to parameterize the query.

Another interesting feature that LINQ to SQL provides is query parameterization. In this instance, the generated SQL query includes a parameter named @p0 that is defined as an nvarchar(5) parameter and assigned a value of %SMI%.

The orderby Clause

LINQ to SQL also provides result ordering via the orderby clause. You can use the orderby keyword in your query to specify the attributes to sort by. Listing 15-16 builds on the query in Listing 15-14 by adding an orderby clause that sorts results by the LastName and FirstName attributes of the Person object.

Listing 15-16. Ordering LINQ to SQL Query Results

```
var query = from p in db.Persons
            where p.LastName.Contains("SMI")
            orderby p.LastName, p.FirstName
            select p;
```

Replacing the query in Listing 15-12 with this query returns all Person objects whose last names contain the letters *smi,* and sorts the objects by their last and first names. The generated SQL query is shown in Listing 15-17. It's similar to the previous query except that LINQ to SQL has added a SQL ORDER BY clause.

Listing 15-17. LINQ to SQL-Generated SQL Query with ORDER BY Clause

```
exec sp_executesql N'SELECT [t0].[BusinessEntityID], [t0].[PersonType], [t0].[NameStyle],
[t0].[Title], [t0].[FirstName], [t0].[MiddleName], [t0].[LastName], [t0].[Suffix], [t0].
[EmailPromotion], [t0].[AdditionalContactInfo], [t0].[Demographics], [t0].[rowguid], [t0].
[ModifiedDate]
FROM [Person].[Person] AS [t0]
WHERE [t0].[LastName] LIKE @p0
ORDER BY [t0].[LastName], [t0].[FirstName]',N'@p0 nvarchar(5)',@p0=N'%SMI%'
```

The join Clause

LINQ to SQL also provides the join clause, which allows you to perform inner joins in your queries. An inner join relates two entities, like Person and EmailAddress in the example, based on common values of an attribute. The LINQ to SQL join operator essentially works the same way as the SQL INNER JOIN operator. Listing 15-18 demonstrates a LINQ to SQL join query.

Listing 15-18. Retrieving Persons and Related E-mail Addresses

```
using System;
using System.Linq;

namespace Apress.Examples
{
    class Listing15_18
    {
        static void Main(string[] args)
        {
            AdventureWorksDataContext db = new AdventureWorksDataContext();
            db.Log = Console.Out;

            var query = from p in db.Persons
                        join e in db.EmailAddresses
                        on p.BusinessEntityID equals e.BusinessEntityID
                        where p.LastName.Contains("SMI")
```

```
                    orderby p.LastName, p.FirstName
                    select new
                    {
                        LastName = p.LastName,
                        FirstName = p.FirstName,
                        MiddleName = p.MiddleName,
                        EmailAddress = e.EmailAddress1
                    };

        foreach (var q in query)
        {
            Console.WriteLine
              (
                "{0}\t{1}\t{2}\t{3}",
                q.FirstName,
                q.MiddleName,
                q.LastName,
                q.EmailAddress
              );
        }
        Console.WriteLine("Press a key to continue...");
        Console.ReadKey();
    }
  }
}
```

THE EQUALS OPERATOR AND NON-EQUIJOINS

C# uses the equals keyword in the LINQ join...on clause instead of the familiar == operator. This is done for clarity. The LINQ from...join pattern maps directly to the Enumerable.Join() LINQ query operator, which requires two delegates that are used to compute values for comparison. The delegate/key on the left side of the operator consumes the outer sequence and the right delegate/key consumes the inner sequence. The decision was made to use the equals keyword to clarify this concept primarily because implementing a full query processor for LINQ would have resulted in significant overhead. In order to perform other types of non-equijoins in LINQ, you can use a combination of the LINQ GroupJoin operator and the where clause.

The LINQ to SQL query in Listing 15-18 uses the join operator to identify the entities to join and the on clause specifies the join criteria. In this example, the Person and EmailAddress entities are joined based on their BusinessEntityID attributes. Because the query needs to return some attributes of both entities, the select clause creates a new anonymous type on the fly. Partial results of the join query are shown in Figure 15-12.

```
var query = from p in db.Persons
            join e in db.EmailAddresses
            on p.BusinessEntityID equals e.BusinessEntityID
            where p.LastName.Contains("SMI")
            orderby p.LastName, p.FirstName
            select new
            {
                LastName = p.LastName,
                FirstName = p.FirstName,
```

```
                    MiddleName = p.MiddleName,
                    EmailAddress = e.EmailAddress1
        };
```

Figure 15-12. *Retrieving Person Names and Related E-mail Addresses*

The SQL query generated by LINQ to SQL includes an SQL INNER JOIN clause, and only retrieves the columns required by the query, as shown in Listing 15-19.

Listing 15-19. LINQ to SQL-generated SQL Query with INNER JOIN Clause

```
exec sp_executesql N'SELECT [t0].[LastName], [t0].[FirstName], [t0].[MiddleName], [t1].
[EmailAddress]
FROM [Person].[Person] AS [t0]
INNER JOIN [Person].[EmailAddress] AS [t1] ON [t0].[BusinessEntityID] = [t1].[BusinessEntityID]
WHERE [t0].[LastName] LIKE @p0
ORDER BY [t0].[LastName], [t0].[FirstName]',N'@p0 nvarchar(5)',@p0 = N'%SMI%'
```

Deferred Query Execution

LINQ to SQL uses a query execution pattern known as *deferred query execution*. When you declare a LINQ to SQL query, .NET creates an *expression tree*. The expression tree is essentially a data structure that acts as a guide that LINQ to SQL can use to execute your query. The expression tree does not contain the actual data retrieved by the query, but rather the information required to execute the query. Deferred query execution causes the execution of the query to be delayed until the data returned by the query is actually needed—when you iterate the results in a foreach loop, for instance. You can view deferred query execution in action by placing breakpoints on the foreach loops of the code samples in the previous sections. LINQ to SQL will not generate and output its SQL code until after the foreach loop iteration begins. This is shown in Figure 15-13.

Figure 15-13. *Deferred Query Execution Test*

Deferred query execution is an important concept that every LINQ to SQL developer needs to be familiar with. If the value of a variable that the query depends on changes between the time the query is declared and the time it is executed, the query can return unexpected results.

From LINQ to Entity Framework

After LINQ was designed, Microsoft released a full blown O/RM framework named Entity Framework (EF). LINQ provides only very basic O/RM implementation, where one table is mapped to one class. EF offers an abstraction level (a Data Access Layer) allowing you to build a conceptual model and work with objects and collections that do not necessarily match the relational schema of the underlying database, and are not tied to a physical implementation. Before EF, developers who wanted to work with an O/RM in .NET were mostly using NHibernate, the port of the Hibernate Java Framework to .NET (and some are still using it, as NHibernate is for now more mature and feature-rich than EF). Microsoft created its own framework and released it in 2008 with the .NET framework 3.5 service pack 1. It wasn't perfect and got a lot of criticism. In 2010, the second version, named Entity Framework 4, was released with the .NET framework 4 (the version number was obviously chosen to meet the .NET framework version) and corrected most of the problems encountered with the first release.

Entity Framework 4 maps database structures to .NET classes that you manipulate in your client application like any other class, with no contact with SQL code and no need for any knowledge of the database structure or physical implementation, matching a business model rather than a physical schema. This model is called the Entity Data Model (EDM). Let's create one right away.

In a Visual Studio C# project, right-click on the project in Solution Explorer. Click on Add → New Item, and select "ADO.NET Entity Data Model" in the Data section. Enter a name for the data model and click on Add. A wizard opens up and asks first whether you want to generate the model from a database, or if you want to create an empty model, as shown in Figure 15-14.

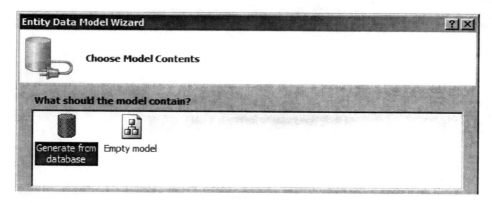

Figure 15-14. *Choose EF Model Contents*

The second choice would create a model-first EF data model that you could use to model your conceptual schema, create EF classes, and generate the database tables later. Choose "Generate from database" and click on Next. The next step allows you to choose or create a data connection to SQL Server. When it is done, you will select the database objects you want to use in your model. You can add tables, views, and stored procedure results, as shown in Figure 15-15.

Figure 15-15. *Database Objects Selection*

We select the following tables:

- HumanResources.Employee
- Person.Person
- Person.BusinessEntity
- Person.EmailAddress
- Person.PersonPhone
- Person.PhoneNumberType

PLURALIZE OR SINGULARIZE GENERATED OBJECT NAMES

The page shown in Figure 15-15 has a checkbox named "Pluralize or singularize generated object names." This allows you to automatically apply English language rules to name entities and entity sets. If the names of your database tables are in plural form, EF would create entity classes in plural that would look confusing in your code. The EntityType generated from the tables kept the plural. Look at this code example.

```
Employees Employee = new Employees();
```

What does the Employees class represent? A single entity, so it should be Employee. But if the database table is named Employees, EF would use this name to build the entity. If "Pluralize or singularize generated object names" is checked, EF will remove the s.

When the tables are selected, click on Finish to let the wizard create the data model. The model generated is shown in Figure 15-16.

Figure 15-16. *The Entity Data Model*

As you can see, EF created one class per table and kept the relationships defined by the foreign keys in our database schema. Some "new" types are not yet supported by Entity Framework, like hierarchyid and spatial types. If you created the EDM from our example, you will get a warning about the OrganizationNode column of the HumanResources.Employee table, which is a hierarchyid type column and cannot be imported into the EDM. To include the string representation of the OrganizationNode column you could create a computed column in HumanResources.Employee as shown in Listing 15-20.

Listing 15-20. Creating a Computed Column to Show Hierarchyid Representation in the EDM

```
ALTER TABLE [HumanResources].[Employee]
ADD OrganizationNodeString AS OrganizationNode.ToString() PERSISTED;
```

■ **Note**   The future release of Entity Framework 5 will integrate spatial data types.

In each class of the EDM, you can see a list of properties that are the tables' columns, but also Navigation Properties that reference the association between entities. For instance, the PersonPhone entity has a navigation property referencing the PhoneNumberType entity, and the PhoneNumberType entity has a navigation property referencing the PersonPhone entity. Each entity that is part of an association is called an end, and the properties that define the values of the association are called roles. If you click on the line joining the two entities in the EDM that represents the association, you will see the assocation's properties as shown in Figure 15-17.

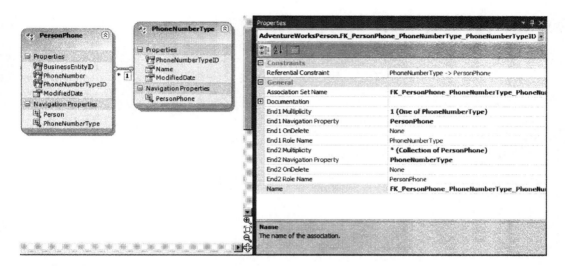

Figure 15-17. *The Properties of an Association between Entities*

The multiplicity of properties allow you to define the cardinality of each role, and the OnDelete properties reflect whether a cascading option has been defined on the foreign key in the database.

■ **Caution**   Do not set the OnDelete to cascade in your EDM if there is no cascading option in the foreign key at the database level. EF will assume that the DELETE is taken care of by the database engine. It will only delete associated objects if they are in memory.

We have said that the EDM is not tied to a physical implementation. Entity Framework maintains three layers for better abstraction. At design time, all the information is stored in an .edmx file, but at run time, EF separates the model into 3 XML files that have different structures, as detailed in Table 15-6.

Table 15-6. *Entity Framework Abstraction Layers*

File extension	Name	Description
.csdl	Conceptual Schema Definition Language	The csdl is used to define the conceptual, database physical implementation agnostic model. It defines entities, relationships, and functions.
.ssdl	Store Schema Definition Language	The ssdl describes the storage model of the conceptual schema. It defines the name of the underlying tables and columns, and the queries used to retrieve the data from the database.
.msl	Mapping Specification Language	The msl maps the csdl attributes to the ssdl columns.

These levels allow you to switch the backend database with minimal change to your client application. The requests you will write to EF will be translated to SQL behind the scene.

Querying Entities

Once you have created an EDM, you can refer to it in your code with what is called an object context, like we have a data context in LINQ to SQL. The EDM will be available as a class inheriting from the ObjectContext class. Let's see it in action in Listing 15-21. The result of the code execution is shown in Figure 15-18.

Listing 15-21. Using an EF Object Context in Your C# Code

```csharp
using System;
using System.Linq;
using System.Text;

namespace EntityFramework
{
    class Program
    {
        static void Main(string[] args)
        {
            using (var ctx = new AdventureWorksEntitiesEmployee())
            {
                var qry = from e in ctx.Employee
                          where e.Gender == "F"
                          select new
                          {
                              e.Person.FirstName,
                              e.Person.LastName,
                              e.BirthDate
                          };

                foreach (var emp in qry.Take(5)) {
                    Console.WriteLine("{0} {1}, born {2}",
                                emp.FirstName,
                                emp.LastName,
                                emp.BirthDate.ToLongDateString()
                    );
                }
                Console.Read();
            }
        }
    }
}
```

Figure 15-18. *The Result of the Code Execution*

The code in Listing 15-21 is a console application. It will return five lines of employees. First, we create an instance of the AdventureWorksEntitiesEmployee class, which inherits from ObjectContext. It will give us access to entities present in the AdventureWorksEntitiesEmployee EDM. The context will allow us to access its entities, to define and execute queries, and to apply modifications to data. We enclose the context instantiation inside a using block in order to ensure that the instance will be freed no matter what happens inside the block.

```
using (var ctx = new AdventureWorksEntitiesEmployee())
{
    ...
}
```

We can use LINQ queries against entities. This functionality is called LINQ to Entities, and it is very much like LINQ to SQL. But where, in LINQ to SQL, we would have written this:

```
var qry = from e in ctx.Employee
          join p in ctx.Person on e.BusinessEntityId equals p.BusinessEntityId
          where e.Gender == "F"
          select new
          {
              p.FirstName,
              p.LastName,
              e.BirthDate
          };
```

In Entity Framework, we can take advantage of navigation properties, which are properties of an entity that give access to the other end of an association. A navigation property returns either one entity or a collection of entities, depending on the cardinality of the relationship. Here, as the association is 0..1, there can be only one person associated with an employee, so it will return only one entity reference, and we can directly use its properties to retrieve the FirstName and LastName. Additionally, to limit the number of properties returned by the query, we create an anonymous type (a class without a name, declared on the fly with a new {...} construct to retrieve only Person.FirstName, Person.LastName and Employee.BirthDate.

```
var qry = from e in ctx.Employee
          where e.Gender == "F"
          select new
    {
        e.Person.FirstName,
        e.Person.LastName,
        e.BirthDate
    };
```

Using the anonymous type improves performance. In Listing 15-22 you can see the T-SQL query generated by EF that we retrieved using SQL Server Profiler.

Listing 15-22. The T-SQL Query Generated by EF

```
SELECT TOP (5)
[Extent1].[BusinessEntityID] AS [BusinessEntityID],
[Extent2].[FirstName] AS [FirstName],
[Extent3].[LastName] AS [LastName],
[Extent1].[BirthDate] AS [BirthDate]
FROM    [HumanResources].[Employee] AS [Extent1]
INNER JOIN [Person].[Person] AS [Extent2] ON [Extent1].[BusinessEntityID]=[Extent2].
[BusinessEntityID]
LEFT OUTER JOIN [Person].[Person] AS [Extent3] ON [Extent1].[BusinessEntityID]=[Extent3].
[BusinessEntityID]
WHERE N'F'=[Extent1].[Gender]
```

You can see that only the needed columns are selected. That reduces the cost of the query and the amount of data that needs to be carried by the query back to the client.

Then, we can simply loop into the query's result, because the query returns an IQueryable desendant object. To limit the number of rows returned, we called the method Take() on the IQueryable, that translates to a SELECT TOP, as you can see in the generated T-SQL in Listing 15-22. That allows you also to see that deferred execution is also working in Entity Framework. Finally, we format the BirthDate column/property to display a user-friendly birth date.

```
foreach (var emp in qry.Take(5)) {
    Console.WriteLine("{0} {1}, born {2}",
        emp.FirstName,
        emp.LastName,
        emp.BirthDate.ToLongDateString()
    );
}
```

To be able to see the result in the console before it disappears, we add a call to Console.Read(), that will make the console wait until a key is pressed.

The context can also give us access directly to entities in the form of an ObjectSet. You can see an ObjectSet as a kind of resultset. You could directly call the ObjectSet and enumerate through it. So the code in Listing 15-21 could be rewritten as in Listing 15-23.

Listing 15-23. Using an EF ObjectSet

```
using System;
using System.Linq;
using System.Text;

namespace EntityFramework
{
    class Program
    {
        static void Main(string[] args)
        {
            using (var ctx=new AdventureWorksEntitiesEmployee())
            {
                foreach (var emp in ctx.Employee.Where(e =>e.Gender == "F").Take(5))
                {
                    Console.WriteLine("{0} {1}, born {2}",
                                        emp.Person.FirstName,
```

```
                            emp.Person.LastName,
                            emp.BirthDate.ToLongDateString()
            );
        }
        Console.Read();
        }
      }
    }
}
```

In the code in Listing 15-23, we directly use the Employee ObjectSet. We can still filter it by using its Where() method. By contrast with the LINQ query approach, this is called method-based query. The Where() method takes a lambda expression as its parameter. Lambda expressions are a way to express parameters with a syntax derived from *Lambda Calculus*, a formal notation in mathematical logic. You can use LINQ queries or method-based querying. Choose what feels more natural to you.

Finally, let's see in Listing 15-24 an example of data modification with Entity Framework. The result is shown in Figure 15-19.

Listing 15-24. Modifying Data in EF

```
using System;
using System.Linq;
using System.Text;

namespace EntityFramework
{
    class Program
    {
        static void Main(string[] args)
        {
            using (var ctx = new AdventureWorksEntitiesEmployee())
            {
                var newP = new BusinessEntity {
                    ModifiedDate = DateTime.Now,
                    rowguid = Guid.NewGuid()
                };

                Console.WriteLine("BusinessEntityID before insert : {0}",
                                newP.BusinessEntityID);

                ctx.BusinessEntities.AddObject(newP);
                ctx.SaveChanges();

                Console.WriteLine("BusinessEntityID after insert :  {0}",
                                newP.BusinessEntityID);
            }

            Console.Read();
        }
    }
}
```

Figure 15-19. *The Result of the Code Execution*

There are several ways to insert new data. We chose to use the object initializer syntax, available since .NET 3.5. In the object initializer block, we affect values to the two properties of the BusinessEntity entity that need to be populated. The ModifiedDate property is a datetime, so we use the DateTime.Now property to set the current date and time; the rowguid property stores a uniqueidentifier, so we use the Guid.NewGuid() method to retrieve a value. When the object is fully populated, we can add it to the entity by using the AddObject() method.

```
var newP = new BusinessEntity {
    ModifiedDate = DateTime.Now,
    rowguid = Guid.NewGuid()
};
```

...

```
ctx.BusinessEntities.AddObject(newP);
```

The changes made to entities are stored in a collection in the context and are applied to the underlying database only when the SaveChanges() method of the context is called. To see what happens with the BusinessEntityId identity column, we return its value before and after the call to SaveChanges(). The key value is automatically set by EF to match the identity value generated by SQL Server. The query issued by EF when we call SaveChanges() is shown in Listing 15-25.

Listing 15-25. The DML Query Generated by EF

```
exec sp_executesql N'insert [Person].[BusinessEntity]([rowguid], [ModifiedDate])
values (@0, @1)
select [BusinessEntityID]
from [Person].[BusinessEntity]
where @@ROWCOUNT > 0 and [BusinessEntityID] = scope_identity()',N'@0 uniqueidentifier,@1
datetime2(7)',@0 = '92EEC64E-BD11-4936-97C3-6528B5D1D97D',@1 = '2012-05-21 15:14:05.3493966'
```

As you can see, a SELECT is issued after the INSERT operation to retrieve the identity value and return it to EF.

We only scratched the surface of Entity Framework. You have to be aware of it, even if you don't do any client coding, because it is the way of the future in .NET data access. The question of whether this a good or bad thing is fortunately—there is a bit of of cowardice here—out of the scope of this book. The thinking behind LINQ and Entity Framework is to abstract out database access, and to hide the T-SQL language from developers, which is considered by many client-side developers as a pain. This trend pushes toward considering DataBase Management Systems as just data stores. In this model, objects like views and stored procedures have less importance, and the craftsmanship of writing good T-SQL queries seems outdated. This has advantages and pitfalls, the more important of the latter being performance issues in complex queries. The best way to address this problem is to get proficient in Entity Framework, and to start on that path, you can read *Pro Entity Framework 4.0* by Scott Klein (Apress, 2010).

Summary

Although the focus of this book is on server-side development, a good database is only useful if the end users can access the data contained within it efficiently. That's where an efficient and well-designed client-side application comes in. In this chapter, we discussed several options available for connecting to SQL Server 2008 from .NET.

We began the chapter with a discussion of the ADO.NET namespaces and the .NET SQL Server Native Client (SqlClient), including connected data access, which requires constant database connectivity, and disconnected datasets, which allow users to cache data locally and connect to a database as needed. Although .NET offers other options for connecting to SQL Server, including OLE DB and ODBC, the primary method of connecting to SQL Server (version 7.0 and higher) is encapsulated in ADO.NET and the System.Data.SqlClient namespace.

We also discussed parameterized queries, including the topics of security and SQL injection. Other topics we covered included the various methods and options that .NET provides to query SQL Server, bulk copy data into SQL Server, and open multiple result sets over a single active database connection.

We rounded this chapter out with a discussion of the O/RM functionalities provided by .NET and Visual Studio. Visual Studio's built-in visual designer and automated class generation can make light work of many O/RM applications. The ability to abstract out database access and to write declarative LINQ to SQL queries directly in procedural code elevates data querying to the level of a first-class programming concept.

EXERCISES

1. [True/False] The System.Data.SqlClient namespace provides optimized access to SQL Server via the SQL Server Native Client library.

2. [Choose one] Which of the following concepts allows for local caching of data, with establishment of database connections on an as-needed basis:

    a. Connected data access

    b. Disconnected datasets

    c. Casual data access

    d. Partial datasets

3. [Choose all that apply] Which of the following are benefits of query parameterization:

    a. Protection against SQL injection attacks

    b. Conversion of lead to gold

    c. Increased efficiency through query plan reuse

    d. Decreased power consumption by at least 25 percent

4. [True/False] Turning on MARS by setting MULTIPLEACTIVERESULTSETS=true in your connection string allows you to open two result sets, but requires at least two open connections.

5. [True/False] Visual Studio includes a drag-and-drop visual O/RM designer.

6. [Choose one] LINQ to SQL uses which of the following query execution patterns:

    a. Instant query execution

    b. Fast-forward query execution

    c. Random query execution

    d. Deferred query execution

CHAPTER 16

■ ■ ■

Data Services

Today's systems are so disparate and large enterprises have a widely heterogeneous environment, with Windows and non-Windows platforms for application development. Developers, whether they are enterprise developers, web developers, ISV (Independent Software Vendor) developers or DBAs, have different needs and different ways of accessing the data that resides in SQL Server. For example ISV developers look for stability in the platform and enterprise developers look for rich development tooling experience and interoperability, whereas web developers want the latest rich development experience. Similarly what a PHP developer needs is very different from what a .NET developer needs. To achieve the rich development experience, developers can choose from various data access libraries such as ADO.NET, SQL Server 2012 Native Client (SNAC), JDBC, ODBC and PHP based on the application requirement. Since SQL Server 2000, the platform has supported interoperability with Windows and non-Windows environments. SQL Server 2000 started supporting Java development using JDBC drivers. PHP application development support was added to SQL Server with SQL Server 2005. With SQL Server 2012, support for ODBC driver for Linux has been added. This simplifies the PHP or other application development on Linux to a greater extent.

The model of choice to address distributed computing and heterogeneous environments is today the Service Oriented Architecture (SOA) paradigm, there have been different ways to generate services from query results over the SQL Server versions. Microsoft is now concentrating on a powerful and very flexible framework named Windows Communication Foundation (WCF). We will see how to use WCF Data Services to provide services and trendy RESTful resources from our databases. Bear with us for the explanation of these concepts.

But firstly, the data access libraries support a new SQL Server 2012 powerful feature named LocalDB (Local Database runtime), that is a very interesting way to ship solutions with an embedded database.

SQL Server 2012 Express LocalDB

Developers always look for simple way to install and embed SQL Server with third party applications or use a small database engine to connect to diverse remote data storage types. When you wanted to meet any of these requirements for creating applications in the past, the only option we had until SQL Server 2012 was to use SQL Server Express Edition. However, developers didn't want to go through tons of screens to install the SQL Server. On top of this they had to worry about the security and management aspect of the SQL Server instance they had just installed as well.

Starting with SQL Server 2012, SQL Server simplifies the experience for developers by introducing LocalDB (Local Database runtime), which was temporarily called Serverless SQL Server during SQL Server 2012 development. The goal of this new feature is to simplify the installation and provide database as a file without any administration overhead while providing the same feature sets as SQL Server Express Edition.

■ **Note** By database as a file, we mean that LocalDB allows using SQL Server, a traditional client-server application, in a local context, more or less like local applications like Microsoft Access or sqlite.

The installation of LocalDB is simplified to a greater extent, with no pre-requisites, no reboots, and no options to select. There is only one global installation, meaning only one set of binaries are installed per major version of the SQL Server for all the LocalDB instances and no constantly running service or agent in the box. The instance of LocalDB is started with the application connects to it and stopped when the application closes the connection. LocalDB can be downloaded from the same page as the old-fashioned SQL Server 2012 Express Edition, at http://www.microsoft.com/en-us/download/details.aspx?id=29062. There are two builds available, ENU\x64\SqlLocalDB.MSI for 64-bit systems and ENU\x86\SqlLocalDB.MSI for 32-bit systems. MSI files are Microsoft Installer packages that you can run by double-clicking and typing them like any executable in a cmd or Powershell session. MSI installations are usually graphical wizard-driven installations. As the LocalDB installation does not require any user choice, you can simply perform a silent install by using the following command:

```
SQLLocalDB.msi /Quiet
```

Once the LocalDB is installed you can create and manage the instances by using SQLLocalDB.exe found in %Program Files%\Microsoft SQL Server\110\Tools\Binn. So, from now on, each time we call SQLLocalDB. exe, it will be in this directory context. As it is not in the path, you need to tell your shell where to find the tool.

■ **Note** The LocalDB runtime, which is nothing other than a specific sqlserver.exe binary, can be found in %Program Files%\Microsoft SQL Server\110\LocalDB\Binn.

You can use the command as shown below to find out the details on the existing instances:

```
SQLLocalDB.exe info
```

To create a LocalDB instance, you can use SQLLocaldb.exe and specify the name of the instance and the version number with the create option. The commands listed below first create an SQL Server 2012 LocalDB instance named SQLSrvWebApp1 and then start the instance. Finally, use the info command to list the existing instances. The results are shown in Figure 16-1.

```
SQLLocalDB.exe create SQLSrvWebApp1 11.0
SQLLocalDB.exe start SQLSrvWebApp1
SQLLocalDB.exe info
```

Figure 16-1. *Query to Create and Start a LocalDB Instance Named SQLSrvWebApp1*

You might have guessed that if you want to drop an instance, you can use the SQLLocalDB.exe delete command.

There are two types of LocalDB instances, Automatic and Named. Automatic instances are created by default. There can be only one automatic instance per major version of SQL Server. For SQL Server 2012, the automatic instance name would be v11.0 (which is the internal version number of the SQL Server 2012 RTM release) and the intent for this instance is that it be public and shared by many applications. Named instances are created explicitly by the user and they are managed by a single application. So, if you have a small web application with the characteristic that it needs to start small and be implemented in the enterprise, the better option is to create a named instance when it is small so that you can isolate and manage the application.

To connect to a LocalDB instance with your SQL server Native Client, OLEDB, or ODBC provider, you simply mention the (localdb) keyword in the connection string. Examples of the connection strings that connect to an automatic instance (first line) and named instance (second line) are shown below:

```
New SQLConnection("Server=(localDB)\v11.0;AttachDBFile=C:\Program Files\Microsoft SQL
Server\Data Files\AppDB1.mdf")'

New SQLConnection("Server=(localDB)\WebApp1;AttachDBFile=C:\Program Files\Microsoft SQL
Server\Data Files\WebApp1DB.mdf")'
```

This code invokes the LocalDB as a child process and will connect to it. The LocalDB runs as an application when you initiate a connection from the client, and if the database is not used by the client application for more than 5 minutes the LocalDB is shut down to save the system resources. LocalDB is supported in ODBC, SQL Native Client and OLEDB client providers. If these client providers encounter "Server=(localdb)\<instancename>" they know to call the LocalDB instance if it already exists or start the instance automatically as a part of the connection attempt.

Likewise, you can connect to a LocalDB instance using SQL Server Management Studio (the Express or full version) or the sqlcmd command line tool, by using the same (localdb) keyword as server name, as shown in the following:

```
sqlcmd -S (localdb)\SQLSrvWebApp1
```

For it to work, you need to make sure that the LocalDB instance is started. You can test it by using the info command along with the instance name, as shown below. The result of the command is shown in Figure 16-2. The instance's state is visible on the State: line.

```
SQLLocalDB.exe info SQLSrvWebApp1
```

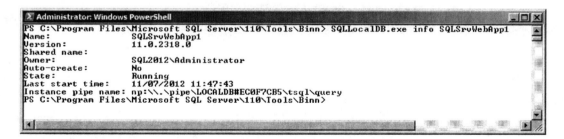

Figure 16-2. *Results of the QLLocalDB.exe Info SQLSrvWebApp1 Command When the Instance Is Stopped*

We can see in Figure 16-2 that our instance is running. If it had stopped, we could have started it using the start command seen earlier before being able to connect to it.

■ **Note**   Connecting to the (localdb) keyword is supported in .NET version 4.0.2 onwards. If you are using an older .NET version, you can connect to a LocalDB instance but you need to use the named pipe address that is returned by the SQLLocalDB.exe info command. We see that address In Figure 16-2. So the server's address in our case is np:\\.\pipe\LOCALDB#ECOF7CB5\tsql\query. That's what we would need to enter in the Server address box for an SSMS connection, or after the –S parameter when calling sqlcmd.

The authentication and security model of LocalDB is simplified. The current user is sysadmin and is the owner of the databases attached to the instance. No other permission is applied. As the LocalDB processes run under the account of a user, this also implies that the database files you want to use on this instance must be in a directory where the user has read and write permissions. Also, while SQL Server hides the physical details of the database storage, LocalDB follows another approach, which is to give access to a database file. A LocalDB connection string supports the AttachDbFileName property that allows attaching a database file during connection. The C# console application in Listing 16-1 illustrates how to use database as a file with LocalDB.

Listing 16-1. Console Application to Connect to a LocalDB Instance

```
using System;
using System.Data.SqlClient;
using System.Text;

namespace localdbClient
{
    class Program
    {
        static void Main(string[] args)
        {
            try
            {
                SqlConnectionStringBuilder builder =
                    new SqlConnectionStringBuilder(@"Server=(localdb)\SQLSrvWebApp1;Integrated
Security=true");

                builder.AttachDBFilename =
@"C:\Users\Administrator\Documents\AdventureWorksLT2012_Data.mdf";

                Console.WriteLine("connection string = " + builder.ConnectionString);

                using (SqlConnection cn = new SqlConnection(builder.ConnectionString))
                {
                    cn.Open();
                    SqlCommand cmd = cn.CreateCommand();
                    cmd.CommandText = "SELECT Name FROM sys.tables;";
                    SqlDataReader rd = cmd.ExecuteReader();

                    while(rd.Read())
                    {
                        Console.WriteLine(rd.GetValue(0));
                    }
                    rd.Close();
                    cn.Close();
                }
```

```
            Console.WriteLine("Press any key to finish.");
            Console.ReadLine();
        }
        catch (Exception ex)
        {
            Console.WriteLine(ex.Message);
            Console.WriteLine("Press any key to finish.");
            Console.ReadLine();
        }
    }
  }
}
```

The interesting element of the code in Listing 16-1 is the connection string builder. We first create a SqlConnectionStringBuilder to connect to the (localdb)\SQLSrvWebApp1 LocalDB, then we use the connection builder's AttachDBFilename property to attach the AdventureWorksLT2012 data file to our LocalDB.

```
SqlConnectionStringBuilder builder =
    new SqlConnectionStringBuilder(@"Server=(localdb)\SQLSrvWebApp1;Integrated Security=true");
builder.AttachDBFilename = @"C:\Users\Administrator\Documents\AdventureWorksLT2012_Data.mdf";
```

The AdventureWorksLT2012_Data.mdf file is in our Documents directory, so we have full permissions over it. When connecting, we will be automatically in the database's context, as we can see by executing the code. A list of the first ten tables inside the AdventureWorksLT database is returned, as shown in Figure 16-3. The generated connection string is also printed in the figure.

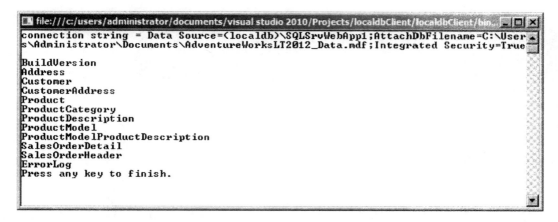

Figure 16-3. *Results of the LocalDB Client Program Execution*

Databases attached to LocalDB can be thought of as personal databases–thus the database as a file approach. You can of course use all T-SQL DDL commands to create a database and the tables in it. You just need to specify a location that you have permissions on for the database files. If you create a database without specifying a location, your user directory will be chosen by LocalDB. For example, the following command

```
CREATE DATABASE ApressDb;
```

will create an .mdf and .ldf file in our personal directory, as shown in Figure 16-4.

Figure 16-4. *The ApressDb Database Files*

You should obviously specify a dedicated location when you create a LocalDb database. The databases created or attached to a LocalDB instance will stay attached until you detach or remove them, even if you attached one during a connection with the AttachDBFilename command. So you theoretically don't need to attach it every time you connect. However, if you used the AttachDBFilename command, the name of the database inside LocalDB will be the full path of the database file. Let's see what a query on the sys.databases catalog view is returning, in Figure 16-5.

```
select name FROM sys.databases;
```

	name
1	master
2	tempdb
3	model
4	msdb
5	ApressDb
6	C:\USERS\ADMINISTRATOR\DOCUMENTS\ADVENTUREWORKSLT2012_DATA.MDF

Figure 16-5. *Database Names in Our LocalDB Instance*

So it is easier to keep the AttachDBFilename option in the connection string that allows attaching the database if it is not already attached, and enter the database context at connection time, thus allowing a smoother experience from the developer's point of view.

Asynchronous Programming with ADO.NET 4.5

Let's take a simple scenario of a requirement in the application to upload multiple files or the need to create reports with pagination. In both these scenarios, using a synchronous model in the application can cause the client and server to slow down considerably and cause higher memory utilization due to the I/O operations. In cases like this, instead of writing the calls synchronously, if you write the calls asynchronously you can improve the user experience; however, the current model has some issues with manageability and debugging capabilities with asynchronous code.

Starting with .NET 4.5 the new Async .NET pattern is extended to ADO.NET. Now the connection operations, `SqlDataReader` and `SqlBulkCopy` can use the asynchronous capabilities. For example, let's take a simple case where we open a connection to SQL Server and run a stored procedure. The sample code shown in Listing 16-2 opens a connection and runs a stored procedure named `dbo.GetProducts` against a LocalDB instance.

Listing 16-2. ADO.NET Code to Run Stored Procedure Synchronously

```
private void ExecuteSP()
{
    SqlConnectionStringBuilder cnString = new SqlConnectionStringBuilder();
    cnString.DataSource = @"(localdb)\v11.0";
    cnString.IntegratedSecurity = true;

    using (SqlConnection cn = new SqlConnection(cnString.ConnectionString))
    {
        cn.Open();
        SqlCommand cmd = new SqlCommand("EXEC dbo.GetProducts", cn);
        cmd.ExecuteReader();
    }
}
```

The above code opens the connection to the database synchronously and runs the stored procedure waiting till the entire resultset is returned. Instead of waiting for the process to complete, it would be more efficient to perform this operation asynchronously. Listing 16-3 shows the above code modified for asynchronous execution. Changes are shown in bold.

Listing 16-3. ADO.NET Code to Run Stored Procedure Asynchronously

```
private async Task ExecuteSP()
{
    SqlConnectionStringBuilder cnString = new SqlConnectionStringBuilder();
    cnString.DataSource = @"(localdb)\v11.0";
    cnString.IntegratedSecurity = true;
    using (SqlConnection cn = new SqlConnection(cnString.ConnectionString))
    {
        await cn.OpenAsync();
        SqlCommand cmd=new SqlCommand("EXEC dbo.GetProducts", cn);
        await cmd.ExecuteReaderAsync();
    }
}
```

If you compare the code from Listings 16-2 and 16-3, the structure of the code has not changed; however, with the inclusion of the keyword `await` and the modification of a few keywords in the code we have retained readability and manageability while adding the asynchronous capability. Every possibility of improving performance on the client side is interesting. Keep in mind of course that the best way to ensure optimal performances in database querying is to improve structure and code on the server side.

ODBC for Linux

For many years and over many SQL Server versions, developers who wanted to access SQL Server from non-Windows environments had only one option: using a free library named OpenTDS that was originally created to access Sybase servers.

■ **Note**   TDS stands for Tabular Data Stream and is the network layer protocol used by Sybase and SQL Server to exchange packets between the database server and the client library. As you might know, SQL Server was in its early days a joint development between Sybase and Microsoft.

Free TDS is fine and works well, but it does do not cover the newer data types and functionalities SQL Server has to offer, like XML, date, time and datetime2 or FILESTREAM data types, or features like MARS (Multiple Active ResultSets). So, Linux developers wanting for a chance to access SQL Server from PHP or any CGI application had to stick to a limited set of functionalities. If you ever wrote PHP code to access SQL Server in a Linux environment, you might have used the integrated PHP MSSQL functions that call the php5-odbc library. It is nothing else than a layer using FreeTDS behind the scenes.

In an effort to provide a wider range of possibilities for accessing SQL Server, Microsoft decided to change its data access strategy that was previously in favor of OLEDB aligning with ODBC for native access to SQL Server. ODBC (Open DataBase Connectivity) is an API first designed by Microsoft that became a kind of de facto standard for heterogeneous database access. It is a set of APIs that allows access to different data sources from many languages and environments.

Along with this change of strategy, Microsoft developed an ODBC driver for Linux that was released in March 2012. You can download it on this page: http://www.microsoft.com/en-us/download/details.aspx?id=28160.

Linux is available though many distributions, with their own core applications, distribution mechanisms and directory organization. At the time of this writing, Microsoft offers 64-bit packages for the Red Hat Enterprise distribution only. A 32-bit version is planned. Red Hat Enterprise does not necessarily have the most widespread distribution, and many companies use other distributions, like Debian, Ubuntu, CentOS, and so on. The Microsoft ODBC driver can be installed from other distributions, providing you have a way to install the libraries the ODBC driver is using.

■ **Caution**   In the Linux world, most of the tools used are open source, and can be compiled directly on the system, to link to the available version of the libraries used in the code, but the ODBC driver for SQL Server is not open source, and only the binaries are available to download. That's why you will need to ensure that you get the proper version of the libraries used by the ODBC driver installed on the Linux box.

We will provide here a short example with Ubuntu Server. Ubuntu is a very popular distribution which is based on Debian, another widespread Linux distribution.

The driver that you can download at the address previously mentioned is compressed in the tar.gz format, the common compression format in Linux. Once downloaded, you can extract it by opening a shell, going to the directory where the compressed file is and executing the following command:

```
tar xvzf sqlncli-11.0.1790.0.tar.gz
```

The tar command will extract the archive into a new directory named here sqlncli-11.0.1790.0 on the version of the ODBC driver.

■ **Note** The xvzf set of options used with the tar command is commonly used to extract tar.gz archives. x means eXtract, and v means Verbose, and they allow the extraction's details to be printed on the shell output; z tells tar that it needs to deal with a gzip archive; and f tells tar that the name of the file to extract will follow.

The archive is extracted into a directory. We will enter it using the cd (change directory) command:

```
cd sqlncli-11.0.1790.0
```

What we will have to do to install the driver on Ubuntu is valid at the time of this writing, with the current driver release, which is sqlncli-11.0.1790.0 for Red Hat Enterprise 6, and the current Ubuntu version, which is 12.04 Precise Pangolin. The driver we are installing is correct at the time of writing but Linux minor and major version upgrades occur regularly. This can mean that the Microsoft driver might be out of date or you may need a later version when a new one is brought out. However we are demonstrating on Ubuntu 12.04 with the 11.0.1790.0 Microsoft driver, and although in future releases the process may vary, we can hopefully guide you in a general way.

According to its documentation, the unixodbc version needed to run the driver is 2.3.0. Using the apt-cache tool that manages the cache of Debian and Ubuntu packages, we check what the current unixodbc version on our system is:

```
apt-cache show unixodbc
```

The show option returns details about a package, and on Debian and Ubuntu, the name of the package is simply unixodbc. The result is shown in Figure 16-6.

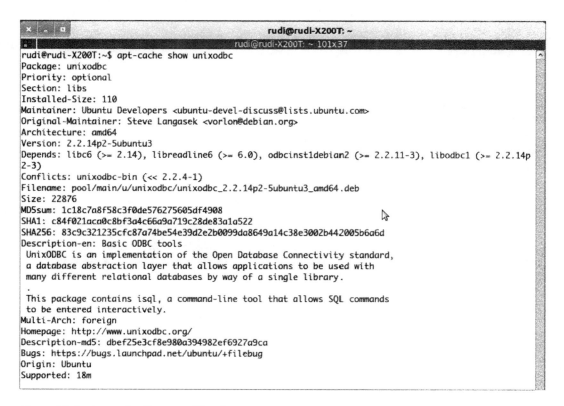

Figure 16-6. *Apt-cache Command Result*

The current version on our Ubuntu is 2.2.14. The libsqlncli downloaded from Microsoft includes a script that downloads and builds the required unixodbc version. So we first uninstall the current unixodbc using the apt-get command, and we install the newer unixodbc using the Microsoft script. Also, we need to prefix our commands with the sudo instruction to execute them with su (super user) privileges, as follows.

```
sudo apt-get remove unixodbc
sudo bash ./build_dm.sh
```

There is a catch here. At the time of this writing, the build_dm.sh script (as well as the install.sh script that we will see very soon) has a flaw: if you open it in a text editor, you will see on its first line that it declares itself as a script written for the sh linux shell, using what is called the *shebang* syntax, as follows.

```
#!/bin/sh
```

This allows the file to be executed without mentioning the interpreter on the command line. The shebang line will be read and the proper interpreter will be called. The problem here is that the script is declared as being an sh script, while it is in fact a bash script. sh and bash are two different Linux shells. So, what we do here for the shell to work is to run it explicitly with bash.

A partial result of the build_dm.sh command is shown in Figure 16-7.

```
The script is provided as a convenience to you as-is, without any express
or implied warranties of any kind.  Microsoft is not liable for any issues
arising out of your use of the script.

Enter 'YES' to have this script continue: YES

Verifying processor and operating system ................................. OK
Verifying wget is installed .............................................. OK
Verifying tar is installed ............................................... OK
Verifying make is installed .............................................. OK
Downloading unixODBC 2.3.0 DriverManager ................................. OK
Unpacking unixODBC 2.3.0 DriverManager ................................... OK
Configuring unixODBC 2.3.0 DriverManager ................................. OK
Building unixODBC 2.3.0 DriverManager .................................... OK
Build of the unixODBC 2.3.0 DriverManager complete.

Run the command 'cd /tmp/unixODBC.22830.6255.24287/unixODBC-2.3.0; make install' to install the drive
r manager.
```

Figure 16-7. *build_dm.sh Command Result*

The unixodbc driver manager was built and copied to a directory in /tmp. The script tells us what to do next: go there and use the make install command to copy the binaries at the right place. What it does not say is that you need administrative privileges to run both commands (shown in the same line in Figure 16-7, separated by a semicolon). So we need to run the commands as follows.

```
sudo cd /tmp/unixODBC.22830.6255.24287/unixODBC-2.3.0
sudo make install
```

Now that the driver manager is installed, we can go to the next step, which is installing the Microsoft driver. The first thing to do is to check the versions of the libraries requested by the driver. We can use the ldd command—ldd returns the shared libraries dependencies of a binary—to check the libraries used by the driver.

```
ldd lib64/libsqlncli-11.0.so.1790.0
```

.so (shared object) is the common extension for shared libraries on Linux. On our system, the command returns the results shown in Figure 16-8.

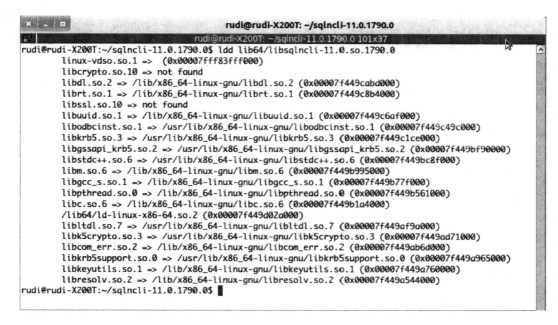

Figure 16-8. *Results of the ldd Command*

In figure 16-8 we see that most of the libraries are found, except the SSL libraries that are libcrypto.so.10 and libssl.so.10. 10 stands for the dynamic shared objects' version number. We need to find out if there are any versions of these libraries available on our system. To do that, we use the find command as follows:

```
find / -name libcrypto.so.* -print
```

As you might have guessed, the find command searches for files. We ask it to start its search at the root of the file system (/), to search for libcrypto.so.* and to print the result. We found this reference: /lib/x86_64-linux-gnu/libcrypto.so.1.0.0. That looks like what we need, but how do we allow our driver to see it? We will create a symbolic link—we could call it a shortcut—with the name requested by the driver, which will be a pointer to the installed library. The following commands do just that:

```
sudo ln -s /lib/x86_64-linux-gnu/libcrypto.so.1.0.0 /lib/x86_64-linux-gnu/libcrypto.so.10
sudo ln -s /lib/x86_64-linux-gnu/libssl.so.1.0.0 /lib/x86_64-linux-gnu/libssl.so.10
```

We use the ln command to create a link, and the -s option specifies that we create a symbolic link.

Now we can install the driver. In the driver's directory, the install.sh shell script allows us to copy the files to the /opt/microsoft/sqlncli location and create the symbolic links in the path to allow the driver and its tools to be recognized on our system. The /opt directory is chosen as the install path because it's where applications not installed with the distribution are supposed to go.

```
sudo bash ./install.sh install --force
```

Once again we use sudo to run the script under administrative privileges and we use bash explicitly. The −force option is needed on our distribution to avoid dependency checks performed by the script to cancel the installation process.

The installation script runs quickly, and when it is finished, you can test the ODBC driver by using the two tools installed with it: a Linux version of the bcp (Bulk Copy) tool, and a Linux version of the sqlcmd shell. As symbolic links are created by the installation script in the path, you can use sqlcmd wherever you are in the file system. An example of starting sqlcmd follows:

```
sqlcmd -S SQL2012 -U apress -P @press!
```

This command connects to the SQL2012 server using the SQL login apress, with password @press!. If you receive an error saying that the library libcrypto.so.10 (or any library used by the ODBC driver) is not found, you might have to investigate and install the library or use the symbolic link technique described above.

Note that here we connect using an SQL Login and not Integrated Security. That's logical, you might think: we are on Linux, not logged in a Windows domain, so how could integrated security work? Well, it can, not fully, but it can. For that, your Linux box must have Kerberos properly configured, which is out of the scope of this book, so please refer to this documentation entry for a high-level description of the requirements for it to work: http://msdn.microsoft.com/en-us/library/hh568450. Note that you cannot impersonate an account, and you are limited to the Linux machine system account.

JDBC

To use the JDBC component, first download it from this page: http://msdn.microsoft.com/en-us/sqlserver/aa937724.aspx. The driver is a JDBC 4 driver that is available to download as a Windows self-extract executable, or a tar.gz compressed file for non-Windows environments. Once the file is uncompressed, you will have a directory with two jar files and other resources like documentation. Put the sqljdbc4.jar file, which is the JDBC 4 driver, in your Java classpath. The classpath is the path where Java will search for classes to run or to import.

Java development is a broad subject so we will not enter into too many details here, but we will provide a short example of the JDBC driver usage, mainly to illustrate the use of the connection string. JDBC connection can be done using a connection string, also named connection URL that is, in the case of SQL Server, very similar to the ADO.NET or ODBC connection strings. The general form of the string is as follows:

```
jdbc:sqlserver://[serverName[\instanceName][:portNumber]][;property=value[;property=value]]
```

Other methods, like setting properties of a Connection object, can be used; we will show here the connection string method. Listing 16-4 shows a short but complete example of a Java class allowing connecting to SQL Server and running a query. To make it more interesting, we assumed that we were in an environment using AlwaysOn Availability Groups, and we added the failoverPartner option in the connection string, in order to allow reconnecting to a mirror in case the first server didn't respond.

■ **Note** If your application accesses the SQL Server with AlwaysOn that listens in multiple subnets with JDBC driver, it is important to set the keyword MultiSubnetFailover=True in the connection string. The reason is that JDBC drivers do not iterate through multiple IP addresses and if the network name listens to multiple IP addresses, JDBC driver spawns parallel connections to the IP addresses and listens to the first one that responds.

Listing 16-4. Java Example Using the Microsoft JDBC Driver

```
import java.sql.*;

public class ApressExample {

        public static void main(String[] args) {
```

```
                String connectionUrl =
"jdbc:sqlserver://SQL2012;integratedSecurity=true;databaseName=AdventureWorks;failoverPartner=
SQL2012B";
                Connection cn = null;
                String qry = "SELECT TOP 10 FirstName, LastName FROM Person.Contact";

                try {
                        cn = DriverManager.getConnection(connectionUrl);
                        runQuery(cn, qry);
                } catch (SQLException se) {
                        try {
                                System.out.println("Connection to principal server failed,
trying the mirror server.");
                                cn = DriverManager.getConnection(connectionUrl);
                                runQuery(cn, qry);
                        } catch (Exception e) {
                                e.printStackTrace();
                        }
                } catch (Exception e) {
                        e.printStackTrace();
                } finally {
                        if (cn != null) try { cn.close(); } catch(Exception e) { }
        }
    }

        private static void runQuery(Connection cn, String SQL) {
                Statement stmt = null;
                ResultSet rs = null;

                try {
                        stmt = cn.createStatement();
                        rs = stmt.executeQuery(SQL);

                        while (rs.next()) {
                                System.out.println(rs.getString(0));
                        }
                        rs.close();
                        stmt.close();
                } catch (Exception e) {
                        e.printStackTrace();
                } finally {
                        if (rs != null) try { rs.close(); } catch(Exception e) {}
                        if (stmt != null) try { stmt.close(); } catch(Exception e) {}
                }
        }
}
```

For this example to work, save it in a file named ApressExample.java, and compile it with the java compiler (javac.exe on Windows) after having made sure that the sqljdbc4.jar file is in the Java classpath. You could also indicate the path of the driver in the javac command line, as shown in the following example:

```
javac.exe -classpath "C:\sqljdbc_4.0\enu\sqljdbc4.jar" c:\apress\ApressExample.java
```

The compilation will result in an `ApressExample.class` file that you can run with java.exe. Once again the JDBC driver will have to be in the classpath for it to work. The classpath is an environment variable, and an example of setting the classpath for the session and running the java class in a cmd session on Windows is shown below. You must be in the directory where the `ApressExample.class` file is for it to work.

```
set classpath=c:\sqljdbc_4.0\enu\sqljdbc4.jar;.;%classpath%
java ApressExample
```

The first line adds the path of the `sqljdbc4.jar` file and the current directory to the classpath environment variable, so it will find the JDBC driver and the `ApressExample` class. The second line runs our code example.

Now that we were able to run our code example, let's come back to its content. The first thing we do in the code is to import the `java.sql` classes in order to have the `Connection`, `Statement`, and all other JDBC classes handy. In the `main()` method of our `ApressExample` class, we define the connection string and set the server's address as well as the mirroring server's address. We choose to be authenticated by Windows, using Integrated Security.

```
String connectionUrl=
"jdbc:sqlserver://SQL2012;integratedSecurity=true;databaseName=AdventureWorks;failoverPartner=
SQL2012B";
```

If you know JDBC, you might be surprised not to find a `Class.forName()` call, as shown in the following snippet:

```
Class.forName("com.microsoft.sqlserver.jdbc.SQLServerDriver");
```

The `Class.forName()` instruction was used to load the JDBC driver and register it to the JDBC `DriverManager`. This is not required anymore if you use JDBC 4, because in JDBC 4 the drivers are able to be loaded magically just by being on the classpath.

The rest of the code is a pretty standard Java example; let's just concentrate on the line that opens the connection:

```
cn = DriverManager.getConnection(connectionUrl);
```

It is enclosed inside a try catch block, in order to catch a connection failure. If such a failure happens, the catch block will run the exact same connection command. This is to allow automatic reconnection in case of a failover. At the second connection attempt the JDBC driver will—once again magically—try with the address defined in the `failoverpartner` option. This second attempt must also be enclosed inside a try catch block in case the other server does not answer either. Because we have to write twice the connection code, we chose here to move the code that uses the connection to run a query in a private method of the class, in order to call it from the `main()` method.

Service Oriented Architecture and WCF Data Services

If you are a die-hard T-SQL developer who didn't venture much into Microsoft client-side code and all the frameworks and libraries, you might crack a smile while reading the few next paragraphs. As T-SQL developers, we are used to dealing with a stable and old-fashioned technology, with no fancy names, which could give the impression that it is so old and solid that it will never change. On the client side, however, things are constantly moving. A history of data access methods and what we call today data services, because of the SOA (Service Oriented Architecture) paradigm, could make a book, and that would be a book full of twists and turns. In the early days of SQL Server, the data access libraries were the native dblib dll and the ODBC API. It was superseded by OLEDB, then by the SQL Server Native Client. Today, we are returning to ODBC to align with a de facto standard, as we have seen in the ODBC for Linux section.

On the data services subject, before the concept ever existed, we were talking about distributed applications, in other words applications broken into components spanned across multiple computers, allowing distant interoperability, components that were exchanging information using a broker like DCOM (Distributed Component Object Model) or CORBA (Common Object Request Broker Architecture) and that were using an RPC (Remote Procedure Call) model. With the release of the .NET framework, Microsoft developed a replacement for creating distributed .NET components named .NET Remoting. But the distributed components model had some shortcomings: mainly, the network protocols they used were not tailored for the web and it was sometimes tricky to allow distant computers behind firewalls to be able to work together. Also you had to implement a unique technology, whether it was DCOM, Corba, .NET Remoting, or others. Moreover, in the case of DCOM and .NET Remoting, it meant that you had to develop on Windows and run Microsoft operating systems and technologies on every end.

So, the Service Oriented Architecture (SOA) paradigm gained attention and popularity because it addressed these limitations. The goal of SOA was to leverage standard and widely used protocols like HTTP or SMTP in order to exchange information between the components of a distributed application, except that in SOA that's not the terminology we use. The components are "services," a term that emphasizes more their loosely coupled and independent nature, and the distributed application model is named Service Oriented Architecture. Using protocols like HTTP allows us to take advantage of existing and proven technologies and infrastructures available on all platforms and designed for the Internet. To ensure that the information exchanged is understood on every platform, text-based structures like XML or JSON (JavaScript Object Notation) are used to generate messages that are created and consumed by these services, which are called Web Services (WS) because of their use of the HTTP protocol. These messages are exchanged mostly using a protocol named SOAP. SOAP was originally an acronym for Simple Object Access Protocol. It is an envelope in which XML messages are enclosed and that defines a set of properties and functionalities for the message. So far so good, but a new model started to gain popularity the last decade, named REST. REST, or Representational State Transfer, is a set of architectural principles for building services, which are called resources. A REST resource is defined by an address, which is an internet address in the form of a URI (Uniform Resource Identifier), a more generic term for what we call an URL in the HTTP protocol. To call the resource, a REST client uses standard HTTP verbs, like GET or PUT, to send or receive messages. So, with REST, you use a model close to what a Web browser would do to call resources, and that makes it interesting mainly because it allows using proven technologies on both sides, and it offers natively the scalability of the web technologies. As REST is more about offering resources than exchanging messages per se, this model is sometimes called Resource Oriented Architecture (ROA), and a system implementing this model is said to be RESTful.

So, with SOA quickly replacing distributed components, some libraries or frameworks were needed in the Microsoft world to build Web Services. The first generation of these tools was called ASP.NET Web Services (ASMX) and was released for .NET 1.0. It was quickly completed by Web Services Enhancement (WSE), which added some SOAP WS additional specifications. That was another programming model to learn, and it was still limited as it didn't implement all the SOA possibilities like the REST model. To build the XML messages, we simply used the .NET xml libraries, or, using SQL Server 2000, we generated directly the XML using the FOR XML clause, and we enclosed it in a SOAP message using our client code. In SQL Server, we also could use an ISAPI extension to provide XML responses directly from SQL server through IIS, without using ASMX. When SQL Server 2005 was released, the ISAPI extension was replaced by an integrated HTTP endpoint capability. SQL Server was then able to act natively as an HTTP server, to receive and send back SOAP messages. Today, this feature is removed from SQL Server 2012, because it didn't offer a complete enough environment to build web services. As a matter of fact, ASMX did not offer all what was needed either. So, Microsoft decided to build a complete and flexible framework to handle all interoperability technologies, which it now calls Connected Systems. That framework is named WCF (Windows Communication Foundation). WCF is integrated into .NET and is the way to go when talking about Web Services, REST, distributed components, or message queuing, in the Microsoft world. WCF offers several layers that provide everything that is needed to create connected systems. They are schematized in Figure 16-9.

Figure 16-9. *The WCF Layers Stack*

The contracts layer comprises the contracts (or interfaces) definition classes that allow services to publish and agree on the content of the information they will exchange. You can define data contracts, message contacts, service contracts, and so on; the service runtime layer offers all the behaviors necessary to implement the services, like transaction behavior, parameter filtering, and so on; the messaging layer offers encoders and channels to handle the more physical and concrete exchange of messages and services; and finally, the activation and hosting layer allows running the services, either as an exe, a windows service, or a COM + application, and so on.

WCF can be used to create Services or remoting applications or to implement message queuing. Here, we will of course concentrate on a specific feature of WCF that provides a very simple way to publish data as REST resources, and that is named WCF Data Services.

■ **Note** Here again, the name of the technology changed a few times in a few years. In 2007, we heard about project Astoria, which aimed to deliver a framework for creating and consuming data services using Service Oriented Architecture. When it was released in 2008 along with .NET 3.5, its final name was ADO.NET Data Services, which was later renamed WCF Data Services.

WCF Data Services supports the concept of REST for accessing your data remotely. As we have briefly said before, REST-style services provide simple URI-based querying, a simpler mechanism than the SOAP protocol. WCF Data Services translates regular HTTP requests into *create, read, update, delete (CRUD)* operations against a data source, and exchanges data by using the OData (Open Data) protocol, an open web protocol for querying and updating data. WCF Data Services uses an HTTP request-to-CRUD operation mapping, as shown in Table 16-1.

Table 16-1. *HTTP Requests to WCF Data Services Operations*

HTTP Request	WCF Data Services Operation
GET	Query the data source; retrieve data.
POST	Create a new entity and insert it into the data source.
PUT	Update an entity in the data source.
DELETE	Delete an entity from the data source.

Creating a WCF Data Service

As with a web service, the first step to creating a WCF Data Service is to create a new ASP.NET Web Application project, as shown in Figure 16-10.

Figure 16-10. *Creating an ASP.NET Web Application in Visual Studio 2010*

Defining the Data Source

Once you have created a web application project, you need to add a source for your data. The easiest way is to add an ADO.NET entity data model (EDM) by right-clicking on the project in Solution Explorer, and choosing Add ➤ New item . . . in Visual Studio and selecting the ADO.NET Entity Data Model template in the Data page of the New Item window, as shown in Figure 16-11, which launches the ADO.NET Entity Data Model wizard.

Figure 16-11. *Adding an ADO.NET EDM Item to Your Web Application*

We have covered Entity Framework in Chapter 15, so we don't need to go into details here. We are generating an EDM from tables in the AdventureWorks database. We choose to include the Production.Product, Production.ProductPhoto, and Production.ProductProductPhoto tables of the AdventureWorks database, as shown in Figure 16-12.

Figure 16-12. *Adding Tables to the EDM*

Once you've added tables to your EDM, you can view them in the Entity Data Model designer as we have seen previously.

Creating the Data Service

The next step after you've defined your EDM is to add a WCF Data Service item to your project through the New item menu option. The Add New Item window is shown in Figure 16-13 with the WCF Data Service template highlighted.

Figure 16-13. *Adding a WCF Data Service*

The WCF Data Service template automatically generates the Data Service landing page, named
ProductPhotoDataService.svc in this example. This is the page you need to call to request the service. Its source
file, named ProductPhotoDataService.svc.cs in this example, uses the System.Data.Services namespace
and contains a class definition for the service that defines access rules for entity sets and service operations. The
class defined in this file requires some modification by hand where you see the automatically generated TODO
comments. You must define the data source class, namely our EF entities class, and at a minimum you must set
the entity access rules. We have done so in Listing 16-5.

Listing 16-5. AdventureWorksDataService Class Definition Using System.Data.Services;

```
using System;
using System.Collections.Generic;
using System.Data.Services;
using System.Data.Services.Common;
using System.Linq;
using System.ServiceModel.Web;
using System.Web;

namespace WCFDataServicesSample
{
    public class ProductPhotoDataService : DataService<AdventureWorksEntities>
    {
        // This method is called only once to initialize service-wide policies.
        public static void InitializeService(DataServiceConfiguration config)
```

```
    {
        config.SetEntitySetAccessRule("Products", EntitySetRights.AllRead);
        config.SetEntitySetAccessRule("ProductPhotoes", EntitySetRights.AllRead);
        config.SetEntitySetAccessRule("ProductProductPhotoes", EntitySetRights.AllRead);
        config.DataServiceBehavior.MaxProtocolVersion = DataServiceProtocolVersion.V2;
    }
  }
}
```

■ **Caution**   You can use the wildcard character (*) to set rights for all entities and service operations at once, but Microsoft strongly recommends against this. Although it's useful for testing purposes, in a production environment this can lead to serious security problems.

In Listing 16-5, we mentioned the Entity Set names that were pluralized by EF, which is why we have the Photoes faulty plural form. Feel free of course to correct it in the entity model source. We've set the access rules to AllRead, meaning that the service allows queries by key or queries for all contents of the entity set. The rights allowed are shown in Table 16-2.

Table 16-2. *Service Entity and Operation Access Rights*

Access Rights	Entity/Operation	Description
All	Both	Allows full read/write access to the entity and full read access to operations.
AllRead	Both	Allows full read access to the entity or operation. It is shorthand for ReadSingle and ReadMultiple access rights combined with a logical OR (|) operation.
AllWrite	Entity	Allows full write access to the entity. It is shorthand for WriteAppend, WriteUpdate, WriteDelete access rights combined with a logical OR (|) operation.
None	Both	Allows no read or write access, and will not appear in the services metadata document.
ReadSingle	Both	Allows for queries by key against an entity set.
ReadMultiple	Both	Allows for queries for the entire contents of the set.
WriteAppend	Entity	Allows new resources to be appended to the set.
WriteDelete	Entity	Allows existing resources to be deleted from the set.
WriteUpdate	Entity	Allows existing resources to be updated in the set.

You can test your WCF Data Service by running it in Debug mode from Visual Studio. Visual Studio will open a browser window with the address set to the start page for your project. Change it to the address of the data service, which is in our example http://localhost:59560/ProductPhotoDataService.svc.

■ **Note** You can also set your WCF Data Service page (.svc extension) as the project start page. In that case you can delete the Default.aspx page in the project since it's not needed.

Your start address and port number will most likely be different. The WCF Data Service will respond to your request with a listing of entities for which you have access, as shown in Figure 16-14.

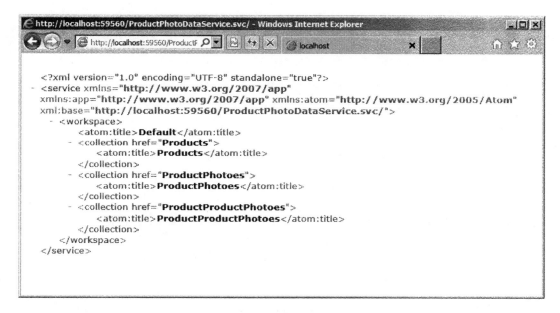

Figure 16-14. *Calling the Page for the WCF Data Service*

■ **Tip** WCF Data Services supports two payload types. The *payload type* is the standard format for incoming request data and outgoing results data. WCF Data Services supports both JavaScript Object Notation (JSON) and the Atom Publishing Protocol for payloads. If you call the page for your WCF Data Service and the results look like a nonsensical syndication feed instead of standard XML, you will need to turn off the feed-reading view in your browser. In Internet Explorer 7, you can uncheck the Tools ➤ Internet Options ➤ Content ➤ Settings ➤ Turn On Feed Reading View option.

Once you've confirmed that the WCF Data Service is up and running, you can query the service using a combination of path expression-style syntax in the URI to locate entities and query string parameters to further restrict and control output. The following are some examples of WCF Data Service queries:

- http://localhost:59560/ProductPhotoDataService.svc/Products: This query retrieves all Product entities.

- http://localhost:59560/ProductPhotoDataService.svc/Products(749): This query retrieves the Product entities with a primary key value of 749. The primary key of the Product entity is ProductID.

- `http://localhost:59560/ProductPhotoDataService.svc/Products?$skip=10&$top=10`:
  This query skips the first ten Product entities and retrieves the following ten (items 11
  through 20) in key order.

- `http://localhost:59560/ProductPhotoDataService.svc/Products?$top=20&$order`
  `by=Name`: This query retrieves the first 20 Product entities ordered (sorted) by the Name
  attribute.

- `http://localhost:59560/ProductPhotoDataService.svc/Products?$filter=ListPrice`
  `gt 1000&$expand = ProductProductPhotoes/ProductPhoto`: This query retrieves all the
  Product entities with a `ListPrice` attribute that is greater than 1,000. The results include
  related `ProductProductPhoto` and `ProductPhoto` entities expanded inline. Note that in
  the expanded option we need to mention first the entity set, and then the entities linked
  to the set, which is why we have `ProductProductPhotoes` and then `ProductPhoto`.

This is just a small sampling of the types of REST-style queries you can create using WCF Data Services. In fact, WCF Data Services supports several query string options, as shown in Table 16-3.

Table 16-3. *Query String Options*

Option	Description
$expand	Expands results to include one or more related entities inline in the results.
$filter	Restricts the results returned by applying an expression to the last entity set identified in the URI path. The $filter option supports a simple expression language that includes logical, arithmetic, and grouping operators, and an assortment of string, date, and math functions.
$orderby	Orders (sorts) results by the attributes specified. You can specify multiple attributes separated by commas, and each attribute can be followed by an optional asc or desc modifier indicating ascending or descending sort order, respectively.
$skip	Skips a given number of rows when returning results.
$top	Restricts the number of entities returned to the specified number.

Creating a WCF Data Service Consumer

Once you have a WCF Data Service up and running, creating a consumer application is relatively simple. For this example, we've created a simple .NET application that calls the service to display the image and details of products selected from a drop-down list.

The first step in building a consumer application is to create classes based on your EDM. Instead of doing it manually, you can generate the creation of these classes by using the Add Service Reference command in Visual Studio that automatically generates C# or Visual Basic classes for use in client applications. For our example, we created an ASP.NET web application and we right-clicked on the project in the Solution Explorer, and we chose the Add Service Reference command. In the Add Service Reference Window, we added the WCF Data Service address and clicked on Go. Visual Studio queried the service's metadata. Figure 16-15 shows the result of this request.

Figure 16-15. *Adding a Service Reference in Visual Studio 2010*

Step two of the process is to create the Default.aspx page of the client application. This page will perform the necessary calls to the service. You are not tied to a web application, however; you can just as easily call ADO.NET Data Services from Windows applications, Silverlight applications, or any other platform that can initiate HTTP requests (although object deserialization on platforms that don't support .NET classes could pose a bit of a challenge). For this client application, we simply added a drop-down list, an image control, and a table to the web form. Then we wired up the page load and drop-down list selection change events. The code is shown in Listing 16-6, with results shown in Figure 16-16.

Listing 16-6. *ASP.NET Client Application Default.aspx Page*

```
using System;
using System.Collections.Generic;
using System.Linq;
using System.Web;
using System.Web.UI;
using System.Web.UI.WebControls;
using WCFdsClient.PhotoServiceReference;
using System.Data.Services.Client;
```

```
namespace WCFdsClient
{
    public partial class _Default : System.Web.UI.Page
    {
        protected void Page_Load(object sender, EventArgs e)
        {
            PopulateDropDown();
        }

        private void PopulateDropDown()
        {
            AdventureWorksEntities ctx = new AdventureWorksEntities(
                new Uri ("http://localhost:59560/ProductPhotoDataService.svc")
                );

            var qry = from p in ctx.Products
                      where p.FinishedGoodsFlag
                      orderby p.Name
                      select p;

            foreach (Product p in qry) {
                ProductDropDown.Items.Add(new ListItem(p.Name, p.ProductID.ToString()));
            }

            string id = ProductDropDown.SelectedValue;
            UpdateImage(id);
        }

        private void UpdateImage(string id) {
            ProductImage.ImageUrl = string.Format("GetImage.aspx?id={0}", id);
        }

        protected void ProductDropDownlist_SelectedIndexChanged(object sender, EventArgs e)
        {
            string id = ProductDropDown.SelectedValue;

            AdventureWorksEntities ctx = new AdventureWorksEntities(
                new Uri("http://localhost:59560/ProductPhotoDataService.svc")
                );

            var qry = from p in ctx.Products
                      where p.ProductID == Convert.ToInt32(id)
                      select p;

            //DataServiceQuery<Product> qry =
ctx.CreateQuery<Product>(string.Format("/Product({0})", id));

            foreach (Product p in qry)
            {
                TableProduct.Rows[0].Cells[1].Text=p.Class;
                TableProduct.Rows[1].Cells[1].Text=p.Color;
                TableProduct.Rows[2].Cells[1].Text=p.Size + " " + p.SizeUnitMeasureCode;
```

```
            TableProduct.Rows[3].Cells[1].Text=p.Weight + " " + p.WeightUnitMeasureCode;
            TableProduct.Rows[4].Cells[1].Text=p.ListPrice.ToString();
            TableProduct.Rows[5].Cells[1].Text=p.ProductNumber;
        }
        UpdateImage(id);
    }

  }

}
```

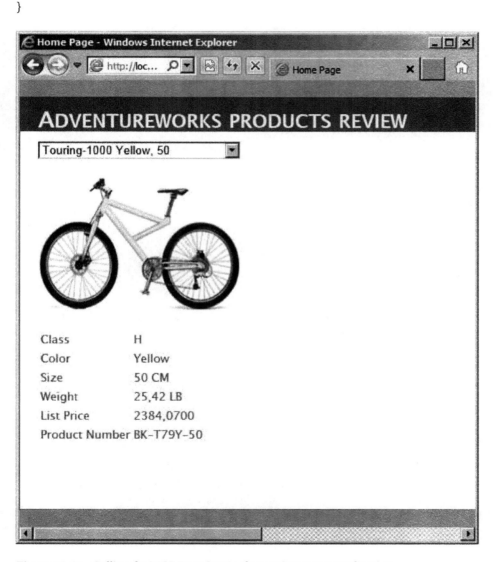

Figure 16-16. *Calling the WCF Data Service from a Consumer Application*

The first part of the code imports the necessary namespaces. The System.Data.Services.Client namespace is required to create WCF Data Services client queries. You will need to add a reference to the System.Data.Services.Client component library to your project. The WCFdsClient.PhotoServiceReference namespace is a reference to our EDM classes' namespace.

```
using WCFdsClient.PhotoServiceReference;
using System.Data.Services.Client;
```

The PageLoad event of the Default.aspx page simply calls a little function called PopulateDropDown that populates the drop-down list with the names and IDs of all "finished goods" products that AdventureWorks keeps in its database:

```
PopulateDropDown();
```

The PopulateDropDown() function begins by creating an instance of the AdventureWorksEntities EDM data context that points to the URI of the WCF Data Service. We have seen data contexts in Chapter 15. Here, in WCF Data Services, the object is a sibling named a DataServiceContext.

```
AdventureWorksEntities ctx = new AdventureWorksEntities(
    new Uri ("http://localhost:59560/ProductPhotoDataService.svc")
);
```

Next, this function uses a LINQ query on the AdventureWorksEntities DataServiceContext that returns a DataServiceQuery. The query filters the Product entities whose FinishedGoodsFlag attributes are set to true. Results are sorted by the Name attribute.

```
var qry = from p in ctx.Products
          where p.FinishedGoodsFlag
          orderby p.Name
          select p;
```

The query returns an IEnumerable result that can be iterated using foreach. In this example, the Name and ProductID attributes are iterated and added to the drop-down list.

```
foreach (Product p in qry) {
    ProductDropDown.Items.Add(new ListItem(p.Name, p.ProductID.ToString()));
}
```

Finally, the product image is updated based on the selected value of the drop-down list:

```
string id = ProductDropDown.SelectedValue;
UpdateImage(id);
```

We've also wired the SelectedIndexChanged event of the drop-down list so that the image and other data being displayed are updated when the user selects a new product. The first thing this function does is retrieve the currently selected value from the drop-down list.

```
string id = ProductDropDown.SelectedValue;
```

Then, as with the PopulateDropDown() function, this function queries the WCF Data Service to retrieve the product selected from the drop-down list.

```
AdventureWorksEntities ctx = new AdventureWorksEntities(
    new Uri("http://localhost:59560/ProductPhotoDataService.svc")
);

var qry = from p in ctx.Products
          where p.ProductID == Convert.ToInt32(id)
          select p;
```

Then, the function iterates the results and updates the display, including the summary information table and the product image.

```
foreach (Product p in qry)
{
    TableProduct.Rows[0].Cells[1].Text = p.Class;
    TableProduct.Rows[1].Cells[1].Text = p.Color;
    TableProduct.Rows[2].Cells[1].Text = p.Size + " " + p.SizeUnitMeasureCode;
    TableProduct.Rows[3].Cells[1].Text = p.Weight + " " + p.WeightUnitMeasureCode;
    TableProduct.Rows[4].Cells[1].Text = p.ListPrice.ToString();
    TableProduct.Rows[5].Cells[1].Text = p.ProductNumber;
}
UpdateImage(id);
```

The UpdateImage() function, called by two of the event handlers in this example, consists of a single line that changes the URL of the product image:

```
ProductImage.ImageUrl = string.Format("GetImage.aspx?id={0}", id);
```

___

■ **Note** In order to actually show the images on a web page, we had to resort to an old ASP.NET trick. Because the images are stored in the database, we had to create a second page in the project called GetImage.aspx to retrieve the appropriate image. This method calls the WCF Data Service and returns the binary product photo image as a JPEG image. We won't go into the details here because they're not essential to understanding WCF Data Services, but the source code is available in the downloadable sample files for the curious.

___

Now that we created a basic WCF Data Service consumer, let us review some of the SQL Server 2012 features supported in ADO.NET 4.5. ADO.NET 4.5 enables support for null bit compression using sparse columns to optimize the data transfer over the wire. Imagine a table with more than half of its columns that are nullable and have null values for all the rows. When you use null bit compression and sparse column schema you will be able to save on the storage as well as optimize the data transfer over the wire as well.

ADO.NET 4.5 also adds support for LocalDB. Remember that LocalDB needs to be started for your code to be able to access it.

Summary

SQL Server 2012 introduces an addition to SQL Server Express named LocalDB that allows using databases as files in applications and simplifies embedding database capabilities in local and easy to deploy applications. At the same time, SQL Server data access libraries keep improving to allow a heterogeneous environment with Linux systems and Java code.

In SQL Server 2005, Microsoft introduced HTTP SOAP endpoints, which allowed developers to expose SPs and UDFs within the database as web service methods. Because it wasn't a full featured and solid enough implementation, and also because Microsoft wants to focus on a unified framework for connected systems, HTTP endpoints have been removed from SQL Server 2012.

We closed the chapter out with an introduction to WCF Data Services. With built-in support for entity data models and the powerful ADO.NET EDM designer, REST-style querying, and both the JSON and Atom payload formats, WCF Data Services can provide a lightweight alternative to SOAP-based web services and a good way to provide interoperability across systems.

EXERCISES

1. [True/False] A LocalDB instance can be run as a Windows service.

2. [True/False] You cannot access an XML data type column if you access SQL Server from a Linux computer.

3. [True/False] HTTP SOAP endpoints can be created in SQL Server 2012.

4. [Fill in the blank] Visual Studio 2010 and 2012 provide a _____ project template to create new web services.

5. [True/False] Visual Studio 2010 includes a graphical EDM designer.

6. [Choose one] WCF Data Services accepts which type of query requests:

    a. SQL queries

    b. XSLT queries

    c. REST-style queries

    d. English language queries

CHAPTER 17

■ ■ ■

Error Handling and Dynamic SQL

Prior to SQL Server 2005, error handling was limited almost exclusively to the @@error system function and the RAISERROR statement, or through client-side exception handling. T-SQL in SQL Server 2012 still provides access to these tools, but it also supports modern structured error handling similar to that offered by other high-level languages such as C++, C#, and Visual Basic. In this chapter, we will discuss legacy T-SQL error-handling functionality and the newer structured error-handling model in T-SQL. This chapter introduces tools useful for debugging server-side code, including T-SQL statements and the Visual Studio IDE.

We will also discuss dynamic SQL in this chapter, which is often more difficult to debug and manage than standard (nondynamic) T-SQL statements. Dynamic SQL, while a useful tool, also has security implications, which we will address.

Error Handling

SQL Server 2012 provides improvements in error handling over SQL Server 2008 and prior releases. In this section, we'll discuss legacy error handling, SQL Server 2008 TRY . . . CATCH structured error handling, as well as the new SQL 2012 THROW statement.

■ **Note** It may seem odd to still be referring in 2012 to an error handling mechanism introduced in SQL Server 2000. The reality is you are still quite likely to encounter the @@error statement in much of your code and, despite certain limitations and restrictions, the @@error statement still proves useful for error handling.

Legacy Error Handling

In SQL Server 2000, the primary method of handling exceptions was through the @@error system function. This function returns an int value representing the current error code. An @@error value of 0 means no error occurred. One of the major limitations of this function is that it is automatically reset to 0 after every successful statement. This means you cannot have any statements between the code that you expect might produce an exception and the code that checks the value of @@error. This also means that after @@error is checked, it is automatically reset to 0, so you can't both check the value of @@error and return @@error from within an SP. Listing 17-1 demonstrates an SP that generates an error and attempts to print the error code from within the procedure and return the value of @@error to the caller.

Listing 17-1. Incorrect Error Handling with @@error

```
CREATE PROCEDURE dbo.TestError (@e int OUTPUT)
AS

BEGIN
  INSERT INTO Person.Person(BusinessEntityID)
  VALUES (1);

  PRINT N'Error code in procedure = ' + CAST(@@error AS nvarchar(10));

  SET @e = @@error;
END
GO

DECLARE @ret int,
  @e int;

EXEC @ret = dbo.TestError @e OUTPUT;
PRINT N'Returned error code = ' + CAST(@e AS nvarchar(10));
PRINT N'Return value = ' + CAST(@ret AS nvarchar(10));
```

The TestError procedure in Listing 17-1 demonstrates one problem with @@error. The result of executing the procedure should be similar to the following:

```
Msg 515, Level 16, State 2, Procedure TestError, Line 4
Cannot insert the value NULL into column 'PersonType', table
'AdventureWorks.Person.Person'; column does not allow nulls. INSERT fails.
The statement has been terminated.
Error code in procedure = 515
Returned error code = 0
Return value = -6
```

As you can see, the error code generated by the failed INSERT statement is 515 when printed inside the SP, but a value of 0 (no error) is returned to the caller via the OUTPUT parameter. The problem is with the following line in the SP:

```
PRINT N'Error code in procedure = ' + CAST(@@error AS nvarchar(10));
```

The PRINT statement automatically resets the value of @@error after it executes, meaning you can't test or retrieve the same value of @@error afterward (it will be 0 every time). The workaround is to store the value of @@error in a local variable immediately after the statement you suspect might fail (in this case the INSERT statement). Listing 17-2 demonstrates this method of using @@error.

Listing 17-2. Corrected Error Handling with @@error

```
CREATE PROCEDURE dbo.TestError2 (@e int OUTPUT)
AS
BEGIN
  INSERT INTO Person.Person(BusinessEntityID)
  VALUES (1);
```

```
SET @e = @@error;

  PRINT N'Error code in procedure = ' + CAST(@e AS nvarchar(10));
END
GO

DECLARE @ret int,
  @e int;
EXEC @ret = dbo.TestError2 @e OUTPUT;
PRINT N'Returned error code = ' + CAST(@e AS nvarchar(10));
PRINT N'Return value = ' + CAST(@ret AS nvarchar(10));
```

By storing the value of @@error immediately after the statement you suspect might cause an error, you can test or retrieve the value as often as you like for further processing. The following is the result of the new procedure:

```
Msg 515, Level 16, State 2, Procedure TestError2, Line 4 Cannot insert the value NULL into
column 'PersonType', table 'AdventureWorks.Person.Person'; column does not allow nulls.
INSERT fails.
The statement has been terminated.
Error code in procedure = 515
Returned error code = 515
Return value = -6
```

In this case, the proper @@error code is both printed and returned to the caller by the SP. Also of note is that the SP return value is automatically set to a nonzero value when the error occurs.

The RAISERROR Statement

The RAISERROR statement is a T-SQL statement that allows you to throw an exception at runtime. The RAISERROR statement accepts a message ID number or message string, severity level, state information, and optional argument parameters for special formatting codes in error messages. Listing 17-3 uses RAISERROR to throw an exception with a custom error message, a severity level of 17, and a state of 127.

Listing 17-3. Raising a Custom Exception with RAISERROR

```
RAISERROR ('This is an exception.', 17, 127);
```

When you pass a string error message to the RAISERROR statement, as in Listing 17-3, a default error code of 50000 is raised. If you specify a message ID number instead, the number must be between 13000 and 2147483647, and it cannot be 50000. The severity level is a number between 0 and 25, with each level representing the seriousness of the error. Table 17-1 lists the severity levels recognized by SQL Server.

Table 17-1. *SQL Server Error Severity Levels*

Range	Description
0–10	Informational messages
11–18	Errors
19–25	Fatal errors

■ **Tip**   Only members of the sysadmin fixed server role of users with ALTER TRACE permissions can specify severity levels greater than 18 with RAISERROR, and the WITH LOG option must be used.

The state value passed to RAISERROR is a user-defined informational value between 1 and 127. The state information can be used to help locate specific errors within your code when using RAISERROR. For instance, you can use a state of 1 for the first RAISERROR statement in a given SP and a state of 2 for the second RAISERROR statement in the same SP. The state information provided by RAISERROR isn't as necessary in SQL Server 2012 since you can retrieve much more descriptive and precise information from the functions available in CATCH blocks.

The RAISERROR statement supports an optional WITH clause for specifying additional options. The WITH LOG option logs the error raised to the application log and the SQL error log, the WITH NOWAIT option sends the error message to the client immediately, and the WITH SETERROR option sets the @@error system function (in a CATCH block) to an indicated message ID number. This should be used with a severity of 10 or less to set @@error without causing other side effects (e.g., batch termination).

RAISERROR can be used within a TRY or CATCH block to generate errors. Within the TRY block, if RAISERROR generates an error with severity between 11 and 19, control passes to the CATCH block. For errors with severity of 10 or lower, processing continues in the TRY block. For errors with severity of 20 or higher, the client connection is terminated and control does not pass to the CATCH block. For these high-severity errors, the error is returned to the caller.

Try . . . Catch Exception Handling

SQL Server 2012 supports the TRY . . . CATCH model of exception handling common in other modern programming languages and first introduced in SQL Server 2008. In the T-SQL TRY . . . CATCH model, you wrap the code you suspect could cause an exception in a BEGIN TRY . . . END TRY block. This block is immediately followed by a BEGIN CATCH . . . END CATCH block that will be invoked only if the statements in the TRY block causes an error. Listing 17-4 demonstrates TRY . . . CATCH exception handling with a simple SP.

Listing 17-4. Sample TRY . . . CATCH Error Handling

```
CREATE PROCEDURE dbo.TestError3 (@e int OUTPUT)
AS
BEGIN

  SET @e = 0;

  BEGIN TRY
  INSERT INTO Person.Address (AddressID)
  VALUES (1);
END TRY

BEGIN CATCH
   SET @e = ERROR_NUMBER();
   PRINT N'Error Code = ' + CAST(@e AS nvarchar(10));
   PRINT N'Error Procedure = ' + ERROR_PROCEDURE();
   PRINT N'Error Message = ' + ERROR_MESSAGE();
END CATCH
```

```
END
GO

DECLARE @ret  int,
  @e int;
EXEC @ret  = dbo.TestError3 @e OUTPUT;
PRINT N'Error code = ' + CAST(@e AS nvarchar(10));
PRINT N'Return value = ' + CAST(@ret AS nvarchar(10));
```

The result is similar to Listing 17-2, but SQL Server's TRY . . . CATCH support gives you more control and flexibility over the output, as shown here:

```
(0 row(s) affected)
Error Code = 544
Error Procedure = TestError3
Error Message = Cannot insert explicit value for identity column in table
'Address' when IDENTITY_INSERT is set to OFF.
Returned error code = 544
Return value = -6
```

The T-SQL statements in the BEGIN TRY . . . END TRY block execute normally. If the block completes without error, the T-SQL statements between the BEGIN CATCH . . . END CATCH block are skipped. If an exception is thrown by the statements in the TRY block, control transfers to the statements in the BEGIN CATCH . . . END CATCH block.

The CATCH block exposes several functions for determining exactly what error occurred and where it occurred. We used some of these functions in Listing 17-4 to return additional information about the exception thrown. These functions are available only between the BEGIN CATCH . . . END CATCH keywords, and only during error handling when control has been transferred to it by an exception thrown in a TRY block. If used outside of a CATCH block, all of these functions return NULL. The functions available are listed in Table 17-2.

Table 17-2. *CATCH Block Functions*

Function Name	Description
ERROR_LINE()	Returns the line number on which the exception occurred.
ERROR_MESSAGE()	Returns the complete text of the generated error message.
ERROR_PROCEDURE()	Returns the name of the SP or trigger where the error occurred.
ERROR_NUMBER()	Returns the number of the error that occurred.
ERROR_SEVERITY()	Returns the severity level of the error that occurred.
ERROR_STATE()	Returns the state number of the error that occurred.

TRY . . . CATCH blocks can be nested. You can have TRY . . . CATCH blocks within other TRY blocks or CATCH blocks to handle errors that might be generated within your exception-handling code.

You can also test the state of transactions within a CATCH block by using the XACT_STATE function. We strongly recommend testing your transaction state before issuing a COMMIT TRANSACTION or ROLLBACK TRANSACTION statement in your CATCH block to ensure consistency. Table 17-3 lists the return values for XACT_STATE and how you should handle each in your CATCH block.

Table 17-3. XACT_STATE Function Return Values

XACT_STATE	Meaning
−1	There is an uncommittable transaction pending. Issue a ROLLBACK TRANSACTION statement.
0	There is no transaction pending. No action is necessary.
1	There is a committable transaction pending. Issue a COMMIT TRANSACTION statement.

The T-SQL TRY . . . CATCH method of error handling has certain limitations attached to it. For one, TRY . . . CATCH can only capture errors that have a severity greater than 10 that do not close the database connection. The following errors are not caught:

- Errors with a severity of 10 or lower *(informational messages)* are not caught.

- Errors with a severity level of 20 or higher *(connection-termination errors)* are not caught, because they close the database connection immediately.

- Most compile-time errors, such as syntax errors, are not caught by TRY . . . CATCH, although there are exceptions (e.g., when using dynamic SQL).

- Statement-level recompilation errors, such as object-name resolution errors, are not caught, due to SQL Server's deferred-name resolution.

Also keep in mind that errors captured by a TRY . . . CATCH block are not returned to the caller. You can, however, use the RAISERROR statement (described in the next section) to return error information to the caller.

TRY_PARSE, TRY_CONVERT, and TRY_CAST

SQL Server 2012 introduces some additional enhancements to the TRY command. The TRY_PARSE, TRY_CONVERT, TRY_CAST functions offer error handling simplicity to some common T-SQL problems. For example the TRY_PARSE function attempts to convert a string value to a date type or numeric type. If the attempt fails then SQL returns a NULL value. In previous versions of SQL Server you would use CAST or CONVERT and need to write code to capture any errors. The syntax for the TRY_PARSE command is as follows:

```
TRY_PARSE ( string_value AS data_type [ USING culture ] )
```

The culture statement allows you specifiy the specific language format used for the conversion. This is set regardless of the default SQL Server collation. If no culture is specified then the command will use the default language on the server. Listing 17-5 shows a few examples. The output is shown in Figure 17-1.

Listing 17-5. Examples of TRY_PARSE

```
DECLARE @fauxdate AS varchar(10)
DECLARE @realdate AS VARCHAR(10)

SET @fauxdate = 'iamnotadate'
SET @realdate = '01/05/2012'

SELECT TRY_PARSE(@fauxdate AS DATE);

SELECT TRY_PARSE(@realdate AS DATE);

SELECT TRY_PARSE(@realdate AS DATE USING 'Fr-FR');

SELECT IIF(TRY_PARSE(@realdate AS DATE) IS NULL, 'False', 'True')
```

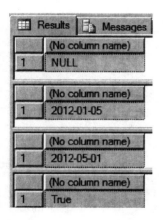

Figure 17-1. *Output of TRY_PARSE Function*

The first query attempts to convert a non-date string to a date and fails by returning NULL. The second query succeeds and returns the date 2012-05-01. The third query returns the same date but collates it to the French date format. The final query shows how you can use conditional processing to return any value you want based on whether the conversion succeeds or fails.

The next function is the TRY_CONVERT function. TRY_CONVERT has the same functionality as the CONVERT function but will return a NULL instead of an error if the conversion fails. You use the TRY_CONVERT function when you want to test the possibility of converting one data type to another data type. The syntax is as follows:

```
TRY_CONVERT ( data_type [ ( length ) ], expression [, style ] )
```

The data_type is the data type you want to convert the expression into and the style determines formatting. Listing 17-6 shows examples. Figure 17-2 shows each output.

Listing 17-6. TRY_CONVERT Examples

```
DECLARE @sampletext AS VARCHAR(10)

SET @sampletext = '123456'

SELECT TRY_CONVERT(INT, @ sampletext);

SELECT TRY_CONVERT(DATE, @ sampletext);

SELECT IIF(TRY_CONVERT(binary, @ sampletext) IS NULL, 'FALSE', 'TRUE');
```

Figure 17-2. *Output of TRY_CONVERT*

We first set the variable to a text value which can easily be converted to an integer. The first TRY_CONVERT successfully performs the conversion but the second fails since the text value cannot implicitly be converted to a date. The final example shows that the conversion succeeded with a return result of TRUE.

The final example is the use of TRY_CAST. TRY_CAST is the technical equivalent of TRY_CONVERT but the format is different. The syntax for TRY_CAST is the following:

```
TRY_CAST (expression AS data_type [ ( length ) ])
```

For demonstration we will use the same examples we used in Listing 17-5 but instead change the syntax to use TRY_CAST. Listing 17-7 shows the differences. The output is the same as in Figure 17-2.

Listing 17-7. Examples Using TRY_CAST

```
DECLARE @sampletext AS VARCHAR(10)

SET @sampletext = '123456'

SELECT TRY_CAST(@sampletext AS INT);

SELECT TRY_CAST(@sampletext AS DATE);

SELECT IIF(TRY_CAST(@sampletext AS BINARY) IS NULL, 'FALSE', 'TRUE');
```

■ **Tip** Though useful keep in mind a couple of things about TRY_PARSE, TRY_CONVERT, and TRY_CAST. Parsing strings can be a costly process so use the function sparingly. Microsoft recommends using TRY_PARSE only for converting strings to date or numeric values. For all other conversions use CAST or CONVERT. Also keep in mind that TRY_CONVERT and TRY_CAST will still throw errors for explicit conversions. These are conversions that are not possible. For a chart of implicit and explicit conversions see Books Online (BOL) at http://msdn.microsoft.com/en-us/library/ms191530.aspx.

Throw Statement

SQL Server 2012 introduces the THROW statement. The THROW statement is similar to what we find in programming languages like C++ and C# and can be used instead of RAISERROR. A primary benefit to using the THROW statement instead of RAISERROR is it does not require an error message ID to exist in sys.messages. The THROW statement can occur either inside a CATCH block or outside the TRY . . . CATCH statements. If no parameters are defined then the THROW statement must be within the CATCH block. Listing 17-8 shows examples of both. We'll use the same INSERT statements as in our previous examples.

Listing 17-8. Examples of the THROW Statement

```
--1. Using THROW without paramaters

        BEGIN TRY
        INSERT INTO Person.Address (AddressID)
        VALUES (1);
    END TRY
    BEGIN CATCH
        PRINT 'This is an error';
        THROW
    END CATCH ;

--2. Using THROW with parameters

  THROW 52000,  'This is also an error',  1

    BEGIN TRY
        INSERT INTO Person.Address (AddressID)
        VALUES (1);
        END TRY
    BEGIN CATCH
        THROW
    END CATCH
```

```
(0 row(s) affected)
This is an error
Msg 544, Level 16, State 1, Line 2
Cannot insert explicit value for identity column in table 'Address' when
IDENTITY INSERT is set to OFF.

MSG 52000, Level 16, State 1, Line 1
```

A couple of things to notice: First off, the only level of severity returned by the THROW statement is 16. The statement doesn't allow for any other level, which is another difference between THROW and RAISERROR. Another thing to notice is that any statement prior to the THROW statement in the CATCH block must end in a semi-colon. This is yet another reason to make sure all your block statements terminate in semi-colons. If you are already used to using the THROW statement in other programming languages then you should find this a helpful addition to SQL Server 2012.

Debugging Tools

In procedural languages like C#, debugging code is somewhat easier than in declarative languages like T-SQL. In procedural languages, you can easily follow the flow of a program, setting breakpoints at each atomic step of execution. In declarative languages, however, a single statement can perform dozens or hundreds of steps in the background, most of which you will probably not even be aware of at execution time. The good news is that the SQL Server team did not leave us without tools to debug and troubleshoot T-SQL code. The unpretentious PRINT statement provides a very simple and effective method of debugging.

PRINT Statement Debugging

The PRINT statement, as demonstrated in Listing 17-9, is a simple and useful server-side debugging tool. Simply printing constants and variable values to standard output during script or SP execution often provides enough information to quickly locate problem code. PRINT works from within SPs and batches, but does not work inside of UDFs, because of the built-in restrictions on functions causing side effects. Consider the sample code in Listing 17-9, in which we are trying to achieve an end result where @i is equal to 10. Because the end result of the code is not @>i = 10, we've added a couple of simple PRINT statements to uncover the reason.

Listing 17-9. Debugging Script with PRINT

```
DECLARE @i int;
PRINT N'Initial value of @i = ' + COALESCE(CAST(@i AS nvarchar(10)), N'NULL');
SET @i + = 10;
PRINT N'Final value of @i = ' + COALESCE(CAST(@i AS nvarchar(10)), N'NULL');
```

The result, shown in Figure 17-3, shows that the desired end result is not occurring because we failed to initialize the variable @i to 0 at the beginning of our script. Because the initial value of @ > i is NULL, our end result is NULL. Once we've identified the issue, fixing it is a relatively simple matter in this example.

Figure 17-3. *Results of PRINT Statement Debugging*

In addition to the simple PRINT statement, you can use the RAISERROR statement with NOWAIT clause to send a message or status indication immediately to the client. While the PRINT statement waits for the buffer to flush, RAISERROR with the NOWAIT clause sends the message immediately.

Trace Flags

SQL Server 2012 provides several trace flags that can help with debugging, particularly when you suspect you have a problem with SQL Server settings. Trace flags can turn on or off specific SQL Server behavior, or temporarily change other server characteristics for a server or session. As an example, trace flag 1204 returns the resources and types of locks participating in a deadlock, and the current command affected.

■ **Tip**   Many trace flags are undocumented, and may only be revealed to you by Microsoft Product Support Services when you report a specific issue; but those that are documented can provide very useful information. BOL provides a complete list of documented SQL Server 2012 trace flags under the title of "Trace Flags."

Turning on or off a trace flag is as simple as using the DBCC TRACEON and DBCC TRACEOFF statements, as shown in Listing 17-10.

Listing 17-10. Turning Trace Flag 1204 On and Off

```
DBCC TRACEON (1204, -1);
GO

DBCC TRACEOFF (1204, -1);
GO
```

Trace flags may report information via standard output, the SQL Server log, or additional log files created just for that specific trace flag. Check BOL for specific information about the methods that specific trace flags report back to you.

SSMS Integrated Debugger

SQL Server 2005 did away with the integrated user interface debugger in SSMS, although it was previously a part of Query Analyzer (QA). Apparently, the thought was that Visual Studio would be the debugging tool of choice for stepping through T-SQL code and setting breakpoints in SPs. Now, in SQL Server 2012, integrated SSMS debugging is back by popular demand. The SSMS main menu contains several debugging actions accessible through the new Debug menu, as shown in Figure 17-4.

Figure 17-4. *The SSMS Debug Menu*

The options are similar to the options available when debugging Visual Studio projects. From this menu, you can start debugging, step into/over your code one statement at a time, and manage breakpoints. Figure 17-5 shows an SSMS debugging session that has just hit a breakpoint inside the body of a SP.

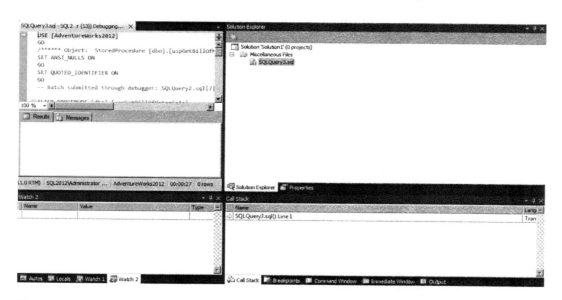

Figure 17-5. *Stepping into Code with the SSMS Debugger*

The SSMS debugger provides several windows that provide additional debugging information, including the Call Stack, Breakpoints, Command, Output, Locals, and Watch windows.

Visual Studio T-SQL Debugger

Visual Studio 2012 also offers an excellent facility for stepping through SPs and UDFs just like any Visual Basic or C# application. You can access Visual Studio's T-SQL debugger through the Server Explorer window. Simply expand the data connection pointing at your SQL Server instance and the SP or function you wish to debug under the appropriate database. Then right-click the procedure or function and select Debug Procedure or Debug Function option from the pop-up context menu. Figure 17-6 demonstrates by selecting the Debug Procedure for the dbo.uspGetBillOfMaterials SP in the AdventureWorks 2012 database.

Figure 17-6. *Debugging the dbo.uspGetBillOfMaterials Procedure*

> ■ **Tip** It's much easier to configure Visual Studio T-SQL debugging on a locally installed instance of SQL Server than to set up remote debugging. BOL offers information about setting up both local and remote SQL Server debugging, in the article "Debugging SQL" (`http://msdn.microsoft.com/en-us/library/ zefbf0t6.aspx`).

If your function or procedure requires parameters, the Run Stored Procedure window will open and ask you to enter values for the required parameters (see Figure 17-7). For this example, we've entered 770 for the `@StartProductID` parameter and 7/10/2005 for the `@CheckDate` parameter required by the `dbo.uspGetBillOfMaterials` procedure.

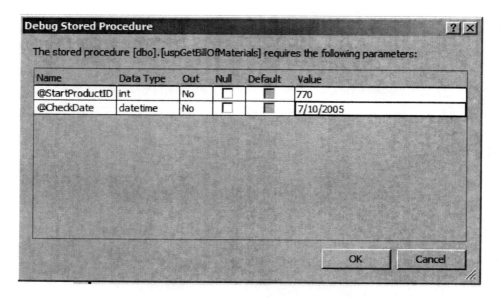

Figure 17-7. Entering Parameter Values in the Run Stored Procedure Window

After you enter the parameters, the procedure will begin running in Debug mode in Visual Studio. Visual Studio shows the script and highlights each line in yellow as you step through it, as shown in Figure 17-8.

Figure 17-8. Stepping Through an SP in Debug Mode

In Debug mode, you can set breakpoints by clicking the left border and using the Continue (F5), Stop Debugging (Shift + F5), Step Over (F10), Step Into (F11), and Step Out (Shift + F11) commands, just like when you debug C# or Visual Basic programs. You can also add watches and view locals to inspect parameter and variable values as your code executes. Any result sets and return values from the SP are shown in the Visual Studio Output window, as in Figure 17-9.

	ProductAssemblyID	ComponentID	ComponentDesc	TotalQuantity	StandardCost	ListPrice	BOMLevel	RecursionLevel
1	770	517	LL Road Seat Assembly	1.00	98.77	133.34	1	0
2	770	738	LL Road Frame - Black, 52	1.00	204.6251	337.22	1	0
3	770	806	ML Headset	1.00	45.4168	102.29	1	0
4	770	811	LL Road Handlebars	1.00	19.7758	44.54	1	0
5	770	818	LL Road Front Wheel	1.00	37.9909	85.565	1	0
6	770	826	LL Road Rear Wheel	1.00	49.9789	112.565	1	0
7	770	894	Rear Derailleur	1.00	53.9282	121.46	1	0
8	770	907	Rear Brakes	1.00	47.286	106.50	1	0

Figure 17-9. The Visual Studio Output Window

Dynamic SQL

SQL Server MVP Erland Sommarskog said it best: dynamic SQL is a curse and a blessing. Put simply, dynamic SQL is a means of constructing SQL statements as strings in your server-side (or even client-side) applications and executing them dynamically on the fly. When used properly, dynamic SQL can be used to generate complex queries at runtime, in some cases to improve performance, and to do tasks that just aren't possible (or are extremely difficult) in standard, nondynamic T-SQL.

The downside is that there are numerous ways to shoot yourself in the foot with dynamic SQL. If not used properly, dynamic SQL can open up security holes in your system big enough to drive a truck through. We will discuss the various methods of executing dynamic SQL, as well as some of the risks and rewards that Erland alludes to.

The EXECUTE Statement

The most basic form of server-side dynamic SQL is achieved by simply passing an SQL query or other instruction as a string to the EXECUTE statement (often abbreviated EXEC). The EXECUTE statement accepts a char, varchar, nchar, or nvarchar constant, variable, or expression that contains valid T-SQL statements. Listing 17-11 shows the most basic form of dynamic SQL with an EXECUTE statement and a string constant.

Listing 17-11. Basic EXECUTE Statement

```
EXECUTE (N'SELECT ProductID FROM Production.Product');
```

As you can see, there is no real advantage to performing dynamic SQL on a string constant. A simple SELECT statement without the EXECUTE would perform the same function and return the same result. The true power of dynamic SQL is that you can build an SQL statement or query dynamically and execute it. Listing 17-12 demonstrates how this can be done.

Listing 17-12. More Complex Dynamic SQL Example

```
DECLARE @min_product_id int = 500;
DECLARE @sql_stmt nvarchar(128) =
    N'SELECT ProductID ' +
    N'FROM Production.Product ' +
    N'WHERE ProductID >= ' + CAST(@min_product_id AS nvarchar(10));
EXECUTE (@sql_stmt);
```

Now that we've given you this simple code sample, let's explore all the things that are wrong with it.

SQL Injection and Dynamic SQL

In Listing 17-12, the variable @sqlstmt contains the dynamic SQL query. The query is built dynamically by appending the minimum product ID to the WHERE clause. This is not the recommended method of performing this type of query, and we show it here to make a point.

One of the problems with this method is that you lose some of the benefits of cached query plan execution. SQL Server 2012 has some great features that can help in this area, including parameter sniffing and the ability to turn on forced parameterization, but there are many exceptions to SQL Server's ability to automatically parameterize queries or clauses. To guarantee efficient reuse of cached query execution plans as the text of your query changes, you should parameterize queries yourself.

But the big problem here is SQL injection. Although not really a problem when appending an integer value to the end of a dynamic query (as in Listing 17-12), SQL injection can provide a back door for hackers trying to access or destroy your data when you concatenate strings to create dynamic SQL queries. Take a look at the innocent-looking dynamic SQL query in Listing 17-13. I will discuss how a hacker could wreak havoc with this query after the listing.

Listing 17-13. Basic Dynamic SQL Query with a String Appended

```
DECLARE @product_name nvarchar(50) = N'Mountain';
DECLARE @sql_stmt NVARCHAR(128) = N'SELECT ProductID, Name ' +
        N'FROM Production.Product ' +
        N'WHERE Name LIKE ''' +
        @product_name + N'%''';
EXECUTE (@sql_stmt);
```

This query simply returns all product IDs and names of all products that begin with the word *Mountain*. The problem is with how SQL Server interprets the concatenated string. The EXECUTE statement sees the following concatenated string (the bold portion reflects the value of the variable that was concatenated into the query).

```
SELECT ProductID, Name
FROM  Production.Product
WHERE Name LIKE 'Mountain%'
```

A simple substitution for @productname can execute other unwanted statements on your server. This is especially true with data coming from an external source (e.g., from the front end or application layer). Consider the following change to Listing 17-13:

```
DECLARE @product_name nvarchar(50) =
    N'''; DROP TABLE Production.Product; --'
```

The EXECUTE statement now executes the following string (again, the portion provided by the variable is shown in bold):

```
SELECT  ProductID,  Name
FROM  Production.Product
WHERE Name LIKE '';
DROP  TABLE Production.Product; --%'
```

The simple dynamic SQL query is now *two* queries, the second of which will drop the Production.Product table from the database! Now consider if the value of the @productname variable had been retrieved from a user interface, like a web page. A malicious hacker could easily issue arbitrary INSERT, UPDATE, DELETE, DROP TABLE, TRUNCATE TABLE, or other statements to destroy data or open a back door into your system. Depending on how secure your server is, a hacker may be able to use SQL injection to grant him or herself administrator rights, retrieve and modify data stored in your server's file system, take control of your server, or access network resources.

The only justification for using the string concatenation method with EXECUTE is if you have to dynamically name the tables or columns in your statements. And this is far rarer than many people think. In fact, the only time this is usually necessary is if you need to dynamically generate SQL statements around database, table, or column names—if you are creating a dynamic pivot table-type query or coding an administration tool for SQL Server, for instance.

If you must use string concatenation with the EXECUTE method, be sure to take the following precautions with the strings being passed in from the user interface:

- Don't ever trust data from the front end. Always validate the data. If you are expecting only the letters A through Z and the numbers 0 through 9, reject all other characters in the input data.

- Disallow apostrophes, semicolons, parentheses, and double hyphens (--) in the input if possible. These characters have special significance to SQL Server and should be avoided. If you must allow these characters, scrutinize the input thoroughly before using them.

- If you absolutely must allow apostrophes in your data, escape them (double them up) before accepting the input.

- Reject strings that contain binary data, escape sequences, and multiline comment markers (/* and */).

- Validate XML input data against an XML schema when possible.

- Take extra special care when input data contains xp_ or sp_, as it may indicate an attempt to run procedures or XPs on your server.

■ **Tip**   If you are concatenating one-part table and object names into SQL statements on the server side, you can use the QUOTENAME function to safely quote them. The QUOTENAME function does not work for two-, three-, and four-part names, however.

Usually, data validations like the ones listed previously are performed on the client side, on the front end, in the application layer, or in the middle tiers of multitier systems. In highly secure and critical applications, it may be important to also perform server-side validations or some combination of client- and server-side validations. Triggers and check constraints can perform this type of validation on data before it's inserted into a table, and you can create UDFs or SPs to perform validations on dynamic SQL before executing it. Listing 17-14 shows a simple UDF that uses the Numbers table created in Chapter 4 to perform basic validation on a string, ensuring that it contains only the letters A through Z, the digits 0 through 9, and the underscore character _, which is a common validation used on usernames, passwords, and other simple data.

Listing 17-14. Simple T-SQL String Validation Function

```
CREATE  FUNCTION  dbo.ValidateString  (@string  nvarchar(4000))
RETURNS int
AS
BEGIN
    DECLARE @result int = 0;
    WITH Numbers (Num)
    AS
    (
        SELECT 1
        UNION ALL
        SELECT Num + 1
        FROM Numbers
        WHERE Num <= LEN(@string)
    )
```

```
    SELECT @result = SUM
    (
        CASE
        WHEN  SUBSTRING(@string,  n.Num,  1)  LIKE N'[A-Z0-9\_]' ESCAPE '\'
        THEN  0
        ELSE 1
        END
    )
    FROM Numbers n
    WHERE n.Num <= LEN(@string)
    OPTION (MAXRECURSION 0);
    RETURN @result;
END
GO
```

The function in Listing 17-14 uses a CTE to validate each character in the given string. The result is the total number of invalid characters in the string: a value of 0 indicates that all the characters in the string are valid. More complex validations can be performed with the LIKE operator or procedural code to ensure that data is in a prescribed format as well.

Troubleshooting Dynamic SQL

A big disadvantage to using dynamic SQL is in debugging and troubleshooting code. Complex dynamic SQL queries can be difficult to troubleshoot, and very simple syntax or other errors can be hard to locate. Fortunately there is a fairly simple fix for that: write your troublesome query directly in T-SQL, replacing parameters with potential values. Highlight the code, and parse—or execute—it. Any syntax errors will be detected and described by SQL Server immediately. Fix the errors and repeat until all errors have been fixed. Then and only then revert the values back to their parameter names and put the statement back in dynamic SQL. Another handy method of troubleshooting is to print the dynamic SQL statement before executing it. Highlight, copy, and attempt to parse or run it in SSMS. You should be able to quickly and easily locate any problems and fix them as necessary.

One of the restrictions on dynamic SQL is that it cannot be executed in a UDF. This restriction is in place because UDFs cannot produce side effects that change the database. Dynamic SQL offers infinite opportunities to circumvent this restriction, so it is simply not allowed.

The sp_executesql Stored Procedure

The sp_executesql SP provides a second method of executing dynamic SQL. When used correctly it is safer than the simple EXECUTE method for concatenating strings and executing them. Like EXECUTE, sp_executesql takes a string constant or variable as a SQL statement to execute. Unlike EXECUTE, the SQL statement parameter must be an nchar or nvarchar.

The sp_executesql procedure offers a distinct advantage over the EXECUTE method: you can specify your parameters separately from the SQL statement. When you specify the parameters separately instead of concatenating them into one large string, SQL Server passes the parameters to sp_executesql separately. SQL Server then substitutes the values of the parameters in the parameterized SQL statement. Because the parameter values are not concatenated into the SQL statement, sp_executesql protects against SQL injection attacks. sp_executesql parameterization also improves query execution plan cache reuse, which helps with performance.

A limitation to this approach is that you cannot use the parameters in your SQL statement in place of table, column, or other object names. Listing 17-15 shows how to parameterize the previous example.

Listing 17-15. Dynamic SQL sp_executesql Parameterized

```
DECLARE @product_name NVARCHAR(50) = N'Mountain%';
DECLARE @sql_stmt NVARCHAR(128) = N'SELECT ProductID, Name ' +
        N'FROM Production.Product ' +
        N'WHERE Name LIKE @name';
EXECUTE  sp_executesql @sql_stmt,
        N'@name NVARCHAR(50)',
        @name = @product_name;
```

■ **Tip** It's strongly recommended that you use parameterized queries whenever possible when using dynamic SQL. If you can't parameterize (e.g., you need to dynamically change the table name in a query), be sure to thoroughly validate the incoming data.

Dynamic SQL and Scope

Dynamic SQL executes in its own batch. What this means is that variables and temporary tables created in a dynamic SQL statement or statement batch are not directly available to the calling routine. Consider the example in Listing 17-16.

Listing 17-16. Limited Scope of Dynamic SQL

```
DECLARE @sql_stmt NVARCHAR(512) = N'CREATE TABLE #Temp_ProductIDs ' +
    N'(' +
    N'    ProductID  int  NOT  NULL  PRIMARY  KEY' +
    N');  ' +
    N'INSERT INTO #Temp_ProductIDs (ProductID) ' +
    N'SELECT ProductID ' +
    N'FROM Production.Product;' ;

EXECUTE (@sql_stmt);

SELECT  ProductID
FROM  #Temp_ProductIDs;
```

The #Temp_ProductIDs temporary table is created in a dynamic SQL batch, so it is not available outside of the batch. This causes the following error message to be generated:

```
(504 row(s) affected)

Msg 208, Level 16, State 0, Line 9

Invalid object name '#Temp_ProductIDs'.
```

The message (504 row(s) affected) indicates that the temporary table creation and INSERT INTO statement of the dynamic SQL executed properly and without error. The problem is with the SELECT statement after EXECUTE. Since the #Temp_ProductIDs table was created within the scope of the dynamic SQL statement, the temporary table is dropped immediately once the dynamic SQL statement completes. This means that once SQL Server reaches the SELECT statement, the #Temp_ProductIDs table no longer exists. One way to work around this issue is to create the temporary table before the dynamic SQL executes. The dynamic SQL is able to access and update the temporary table created by the caller, as shown in Listing 17-17.

Listing 17-17. Creating a Temp Table Accessible to Dynamic SQL

```
CREATE  TABLE  #Temp_ProductIDs
(
    ProductID int NOT NULL PRIMARY KEY
);

DECLARE @sql_stmt NVARCHAR(512) = N'INSERT INTO #Temp_ProductIDs (ProductID) ' +
        N'SELECT ProductID ' +
        N'FROM Production.Product;' ;

EXECUTE (@sql_stmt);

SELECT  ProductID
FROM  #Temp_ProductIDs;
```

Table variables and other variables declared by the caller are not accessible to dynamic SQL, however. Variables and table variables have well-defined scope. They are only available to the batch, function, or procedure in which they are created, and are not available to dynamic SQL or other called routines.

Client-Side Parameterization

Parameterization of dynamic SQL queries is not just a good idea on the server side; it's also a great idea to parameterize queries instead of building dynamic SQL strings on the client side. Apart from the security implications, query parameterization provides cached query execution plan reuse, making queries more efficient than their concatenated string counterparts. Microsoft .NET languages provide the tools necessary to parameterize queries from the application layer in the System.Data.SqlClient and System.Data namespaces. We discussed parameterization on the client side in Chapter 15.

Summary

SQL Server has long supported simple error handling using the @@error system function to retrieve error information and the RAISERROR statement to throw exceptions. SQL Server 2012 continues to support these methods of handling errors, but also provides modern, structured TRY . . . CATCH and THROW exception handling similar to other modern languages. T-SQL TRY . . . CATCH exception handling includes several functions that expose error-specific information in the CATCH block. SQL Server 2012 also introduced a more streamlined error handling approach to common programming senarios by introducing TRY_PARSE, TRY_CONVERT, and TRY_CAST functions.

In addition to the SSMS integrated debugger, which can be accessed through the Debug menu, SQL Server itself and Visual Studio provide tools that are useful for troubleshooting and debugging your T-SQL code. These include simple tools like the PRINT statement and trace flags, and even more powerful tools like Visual Studio debugging, which lets you set breakpoints, step into code, and use much of the same functionality that is useful in debugging C# and Visual Basic programs.

Also in this chapter, we discussed dynamic SQL, a very useful and powerful tool in its own right, but often incorrectly used. Misuse of dynamic SQL can expose your databases, servers, and other network resources, leaving your IT infrastructure vulnerable to SQL injection attacks. Improper use of dynamic SQL can also impact application performance. SQL injection and query performance are the two most compelling reasons to take extra precautions when using dynamic SQL.

In the next chapter, we will give an overview of SQL Server 2012 query performance tuning.

EXERCISES

1. [Fill in the blank] The _____ system function automatically resets to 0 after every successful statement execution.

2. [Choose one] Which of the following functions, available only in the CATCH block in SQL Server, returns the severity level of the error that occurred:

   a. ERR_LEVEL()

   b. EXCEPTION_SEVERITY()

   c. EXCEPTIONALEVEL()

   d. ERROR_SEVERITY()

3. [True/False] The RAISERROR statement allows you to raise errors in SQL Server.

4. [True/False] Visual Studio provides integrated debugging, which allows you to step into T-SQL functions and SPs and set breakpoints.

5. [Choose all that apply] The potential problems with dynamic SQL include which of the following:

   a. Potential performance issues

   b. SQL injection attacks

   c. General exception errors caused by interference with graphics drivers

   d. All of the above

CHAPTER 18

Performance Tuning

In most production environments, database and server optimization has long been the domain of DBAs. This includes server settings, hardware optimizations, index creation and maintenance, and many other responsibilities. SQL developers, however, are responsible for ensuring that their queries perform optimally. SQL Server is truly a developer's DBMS, and as a result the developer responsibilities can overlap with those of the DBA. This overlap includes recommending database design and indexing strategies, troubleshooting poorly performing queries, and making other performance enhancement recommendations. In this chapter, we will discuss various tools and strategies for query optimization and performance enhancement and tuning the queries.

SQL Server Storage

SQL Server is designed to abstract away many of the logical and physical aspects of storage and data retrieval. In a perfect world, you wouldn't have to worry about such things—you would be able to just "set it and forget it." Unfortunately, the world is not perfect, and how SQL Server stores data can have a noticeable impact on query performance. Understanding SQL Server storage mechanisms is essential to properly troubleshooting performance issues. With that in mind, we're going to give a brief overview of how SQL Server stores your data.

■ **Tip** This section will give only a summarized description of how SQL Server stores data. The best detailed description of the SQL Server storage engine internals is in the book *Inside Microsoft SQL Server 2012 Internals*, by Kalen Delaney et al. (Microsoft Press, 2012).

Files and Filegroups

SQL Server stores your databases in files. Each database consists of at least two files, a database file with an .mdf extension and a log file with an .ldf extension. You can also add additional files to a SQL Server database, normally with an .ndf extension.

Filegroups are logical groupings of files for administration and allocation purposes. By default, SQL Server creates all database files in a single primary filegroup. You can add additional filegroups to an existing database or specify additional filegroups at creation time. One of the big performance benefits of using multiple filegroups comes from placing the different filegroups on different physical drives. It's common practice to increase performance by placing data files on a separate filegroup and physical drive from nonclustered indexes. It's also common to place log files on a separate physical drive from both data and nonclustered indexes.

Understanding how physical separation of files improves performance requires an explanation of the read/write patterns involved with each type of information that SQL Server stores. Your actual database data will generally utilize a random access read/write pattern. The hard drive head is constantly repositioning itself to read and write user data to the database. Nonclustered indexes, likewise, are also usually random access in nature. The hard drive head repositions itself all over the place to traverse the nonclustered index. Once nodes that match the query criteria are found in the nonclustered index, if columns must be accessed that are not in the nonclustered index, the hard drive must again reposition itself to locate the actual data stored in the data file. The transaction log file has a completely different access pattern from both data and nonclustered indexes. SQL Server writes to the transaction log in a serial fashion. These conflicting access patterns can result in "head thrashing," or constant repositioning of the hard drive head to read and write these different types of information.

Dividing your files by type and placing them on separate physical drives helps improve performance by reducing head thrashing and allowing SQL Server to perform I/O activities in parallel.

You can also place multiple data files in a single filegroup. When you create a database with multiple files in a single filegroup, SQL Server uses a proportional fill strategy across the files as data is added to the database. This means that SQL Server tries to fill all files in a filegroup at approximately the same time. Log files, which are not part of a filegroup, are filled using a serial strategy. If you add additional log files to a database, they will not be used until the current log file is filled.

■ **Tip** You can move a table from its current filegroup to a new filegroup by dropping the current clustered index on the table and creating a new clustered index, specifying the new filegroup in the CREATE CLUSTERED INDEX statement.

Space Allocation

SQL Server uses a random access file to locate the data that reside in a specific location rather than reading the data from the beginning when reading the data. To enable the random access file, the system should have consistently sized allocation units in the file structure. SQL Server allocates space in the database in units called extents and pages to accomplish this. A page is an 8-KB block of contiguous storage. An extent consists of 8 logically contiguous pages, or 64 KB of storage. SQL Server has two types of extents: uniform extents, which are owned completely by a single database object, and mixed extents, which can be shared by up to eight different database objects. When a new table or index is created the pages are allocated from mixed extents. When the table or index grows beyond 8 pages, then the allocations are done in uniform extents to make the space allocation efficient.

This physical limitation on the size of pages is the reason for the historic limitations on data types such as varchar and nvarchar (up to 8,000 and 4,000 characters, respectively) and row size (8060 bytes). It's also why special handling is required internally for LOB data types such as varchar(max), varbinary(max), and xml, since the data they contain can span many pages.

SQL Server keeps track of allocated extents with two types of allocation maps known as *global allocation map (GAM)* pages and *shared global allocation map (SGAM)* pages. GAM pages use bits to track all extents that have been allocated. SGAM pages use bits to track mixed extents with one or more free pages available. Index Allocation Map (IAM) tracks all the extents used by the index or table, and they are used to navigate through the data pages. Page Free Space (PFS) tracks the free space on each page that stores LOB values. The combination of the GAM and SGAM pages allows SQL Server to quickly allocate free extents, uniform/full mixed extents, and mixed extents with free pages as necessary whereas IAM and PFS are used to decide when the object needs the extent allocation.

The behavior of the SQL Server storage engine can have a direct bearing on performance. For instance, consider the code in Listing 18-1, which creates a table with narrow rows. Note that SQL Server can optimize storage for variable-length data types like varchar and nvarchar, so we've forced the issue by using fixed-length char data types for this example.

Listing 18-1. Creating a Narrow Table

```
CREATE TABLE dbo.SmallRows
(
    Id   int NOT NULL,
    LastName nchar(50) NOT NULL,
    FirstName nchar(50) NOT NULL,
    MiddleName nchar(50) NULL
);

INSERT  INTO  dbo.SmallRows
(
    Id,
    LastName,
    FirstName,
    MiddleName
)
SELECT
    BusinessEntityID,
    LastName,
    FirstName,
    MiddleName
FROM Person.Person;
```

The rows in the dbo.SmallRows table are 304 bytes wide. This means that SQL Server can fit about 25 rows on a single 8-KB page. You can verify this with the undocumented sys.fn_PhysLocFormatter function, as shown in Listing 18-2. Partial results are shown in Figure 18-1. The sys.fn_PhysLocFormatter function returns the physical locator in the form (file:page:slot). As you can see in the figure, SQL Server fits 25 rows on each page (rows are numbered 0 to 24).

■ **Note** The sys.fn_PhysLocFormatter function is undocumented and not supported by Microsoft. We've used it here for demonstration purposes, as it's handy for looking at row allocations on pages; but don't use it in production code.

Listing 18-2. Looking at Data Allocations for the SmallRows Table

```
SELECT
    sys.fn_PhysLocFormatter(%%physloc%%) AS [Row_Locator],
    Id
FROM dbo.SmallRows;
```

	Row_Locator	Id
22	(1:4639:21)	1770
23	(1:4639:22)	4194
24	(1:4639:23)	305
25	(1:4639:24)	16691
26	(1:5375:0)	4891
27	(1:5375:1)	10251
28	(1:5375:2)	16872
29	(1:5375:3)	10293
30	(1:5375:4)	4503
31	(1:5375:5)	4970

Figure 18-1. *SQL Server Fits 25 Rows per Page for the dbo.SmallRows Table*

By way of comparison, the code in Listing 18-3 creates a table with wide rows—3,604 bytes wide to be exact. The final SELECT query in Listing 18-3 retrieves the row locator information, demonstrating that SQL Server can only fit two rows per page for the dbo.LargeRows table. The results are shown in Figure 18-2.

Listing 18-3. Creating a Table with Wide Rows

```
CREATE TABLE dbo.LargeRows
(
    Id   int NOT NULL,
    LastName nchar(600) NOT NULL,
    FirstName nchar(600) NOT NULL,
    MiddleName nchar(600) NULL
);

INSERT  INTO  dbo.LargeRows
(
    Id,
    LastName,
    FirstName,
    MiddleName
)
SELECT
    BusinessEntityID,
    LastName,
    FirstName,
    MiddleName
FROM Person.Person;

SELECT
    sys.fn_PhysLocFormatter(%%physloc%%) AS [Row_Locator],
    Id
FROM dbo.LargeRows;
```

	Row_Locator	Id
210	(1:528:1)	13851
211	(1:529:0)	3288
212	(1:529:1)	1149
213	(1:530:0)	19175
214	(1:530:1)	7592
215	(1:531:0)	7350
216	(1:531:1)	335
217	(1:532:0)	13575
218	(1:532:1)	7293
219	(1:533:0)	20742

Figure 18-2. SQL Server Fits Only Two Rows per Page for the dbo.LargeRows Table

Now that we have created two tables with different row widths, the query in Listing 18-4 queries both tables with STATISTICS IO turned on to demonstrate the difference this makes to your I/O.

Listing 18-4. I/O Comparison of Narrow and Wide Tables

```
SET  STATISTICS IO ON;
SELECT
    Id,
    LastName,
    FirstName,
    MiddleName
FROM dbo.SmallRows;

SELECT
    Id,
    LastName,
    FirstName,
    MiddleName
FROM dbo.LargeRows;
```

The results returned, as shown following, demonstrate a significant difference in both logical reads and read-ahead reads:

```
(19972 row(s) affected)
```

```
Table 'SmallRows'. Scan count 1, logical reads 799, physical reads 0, read-ahead reads 8, lob
logical reads 0, lob physical reads 0, lob read-ahead reads 0.
```

```
(19972 row(s) affected)
```

Table 'LargeRows'. Scan count 1, logical reads 9986, physical reads 0, read-ahead reads 10002, lob logical reads 0, lob physical reads 0, lob read-ahead reads 0.

The extra I/Os incurred by the query on the dbo.LargeRows table significantly affect the query plan estimated I/O cost. The query plan for the dbo.SmallRows query is shown in Figure 18-3, with an estimated I/O cost of 0.594315.

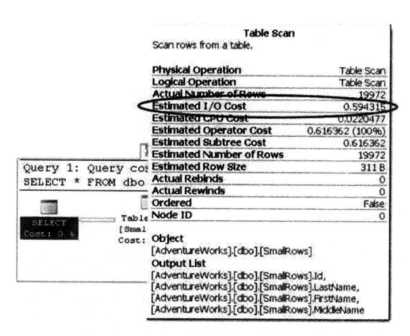

Figure 18-3. *Estimated I/O Cost for the dbo.SmallRows Query*

The query against the dbo.LargeRows table is significantly costlier with an estimated I/O cost of 7.39942—nearly 12.5 times greater than the dbo.SmallRows query. Figure 18-4 shows the higher cost for the dbo.LargeRows query.

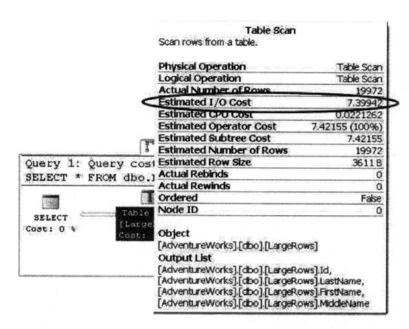

Figure 18-4. *Estimated I/O Cost for the dbo.LargeRows Query*

As you can see from these simple examples, SQL Server has to read significantly more pages when a table is defined with wide rows. This increased I/O cost can cause a significant performance drain when performing SQL Server queries, even those queries that are otherwise highly optimized. One way to minimize the cost of I/O is to minimize the width of columns where possible, and always use the appropriate data type for the job. In the examples given, a variable-width character data type (varchar) would have significantly reduced the storage requirements of the sample tables. Although I/O cost is often a secondary consideration for developers and DBAs, and is often only addressed after slow queries begin to cause drag on a system, it's a good idea to keep the cost of I/O in mind when initially designing your tables.

Partitions

Partitioning the tables and indexes by range was introduced in SQL Server 2005. This functionality allows the data to be partitioned into rowsets based on the partitioning column value and the partitions can be placed into one more filegroups in the database to improve the performance of the query and manageability while treating them as a single object.

Partitioning is defined by a partition scheme which maps the partitions defined by the partition function to a set of files or filegroups that you define. The partition function specifies how the index or the table is partitioned. The column value that is used to define the partition can be of any data type except LOB data or timestamp. SQL Server 2008 supports 1,000 partitions by default and this meets most application needs; however there are cases where due to industry regulations you need to retain the daily data for more than 3 years and in those cases, we need the database to support more than 1,000 parititions. SQL Server 2008 R2 introduced the support for 15 K partitions; however, you need to run a stored procedure to enable this support. SQL Server 2012 provides support for 15,000 partitions by default and also provides native support for high availability and disaster recovery features such as AlwaysOn, replication, database mirroring, and log shipping as well.

Partitioning is useful to group the data from a large table into smaller chunks so that the data can be maintained independently for database operations such as speeding up queries, primarily with scans or loading data or reindexing to name a few. Partitioning can improve the query performance when the partitioning key is part of the query and the system has enough processors to process the query. Not all tables need to be partitioned; you should consider characteristics such as how large the table is, how it is being accessed and the query performance against the tables before considering whether to partition the data.

So, the first step to partitioning a table is to determine how the rows in the table will be divided between the partitions using a function called a partition function. To effectively design a partition function you need to specify logical boundaries. If you specify two boundaries, then three partitions are created and depending on whether the data is being partioned left or right the upper and lower boundary condition is set.

The partition function defines logical boundaries and the partition scheme defines the physical location, meaning filegroups, for them. Once the partition function is defined to set the logical boundary and the partition scheme is defined to map the logical boundary to filegroups, you can create the partitioned table. As with the table, you can partition the indexes as well. Partitioning the clustered index must have the partition key specified in the clustered index. Partitioning nonclustered index does not require the partition key; if the partition key is not specified, then SQL Server will include them in the indexes. The indexes that are defined with the partitioned tables can be aligned or nonaligned. The index is aligned if the table and the index logically have the same partition strategy.

In general, partitioning is most useful when the data has a time component. Generally large tables such as order details where most of the DML operations are performed on the current month's data and previous months are simply used for selects may be good candidates to partition by month. This enables the queries to modify the data found in a single partition rather than scanning though the entire table to locate the data to be modified, hence enhancing the query performance.

Partitions can be split or merged easily in a sliding window scenario. Partitions can be split or merged only if all the indexes are aligned and the partition scheme and functions match. Partition alignment does not mean that both the objects have to use the same partition function, but if both objects have the same partition scheme, functions, and boundaries, they are considered to be aligned. When both the objects have the same partitioning scheme or file groups, they are storage aligned. Storage alignment can be physical or logical, and in both cases the performance of the queries is improved.

Data Compression

In addition to minimizing the width of columns by using the appropriate data type for the job, SQL Server 2012 provides built-in data compression functionality. By compressing your data directly in the database, SQL Server can reduce I/O contention and minimize storage requirements. There is some CPU overhead associated with compression and decompression of data during queries and DML activities, but data compression is particularly useful for historical data storage where access and manipulation demands are not as high as they might be for the most recent data. We will discuss the types of compression that SQL Server supports as well as the associated overhead and recommended usage of each.

Row Compression

SQL Server 2005 introduced an optimization to the storage format for the decimal data type in SP 2. The vardecimal type provided optimized variable-length storage for decimal data, which often resulted in significant space savings—particularly when your decimal columns contained a lot of zeros. This optimization is internal to the storage engine, so it's completely transparent to developers and end users. In SQL Server 2008, this optimization was expanded to include all fixed-length numeric, date/time, and character data types in a feature known as row compression.

■ Note The `vardecimal` compression options and SPs to manage this feature, including sp_db_vardecimal_ storage_format and sp_estimated_rowsize_reduction_for_vardecimal, are deprecated, since SQL Server 2012 rolls this functionality up into the new row compression feature.

SQL Server 2012 provides the useful `sp_estimate_data_compression_savings` procedure to estimate the savings you'll get from applying compression to a table. Listing 18-5 estimates the space you'll save by applying row compression to the `Production.TransactionHistory` table. This particular table contains fixed-length `int`, `datetime`, and `money` columns. The results are shown in Figure 18-5.

Listing 18-5. Estimating Row Compression Space Savings

```
EXEC sp_estimate_data_compression_savings 'Production',
    'TransactionHistory',
    NULL,
    NULL,
    'ROW';
```

Figure 18-5. *Row Compression Space Savings Estimate for a Table*

■ Note We changed the names of the last four columns in this example so they would fit in the image. The abbreviations are `size_cur_cmp` for `Size with current compression setting (KB)`, `size_req_cmp` for `Size with requested compression setting (KB)`, `size_sample_cur_cmp` for `Sample size with current compression setting (KB)`, and `size_sample_req_cmp` for `Sample size with requested compression setting (KB)`.

The results shown in Figure 18-5 indicate the current size of the clustered index (`indexid = 1`) is about 6.1 MB, while the two nonclustered indexes (`indexid = 1` and 2) total about 2.9 MB. SQL Server estimates that it can compress this table down to a size of about 4.0 MB for the clustered index and 2.6 MB for the nonclustered indexes.

■ Tip If your table does not have a clustered index, the heap is indicated in the results with an `index_id` of 0.

You can turn row compression on for a table with the `DATACOMPRESSION = ROW` option of the `CREATE TABLE` and `ALTER TABLE` DDL statements. Listing 18-6 turns on row compression for the `Production.TransactionHistory` table.

Listing 18-6. Turning on Row Compression for a Table

```
ALTER TABLE Production.TransactionHistory REBUILD
WITH (DATA_COMPRESSION = ROW);
```

You can verify that the ALTER TABLE statement has applied row compression to your table with the sp_spaceused procedure, as shown in Listing 18-7. The results are shown in Figure 18-6.

Listing 18-7. Viewing Space Used by a Table after Applying Row Compression

```
EXEC sp_spaceused N'Production.TransactionHistory';
```

name	rows	reserved	data	index_size	unused
1 TransactionHistory	113449	7384 KB	4152 KB	2976 KB	256 KB

Figure 18-6. *Space Used by the Table after Applying Row Compression*

As you can see in the figure, the size of the data used by the Production.TransactionHistory table has dropped to about 4.0 MB. The indexes are not automatically compressed by the ALTER TABLE statement. To compress the nonclustered indexes, you need to issue ALTER INDEX statements with the DATA_COMPRESSION = ROW option. You can use the DATACOMPRESSION = NONE option to turn off row compression for a table or index.

Row compression uses variable-length formats to store your fixed-length data, and SQL Server stores an offset value in each record for every variable-length value it stores. Prior to SQL Server 2008, this offset value was fixed at 2 bytes of overhead per variable-length value. SQL Server 2008 introduced a new record format that uses a 4-bit offset for variable-length columns that are 8 bytes in length or less.

Page Compression

SQL Server 2012 also has the capability to compress data at the page level using two methods: *column-prefix compression* and *page-dictionary compression.* Where row compression is good for minimizing the storage requirements for highly unique fixed-length data at the row level, page compression helps minimize the storage space required by duplicated data stored in pages.

The column-prefix compression method looks for repeated prefixes in columns of data stored on a page. Figure 18-7 shows a sample page from a table with repeated prefixes in columns underlined.

BusinessEntityID	FirstName	LastName
18069 (0x00004695)	Alexander	Smith
15854 (0x00003DEE)	Alexandra	Smith
16058 (0x00003EBA)	Alexis	Smith
18863 (0x000049AF)	Andrew	Smith
18118 (0x000046C6)	Austin	Smith

Figure 18-7. *Page with Repeated Column Prefixes Identified*

To compress the column prefixes identified in Figure 18-7, SQL Server creates an *anchor record.* This is a row in the table just like any other row, except that it serves the special purpose of storing the longest value in the column containing a duplicated column prefix. The anchor record is later used by the storage engine to re-create the full representations of the compressed column values when they are accessed. This special type of record is accessible only internally by the storage engine and cannot be retrieved or modified directly by normal queries or DML operations. Figure 18-8 shows the column prefix-compressed version of the page from Figure 18-7.

BusinessEntityID		FirstName	LastName
Anchor Record 18069 (0x00004695)		Alexander	Smith
[NULL]	[NULL]	[NULL]	[NULL]
[2]15854	[2]3DEE)	[7]ra	[NULL]
[2]16058	[2]3EBA)	[4]is	[NULL]
[2]18863	[2]49A7)	[1]ndrew	[NULL]
[3]198	[3]C6)	[1]ustin	[NULL]

Figure 18-8. *Page with Column-Prefix Compression Applied*

There are several items of note in the column prefix-compressed page shown in Figure 18-8. First is that the anchor record has been added to the page. Column-prefix compression uses byte patterns to indicate prefixes, making the column-prefix method data type-agnostic. In this instance, the BusinessEntityID column is an int data type, but as you can see it takes advantage of data type compression as well. We've shown the BusinessEntityID column values in both int and varbinary format to demonstrate that they are compressed as well.

The next interesting feature of column-prefix compression is that SQL Server replaces the prefix of each column with an indicator of how many bytes need to be prepended from the anchor record value to re-create the original value. NULL is used to indicate that the value in the table is actually the full anchor record value.

■ **Note** The storage engine uses metadata associated with each value to indicate the difference between an actual NULL in the column and a NULL indicating a placeholder for the anchor record value.

In the example given, each column of the first row is replaced with NULLs that act as placeholders for the full anchor record values. The second row's BusinessEntityID column indicates that the first two bytes of the value should be replaced with the first two bytes of the BusinessEntityID anchor record column. The FirstName column of this row indicates that the first seven bytes of the value should be replaced with the first seven bytes of the FirstName anchor record column, and so on.

Page-dictionary compression is the second type of compression that SQL Server uses to compress pages. Page-dictionary compression creates an on-page dictionary of values that occur multiple times across any columns and rows on the page. It then replaces those duplicate values with indexes into the dictionary. Consider Figure 18-9, which shows a data page with duplicate values.

BusinessEntityID		FirstName	LastName
1585	(0x00003DEB)	Maurizio	Macagno
3150	(0x00000C4E)	Adriana	Arthur
17387	(0x000043EB)	Austin	Martin
10935	(0x00002AB7)	Arthur	Martin
16756	(0x00004174)	Martin	Fernandez

Figure 18-9. *Uncompressed Page with Duplicate Values across Columns and Rows*

The duplicate values Arthur and Martin are added to the dictionary and replaced in the data page with indexes into the dictionary. The value Martin is replaced with the index value (0) everywhere it occurs in the data page, and the value Arthur is replaced with the index value (1). This is demonstrated in Figure 18-10.

BusinessEntityID		FirstName	LastName
Dictionary	(0)=Martin, (1)=Arthur		
1585	(0x00003DEB)	Maurizio	Macagno
3150	(0x00000C4E)	Adriana	(1)
17387	(0x000043EB)	Austin	(0)
10935	(0x00002AB7)	(1)	(0)
18756	(0x00004174)	(0)	Fernandez

Figure 18-10. Page Compressed with Page-dictionary Compression

When SQL Server performs page compression on data pages and leaf index pages, it first applies row compression, and then it applies page-dictionary compression.

■ **Note**   For performance reasons, SQL Server does not apply page-dictionary compression to non-leaf index pages.

You can estimate the savings you'll get through page compression with the sp_estimate_data_compression_savings procedure, as shown in Listing 18-8. The results are shown in Figure 18-11.

Listing 18-8. Estimating Data Compression Savings with Page Compression

```
EXEC  sp_estimate_data_compression_savings 'Person',
    'Person',
    NULL,
    NULL,
    'PAGE';
```

Figure 18-11. Page Compression Space Savings Estimate

As you can see in Figure 18-11, SQL Server estimates that it can use page compression to compress the Person.Person table from 29.8 MB in size down to about 18.2 MB, a considerable savings. You can apply page compression to a table with the ALTER TABLE statement, as shown in Listing 18-9.

Listing 18-9. Applying Page Compression to the Person.Person Table

```
ALTER TABLE Person.Person REBUILD
WITH (DATA_COMPRESSION = PAGE);
```

As with row compression, you can use the sp_spaceused procedure to verify how much space page compression saved you.

Page compression is great for saving space, but it does not come without a cost. Specifically you pay for the space savings with increased CPU overhead for SELECT queries and DML statements. So when should you use page compression? Microsoft makes the following recommendations:

- If the table or index is small in size, then the overhead you incur from compression will probably not be worth the extra CPU overhead.

- If the table or index is heavily accessed for queries and DML actions, the extra CPU overhead can significantly impact your performance. It's important to identify usage patterns when deciding whether or not to compress the table or index.

- Use the sp_estimate_data_compression_savings procedure to estimate the space savings. If the estimated space savings is insignificant (or nonexistent), then the extra CPU overhead will probably outweigh the benefits.

Sparse Columns

In addition to row compression and page compression, SQL Server provides *sparse columns,* which let you optimize NULL value storage in columns. The trade-off (and you knew there would be one) is that the cost of storing non-NULL values goes up by 4 bytes for each value. Microsoft recommends using sparse columns when it will result in at least 20 to 40 percent space savings. For an int column, for instance, at least 64 percent of the values must be NULL to achieve a 40 percent space savings with sparse columns. Sparse column is a column attribute that provides storage optimization, meaning when NULL values are stored in the column it takes up 0 bytes.

To demonstrate sparse columns in action, we'll use a query that generates columns with a lot of NULLs in them. The query shown in Listing 18-10 creates a pivot-style report that lists the CustomerID numbers associated with every sales order down the right-hand side of the results, and a selection of product names from the sales orders. The intersection of each CustomerID and product name contains the number of each item ordered by each customer. A NULL indicates that a customer did not order an item. Partial results of this query are shown in Figure 18-12.

Listing 18-10. Pivot Query that Generates Columns with Many NULLs

```
SELECT
    CustomerID,
    [HL Road Frame - Black, 58],
    [HL Road Frame - Red, 58],
    [HL Road Frame - Red, 62],
    [HL Road Frame - Red, 44],
    [HL Road Frame - Red, 48],
    [HL Road Frame - Red, 52],
    [HL Road Frame - Red, 56],
    [LL Road Frame - Black, 58]
FROM
(
    SELECT soh.CustomerID, p.Name AS ProductName,
        COUNT
        (
        CASE WHEN sod.LineTotal IS NULL THEN NULL
        ELSE 1
        END
```

```
          )  AS  NumberOfItems
          FROM Sales.SalesOrderHeader soh
          INNER JOIN Sales.SalesOrderDetail sod
          ON soh.SalesOrderID = sod.SalesOrderID
          INNER JOIN Production.Product p
          ON   sod.ProductID = p.ProductID
          GROUP BY
          soh.CustomerID,
          sod.ProductID,
          p.Name
)  src
PIVOT
(
    SUM(NumberOfItems) FOR ProductName
    IN
    (
    "HL Road Frame - Black, 58",
    "HL  Road  Frame  -  Red, 58",
    "HL  Road  Frame  -  Red, 62",
    "HL  Road  Frame  -  Red, 44",
    "HL  Road  Frame  -  Red, 48",
    "HL  Road  Frame  -  Red, 52",
    "HL  Road  Frame  -  Red, 56",
    "LL Road Frame - Black, 58"
    )
)  AS  pvt;
```

	CustomerID	HL Road Frame - Black, 58	HL Road Frame - Red, 58	HL Road Frame - Red, 62	HL Road Frame - Red, 44
19112	30111	NULL	NULL	NULL	NULL
19113	30112	NULL	NULL	1	2
19114	30113	NULL	NULL	NULL	NULL
19115	30114	NULL	NULL	NULL	NULL
19116	30115	NULL	NULL	NULL	NULL
19117	30116	NULL	NULL	NULL	NULL
19118	30117	NULL	NULL	2	2
19119	30118	NULL	NULL	NULL	NULL

Figure 18-12. *Pivot Query that Returns the Number of Each Item Ordered by Each Customer*

Listing 18-11 creates two similar tables to hold the results generated by the query in Listing 18-10. The tables generated by the CREATE TABLE statements in Listing 18-11 have the same structure, except that the SparseTable includes the keyword SPARSE in its column declarations, indicating that these are sparse columns.

Listing 18-11. Creating Sparse and Nonsparse Tables

```
CREATE TABLE NonSparseTable
(
    CustomerID int NOT NULL PRIMARY KEY,
    "HL Road Frame - Black, 58" int NULL,
    "HL  Road  Frame  -  Red,  58"  int NULL,
    "HL  Road  Frame  -  Red,  62"  int NULL,
```

```
    "HL    Road    Frame    -    Red,    44"    int NULL,
    "HL    Road    Frame    -    Red,    48"    int NULL,
    "HL    Road    Frame    -    Red,    52"    int NULL,
    "HL    Road    Frame    -    Red,    56"    int NULL,
    "LL Road Frame - Black, 58" int NULL
);
CREATE    TABLE    SparseTable
(
    CustomerID int NOT NULL PRIMARY KEY,
    "HL    Road    Frame    -    Black,    58"    int    SPARSE    NULL,
    "HL    Road    Frame    -    Red,    58"    int    SPARSE NULL,
    "HL    Road    Frame    -    Red,    62"    int    SPARSE NULL,
    "HL    Road    Frame    -    Red,    44"    int    SPARSE NULL,
    "HL    Road    Frame    -    Red,    48"    int    SPARSE NULL,
    "HL    Road    Frame    -    Red,    52"    int    SPARSE NULL,
    "HL    Road    Frame    -    Red,    56"    int    SPARSE NULL,
    "LL    Road    Frame    -    Black,    58"    int    SPARSE    NULL
);
```

After using the query in Listing 18-10 to populate these two tables, you can use the sp_spaceused procedure to see the space savings that sparse columns provide. Listing 18-12 executes sp_spaceused on these two tables, both of which contain identical data. The results shown in Figure 18-13 demonstrate that the SparseTable takes up only about 25 percent of the space used by the NonSparseTable since NULL values in sparse columns take up no storage space.

Listing 18-12. Calculating the Space Savings of Sparse Columns

```
EXEC sp_spaceused N'NonSparseTable';
EXEC sp_spaceused N'SparseTable';
```

Figure 18-13. *Space Savings Provided by Sparse Columns*

Sparse Column Sets

In addition to sparse columns, SQL Server provides support for XML sparse column sets. An XML column set is defined as an xml data type column, and it contains non-NULL sparse column data from the table. An XML sparse column set is declared using the COLUMNSET FOR ALLSPARSECOLUMNS option on an xml column. As a simple example, the AdventureWorks Production.Product table contains several products that do not have associated size, color, or other descriptive information. Listing 18-13 creates a table called Production.SparseProduct that defines several sparse columns and a sparse column set.

Listing 18-13. Creating and Populating a Table with a Sparse Column Set

```
CREATE TABLE Production.SparseProduct
(
    ProductID int NOT NULL PRIMARY KEY,
    Name    dbo.Name   NOT  NULL,
    ProductNumber nvarchar(25) NOT NULL,
    Color nvarchar(15) SPARSE NULL,
    Size  nvarchar(5)  SPARSE  NULL,
    SizeUnitMeasureCode nchar(3) SPARSE NULL,
    WeightUnitMeasureCode nchar(3) SPARSE NULL,
    Weight decimal(8, 2) SPARSE NULL,
    Class nchar(2) SPARSE NULL,
    Style nchar(2) SPARSE NULL,
    SellStartDate datetime NOT NULL,
    SellEndDate datetime SPARSE NULL,
    DiscontinuedDate datetime SPARSE NULL,
    SparseColumnSet xml COLUMN_SET FOR ALL_SPARSE_COLUMNS
);
GO

INSERT INTO Production.SparseProduct
(
    ProductID,
    Name,
    ProductNumber,
    Color,
    Size,
    SizeUnitMeasureCode,
    WeightUnitMeasureCode,
    Weight,
    Class,
    Style,
    SellStartDate,
    SellEndDate,
    DiscontinuedDate
)
SELECT
    ProductID,
    Name,
    ProductNumber,
    Color,
    Size,
    SizeUnitMeasureCode,
    WeightUnitMeasureCode,
    Weight,
    Class,
    Style,
    SellStartDate,
    SellEndDate,
    DiscontinuedDate
FROM  Production.Product;
GO
```

You can view the sparse column set in XML form with a query like the one in Listing 18-14. The results in Figure 18-14 show that the first five products do not have any sparse column data associated with them, so the sparse column data takes up no space. By contrast, products 317 and 318 both have Color and Class data associated with them.

Listing 18-14. Querying XML Sparse Column Set as XML

```
SELECT TOP(7)
ProductID,
SparseColumnSet FROM Production.SparseProduct;
```

	ProductID	SparseColumnSet
1	1	NULL
2	2	NULL
3	3	NULL
4	4	NULL
5	316	NULL
6	317	\<Color>Black\</Color>\<Class>L \</Class>
7	318	\<Color>Black\</Color>\<Class>M \</Class>

Figure 18-14. *Viewing Sparse Column Sets in XML Format*

Although SQL Server manages sparse column sets using XML, you don't need to know XML to access sparse column set data. In fact, you can access the columns defined in sparse column sets using the same query and DML statements you've always used, as shown in Listing 18-15. The results of this query are shown in Figure 18-15.

Listing 18-15. Querying Sparse Column Sets by Name

```
SELECT
    ProductID,
    Name,
    ProductNumber,
    SellStartDate,
    Color,
    Class
FROM  Production.SparseProduct
WHERE ProductID IN (1, 317);
```

	ProductID	Name	ProductNumber	SellStartDate	Color	Class
1	1	Adjustable Race	AR-5381	2002-06-01 00:00:00.000	NULL	NULL
2	317	LL Crankarm	CA-5965	2002-06-01 00:00:00.000	Black	L

Figure 18-15. *Querying Sparse Column Sets with SELECT Queries*

Sparse column sets provide the benefits of sparse columns, with NULLs taking up no storage space at all. However, the downside is that non-NULL sparse columns that are a part of a column set are stored in XML format, adding some storage overhead as compared with their nonsparse, non-NULL counterparts.

Indexes

Your query performance may begin to lag over time for several reasons. It may be that database usage patterns have changed significantly over time, or the amount of data stored in the database has increased significantly over time, or the database has fallen out of maintenance. Whatever the reason, the knee-jerk reaction of many developers and DBAs is to throw indexes at the problem. While indexes are indeed useful for increasing performance, they do consume resources, both in storage and maintenance. Before creating new indexes all over your database, it's important to understand how they work. In this section, we will give an overview of SQL Server's indexing mechanisms.

Heaps

In SQL Server parlance, a heap is simply an unordered collection of data pages with no clustered index. SQL Server uses *index allocation map (IAM)* pages to track *allocation units* of the following types:

- Heap or B-tree (a.k.a. "hobt") allocation units, which track storage allocation for tables and indexes

- LOB allocation units, which track storage allocation for LOB data

- Small LOB (SLOB) allocation units, which track storage allocation for row overflow data

As any DBA will tell you, a *table scan,* which is SQL Server's "brute force" data retrieval method, is a bad thing (though not necessarily the worst thing that can happen). In a table scan, SQL Server literally scans every data page that was allocated by the heap. Any query against the heap causes a table scan operation. To determine which pages have been allocated for the heap, SQL Server must refer back to the IAM. A table scan is known as an *allocation order scan* since it uses the IAM to scan the data pages in the order in which they were allocated by SQL Server.

Heaps are also subject to fragmentation, and the only way to eliminate fragmentation from the heap is to copy the heap to a new table or create a clustered index on the table or performing periodic maintenance to keep the index from being fragmented. Forward pointers introduce another performance-related issue to heaps. When a row with variable length column is updated with row length larger than the page size, the updated row may have to be moved to a new page. When SQL Server must move the row in a heap to a new location, it leaves a forward pointer to the new location at the old location. If the row is moved again, SQL Server leaves another forward pointer, and so on. Forward pointers result in additional I/Os, making table scans even less efficient (and you thought it wasn't possible!).

Table scans are not essentially bad if you have to perform row based operations or if you are querying against tables with small data sets such as lookup tables, where adding an index creates maintenance overhead.

■ **Tip** Querying a heap with no clustered or nonclustered indexes always results in a costly table scan.

Clustered Indexes

If a heap is an unordered collection of data pages, how do you impose order on the heap? The answer is a clustered index. A clustered index turns an unordered heap into a collection of data pages ordered by the specified clustered index columns. Clustered indexes are managed in the database as B-tree structures.

The top level of the clustered index B-tree is known as the root node, the bottom level nodes are known as leaf nodes, and all nodes in between the root node and leaf nodes are collectively referred to as intermediate nodes. In a clustered index, the leaf nodes contain the actual data rows for a table, and all leaf nodes point to the next and previous leaf nodes, forming a doubly linked list. The clustered index holds a special position in SQL Server indexing because its leaf nodes contain the actual table data. Since the page chain for the data pages can be ordered only one way, there can only be one clustered index defined per table. The query optimizer uses the clustered index for seeks, because the data can be found directly at the leaf level if a clustered index is used. The clustered index B-tree structure is shown in Figure 18-16.

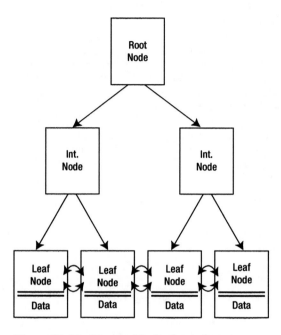

Figure 18-16. *Clustered Index B-tree Structure*

GUARANTEED ORDER

Despite the fact that the data pages in a clustered index are ordered by the clustered index columns, you cannot depend on table rows being returned in clustered index order unless you specify an ORDER BY clause in your queries. There are a couple of reasons for this, including the following:

- Your query may join multiple tables and the optimizer may choose to return results in another order based on indexes on another table.

- The optimizer may use an allocation order scan of your clustered index, which will return results in the order in which data pages were allocated.

The bottom line is that the SQL query optimizer may decide that, for whatever reason, it is more efficient to return results unordered or in an order other than clustered index order. Because of this, you can't depend on results always being returned in the same order without an explicit ORDER BY clause. We've seen many cases of developers being bitten because their client-side code expected results in a specific order, and after months of receiving results in the correct order, the optimizer decided that returning results in a different order would be more efficient. Don't fall victim to this false optimism—use ORDER BY when ordered results are important.

Many are under the impression that a clustered index scan is the same thing as a table scan. In one sense they are correct—when SQL Server performs an *unordered clustered index scan*, it refers back to the IAM to scan the data pages of the clustered index using an allocation order scan, just like a table scan.

However, SQL Server has another option for clustered indexes, the *ordered clustered index scan*. In an ordered clustered index scan, or leaf-level scan, SQL Server can follow the doubly linked list at the leaf node level instead of referring back to the IAM. The leaf-level scan has the benefit of scanning in clustered index order. Table scans do not have the option of a leaf-level scan since the leaf-level pages are not ordered or linked. Clustered indexes also eliminate the performance problems associated with forward pointers in the heap, although you do have to pay attention to fragmentation, page splits, and fill factor when you have a clustered index on your table. Fill factor determines how many rows can be filled in the index page. When the index page is full and new rows need to be inserted, SQL Server will create a new index page and transfer rows to the new page from the previous page which is called as page split. The page splits can be reduced by setting the proper fill factor to determine how much free space there is in the index pages.

So when should you use a clustered index? As a general rule, we like to put a clustered index on nearly every table we create although it is not a requirement to have clustered indexes for all the tables. Although you will have to decide on which columns you wish to create in your clustered indexes, here are some general recommendations for columns to consider in your clustered index design:

- Columns that provide a high degree of uniqueness. Monotonically increasing columns, such as IDENTITY or SEQUENCE columns, are ideal as they also reduce the overhead associated with page splits that result from insert and update operations.

- Columns that return a range of values using operators like >=, <, and BETWEEN. When you use a range query on clustered index columns, after the first match is found, the remaining values are guaranteed to be linked/adjacent in the B-tree.

- Columns that are used in queries that return large result sets of data from those columns.

- Columns that are used in the ON clause of a JOIN. Usually, these are primary key or foreign key columns. SQL Server creates a unique clustered index on the column when the primary key is added to the table.

- Columns that are used in GROUP BY or ORDER BY clauses. A clustered index on these columns can help SQL Server improve performance when ordering query result sets.

You should also make your clustered indexes as narrow as possible (often a single int or uniqueidentifier column), since this decreases the number of levels that must be traversed and hence reduces I/O. Another reason is that they are automatically appended to all nonclustered indexes on the same table as row locators, so keeping the clustered index key small will reduce the size of nonclustered indexes as well.

Nonclustered Indexes

Nonclustered indexes provide another tool for indexing relational data in SQL Server. Like clustered indexes, SQL Server stores nonclustered indexes as B-tree structures. Unlike clustered indexes, however, each leaf node in a nonclustered index contains the nonclustered key value and a row locator. The table rows are stored apart from the nonclustered index—in the clustered index if there is one defined on the table or in a heap if the table has no clustered index. Figure 18-17 shows the nonclustered index B-tree structure. Recall from the previous section on Clustered Indexes that data rows can only be stored in one sorted order and this is achieved via a clustered index. Order can only be achieved via the clustered index.

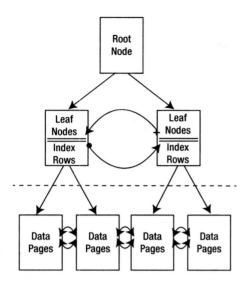

Figure 18-17. *Nonclustered Index B-tree Structure*

If a table has a clustered index, all nonclustered indexes defined on the table automatically include the clustered index columns as the row locator. If the table is a heap, SQL Server creates row locators to the rows from the combination of the file identifier, page number, and slot on the page. Therefore, if you add a clustered index at a later date, be aware that you will need to rebuild your non-clustered indexes to use the clustered index column as row locator rather than file identifier.

Nonclustered indexes are associated with the RID lookup and key lookup operations. *RID lookups* are bookmark lookups into the heap using row identifiers (RIDs), while *key lookups* are bookmark lookups on tables with clustered indexes. Once SQL Server locates the index rows that fulfill a query, if the query requires more columns than the nonclustered index covers, then the query engine must use the row locator to find the rows in the clustered index or the heap to retrieve necessary data. These are the operations referred to as a RID and key lookups, and they are costly operations—so costly, in fact, that many performance-tuning operations are based on eliminating them.

■ **Note**   In prior versions of SQL Server, we had the bookmark lookup operation. In SQL Server 2012, this operation has been split into two distinct operations, the RID lookup and the key lookup, to differentiate between bookmark lookups against heaps and clustered indexes.

One method of dealing with RID and key lookups is to create *covering indexes.* A covering index is a nonclustered index that contains all of the columns necessary to fulfill a given query or set of queries. If a nonclustered index does not cover a query, for each row, SQL Server has to look up the row to retrieve values for the columns that are not included in the nonclustered index. By performing the lookup using RID there is extra I/O for each row in the resultset. Whereas, when you define a covering index, the query engine can determine that all the information it needs to fulfill the query is stored in the nonclustered index rows, so it does not need to perform a lookup operation.

SQL Server offers the option to INCLUDE columns in the index. An included column is not an index key, so it allows the columns to appear on the leaf pages of the nonclustered index and hence improve the query performance.

■ **Tip** Prolific author and SQL Server MVP Adam Machanic defines a clustered index as a covering index for every possible query against a table. This definition provides a good tool for demonstrating that there's not much difference between clustered and nonclustered indexes, and it helps to reinforce the concept of index covering.

The sample query in Listing 18-16 shows a simple query against the Person.Person table that requires a bookmark lookup, which is itself shown in the query plan in Figure 18-18.

Listing 18-16. Query Requiring a Bookmark Lookup

```
SELECT
BusinessEntityID,
LastName,
FirstName,
MiddleName,
Title FROM Person.Person WHERE LastName = N'Duffy';
```

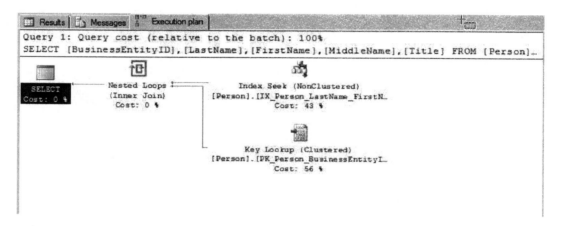

Figure 18-18. *Bookmark Lookup in the Query Plan*

So why is there a bookmark lookup (referenced as a key lookup operator in the query plan)? The answer lies in the query. This particular query uses the LastName column in the WHERE clause to limit results, so the query engine decides to use the IX_Person_LastName_FirstName_MiddleName nonclustered index to fulfill the query. This nonclustered index contains the LastName, FirstName, and MiddleName columns, as well as the BusinessEntityID column, which is defined as the clustered index. The lookup operation is required because the SELECT clause also specifies that the Title column needs to be returned in the result set. Since the Title column is not included in the covering index, SQL Server has to refer back to the table's data pages to retrieve it.

Creating an index with the Title column included in the nonclustered index as shown in Listing 18-17 removes the lookup operation from the query plan for the query in Listing 18-16. As shown in Figure 18-19, the IX_Covering_Person_LastName_FirstName_MiddleName index covers the query.

■ **Tip** Another alternative to eliminate this costly lookup operation is to modify the nonclustered index used in the example to include the `Title` column, which would create a covering index for the query.

Listing 18-17. Query Using a Covering Index

```
CREATE NONCLUSTERED INDEX [IX_Covering_Person_LastName_FirstName_MiddleName] ON
[Person].[Person]
(
        [LastName] ASC,
        [FirstName] ASC,
        [MiddleName] ASC
) INCLUDE (Title)
WITH (PAD_INDEX = OFF, STATISTICS_NORECOMPUTE = OFF, SORT_IN_TEMPDB = OFF, DROP_EXISTING = OFF,
ONLINE = OFF, ALLOW_ROW_LOCKS = ON, ALLOW_PAGE_LOCKS = ON) ON [PRIMARY]
GO
```

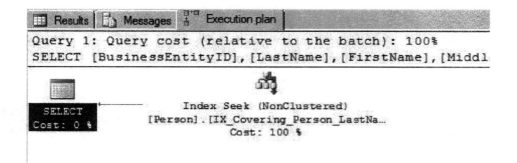

Figure 18-19. *The Covering Index Eliminates the Lookup Operation*

You can define up to 999 nonclustered indexes per table. You should carefully plan your indexing strategy and try to minimize the number of indexes you define on a single table. Nonclustered indexes can require a substantial amount of additional storage, and there is a definite overhead involved in automatically updating them whenever the table data changes. When deciding how many indexes to add to a table, consider the usage patterns carefully. Tables with data that does not change—or rarely changes—may derive greater benefit from having lots of indexes defined on them than tables whose data is modified often.

Nonclustered indexes are useful for the following types of queries:

- Queries that return one row, or a few rows, with high selectivity.

- Queries that can use an index with high selectivity (generally above 95 percent). Selectivity is a measure of the unique key values in an index. SQL Server will often ignore indexes with low selectivity.

- Queries that return small ranges of data that would otherwise result in a clustered index or table scan. These types of queries often use simple equality predicates (=) in the WHERE clause.

- Queries that are completely covered by the nonclustered index.

Filtered Indexes

In SQL Server 2012, filtered indexes provide a way to create more targeted indexes that require less storage and can support more efficient queries. Filtered indexes are optimized nonclustered indexes that allow you to easily add filtering criteria to restrict the rows included in the index with a WHERE clause. A filtered index improves the performance of queries since the index is smaller than a nonclustered index and the statistics are more accurate since they cover only the rows in the filered index. Adding a filtered index to the table where a nonclustered index is unnecessary reduces disk storage for the nonclustered index and the statistics update the cost as well. Listing 18-18 creates a filtered index on the Size column of the Production.Product table that excludes NULL.

Listing 18-18. Creating and Testing a Filtered Index on the Production.Product Table

```
CREATE NONCLUSTERED INDEX IX_Product_Size
ON Production.Product
(
Size,
SizeUnitMeasureCode )
WHERE Size IS NOT NULL;
GO
SELECT
ProductID,
Size,
SizeUnitMeasureCode FROM Production.Product WHERE Size = 'L';
GO
```

■ **Tip**   Filtered indexes are particularly well suited for indexing non-NULL values of sparse columns.

Optimizing Queries

One of the more interesting tasks that SQL developers and DBAs must perform is optimizing queries. To borrow an old cliché, query optimization is as much art as science. There are a lot of moving parts within the SQL query engine, and your task is to give the optimizer as much good information as you can so that it can make good decisions at runtime.

Performance is generally measured in terms of *response time* and *throughput,* defined as follows:

- Response time is the time that it takes for SQL Server to complete a task, such as a query.

- Throughput is a measure of the volume of work that SQL Server can complete in a fixed period of time, such as the number of transactions per minute.

There are several other factors that affect your overall system performance but are outside the scope of this book. Application responsiveness, for instance, depends on several additional factors like network latency and UI architecture, both of which are beyond SQL Server's control. In this section, we will talk about how to use query plans to diagnose performance issues.

Reading Query Plans

When you submit a T-SQL script or statement to the SQL Server query engine, SQL Server compiles your code into a query plan. The query plan is composed of a series of physical and logical operators that the optimizer has chosen to complete your query. The optimizer bases its choice of operators on a wide array of factors like data distribution statistics, cardinality of tables, and availability of useful indexes. SQL Server uses a cost based optimizer, meaning the execution plan it chooses will have the lowest estimated cost.

SQL Server can return query plans in a variety of formats. Our preference is the graphical query execution plan, which we've used in examples throughout the book. Figure 18-20 shows a query plan for a simple query that joins two tables.

Figure 18-20. *Query Execution Plan for an Inner Join Query*

You can generate a graphical query plan for a given query by selecting the Query ➤ Include Actual Execution Plan option from the SSMS menu, and then running your SQL statements. Alternatively, you can select Query ➤ Display Estimated Execution Plan without running the query.

A graphical query plan is read from right to left and top to bottom. It contains arrows indicating the flow of data through the query plan. The arrows show the relative amount of data being moved from one operator to the next, with wider arrows indicating larger numbers of rows, as shown in Figure 18-20. You can position the mouse pointer on top of any operator or arrow in the graphical query plan to display a pop-up with additional information about the operator or data flow between operators, such as the number of rows being acted upon and the estimated row size. You can also right-click an operator or arrow and select Properties from the pop-up menu to view even more descriptive information.

You can also right-click in the Execution Plan window and select Save Execution Plan As to save your graphical execution plan as an XML query plan. Query plans are saved with a .sqlplan file extension and can be viewed in graphical format in SSMS by double-clicking the file. This is particularly useful for troubleshooting queries remotely, since your users or other developers can save the graphical query plan and e-mail it to you, and you can open it up in a local instance of SSMS for further investigation.

ACTUAL OR ESTIMATED?

Estimated execution plans are useful in determining the optimizer's intent. The word *estimated* in the name can be a bit misleading since all query plans are based on the optimizer's estimates of your data distribution, table cardinality, and more.

There are some differences between estimated and actual query plans, however. Since an actual query plan is generated as your T-SQL statements are executed, the optimizer can add additional information to the query plan as it runs. This additional information includes items like actual rebinds and rewinds, values that return the number of times init() method is called in the plan and actual number of rows. When dealing with temporary objects, actual query plans have better information available concerning which operators are being used as well. Consider the following simple script that creates, populates, and queries a temporary table:

```
CREATE TABLE #tl (
BusinessEntityID int NOT NULL,
LastName nvarchar(50),
FirstName nvarchar(50),
MiddleName nvarchar(50) );
CREATE INDEX tl_LastName ON #tl (LastName);
INSERT INTO #tl (
BusinessEntityID,
LastName,
FirstName,
MiddleName )
SELECT
BusinessEntityID,
LastName,
FirstName,
MiddleName FROM Person.Person;
SELECT
BusinessEntityID,
LastName,
FirstName,
MiddleName FROM #tl WHERE LastName = N'Duffy';
DROP TABLE #tl;
```

In the estimated query plan for this code, the optimizer indicates that it will use a table scan, as shown following, to fulfill the SELECT query at the end of the script:

The actual query plan, however, uses a much more efficient nonclustered index seek with a bookmark lookup operation to retrieve the two relevant rows from the table, as shown here:

The difference between the estimated and actual query plans in this case is the information available at the time the query plan is generated. When the estimated query plan is created, there is no temporary table and no index on the temporary table, so the optimizer guesses that a table scan will be required. When the actual query plan is generated, the temporary table and its nonclustered index both exist, so the optimizer comes up with a better query plan.

In addition to graphical query plans, SQL Server supports XML query plans and text query plans, and it can report additional runtime statistics. This additional information can be accessed using the statements shown in Table 18-1.

Table 18-1. *Query Plan Generation Statements*

Statement	Description
SET SHOWPLAN_ALL ON/OFF	Returns a text-based estimated execution plan without executing the query
SET SHOWPLAN_TEXT ON/OFF	Returns a text-based estimated execution plan without executing the query
SET SHOWPLAN_XML ON/OFF	Returns an XML-based estimated execution plan without executing the query
SET STATISTICS IO ON/OFF	Returns statistics information about logical I/O operations during execution of a query
SET STATISTICS PROFILE ON/OFF	Returns actual query execution plans in result sets following the result set generated by each query executed
SET STATISTICS TIME ON/OFF	Returns statistics about the time required to parse, compile, and execute statements at runtime

Once the query is compiled, it can be executed and the execution need not necessarily happen after the query is compiled. So, if the query is executed several days after it has been compiled, the underlying data might have changed and the plan that has been compiled may not be optimal during the execution time. So, when this query is being executed SQL Server first checks to see if the plan is still valid. If the query optimizer decides that the plan is suboptimal, a few statements or the entire batch will be recompiled to produce a different plan. These compilations are called recompilations and although sometimes it is necessary to recompile the queries, this process can slow down the query or batch executions considerably, and so it is optimal to reduce recompilations.

Some of the causes for recompilations are:

- Schema changes such as adding or dropping columns, constraints, indexes, statistics, etc.

- Running sp_recompile on stored procedure or trigger.

- Using Set options after the batch has started such as ANSI_NULL_DFLT_OFF, ANSI_NULLS, ARITHABORT, etc.

One of the main causes for excessive recompilations is the use of temporay tables in the queries. If you create a temporary table in StoredProcA and reference the temporary table in a statement in StoredProcB, then the statement must be recompiled every time StoredProcA runs. Table variable may be a good option to replace a temporary table for a small number of rows.

Sometimes you see suboptimal query performance, and there are few causes for this. One of the common causes is using nonSearch ARGumentable (nonSARGable) expressions in the where clauses or joins which prevents SQL Server from using the index. Using these expressions can slow down the queries significantly as well. Some of the nonSARGable expressions are inequality expression comparisions, functions, implicit datatype conversions, and the LIKE keyword. Often these expresions can be rewritten to use an index. Consider a simple script below that finds person names starting with 'C.'

```
SELECT Title, FirstName, LastName  FROM person.person WHERE SUBSTRING(FirstName, 1,1)='C'
```

The above query will cause a table scan, whereas if the query is rewritten as follows, the optimizer will use clustered seek if a proper index exists in the table, hence improving performance.

```
SELECT Title, FirstName, LastName  FROM person.person WHERE FirstName LIKE 'C%'
```

Sometimes you do have to use functions in the queries for calculations, and in these cases if you replace the function with an indexed computed column then the SQL Server query optimizer can generate a plan that will use an index. SQL Server can match an expression to the computed column to use statistics; however, the expression should match the computed column definition exactly.

Methodology

The methodology that has served us well when troubleshooting performance issues involves the following eight steps:

1. *Recognize the issue:* Before you can troubleshoot a performance issue, you must first determine that there is an actual issue. The recognition of an issue can begin with something as simple as end users complaining that their applications are running slowly.

2. *Identify the source:* Once you've recognized that there is an issue, you need to identify the problem as an SQL Server-related problem. For instance, if you receive reports of database-enabled applications running slowly, it's important to narrow down the source of the problem. If the issue is a network bandwidth or latency issue, for instance, it can't be resolved through simple query optimizations. If it's a T-SQL issue, you can use tools like SQL Profiler and query plans to identify the problematic code.

3. *Review baseline:* Once you have identified the issue and the source, evaluate the baseline. For instance, if the end user is complaining that the application runs slowly, you need to understand the definition of slow and also if it is reproducible. Slow could mean the reports are not rendered within 1 minute or slow could mean that the reports are not rendered within 10 milliseconds. Without a proper baseline you have nothing to compare to and cannot really acertain if the issue exists or not.

4. *Analyze the code:* Once you've identified T-SQL code as the source of the problem, it's time to dig deeper and analyze the root cause of the problem. The operators returned in graphical query plans provide an excellent indicator of the source of many problems. For example, you may spot a costly clustered index scan operator where you expected a more efficient nonclustered index seek.

5. *Define possible solutions:* After the issues have been identified in the code, it's time to come up with potential solutions. If bookmark lookup operations are slowing down your query performance, for instance, you may determine that adding a new nonclustered index or modifying an existing one is a possible fix for the issue. Another possible solution might be changing the query to return fewer columns that are already covered by an index.

6. *Evaluate the solutions:* A critical step after defining your possible solutions is to evaluate the practicality of those solutions. Many things affect whether or not a solution is practical. For instance, you may be forbidden to change indexes on the production servers, in which case adding or modifying indexes to solve an issue may be impractical. On the other hand, your client applications may depend on all of the columns currently being returned in the query's result sets, so changing the query to return fewer columns may not be a workable solution.

   During this step of the process, you also need to determine the impact of your solutions on other parts of the system. Adding or modifying an index on the server to solve a query performance problem might fix the problem for a single query, but it might introduce new performance problems for other queries or DML statements. These conflicting needs should be evaluated.

7. *Implement the solution:* This step of the process is where you actually apply your solution. You will most likely have a subprocess here, in which you apply the solution first to a development environment, and then to a quality assurance (QA) environment, and finally promote it to the production environment.

8. *Examine the impact of the solution:* After implementing your solution, you should revisit it to ensure that it actually fixes the problem. This is a very important step that many people largely ignore, only revisiting their solutions when another issue occurs. By scheduling to revisit your solution, you can take a proactive approach and head off problems before they affect your end users.

Scalability is another important factor to consider when writing T-SQL. Scalability is a measure of how well your code works under increasing demands. For instance, a query may provide acceptable performance when the source table contains 100,000 rows and 10 end users simultaneously querying. However, the same query may suffer performance problems when the table grows to 1,000,000 rows and the number of end users grows to 100. Increasing stress on a system tends to uncover scalability and performance issues that weren't previously apparent in your code base. As pressure on your database grows, it's important to monitor changing access patterns and increasing demands on the system to proactively handle issues before they affect end users.

It's important to also understand when an issue is not really a problem, or at least not one that requires a great deal of attention. As a general rule, we like to apply the 80/20 rule when optimizing queries. That is to say, as a rule of thumb, focus your efforts on optimizing the 20 percent of code that is executed 80 percent of the time. If you have an SP that takes a long time to execute but is only run once a day, and a second procedure that takes a significant amount of time but is run 10,000 times a day, you'd be well served to focus your efforts on the latter procedure.

Waits

Your main goal in designing and writing the application is to enable the users get accurate resultsets in an efficient way. So, when you come across a performance issue, the first place to start with is the actual query itself. For any given session, the query or the thread can be in one of two states: it is either running or it is waiting on something. When the query is running it could be compiling or executing; and when the query is waiting, it can be waiting for I/O, Network, Memory, Locks or Latches, etc., or it can be forced to wait to make sure the process yields for other processes. Whatever the case may be, when the query is waiting on the resource SQL Server logs the wait type for the resource the query is waiting on. You can then use this information to understand why the query performance is affected.

To better help you understand the resource usage, there are three performance metrics that can play role in the query performace—CPU, Duration, and Logical Reads. CPU is essentially the worker time spent to execute the query; Duration is the time the worker thread takes to execute the query, which also includes the time it takes to wait for the resources as well as time it takes to execute the query; and Logical Reads are the number of data pages read by the query execution from the buffer pool or the memory. If the page does not exist in the buffer pool then SQL Server performs a physical read to read the page into the buffer pool. Since we are measuring the performance on the query, logical reads are considered to measure the performance and not physical reads. The wait time can be simply calculated by the formula Duration-CPU.

Waitstats is one of the methodologies that will help you identify opportunities to tune the query performance, and SQL Server 2012 has 649 wait types. Let's say in your application you have some users read from the table and some users write to the same table as well. At any given time, if rows are being inserted into the table, the query that is trying to read those rows has to stop processing since the resource is unavailable. Once the row insertion is completed, the read process gets a signal that the resource is available now for this process, and once a scheduler is available to process the read thread, the query is processed. The time SQL Server spends to acquire the system resource in this example is called a wait. The time SQL Server spends waiting for the process to be signed when the resource is available is called resource wait time. Once the process is signaled the process has to wait for the scheduler to be available for the process to continue, and this wait time is called signal wait time. Both resource wait time and signal wait time combined together gives the wait time in milliseconds.

The wait types can be queried using DMVs sys.dm_os_waiting_tasks and sys.dm_os_wait_stats and sys.dm_exec_requests. sys.dm_os_waiting_tasks and sys.dm_exec_requests return the details on what the tasks are waiting on currently, whereas sys.dm_os_wait_stats lists the aggregate of the waits since the instance has been last restarted, So, you need to check the sys.dm_os_waiting_tasks for the query performance analysis.

Let's review how waits can help you tune queries with a common example. You might have come across the situation where you are trying to insert a set of rows to the table and the insert process hangs and is not responsive. When you query sp_who2, it does not show any blocking; however, the insert process waits for a long time before it completes. Let's see how we can use waitstats to debug this scenario. Listing 18-19 is the script that inserts rows to the waitsdemo table we created in Adventureworks with user session id 54.

Listing 18-19. Script to Demonstrate Waits

```
use adventureworks
go
CREATE TABLE [dbo].[waitsdemo](
        [Id] [int] NOT NULL,
        [LastName] [nchar](600) NOT NULL,
        [FirstName] [nchar](600) NOT NULL,
        [MiddleName] [nchar](600) NULL
) ON [PRIMARY]

GO
```

```
declare @id int = 1
while (@id <= 50000)
begin
        insert into waitsdemo
                select @id,'Foo', 'User',NULL
        SET @id = @id + 1
end
```

Now, to identify the issue of why the insert query is being blocked, let's query the DMVs sys.dm_exec_requests and sys.dm_exec_sessions to see the processes that are currently executing and also query the DMC sys.dm_os_waiting_tasks to see the list of processes that are currently waiting. The DMV queries are listed in Listing 18-20 and partial results are shown in Figure 18-21. In our example, the insert query using session id 54 is waiting on the shrinkdatabase task with session id 98.

Listing 18-20. DMV to Query Current Processes and Waiting Tasks

```
--List waiting user requests
SELECT
er.session_id, er.wait_type, er.wait_time,
er.wait_resource, er.last_wait_type,
er.command,et.text,er.blocking_session_id
FROM sys.dm_exec_requests AS er
JOIN sys.dm_exec_sessions AS es
ON es.session_id = er.session_id
AND es.is_user_process = 1
CROSS APPLY sys.dm_exec_sql_text(er.sql_handle) AS et
GO
--List waiting user tasks
SELECT
wt.waiting_task_address, wt.session_id, wt.wait_type,
wt.wait_duration_ms, wt.resource_description
FROM sys.dm_os_waiting_tasks AS wt
JOIN sys.dm_exec_sessions AS es
ON wt.session_id = es.session_id
AND es.is_user_process = 1
GO
-- List user tasks
SELECT
t.session_id, t.request_id, t.exec_context_id,
t.scheduler_id, t.task_address,
t.parent_task_address
FROM sys.dm_os_tasks AS t
JOIN sys.dm_exec_sessions AS es
ON t.session_id = es.session_id
AND es.is_user_process = 1
GO
```

	session_id	wait_type	wait_time	wait_resource	last_wait_type	command	text
1	54	WRITELOG	0		WRITELOG	INSERT	declare @id int = 1,@FirstName nchar(100) = 'Too',@LastName nchar(100) = 'User' while (@id <= 50000) begin insert into
2	57	NULL	0		MISCELLANEOUS	SELECT	select er.session_id, er.wait_type, er.wait_time, er.wait_resource, er.last_wait_type, er.command,st.text, er.blocking_session_i
3	98	PAGEIOLATCH_SH	84	7:1:38527	PAGEIOLATCH_SH	DbccFilesCompact	DBCC SHRINKDATABASE(N'AdventureWorks')

	waiting_task_address	session_id	wait_type	wait_duration_ms	resource_description
1	0x00000004FB02DC38	54	WRITELOG	10	NULL

	session_id	request_id	exec_context_id	scheduler_id	task_address	parent_task_address
1	54	0	0	3	0x00000004FB02DC38	NULL
2	57	0	0	4	0x00000004FB035C38	NULL
3	98	0	0	5	0x00000004E5FC4558	NULL

Figure 18-21. Results of sys.dm_os_waiting_tasks

The above results show that process 54 is indeed waiting and the wait type is writelog which means that the I/O to the log files is slow. When you correlate this to the session_id 98 which is shrinkdatabase task, you can identify that the root cause for the performance issue with the insert query is the shrinkdatabase process. Once the shrinkdatabase operation completes the insert query starts to process as shown in Figure 18-22.

	session_id	wait_type	wait_time	wait_resource	last_wait_type	command	text	blocking_session_id
1	54	WRITELOG	0		WRITELOG	INSERT	declare @id int = 1,@FirstName nchar(100) = ...	0
2	57	NULL	0		MISCELLANEOUS	SELECT	select er.session_id, er.wait_type, er.wait_time, ...	0

	waiting_task_address	session_id	wait_type	wait_duration_ms	resource_description
1	0x00000004FB02D868	54	WRITELOG	2	NULL

	session_id	request_id	exec_context_id	scheduler_id	task_address	parent_task_address
1	54	0	0	3	0x00000004FB02D868	NULL
2	57	0	0	4	0x00000004FB035868	NULL

Figure 18-22. Results of DMV to Show the Blocking Thread

Not all wait types need to be monitored constantly. Some of the wait types like broker_*, clr_* can be ignored if you are not using service broker or CLR in your datbases. We have only touched the tip of the iceberg with this example, waits can be a much more powerful mechanism in helping to identify and resolve query performance issues.

Extended Events

Extended Events (XEvents) is a diagnostic system that can help you troubleshoot performance problems with the SQL Server. It was first introduced in SQL 2008 and then went through a complete makeover in SQL Server 2012 with additional event types and new user interface and templates similar to SQL Server Profiler. Let's review the Extended Events user interface first and then use a case to see how we can troubleshoot with Extended Events. The XEvents user interface is integrated with Management Studio, and there is a separate node in the tree called Extended Events. To start a new Extended Events session, expand the Management node and then expand Extended Events. Right click Sessions and then click New Session. Figure 18-23 shows the Extended Events user interface.

Figure 18-23. *Extended Events New Session*

XEvents offers a rich diagnostic framework that is highly scalable and offers the capability to collect little or large amounts of data in order to troubleshoot a given performance issue. XEvents has the same capabilities as SQL Profiler, and so you may ask why should you use XEvents and not SQL Profiler. Anybody who has worked with SQL Server can tell you that SQL Profiler adds significant resource overhead when tracing the server, which can sometimes bring the server to its knees. The reason for the overhead with SQL Profiler is that when you use SQL Profiler to trace the activities on the server, all the events are streamed to the client and the events are filtered based on the criteria set by you on the client side, which needs lot of resources to process the events. Whereas, with XEvents, the filtering happens on the server side, so the events that are needed are not sent to the client—hence better performance with a process that is less chatty. Another reason to start using XEvents is simply because SQL Profiler has been marked for deprecation.

Extended events sessions can be based on predefined templates or you can create the session by choosing specific events. You can also autostart an XEvents session on server startup, one of the features that is not available in SQL Profiler. Figure 18-24 shows the autostart option.

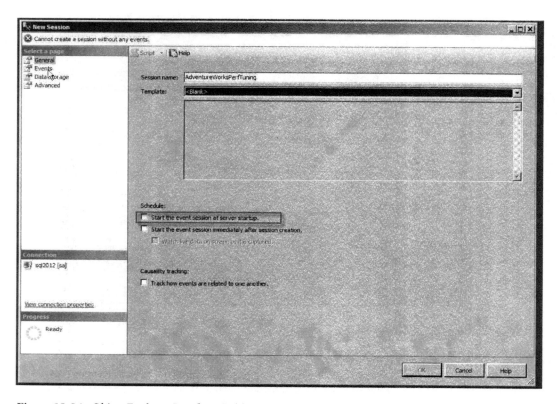

Figure 18-24. *Object Explorer Database Table Pop-up Context Menu*

The Event library lists all the events that are searchable as well, and they are categorized and grouped based on the events. You are able to search the events based on names and/or descriptions. Once you select the events you want to track, you are able to set the filter criteria. After the filters have been defined, you can select the fields you want to track. The common fields that are tracked are selected by default. Figure 18-25 shows a sample session to capture the SQL statements for performance tuning.

Figure 18-25. Sample Extended Events Session Configuration for SQL Performance Tuning

Once all of the criteria have been defined, you can set the target depending on what you want to do with the data, whether you want to capture the data to a file, forward it to in-memory targets, or write it to a live reader. Figure 18-26 shows the possible targets for the session.

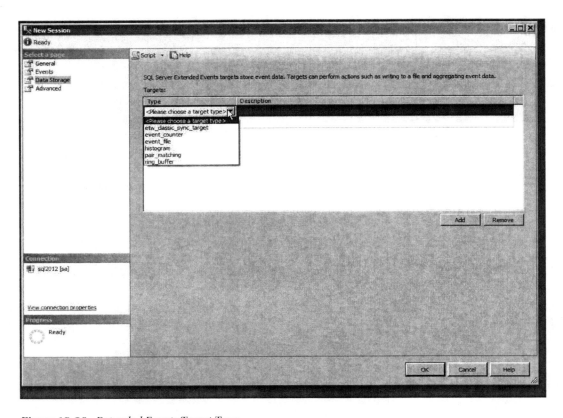

Figure 18-26. *Extended Events Target Type*

Figure 18-27 shows the results of the Extended Events streaming the live data of the SQL statements for the performance tuning session.

Figure 18-27. Sample Data from the Extended Events Session for SQL Performance Tuning

Now let's take a common problem: a business user is complaining that the application is slow and there is a lot of blocking. You need to figure out where the problem is, given the application is third-party software. The challenge is to identify a piece of application functionality and the queries behind this functionality that are causing the performance issue. So you have multiple areas to investigate, including clients, network, blocking, CPU, and I/O issues. One way to approach the problem is to run the tool Performance Monitor (perfmon) and start a profiler trace, and try to tie in the application issue to the server metrics, but there is no direct way to get the details on the query chain of the lead blocker that causes and follows the blocking issue without using XEvents.

If the application is built on the latest ODBC drivers or the new ADO.NET 4.5, the application is going to attach an identifier called ConnectionId which is a guide to the server when the connections are made which makes the process of tracing or correlating activities between client and server much simpler. Along with this, the client will send another identifier called ActivityId which provides information on the process that is currently executing. With the ConnectionId and ActivityId we will now have the information required to build a complete image of the activities that take place in the server, and we can effectively trace it with the server activities to identify the bottlenecks.

Extended Events makes common problems like page splits or locking much easier to identify and resolve with proper code changes. For tracking page splits, you can set up an Extended Events session using a script as shown in Listing 18-21.

Listing 18-21. Extended Event Session Script to Troubleshoot Login Timeouts

```
CREATE EVENT SESSION [Troubleshoot page split] ON SERVER
ADD EVENT sqlserver.page_split(

ACTION(sqlserver.client_app_name,sqlserver.database_id,sqlserver.database_name,sqlserver.plan_
handle,sqlserver.server_instance_name,sqlserver.server_principal_name,sqlserver.server_principal_
sid,sqlserver.session_id,sqlserver.session_nt_username,sqlserver.sql_text,sqlserver.transaction_
id,sqlserver.username)),
ADD EVENT sqlserver.rpc_completed(

ACTION(sqlserver.client_app_name,sqlserver.database_id,sqlserver.database_name,sqlserver.plan_
handle,sqlserver.server_instance_name,sqlserver.server_principal_name,sqlserver.server_principal_
sid,sqlserver.session_id,sqlserver.session_nt_username,sqlserver.sql_text,sqlserver.transaction_
id,sqlserver.username)),
ADD EVENT sqlserver.rpc_starting(

ACTION(sqlserver.client_app_name,sqlserver.database_id,sqlserver.database_name,sqlserver.plan_
handle,sqlserver.server_instance_name,sqlserver.server_principal_name,sqlserver.server_principal_
sid,sqlserver.session_id,sqlserver.session_nt_username,sqlserver.sql_text,sqlserver.transaction_
id,sqlserver.username)),
ADD EVENT sqlserver.sp_statement_completed(

ACTION(sqlserver.client_app_name,sqlserver.database_id,sqlserver.database_name,sqlserver.plan_
handle,sqlserver.server_instance_name,sqlserver.server_principal_name,sqlserver.server_principal_
sid,sqlserver.session_id,sqlserver.session_nt_username,sqlserver.sql_text,sqlserver.transaction_
id,sqlserver.username)),
ADD EVENT sqlserver.sp_statement_starting(

ACTION(sqlserver.client_app_name,sqlserver.database_id,sqlserver.database_name,sqlserver.plan_
handle,sqlserver.server_instance_name,sqlserver.server_principal_name,sqlserver.server_principal_
sid,sqlserver.session_id,sqlserver.session_nt_username,sqlserver.sql_text,sqlserver.transaction_
id,sqlserver.username))
ADD TARGET package0.event_file(SET filename=N'C:\Temp\Troubleshoot page split.xel')
WITH (MAX_MEMORY=4096
KB,EVENT_RETENTION_MODE=ALLOW_SINGLE_EVENT_LOSS,MAX_DISPATCH_LATENCY=30 SECONDS,MAX_EVENT_SIZE=0
KB,MEMORY_PARTITION_MODE=NONE,TRACK_CAUSALITY=OFF,STARTUP_STATE=OFF)
GO
```

Now you can start the Extended Events session that was created using Listing 18-21and start identifying the queries and the session details that cause these page splits. This will help you narrow down the issue very quickly and troubleshoot what is causing the page splits.

Summary

SQL Server stores data in 8-KB pages that it allocates in contiguous groups of 8 pages each, which are known as extents. In a perfect world, SQL Server's logical and physical storage mechanisms would not make a difference to you as a developer. In the real world, however, an understanding of storage engine operation is important to maximizing performance. We began this chapter with an overview of the SQL Server storage engine and how it affects performance.

Indexes are the primary means of increasing query performance on SQL Server. We continued the discussion by addressing the concepts of heaps, clustered indexes, and nonclustered indexes, with details of how each affects the overall performance of your queries and DML statements.

Optimizing queries depends on maximizing two critical aspects: response time and throughput. SQL Server provides query plans and statistics, in addition to other external tools, to help diagnose performance issues. We wrapped up this chapter with a suggested methodology for dealing with performance issues. Using a methodology like the eight-step process described here will help you quickly narrow down the source of performance issues; define, evaluate, and implement solutions; and take a proactive approach in addressing future performance-related issues.

Using troubleshooting techniques such as waitstats and DMVs will help you narrow down the performance issues and will provide you information to derive a complete picture of what is going on in the system. Combining this with high performance event monitoring infrastructure such as Extended Events provides proactive monitoring capabilities for the servers that allow you to identify issues and resolve them in timely fashion.

We hope that you've enjoyed reading this book as much as we've enjoyed bringing it to you. We wish you all the best in your T-SQL development efforts, and we hope you find this book helpful in your development endeavors.

EXERCISES

1. [Choose all that apply] SQL Server 2012 uses which of the following types of files to store database information:

   a. Data files (.mdf extension)

   b. Transaction log files (.ldf extension)

   c. Additional data files (.ndf extension)

   d. Rich text files (.rtf extension)

2. [True/False] SQL Server stores data in 8-KB storage units known as pages.

3. [Choose one] Eight contiguous 8-KB pages of storage in SQL Server are known as which of the following:

   a. A filegroup

   b. A chunk

   c. An extent

   d. A file

4. [Fill in the blank] A heap is an _____ collection of data pages.

5. [Fill in the blank] Clustered indexes and nonclustered indexes are managed by SQL Server as _____ structures.

6. [Fill in the blank] _____ sessions can be used to trace waits.

7. [Fill in the blank] Optimized nonclustered index is _____.

8. [Choose all that apply] SQL Server performance is measured using which of the following terms:

   a. Throughput

   b. Luminescence

   c. Response time

   d. All of the above

■ ■ ■

Exercise Answers

This appendix contains the answers to the exercises at the end of each chapter. The answers are grouped by chapter and numbered to match the associated exercises in the corresponding chapter.

Chapter 1

1. Imperative languages require you to provide the computer with step-by-step directions to perform a task—essentially, you tell the computer *how* to achieve the end result. Declarative languages allow you to tell the computer what the end result should be and trust the computer to take appropriate action to achieve it. Instead of telling the computer how to achieve the result, in declarative languages you tell the computer *what* the end result should be.

2. *ACID* stands for "atomicity, consistency, isolation, durability." These represent the basic properties of a database that guarantee reliability of data storage, processing, and manipulations.

3. The five index types that SQL Server supports are clustered indexes, nonclustered indexes, XML indexes, spatial indexes, and full-text indexes.

4. All of the following are restrictions on all SQL Server UDFs: (1) they cannot perform DML or DDL statements, (2) they cannot change the state of the database (no side effects), (3) they cannot use dynamic SQL, and (4) they cannot utilize certain nondeterministic functions.

5. False. All newly declared variables are set to NULL on creation. You should always initialize newly created variables immediately after creation.

Chapter 2

1. SSDT is an integrated project oriented development environment for database and application development.

2. The correct answers are A, B, C and D. SQL Server 2012 SSMS provides integrated Object Explorer, and IntelliSense. Code snippets and customizable keyboard mapping scheme.

3. SSIS is considered an ETL (extract, transform, load) tool.

4. True. SQLCMD scripting variables can be set via command-line options and environment variables, and in script via the SQLCMD :setvar command.

5.	The correct answer is D, all of the above. BCP can generate format files that can be used with the SSIS Bulk Insert task, with the T-SQL BULK INSERT statement, or with BCP itself. BCP can also import data into tables without a format file and export data from a table to a file.

6.	You can query the Extended Events trace files directly. With SQL Profiler trace, you have to load the captured trace data to a table and then you can query them. Direct querying against Profiler trace data is not supported.

7.	SQL Server 2005, SQL Server 2008, SQL Server 2008 R2, SQL Server 2012, and SQL Azure.

Chapter 3

1.	True. SQL 3VL supports the three Boolean results true, false, and unknown.

2.	The correct answer is A. In SQL, NULL represents an unknown or missing value. NULL does not represent a numeric value of 0 or a zero-length string.

3.	False. SQL's BEGIN...END construct defines a statement block, but does not limit the scope of variables declared within the statement block. This is contrary to the behavior of C#'s curly braces ({ }).

4.	The BREAK statement forces a WHILE loop to terminate immediately.

5.	False. TRY...CATCH can't capture syntax errors, errors that cause a broken connection, or errors with severity of 10 or less, among others.

6.	SQL CASE expressions come in both *simple* and *searched* CASE expression forms.

7.	The correct answers are A and B. T-SQL provides support for read-only cursors and forward-only cursors. There is no such thing as a backward-only cursor or a write-only cursor.

8.	The following code modifies the example in Listing 4–13 to return the total sales (TotalDue) by region in pivot table format. The required change to the code is shown in bold.

```
-- Declare variables DECLARE @sql nvarchar(4000);
DECLARE @temp_pivot table (TerritoryID int NOT NULL PRIMARY KEY, CountryRegion nvarchar(20) NOT
NULL, CountryRegionCode nvarchar(3) NOT NULL);
-- Get column names from source table rows INSERT INTO @temp_pivot (TerritoryID,
CountryRegion,
CountryRegionCode) SELECT TerritoryID,
Name,
CountryRegionCode FROM Sales.SalesTerritory GROUP BY TerritoryID, Name, CountryRegionCode;
-- Generate dynamic SOL query SET @sql=N'SELECT'+SUBSTRING(
(
SELECT N', SUM(CASE WHEN t.TerritoryID='+CAST(TerritoryID AS NVARCHAR(3)) +
N' THEN soh.TotalDue ELSE 0 END) AS '+QUOTENAME(CountryRegion) AS "*"
FROM @temp_pivot
FOR XML PATH('') ), 2, 4000) +
N' FROM Sales.SalesOrderHeader soh '+N' INNER JOIN Sales.SalesTerritory t '+N' ON
soh.TerritoryID=t.TerritoryID; ' ;
-- Print and execute dynamic SOL PRINT @sql;
EXEC (@sql);
```

Chapter 4

1. SQL Server supports three types of T-SQL UDFs: *scalar UDFs, multistatement TVFs,* and *inline TVFs.*

2. True. The RETURNS NULL ON NULL INPUT option is a performance-enhancing option that automatically returns NULL if any of the parameters passed into a scalar UDF are NULL.

3. False. The ENCRYPTION option performs a simple code obfuscation that is easily reverse-engineered. In fact, there are several programs and scripts available online that allow anyone to decrypt your code with the push of a button.

4. The correct answers are A, B, and D. Multistatement TVFs (as well as all other TVFs) do not allow you to execute PRINT statements, call RAISERROR, or create temporary tables. In multistatement TVFs, you can declare table variables.

5. The following code creates a deterministic scalar UDF that accepts a float parameter, converts it from degrees Fahrenheit to degrees Celsius, and returns a float result. Notice that the WITH SCHEMABINDING option is required to make this scalar UDF deterministic.

```
CREATE FUNCTION dbo.FahrenheitToCelsius (@Degrees float)
RETURNS float
WITH SCHEMABINDING
AS
BEGIN
RETURN (@Degrees - 32.0) * (5.0 / 9.0); END;
```

Chapter 5

1. False. The SP RETURN statement can return only an int scalar value.

2. One method of proving that two SPs that call each other recursively are limited to 32 levels of recursion in total is shown following. Differences from the code in the original listing are shown in bold.

```
CREATE PROCEDURE dbo.FirstProc (@i int)
AS
BEGIN
PRINT @i;
SET @i+= 1;
EXEC dbo.SecondProc @i;
END; GO
CREATE PROCEDURE dbo.SecondProc (@i int)
AS
BEGIN
PRINT @i;
SET @i+= 1;
EXEC dbo.FirstProc @i; END; GO
EXEC dbo.FirstProc 1;
```

3.   The correct answer is D. Table-valued parameters must be declared READONLY.

4.   The correct answers are A and B. You can use the sprecompile system SP or the WITH
      RECOMPILE option to force SQL Server to recompile an SP FORCE RECOMPILE and DBCC
      RECOMPILEALLSPS are not valid options/statements.

Chapter 6

1.   True. In DDL triggers, the EVENTDATA function returns information about the DDL
      event that fired the trigger.

2.   True. In a DML trigger, an UPDATE event is treated as a DELETE followed by an INSERT,
      so both the deleted and inserted virtual tables are populated for UPDATE events.

3.   The correct answers are A, C, and E. SQL Server 2012 supports logon triggers, DDL
      triggers, and DML triggers.

4.   The SET NOCOUNT ON statement prevents extraneous rows affected messages.

5.   The correct answer is A. The COLUMNSUPDATED function returns a varbinary string
      with bits set to represent affected columns.

6.   True. @@ROWCOUNT at the beginning of a trigger returns the number of rows affected by
      the DML statement that fired the trigger.

7.   False. You cannot create any AFTER triggers on a view.

Chapter 7

1.   True. Symmetric keys can be used to encrypt data or other symmetric keys.

2.   The correct answers are A, B, and E. SQL Server 2012 provides native support for
      DES, AES, and RC4 encryption. Although the Loki and Blowfish algorithms are real
      encryption algorithms, SQL Server does not provide native support for them.

3.   False. SQL Server 2012 T-SQL provides no BACKUP ASYMMETRIC KEY statement.

4.   You must turn on the *EKM provider enabled* option with spconfigure to activate EKM
      on your server.

5.   False. TDE automatically encrypts the tempdb database, but it does not encrypt the
      model and master databases.

6.   True. SQL Server automatically generates random initialization vectors when you
      encrypt data with symmetric encryption.

Chapter 8

1.   True. When a CTE is not the first statement in a batch, the statement preceding it
      must end with a semicolon statement terminator.

2.   The correct answers are A, B, and D. Recursive CTEs require the WITH keyword, an
      anchor query, and a recursive query. SQL Server does not support an
      EXPRESSION keyword.

3. The MAXRECURSION option can accept a value between 0 and 32767.

4. The correct answer is E, all of the above. SQL Server supports the ROWNUMBER, RANK, DENSE_RANK, and NTILE functions.

5. False. You cannot use ORDER BY with the OVER clause when used with aggregate functions.

6. True. When PARTITION BY and ORDER BY are both used in the OVER clause, PARTITION BY must appear first.

7. The names of all columns returned by a CTE must be *unique*.

8. The default framing clause is RANGE BETWEEN UNBOUNDED PRECEDING AND CURRENT ROW.

9. True. When Orderby is not specified then there is no starting or ending point for the boundary. So entire partition is used for the window frame.

Chapter 9

1. False. European language accents fit in the ANSI encoded characters. You need UNICODE for non-Latin characters.

2. The correct answers are A, C, and D. image and (n)text are deprecated since SQL Server 2005.

3. False. The date data type does not store time zone information. Use the datetimeoffset data type if you need to store time zone information with your date/time data.

4. The hierarchyid data type uses the materialized path model to represent hierarchies in the database.

5. The correct answer is B. The geography data type requires Polygon objects to have a counterclockwise orientation. Also, spatial objects created with the geography data type must be contained in a single hemisphere.

6. The correct answer is B. The SWITCHOFFSET function adjusts a given datetimeoffset value to another specified time offset.

7. True. FILESTREAM functionality utilizes NTFS functionality to provide streaming BLOB data support.

8. The column is named path_locator. It is a hierarchyid type column.

Chapter 10

1. True. Stoplists and full-text indexes are stored in the database.

2. The correct answer is C. You can create a full-text index using the wizard in SSMS or the T-SQL CREATE FULLTEXT INDEX statement.

3. The FREETEXT predicate automatically performs word stemming and thesaurus *replacements* and *expansions*.

4. Stoplists contain stopwords, which are words that are *ignored* during full-text querying.

5. True. The `sys.dmftsparser` dynamic management function shows the results produced by word breaking and stemming.

Chapter 11

1. The correct answers are A, B, C, and D. The SQL Server FOR XML clause supports the FOR XML RAW, FOR XML PATH, FOR XML AUTO, and FOR XML EXPLICIT modes. FOR XML RECURSIVE is not a valid FOR XML mode.

2. `OPENXML` returns results in *edge* table format by default.

3. True. The `xml` data type `query()` method returns results as untyped `xml` instances.

4. The correct answer is C. A SQL Server primary XML index stores your `xml` data type columns in a preshredded relational format.

5. True. When you haven't defined a primary XML index on an `xml` data type column, performing XQuery queries against the column causes SQL Server to perform on-the-fly shredding of your XML data. This can result in a severe performance penalty.

6. True. Additional XML functionality, available through the .NET Framework, can be accessed via SQL Server's SQL CLR integration.

Chapter 12

1. True. The `FOR XML PATH` clause supports a subset of the W3C XPath recommendation for explicitly specifying your XML result structure.

2. The correct answer is A. The at sign (@) is used to identify attribute nodes in both XPath and XQuery.

3. The context item (indicated by a single period) specifies the current *node* or scalar *value* being accessed at any given point in time during query execution.

4. The correct answers are A, B, and D. You can declare XML namespaces for SQL Server XQuery expressions with the `WITH XMLNAMESPACES` clause, the `declare default element namespace` statement, or the `declare namespace` statement. There is no `CREATE XML NAMESPACE` statement.

5. In XQuery, you can dynamically construct XML via *direct* constructors or *computed* constructors.

6. True. SQL Server 2012 supports all five clauses of FLWOR expressions: `for`, `let`, `where`, `order by`, and `return`. Note that SQL Server 2005 did not support the `let` clause.

7. `_SC` collation enables SQL Server to be UTF-16 aware.

8. The correct answers are B, C, and D. XQuery provides three types of comparison operators: general comparison operators, node comparison operators, and value comparison operators.

Chapter 13

1. "Metadata" is "data that describes *data.*"

2. *Catalog views* provide insight into database objects and server-wide configuration options.

3. The correct answer is B. Many catalog views are defined using an inheritance model. In the inheritance model, catalog views inherit columns from other catalog views. Some catalog views are also defined as the union of two other catalog views.

4. True. Dynamic management views and functions provide access to internal SQL Server data structures that would be otherwise inaccessible. DMVs and DMFs present these internal data structures in relational tabular format.

5. The correct answers are A and C. INFORMATION_SCHEMA views provide the advantages of ISO SQL standard compatibility and, as a consequence, cross-platform compatibility.

Chapter 14

1. The correct answers are A, B, C, D and E. SQL Server 2012 provides support for SQL CLR UDFs, UDAs, UDTs, SPs, and triggers.

2. False. SQL Server 2012 expands the limit on MaxByteSize for UDAs and UDTs to over 2 billion bytes. In SQL Server 2005, there was an 8000-byte limit on the size of UDAs and UDTs.

3. The correct answer is D. SAFE permissions allow SQL CLR code to execute managed .NET code. EXTERNALACCESS permissions are required to write to the file system, access network resources, and read the computer's registry.

4. True. SQL CLR UDAs and UDTs must be declared with the Serializable attribute.

5. A SQL CLR UDA that is declared as Format.UserDefined must implement the IBinarySerialize interface.

6. The correct answers are A, C, D, and E. A SQL CLR UDA is required to implement the following methods: Init, Terminate, Merge, and Accumulate. The Aggregate method is not a required method for UDAs.

Chapter 15

1. True. The System.Data.SqlClient namespace provides support for the SQL Server Native Client library, which provides optimized access to SQL Server.

2. The correct answer is B. Disconnected datasets cache required data locally and allow you to connect to a database only as needed.

3. The correct answers are A and C. The benefits of query parameterization include protection against SQL injection attacks and increased efficiency through query plan reuse.

4. False. When you turn on MARS, you can open two or more result sets over a single open connection. MARS requires only one open connection.

5. True. Visual Studio provides a visual O/RM designer with a drag-and-drop interface.

6. The correct answer is D. LINQ to SQL uses deferred query execution, meaning that it does not execute your query until the data returned by the query is actually needed.

Chapter 16

1. False. A LocalDB instance cannot run as a service.

2. False, you can access XML columns from Linux by using the Microsoft ODBC driver for Linux.

3. False. HTTP SOAP endpoints are deprecated in SQL Server 2008.

4. Visual Studio 2010 and 2012 provides the *ASP.NET Web Service* template for creating new web services.

5. True. Visual Studio includes a built-in graphical EDM designer beginning with SP 1.

6. The correct answer is C. WCF Data Services accepts REST-style queries in requests.

Chapter 17

1. The @@error system function automatically resets to 0 after every successful statement execution.

2. The correct answer is D. The ERROR_SEVERITY() function, available only in the CATCH block in SQL Server, returns the severity level of the error that occurred.

3. True. The RAISERROR statement allows you to raise errors in SQL Server.

4. True. Visual Studio provides integrated debugging of T-SQL functions and SPs. Using Visual Studio, you can step into T-SQL code and set breakpoints.

5. The correct answers are A and B. The potential problems with dynamic SQL include performance issues caused by lack of query plan reuse, and exposure to SQL injection attacks.

Chapter 18

1. The correct answers are A, B, and C. SQL Server 2012 uses data files with an .mdf extension, transaction log files with an .ldf extension, and additional data files with an .ndf extension.

2. True. SQL Server stores data in 8 KB storage units known as pages.

3. The correct answer is C. Eight contiguous 8 KB pages of storage in SQL Server are known as an extent.

4. A heap is an *unordered* collection of data pages.

5. Clustered indexes and nonclustered indexes are managed by SQL Server as *B-tree* structures.

6. Extended events sessions can be used to trace waits.

7. Optimized nonclustered index is called filtered index.

8. The correct answers are A and C. SQL Server performance is measured in terms of throughput and response time.

APPENDIX B

■ ■ ■

XQuery Data Types

SQL Server 2012 supports the data types defined in the XQuery Data Model (XDM). The supported data types are listed with their definitions in Table B-1. The diagram in Figure B-1 is a quick reference showing the relationships between the XDM data types.

Table B-1. *XQuery Data Types*

Type	Description
Base Types	
xs:anySimpleType	This is the base type for all simple built-in types.
xs:anyType	This is the base type for xs:anySimpleType and complex built-in types.
Date/Time Types	
xs:date	This type represents a Gregorian calendar–based date value exactly one day in length, represented in the format yyyy-mm-dd[*time_offset*]. *time_offset* can be a capital Z for *zero-meridian* (UTC), or in the format +/-hh:mm to represent a UTC offset. An example of a valid xs:date is 2006-12-25Z, which represents December 25, 2006, UTC time.
xs:dateTime	This type represents a Gregorian calendar-based date and time value with precision to 1/1000th of a second. The format is yyyy-mm-ddThh: mm:ss.sss[*time_offset*]. Time is specified using a 24-hour clock. As with xs:date, *time_offset* can be a capital Z (UTC) or a UTC offset in the format +/-hh:mm. A valid xs:dateTime value is 2006-10-30T13:00: 59.500-05:00, which represents October 30, 2006, 1:00:59.5 PM, US Eastern Standard time. Unlike SQL Server 2005, in SQL Server 2012 the xs:dateTime type maintains the time zone information you assign instead of automatically converting all date/time values to a single time zone. The time zone is also not mandatory in SQL Server 2012.
xs:duration	This type represents a Gregorian calendar–based temporal (time- based) duration, represented as PyyyyYmmMddDThhHmmMss.sssS. P0010Y03M12DT00H00M00.000S, for instance, represents 10 years, 3 months, 12 days.
xs:gDay	This type represents a Gregorian calendar–based day. The format is dd[*time_offset*] (notice the three preceding hyphen [-] characters). The *time_offset* is optional. A valid xs:gDay value is 09Z, which stands for the ninth day of the month, UTC time.

(continued)

Table B-1. (*continued*)

Type	Description
xs:gMonth	This type represents a Gregorian calendar–based month. The format is --mm[*time_offset*] (notice the two preceding hyphen characters). *time_offset* is optional. A valid xs:gMonth value is -12, which stands for December.
xs:gMonthDay	This type represents a Gregorian calendar–based month and day. The format is --mm-dd[*time_offset*] (notice the two preceding hyphens). The *time_offset* for this data type is optional. A valid xs:gMonthDay value is --02-29 for February 29.
xs:gYear	This type represents a Gregorian calendar–based year. The format is yyyy[*time_offset*]. The *time_offset* is optional. The year can also have a preceding hyphen character indicating a negative (BCE—"before the Christian Era") year as opposed to a positive (CE—"Christian Era") date. A valid xs:gYear value is -0044 for 44 BCE. Notice that all four digits are required in the year representation, even for years that can be normally represented with less than four digits.
xs:gYearMonth	This type represents a Gregorian calendar–based year and month. The format is yyyy-mm[*time_offset*]. The *time_offset* for this data type is optional and can be Z or a UTC offset. A valid xs:gYearMonth value is 2001-01 for January 2001.
xs:time	This type represents a time value with precision to 1/1000th of a second, using a 24-hour clock representation. The format is hh:mm:ss.sss [*time_offset*]. As with other temporal data types, *time_offset* can be Z (UTC) or a UTC offset in the format +/-hh:mm. A valid xs:time value is 23:59:59.000-06:00, which represents 11:59:59 PM, US Central Standard time. The canonical representation of midnight in 24-hour format is 00:00:00.

Binary Types

Type	Description
xs:base64Binary	This type represents Base64-encoded binary data. Base64-encoding symbols are defined in RFC 2045 (www.ietf.org/rfc/rfc2045.txt) as A through Z, a through z, 0 through 9, +, /, and the trailing = sign. Whitespace characters are also allowed, and lowercase letters are considered distinct from uppercase letters. An example of a valid xs:base64Binary value is QVByZXNzIEJvb2tzIEFuZCBTUUwgU2V☐ydmVyIDIwMDU=.
xs:hexBinary	This type represents hexadecimal-encoded binary data. The symbols defined for encoding data in hexadecimal format are 0 through 9, A through F, and a through f. Upper- and lowercase letters A through F are considered equivalent by this data type. An example of a valid xs:hexBinary value is 6170726573732E636F6D.

Boolean Type

Type	Description
xs:Boolean	This type represents a Boolean binary truth value. The values supported are true (1) and false (0). An example of a valid xs:boolean value is true.

Numeric Types

Type	Description
xs:byte	This type represents an 8-bit signed integer in the range –128 to +127.
xs:decimal	This type represents an exact decimal value up to 38 digits in length. These numbers can have up to 28 digits before the decimal point and up to 10 digits after the decimal point. A valid xs:decimal value is 8372.9381.

(*continued*)

Table B-1. (*continued*)

Type	Description
xs:double	This type represents a double-precision floating point value patterned after the IEEE standard for floating point types. The representation of values is similar to xs:float values $nE[+/-]e$, where n is the mantissa followed by the letter E or e and an exponent e. The range of valid values for xs:double are approximately $-1.79E+308$ to $-2.23E-308$ for negative numbers, 0, and $+2.23E-308$ to $+1.79E+308$ for positive numbers.
xs:float	This type represents an approximate single-precision floating point value per the IEEE 754–1985 standard. The format for values of this type is nEe, where n is a decimal mantissa followed by the letter E or e and an exponent. The value represents $n \cdot 10^e$. The range for xs:float values is approximately $-3.4028e+38$ to $-1.401298E-45$ for negative numbers, 0, and $+1.401298E-45$ to $+3.4028e+38$ for positive numbers. The special values $-INF$ and $+INF$ represent negative and positive infinity. SQL Server does not support the XQuery-specified special value NaN, which stands for "not a number." A valid xs:float value is $1.98E+2$.
xs:int	This type represents a 32-bit signed integer in the range -2147483648 to $+2147483647$.
xs:integer	This type represents an integer value up to 28 digits in length. A valid xs:integer value is 76372.
xs:long	This type represents a 64-bit signed integer in the range -9223372036854775808 to $+9223372036854775807$.
xs:negativeInteger	This type represents a negative nonzero integer value derived from the xs:integer type. It can be up to 28 digits in length.
xs:nonNegativeInteger	This type represents a positive or zero integer value derived from the xs:integer type. It can be up to 28 digits in length.
xs:nonPositiveInteger	This type represents a negative or zero integer value derived from the xs:integer type. It can be up to 28 digits in length.
xs:positiveInteger	This type represents a positive nonzero integer value derived from the xs:integer type. It can be up to 28 digits in length.
xs:short	This type represents a 16-bit signed integer in the range -37268 to $+32767$.
xs:unsignedByte	This type represents an unsigned 8-bit integer in the range 0 to 255.
xs:unsignedInt	This type represents an unsigned 32-bit integer in the range 0 to $+4294967295$.
xs:unsignedLong	This type represents an unsigned 64-bit integer in the range 0 to $+18446744073709551615$.
xs:unsignedShort	This type represents an unsigned 16-bit integer in the range 0 to $+65535$.
String Types	
xs:ENTITIES	This type is a space-separated list of ENTITY types.
xs:ENTITY	This type is equivalent to the ENTITY type from the XML 1.0 standard. The lexical space has the same construction as an xs:NCName.

(*continued*)

Table B-1. (*continued*)

Type	Description
xs:ID	This type is equivalent to the ID attribute type from the XML 1.0 standard. An xs:ID value has the same lexical construction as an xs:NCName.
xs:IDREF	This type represents the IDREF attribute type from the XML 1.0 standard. The lexical space has the same construction as an xs:NCName.
xs:IDREFS	This type is a space-separated list of IDREF attribute types.
xs:language	This type is a language identifier string representing natural language identifiers as specified by RFC 3066 (www.ietf.org/rfc/rfc3066.txt). A complete list of language codes is maintained by the IANA registry at www.iana.org/assignments/language-subtag-registry. Language identifiers must conform to the regular expression pattern [a-zA- Z]{1,8}(-[a-zA-Z0-9]{1,8})*. An example of a valid language identifier is tlh, which is the identifier for the Klingon language.
xs:Name	This type is an XML name string. A name string must match the XML- specified production for Name. Per the standard, a Name must begin with a letter, an underscore, or a colon, and may then contain a combination of letters, numbers, underscores, colons, periods, hyphens, and various other characters designated in the XML standard as *combining characters* and *extenders*. Refer to the XML standard at www.w3.org/TR/2000/WD-xml-2e-20000814#NT-Name for specific information about these additional allowable Name characters.
xs:NCName	This type is a noncolonized name. The format for an xs:NCName is the same as for xs:Name, but without colon characters.
xs:NMTOKEN	This type is an NMTOKEN type from the XML 1.0 standard. An xs:NMTOKEN value is composed of any combination of letters, numbers, underscores, colons, periods, hyphens, and XML combining characters and extenders.
xs:NMTOKENS	This type is a space-separated list of xs:NMTOKEN values.
xs:normalizedString	This type is an XML *whitespace-normalized* string, which is one that does not contain the whitespace characters #x9 (tab), #xA (line feed), or #xD (carriage return).
xs:string	This type is an XML character string.
xs:token	This type is an XML whitespace-normalized string with the following additional restrictions on #x20 (space) characters: (1) it can have no leading or trailing spaces, and (2) it cannot contain any sequences of two space characters in a row.

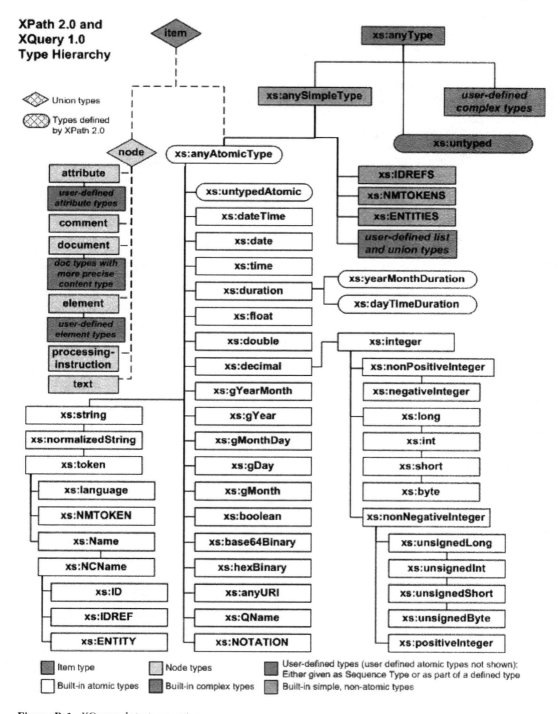

Figure B-1. *XQuery data type system*

APPENDIX C

Glossary

ACID

This is an acronym for *atomicity, consistency, isolation, durability*. These four concepts of transactional data stores, including SQL databases, ensure data integrity.

Adjacency list model

This is the representation of all arcs or edges of a graph as a list. In SQL, this is often implemented as a self-referential table in which each row maintains a pointer to its parent node in the graph.

ADO.NET Data Services

Also known as "Project Astoria," ADO.NET Data Services provides middle-tier support for accessing SQL Server databases through REST-style queries and entity data models (EDMs).

Anchor query

This is the nonrecursive query specified in the body of a CTE.

Application programming interface (API)

This is a well-defined interface provided by an application or service to support requests and communications from other applications.

Assembly

In SQL Server, a .NET assembly is a compiled SQL CLR executable or DLL.

Asymmetric encryption

Asymmetric encryption is encryption that requires two different keys: one to encrypt data and another to decrypt it. The most common form of asymmetric encryption is public key encryption, in which the two keys are mathematically related.

Atomic data types, list data types, and union data types

Atomic data types are indivisible data types that derive from the `xs:anyAtomicType` type. Examples include `xs:boolean`, `xs:date`, and `xs:integer`. List data types are types that are constructed of sequences of other types. Union data types are constructed from the *ordered union* of two or more data types, or a restricted subset of a data type. The XML Schema 1.1 Part 2: Data types specification working draft (`www.w3.org/TR/xmlschemall-2/#ordinary-built-ins`) defines no built-in union data types.

Axis

An axis specifier indicates the relationship between the nodes selected by the location step and the context node. Examples of axis specifiers include `child`, `parent`, and `ancestor`.

Bulk Copy Program (BCP)

This is a command-line utility supplied with SQL Server for the purpose of quickly loading large datasets into tables.

Catalog view

A catalog view returns a SQL Server database and server-specific metadata.

Certificate

A certificate is an electronic document consisting of an asymmetric key with additional metadata such as an expiration date and a digital signature that allows it to be verified by a third-party like a certificate authority (CA).

Check constraint

A check constraint is a condition placed on a table that restricts the range of valid values for one or more columns.

Closed-world assumption (CWA)

The CWA is a logic formalism that states what is not known to be true is false. SQL databases violate the CWA through the introduction of `NULL`s.

Clustered index

This is an index that contains a table's row data in its leaf-level nodes.

Comment

XQuery comments are denoted by the `(:` and `:)` delimiters in XQuery queries. XQuery comments are ignored during processing. They should not be confused with XML *comment nodes,* which are designated with `<!--` and `-->` delimiters.

  T-SQL allows single-line comments that begin with `--` or multiline comments enclosed in `/*` and `*/` delimiters.

Computed constructor

Computed constructors provide an alternative way to create XML nodes by specifying the type of node to be created through the use of special keywords.

Content expression

A content expression is part of a computed constructor, enclosed in braces, that generates XML node content.

Context item expression

This expression evaluates to the context node.

Context node

The context node is the node currently being processed. Each node of each set/sequence returned by a step in a location path is used in turn as a context node. Subsequent steps define their axes in relation to the current context node. For instance, with the sample XPath expression /Root/Person/Address, the Root node is the first context node. All Person nodes returned below Root become the context node in turn, and the Address nodes are retrieved relative to these context nodes.

Database encryption key

This is an encryption key used by Transparent Data Encryption to encrypt entire SQL Server databases.

Database master key

This is a database-level encryption key used to secure other keys in the database.

Data domain

The data domain for a column includes all valid values that may be stored in that column. The data domain can be restricted through the use of data types, check constraints, referential integrity/foreign key constraints, and triggers.

Data page

A data page is the smallest unit of storage that SQL Server can allocate. The data page consists of 8 KB of logically contiguous storage.

Datum

A geodetic datum is a set of reference points against which position can be measured. A datum is often associated with a model of the shape of the earth to define a geographic coordinate system.

Empty sequence

This is an XPath 2.0/XQuery 1.0 sequence containing zero items.

Entity data model (EDM)

An EDM is an abstract logical representation of a physical database, used to implement database connectivity in the middle or client tiers.

Extended Events (XEvents)

XEvents is a lightweight diagnostic system that can help you troubleshoot the performance problems with the SQL Server.

Extensible key management (EKM)

EKM is a SQL Server 2012 encryption option that allows you to physically store encryption keys on third-party hardware security modules (HSMs).

Extent

An extent is SQL Server's basic allocation unit of storage. An extent is 64 KB in size and consists of eight logically contiguous data pages, each page being 8 KB in size.

Extract, Transform, Load (ETL)

ETL processes involve pulling data from disparate data sources, cleaning and scrubbing the data, manipulating it (transform), and storing it in the database.

Facet

A facet is a schema component used to constrain data types. A couple of commonly used facets are `whiteSpace`, which controls how whitespace in string values is handled, and `length`, which restricts values to a specific number of units in length.

Filter expression

This is a primary expression followed by zero or more predicates.

FLWOR expression

FLWOR is an acronym for the XQuery keywords `for`, `let`, `where`, `order by`, and `return`. FLWOR expressions support iteration and binding variables.

Foreign key constraint

A foreign key constraint is a logical coupling of two SQL tables through the values of specified columns.

Full-text catalog

A full-text catalog is a logical grouping of SQL Server full-text indexes for management purposes.

Full-text index

A full-text index enables advanced text-based searches to be performed against a database table.

Full-text search (FTS)

FTS is the SQL Server 2012 implementation of SQL Server full-text search engine with the SQL Server query engine.

Functions and Operators (F&O)

This is XQuery 1.0 and XPath 2.0 Functions and Operators specification, available at www.w3.org/TR/xquery-operators/.

General comparison

This is an existentially quantified XQuery comparison that may be applied to operand sequences of any length. In general comparisons, the nodes are atomized and the atomic values of both operands are compared using value comparisons. If any of the value comparisons evaluate to true, the result is true.

Geography Markup Language (GML)

GML is a standard for the representation of geographic data using XML.

Grouping set

A grouping set is a SQL Server 2012 feature that allows you to define sets of grouping columns in your queries.

Hash

A hash is the result of applying a mathematical function or transformation on data to generate a smaller "fingerprint" of the data. Generally, the most useful hash functions are one-way collision-free hashes that guarantee a high level of uniqueness in their results.

Heap

A heap is an unordered collection of data pages. Any table without a clustered index is a heap.

Heterogeneous sequence

A heterogeneous sequence is an XQuery sequence of atomic values of different types and/or XML nodes. SQL Server XQuery does not support heterogeneous sequences consisting of atomic values and nodes.

Homogenous sequence

A homogeneous sequence is an XQuery sequence consisting entirely of nodes or entirely of singleton atomic values of compatible data types.

Indirect recursion

Indirect recursion is recursion by a trigger that occurs when a trigger fires, causing another trigger of the same type to fire, which causes the first trigger to fire again.

Inflectional form

SQL Server integrated full-text search (FTS) can search for inflectional forms of a word, including verb tenses and plural forms of nouns.

Initialization vector (IV)

An IV is a block of bits that is used to obfuscate the first block of data during the encryption process.

Language Integrated Query (LINQ)

LINQ adds native data source-agnostic querying capabilities to .NET languages using a declarative syntax.

Location path

A *path* is an XPath or XQuery expression that addresses a specific subset of nodes in an XML document. A location path is a series of *steps* separated by the solidus (forward slash) character, evaluated from left to right. Each step generates a sequence of items. Location paths can be relative or absolute. *Absolute* location paths begin with a single solidus character; *relative* location paths do not.

Logon triggers

Logon triggers fire in response to a server LOGON event.

Materialized path model

In the materialized path model for storing hierarchical data, the entire path to the root node is stored with each node in the hierarchy.

Multiple Active Result Sets (MARS)

MARS allows you to simultaneously open multiple result sets on a single open connection.

Nested sets model

In the nested sets model, hierarchical data is represented as a collection of sets containing other sets. The lower and upper bounds of each set define the contents of the set.

Node

XPath 2.0 and XQuery 1.0 treat XML data as a hierarchical tree structure, similar to (but not exactly the same as) the Document Object Model (DOM) that web programmers often use to manipulate HTML and XML. XPath and XQuery XML trees are composed of the seven types of nodes defined in the W3C XQuery 1.0 and XPath 2.0 Data Model (XDM), full descriptions of which are available at www.w3.org/TR/xpath-datamodel/#node-identity. These node types include the following:

- Attribute nodes, which represent XML attributes
- Comment nodes, which encapsulate XML comments
- Document nodes, which encapsulate XML documents
- Element nodes, which encapsulate XML elements
- Namespace nodes, which represent the binding of a namespace URI to a namespace prefix (or the default namespace)
- Processing instruction nodes, which encapsulate processing instructions
- Text nodes, which encapsulate XML character content

XPath 1.0 defines the node types it uses in Part 5 of the XPath 1.0 specification. The main difference between XPath 1.0 nodes and XDM nodes is that XPath 1.0 defines the *root node* of a document in place of the *document nodes* of the XDM. Another major difference is that in the XDM, element nodes are either explicitly or implicitly (based on content) assigned type information.

Node comparison

A node comparison in XQuery compares nodes by their document order or identity.

Node test

A node test is a condition that must be true for each node generated by a step. A node test can be based on the name of the node, the kind of node, or the type of node.

Nonclustered index

A nonclustered index is an index that stores the clustering key or row ID to the row data in its leaf nodes, depending on whether the table is a clustered table or a heap.

Optional occurrence indicator

The ? character, when used in conjunction with the cast as keywords, is referred to as the optional occurrence indicator. It indicates that the empty sequence is allowed.

Object-relational mapping (O/RM)

O/RM is a technique for mapping data between relational databases and object-oriented programming languages.

Open-world assumption (OWA)

The OWA is a logic formalism that states that the truth of a statement is independent of whether it is known to be true.

Parameterization

Parameterization is the act of using named or positional markers in place of constant values in a T-SQL query or statement. The actual values are passed to SQL Server independently of the actual query.

Path expression

See *location path*.

Predicate

AT-SQL predicate is an expression that evaluates to a SQL truth value. Predicates are used to control program flow and to limit the results of queries and the effect of statements.

An XQuery predicate is an expression enclosed in brackets ([ ]) that is used to filter a sequence. The predicate expressions are generally comparison expressions of some sort (equality, inequality, etc.).

Predicate truth value

In XQuery, a predicate truth value is a Boolean value derived from the result of an expression through a set of rules defined in the XQuery recommendation.

Primary expression

This is the basic *primitive* of the XQuery language. A primary expression can be a literal, a variable reference, a context item expression, a data type constructor, or a function call.

Query plan

A query plan is a sequence of logical and physical operators and data flows that the SQL query optimizer returns for use by the query processor to retrieve or modify data.

Recompilation

Recompilation is the process of compiling a new query plan for a given query, statement, or stored procedure (SP) when a plan already exists in the query plan cache. Recompilation can be triggered by SQL Server due to changes that have occurred since the prior query plan was generated for the statement, or it can be forced by user actions and T-SQL options.

Recursion

Recursion is a method of defining functions, CTEs, procedures, or triggers in such a way that they call themselves or cause themselves to be called multiple times.

Row constructor

A row constructor is a SQL Server 2012 feature that allows you to specify multiple rows in a single VALUES clause of the INSERT statement.

Scalar function

A scalar function returns a single atomic value as its result.

Searched CASE expression

A searched CASE expression allows you to specify one or more SQL predicates in WHEN clauses.

Sequence

XPath 2.0 and XQuery 1.0 define a sequence as an ordered collection of zero or more items. The term *ordered* is important here, as it differentiates a sequence from a *set*, which, as most T-SQL programmers know (or quickly come to realize), is unordered. XPath 1.0 defined its results in terms of *node sets*, which are unordered and cannot contain duplicates. XQuery changes this terminology to *node sequences*, which recognize the importance of node order in XML and can contain duplicates.

Server certificate

A server certificate is a certificate created in the master database for purposes of encrypting an entire database via transparent data encryption (TDE).

Service master key (SMK)

The SMK is an encryption key managed at the SQL Server service level. The SMK is used to encrypt all other keys in the SQL Server encryption key hierarchy.

Shredding

This is the process of converting XML data to relational style rows and columns.

Simple CASE expression

A simple CASE expression is defined with constants or value expressions in its WHEN clauses. The simple CASE evaluates to a series of simple equality expressions.

SOAP

SOAP, the Simple Object Access Protocol, is an XML-based protocol designed for exchanging structured information in distributed, decentralized environments.

Spatial data

Spatial data is used to represent objects and points on the earth.

Spatial index

A spatial index is a mechanism for increasing the efficiency of geographic calculations like the distance between points, or whether an object contains another point or object.

SQL Server Data Tools

SQL Server Data Tools provides integrated environment for database and application development.

SQL injection

SQL injection is a technique that exploits security vulnerabilities in the application layer and middle tier, allowing users to execute arbitrary SQL statements on a server.

Step

A step in XQuery is composed of an axis, a node test, and zero or more predicates. Each step is a part of a path expression that generates a sequence of items and then filters the sequence.

Table type

This is an alias type that defines a table structure for use with table-valued parameters.

Three-valued logic (3VL)

The SQL language supports 3VL with three truth values: true, false, and unknown.

Transparent data encryption (TDE)

TDE is a SQL Server 2012 feature that allows you to encrypt an entire database at once.

Untyped XML

This is an XML data instance that is not associated with an XML schema collection.

User-defined aggregate (UDA)

A UDA is a SQL CLR routine that applies a function or calculation to an entire set of values.

User-defined type (UDT)

A UDT is a SQL CLR-based data type.

Value comparison

This is a comparison of single values in XQuery.

Well-formed XML

This is XML data that follows the W3C XML recommendation for well-formed data. It includes a single root element and properly nested elements, and is properly entitized.

Well-known text (WKT)

WKT format is a plain-text format for defining geospatial data.

Windowing functions

Windowing functions are functions that can partition and possibly order datasets before they are applied to the dataset partitions.

World Wide Web Consortium (W3C)

The W3C is a standards body with the stated mission of "developing interoperable technologies . . . to lead the Web to its full potential."

XML

XML is the acronym for Extensible Markup Language, a restricted form of SGML (Standardized General Markup Language) designed to be easily served, received, and processed on the Web.

XML Schema

Part 2 of the XML Schema 1.1 standard defines XML Schema data types, which are the basic data types utilized by XQuery.

XPath

XPath, or XML Path Language, is an expression language designed to allow processing of values that conform to the XPath Data Model (XDM).

XQuery

XQuery, or XML Query Language, is an XML query language designed to retrieve and interpret data from diverse XML sources.

XQuery/XPath Data Model (XDM)

The XQuery 1.0 and XPath 2.0 Data Model is defined by the W3C at
www.w3.org/TR/2006/PR-xpath-datamodel-20061121/. See *XQuery*.

XSL

XSL, or Extensible Stylesheet Language, is a language for expressing style sheets, consisting of a language for transforming XML documents and an XML vocabulary for specifying formatting semantics. See *XSLT*.

XSLT

XSLT, or XSL Transformations, is a language for transforming XML documents into other XML documents. For instance, XSLT can be used to transform an XML document into an XHTML document. See *XSL*.

■ ■ ■

SQLCMD Quick Reference

SQLCMD is the standard text-based tool for executing batches of T-SQL on SQL Server. As a text-based tool, SQLCMD provides a lightweight but powerful tool for automating T-SQL batches. This appendix is designed as a quick reference to SQLCMD. The descriptions of many of the features and the functionality given here differ from BOL in some instances. The descriptions provided in this appendix are based on extensive testing of SQLCMD.

Command-Line Options

SQLCMD provides several command-line options to provide flexibility in connecting to SQL Server and executing T-SQL batches in a database. The full format for SQLCMD is shown here:

```
sqlcmd [ [-U login_id ] [-P password ] | [-E] ] [-C]
[-S server [\instance] ] [-d db_name] [-H workstation]
[-l login timeout] [-t query timeout] [-h headers] [-s column_separator] [-w column_width]
[-a packet_size] [-I] [-L[c] ] [-W] [-r[o|1]] [-q "query"] [-Q "query" and exit]
[-c batch_term] [-e] [-m error Level] [-V Severity Level] [-b] [-N]  [-K]
[-i input_file [,input_file2 [, ...] ] ] [-o output_file] [-u]
[-v var = "value" [,var2 = "value2"] [,...] ] [-X[1 ] [-x] [-?]
[-z new_password] [-Z new_password] [-f codepage | i:in_codepage [,o:out_codepage] ]
[-k[1|2] ] [-y display_width] [-Y display_width]
[-p[1 ] [-R] [-A]
```

The available command-line options are listed in Table D-1. The SQLCMD command-line options are case sensitive, so, for example, -v is a different option from -V.

Table D-1. *SQLCMD Command-Line Options*

Option	Description
-?	The -? option displays the SQLCMD help/syntax screen.
-A	The -A option tells SQLCMD to log into SQL Server with a dedicated administrator connection. This type of connection is usually used for troubleshooting.
-a packet_size	The -a option requests communications with a specific packet size. The default is 4096. packet_size must be within the range 512 to 32767.

(continued)

Table D-1. (*continued*)

Option	Description
-b	The -b option specifies that SQLCMD exits on an error and returns an ERRORLEVEL value to the operating system. When this option is set, a SQL error of severity 11 or greater will return an ERRORLEVEL of 1; an error or message of severity 10 or less will return an ERRORLEVEL of 0. If the -V option is also used, SQLCMD will report only the errors with a severity greater than or equal to the severity_level (level 11 or greater) specified with the -V option.
-c batch_term	The -c option specifies the batch terminator. By default, it is the GO keyword. Avoid using special characters and reserved words as the batch terminator.
-C	The –C option specifies that the server certificate can be trusted implicitly without validation used by the client.
-d db_name	The -d option specifies the database to use after SQLCMD connects to SQL Server. Alternatively, you can set this option via the SQLCMDDBNAME environment variable. If the database specified does not exist, SQLCMD exits with an error.
-E	The -E option uses a trusted connection (Windows authentication mode) to connect to SQL Server. This option ignores the SQLCMDUSER and SQLCMDPASSWORD environment variables, and you cannot use it with the -U and -P options.
-e	The -e option prints (echoes) input scripts to the standard output device (usually the screen by default).
-f codepage | i:in_codepage [,oout_codepage]	The -f option specifies the code pages for input and output. If i: is specified, in_codepage is the input code page. If o: is specified, out_codepage is the output code page. If i: and o: are not specified, the codepage supplied is the code page for both input and output. To specify a code page, use its numeric identifier. The following code pages are supported by SQL Server 2005:

Code Page Number	Code Page Name
437	MS-DOS US English
850	Multilingual (MS-DOS Latin1)
874	Thai
932	Japanese
936	Chinese (Simplified)
949	Korean
950	Chinese(Traditional)
1250	Central European
1251	Cyrillic
1252	Latin1 (ANSI)
1253	Greek
1254	Turkish
1255	Hebrew
1256	Arabic

(*continued*)

Table D-1. (*continued*)

Option	Description
	1257 Baltic
	1258 Vietnamese
-H workstation	The -H option sets the workstation name. You can use -H to differentiate between sessions with commands such as sp_who.
-h headers	The -h option specifies the number of rows of data to print before a new column header is generated. The value must be from –1 (no headers) to 2147483647. The default value of 0 prints headings once for each set of results.
-I	The -I option sets the connection QUOTED_IDENTIFIER option to ON. Turning the QUOTED_IDENTIFIER option on makes SQL Server follow the ANSI SQL-92 rules for quoted identifiers. This option is set to OFF by default.
-i input_file [,input_file2] [,...]	The -i option specifies that SQLCMD should use files that contain batches of T-SQL statements for input. The files are processed in order from left to right. If any of the files don't exist, SQLCMD exits with an error. You can use the GO batch terminator inside your SQL script files.
-k [1|2]	The -k option removes control characters from the output. If 1 is specified, control characters are replaced one for one with spaces. If 2 is specified, consecutive control characters are replaced with a single space.
-K	The –K option specifies the intent of the application workload that is connecting to the server that is a secondary replica in AlwaysOn availability group. The only value that can be specified currently is ReadOnly.
-L [c]	The -L option returns a listing of available SQL Server machines on the network and local computer. If the -Lc format is used, a "clean" listing is returned without heading information. The listing is limited to a maximum of 3,000 servers. Note that because of the way SQL Server broadcasts to gather server information, any servers that don't respond in a timely manner will not be included in the list. You cannot use the - L option with other options.
-l timeout	The -l option specifies the login timeout. The timeout value must be from 0 to 65534. The default value is 8 seconds, and a value of 0 is no timeout (infinite).
-m error_level	The -m option defines an error message customization level. Only errors with a severity greater than the specified level are displayed. If error_level is –1, all messages are returned, even informational messages.
-N	The client connection will be encrypted.
-o output_file	The -o option specifies the file to which SQLCMD should direct output. If -o is not specified, SQLCMD defaults to standard output (usually the screen).
-P password	The -P option specifies a password to log into SQL Server when using SQL authentication mode. If -P is omitted, SQLCMD looks for the SQLCMDPASSWORD environment variable to get the password to log in. If the SQLCMDPASSWORD environment variable isn't found, SQLCMD will prompt you for the password to log in using SQL authentication mode. If neither -P nor -U is specified and the corresponding environment variables aren't set, SQLCMD will attempt to log in using Windows authentication mode.

(*continued*)

Table D-1. (*continued*)

Option	Description
-p [1]	The -p option prints performance statistics for each result set. Specifying 1 produces colon-separated output.
-Q "query" and -q "query"	The -Q and -q options both execute a SQL query/command from the command line. -q remains in SQLCMD after query completion. -Q exits SQLCMD after completion.
-R	The -R option specifies client regional settings for currency and date/time formatting.
-r [0|1]	The -r option redirects error message output to the standard error output device—the monitor by default. If 1 is specified, all error messages and informational messages are redirected. If 0 or no number is specified, only error messages with a severity of 11 or greater are redirected. The redirection does not work with the -o option; it does work if standard output is redirected with the Windows command-line redirector (>).
-S server [\instance]	The -S option specifies the SQL Server server or named instance to which SQLCMD should connect. If this option is not specified, SQLCMD connects to the default SQL Server instance on the local machine.
-s column_ separator	The -s option sets the column separator character. By default, the column separator is a space character. separator can be enclosed in quotes, which is useful if you want to use a character that the operating system recognizes as a special character, such as the greater-than sign (>).
-t timeout	The -t option specifies the SQL query/command timeout in seconds. The timeout value must be in the range 0 to 65535. If -t is not specified, or if it is set to 0, queries/commands do not time out.
-U login_id	The -U option specifies the user login ID to log into SQL Server using SQL authentication mode. If the -U option is omitted, SQLCMD looks for the SQLCMDUSER environment variable to get the login password. If the -U option is omitted, SQLCMD attempts to use the current user's Windows login name to log in.
-u	The -u option specifies that the output of SQLCMD will be in Unicode format. Use this option with the -o option.
-V severity_ level	The -V option specifies the lowest severity level that SQLCMD reports back. Errors and messages of severity less than severity_level are reported as 0. severity_level must be in the range 1 to 25. In a command-line batch file, -V returns the severity level of any SQL Server errors encountered via the ERRORLEVEL so that your batch file can take appropriate action.
-v var = "value" [,var2 = "value2"] [,...]	The -v option sets scripting variables that SQLCMD can use in your scripts to the specified values. Scripting variables are described later in this appendix.
-W	The -W option removes trailing spaces from a column. You can use this option with the -s option when preparing data that is to be exported to another application. You cannot use -W in conjunction with the -Y or -y options.
-w column_width	The -w option specifies screen width for output. The width value must be in the range 9 to 65535. The default of 0 is equivalent to the width of the output device. For screen output, the default is the width of the screen. For files, the default width is unlimited.

(*continued*)

Table D-1. (*continued*)

Option	Description
-X [1]	The -X option disables options that can compromise security in batch files. Specifically, the -X option does the following:
	• Disables the SQLCMD : ! ! and : ED commands.
	• Prevents SQLCMD from using operating system environment variables.
	• Disables the SQLCMD startup script.
	If a disabled command is encountered, SQLCMD issues a warning and continues processing. If the optional 1 is specified with the -X option, SQLCMD exits with an error when a disabled command is encountered. Descriptions of SQLCMD commands, script variables, environment variables, and the startup script are detailed later in this appendix.
-x	The -x option forces SQLCMD to ignore scripting variables.
-Y display_width	The -Y option limits the number of characters returned for the char, nchar, varchar (8000 bytes or less), nvarchar (4000 bytes or less), and sql_variant data types.
-y display_width	The -y option limits the number of characters returned for variable- length data types such as varchar(max), varbinary(max), xml, text, and fixed-length or variable-length user-defined types (UDTs).
-Z new_password and -z new_ password	When used with SQL authentication (the -U and -P options), the -Z and -z options change the SQL login password. If the -P option is not specified, SQLCMD will prompt you for the current password. -z changes the password and enters interactive mode. -Z exits SQLCMD immediately after the password is changed.

Scripting Variables

SQLCMD supports scripting variables, which allow you to dynamically replace script content at execution time. This allows you to use a single script in multiple scenarios. By using scripting variables, for instance, you can execute a single script against different servers or databases without modification. SQLCMD allows you to set your own custom scripting variables with the -v command-line option. If more than one scripting variable is specified with the same name, the variable with the highest precedence (according to the following list) is used:

1. System-level environment variables have the highest precedence.

2. User-level environment variables are next.

3. Variables set via the command shell SET option are next.

4. Variables set via the SQLCMD -v command-line option are next.

5. Variables set inside a SQLCMD batch via the : SETVAR command have the lowest precedence.

■ **Note** The -X and -x options disable startup script execution and environment variable access, respectively. -x also prevents SQLCMD from dynamically replacing scripting variable references in your code with the appropriate values. This is a feature designed for secure environments where scripting variable usage could compromise security.

SQLCMD also provides several predefined scripting variables, which are listed in Table D-2. You can set the predefined read-only SQLCMD scripting variables via the command shell SET option or through SQLCMD command-line options; you cannot alter them from within a SQLCMD script with :SETVAR.

Table D-2. *SQLCMD Scripting Variables*

Name	Default	Read/Write	Description
SQLCMDCOLSEP		Read/write	Column separator character. See the -s command-line switch (in Table D-1).
SQLCMDCOLWIDTH	0	Read/write	Output column width. See the -w command-line switch.
SQLCMDDBNAME		Read-only	Default database name. See the -d command-line switch.
SQLCMDERRORLEVEL	0	Read/write	Level of error message customization. See the -m command-line switch.
SQLCMDHEADERS	0	Read/write	Number of lines to print between result set headers. See the -h command-line switch.
SQLCMDINI		Read-only	SQLCMD startup script.
SQLCMDLOGINTIMEOUT	8	Read/write	Login timeout setting (in seconds). See the -l command-line switch.
SQLCMDMAXFIXEDTYPEWIDTH	256	Read/write	Fixed-width data type display limit. See the -Y command-line switch.
SQLCMDMAXVARTYPEWIDTH	0	Read/write	Variable-length data type display limit. See the -y command-line switch.
SQLCMDPACKETSIZE	4096	Read-only	Packet size being used for SQL communications. See the -a command-line switch.
SQLCMDPASSWORD		N/A	SQL Server login password. See the -P command-line switch.
SQLCMDSERVER	server name	Read-only	SQL Server/instance name. See the -S command-line switch.
SQLCMDSTATTIMEOUT	0	Read/write	Query/command timeout setting (in seconds). See the -t command-line switch.
SQLCMDUSER		Read-only	SQL Server login username. See the -U command-line switch.
SQLCMDWORKSTATION		Read-only	SQL Server workstation name. See the -H command-line switch.
SQLCMDEDITOR	" "	Read-only	SQLCMD default editor.

Commands

SQLCMD recognizes a set of commands that are not part of T-SQL. These SQLCMD commands are not recognized by other query tools; they're not even recognized by SSMS (except when running it in SQLCMD mode). SQLCMD commands all begin on a line with a colon (:) to identify them as different from T-SQL statements. You can intersperse SQLCMD commands within your T-SQL scripts. Table D-3 lists the SQLCMD commands available.

■ **Tip** For backward compatibility with older osql scripts, you can enter the following commands without a colon prefix: !!, ED, RESET, EXIT, and QUIT. Also, SQLCMD commands are case insensitive, they must appear at the beginning of a line, and they must be on their own line. A SQLCMD command cannot be followed on the same line by a T-SQL statement or another SQLCMD command.

Table D-3. *SQLCMD Commands*

Command	Description
:!! command	The :!! command invokes the command shell. It executes the specified operating system command in the command shell.
:CONNECT server [\instance]	The :CONNECT command connects to a SQL Server instance.
[-ltimeout] [-Uuser [-Ppassword]]	The server name (server) and instance name (\instance) are specified in the command. When :CONNECT is executed, the current connection is closed. You can use the following options with the :CONNECT command: the -l option specifies the login timeout (specified in seconds; 0 equals no timeout); the -U option specifies the SQL authentication username; the -P option specifies the SQL authentication password.
:ED	The :ED command starts the text editor to edit the current batch or the last executed batch. The SQLCMDEDITOR environment variable defines the application used as the SQLCMD editor. The default is the Windows EDIT utility.
:ERROR destination	The :ERROR command redirects error messages to the specified destination. destination can be a file name, STDOUT for standard output, or STDERR for standard error output.
:EXIT [()|(query)]	The :EXIT command has three forms: :EXIT alone immediately exits without executing the batch and with no return code. :EXIT() executes the current batch and exits with no return code. :EXIT(query) executes the batch, including the query specified, and returns the first value of the first result row of the query as a 4-byte integer to the operating system.
GO [n]	GO is the batch terminator. The GO batch terminator executes the statements in the cache. If n is specified, GO will execute the statement *n* times.
:HELP	The :HELP command displays a list of SQLCMD commands.
:LIST	The :LIST list command lists the contents of the current batch of statements in the statement cache.

(continued)

Table D-3. (*continued*)

Command	Description
:LISTVAR	The :LISTVAR command lists all the SQLCMD scripting variables (that have been set) and their current values.
:ON ERROR action	The :ON ERROR command specifies the action SQLCMD should take when an error is encountered. action can be one of two values: EXIT stops processing and exits, returning the appropriate error code. IGNORE disregards the error and continues processing.
:OUT destination	The :OUT command redirects output to the specified destination. destination can be a file name, STDOUT for standard output, or STDERR for standard error output. Output is sent to STDOUT by default.
:PERFTRACE destination	The :PERFTRACE command redirects performance trace/timing information to the specified destination. destination can be a file name, STDOUT for standard output, or STDERR for standard error output. Trace information is sent to STDOUT by default.
:QUIT	The :QUIT command quits SQLCMD immediately.
:R filename	The :R command reads in the contents of the specified file and appends it to the statement cache.
:RESET	The :RESET command resets/clears the statement cache.
:SERVERLIST	The :SERVERLIST command lists all SQL Server instances on the local machine and any servers broadcasting on the local network. If SQLCMD doesn't receive timely responses from a server on the network, it may not be listed.
:SETVAR var [value]	The :SETVAR command allows you to set or remove SQLCMD scripting variables. To remove a SQLCMD scripting variable, use the :SETVAR var format. To set a SQLCMD scripting variable to a value, use the :SETVAR var value format.
:XML ON|OFF	The :XML command indicates to SQLCMD that you expect XML output from SQL Server (i.e., the SELECT statement's FOR XML clause). Use :XML ON before your SQL batch is run and :XML OFF after the batch has executed (after the GO batch terminator).

Index

CPSIA information can be obtained at www.ICGtesting.com
Printed in the USA
LVOW11s1502220114

370531LV00002B/8/P